MW01075055

O'HARA'S FUNDAMENTALS OF CRIMINAL INVESTIGATION

ABOUT THE AUTHOR

DeVere Woods received his bachelor's degree from Michigan State University, master's degree from Saginaw Valley State University, and doctoral degree from Michigan State University. He was a police officer in the state of Michigan where he served as a patrol officer, detective, crime scene investigator, shift commander, and division commander. Dr. Woods is a former consultant for the National Center for Community Policing at Michigan State University and former international consultant for the research division of the National Police of El Salvador. He is now chair of the Department of Criminology and Criminal Justice at Indiana State University. He is a member of the International Homicide Investigators Association and the International Association for Identification. His many publications include articles on community policing, criminal investigation, and other policing issues.

Eighth Edition

O'Hara's Fundamentals of Criminal Investigation

By

DeVERE D. WOODS Jr., Ph.D.

CHARLES C THOMAS • PUBLISHER, LTD.
Springfield • Illinois • U.S.A.

Published and Distributed Throughout the World by

CHARLES C THOMAS • PUBLISHER, LTD.
2600 South First Street
Springfield, Illinois 62704

ISBN 978-0-398-08845-3 (hard)
ISBN 978-0-398-08846-0 (ebook)

Library of Congress Catalog Card Number: 2012027099

First Edition, 1956
Second Edition, 1970
Third Edition, 1973
Fourth Edition, 1976
Fifth Edition, 1980
Revised Fifth Edition, 1988
Sixth Edition, 1994
Seventh Edition, 2003
Eighth Edition, 2013

With THOMAS BOOKS *careful attention is given to all details of manufacturing
and design. It is the Publisher's desire to present books that are satisfactory as to their
physical qualities and artistic possibilities and appropriate for their particular use.*
THOMAS BOOKS *will be true to those laws of quality that assure a good name
and good will.*

Printed in the United States of America
MM-R-3

Library of Congress Cataloging-in-Publication Data

Woods, Devere D.
    O'Hara's fundamentals of criminal investigation / by Devere D. Woods, Jr. – 8th ed.
    p. cm.
    Rev. ed. of: Fundamentals of criminal investigation / Charles E. O'Hara and
Gregory L. O'Hara. 7th ed. c2003.
Includes bibliographical references and index.
    ISBN 978-0-398-08845-3 (hard) – ISBN 978-0-398-08846-0 (ebook)
    1. Dundamentals of criminal investigation. II. Title. III. Title: Fundamentals of
criminal investigation.

HV8073.O39 2013
363.25–dc23   2012027099

To
Marty

PREFACE TO THE EIGHTH EDITION

THE EIGHTH EDITION is the most extensive revision so far. It continues the tradition of concentrating on the essential elements of a criminal investigation but restructures the presentation. In addition to revising the material, many chapters have been merged to consolidate similar topics. All the relevant material that previous users have come to rely on is more efficiently presented and updated. Advancements in forensic science, practices of criminalistics, computerization, electronic databases, and the Internet have greatly changed investigative practices.

When Charles O'Hara wrote the first edition of this text in 1956, gathering information was a laborious and tedious process. Today, most investigators can gather a wealth of background information by accessing an electronic database, Internet search engine, or social networking site. Despite all of these technological advancements, much of the role of criminal investigators remained unchanged. The time honored methods of collecting information are still effective and used in addition to electronic searches. Investigators still structure investigations around the elements of specific crimes. They are responsible for collecting evidence; documenting the crime scene through notes, reports, photographs and sketches; interrogating suspects; and developing information from interviews, public sources, informants, surveillance, and undercover work. They also work closely with crime scene and forensic specialists. All of these activities should be performed with the view of eventually presenting the evidence in court.

While investigators are concerned with proving the guilt of a suspect, they must also protect the innocent. The primary function of investigators is to uncover facts. Objectivity and a professional attitude should characterize investigators. Part of a professional attitude is the respect for the constitutional rights of suspects, informants, witnesses, and any citizen contacted during the course of an investigation. Criminal investigators should reflect the democratic ideals of their country and the professional standards of their occupation.

Charles and Gregory O'Hara's Fundamentals of Criminal Investigation has served as the "Bible" of criminal investigation for many years. It is the book I used to learn criminal investigation. I read the text as an undergraduate student, and it was my prime source of information when studying for my detective sergeant examination. It was the book I always recommended to young officers preparing for promotional exams. I have always credited it with having a major effect on my career.

When asked to revise this text, I naturally hesitated. How do you rewrite the standard for investigation? How do you update your mentor? For those concerned by the extensive structural changes to the text, I understand your apprehension. My purpose is to reposition the work of Charles and Gregory O'Hara for a new generation of criminal investigators. I do not seek to replace their work, but rather to share what I learned from them with those about to take on one of the most important roles in our society—the criminal investigator.

Careers are much like investigations; they are collaborations. What we achieve or accomplish is seldom from personal effort alone. Many others have helped us along the way. For the many people who have supported my efforts, I extend my sincere appreciation. Though far too many to name, a few must be acknowledged here. First, I want to acknowledge my family for all they have done. I thank my wife Marty for her support, assistance, and editing skills. I could not have completed this project without her. I thank my parents, Don and Ida Woods, for all their sacrifices and support to make my life better. Dean Woods and Sarah Woods Greene have always been there for me and believed in me when others did not. Matthew Woods has always looked after things when I was away and made it good to return home. Robert and Martha Bridges always made me feel part of the family. Ralph Turner, Michigan State University, provided inspiration and taught me the importance of investigation. Don Bachand, Saginaw Valley State University, gave me the focus and push I needed to complete my master's degree. Robert Trojanowicz, Michigan State University, convinced me to pursue my doctoral degree and changed my life. He was a good friend and good person who left us too soon but will never be forgotten. John Murray, Indiana State University, supported and encouraged me through this project and has provided a great working environment. Finally, I thank Michael Thomas for offering me this project. It was an opportunity and a pleasure working with the Charles C Thomas, Publisher organization.

D.D.W.

INTRODUCTION

THE PURPOSE OF THIS BOOK is to help readers master the basic, fundamental concepts of criminal investigation. No book could cover every aspect or nuance of investigation. Rapid advances in forensic science bring constant change, but the core concepts of good criminal investigation endure. After building a good foundation, investigators can, with the help of other literature and experience, develop their skills in specialized fields of crime detection or investigation.

Even as forensic science rapidly advances, criminal investigation continues to straddle both art and science. You cannot learn to become an accomplished investigator through books or courses alone. Techniques, such as interrogation and surveillance, are acquired substantially through patient practice, self-evaluation, and continued experience. Many skills are best learned from other investigators. Students can, however, bypass months of aimless apprenticeship by applying the basic tools of investigation and continually honing their skills. The science and study of investigative practices continue to inform and explain the art of criminal investigation. The professional investigator continues to study to learn what works, why it is effective, and how it can be improved.

This book will introduce students to the techniques and processes of investigation and provide a foundation upon which to build. In each area a broad overview is presented so readers can pursue further studies. Some offenses have been chosen for extensive discussion because of their serious nature and the frequency with which they occur. Investigators who understand the principles used to investigate these crimes can apply them to the investigation of other crimes.

The presentation of material is directed to the beginning student of investigation, but experienced investigators and supervisors will also find this text useful. Investigators will find this book a valuable resource and reference. Administrators, with little investigative experience, will find the discussion useful to better understand the work of their subordinates. The focus is on the practical application of investigation by police investigators, private investigators, or federal agents.

The many recommendations found in these chapters are guides and starting points. They are not the only effective procedures. Investigators need to start with accepted practices and adapt them to the circumstances at hand. When learning or moving into uncharted territory, it is useful to be guided by procedures until your judgment and understanding grow. Applying this discipline until your mastery and judgment are sufficient to move beyond preliminary guidance is an important step to becoming a successful investigator

CONTENTS

Part I
OVERVIEW OF CRIMINAL INVESTIGATION

Chapter

Part II
CRIME SCENE PROCEDURES
AND PHYSICAL EVIDENCE

Part III
OBTAINING INFORMATION

Part IV
SELECTED PROPERTY OFFENSES

Part V
SELECTED VIOLENT CRIMES

Part VI
THE INVESTIGATOR IN COURT

O'HARA'S FUNDAMENTALS OF CRIMINAL INVESTIGATION

Part I

OVERVIEW OF CRIMINAL INVESTIGATION

Chapter 1

METHODS OF INVESTIGATION

1. Nature of Investigation

CRIMINAL INVESTIGATORS collect facts to identify, locate, and prove the guilt of the perpetrators of crimes. Criminal investigation is practiced as an art and has yet to develop into a science guided by strict rules or theories. There is much to learn about the investigative process. How are crimes solved? When crimes are solved, what proportion of success is attributed to the characteristics and actions of investigators and what proportion is attributed to the characteristics and actions of perpetrators? Until we can answer these questions, we cannot establish a science of investigation. Intuition, circumstance, and chance continue to affect the choice of methods and decisions of investigators.

Even though investigation has not achieved the status of a science, it is useful to study and evaluate it as if it were. This premise of a science of investigation, complete with general principles and special theorems to guide investigators in solving cases, can help to build a structure for improving the quality and reliability of the criminal investigation process.

The tools of investigators are referred to as the three "I's," namely, Information, Interrogation, and Instrumentation. By applying the three "I's," investigators gather the facts to establish the guilt or innocence of suspects.

At the present time, there are no normative criteria for judging the success or failure of an investigation. The fact that the crime remains unsolved does not indicate a deficiency in the investigation, nor does a conviction of the accused necessarily mean that the investigation was conducted in an intelligent manner. An investigation may be considered a success if all the available, relevant and material information is uncovered. There is, however, no way of knowing the true extent of information available.

It is a common misconception that every crime can be solved, that sufficient evidence is always available to identify the criminal, and that there are always clues at the crime scene that will lead to the perpetrator. These misconceptions, fueled by the popular entertainment media, may lead to public disdain of inability by police to solve a particular crime.

Many crimes are not solved because there is insufficient evidence. The absence of eyewitnesses, discernible motives, and physical evidence often prohibit a solution. Sometimes the *corpus delicti,* or the fact that a crime was committed, cannot be established and then even a confession is of little value.

To the general public, an investigation consists of merely discovering the identity of suspects and apprehending them. A complete investigation entails much more than identifying and capturing perpetrators. Investigators must also develop and present sufficient evidence in a court to warrant a conviction. Finding the perpetrators is frequently the simplest phase of the investigation. Obtaining, within the rules of the justice system, sufficient evidence to support the charge is often an exceedingly complex task.

To simplify the presentation in this book, we will assume that most crimes can be solved. The methods described throughout the text are usually effective in finding a solution. The investigation will be considered successful if the available physical evidence was competently handled, witnesses intelligently interviewed, suspects (if willing) effectively interrogated, all logical leads properly developed, and the case comprehensively and accurately reported. The verdict of the court in regard to the guilt of the accused will not be considered sufficient to determine the success or failure of the investigation.

2. Information

Information is the basis of any criminal investigation. The word "information" is used here to describe the knowledge that investigators gather from people through interviews, questioning, or conversation. Some information is acquired from regular sources such as conscientious and public-spirited citizens, company records, and the files of other agencies. Other information is gathered by investigators from cultivated sources such as paid informants, service industry workers, former criminals, or acquaintances. The use of informants varies widely with law enforcement agencies. Many agencies use paid informants in major cases. Some agencies routinely gather information through their community policing programs.

Of the three "I's," information is by far the most important. By simply questioning a knowledgeable and sometimes anonymous individual, the identity of perpetrators, and possibly their motive, may be revealed. This information then guides the subsequent steps of the investigation. Conducting an investigation is sometimes like working a mathematical problem backwards with the solution known but with proof yet to be derived.

Commonly, offenses committed by career criminals are solved with information derived from the criminal subculture. A homicide may be solved by a tip from a paroled convict or drug addict, or a few snatches of conversation gleaned by a curious bartender. Economic crime is ordinarily motivated by a desire for economic gain (e.g. larceny, robbery, and burglary), while assault and homicide are often the by-product of disputes over divisions of spoils. Crimes motivated by greed, when perpetrated by professional criminals, are frequently solved by information from informants and information derived from the criminal subculture.

Crimes motivated by passion, love, hate, or desires for revenge (often committed in the heat of the moment by otherwise law-abiding citizens) are not likely to be solved through tips from an informant immersed in the criminal culture. Senseless crimes committed by deranged individuals are also unlikely to be solved by information from informants.

3. Interrogation

Interrogation, the second "I," includes the skillful questioning of witnesses or suspects. Successful interrogation depends on locating knowledgeable suspects and developing well-crafted strategies for questioning them. The term interview will be used throughout the text to describe the simple questioning of a person who has no personal reason to withhold information and therefore may be expected to divulge information freely. An interrogation involves skillful questioning to extract information from a resistant individual. The ability to obtain information by questioning is an important talent for investigators.

Novice investigators may overlook the most obvious approach to solving a crime, namely, asking the suspect if he or she committed the offense. The approach is so elementary that it is frequently neglected by beginners too eager to use more refined techniques. The guilty person is in possession of most of the information necessary for a successful prosecution. If questioned intelligently, he or she can usually be induced to talk. The accused should be asked to supply details from which his or her actions and intentions can be deduced. Even evasive or untruthful statements give indications of motive and state of mind. A confession that includes details that could not be known by an innocent party is a convincing form of proof.

Why, if silence so greatly favors the criminal, do suspects agree to talk to police even after being properly given the *Miranda* warnings? Many people possess an irresistible desire to talk. They cannot, when reputation and character are being seriously questioned, resist the temptation to defend themselves by stating the truth or resorting to extravagant falsehoods. A guilty person under questioning by the police is often very frightened and will seek comfort, however indirectly, in communication with another. Only an exceptionally strong personality or an experienced criminal can withstand prolonged, skillful interrogation.

Investigators should view suspects or reluctant witnesses as people who will yield information if questioned with sufficient skill and patience. Becoming a proficient interrogator takes years of work. Investigators who possess common sense and a capacity for perseverance can eventually become reasonably effective. Investigators armed with insight into personalities and knowledge of practical psychology will excel in the art of interrogation. Through the application of study and observation, investigators develop their ability to establish rapport quickly with a wide variety of criminal types. Finally, investigators must be quick-witted. Interrogation is an intellectual game that is often won by the player who is mentally faster and who can rapidly take advantage of an opening or an indicated weakness. As in any other game or skill, the art of interrogation must be practiced constantly in order to improve or maintain proficiency. A period of inactivity of even a few months will result in a marked decline in effectiveness.

4. Instrumentation

The third "I" is the application of the instruments and methods of science and computer analysis to the detection of crime. This area is represented by criminalistics, crime scene investigation, and computer-assisted analysis. Physics, chemistry, biology, pathology, statistics, and the other natural sciences aid investigative efforts. Scientific procedures may help establish *corpus delicti* or link suspects to crimes.

Instrumentation, however, is more than criminalistics. It includes the technical methods used to track fugitives or further investigations. Computerized fingerprint and criminal record systems, DNA analysis, *modus operandi* files, polygraph examinations, communication systems, surveillance equipment, searching apparatus (x-ray unit, metal detector, thermal imagers, etc.) and other investigative tools are contained within the scope of instrumentation.

There has been a tendency to place too great a value on the contribution of the instrumentation to the detection of crime. The inexperienced are especially prone to place their faith in technical methods to the neglect of the more basic and generally more effective procedure. Several reasons may be given to account for this. The popularity of television crime dramas has fostered an unrealistic view of forensic science in the minds of the public. This misperception, known as the CSI effect, fosters the view that every case can be solved by analyzing physical evidence, laboratory tests are nearly instantaneous, and expense is never an issue. This view is particularly problematic when held by jurors who refuse to convict unless evidence of scientific analysis is presented that removes all doubt of guilt. Jurors become suspicious when a case lacks the scientific analysis they are accustomed to seeing in their favorite television show. Investigators must ensure all relevant physical evidence was collected and analyzed, and prosecutors must explain why exotic or expensive laboratory analysis was not employed.

In many cases there is limited physical evidence, and forensic analysis is relatively unimportant. Little physical evidence may be left after a larceny or robbery. In a homicide, however, physical evidence is often of paramount importance. The use of information and interrogation is applicable to nearly all cases, but instrumentation is found most effective in cases where physical evidence is abundant.

The introduction of DNA analysis has greatly enhanced the importance of instrumentation for investigators. DNA is the genetic material in our cells that determines our individual characteristics and thus can be used to identify an individual. DNA profiles can be computerized and stored in national information systems so that criminals can no longer escape detection by moving to a different jurisdiction. Serial offenders can be identified and linked to several crime scenes. Individuals arrested for minor offenses can often be linked to major crimes.

Investigators need to be thoroughly trained in the resources of instrumentation and forensic science. The ability to anticipate the proper technique or apparatus to use can determine success. Knowledge of the limitations of technical methods is also important. Excessive reliance on instruments may result in neglect of other and more suitable investigative procedures.

5. Ethics of Investigation

The mission of criminal investigators is to uncover facts to help determine the truth, not to amass convictions. Investigators are social agents empowered to protect society from predators. They must limit themselves to using only appropriate methods to guard against becoming predators themselves. Means and methods are as important as results. Bending or breaking rules in an effort to enforce the law is a dangerous and misguided strategy. Investigators must maintain the values of justice, or social control mechanisms (both individual and social) will not function. Investigators cannot accept doing wrong for the "right reasons." Investigators cannot accept dishonesty and ethical breaches for themselves or others. They have an obligation to their profession to maintain social trust and to ferret out and identify unethical practices wherever they occur.

Arrests and convictions will always be an objective not a goal. A good investigator seeks truth most of all. No matter how strongly we feel an outcome is correct, it cannot be achieved by improper means. The means cannot be justified by our desire for results. Truth cannot be validated without examination of the means by which it was derived. Our perception of a truth we hold today may change by the addition to, or alteration of, the facts tomorrow.

6. Phases of the Investigation

Criminal investigation consists of identifying perpetrators, tracking and locating perpetrators, and developing facts to prove guilt in court. The three phases are not necessarily separated and are usually fused throughout the investigation. Moreover, the same evidence can often be used for all three objectives. Throughout all phases of the investigation, the three "I's" are constantly employed.

7. Identifying the Criminal

In the first phase the criminal is identified, i.e., some person is identified as the perpetrator of the criminal acts. Ordinarily the identity of the criminal is discovered in one or more of the following ways: confession, eyewitness testimony, or circumstantial evidence.

a. **Confession**. Admission or confession by a suspect is a major objective of every investigation. The confession is, of course, an excellent means of identifying the criminal. To prove guilt at the trial, a confession must be supported by other corroborative evidence. The *corpus delicti* must be separately established in order to support a conviction. A confession may be recanted in court, and the defense counsel may successfully argue it was made under duress and coercion unless it can be shown to be voluntary (*Miranda* warnings and so forth).

b. **Eyewitness**. The ideal identification consists of the testimony of several objective persons who are familiar with the appearances of the accused and who witnessed the commission of the crime. Where witnesses and suspects are strangers and the observation was limited to a few seconds, the validity of the identification depends upon the ability of witnesses to observe and remember the suspects' appearance, the conditions of visibility and observation, and the period of time between the crime and the identification.

c. **Circumstantial Evidence**. Identification may be established indirectly by proving facts or circumstances from which the identity of the perpetrator can be inferred. Evidence of this nature usually falls into one of the following classes.

1) *Motive*. A motive may be inferred from circumstances and statements of witnesses. For example, a person with financial need may commit a property theft and a quarrel or argument would be relevant in a crime of violence.

Closely related to motive is state of mind. Evidence relating to motive or state of mind is usually obtained by interviewing witnesses, a study and reconstruction of the crime scene, and the prior and subsequent acts of the suspect.

2) *Opportunity*. It must have been physically possible for suspects to commit the crime. Suspects must have had access to the place of the crime, had the means to commit the crime, and not have alibis.

3) *Associative Evidence*. Evidence may serve to identify perpetrators through the transfer of trace evidence, possession of property, pattern evidence found at the crime scene, or testimonial or physical evidence placing them in proximity to the crime scene. Perpetrators may leave some clue at the scene such as a weapon, tool, garment, fingerprint, or foot impression, or may unwittingly carry from the scene evidence in the form of glass, paint, hair, or blood. In crimes of personal gain, the fruits of the crime may be possessed by suspects. Crimes of violence will often leave evidence of physical struggle.

8. Tracking and Locating the Criminal

The second phase of the investigation is to locate the offender. Obviously many of the steps used to identify suspects will also lead to their location. Usually criminals are not hiding, they are simply unknown. Generally, professional criminals do not operate near their residence and unless identified, merely return home. Amateur criminals usually commit crimes of opportunity. It is to their advantage to remain in their normal environment, since flight might betray guilt. In cases where it is necessary to track a hiding fugitive, the tips, interview techniques and general information described earlier will be most useful.

9. Proving the Guilt

Apprehending the criminal does not complete the investigation. The third stage of the investigation, proving guilt, is often the most difficult phase. Investigators must gather the facts necessary to prove the guilt of the accused. A confession and a good theory of the case are not enough. The court requires that guilt be proved beyond a reasonable doubt using evidence presented in accordance with procedures that assure quality and trustworthiness.

The final test of a criminal investigation is the presentation of evidence in court. It must be shown in an orderly and logical fashion that: a crime was committed; the perpetrator was identified and associated with the crime scene; witnesses are competent and credible; the physical evidence is appropriately identified and relevant; and the chain of custody was maintained.

10. Elements of the Offense

Early in a criminal trial the prosecution must prove the *corpus delicti,* or fact that a crime was committed. Unless it can be shown that a crime has been committed, there is little basis for testing the guilt or innocence of the accused and the court will dismiss the case. The *corpus delicti* is proved by facts that form the basis of the crime. Preferably this should be established by direct and positive proof, but circumstantial evidence will suffice if it is clear and cogent. In general it may be said that a confession in itself is worthless without evidence to establish *corpus delicti.*

In addition to establishing the *corpus delicti* and identifying the perpetrator, the accused must be shown to be a responsible agent in the commission of the crime. It is not necessary to show that the accused willed the particular effect in its final form. It is sufficient to show that his or her objective could not have been accomplished without violating the law.

Finally, the prosecutor must demonstrate that all elements of the crime have been fulfilled. For example, the elements of common law burglary are: the accused broke into a dwelling, in the night-time, in order to commit a crime therein. A charge of burglary can be supported if proof of these elements of burglary is presented. To understand the elements of criminal offenses, investigators must study the penal law of their jurisdiction.

An outline of the elements of the crime also provides a convenient framework for investigators developing a case. The elements should be kept constantly in mind, to ensure all appropriate leads are followed and relevant evidence is collected.

a. **Intent**. Investigators must develop facts indicating the frame of mind of the accused. It must be shown that the accused knew what he or she was doing. Consciousness of the unlawfulness of the act is not essential, since ignorance of the law is no defense. In some crimes intent is an essential element. In others, it is merely necessary to show that the accused was aware of the consequences of his or her acts. Some crimes include the additional element of malice, or the intent to do injury to another. Legal malice does not necessarily imply hate or ill will. It is a mental state in which an individual acts, without legal excuse or justification, to injure another. Malice is often inferred from the facts developed by the investigation.

Motive, or that which induces the criminal to act, must be distinguished from intent. The motive may be the desire to obtain revenge or personal gain, while the intent is the accomplishment of the act. Motive need not be shown in order to obtain a conviction, but intent must always be proved where it is an element of the offense. Although proof of motive is not often required, if motive is not established it can bring into question whether the accused committed the crime. In cases that depend upon circumstantial evidence, proof of motive is especially important. The significance of motive varies widely with the nature of the crime. In some cases, investigators should look into the life history of the victim (e.g. relationships, conflicts). When interviewing witnesses, investigators should encourage them to gossip. Motive is a nebulous matter and difficult to detect in a strict recitation of facts.

11. Role of Reason

Investigators are not just collectors of facts. They must also construct hypotheses and draw conclusions relating to the identity of perpetrators and how crimes were committed. Reason, logic, good judgment, and common sense should guide this process, even when investigators are engaging in speculation. Investigators, faced with a complex crime, may be compared to research scientists, employing the same resources of reason and resorting, where necessary, to imagination, ingenuity, and intuition.

Investigation should be guided by both inductive and deductive reasoning. Inductive reasoning guides investigators from the particular to the general. Investigators use specific observations to generalize an explanation for the events under examination. For example, from the observation of a broken window, an open door, and overturned desk drawers, investigators might conclude by inductive reasoning that a burglary had taken place. By comparing the details of two burglaries, investigators could theorize that both crimes were probably committed by the same person. This type of thinking, forming a general theory from the examination of particular details, is inductive reasoning.

In deductive reasoning, investigators proceed from the general to the particular. Investigators begin with a general theory, apply it to a particular crime, and determine whether the crime can be explained by the theory. For example, investigators might apply the theory that one can determine that a burglar is experienced if the crime scene evidence reflects planning and execution. Investigators would analyze the crime scene to determine if this theory applied to a particular instance. If the residents were not at home and there were valuables on the premises, it might indicate that the burglary was well-"cased" and well-planned. If the burglar easily entered and exited, left few clues, searched methodically and removed valuables selectively, it would indicate that the crime was well-executed. From these observations, investigators could determine that this crime scene was consistent with the theory, and that this particular burglary was probably committed by an experienced burglar. When investigators apply a general theory to a particular instance to see if it fits, they are practicing deductive reasoning.

In practice, investigators shift continually between inductive and deductive thinking. At one moment, investigators may be theorizing that a burglary has taken place by examining the details of the crime scene (induction). At the next moment, they may be applying the general definition of what constitutes a burglary to see if the elements are present in this particular crime scene (deduction). In both inductive and deductive reasoning, the passage from point to point must be managed by logical steps, a requirement that is not easily satisfied. The use of correct reasoning requires a constant vigilance against the pitfalls of false premises, logical fallacies, unjustifiable inferences, ignorance of conceivable alternatives, and failure to distinguish between the factual and the probable.

12. Representative Approach

No single method of reasoning may be said to be the only correct procedure for arriving at a solution. Investigators must critically review the crime to determine its nature, and then comprehensively collect information from the crime scene, witnesses, and observations. The information is then analyzed to establish proof and create hypotheses of the crime. Hypotheses are compared to existing and developing evidence. Various possibilities are eliminated systematically by considering opportunity, motive, past record, observed reactions, and corroboration of alibis. A hypothesis is selected on the basis of consistency with known facts and its degree of probability. The best hypothesis must be objectively tested and modified or rejected when contrary evidence is uncovered. Investigators must not permit observations and interpretations to be biased in favor of the hypothesis.

13. Chance

Many investigative situations cannot be solved by reason and logic alone. Enterprise, initiative, perseverance, ingenuity, and an insatiable curiosity are among the characteristics needed in addition to a rational and comprehensive method. Chance can also play an important part in the solution of crimes. This is not to imply that investigation should be left to happenstance, but rather to remind investigators to be prepared for a fortuitous development. Training the powers of observation and remaining prepared for the unexpected will allow investigators to take advantage of fortuitous clues that may resolve the case. Chance may provide the opportunity, but an open mind is required to grasp an opportunity, and a prepared mind is needed to interpret it.

14. Intuition

Since investigation is an art that incorporates a developing science, consideration must be given to the study of intuition–the sudden and unexpected insight that cannot be overtly developed by logic and reason. Proceeding on a "hunch" is common in police work. Some investigators receive inspiration or illumination when method alone will not yield a solution. The key idea may come suddenly when the investigator is not consciously thinking of the case, or it may arrive dramatically while weighing the available information. It may spring involuntarily to the conscious mind from the subconscious that is saturated with the data of a case and the many facets of the problem. Until we can better explain the functioning of the human mind, we should merely accept intuition as a gift. Relaxation and even distraction can sometimes facilitate this phenomenon and should be sought when problems appear unsolvable. Since there is no evidence that crimes are intrinsically soluble, investigators can expect in many cases that sheer plodding work and deductive reasoning will not be fruitful. The answer may lie in intuition or chance.

15. Summary

This chapter has been devoted to describing the nature and process of criminal investigation. The tools and methods of investigation are the three "I's"–Information, Interrogation, and Instrumentation. An investigation consists of three phases: identifying the perpetrator, locating the perpetrator, and proving his or her guilt. To successfully prosecute a case in court, evidence must be sufficient to prove guilt beyond a reasonable doubt. Investigators must establish that a crime has been committed (*corpus delicti*), by criminal action, show that all elements of the offense are present, and establish a causal connection between the acts of the accused and commission of the crime.

The completed investigation is the end product of teamwork. The patrol officer who discovers the crime and protects the scene, the detective who is assigned to the case, the investigators who assist in running leads, the supervisors who aid administratively, the technical services (who preserve, examine, and record the evidence), and the state's attorney who provides overall guidance and presents the case in court. All of these are members of the team who solve the case.

A prejudiced investigator is a contradiction in terms. A biased inquiry cannot comprehensively consider all relevant facts but results in a polarized view of selected, predetermined data. It is not an objective search for the truth but a proffering of a preferred hypothesis by adducing the most favorable facts and examining only the data that contribute to its support. Investigators must seek facts and determine the truth in an ethical manner. Their first obligation is to the integrity of their profession, not to procure convictions through any means.

ADDITIONAL READING

Criminal Investigation

Becker, R.F.: *Criminal Investigation.* New York: Panel, 1999.

Bennet, W.W. and Hess, K.M.: *Criminal Investigation* (5th ed.). St. Paul: West Publishing, 1997.

Berg, B.L. and Horgan, J.J.: *Criminal Investigation* (3rd ed.). New York, Macmillan, 1998.

Brown, M.F.: *Criminal Investigation: Law and Practice.* Woburn, MA: Butterworth-Heinemann, 1998.

Burstein, H.: *Criminal Investigation: An Introduction.* Englewood Cliffs, NJ: Prentice Hall, 1998.

Dempsey, J.S.: *An Introduction to Public and Private Investigation.* St. Paul: West Publishing, 1996.

Dutelle, A.W.: *An Introduction to Crime Scene Investigation.* Boston: Jones and Bartlett, 2011.

Fisher, B.A.J.: *Techniques of Crime Scene Investigations* (6th ed.). Boca Raton, FL: CRC Press, 1999.

Gilbert, J.N.: *Criminal Investigation* (5th ed.). Englewood Cliffs, NJ: Prentice Hall, 2000.

Golec, A.M.: *Techniques of Legal Investigation* (3rd ed.). Springfield, IL: Thomas, 1995.

Kenny, J.P. and More, H.W.: *Principles of Investigation* (2nd ed.). St. Paul, West Publishing, 1994.

Kinnee, K.B.: *Practical Investigation Techniques.* Boca Raton, Fla.: CRC Press, 1994.

Lyman, M.D.: *Criminal Investigation* (2nd ed.). Englewood Cliffs, NJ: Prentice Hall, 1998.

Osterburg, J.W. and Ward, R.H.: *Criminal Investigation: A Method for Reconstructing the Past* (3rd ed.). Cincinnati: Anderson, 2000.

Palmiotto, M.J.: *Criminal Investigations* (2nd ed.). Bethesda, MD: Austin and Winfield, 1999.

Pena, M.: *Criminal Investigation* (5th ed.). Incline Village, NV: Copperhouse, 2000.

Robbins, R.K.: *Criminal Investigation Procedures.* Berkeley, CA: McCutchan, 1993.

Shelton, D.: The 'CSI Effect': Does it Really Exist? *NIJ Journal,* No. 259, March 2008.

Swanson, C.R., Jr., Chamelin, N.C., and Territo, L.: *Criminal Investigation* (7th ed.). New York: McGraw Hill, 1999.

Trojanowicz, R. and Bouquerx, B.: *Community Policing: A Contemporary Perspective.* Cincinnati: Anderson, 1990.

Using DNA to Solve Cold Cases, *NIJ Special Report,* NCJ 194197, US Department of Justice, July 2, 2002.

Weston, P.B., Wells, K.M., and Lushbaugh, C.: *Criminal Investigation: Basic Perspectives* (8th ed.). Englewood Cliffs, NJ: Prentice Hall, 1999.

Wilson, J.B.: Criminal Investigations: *A Behavioral Approach.* Prospect Heights, IL: Waveland Press, 1993.

Criminal Investigation Web Sites

About Crime and Punishment: www.crime.about.com

Alcohol, Tobacco, Firearms and Explosives: www.atf.gov

Bureau of Justice Statistics: www.ojp.usdoj.gov/bjs

Crime and Clues: www.crimeandclues.com

Crime Scene Investigation: www.crime-scene-investigator.net

Crime Scene Investigations: www.feinc.net/cs-inv-p.htm

Criminal Investigation on Line: www.ciol.org

Criminal Offender Profiling, Victimology, Serial Killers, and Forensic Psychology: www.criminalprofiling.com

Department of Justice: www.usdoj.gov

Drug Enforcement Agency: www.usdoj.gov/dea

FBI: www.fbi.gov

Investigative Resources: www.officer.com/

National Criminal Justice Reference Service: www.ncjrs.org

National Institute of Justice: www.ojp.usdoj.gov/nij
Secret Service: www.treas.gov/usss

Chapter 2

THE INVESTIGATIVE REPORT

THE INVESTIGATOR'S NOTEBOOK

THE INVESTIGATOR is responsible for piecing the various parts of an investigation into a cohesive whole. Investigators must interview complainants, search crime scenes, collect and transmit the evidence, interview witnesses, interrogate suspects, and perform the innumerable minor chores attached to an investigation. Many of the details associated with a case may not be essential to the report but may become important when the case goes to trial. The amount of information investigators encounter over multiple cases make it impossible to rely on memory alone. A good report and a good investigation begin with good notes.

a. **Repository for Details**. Investigators need a means of storing information, whether it is a notebook, voice recorder, or some other electronic device. Each recording method comes with unique advantages and disadvantages. Notebooks are cheap, easily stored, and information can be recorded privately even in the presence of others, but they occupy the investigator's hands. Voice recorders can be operated hands-free and can record more detail, but observations cannot be recorded privately while in the presence of others, information must be transcribed, and they are more difficult to search for specific information. Many other electronic recording devices occupy the investigator's hands and may present issues of secure, long-term data storage. Regardless of the device used, investigators may need to present the original recording medium in court. The remaining discussion will focus on the most common means of recording notes, the notebook, but the principles of information collection are the same for any recording mechanism.

Adequate notes are a prerequisite to the future recording, evaluation, and presentation of the information developed in an investigation. The passing of time obscures the investigator's memory. A few notes taken during or immediately after an interview or a search will aid in recalling the entire interview or the circumstances surrounding a search. Many seemingly inconsequential details become important in the light of later developments. The demands placed on investigators while conducting investigations make it difficult to evaluate the significance of information as it is received. The notebook serves as a repository of data for investigators to later carefully analyze and assess facts and observations.

b. **Basis of the Report**. The investigative report will be drafted from the raw material contained in the investigator's notebook. At the outset of the investigation it is rarely possible to determine which investigative steps are significant and should be included in the report. Investigators must record data without knowing its ultimate value to the investigation. Often information pertaining to a number of potential suspects is gathered until the perpetrator is identified.

c. **To Supplement Sketches and Photographs**. Sketches and photographs supplement but do not replace good notes. A crime scene sketch shows the relationship between what is perceived to be relevant evidence. Photographs contain more detail but may distort distances between objects. The notebook should provide the true location and condition of objects, the nature and appearance of hidden objects, relevant details pertaining to various articles, the odor and general atmosphere of the area, and an inventory of articles of value.

d. **Documentary Evidence**. Investigators often use their notebooks to refresh their memories while testifying in court. Defense counsel may, under these circumstances, examine the entire notebook. This possibility should prompt investigators to ensure that notes are carefully and accurately recorded. Under examination by defense counsel investigators must be able to account for all entries in their notebooks. Cryptic, vague, or illegible inscriptions tend to undermine the validity of the notes and the credibility of the witness. One of the conditions sometimes placed on the use of notes in court is that they be original notes that were taken contemporaneously with the actions they record.

2. Materials

There are ordinarily no official requirements to maintaining a notebook, but experience suggests some useful practices. Recording in ink is preferred to pencil for both permanence and ensuring the entries have not been altered. A bound notebook creates a more favorable impression because pages can be easily removed from a loose-leaf notebook. Ideally, the notebook should contain the notes of only one investigation so that an in-court examination does not involve the disclosure of information pertaining to separate investigations.

3. Recording Notes

Notes are gathered and recorded in chronological order as investigative actions are taken or information is received, and not necessarily in logical order. The information is later sorted into a logical investigative report. Notebook entries should be recorded in a complete, accurate, and legible fashion so that another investigator could take over the investigation and interpret the entries. Improper abbreviations and highly personal, unintelligible codes should be avoided.

When documenting an interview, investigators should preface the notes with the case identifier, identity of the person interviewed, and names of any others present. Important statements should be recorded verbatim, if possible. The extent of the notes will depend upon the importance of the interview and the ability of the investigator to reconstruct an interview. If the matter under investigation is sensitive, the interviewee may be less candid if it becomes obvious investigators are recording the statement. In an interrogation, it is poor technique to draw out a notebook as soon as the suspect begins to make admissions. The flow of information frequently dries up at the sight of a notebook. In other interviews, such as a routine personnel background check, there is usually no objection to the open use of the notebook.

REPORT WRITING

4. Importance

The effectiveness of investigators and the quality of investigations are judged in large measure by investigative reports. If an otherwise satisfactory investigation is poorly reported, the reputations of investigators suffer. Investigators are part of a team, and their information must be available to the other members. The information is of little use when confined to investigators' notebooks or memories. The report validates the complaint, presents the general nature and magnitude of the case, guides additional investigative steps, provides a means for supervision and evaluation, is the foundation for crime reporting and analysis, and is used to support administrative planning and resource management.

An agency covering a large geographic area relies heavily on the submission of effective reports. An investigation may be nationwide in scope involving multiple offices and investigators. The only way to intelligently manage such a case is through competent reporting.

Investigators should avoid preparing superficial reports for cases they consider unlikely to be solved. One never knows which case may eventually become linked to another. A superficial report can become the weak link in an important series of investigations. Investigators may then be the subject of ridicule from colleagues and subjected to intensive scrutiny from defense counsel. Police reports are read by other officers and investigators, supervisors, prosecutors, defense attorneys, judges, jurors, insurance agency personnel, victim advocates, civil counsel, probation or parole officers, and the press.

5. Purpose of an Investigative Report

Investigators must keep in mind the purpose and audience of their reports. A report is an official business record pertaining to an investigation. The report provides other investigators with information necessary to advance an investigation. It may be used to initiate a criminal, corrective, or disciplinary action.

6. Nature of the Report

A report is an objective statement of the investigator's findings. It is an official record of the information relevant to the investigation. A case may not go to trial for months after the completion of the investigation. A report may be used to supplant loss of memory, missing notebooks, or an unavailable investigator. Reports should be well written. Poor grammar or sentence structure, misspellings, or improperly used words can be used to discredit the investigator.

7. Qualities

The effective report writer should strive to be accurate, clear, and brief. Avoid jargon and uncommon abbreviations. The report should be objective and impartial. The purpose of the report is not to convict but to describe or narrate. The report is not the place for the investigator's opinions. It should contain only the facts and relevant information. Everything relevant to the proof or disproof of the crime must be included.

a. **Accuracy**. The report should be a true representation of the facts to the best of the investigator's ability. Information both favorable and unfavorable to the suspect should be included. Statements and opinions of subjects and witnesses should be clearly presented as such. Persons referenced should be adequately identified, and information obtained should be verified by other witnesses, documents, or records.

b. **Completeness**. The report should address questions of who, what, when, where, and how. The reports should present the elements of the offense and the facts that support them. Every lead should be addressed, and negative results from leads should be indicated. Where a lead is not developed, reasons for this lack of action should be given. The report should include important statements, letters, findings of other agencies, and laboratory reports.

c. **Clarity**. The report should develop logically. The order of presentation is not fixed but is determined by the nature of the case. Chronological order is best suited to certain parts of the investigation, while others should be associated with a place, person, or event.

8. Sequence of Reports

In general, all investigative effort should be reported. Activities that are not documented are often assumed to have not been done. Obviously, trivial or irrelevant findings should not be included. The report, however, should include negative as well as positive findings to remove unwarranted and misleading suspicion. An investigation often requires one or more supplemental reports. Reports should be submitted in a timely manner so that progress can be assessed and additional investigation directed. In major cases, status reports may be necessary even when no new significant information has been uncovered. A closing report will be submitted when all leads are developed, and the case warrants no further investigation.

9. Parts of a Report

The report requirements of investigative agencies vary greatly, but usually all reports will contain the following parts:

a. **Administrative Data** is used to properly identify and file cases. Included in this area is the date of the report, file or complaint number, offense or criminal code designation, the suspect's name (if known), address, date of birth and physical description, complainant's identifying and contact information, victim's identifying and contact information, witnesses' identifying and contact information, identity of investigating officers, and the investigating unit or office. The status of the case should also be included. The case may be open or pending if the matter is still under investigation or closed if the investigation is complete, there are no active leads, the complaint is determined to be unfounded, or if *corpus delicti* cannot be established.

b. **Synopsis**. Each report should include a synopsis or brief description of the actions of the perpetrator and a summary of the major investigative steps. The purpose of the synopsis is to provide a brief, informative summary of the nature and important events of the case.

A synopsis facilitates case review and the filing of charges by helping the reader understand the nature of the incident and information included in the report. This is done in a short narrative (usually one or two paragraphs). The synopsis should include an estimate of the value of property stolen or damaged; perpetrator's name, race, date of birth (DOB), address (if known), and status (arrested/at large); and the victim's name and address. The following is an example of a synopsis in a burglary case.

"Investigation revealed that on April 15, 2012, JOHN JONES entered the home of THOMAS BROWN at 6854 Dento Rd. and stole a camera and watch. On 24 April JONES was apprehended at the Greyhound bus terminal in Center City.

JOHN JAMES JONES, W/M, DOB 16 April 1990, 1313 Main Street, Our Town.

Value of property reported stolen: $410.

Value of property recovered: $410.

JONES presently is in the George County Jail."

c. **Details of the Report**. The details section of the report is a narrative account of the investigation. It should be arranged logically so the reader can comprehend the nature of the case and evidence developed. Each paragraph should normally contain a separate investigative step. All pertinent details uncovered by the investigation should be reported and investigators should reference relevant exhibits, evidence, observations, and statements. Jargon and uncommon abbreviations should be avoided, as well as the informalities common in electronic messaging. Headings should be used to provide transitions between actions and events, and to facilitate reviewing and retrieval of information from the report.

d. **Conclusions and Recommendations**. Investigators' opinions, conclusions, and recommendations as to the status of the case and the disposition of physical evidence should be expressed under this heading. Because of investigators' proximity to the sources of information, they are in a better position than a reviewer to judge the credibility of statements in the report. Great weight, therefore, is usually given to investigators' conclusions. It is, of course, incumbent upon investigators to justify or account for any conclusions that are not consistent with the report or not clearly supported by the facts. (Some investigative agencies do not permit investigators to submit conclusions or recommendations.)

e. **Undeveloped Leads**. An undeveloped lead is a possible source of pertinent information that may contribute to the investigation. Any undeveloped lead known to investigators should be listed here. Investigators should try to make each lead specific, stating exactly what information is to be expected from the lead.

f. **Enclosures**. Photographs and sketches of crime scenes, identification photographs, and photocopies of checks are among the exhibits or enclosures that can support a report. Each enclosure should be assigned an identifying number or letter of the alphabet along with a brief description so it can be referenced in the body of the report.

g. **Style**. Clear, simple language should be employed. The use of confusing pronouns should be avoided. Use names, when known, rather than labels such as suspect or witness. Although interviews or statements are often similar, avoid monotonously repeating phrases (unless verbatim language is relevant). Unless third person reporting is required by your agency, write in first person. Most people find it easier and more effective to write in first person. Unless carefully crafted, third person accounts can confuse the reader and drain life from the manuscript.

10. Initial Report

The initial report should set forth the basis of the investigation, i.e., how the case arose, whether by complaint or observation, and on what authority the investigation was begun. The complainant should be interviewed and the crime established. Describe the evidence found at the scene of the crime, the actions of searching and processing, and the physical layout of the scene. Other details about which relevance is not immediately known should be recorded in a notebook. Describe any interviews. Any proposed leads should be documented at the end of the report.

11. Progress or Supplemental Report

In simple cases the initial report can be the final report. In most cases, however, the investigation will require an extended period of time. Progress reports should be filed as actions are taken or to keep supervisors of the investigative team apprised of the progress of the case. These reports might be submitted at fixed intervals of time or as developments occur. Progress reports may also set out new lines of inquiry.

12. Closing Report

When an investigation is terminated a closing report should be submitted. This is done when a case is successfully concluded, all leads are exhausted and there appear to be no further steps to be taken, or on orders from a higher authority. The submission of the closing report does not preclude the reopening of the case or the receiving of new information. The closing report should summarize the results of the investigation and should indicate the status of the case.

13. Miscellaneous

In addition to the information presented for writing a report, the following suggestions are given to assist in reporting commonly occurring details.

a. **Informants**. To avoid disclosing the identity of a confidential informant, the informant should be referred to by a symbol such as "I-2." Accompanying information should not suggest the informant's identity by revealing occupation, location, habits, or other clues.

b. **Minors**. When interviewing a minor, document the consent of the parents and the child's competency as a witness.

c. **Statements**. A statement of a subject should be set forth verbatim, when possible. Investigators may also report the substance of a witness interview or may collect the information in a written statement prepared by the witness. The report should identify the time and place where the statement was taken and location of any written statement by the subject or any recordings of the interview.

d. **Records**. Investigators may use a variety of business records, such as invoices, attendance reports, phone logs, deeds, tax statements, etc. When a business or official record is relevant, the following data should be reported to identify the document: title, location, identity of the person who revealed it, date, and content. If the record is to become evidence in the case, the name of the custodian should be given so the person can be subpoenaed to testify.

e. **Events Witnessed by Investigators**. The time and place of significant events witnessed by investigators should be reported.

f. **Description of Persons and Property**. Describing persons or objects is covered in Chapter 7.

14. Summary

The investigator's notes are a repository of information pertaining to the investigation. Note taking should start immediately upon commencing an investigation and continue until the investigation is complete. Notes should be contemporaneous to the events they record.

A report of investigation is an official business record. It should contain information relevant to prove or disprove the allegations. Every step, whether fruitful or not, should be recorded to show that no logical measure was overlooked and to demonstrate the investigation was unbiased. Reports should strive for clarity and accuracy. Investigative reports may be viewed by many people as a way to evaluate the quality of the investigation. A poorly crafted report may be used to embarrass and discredit the investigator.

ADDITIONAL READING

Coumoundouros, J.: Computerized Report Entry Systems. *Police Chief, 60* (9), 1993.

Cox, C.R. and Brown, J. G.: *Report Writing for Criminal Justice Professionals.* Cincinnati: Anderson, 1991.

Fox, R.H. and Cunningham, C.L.: *Crime Scene Search and Physical Evidence Handbook.* Boulder, CO: Paladin Press, 1988.

Gammage, A.Z.: *Basic Police Reporting* (2nd ed.). Springfield, IL: Thomas, 1974.

George, D.: Computer-Assisted Report Entry: Toward a Paperless Police Department. *Police Chief, 57* (3), 1990.

Hess, K.M. and Wrobleski, H.M.: *For the Record: Report Writing in Law Enforcement.* New York: Wiley, 1978.

Kakonis, T.E. and Hanzek, D.: *A Practical Guide to Police Report Writing.* New York: McGraw-Hill, 1978.

Kelly, P.T.: Increasing Productivity by Taping Reports, *Police Chief, 57* (3), 1990.

Lesce, T.: Lap Computers Aid Report Writing. *Law and Order, 35* (2), 1987.

Levie, R.C. and Ballard, L.E.: *Writing Effective Reports on Police Investigations: Concepts, Procedures, Samples.* Boston: Allyn and Bacon, 1978.

Romig, C.H.A.: The Improvement of Investigative Reports. *Law and Order, 26* (3), 1978.

Seay, W.T.: Report Writing: Do It Right the First Time! *FBI Law Enforcement Bulletin, 57* (12), 1988.

Part II

CRIME SCENE PROCEDURES AND PHYSICAL EVIDENCE

Chapter 3

CRIME SCENE PROCEDURES

CRIME SCENE SEARCH

1. Overview

S EARCHING THE SCENE of the crime for physical evidence can be the most important part of an investigation. Advances in technology and the analysis of evidence, such as DNA, have transformed crime scene procedures. For some crimes, finding a scene to investigate can be problematic. Offenses such as embezzlement and fraud may leave little to find even if the crime scene is located. Crimes of violence, however, result in an interaction between the perpetrator and the environment. Evidence in the form of clothing, shoe impressions, fingerprints, bloodstains, overthrown furniture, disturbed articles, and tool marks may be found.

Investigators should view all crimes as an interaction between the perpetrator and the environment. The criminal's actions affect the scene, and the scene imparts traces to the criminal. Investigators must be able to visualize the interaction between the perpetrator and the scene. Trace evidence such as dust, paint, seeds, and soil may adhere to the clothing of suspects, while they leave behind latent prints and biological traces such as hair, fiber or DNA. Samples of the trace material must be gathered from the scene in anticipation of finding these traces on suspects.

2. Preliminary

Upon arriving at a crime scene, the first responder must determine if suspects are still in the area. If suspects are present, they must be arrested or controlled. Next, aid is rendered to anyone who is injured, and the perimeters of the scene is determined and secured. Creating an inner and outer perimeter is preferable, for it creates a buffer between the scene and those not involved in the investigation. Witnesses should be separated and identified. If time and resources do not permit a comprehensive interview, preliminary statements should be taken. A place should then be selected outside of the inner perimeter for a "command center." Equipment, evidence, and trash generated by the investigation can be placed in this designated area.

Once the scene is secure, only individuals who are processing the evidence should be admitted. All others must be excluded from the crime scene. A log should be maintained of anyone entering the scene. Everyone listed in the log is subject to subpoena. Officers and supervisors not processing evidence may need to be briefed but should not enter the scene. Spectators, newspaper photographers, reporters, and others who are not officially connected with the investigation should be kept at a distance.

3. Assignment of Duties

The nature of the crime, agency policy, and available resources will determine the assignment of duties. For some agencies a team of specialists will process the scene while investigators conduct interviews and follows up on leads. In other circumstances, investigators perform all of the crime scene duties. Regardless, the steps to an effective investigation remain the same; only the division of labor varies.

Someone must take responsibility for overseeing the investigation. The *officer in charge* directs and coordinates, assigns duties, and assumes responsibility for the effectiveness of the search. This is not necessarily the highest ranking officer at the scene. The *photographer* photographs the scene and individual pieces of evidence as they are discovered. The *sketcher* prepares a rough sketch at the scene and later a finished drawing. The *master note taker,* sometimes called the scribe, chronicles the scene investigation by recording observations and descriptions given by the others, notes the time that evidence is discovered and by whom, and maintains an orderly log of the proceedings. The *evidence collector* collects, preserves, and tags articles of evidence. The *measurer* makes overall measurements of the scene and location of each article of evidence or significant object. The search of a large crime scene area may require creating search teams headed by a section leader. If a searcher discovers an object of significance, it is called to the attention of the section leader who will note the discovery and make the necessary arrangements for its collection, preservation, or transportation.

4. The Survey

The individual responsible for the scene investigation may make a preliminary assessment or walk through to determine the resources that will be required. Before entering the scene, as much information as possible should be gathered from the perimeter. Attempt to determine the most likely places the perpetrator entered and exited the scene and avoid them if possible. Be careful not to damage any foot impressions or trace evidence. Evidence is not collected at this time but if transient evidence (evidence that can be easily damaged or may not survive for long, e.g., a wet shoe print) is discovered, it should be collected as soon as possible.

5. The Search

General photographs of the scene should precede the search. Next, a search method is selected. The search plan should cover the entire scene. The plan must be strictly followed to ensure all evidence will be discovered. The crime you think you are investigating during the search may turn out to be something quite different. There is only one opportunity to properly search a crime scene. Investigators must keep in mind that every step of an investigation may be scrutinized by a judge and jury. Methodical notes should supplement the crime scene sketches and photographs. As a basic guide, investigators should examine the scene to establish the *corpus delicti* and the identity of the guilty person.

6. The Mechanics of the Search

The choice of a search method may be dictated by the size and nature of the scene. The choice of method is less important than ensuring a thorough search. Whether a search is conducted by one or more persons, responsibilities must be well-defined. For convenience, the following examples will assume that three people are performing the search.

a. **Strip Method**. In this method, the search area is blocked out in the form of a rectangle. The three searchers, A, B, and C, proceed slowly at the same pace along paths parallel to one side of the rectangle. When a piece of evidence is found, the finder announces the discovery and all halt until the evidence is collected. A photographer is called if necessary. The evidence is packaged and tagged and the search proceeds at a given signal. At the end of the rectangle, the searchers turn and proceed back along new lanes as shown in Figure 3-1. A modification of this plan is the grid or double strip method. Here, the rectangle is traversed first parallel to the base and then parallel to a side (see Figure 3-2).

b. **Spiral Method**. The three searchers follow each other in a spiral path beginning on the outside and spiraling in toward the center (see Figure 3-3).

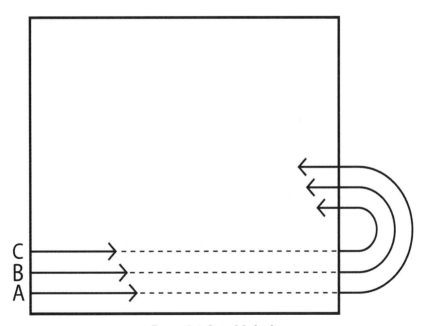

Figure 3-1. Strip Method.

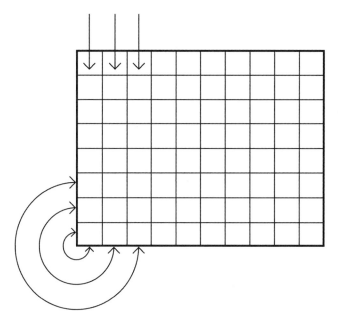

Figure 3-2. Grid or Double Strip Method.

Figure 3-3. Spiral Method.

c. **Zone Method**. One searcher is assigned to each subdivision of a quadrant. When quadrants are large, they may be further subdivided (see Figure 3-4).

e. **Wheel Method**. In this method, the area is considered as being approximately circular. The searchers begin at the parameter and proceed to the center along radii or spokes. The procedure should be repeated several times depending on the size of the circle and the number of searchers. One shortcoming of this method is the great increase of relative area to be observed as the searcher departs from the center (see Figure 3-5).

7. Precautions

An effective search requires both imagination and thoroughness. For example, when searching indoor crime scenes, do not overlook cracks in the floor, ceiling and walls, new paint or plaster, light fixtures, closets, clothing, shades, draperies, door locks, casings, sills, stairs, banisters, under furniture, behind doors, and in trash containers. Also look in toilets (and tanks), fuse/circuit breaker boxes, pipe runs, washing machines, vacuum cleaners, and so forth. Investigators should not run water, flush toilets, or use the telephone at the scene.

8. Evaluation

During the search, physical evidence is collected with little analysis of its relation to the crime. Up to this point evidence is viewed singularly or in small groups. When the search is completed, investigators should give thought to the significance of all the evidence and refine the theory of the crime. Are logical patterns emerging? What exactly does the evidence prove or partly prove? What is missing or unusual by its presence? What additional evidence must be sought to supplement the proof or identify of the perpetrator? Does the case theory best explain this set of evidence, or are there other or better explanations?

Next investigators move to establish the elements of proof and to identify and locate suspects. This involves reconstructing the crime. Investigators attempt to determine from the appearance of the scene and the location of objects what actually occurred. The

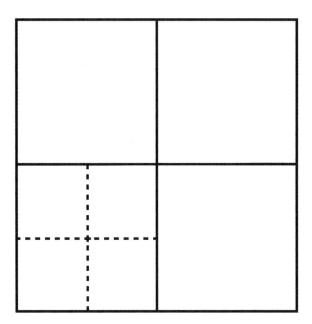

Figure 3-4. Zone Method.

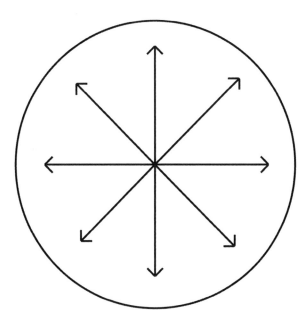

Figure 3-5. Wheel Method.

movements and methods of criminals help determine the *modus operandi*. From a study of the evidence, it is often possible to make useful inferences that may be synthesized into a reasonable theory.

a. **Physical Reconstruction**. If possible, investigators should reconstruct the physical appearance of the scene from the description of witnesses and the physical evidence. If the lighting and weather conditions are relevant, they should be reflected in the reconstruction. Witnesses should be asked to reenact their movements while stand-ins assume the positions of the participants.

b. **Mental Reconstruction**. After reenacting the crime, the consistency of the accounts of the witnesses can be evaluated. Investigators should test the case theory for logic and consistency. Examine events from the point of view of the criminal. No assumptions should be made concerning actions that are not supported by evidence. The theory finally developed by investigators should guide investigative action but not blind the investigator to new facts or inconsistencies.

9. Equipment

The equipment necessary for a proper search of a crime scene is dictated by the nature of the scene and the offense. Some items, though, are useful for investigating a variety of crimes. A quality flashlight and magnifier are useful for searching. Equipment for sketching and photographing the scene are needed (sketching and photographic equipment is covered in a later section). Investigators should also have a basic fingerprint kit (brushes, powders, and lifting tape) and evidence collection kit (disposable scalpels, forceps, cotton swabs, containers such as glass jars, plastic vials, paper and plastic bags, filter paper, envelopes, pillboxes, and cardboard boxes, scriber and marking pen, labels and sealing tape). In addition, various small hand tools are often needed. Finally, investigators must have access to personal protection equipment (gloves, shoe covers, Tyvek suits, eye protection, and respirators) to function in a variety of hazardous environments.

CRIME SCENE SKETCH

10. General

The crime scene sketch plays an important role in an investigation. A sketch gives perspective to the important items in a crime scene. In a photograph, the distances between the various objects may be distorted. Certain objects may not be visible or clearly identified in a photograph. A drawing or crime scene sketch is the simplest and most effective way of showing actual measurements and identifying significant items and their placement in the scene. Sketches are divided generally into rough sketches and finished drawings.

a. **Rough Sketch**. The rough sketch is made at the scene by an investigator. It need not be drawn to scale, but objects should be proportional and appropriate measurements shown. The rough sketch may be used as a basis for the finished drawing. No changes should be made to the original sketch after leaving the scene.

b. **Finished Drawing**. The finished drawing is made primarily for courtroom presentation. It is generally based on the rough sketch and drawn to scale.

c. **Materials**. A sketch of a crime scene may be made with little more than a pencil, a sheet of paper, and a straight edge. On the other hand, a finished drawing will require more advanced equipment or computer software. The following materials will be found useful for sketching and drawing.

1) *Rough Sketching*. For a rough sketch it is best to use a soft lead pencil. Graph paper is excellent for sketching as it provides a guide for lines and proportions. A clipboard, compass (to accurately indicate directions), and measuring devices complete the sketching kit.

2) *Finished Drawing*. The finished drawing is made from the rough sketch. Since the drawing is made to scale, knowledge of drafting and access to drafting equipment is necessary to insure accuracy. (Computer-aided drawings are covered later.)

11. Elements of Sketching

The following considerations apply to most sketches:

a. **Measurements**. Measurements must be accurate. Each measuring device should have a unique identification number and the number recorded in the investigator's notes or sketch. Measurements to a movable object must be taken from an immovable object. Whenever possible, measurements should be verified by another person.

b. **Compass Direction**. Compass direction should be indicated to properly orient the sketch. Normally, an arrow pointing north should appear at the top of the sketch.

c. **Essential Items**. The sketch should portray items important to the investigation. Simplicity is essential, and sketches should be limited to only relevant material. For example, the sketch might include an outline of the room with the doors, windows, chimney, and other large fixed objects. Templates of common crime scene objects (furniture, plumbing fixtures, weapons, and human figures) are available in different sizes to fit the scale of the drawing. The distances between key items and features should be recorded.

d. **Scale or Proportion**. The scale of a drawing will normally depend upon the area to be portrayed and the amount of detail to be shown. The actual or approximate scale of a sketch should always be included.

e. **Legend**. The legend is an explanation of symbols used to identify objects in the sketch. Excessive writing on the sketch generally will result in a clutter that obscures essential items.

f. **Title**. The title of a sketch should contain the case identification (case file number and offense), identification of victim or scene portrayed, location, date and hour made, and name of the person drawing the sketch.

12. Cross-Projection Sketch

Most sketches will show the scene in two dimensions, such as a floor plan. When it is necessary to demonstrate the correlation of evidence in three dimensions, a cross-projection sketch is used. A cross-projection sketch of a room is like a cardboard box whose edges have been cut and the sides flattened. Walls, floor, and ceiling are depicted in one drawing (see Figure 3-7).

13. Measuring Methods

When portraying large areas, it may be necessary to employ the skills of a surveyor. Most scenes, however, can be recorded using one of the following methods.

a. **Rectangular Coordinates**. The simplest way to locate points on a sketch is to give the distances from two perpendicular lines. If the crime scene is a room, the objects can be mapped by using perpendicular walls as the reference lines. A chair, for example, can then be located by measuring its distance from each wall.

b. **Triangulation**. In this method, an object is located by measuring the distances along two straight lines between two fixed reference points. In an indoor scene, the distance from one corner of the room to the object and the distance from the adjacent corner to the object can be used to fix its position. In an outdoor setting, the distance between the object and two fixed points, such as telephone poles or trees, would locate that object. Be sure to record the distance between the reference points.

c. **Base Line**. Base line measurements require a reference point and a straight line (floor seam, wall, edge of sidewalk or street). It is useful to run a measuring tape from the reference point along the base line. A line perpendicular to the base line is used to measure the distance from the base line to the object. An object is located with two measurements, the distance along the base line from the starting point to the point where the perpendicular line meets, and the distance from this point to the object.

d. **Polar Coordinates**. A point can also be mapped by giving its distance and directional angle from a reference point to an object. The system is particularly useful for outdoor scenes. The angle is determined by using a compass.

4. Computer Method

An accurate and detailed crime scene sketch can also be made using computer software. Various programs are available that include templates of common crime scene objects that can be insert-

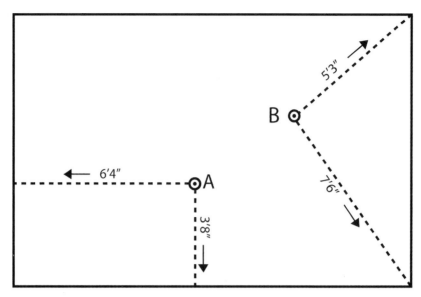

Figure 3-6. Locating points in an indoor crime scene sketch. Using the rectangular coordinates method, point A is located by measuring from A to each of two perpendicular walls. Using the triangulation method, point B is located by measuring from B to two adjacent corners of the room. The corners serve as the two fixed points.

ed into the sketch (see Figure 3-8). After a short tutorial, computer crime scene software is often easy to use and multiple copies can be printed in various sizes.

PHOTOGRAPHING THE CRIME SCENE

15. Use of Photography

The essence of photography is visual communication. Investigators photograph the crime scene to convey relevant events. The type of crime, its seriousness and circumstances will determine the number and nature of photographs. In general, a photographic record is made of the elements of the crime and any relevant activities. The complexity of the crime, the size of the scene, and the amount of physical evidence are other considerations affecting the number of photographs needed.

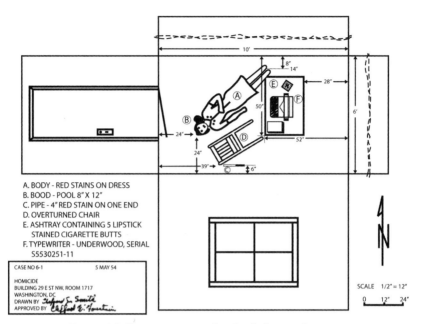

A. BODY - RED STAINS ON DRESS
B. BOOD - POOL 8" X 12"
C. PIPE - 4" RED STAIN ON ONE END
D. OVERTURNED CHAIR
E. ASHTRAY CONTAINING 5 LIPSTICK
   STAINED CIGARETTE BUTTS
F. TYPEWRITER - UNDERWOOD, SERIAL
   S5530251-11

CASE NO 6-1   5 MAY 54

HOMICIDE
BUILDING 29 E ST NW, ROOM 1717
WASHINGTON, DC
DRAWN BY
APPROVED BY

SCALE   1/2" = 12"

0   12"   24"

Figure 3-7. Cross-projection sketch of a homicide scene.

As a general rule, it is better to take too many photographs rather than too few. In most cases, the investigator has only one opportunity to photograph the crime scene in its original condition before the physical evidence is collected and removed. A seemingly insignificant object may later become important to the case. Its appearance and position in the crime scene photograph might have great significance. While investigators may not be able to determine the value of every artifact in the crime scene, photographs can record the scene in its unaltered condition.

16. Purpose of Crime Scene Photographs

a. **To Provide a Permanent Record**. The crime scene photographs provide a permanent record of how the crime scene appeared shortly after the crime was committed, before the objects of evidence were moved or otherwise disturbed. Along with the report and the crime scene sketch, photographs are part of the official record of the investigation. They are used throughout the investigation, prosecution, and trial. If a conviction is appealed, pictures can help reconstruct the crime years later.

b. **To Understand the Crime**. Verbal descriptions of the crime scene are more understandable when illustrated with photographs. Photos help those who have not visited the scene better understand the crime.

c. **For Investigative Purposes**. Crime scene photographs help establish the *corpus delicti* and reproduce the scene. Photographs can be used to verify the story of a witness or a suspect. Does a witness's or suspect's account of the crime correspond to the condition and arrangement of objects, furniture, doors, and windows depicted in the crime scene photographs? Photographs are used to refresh investigators' memories, reconstruct the crime, and reduce the need to handle physical evidence. Witnesses can be shown photographs to reduce unnecessary handling and protect physical evidence from possible alteration. Crime scene photographs are a primary means of conveying information to the judge and jury.

17. Evidence Rules Relating to Photographs

For photographs to be admissible in court, the photographer, or someone familiar with the crime scene, must testify that the pictures faithfully represent the subject matter. The photograph must not mislead the viewer in any significant aspect. A few basic precautions must be observed to insure the admissibility of photographs in court. The object represented should be material and relevant. (That is, the image should tend to establish a fact that is both significant and related to an issue in the case.) The photograph should not unduly incite prejudice or sympathy. Pictures of severe injuries may arouse fear, anger, and indignation in the minds of jurors. As long as the intent of the photograph is to document the relevant facts of the case and not to prejudice the jurors against the defendant, it will be admissible as evidence. Photographs should be free of distortion and should not misrepresent the scene or objects they depict.

Distortions in photographs may occur for a variety of reasons. *Incorrect point of view* occurs when the camera is aimed to obscure essential objects and emphasize others. *Improper perspective* results

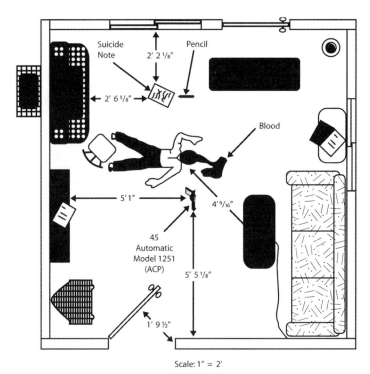

Scale: 1" = 2'

Figure 3-8. A computer-generated crime scene sketch. (Courtesy of Visatex Corp.)

from tilting the camera upward or downward to distort the size and distance of objects. Photographs have the proper perspective when the size and distance of objects appear normal to the average viewer. This can be accomplished by keeping the camera at eye level with the lens pointed at a 90-degree angle to an opposing wall. Another source of distortion results when the focal length of the lens is inappropriate for the print-viewing distance of the photo. A long focal length can compress the portrayal of distance while a short focal length expands it. Anything in a photograph that misrepresents the scene can nullify the photograph as evidence.

18. Photographing the Crime Scene

When photographing a crime scene investigators should create a series of shots that comprehensively cover the events and scene.

The photographer should show the relationships of significant objects to one another. Locations of articles should be clearly seen with reference to recognizable backgrounds. Since at the time the photograph is taken, investigators may not know the significance of all articles of evidence, comprehensive coverage is required.

Digital photography has all but replaced film for general crime scene photography. As the quality of digital imaging has improved, film photography has been relegated to specialized forensic techniques. As with film photography, the quality of the camera, lens, and the photographer's experience all affect the quality of the photograph. Inexpensive cameras are more likely to have imperfections in the lens and a limited imaging array. A cheap camera in the hands of an untrained photographer is not likely to provide useful results.

The highly automated cameras commonly used today can lead to photographers overestimating their photographic abilities. Cameras are designed to capture the images of a normal scene. Forensic photography requires producing images of unusual scenes. This requires the photographer to be smarter than the camera and to override the default exposure setting. Once images are recorded, they should be securely stored in their original format. While beyond the scope of this text, it is recommended that investigators become familiar with the principles of photography.

The following suggestions pertain to photographing a major scene. Homicide was selected because it encompasses many of the techniques that are applicable to other crimes.

a. **Overall Photographs**. Several photographs should be taken to record an overview of the scene. Mid-range and close-up photos are necessary for each item of evidence.

b. **Photographs of the Deceased**. A body should be photographed from several angles. Midrange photographs should show the relationship of the body to surrounding furniture or items of evidence.

c. **Photographs of Evidence**. Take midrange and close-up photographs of evidence (weapons, bloodstains, hair, fibers, papers, etc.) before they are moved.

d. **Markers in the Field of View**. Markers are devices placed in the field of view to aid in interpreting a photograph. In court exhibits, markers draw attention to evidence and help jurors understand its relationship to the crime. To avoid accusations of tampering, it is best to take photographs before and after placing markers in the scene. The scene can then be shown in its original state as well as with the markers in place. Markers must not misrepresent the evidence or conceal any significant part of it. Some common markers include:

1) *Rulers*. Including a ruler or measuring device in the photograph helps to demonstrate the size of objects and the distance between objects. Place a small ruler in the field of view to indicate size when the image is printed or enlarged.

2) *Location Markers*. Number or letter placards are placed adjacent to evidence to show its location and relationship to other evidence. Alternatively, arrows, numbers, or labels can be inserted into a photographic exhibit.

(3) *Identifying Data*. A small sign placed in the field of view can be used to identify a photograph. The information will usually include the date, time, and location of the crime scene as well as the photographer's name. The data should not indicate the type of offense to avoid objection in court that it will prejudice the jury.

e. **Special Techniques**. A wide-angle lens may be used to include more of the contents of a room in the field of view. When a photograph will be used to make comparisons, such as a footwear impression, capture as much information as possible by "filling the frame." For example, compose the photo so that the toe of the impression is placed in one corner and the heel in the corner diagonally across the frame. This will maximize the information recorded in the image. In addition, the surface plane of the impression should be parallel to the plane of the back of the camera. This will minimize distortion. Evidence such as a fingerprint or a tool mark should be recorded by macro photographs to create an image greater than life size.

f. **Photographing the Environs**. The crime scene should not be limited to the area immediately surrounding the body or the apparent target of the perpetrator. If the homicide took place in a house, all rooms and areas that may have been used in approach, pursuit, flight, or struggle should be considered part of the scene. The nature of the crime will determine what needs to be photographed.

g. **Photographing the Body After Removal**. Additional photographs of the body may be required after the body has been removed from the scene. If the identity of the deceased is unknown, photograph the face and any identifying scars, tattoos, or deformities. The face should be photographed from both sides and from the front as normally done for identification photographs. Significant wounds should be photographed with and without a ruler in the field of view.

h. **Photographic Log**. A complete record of each photograph is useful for later identifying photographs. While the sole requirement for introducing a photograph into a court of law is that it is an accurate and truthful representation of the scene, recording how a photograph was created can be useful. This task was much easier when photographers manually adjusted all camera settings. As cameras became more automated, cameras adjusted setting immediately before exposure and recording exposure setting became problematic. A photo log should contain identifying data such as the offense; identity of the photographer; date and time; make, model, and serial number of camera; and the focal length of lens or lenses. Next, photographs are listed describing what is depicted. Additional information such as camera position and exposure settings are desirable but are becoming less common. Any special editing or enhancing techniques need to be reported as well as the chain of custody for the original images.

19. Selection of Point of View

The camera should be carefully placed to provide a perspective that is both normal and informative. Using an incorrect photographic angle often results in a distorted and false impression of the scene. Photos are normally taken at eye level. This is particularly important if the photograph purports to show what a witness could have seen from his or her vantage point.

20. Digital Video

When faced with an extensive crime scene, a digital video camera or camcorder can be an invaluable aide to investigators. A video of the crime scene can provide background and continuity to a collection of photographs by showing the relationship of what may appear to be unrelated pictures. By panning across a room, articles of evidence that have been overlooked or have not been recognized as significant can be recorded. At arson or homicide crime scenes, a video of a crowd of spectators may be used to identify witnesses or even suspects.

Shooting the crime scene with a video recorder is similar to the procedure for still photographs. First, general views are taken by panning across the crime scene. Be careful to pan slowly. Then take close-ups of the physical evidence. It is generally recommended that any narration occur at the beginning of the video to identify the scene, and that audio then be turned off to avoid capturing inadvertent comments.

If a video of the crime scene is made, it should be made in addition to the photographs. The video should not replace photographs but supplement them. In addition, it should be remembered that jurors are used to viewing professional quality video in the form of television and movies. Poor quality police video can appear amateurish and cast doubt on the quality of the investigation.

21. "Posed" Photographs and Markers

It is sometimes desirable to supplement the statement of a witness with posed photographs. A person with the same general physical appearance and dress is depicted as the suspect. He or she should be directed by the witness to the same spot and position as the suspect. The photograph should be taken from the point of view of the witness. If there are multiple witnesses, several photographs should be made to represent the statement of each witness.

ADDITIONAL READING

Crime Scene Search

Becker, R.F.: *The Underwater Crime Scene.* Springfield, IL: Thomas, 1995.

Berry, G.N.: The Uniformed Crime Investigator: A Unique Strategy to Protect and Serve. *FBI Law Enforcement Bulletin, 53* (3), 1984.

Bevel, T.: Crime Scene Reconstruction. *Journal of Forensic Identification, 41* (248), 1991.

Buckwalter, A.: *Search for Evidence.* Stoneham, A: Butterworth, 1984.

Burke, T.W. and O'Rear, C.E.: Forensic Diving: The Latest in Underwater Investigation. *FBI Law Enforcement Bulletin, 67* (4), 1998.

Clede, B.: Forensic Determinations Depend on Training. *Law and Order, 36* (3), 1988.

Crawford, K.A.: Crime Scene Searches: The Need for Fourth Amendment Compliance. *FBI Law Enforcement Bulletin, 68* (1), 1999.

Crime Scene Investigation: A Guide for Law Enforcement. Washington, D.C.: National Institute of Justice, 2000.

Fisher, B.A.J., Svensson, A. and Wendel, O.: *Techniques of Crime Scene Investigation* (4th ed.). New York: Elsevier, 1987.

Fox, R.H. and Cunningham, C.L.: *Crime Scene Search and Physical Evidence Handbook.* Boulder, CO: Paladin Press, 1988.

Garrison, D.H., Jr.: Protecting the Crime Scene. *FBI Law Enforcement Bulletin, 63* (9), 1994.

Gifford, W.D.: A Crime Scene Vehicle for the 21st Century. *FBI Law Enforcement Bulletin, 63* (11), 1994.

Glidden, R.C.: Establishing a Crime Scene Unit. Law and Order, 38 (6), 1990.

Graham, R.K.: Metal Detection: The Crime Scene's Best Kept Secret. *FBI Law Enforcement Bulletin, 64* (2), 1995.

Hoving, G.L.: *Crime Scene Investigation: A Manual for Patrol Officers.* San Luis Obispo, CA: Concepts in Criminal Justice, 1985.

Scene of the Crime: U.S. Government Forensic Handbook. Boulder, CO: Paladin Press, 1992.

Schultz, D.O. and Scheer, S.: *Crime Scene Investigation.* Englewood Cliffs, NJ: Prentice-Hall, 1977.

Tackett, E.: *Underwater Crime Scene Investigation.* Fountain Valley, CA: Lasertech, 1987.

Urlacher, G.F. and Duffy, R.J.: The Preliminary Investigation Process. *FBI Law Enforcement Bulletin, 59* (3), 1990.

Will, J.W.: Sonar: Underwater Search and Recovery. *FBI Law Enforcement Bulletin, 56* (5), 1987.

Crime Scene Sketch

Breuninger, P.G.: Crime Scene Reconstruction Using 3-D Computer-Aided Drafting. *Police Chief, 62* (10), 1995.

Computer-aided Drafting for Law Enforcement. *FBI Law Enforcement Bulletin, 60* (2), 1991.

Fox, R.H. and Cunningham, C.L.: *Crime Scene Search and Physical Evidence Handbook.* Boulder, CO: Paladin Press, 1988.

Kehl, E.: Sketching the Crime Scene. *Forensic Photography, 4* (11), 1976.

Samen, C.C.: Crime Scene Investigation, Part III. *Law and Order, 19* (10), 1971.

Scott, J.D.: *Investigative Methods.* Reston, VA: Reston Publishing, 1978.

Photography

Auten, J.: Traffic Collision Investigation: Photographing the Crime Scene. *Law and Order, 35* (1), 1988.

Chernoff, G. and Herschel, S.: *Photography and the Law.* New York: Amphoto, 1978.

Dey, L.M.: Night Crime-Scene Photography. *Law and Order, 21* (4), 1973.

Duckworth, J.E.: *Forensic Photography.* Springfield, IL: Thomas, 1983.

Geberth, V.J.: A Return to the Scene of the Crime: Using Videotape in Homicide Investigations. *Law and Order, 44* (3), 1996.

Giacoppo, M.: The Expanding Role of Video in Court. *FBI Law Enforcement Bulletin, 60* (11), 1991.

Harman, A.: Videotaping by Police. *Law and Order, 36* (9), 1988.

Kilpack, L.: Use of Video Camera for DUI Investigation. *FBI Law Enforcement Bulletin, 56* (5), 1987.

MacFarlane, B.A.: Photographic Evidence: Its Probative Value at Trial and the Judicial Discretion to Exclude it from Evidence. *Criminal Law Quarterly, 16* (149), 1974.

Mayer, R.E.: Minilabs in Law Enforcement. *Law and Order, 38* (7), 1990.

——: Versatile Compact 35mm Cameras. *Law and Order, 38* (5), 1990.

McEvoy, R.T., Jr.: Surveillance Photography: What You Need to Know. *Law Enforcement Technology,* February/March, 1986.

Mestel, G.S.: Video Camcorders Offer a New Edge in Crime Scene Documentation. *Police Chief, 54* (12), 1987.

O'Brien, K.P. and Sullivan, R.C.: *Criminalistics: Theory and Practice* (3rd ed.). Boston: Allyn and Boston, 1980.

O'Hara, C.E.: *Photography in Law Enforcement.* Rochester, Eastman Kodak, 1963.

Poutney, H.: *Police Photography.* New York: Elsevier, 1971.

Redsicker, D.R.: *The Practical Methodology of Forensic Photography.* New York: Elsevier, 1991.

Samen, C.C.: Major Crime Scene Investigation – Basic Photography, Part II. *Law and Order, 19* (9), 1971.

Sansome, S.J.: *Police Photography: Law Enforcement Handbook.* Cincinnati: Anderson, 1977.

Schmidt, J.: A Changing Picture: Instant Photography in Policing. *Police Chief, 58* (12), 1991.

Scott, C.C.: *Photographic Evidence* (2nd ed., 3 vols.). St. Paul: West Publishing, 1969.

Siljander, R.P. and Fredrickson, D.D.: *Applied Police and Fire Photography* (2nd ed.). Springfield, IL: Thomas, 1997.

Unsworth, S.H. and Forte, R.M.: Waltham Police Benefit from Focus on Instant Photography. *Law and Order, 39* (9), 1991.

Young, P.A.: Night Photography. *Police Research Bulletin, 28* (21), 1976.

Chapter 4

FINGERPRINTS

1. Introduction

INVESTIGATORS HAVE LONG SEARCHED for a means to identify individuals. Early attempts included tattooing, branding, physical description, measuring, and photographing. The latter three methods are still in use. In the early twentieth century, fingerprints became the dominate means of identification. Advances in electronic fingerprint databases and automated searching have greatly enhanced investigative capabilities.

An intricate set of ridges on the palmar surfaces of the hands and on the soles of the feet are found in both men and apes. They function to improve grip like the tread of a tire. These ridges are formed in the dermal layer of skin during the third or fourth fetal month and remain throughout life. They change only in size during growth. The patterns of loops, arches, and whorls remain unchanged throughout life.

Identification is made by comparing details of the ridges. A number of points of minutia must correspond with no unexplainable discrepancies for a match to be declared. There was once thought to be a minimum number of corresponding characteristics necessary to establish identification. In 1973, the International Association for Identification, after examining this issue for three years, decided there was no scientific basis for this requirement. Identification is established when an experienced examiner determines there is sufficient similarity between two prints. The success of fingerprint identification stems from the print's attributes of permanence, universality, uniqueness, ease of recording, and simplicity of classification.

a. **Permanence**. Although cuts, burns, and skin diseases may produce temporary disfigurement of the ridge pattern, the ridges will ordinarily resume their original appearance on healing. Permanent destruction of the ridges occurs when the damage extends into the dermal layer of skin.

b. **Universality**. Criminals have occasionally mutilated their fingertips to destroy the fingerprints. Where fingers have been mutilated, the scars serve equally well in identifying the individual.

c. **Uniqueness**. Throughout the history of fingerprint examination, no two persons have been found to share the same fingerprint. In addition, the statistical probability of two individuals sharing the same fingerprint characteristics is negligible when compared to the world population.

d. **Simplicity of Recording**. Fingerprints are easily recorded by merely inking a finger and pressing it against paper. This procedure is not complex but does require practice to produce usable inked impression. Unfortunately, some investigators never put forth sufficient effort to master the technique. As a consequence, many fingerprint cards are submitted to identification bureaus with poorly recorded prints that are unsuitable for classification. Today many of these issues are overcome through the electronic scanning of fingerprints. Though scanning is replacing the ink and paper method of recording fingerprints, there are still benefits to learning the older method. It helps the investigator develop a better appreciation of what is needed to record an acceptable print. The skill also allows investigators to record fingerprints when an electronic scanner is not available. The proper procedures for learning to record inked impressions are readily available from many sources including the Internet.

e. **Simplicity of Classification**. The traditional manner of classifying fingerprints requires extensive training but is reasonably reliable and not overly complex. Electronic scanning has reduced the labor required to record and file fingerprints.

2. The Nature of a Fingerprint

No two objects are alike. Fingerprints, paper clips, sheets of paper, or blades of grass cannot be found in identical pairs. Close examination will always reveal differences. The fingerprint pattern is a configuration of ridges and intervening depressions or valleys. The ridges are dotted irregularly with pores, the orifices from which perspiration is emitted. When the fingerprint pattern is recorded, the minute details of the ridge structure display both characteristic and unique qualities making classification and identification possible.

3. Sole Prints

Identifiable friction ridge detail is found on the fingers, toes, palms, and soles of the feet. Though not as common as fingerprints, palm and sole prints can be used to link a suspect to a crime scene. Although there is no generally accepted system to classify prints, they can nevertheless be compared to prints of a suspect.

Infant footprints are commonly recorded for identification. Sole prints of babies are taken shortly after birth to identify the child in the event of a baby "switch." The importance of infant footprints has been demonstrated in both civil and criminal cases.

a. **Infant Footprints**. Both the ridge areas and flexure lines can be used to identify an infant, with identification based on ridge structure preferred. Sometimes the child's foot does not present any legible ridge areas, but the flexure lines of the sole are sufficient in quantity, complexity, and variance to permit identification. Most hospitals are required by law to record inked impressions of newborn's footprints, but these are often inadequate because of unsatisfactory printing techniques. Police departments can aid in a hospital's identification program by providing training in printing technique and periodically reviewing the hospital's files.

b. **Latent Sole Prints**. Latent sole prints are prints made with the bare foot. If the sole print is clearly visible, it should be photographed before further treatment. Occasionally a relatively invisible, or truly latent, sole print can be developed by the methods used for latent fingerprints. Large tile bathroom floors, paper on floors, polished wood, and similar surfaces are receptive to such prints. After development the print should be photographed with the print diagonally filling the camera frame to record maximum detail.

4. Deceased Persons

To establish identity, the investigator may need to fingerprint a deceased person. The technique used will depend upon the condition of the corpse. In extreme cases it may be necessary to amputate the hands or fingers of the person and forward them to a forensic laboratory. Authorization for removing the hands or fingers is determined by law and directed by the medical examiner or coroner. The action taken by the investigator in printing a deceased person should be guided by the fragility of the skin of the fingers. Nondestructive methods such as photography should precede any removal or printing action that might damage the friction ridges. In severe cases, preserve the fingers intact and transport the body to a physician or forensic laboratory.

a. **Recently Dead**. If death has taken place within the last ten hours and rigor mortis has not set in, the prints can be recorded by scanning or using the spoon method. (It should be noted that the presence of an assistant greatly simplifies this procedure.) To record prints using the spoon method, a fingerprint card is cut into strips containing the spaces for the fingers of each hand. The strip is inserted into a curved holder or "spoon," and the fingerprints recorded in the appropriate space. If the fingers are clenched, they will need to be manipulated or soaked in warm water until relaxation is felt.

If fingerprinting of the deceased is not accomplished at the crime scene, paper bags should be placed over the victim's hands before transporting. This protects any evidential material that may be on the hands. Traces such as blood, fibers, hair, and debris should be removed from the victim's hands before fingerprinting.

If the fingers are wrinkled from immersion in water, it may be necessary to fill out the finger before a satisfactory impression can be made. This can be done by means of a hypodermic needle and a suitable filling fluid such as warm water or glycerin. The fluid is injected in the finger in sufficient quantity to restore its normal contour. A piece of string may be tied around the finger at a point immediately above the hole to prevent the fluid from leaking out.

b. **Advanced Decomposition**. When a body is decomposing, specialized techniques are needed. If the epidermis or outer skin is destroyed, the dermal layer can be recorded, since the dermal layer of skin has the same ridge outline in a less pronounced form. Remaining fragments of the outer layer should first be removed. If the resulting prints are not satisfactory, it is often because the ridge detail is too fine to record. In this situation, photograph the finger-print using careful lighting to emphasize the ridge outlines. Sig-nificantly decomposed bodies should be sent to a forensic labora-tory or the medical examiner. Exercise great care to avoid damag-ing the remaining evidence.

c. **Desiccation and Charring**. Desiccated and shriveled skin presents the problem of smoothing out the print surface. This may be done by first softening the skin and then attempting to fill it out by the previously described methods. Charred skin is quite brittle and should be first photographed. Inking and rolling should not be attempted if there is any indication the skin will crumble on manip-ulation.

d. **Drowned Persons**. The prints of "floaters" or persons sub-jected to prolonged immersion can sometimes be taken by actual removal of the skin. The operator places the removed skin over his or her own finger (which is first protected by a rubber glove) and proceeds to print as though it were his or her own finger.

5. **Dusting-Tape Method**. For extremely fine or worn ridge detail, the dusting-tape method has been found to be superior to the inked method of recording print. Ordinary black fingerprint pow-der is applied to the fingers of the deceased using a fingerprint brush or cotton ball. A piece of white-backed, opaque, pressure-sensitive tape is then applied to the dusted ridges of each finger, peeled off and pressed against a piece of glass or transparent vinyl.

LATENT FINGERPRINTS

5. General

The search for fingerprints should be conducted before moving any of the objects at the scene. There are three types of finger-prints–latent, plastic, and visible. Latent fingerprints are hidden or relatively invisible and must be developed, photographed, and pos-sibly lifted. Plastic fingerprints are impressions of the friction ridges in a soft object such as soap, butter, putty, or melted wax, and are most often photographed. Visible fingerprints are made when the fingers are covered with a substance, such as paint, blood, grease, ink, or dirt. They should be first photographed before attempting to further develop them.

6. Searching for Fingerprints

The process of searching for fingerprints can be flexible as long as it is methodical. For a thorough search, the investigator needs to consider the *modus operandi* of the culprit as well as the surfaces capable of retaining fingerprint. A plan as simple as working clockwise around a room to process articles and surfaces is sufficient if carefully followed. Special attention should be paid to points of entrance and departure, and particularly objects such as doorknobs, window sills, door panels, windowpanes, and porch railings.

a. **Searching for Latent Fingerprints**. Identifiable latent fingerprints may not be found at the scene due to the delicate nature of the print. To deposit a fingerprint on a surface, optimum conditions must be present. The surface must be able to retain the print without absorbing and spreading it. Hard, glossy objects such as glass and enamel-painted walls and doors are ideal surfaces. Dirty surfaces and absorbent materials do not readily bear prints. The fingerprint, moreover, must be deposited with the right amount of pressure. Excessive pressure tends to spread the print and collapse the ridges. Any movement of the finger will result in a smear. Hot, cold, or wet surfaces may not retain the print. The fingers of the person depositing the prints must have a certain degree of moisture or body oils on the ridges. When all these requirements are fulfilled, a good latent fingerprint is deposited.

Despite the obstacles to depositing a print, the value of a print as evidence warrants the effort to search. No general rules can be given concerning the finding of fingerprints. Although prints are seldom found on certain types of surfaces, the fact that such impressions are sometimes discovered necessitates exhausting all possibilities.

Some typical surfaces to be searched for particular crimes include:

1. ***Suspected poisoning***. Glasses, bottles, cups, saucers, spoons, medicine cabinets, bathroom, kitchen, etc.

2. **Shooting.** Firearms, unfired cartridges, ammunition boxes, desk or cupboard where ammunition or firearm was habitually kept, etc.
3. **Cutting or stabbing.** All sharp pointed or edged instruments, broken glass, or crockery.
4. **Automobile used in the commission of a crime and abandoned.** Rearview mirror, seatbelt buckle, seat adjustment lever, edges of doors, radio or GPS display, all glass and smooth surfaces, hood and trunk.
5. **Burglary and larceny.** Areas necessary for access and containers, closets and objects probably handled in searching for valuables.

7. Locating Prints

The investigator should attempt to locate latent prints before beginning any processing. The beam from a strong light held at an acute angle to a surface may reveal impressions that are not otherwise visible. Manipulating an object to view it from different angles may produce a like effect. Breathing on a surface may cause fingerprints to be visible on certain types of materials.

7. Developing the Print

The latent fingerprint must be converted into a visible image before it can be compared or identified. Typically the latent print consists of a residue of 98 percent water and two percent organic and inorganic materials. Some prints may contain body oils and other contaminants. Moisture from the print will evaporate at a rate based upon the temperature and relative humidity. Some method of developing latent fingerprints must be used to provide a contrast between the ridge lines and the background. The selection of a development technique should consider the nature of the surface and choice of print residue to develop. Each development method targets a specific material in the residue (e.g., moisture, amino acid, salt, oil, etc.) to develop. It may be necessary to experiment on a similar surface to determine the most effective method. Some common methods of development include powder, vapor, liquid, and laser light.

a. **Powder**. Powder is commonly used to develop latent prints on hard, dry, and smooth surface. The powder adheres to the moisture in the print to display the ridges. Fingerprint powder comes in a variety of colors to provide contrast between the ridges and background surface with light colored powder used on dark surfaces and dark colored powder used on light surfaces. Fluorescent powder is designed to develop latent fingerprints on a multicolored background. Illumination by means of ultraviolet light causes the powder to fluoresce while the colors in the background remain only faintly visible. A good contrast between the print and the background surface makes it easier to photograph the print.

Brushing the powder onto the object is the most common method of applying powder, although it can also be sprayed with an atomizer or sifted onto the object. Brushing requires a good quality fingerprint brush and the appropriate powder. One brush should be used for each color powder. Powder should be used sparingly. A small quantity is placed on a piece of paper and is picked up with the tips of the bristles as required. It is poor practice to push the brush into the bottles, as this tends to lump the powder and

Figure 4-1. The Zephyra II fingerprint brush features a soft fiberglass bundle composition. (Courtesy of ACE Fingerprint Equipment Laboratories, Inc.)

damage the brush. The brush is used to distribute the powder in a circular motion lightly across the fingerprint until the characteristic outlines of the ridges become visible. More powder is added, if necessary, and the desired density built up gradually. As soon as development is completed, the surplus powder is tapped from the brush, which is now used to "clean" the impression by sweeping excess powder from between the ridges.

Powders differ in their application characteristics. Black powder is course and abrasive. It requires the use of more powder and less brushing. Too much brushing can destroy the print. Light colored powders tend to have a very fine grain and require more brushing. If too much powder is applied to the print, the powder may fill the furrows between the ridges making it impossible to develop the ridge structure. Some technicians select a powder based upon its developing characteristics rather than its contrasting color. If properly lighted, an acceptable photograph can usually be made to distinguish the ridge structure from the background.

b. **Ferromagnetic Mixtures**. The Magna-Brush® functions as a brush but is less likely to damage the fingerprint because only the powder touches the surface. Magnetic powder is composed of fingerprint powder and very fine magnetic particles. When a magnetic wand is inserted into the powder, a ball of powder adheres to the end of the wand creating a "brush." The manner of developed is similar to that used in the conventional brush method. Because there are no bristles, the method is less destructive and more effective on problem surfaces such as disposable drink cups, wood, plastic, cardboard, and so forth.

c. **Small Particle Reagent (SPR)**. SPR is a molybdenum sulfide and detergent solution. When sprayed on the surface, the molybdenum grains cling to fats in the print. Excessive reagent is washed away with distilled water and prints are then photographed and lifted. SPR is effective on wet or dirty surfaces.

d. **Chemical Development**. Absorbent surfaces such as paper, cardboard, and wood require a different method of processing. Chemicals are selected for their ability to react with organic and inorganic materials in the print residue and make the ridge structure visible through staining. The chemical is generally applied to the object by fuming, immersion, or spraying. Most of these methods involve the use of toxic agents and should only be used by trained technicians in an appropriate laboratory setting. New methods emerge regularly, so this discussion is limited to the most common techniques.

e. **Fuming**. Developing a fingerprint by exposing it to a chemical vapor is called fuming. The two most frequently used fuming techniques are the iodine method, which is excellent on porous surfaces such as paper and cardboard, and the cyanoacrylate method, which works well on nonporous surfaces such as glass, metal, plastic, and leather.

1) *Iodine*. Exposing paper or cardboard to a flow of iodine vapor will make latent prints visible. Iodine vapors can be generated by gently heating iodine crystals in a glass tank or using a portable iodine fuming pipe. The fuming pipe operator blows into a tube containing iodine crystals and the warmth of the operator's breath provides a stream of vapor that can be directed as desired. The iodine's effect is temporary so fingerprints should be photographed as soon as maximum contrast is visible.

2) *Cyanoacrylate (Super Glue)*. The cyanoacrylate method is a fuming technique, invented by the Japanese National Police in 1978. It is effective in developing fingerprints on nonporous materials such as glass, metal, tin foil, wax paper, plastic bags, disposable drinking cups, and also leather. It is often referred to as the Super Glue method because that product is composed of approximately 98 percent cyanoacrylate ester.

The object to be processed is placed in an airtight glass or plastic container in such a way as to insure that all of its sides are exposed to the vapor. The fuming process is accelerated by heating a few drops of glue or by adding the glue to cotton dipped in a sodium hydroxide solution. In about one-half hour to an hour, a gray and white image will appear as the glue vapor adheres to the friction ridges of the print. Hand held wands are also available to vaporize the superglue for field and laboratory use. When it is fully visible, the fingerprint is photographed and then developed with powder. The resulting print can be lifted several times because the glue has hardened the impression.

Figure 4-2. (A) Latent fingerprint on a multi-colored paper surface developed with iodine fumes. Note that much of the print detail is lost as a result of the dark portions of the background. (B) Photograph of the same print after being lifted. (Courtesy of Raymond B. Siljander and Darin D. Fredrickson from *Applied Police and Fire Photography*, 2nd ed.)

f. **Spraying or Immersion**. A variety of substances have been proposed for the chemical development of latent fingerprints on paper and wood. Ninhydrin and Physical Developer are widely used.

1) *Ninhydrin*. Ninhydrin is widely used to develop prints on paper. When sprayed over the document it reacts with amino acids. Care should be exercised to guard against over-spraying, since the excess may dissolve the prints. After optimal spraying, the document is heated in an oven at a temperature between 80° and 140° C until pink areas are observed. With the passage of time the fingerprints will acquire a deeper shade of pink, improving in contrast for photographic purposes even after several days. Ninhydrin can also be applied by immersing the document in a tray of the solution.

2) ***Physical Developer***. Physical Developer is a silver nitrate. reagent commonly used if ninhydrin fails to develop prints. It is particularly useful for developing prints on porous surfaces that had once been wet. Because Physical Developer removes the proteins from the surface, it should be used after trying ninhydrin or iodine fuming.

3) ***DSO***. DSO (1,8-diazafluorenone) has proven more sensitive than ninhydrin on porous surface. It stains prints to fluoresce when exposed to an Alternative Light Source.

e. **Alternative Light Source**. An Alternative Light Source (ALS) is an intense light that is passed through a combination of filters to separate it into its component wavelengths (a laser is one type). In general, when the correct wavelength is used, a fingerprint or biological stain will fluoresce. The use of ALS to illuminate fingerprints is a recent advancement in print processing. Laser detection was pioneered in 1976 in a joint venture of the Ontario Provincial Police and the Xerox Research Center. In this method, a concentrated beam of blue laser light produced by an argon ion laser is directed on the area to be examined. Fingerprint residues will become luminescent in the presence of laser light. These fingerprint residues will absorb the light and reemit it at a different wavelength. With the use of specially filtered goggles, the latent print becomes visible as a yellow-orange luminescence. Using a similarly filtered lens, the print can then be photographed.

The ALS method requires no pretreatment of the specimen, but chemicals may be applied to enhance the image. It is non-destructive, and will not alter the evidence, so it can be used prior to the application of powder and chemical methods. ALS detection is especially useful on difficult surfaces, such as styrofoam, cloth, skin, and places where conventional methods will not work. This method is also helpful with old prints. Using the laser technique, the FBI was able to detect a fingerprint of a Nazi war criminal on a postcard dating from the 1940s.

9. Photography

Latent fingerprints should be photographed after being developed and before any other measures are taken to preserve them.

Table 4-1. Latent Fingerprint Development.

Property of	Method	Operation	Effect	Color	Surfaces
Moister	Powder	Brush or Spray	Adhere to Ridges	Color of Powder	Smooth, Glazed or Sized
Fatty Material	Iodine Reagent	Fuming	Darkens Ridges	Brown	Paper & Wood
Chloride Ion	Silver Nitrate	Immersion & Exposure to Light	Sensitive to Sunlight & U.V.	Dark Brown	Paper & Wood
Amino Acids	Ninhidrin	Spray or Immersion	Organic Reagent	Pink	Old prints on a variety of surfaces

Photographs may be taken with a fingerprint camera or other high resolution camera.

A fingerprint camera is a specially designed, fixed focus camera used to copy fingerprints that are developed on a flat or nearly flat surface. If the surface is curved beyond the capabilities of the fingerprint camera to record a sharp image, another type should be used. The fingerprint camera produces a copy of the latent print at its natural size, that is, a one to one replication. The basic fingerprint camera is easy to use, requiring only a minimum of photographic training and experience.

Other high resolution cameras, in the hands of an experienced photographer, can be used to produce quality images. Cameras with larger sensor arrays, or film formats, record more detail and produce better quality images.

10. Handling and Transporting

Handling and removing objects bearing fingerprints must be done with great care. Gloves should be worn and articles should be touched only where there is little likelihood of disturbing a latent fingerprint. Never wrap an object in a handkerchief or a towel.

Cellophane sheets or envelopes may be used for protecting papers. Fired bullets and cases should be placed separately in small boxes or vials. Small objects such as these should not be placed in paper bags. After photographing the latent prints, objects bearing fingerprints should be marked for identification and packed to protect prints.

If it is inconvenient to move an object because of its size or weight, it may be necessary to detach the part bearing the fingerprint. For example, doors, windows, furniture legs, or drawers may need to be removed. Under ordinary circumstances, the fingerprint should be left on the surface where it was found.

11. Elimination Prints

When fingerprints are found at the scene of the crime, the investigator will need to eliminate the prints of persons who have legitimate access to the scene. This may include members of the household, employees of a business, or even police officers and other emergency responders. If elimination prints cannot be recorded at the scene, arrangements should be made to acquire these prints later.

12. Lifting

Lifting is the process of physically removing latent fingerprints from their original surface. Under ideal conditions, a skilled technician can lift most latent prints. There are, however, dangers involved and prints can be ruined. It is always a good practice to first photograph the print before any attempt is made to lift it.

a. **Techniques**. Most prints are lifted using transparent tape. Once developed, the tape should be anchored to the surface adjacent to the latent print. The tape is then carefully slid over the print to avoid air bubbles. After covering the print, firmly rubbing the tape will help eliminate air bubbles and increase the adhesiveness of the tape. The tape is then carefully peeled back and reapplied to a fingerprint backer. Rubber fingerprint lifters are less common but still used to lift latent fingerprints. The process is similar to using tape but the lifted image is viewed in reversed. When using a clear backer, a small tab or paper, inscribed with pertinent identifying data, can also be attached to the tape.

13. Palm Prints

Palm prints are commonly found at crime scenes. The perpetrator may deposit a palm print by leaning on a table or crawling through a window. Palm print identification is similar to that of fingerprints. The permanent, unalterable pattern of friction ridges and flexure lines on the palm varies with the individual. When two patterns are found to correspond in a sufficient number of characteristics and no unexplainable discrepancies, the expert may conclude that they were made by the same hand. Palm prints are developed and photographed in the same manner as fingerprints. When obtaining comparison prints from a suspect, be sure to capture the entire palm area.

14. Poroscopy

Identification through poroscopy remains controversial and is presented here for historical and educational purposes. The friction ridges of the palms and fingers of the hand contain pores. Each ridge is dotted by pores which differ in position, shape, and size. Poroscopy uses the pore pattern to identify the suspect when only a few friction ridges are found. Since the pores are permanent and appear in an infinite variety of patterns, an identification in this manner has the same theoretical validity as that of a fingerprint. The technique is not commonly used because the outlines of the pores are so delicate that they are generally not clearly visible in latent prints.

a. **Poroscopy Controversy**. Since pore prints are extremely delicate and easily destroyed, they are difficult to record. Pore location and shape may be distorted in the development process. Fingerprint powder, dirt, or other contaminants may hide or alter the shape of a pore, as can recording them using ink. Though once considered a promising identification technique, many question its validity and reliability. The research on poroscopy has yet to reach scientific acceptance.

Figure 4-3. A fingerprint with the pores are visible. The wide variation in the shape of the pore is apparent.

15. Earprints

Much as the case with poroscopy, earprint identification was once considered a promising means of identification. Today, the science of earprint identification is questioned and convictions are being overturned by the courts. As with poroscopy, this section is presented for historic and educational purposes.

At his trial in Lusanne, Switzerland, in 1990, George Roman, a suspect in more than 30 burglaries, was convicted on the basis of earprint evidence found at the scene of the crime. Before entering an apartment, Roman would place his ear against the door to listen for activity inside. In this way, he would make sure that no one was at home at the time of his entry. As a result, his earprints were recovered and identified by the police in 11 of the cases.

a. **Latent Earprints**. While dusting for fingerprints, sometimes a visible outline of an ear is recognized. It is usually found on an outside door or window, or occasionally on a safe door. Latent earprints are produced by the deposit of a thin layer of perspiration and body oils when the ear is pressed against a hard glossy surface.

They are imprints of the flesh lines that form the anatomical structure of the external ear.

Latent earprints are developed with fingerprint powders; magnetic powders work especially well. After developing the print, it is photographed and can then be lifted in the same manner as a fingerprint.

b. **Comparison Prints**. When taking comparison prints from a suspect or someone associated with the crime scene, it is necessary to try to duplicate the amount of pressure which produced the original earprint. Usually several prints are made using varying degrees of pressure. When dealing with partial prints, reproduce only that part of the ear which appears in the original.

c. **Value as Evidence**. At present, earprint identification is questioned and criminal convictions being overturned. Until more scientific study is completed, investigators should continue to collect earprints found at crime scenes but their use for identification is limited.

CLASSIFICATION OF FINGERPRINTS

16. Introduction

Once fingerprints were recognized as a means of identifying people, it became necessary to develop a system for filing and retrieving them. For many years, the Henry System was the most commonly used method of fingerprint classification in English-speaking countries. Over the years, other systems have emerged to better facilitate electronic filing and retrieving. Most of these systems, though, were based on the principles of the Henry System and it remains beneficial to understand the basis of the it.

Basically, the challenge of fingerprint classification is to create a means of indexing fingerprint records. Three common elements include: types of ridges; the location of the ridges; and a method of counting the lines. To count ridges, a point of reference, or starting point, is needed.

17. Ridge Characteristics

The ridges are the basic elements of classification. Some common ridge characteristics are displayed in Figure 4-4. These characteristics are used when comparing two fingerprints to make an identification. An identification can be made when a sufficient number of ridge characteristics are present in both prints with no unexplainable discrepancies found.

18. Basic Features and Terminology

While it is beyond our purpose to teach the complete Henry System of classification, it is useful to understand some basic characteristics and terminology. The characteristics that define a print are found in the *Pattern Area* (Figure 4-5). This is simply that part of the fingerprint that contains the ridges necessary to determine classification. The pattern area is bounded by the *Type Lines* (Figure 4-6). These ridges begin as parallel lines then diverge to surround the pattern area.

Loop and whorl patterns have deltas. A Delta is the first ridge structure located at the divergence of the type lines. Loops have one delta and whorl patterns may have two or more deltas. The delta is the starting point from where ridges are counted.

A *Core* is the approximate center of the pattern area. For a loop pattern, it is located on or within the innermost looping ridge in the area of the shoulders.

19. Pattern Types

There are three basic pattern types: arches, loops, and whorls. Each pattern type is further defined into subcategories.

a. **Arches**. The arch category contains plain and tented arches and makes up about five percent of fingerprint patterns. A *Plain Arch* consists of a series of ridges that enter from one side of the pattern and flow without interruption across the pattern with a slight rise in the center. There are no recurving ridges in the pattern. A *Tented Arch* is similar to the plain arch except that there is a sharp or

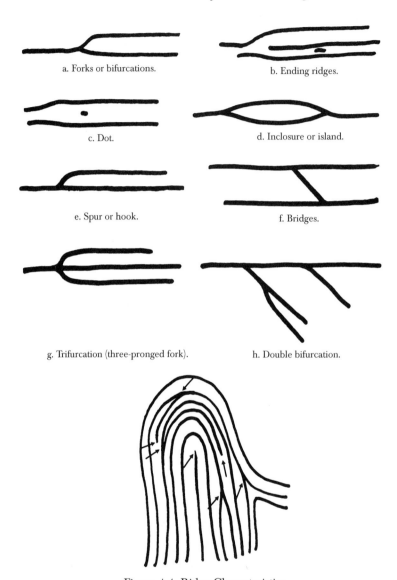

a. Forks or bifurcations.

b. Ending ridges.

c. Dot.

d. Inclosure or island.

e. Spur or hook.

f. Bridges.

g. Trifurcation (three-pronged fork).

h. Double bifurcation.

Figure 4-4. Ridge Characteristics.

Figure 4-5. Pattern area or working.

Figure 4-6. Type lines.

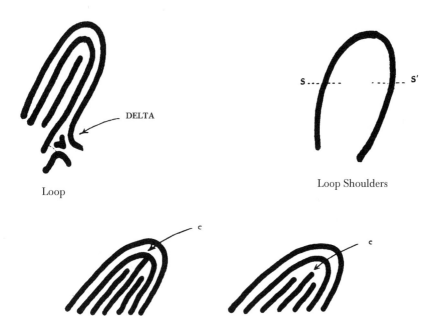

Loop

Loop Shoulders

Figure 4-7. Locating the delta, shoulders and core of loop patterns.

Figure 4-8. Locating the core for an even number of rods.

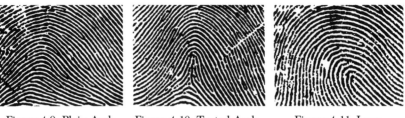

Figure 4-9. Plain Arch.   Figure 4-10. Tented Arch.   Figure 4-11. Loop.

angular rise in the center of the pattern. A very sharp peak is noted in most tented arches and a definite angle is formed by the upward thrust of the ridges.

b. **Loops**. Loops are the most common pattern type making up about 60 percent of fingerprint patterns. A loop is formed by one or more ridges entering at one side of the pattern, continuing up to the center of the pattern, and recurving around and between the core and delta, then flowing in the opposite direction and terminating on the same side from which they entered. Loops are further classified by their *ridge count,* or the number of ridges passing between the core and delta. *Radial loops* are those that have a flow of ridges starting and terminating in the direction of the thumb of the same hand on which they are found. *Ulnar Loops* denote a pattern

Figure 4-12. Downward slope of radial loop, recurving toward the thumb.

Figure 4-13. Radial and ulnar loops (the directions will vary depending on whether it is the left or right hand).

where ridges flow in the direction of the little finger of the hand. It should be noted that loops are divided into radial and ulnar according to the way they flow on the hands and not according to the arrangement on the fingerprint card.

c. **Whorls**. Whorls account for approximately 35 precent of fingerprint patterns. A *Plain Whorl* is a pattern in which one or more ridges appear to revolve around a center point often making a complete circuit. All whorls have two or more deltas, located below and to the right and left of the center of the pattern. In the plain whorl pattern an imaginary straight line drawn between deltas will cut one or more of the recurving ridges that completely encircle the core. A *Central Pocket Loop Whorl* closely resembles an ordinary loop, but has a recurving ridge or ridges in the center of the pattern, which forms a pocket within the loop. A *Double Loop Whorl* consists of two separate but not necessarily unconnected loop formations. There are two distinct sets of shoulders and two deltas. An *Accidental Whorl* is an unusual ridge pattern that does not conform to any of the rules that would apply to the other patterns. This accidental formation is a natural condition and is not caused by any injury to the finger. Whorl patterns are further defined by tracing the ridge flow from the left to right delta and counting the number of intervening ridges.

20. Henry Classification

The Henry System of classification assigns a formula to a set of fingerprint impressions based on pattern types and their location. This formula consists of letters and numbers written above and below a horizontal line. All ten fingers are used. The formula will include a key and major division and the primary, secondary, subsecondary, and final. The following is an illustration of a typical classification:

Key	Major	Primary	Secondary	Sub-Secondary	Final
17	L	1	U	III	4
	S	1	U	IIO	

The components of the formula are determined by the pattern types, the location of whorl patterns, ridge counts and ridge traces.

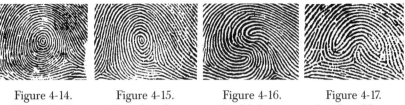

| Figure 4-14. | Figure 4-15. | Figure 4-16. | Figure 4-17. |
| Plain whorl. | Central pocket. | Double loop. | Accidental loop. |

21. NCIC Fingerprint Classification System

The National Crime Information Center (NCIC) computerized Wanted Persons File contains outstanding warrants and criminal histories. In November, 1971, a file known as Computerized Criminal History (CCH) was added to the NCIC data base. The file contains personal descriptions of individuals arrested for serious crimes and the disposition of the arrest. Developed in conjunction with local, state, and federal NCIC participants, this file was designed to meet the needs of criminal justice agencies for prompt criminal his-

1. Thumb	2. Index	3. Middle	4. Ring	5. Little
a	W	\	w	t

6. Thumb	7. Index	8. Middle	9. Ring	10. Little
r	/	/	w	/

Figure 4-18. Right (top) and Left (bottom) hand with pattern types (a = arch, w = whorl, \ or / = ulnar loop, t = tented arch, r = radial loop).

Figure 4-19. Ridge counting a loop pattern.

tory information. Included in this data is the subject's NCIC FPC (Finger Print Classification). The NCIC FPC is not a positive identifier, but it can aid in establishing the identity of an individual, particularly when a subject possesses a common name.

The FPC consists of a twenty-character field. Two characters are to be used for each finger starting with the right thumb and ending with the left little finger.

An example of the NCIC FPC for a set of fingerprints made up of all ulnar loops might thus read: 12101116141109111713. The same fingerprints with #2 and #7 fingers being radial loops would appear as follows: 12601116141159111713. For a set of fingerprints that contains the following: #1 finger is an ulnar loop with 12 ridge counts, #2 finger has been amputated, #3 finger is a plain arch, #4 finger is a central pocket loop with outer tracing, #5 finger is an ulnar loop with 4 counts, #6 finger is completely scarred, #7 finger is a radial loop with 9 ridge counts, #8 finger is a tented arch, #9 finger is a double loop with a meeting tracing, and #10 finger is an ulnar loop with 10 ridge counts. Applying the foregoing rules, the correct NCIC FPC would be: 12XXAACO04SR59TTdM10.

22. Automated Fingerprint Identification System (AFIS)

In 1985, California unveiled a new automated fingerprint identification system. It was first used to identify a latent print found on an orange Toyota in Los Angeles two days before. The print was thought to have been left by the "Night Stalker," a brutal serial killer who had terrorized Los Angeles for seven months, and was

Table 4-2. NCIC Fingerprint Code.

Pattern Type	Pattern Subgroup	NCIC FPC Code
ARCH	Plain ARCH	AA
	Tented ARCH	TT
LOOP	Radial LOOP	2 numeric characters. Determine actual ridge count and add fifty (50). E.G., if the ridge count of a radial loop is 16, add 50 to 16 for a sum of 66. Enter this sum (66) in the appropriate finger position of the FPC field.
	Ulnar LOOP	2 numeric characters indicating actual ridge count (less than 50). If the ridge count is less than 10, precede actual count with a zero. E.g., ridge count of 14, enter as 14; ridge count of 9, enter as 09.
WHORL	Plain WHORL	Enter "P" followed by tracing of whorl.
	Inner tracing	PI
	Meeting tracing	PM
	Outer tracing	PO
	Central Pocket Loop WHORL	Enter "C" followed by tracing of whorl.
	Inner Tracing	CI
	Meeting tracing	CM
	Outer tracing	CO
	Double1 Loop WHORL	Enter "d" followed by tracing of whorl. In double loop whorl pattern the small letter "d" is utilized when classifying prints in lieu of the capital "D" in order to make the handwritten character more distinguishable from the handwritten letter O. When entered in a computer data base or when the NCIC FPC is otherwise typed or printed out, the capital "D" will be used instead of the small letter "d" to avoid the complications involved in having to provide both upper (capital letter) and lower (small letter) case character sets.
	Inner tracing	dI
	Meeting tracing	dM
	Outer tracing	Enter "X" followed by tracing of whorl.
	Accidental WHORL	XI
	Inner tracing	XI
	Meeting tracing	XM
	Outer tracing	XO

Table 4-2—Continued

Pattern Type	Pattern Subgroup	NCIC FPC Code
	MISSING/ AMPUTATED FINGER[2]	XX
	COMPLETELY SCARRED OR MUTILATED PATTERN[3]	SR

1. In double loop whorl patterns the small letter d is utilized in lieu of the capital D in order to make it more distinguishable from the handwritten letter O.
2. Used only in instances of missing and totally/partly amputated fingers making it impossible to accurately classify an impression according to the above instructions for NCIC FPC. It is recognized that under the Henry System of classifying fingerprints, if a finger is missing or amputated, it is given a classification identical with the opposite finger; however, this should not be done in the NCIC FPC, since the precise identity of the finger or fingers missing/amputated is not preserved.
3. Used only in instances in which the fingerprint cannot be accurately classified due to complete scarring or mutilation and a classification print cannot be obtained. As in the case of missing and amputated fingers, the procedure for assigning the classification of the opposite finger, as is done under the Henry System of classifying fingerprints, *should not be used* for the NCIC FPC>

believed to be responsible for the deaths of fifteen women. A few minutes after the fingerprint was entered into the system to be compared with the 380,000 prints stored in its memory, it printed out a list of suspects with a similar fingerprint. At the head of the list was the name of Richard Ramirez, a 25-year-old drifter who had previous convictions for drug offenses and auto thefts. Los Angeles Police fingerprint experts confirmed the match and Ramirez was successfully prosecuted.

The identification of single fingerprints found at crime scenes has always been a laborious and time-consuming job for identification experts. In what is called a "cold search," where there is little except the latent fingerprint, the examiner would use a magnifying glass to search through reams of fingerprint cards, comparing the latent print with those on file. In a typical case, examiners would first examine the prints of those suspects living in the area of the crime scene and expand in a widening circle to adjacent neighborhoods. In a large city with a mobile criminal population, this system was rarely successful. Because "cold searching" was so time consuming and unproductive, latent fingerprints found at the crime scene were used primarily to confirm the identification if a suspect was identified. Now, with AFIS, crime scene prints are simply entered into the computer to search the database.

An AFIS consists primarily of two instruments, a scanning machine, which translates the images of the fingerprint into a numerical code, and a computer, which compares the numerical code of the print with those on file. The computer compares the codes, not the images of the fingerprints. Ultimately, the goal is to maintain all fingerprints only in digital form rather than in images. This technology has evolved into the Integrated Automated Fingerprint System (IAFIS) and in July 1999 become the national fingerprint and criminal history repository maintained and operated by the FBI. The average response time for a criminal fingerprint request to IAFIS is ten minutes.

a. **Recording**. A scanner uses a beam of light to record what are referred to as "minutiae." The minutiae are the ridge details such as ridge ends or splits. Information is recorded digitally consisting of the *type* (whether the minutia is on a ridge line that either splits or ends), *location* (the position of the minutia with respect to marks such as the "core," or center of the fingerprint pattern), *direction* (the angle of the ridge line on which the minutia is located with respect to the "axis,"–or fingerprint pattern direction), and *ridge count* (the number of ridge lines that are counted between the minutia and each of the four closest minutiae).

This information is recorded for each minutia. The scanner has the capability to process up to 100 minutiae for each fingerprint, although the computer can make an identification using as little as eight minutiae. Blurred areas of a fingerprint are ignored.

b. **Comparing**. The computer will compare the numerical code of the "questioned" print with the numerical code of the "known" prints on file. It will then list and rank, in probable order, the names of the people whose fingerprints most closely resemble the "questioned" print. A technician will make a decision on a possible match. It is claimed that AFIS has a 97 percent accuracy rate.

ADDITIONAL READING

Fingerprint Recording

Collins, C.G.: *Fingerprint Science: How to Roll, File and Use Fingerprints* (2nd ed.). Costa Mesa, CA: Custom Publishing, 1989.

Federal Bureau of Investigation. *The Science of Fingerprints: Classification and Uses* (Rev. ed.). Washington, D.C.: U.S. Government Printing Office, 1984.

Olsen, R.D., Sr.: *Scott's Fingerprint Mechanics.* Springfield, IL: Thomas, 1978.

Palm Prints and Sole Prints

See Chapter 5, Additional Reading, "Palm Prints and Sole Prints."

Latent Fingerprints

Allison, H.C.: *Personal Identification.* Boston: Holbrook Press, 1973.

Andrae, D.: Recovering Fingerprints from Skin. *Law and Order, 43* (11), 1995.

Bridges, B.C.: *Practical Fingerprinting.* Rev. by C.E. O'Hara. New York: Funk & Wagnalls, 1963.

Brooks, A.J., Jr.: Frequency of Distribution of Crime Scene Latent Prints. *Journal of Police Science and Administration, 3* (292), 1975.

——: Techniques for Finding Latent Prints. *Fingerprint and Identification Magazine, 54* (5), 1972.

Clements, W.W.: *The Study of Latent Fingerprints.* Springfield, IL: Thomas, 1987.

Cowger, J. F.: *Friction Ridge Skin: Comparison and Identification of Fingerprints.* New York: Elsevier, 1983.

Crown, D.A.: The Development of Latent Fingerprints with Ninhydrin. *Journal of Criminal Law, Criminology and Police Science, 60* (258), 1969.

Dutelle, A. *An Introduction to Crime Scene Investigation.* Boston: Jones and Bartlett, 2011.

Federal Bureau of Investigation. *The Science of Fingerprints: Classification and Uses* (Rev. ed.). Washington, D.C.: U.S. Government Printing Office, 1984.

Futrell, I.R.: Hidden Evidence: Latent Prints on Human Skin. *FBI LawEnforcement Bulletin, 65* (4), 1996.

Gideon, H.J. and Epstein, G.: Latent Impressions on Questioned Documents. *Police Chief, 39* (8), 1972.

Grasman, H.J.: New Fingerprint Technology Boosts Odds in Fight Against Terrorism. *Police Chief, 64* (1), 1997.

Lambourne, G.: Glove Print Identification: A New Technique. *Police Journal, 48* (219), 1975.

Lee, H.C. and Gaensslen, R. F. (Eds.): *Advances in Fingerprint Technology.* New York: Elsevier, 1991.

Micik, W.: Latent Print Techniques. *Fingerprint and Identification Magazine, 56* (4), 1974.

Moenssens, A.A.: *Fingerprint Techniques.* Philadelphia: Chilton Book, 1971.

Nutt, J.: Chemically Enhanced Bloody Fingerprints. *FBI Law Enforcement Bulletin, 54* (2), 1985.

Ogle, R. *Crime Scene Investigation and Reconstruction.* Upper Saddle River, NJ: Pearson Prentice Hall, 2007.

Olsen, R.D., Sr.: *Scott's Fingerprint Mechanics.* Springfield, IL: Thomas, 1978.

Petersilia, J.: *Processing Latent Fingerprints—What are the Payoffs?* Santa Monica, CA: Rand Corp., 1976.

Saferstein, R. *Criminalistics: An Introduction to Forensic Science.* Boston: Prentice Hall, 2011.

Trowell, F.: A Method for Fixing Latent Fingerprints Developed with Iodine. *Journal of the Forensic Science Society, 15* (189), 1975.

Wilson, J.C.: Developing Latent Prints on Plastic Bags. *Fingerprint and Identification Magazine, 56* (6), 1974.

Laser Detection of Latent Prints

Burt, J.A. and Menzel, E.R.: Laser Detection of Latent Fingerprints: Difficult Surfaces. *Journal of Forensic Sciences, 30* (364), 1985.

Creer, K.E.: Operational Experience in the Detection and Photography of Latent Fingerprints by Argon Ion Laser. *Forensic Science, 23* (149), 1983.

Herod, D.W. and Menzel, E.R.: Laser Detection of Latent Fingerprints: Ninhydrin Followed by Zinc Chloride. *Journal of Forensic Sciences, 27* (513), 1982.

Goodroe, C.: Laser Based Evidence Collection and Analysis. *Law and Order, 35* (9), 1989.

Menzel, E.R.: *Fingerprint Detection with Lasers* (2nd rev. ed.). New York: Dekker, 1999.

Menzel, E.R., et al.: Laser Detection of Latent Fingerprints: Treatment of Glue Containing Cyanoacrylate Ester. *Journal of Forensic Sciences, 28* (307), 1983.

Ridgely, J.E.: Latent Print Detection by Laser. *FBI Law Enforcement Bulletin, 54* (6), 1985.

Classification of Fingerprints

Allison, H.C.: *Personal Identification.* Boston: Holbrook Press, 1973.

Bridges, B.C.: *Practical Fingerprinting.* Rev. by C.E. O'Hara. New York: Funk & Wagnalls, 1963.

Clements, W.W.: *The Study of Latent Fingerprints.* Springfield, IL: Thomas, 1987.

Collins, C.G.: *Fingerprint Science: How to Roll, Classify, File and Use Fingerprints* (2nd ed.). Costa Mesa, CA: Custom Publishing, 1989.

Cowger, J. F.: *Friction Ridge Skin: Comparison and Identification of Fingerprints.* New York: Elsevier, 1983.

Federal Bureau of Investigation. *The Science of Fingerprints: Classification and Uses* (Rev. ed.). Washington, D.C.: U.S. Government Printing Office, 1984.

The Fingerprint Identification System. Boulder, CO: Paladin Press, 1988.

Olsen, R.D., Sr.: *Scott's Fingerprint Mechanics.* Springfield, IL: Thomas, 1978.

Automated Fingerprint Systems

Brotman, B.J. and Pavel, R.K.: Identification: A Move Toward the Future. *FBI Law Enforcement Bulletin, 60* (7), 1991.

Fjetland, R. and Robbins, C.: The AFIS Advantage: A Milestone in Fingerprint Identification Technology. *Police Chief, 56* (6), 1989.

Hildreth, R.: The Tenprinter. *Law and Order, 37* (7), 1989.

IAFIS. http://www.fbi.gov/about-us/cjis/fingerprints_biometrics/iafis/iafis

Lucchesi, C.L.: Resolving AFIS Issues on an International Scale. *Police Chief, 65* (9), 1998.

Pilant, L.: The State of the Art in AFIS. *Police Chief, 65* (9), 1998.

Rundell, P.: AFIS Today: An Overview. *Law and Order, 35* (7), 1987.

SEARCH Group, Inc.: *Automated Fingerprint Identification Systems: Technology and Policy Issues.* Washington,D.C.: U.S. Department of Justice, 1987.

Shonberger, M.F.: Miami Police and A.F.I.S. Complete First Decade. *Law and Order, 38* (11), 1990.

Slahor, S.: Leading the Way. *Law and Order, 38* (7), 1990.

Smith, K.: Integrated Automated Fingerprint Identification System. *Police Chief, 65* (5), 1998.

What Is an AFIS? *Police Chief, 56* (6), 1989.

Chapter 5

IMPRESSIONS, TRACE
EVIDENCE AND FIREARMS

IMPRESSION

1. Overview

NO TWO PHYSICAL OBJECTS are alike in all detail, and the impressions made by footwear, tires, or tools might link the perpetrator to a crime. Impression may share common or unique characteristics. Class characteristics identify the kind, make, or model of the object that produced the impression. All objects within the class will contain similar characteristics. For example, all tire prints of a specific brand and model will display the same size and tread pattern. *Individual* characteristics serve to identify the specific object that caused the impression. Examples include the individual striations in tool marks that correspond with the defects of the tool, or nicks and cuts in a tire impression that match the defects in a specific tire.

Individual characteristics are of greater probative value than simple class characteristics but are more difficult to discover. Class characteristics, however, can help associate or exclude individuals or objects from a crime scene. Although class characteristics cannot positively link an impression to a specific object, they can narrow the field of objects to be considered. If one considers the thousands of makes and models of shoes available, the identification of a shoe print as being from a type that is worn by less than one percent of the population is an important clue. If another class characteristic, the size of the shoe, can be determined, it would further limit the number of people who could have made the shoe print.

2. Casting

Casting is a method of recording impression evidence by reproducing its three dimensional form. Ordinarily, a cast is created for comparison to an object suspected to have made the impression. Linking an object to an impression implies the person in possession of the object was at the crime scene. Impressions made by shoes, tires, teeth, and tools can be reproduced by casting.

Casts and photographs both play an important part in the accurate recording of an impression. A photograph will often provide more overall detail, but a cast may better capture three dimensional details. Characteristics found at different depths within the same impression are often difficult to photograph.

3. Foot Impression

Shoes are usually mass-produced so the probative value of any class characteristics is limited. Individual characteristics such as marks of wear and other defects are usually helpful in identifying a specific shoe.

If a number of consecutive footprints are found, it is sometimes possible to detect distinctive characteristics that may aid the investigation. For example, the angle of walk, the length of step, and any infirmities that are characteristic of the person may be reflected in the impressions. However, such characteristics are merely indicative and not a means of positive identification.

a. **Surface Footprints**. A surface footprint is made when material is transferred from the foot or shoe to the walking surface. It is a layer dust, liquid, mud, or perspiration. Shoe prints are the most common. These are often found at burglaries where the perpetrator stepped on scattered papers or other clean surfaces. Floors should be examined for latent footwear prints using oblique lighting. If no prints are apparent, latent prints may still be developed using fingerprint powder and a brush. A shoe print found on any surface should first be photographed, using oblique lighting, with the camera plane directly over the print and parallel to the surface. A scale should be included in the photograph. If a foot print is found in dust, it can also be lifted using an electrostatic lifting device. In this process, a mylar sheet is placed over the print, then an electronic charge is applied. The dust attaches to the mylar film and records the print.

Often general class characteristics can determine whether to exclude a suspect's shoes or to conduct a more extensive examination. When a shoe appears similar to the crime scene print, it should be forwarded to the laboratory for comparison.

b. **Sole Prints**. Prints made with the bare feet are called sole prints. If a print is found, it should first be photographed and then developed as a latent print. Large tile bathroom floors, paper on floors, polished wood, and similar surfaces are good for such prints. Comparison prints of a suspect can be obtained by the regular method used for fingerprints.

4. Casting Footwear Impressions

Although a cast can be made from a number of materials, dental stone has become the most widely used and is available through most forensic suppliers. It is simple to prepare, provides a durable cast, is capable of reproducing fine detail, and does not need reinforcing. Plaster-of-paris, is still used by some investigators because it is readily available at any hardware supply store.

a. **Preparation**. Before casting the impression, several photographs should be made. First, an overview photograph should show the location of the impression in the crime scene. Next, a mid-range photograph should show the impression and its immediate surroundings. Then, close-up pictures should be taken both with and without a ruler in the field of view and with the camera parallel to the base surface of the impression. A ruler, placed alongside the impression and depressed into the surface at the same depth as the impression, permits an accurate guide for creating enlargements of the photographs. The camera should be held by a tripod placed over the impression with the impression filling the camera frame. A light source held at various oblique angles is helpful in revealing detail. Relatively large particles of extraneous matter should be removed to prevent the obscuring of parts of the impression.

If the surface consists of a soft substance such as dust, sand, or flour, a quick-drying fixative agent (plastic spray, shellac, or hair spray may substitute) should be applied prior to casting. The spray should be directed against a piece of cardboard and permitted to settle over the impression. When the fixative is dry, a release agent (aerosol cooking oil or a non-stick spray may substitute) may be sprayed over the surface to facilitate separation of cast from the fixative. If the impression is in snow, several coats of a "snow print wax" should be used.

Estimate the amount of material required for cast (approximately 2 pounds of casting material to 12 oz. of water) and mix with water in a glass, porcelain, or rubber container. Stir thoroughly until the mixture has the consistency of cream. Additional casting material or water is added to achieve the proper consistency.

b. **Making the Cast.** Pour the casting mixture into the impression from a low height. The fall of the liquid should be broken by means of a flat piece of wood. A depth of one-half inch is sufficient for dental stone. Plaster-of-paris must be poured to a depth of one-half inch, then reinforced (with screen, cross-patterned wood strips, etc.) and then another one-half inch of plaster-of-paris added.

The cast should be allowed to set for approximately thirty minutes. In hardening, the plaster first becomes warm then cools on setting. Before the plaster has completely set, it should be marked for identification. The date, case number, and initials of the investigator can be scratched on the upper surface.

After hardening, the cast should be removed and permitted to dry further for several hours. Check with your forensic laboratory before attempting to clean the cast. Once it has completely dried, it can then be washed and lightly brushed in water to remove the adhering debris. If done incorrectly, the cast can be damaged during the cleaning process, so it is often best to submit the cast without cleaning.

5. Tire Impressions

Criminals often use a vehicle to escape from the scene of the crime. Even if the area is paved, there may be opportunities to find tire impressions. If the perpetrator turns too sharply or drives over a soft surface a tire impression may be created. Unless the car was turned or traveled backwards only the rear tire tracks will be visi-

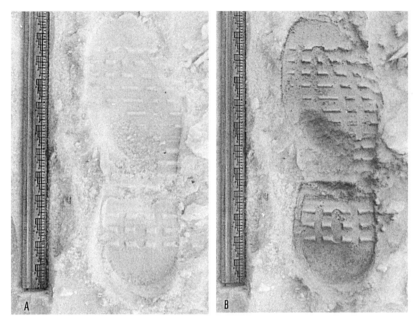

Figure 5-1. Left, footprint in snow on an overcast day. Note the obvious lack of detail. Right, same print after having black fingerprint powder lightly applied with a blower. (Courtesy of Raymond P. Siljander and Darin D. Fredrickson from *Applied Police and Fire Photography,* 2nd ed.)

ble. For a few vehicles, though, the rear wheels are farther apart than the front, and part of the front tire tracks may be visible.

a. **Direction of Travel**. If fluids are dripping from the vehicle, the drops will be tapered toward the direction of travel. On unpaved roads small masses of dirt may be thrown up by the side of the wheels so that they taper in the direction of travel.

b. **Measurements and Recording**. The distance between the wheels should be measured as well as the breadth of the tire track. The tire impression should be photographed and cast in the same manner as a footwear impression.

c. **Tire Tread File**. Many forensic laboratories maintain databases of tire manufacturers' tread patterns to determine the make and model of a tire from a tire impression.

6. Tool Marks

Tools used to commit a crime may leave behind identifiable markings. A screwdriver used to pry a door, pliers used to twist a bolt, or bolt cutters used to remove a lock may leave behind markings that link them to the crime. A tool's working face is seldom smooth and unmarred. Examining a tool under low-power magnification will reveal many imperfections. If there are a sufficient number of imperfections, an expert may be able to match the instrument to the tool mark. The underlying theory of tool mark identification also applies to firearms. Bullets and shell casings frequently bear characteristic markings of the weapon that fired them. Experts can usually determine whether bullets and shell cas-

Figure 5-2. A tire impression photographed before casting. The careful selection of the right angle of illumination serves to emphasize the pattern.

ing found at the crime scene were discharged from the suspect's firearm. Tools, like firearms, differ in size, width, thickness, and general shape. Even for tools having the same class characteristics, minute differences will exist from the accidental defects in the manufacturing process, uneven wear, unusual use or abuse, sharpening, or modifications made by the owner. When the tool is used, these defects or imperfections can be observed in the surface of the object they encountered. Depending upon the number of imperfections found, a tool mark expert may be able to associate a tool to a crime scene, link a series of crimes to a single tool, help establish *modus operandi,* identify the type of tool that could have made the mark, or determine that a tool could not have made the marks in question.

a. **Types of Tool Marks**. Tool impressions will vary depending upon whether the tool was moved along the surface or pressed into it. If a tool such as a screwdriver is used simply as a lever, the resulting tool mark will be an impression. If the blade of a screwdriver is scraped across a surface, striations are created. If forced into a narrow space and then used as a lever, both types of marks may be imparted to the surface.

b. **Handling of Tool Mark Evidence**. Tool impressions are commonly found in burglary investigations. They are most likely found at the point of entry or on rifled drawers and strongboxes. Doors, windows, transoms, and skylights should be examined for signs of forced entry. Broken, forced, or cut locks, latches, and bolts should be studied for marks, along with desks, cabinets, safes, and cash boxes. Tool impressions and tools should be documented in reports, sketched, and photographed.

Protect the evidence until the examination or collection is complete. Never attempt to fit a tool into an impression. Doing so may damage the impression and diminish the value of any trace evidence adhering to the tool's surface. Normally, doors and windows should be fingerprinted before collecting tool marks. After photographs and sketches have been made, the object should be marked with the investigator's initials, date, and case number. The evidence should also be marked to show the inside, outside, top and bottom surfaces, and the area bearing the tool impression.

Then transport the object and any suspected tool to the laboratory for comparison. Where it is impractical to remove the original evidence, the investigator can photograph and cast the tool mark.

c. **Photographing Tool Marks**. Before casting, molding, or removing a tool mark, it should be carefully photographed to record its original condition. First, photograph the tool mark showing its location. Next, close-up photographs are made to show minute details of the mark. The close-up photo should be taken using oblique lighting from various angles with the plane of the camera parallel to the plane of the surface. In both photographs a ruler should be placed in the field of view and to one side, to provide laboratory technicians with a reference scale for examination and comparison.

d. **Casting Tool Marks**. Dental stone and plaster-of-paris will not capture the fine detail of tool marks. There are a number of materials suitable for casting such as silicone rubber, dental impression creams, moulage, modeling clay, and thermosetting plastics. These products produce a high quality reproduction that does not adhere to the mark and is flexible enough to be removed easily from the impression.

7. Number Restoration by Chemical Etching

Manufacturers use serial numbers to monitor quantity, quality, and location as their products move through production, distribution, and warranty coverage. The serial numbers, along with the information contained in the manufacturer's and dealer's records, are instrumental in determining the ownership of the questioned property. To disguise the ownership or origin, criminals sometimes remove (by filing or grinding) or alter the serial numbers on stolen equipment. Serial numbers stamped into metal can be found on motor vehicles and their parts, bicycles, construction equipment, firearms, appliances, office machines, and many other products. When these numbers are removed or altered, it is sometimes possible to restore them by chemical etching.

The removal of serial numbers from automobiles, firearms, and other equipment is against the law in most states. However, for the investigator to prove the more serious crime of theft, it is necessary to establish the ownership of the stolen object. This can often be accomplished if the serial number can be restored.

a. **Theory of Chemical Etching**. When the serial number is stamped into metal, the force exerted on the surface compresses the molecular structure of the metal directly below the numbers. This region becomes permanently stressed to a depth of from one-half to several times that of the printed number depending on the type of metal involved. This alters the structure of the metal and it reacts differently to chemical treatment. If the serial number has been filed away, the imprint of the number may still be restored by the application of a dilute acid or base etching solution. This solution will dissolve the compressed metal at a faster rate than the surrounding metal, making the outline of the numbers visible. Deep filing or grinding, pounding with a hammer, welding it or heating with a torch, or stamping over the original number, may destroy or alter the effects of the original stamping process and the numbers can no longer be retrieved.

b. **Technique**. Because every metal reacts at a different rate, there are formulas for redeveloping serial numbers. The etching solution should not be so strong that the numbers do not have time to develop. The time it will take for the numbers to become visible may vary from a few minutes to an hour or longer.

Photograph the object and area where the numbers should appear. Clean the surface with a solvent. Polish the surface with an emery cloth to a mirror-like finish. Then apply the etching solution with a cotton swab. When the numbers appear, photograph them immediately. The numbers may be visible for only a short time. Add water to halt the chemical reaction and record the numbers or partial numbers. Cast iron and steel react best to a solution of hydrochloric acid (120 cc), distilled water (190 cc), ethyl alcohol (75 cc) and copper chloride (15 g). Aluminum responds best to a solution of sodium hydroxide (11 g) and distilled water (99 cc).

8. Bite Marks

Bite marks may be found in homicide, assault cases, and sometimes burglary (when the perpetrator partially eats food from the scene). Teeth differ naturally in size, shape, spacing, and direction of growth. There are ridges on the edges of teeth as well as grooves on the front and back. These ridges and grooves are different in each individual and continually change due to wear. In addition, teeth acquire additional distinctive characteristics through breakage, loss, fillings, and other dental work. These natural differences and acquired alterations combine to make every set of teeth significantly different.

A bite mark may provide sufficient detail to compare to the dental impression of a suspect. The comparison of bite marks is performed by a *forensic odontologist,* a dentist trained in the recovery and analysis of dental evidence. If several points of similarity are discovered with no unresolved differences, identification can be made. Bite mark evidence may also exclude a suspect.

a. **Bite Marks on Food**. Criminals sometimes sample food at the crime scene leaving teeth impressions on a discarded portion. Fruit, cheese, and chocolate have a consistency that is especially receptive to retaining impressions. Due to the perishable nature of the evidence, it is necessary to photograph and cast the bite marks as soon as possible.

1) *Photography*. Bite marks on food are photographed in a manner similar to tool marks. One photograph locates the object bearing the bite mark, showing its position and background in the crime scene. Then a close-up (preferably at least one-to-one in size), records the details of the bite mark. Oblique lighting is helpful in highlighting the teeth indentations. A ruler should be included in some of the photographs to compare the size of the bite mark with the size of a dental impression obtained from a suspect.

2) *Casting*. A cast will sometimes record fine details missed by a photograph. Casting may be done with a silicone rubber casting compound or some other dental impression material. Often due to the fragile nature of the evidence, only one cast can be made because the process alters the details of the impression.

b. **Bite Marks on Skin**. Bite marks occur most frequently in homicide and assault cases. They appear in a variety of forms including the characteristic doughnut and double-horseshoe patterns. If the teeth have not broken the skin, the bite mark can appear as a bruise. When biting may have occurred, a visual inspection of the entire body is appropriate. Bites that occurred over clothing may be found on the skin underneath. Victims sometimes bite perpetrators and these marks can be used to link the suspect to the victim.

1) ***Occurrence***. Bite marks are common in a variety of criminal cases. In child abuse cases, an enraged parent or guardian might retaliate with a single bite. This type of abuse stems from frustration with a perceived misbehavior by the child, often associated with diaper changing or toilet training.

Bite marks are also associated with homicide. Sexual homicide generally involves multiple bite wounds, often done slowly and sadistically, on or near the genital area. The biting is characteristically followed by a sucking of the skin. The sucking will leave a bruised area of tissue or, in the more severe cases, a hematoma (an accumulation of blood in the tissues following a rupture of the blood vessels) in the center of the bite mark. Because the biting is done slowly and deliberately, it will often leave fine details on the skin. In non-sexual homicides, bite marks may result from the victim fending off the attacker. The assailant will sometimes have a single bite mark on the hands, arms, neck, or face.

2) ***Photography***. A bite mark, as with any bruise, will change color and appearance with the passage of time. They frequently become more distinct after a day or two. When possible, photograph bite marks (on both live and deceased victims) at 24-hour intervals for a period of five days. In homicide cases, the body should be refrigerated but not embalmed during this period. Embalming tends to wash out the color of the bite wound.

Both orientation and close-up photos should be taken. Orientation photographs show the position of the bite mark on the body. Close-up photographs show the details of the bite mark. A ruler should be included in some of the close-up pictures to indicate the size of the impression. (The American Board of Forensic Odontology has designed a scale especially for photographing bite marks.) To avoid distortion, position the camera perpendicular to the bite mark. Because of the elasticity of the skin, the shape and appearance of the bite mark will sometimes change, depending on whether the victim is standing, sitting, or lying down. When possible, place the victim in the same position as when the bite occurred.

3) ***Swabbing***. Saliva around the wound may be used for DNA analysis to identify the perpetrator. Collect samples using cotton swabs and distilled water or a saline solution. Swab the skin in concentric circles working toward the center of the bite mark. Replace swabs frequently. Swabs should be allowed to dry and then placed in sealed, sterile test tubes to be sent to the laboratory for analysis. Control-swabs of the body areas should be included. Collect blood and saliva specimens for comparison from the victim as well as from any suspect in custody.

4) ***Casting and Analysis***. The casting of bite marks is usually preformed by a forensic odontologist or an experienced laboratory technician. Casts are generally made with silicone rubber casting compound or other dental impression material. When a suspect is in custody, dental impressions and photographs are obtained either by the informed consent of the suspect or by court order. If possible, obtain the suspect's dental records. Forensic odontologists compare these materials with the photographs, casts, and models of the bite mark.

BROKEN GLASS

9. Overview

It is not unusual to find broken glass at a crime scene. Broken glass is commonly found at the scene of burglary, arson, shootings, and motor vehicle homicide. The analysis of glass may help resolve some investigative problems. *The direction of impact* can be an issue in burglary and arson cases when it is important to determine whether a window was broken from the inside or the outside. An *analysis of bullet* holes in cases involving firearms may determine the direction and angle of the shot, and sequences of shots when several shots were fired. A *fracture match* in a hit-and-run case may link a fragment of glass found on the victim to the headlight glass of the suspect's vehicle. A *comparison of particles* of glass in a burglary case might match minute particles of glass discovered on the suspect to glass found at the scene. Comparing density and refractive index will indicate whether fragments may have originated from the same source.

10. Types of Glass

Glass is primarily a composite of the oxides of silicon, sodium and calcium. It is formed when silica sand (silicon dioxide, SiO_2), soda ash (sodium carbonate, $Na2CO_3$) and limestone (calcium carbonate, $CaCO_3$) are melted at high temperature and then mixed together until they fuse. Glass manufactures have hundreds of different glass formulas. These different compositions are achieved by varying the proportions of silicon, sodium and calcium oxides or by substituting or adding other metal oxides. For example, lead monoxide is added to produce "crystal" tableware. Boron oxide is added to create heat and corrosion-resistant glass used in headlight lamps, pyrex cookware and laboratory containers. Other oxides are added to color the glass.

Some common forms of glass include *window glass* (soda-lime-silica glass), *plate glass* (break resistant soda-lime-silica glass), *tempered glass* (compressed, rapidly heated and cooled break-resistant glass designed to fragment or "dice" into thousands of tiny cubes with few sharp edges or splinters when broken), *safety glass* (laminated glass used in windshields), *headlight glass* (borosilicate glass that is heat and corrosion resistant), and *bottle glass* (soda-lime-silica with a metal oxide for color).

11. Determining the Direction of Impact

The act of breaking a window leaves behind telltale signs of the process. The glass fragments found around the window frame will indicate from which side the breaking force was applied. This information can be important to an investigation. For example, an investigator at the scene of a burglary may need to eliminate the possibility of an "inside job." Employees who steal from their workplace may break a window to create the appearance that the thief entered the building from the outside. To avoid being seen by people in the neighborhood, they might break the window from the inside. Determining that the window was broken from the inside changes the course of the investigation.

There is a common misperception that the direction of impact can be determined by the location of glass pieces around a window frame. A large amount of glass found on the floor or ground on one side of a broken window does not necessarily mean that the force which broke the window came from the opposite side. There are many factors that affect the distribution of glass fragments.

Glass will break first on the side opposite the point of impact. When force is applied, glass bends on the impact side causing the opposite side to stretch. Bending compresses the glass molecules together, while stretching separates the molecules, creating a state of tension. When the elastic limit is reached, the glass will crack. It will break first in the area where the most stretching has occurred, on the side opposite the point of impact (Figure 5-3).

a. **Fracture Patterns**. The spider web-like cracks in a broken window reveals how the damage occurred (see Figure 5-4). Though not present in every broken window, when found they can explain how the glass was broken. The spoke-like cracks emanating from the area of impact are called *radial fractures*. When the glass is stretched to its limit, it will crack first along lines radiating outward on the side opposite the impact. *Concentric fractures* are secondary cracks on the side of impact. The stretching that causes the radial fractures around the breaking point will cause other areas of the glass to bend in toward the side of impact and result in a series of concentric fractures.

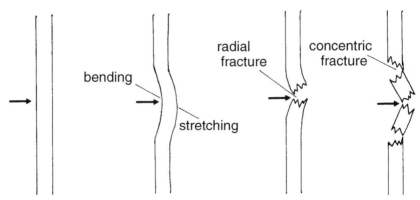

Figure 5-3. Side view of the breaking of a piece of glass. The arrow indicates the direction of impact.

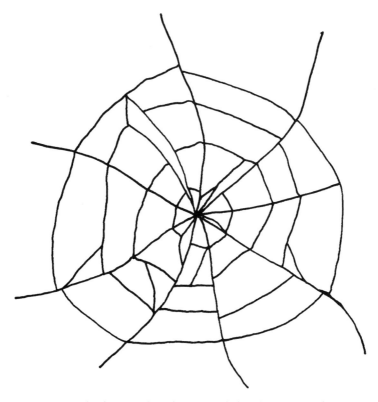

Figure 5-4. A broken window showing radial and concentric fractures.

Concentric fractures form a set of circular patterns around a central point connecting the radial lines around the point of impact. A crack will not cross a pre-existing crack. Because the radial cracks occur prior to the concentric ones, all of the concentric lines are stopped at both ends when they meet the radial lines. Thus, concentric fractures are a series of interrupted lines in a circular pattern around the point of impact.

Rib marks are curved lines of stress that are visible on the edge of a piece of broken glass. These lines run almost parallel to one surface and then curve to become nearly perpendicular to the opposite surface. They are called rib marks because the series of curved lines together resembles a rib cage. Rib marks are always

Figure 5-5. Spider web fracture of the windshield caused by impact of the driver's head. The head did not go through the hole. (Courtesy of Werner U. Spitz, M.D., from *Medicolegal Investigation of Death,* 3rd ed.)

perpendicular to the side of the glass that broke first (Figure 5-6.).

b. **Reassembling the Glass**. A reliable determination of the direction of impact cannot be made from a single isolated piece of broken glass. If radial or concentric fracture lines cannot be determined from glass remaining in the frame, fragments must be collected and reassembling or partially reassembled to establish whether the glass fragment was facing inside or outside and whether the edge being examined is a radial or a concentric fracture. Dirt on the window, water spots and putty marks are helpful in distinguishing the outside surface. When the window is sufficiently reconstructed, the investigator can identify the radial and concentric fractures. An examination of the fractures or rib marks will indicate the direction of the blow.

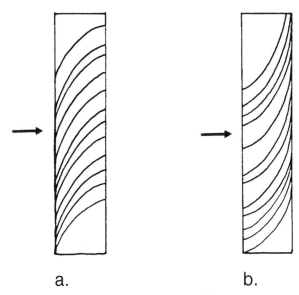

a.   b.

Figure 5-6. Rib marks: (a) on a radial fracture; (b) on a concentric fracture. The arrows indicate the direction of impact.

12. Determining the Direction of Impact

When a significant portion of the glass remains in a window frame and radial and concentric fracture lines are observed, determining the direction of the force is a simple matter of examining the glass to identify the fracture marks. This can be determined by lightly rubbing your fingernail across the fracture line. You will be able to feel the fracture on one side of the glass but not the other. Radial fractures occur first on the side opposite the impact. Concentric factures occur on the side the force was applied. For example if the concentric fractures are on the inside of the window and radial fracture on the outside, then window was broken from the inside.

You can also determine the direction of the force by examining the rib marks. You must first determine if you are examining a radial or concentric fracture line. Radial fractures have rib marks that are perpendicular to the side opposite the side of impact. Concentric fractures have rib marks that are perpendicular to the side of impact.

a. **Exceptions to this Procedure**. The direction of force cannot be determined in some situations. Glass that falls on a hard surface and breaks again will have an additional set of cracks which will complicate the examination. Glass may not bend if the window is small or the glass is too loosely secured. Tempered glass will "dice" on impact rather than form radial and concentric cracks. Windows broken by heat, wind, or an explosion do not have a point of impact. A glass window subjected to the intense heat of a fire will crack with characteristic long, wavy lines. The edge of these glass fragments will be smooth and without the rib marks indicating a point of impact. The pieces of glass tend to fall inward toward the fire sometimes creating the deceptive appearance of the window being pushed in from the outside by an intruder. If safety glass is not hit with sufficient force to complete the fracture, the radial and concentric cracks will not extend all the way through to the other side of the glass. Safety glass, though, often bends and remains bent when struck. Placing a long ruler across the surface of the glass may reveal a concave area on the impact side.

b. **Hackle Marks**. When glass is broken by a sudden powerful force, hackle marks are created and can indicate the direction of

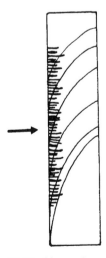

Figure 5-7. Hackle marks on a radial edge.

impact (Figure 5-7). Hackle marks are minute irregular lines found on the edge of a piece of broken glass that are formed when two glass surfaces scrape against each other causing small particles to flake off and fly backwards. When viewed under low magnification, they appear as short lines of varying length located on the edge nearest the impact surface and running in the direction of the force. On a radial edge, they are at right angles to the rib marks.

13. Bullet Holes in Glass

It is often difficult to determine whether window glass has been broken by a bullet or by some other projectile, such as a small stone. When a bullet penetrates glass, it leaves a small, clean-cut entrance hole and a much larger saucer-shaped exit hole as it pushes the glass particles ahead of it (Figure 5-8). A pebble thrown from the tire of a passing car can cause a similar hole in a windshield. Finding the projectile may solve the problem. If a bullet is discovered, sometimes minute glass particles can be found embedded in its nose. Bullets will generally leave a more symmetrical system of radial and concentric cracks in the immediate area surrounding the hole.

If a shot is fired from close range, gunshot residue particles may be found on the pieces of glass. When a shot is fired from long range, a bullet may lose its velocity before it reaches the window. It may turn end over end and enter the glass sideways, making it difficult to determine whether the window was broken by a stone or a bullet.

a. **Determining the Angle of the Gunfire**. When a bullet enters a window, it pushes the glass particles ahead of it creating the saucer-shaped depression as well as the chipping around the exit hole. When the bullet strikes the glass at right angles, the chipping will be distributed uniformly. If the bullet is fired from the right side of the glass (see Figure 5-8), it will leave an elliptical hole with little chipping on the left side. As the angle of fire becomes more acute, there will be more chipping on the opposite side. The angle of fire can be approximated by observing the hole. Test firing bullets from a known angle into similar glass using the same type of weapon and ammunition may provide a more precise determination.

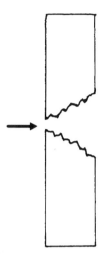

Figure 5-8. Bullet hole in glass.

b. Which Bullet Hole Was Made First? In cases involving an exchange of gunfire coming from opposite sides of a window, it is often important to know which shot was fired first. A radial fracture caused by a bullet will travel across the glass unless it is interrupted by a previously formed fracture. The first bullet hole will have radial cracks that are complete and uninterrupted. The second bullet will cause radial cracks that will be terminated by the radial and concentric cracks formed by the first bullet. If there is a third bullet, its radial lines will be interrupted by those lines emanating from the first and second bullet holes (Figure 5-9).

c. Determining the Type of Weapon or Ammunition. Some guns and ammunition produce characteristic bullet holes in glass. Test firing different weapons into similar glass under similar conditions may indicate the type of weapon or caliber of ammunition that was used. This may be useful in cases where the spent bullets, the cartridges, and the weapon have not been located and a particular type of weapon or caliber of ammunition is suspected.

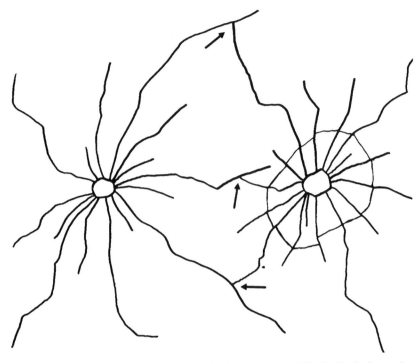

Figure 5-9. Bullet holes from two shots fired in sequence. The bullet hole on the left was made first. The arrows show where the fracture lines of the second bullet terminate at the lines caused by the first.

14. Fracture Matches

In some cases it may be important to show that pieces of glass were once joined together such as part of the same window, headlight or other glass object. Shards of glass may be found adhering to the perpetrator's clothing or embedded in his or her shoes. They may also be found embedded in the victim or at the scene of a hit and run. The phrase "fracture match" is used here to describe this precise meshing of the two glass fragments. Others refer to this process as a "physical match," "edge match," or "mechanical fit." Regardless of terminology it is a jigsaw puzzle-like fit of broken pieces. Broken glass, more so than other objects, has edges that are slightly ridged and uneven. Because of this, a glass piece broken from an adjacent piece will tend to lock as the rib marks mesh into place and resist any movement when fitted together with its complementary piece.

If a fracture match is contemplated, all broken pieces should be collected and packaged to avoid additional breakage. Glass from different locations should then be placed in separate containers and labeled. The containers are then transported to the laboratory where "known" samples (pieces whose origins can be determined) and "questioned" samples (pieces whose origins need to be determined) will be compared.

Examiners first screen the pieces to be certain they are similar in color, thickness, curvature, texture, surface pattern, and other obvious physical characteristics. The pieces are then carefully joined together and gentle pressure is applied to make sure there is "the feel" of a proper fit. Next, the edges of both pieces are examined under a low-power comparison microscope and then photographed with the rib marks and hackle marks (if present) of both pieces properly aligned to provide a positive identification of the "questioned" glass.

15. Glass Physical Properties

When a window is broken with a heavy metal instrument, such as a tire iron or hammer, minute glass particles can fly backwards up to a distance of ten feet. These minute particles may adhere to a burglar's clothing or may be stepped on and embedded in the soles or heels of his or her shoes. When a suspect is apprehended, these glass particles may link the perpetrator to the crime scene.

While laboratory glass examination can seldom individualize glass on physical properties alone, determining the class characteristics of glass can narrow or eliminate some sources. Two of the more useful physical properties for comparing glass are those of density and refraction.

Density is a measurement of the weight of a substance in relation to the volume it occupies. Lead has a greater density than glass; it has more weight per unit of volume it occupies. The density of a substance is also a measure of its buoyancy. A substance will float or sink in a liquid depending on its density in comparison with the liquid. When a substance is placed in a liquid having the same density as itself, it will remain suspended, neither floating nor sinking. This phenomenon provides a convenient method of determining density as well as comparing the relative density of two glass particles.

Refractive Index is the measurement of the bending of light as it passes through a substance. When light passes from air through water, from a substance of lesser density through a substance of greater density, the velocity of the light is reduced. The light refracts or bends as it slows. Light will not bend when it travels between substances having the same refractive index. The refractive index of both the "known" glass particle and the "questioned" glass particle can be determined and compared.

16. Collection of Glass Evidence

When collecting glass evidence, consider the type of analysis that will be preformed. If trying to determine the direction from which a window was broken, then all of the glass from the pane should be collected. For other purposes, such as particle comparison, only a small sample of glass pieces will be required. Before moving glass evidence, describe the crime scene in the notes and sketches, and then photograph.

A variety of evidence may adhere to glass. The smooth surface of glass may yield excellent fingerprints. Blood is frequently found on broken glass. The investigator should also be alert for hair, fibers, dirt, or other debris adhering to the glass.

Care must be taken in handling glass fragments to avoid smudging fingerprints or disturbing evidence on the glass. Hold glass pieces with the fingers on the edges rather than on the flat surfaces. To avoid being cut, gloves made of rubber or cloth may be worn. For small pieces and particles, rubber-tipped tweezers or metal tweezers with adhesive tape placed over the tips should be used to avoid scratching the glass. Evidence should be packaged and marked in a manner that does not alter or destroy possible evidence. Smaller glass pieces and particles can be placed in a small container, such as a pillbox, and then sealed and labeled.

To avoid confusion and evidence contamination, glass from different locations should be placed in separate containers. Wrap each piece of glass separately in tissue paper or cotton and pack them tightly in a container so that the contents will not shift and break. If the evidence containers are to be shipped, they should be marked "Fragile."

MISCELLANEOUS TRACE EVIDENCE

17. Hair

Hair can be valuable forensic evidence. It is composed of the protein keratin and consists of three primary layers; the *cuticle* or outer covering, the *medulla* or innermost layer, and the *cortex,* the middle layer that contains the pigment cells. In its active growth state, the *anagen phase,* deposits are made to the follicle. As growth slows the hair enters the *catagen phase.* During the *telogen phase* growth is ceased and the hair follicle is in a resting period. Hair is frequently found at crime scenes due to natural shedding during the telogen phase or from forcible removal.

Hair provides a wealth of information. Analysis generally begins by determining if it is human or animal, and if animal, what species. Human hair can reveal the race of the individual (best determined by head hair), the area of the body it came from, the manner it was removed (shed, cut or forcibly), if dyed or bleached, contaminants on the hair shaft (shampoo, other chemicals, gunshot residue, etc.), if drugs were ingested and how long ago, and whether the individual was a smoker. Because hair is so resilient, useful determinations can be made long after other tissue has decomposed.

Advances in DNA technology have mostly relegated traditional microscopic examination to an exclusionary process. If the hair follicle remains attached to the hair shaft, DNA analysis is appropriate. If there is no follicular material, mtDNA is appropriate.

Crime scene hairs should be carefully collected and packaged. Samples from victims and suspects should include combed and plucked hairs.

18. Fibers

Due to the conformity of mass production, a fiber can rarely be linked to a source garment. Unless the fabric is torn and suitable for a fracture match, inclusion or exclusion rests solely with class characteristics. There are a variety of types of fibers such as animal fiber (wool), vegetable fiber (cotton), synthetic fiber (polyester, nylon), mineral fiber (glass wool, asbestos), and blends (polyester and cotton).

Fibers are one of the most common forms of trace evidence submitted to forensic laboratories. Analysis involves physical, chemical and microscopic characteristics, and may include color, type of fabric, dye, direction of twist, and thread count.

Fibers are often collected using forceps, cellophane tape, vacuuming, or mechanical dislodging (shaking over a clean paper-covered surface). Evidence should be properly labeled and packaged separately in paper bindles.

19. Paint

Paint evidence is generally associated with hit-and-runs and forced entries but may be found in other crimes as well. Paint and other protective coatings are principally composed of a mixture of pigment, binder, solvent and additives. Unless a fracture match is possible, single layer paint chips cannot be identified to an individual source. Multi-layer paint chips are more unique and increase the probability of identifying a source.

Paint analysis may involve examination of color, chemical composition, number of coats, texture, and weathering through microscopic, spectroscopic, and chemical analysis. Forensic laboratories have access to databases to identify paint by its color and chemical composition.

Paint evidence may be in the form of smears, chips, or chalking of old paint. Chips should be packaged in paper bindles. Do not use tape to collect chips because the adhesive may interfere with the chemical analysis. Paint evidence on tools should be carefully wrapped and the entire tool submitted to the lab. Comparison samples should be collected by scraping or chipping from the area of damage and submitted in paper bindles.

20. Soil

Soil is a highly variable mixture of weathered and decaying rock, organic material, and synthetic materials (paint chips, rubber, glass, asphalt, etc.). Forensic laboratories vary greatly in their abilities to analyze soil. The analysis can be complex and time consuming, and may consist of examination of the texture, general appearance, and color. Microscopic examination often identifies miscellaneous material. Analysis generally includes particle size, distribution, and density gradient, as well as chemical and elemental composition. While still a developing technique, some examiners are exploring the use of bacterial DNA studies to identify soil. While most soil analysis generally results in a determination of class characteristics, in some cases the complexity of the sample can approach identification.

Soil evidence is commonly found on footwear, clothing, and vehicles in the form of loose particles or mud. It is easily transferred to suspects and victims. Comparison samples should be collected at the scene and several feet away. Four to five samples should come from the immediate scene along with samples from 20 to 50 feet away in each direction. Each comparison sample should consist of two to three tablespoons of top soil (do not dig more than 1 inch deep). Samples should also be taken from around the suspect's home and place of work, and any area connected to an alibi.

FIREARMS

21. Overview

The United States is the birthplace of the revolver, and the possession of firearms has long been engrained in the culture. Easy access and high levels of ownership result in firearms playing a frequent role in crime in the United States. Some crimes are solved by tracing or otherwise establishing ownership of a firearm. For other crimes a bullet, cartridge case, firearm wound, or bullet trajectory plays a key role in the investigation. Since criminals often use the same firearm in a series of crimes, identifying a firearm may prove important to solving multiple crimes. Moreover, charging a suspect with illegally possessing or carrying a firearm may lead to other evidence useful in an investigation.

22. National Integrated Ballistic Information Network

As is the case with fingerprints, the science of ballistics and firearm identification has greatly benefited from advances in recording evidence and searching databases. National Integrated Ballistic Information Network (NIBIN) is the principal repository of ballistic information. The NIBIN system deploys equipment to federal, state, and local law enforcement agencies for imaging and comparing bullets and cartridge cases maintained by the Bureau of Alcohol, Tobacco, Firearms and Explosives.

A firearms trace will not always be successful or produce the identity of the user. A firearm may not be traceable if manufactured before accurate records were kept. If the gun was lost or stolen, the trace will lead only to the lawful owner. Sometimes a theft of the firearm has not been reported to the police, or if it has, the theft has not been entered into the local or the National Crime Information Center's stolen gun file.

23. Investigative Problems

Examination by a firearms expert is appropriate whenever it is suspected that a firearm has been used in a crime, especially in connection with cases of robbery, assault, suicide, and homicide.

The investigation may center on identification, or may attempt to answer a variety of questions. What type of weapon fired the evidence bullet? What type of firearm could have fired cartridge casings found at the scene? Can a bullet or cartridge casing be identified as having been fired from a specific firearm? Were filler wads found at the scene fired by a shotgun such as the one in question?

Only a small percentage of forensic firearm examinations are limited to identification. The examination may focus on workability or functioning condition of the weapon. For other cases, the trajectory and distance of a shot might be important. The discharge distance may help distinguish a suicide from a murder. The approximate discharge distance can be estimated from a study and comparison of powder patterns on clothing and skin or, in the case of shotguns, from an examination of the shot pattern.

24. Describing the Firearm

Firearms related to a criminal investigation must be marked, labeled, and described so that it can be identified in any subsequent legal action. At a minimum the description should include the *caliber, make, model, type, serial number,* and *finish.* The caliber is the diameter of the bore. Some common handgun calibers include .22, .25, .38, .380, .40, .45, and 9 mm. The make is the manufacturer's name and is usually stamped on the barrel or frame. Common makes include Colt, Smith and Wesson, Ruger, Glock, Walther, H&K, and Remington. Since two firearms of the same caliber and make can have identical serial numbers, designation of the model is essential. The model may be a name or number. The type describes the manner of operation, such as *revolver, automatic, semi-automatic,* and *single shot.* Some knowledge of firearms is required in distinguishing certain types. Serial numbers are located in various areas on the weapon. On some firearms the serial numbers are not visible unless the weapon is disassembled. The finish describes the color and surface of the firearm. The most common examples are *blue, nickel, stainless,* and *parkerized* (the dull gray appearance of military handguns).

If the weapon is difficult to describe, include other characteristics such as *barrel length, overall length,* and the number of chambers or magazine capacity. Barrel length of a revolver is measured from the muzzle to the front end of the cylinder. The barrel length of an automatic is measured from the muzzle to the face of the breech. Items such as "ducks-bill hammer," "ramped sights," or a broken trigger guard should be recorded. With foreign-made automatics, document any markings stamped on the side or frame, since these often are indications of the model and place of manufacture. Too much information rather than too little should be the rule in describing firearms. Size, model, make and serial number may not properly identify a firearm. The description ".32, H. & R., Serial #

12345," for example, is inadequate, since the description may fit eight or more different firearms. Finally, consider the Remington .41 cal. Derringer. It has been estimated that about 250,000 were distributed, yet most of these weapons have only three-digit serial numbers.

25. Firearms Identification

The term firearms identification primarily relates to matching bullets or cartridge cases to a particular type of firearm or to an individual firearm. Determining the type of firearm is generally more likely than determining the specific weapon. The class and individual characteristics of bullets and casings form the basis of the examination.

a. **Bullets**. The manufacturing process ensures some uniformity in physical properties or general characteristics of bullets. Many of these properties remain after firing and serve to indicate the firearm. When a bullet is fired, it acquires additional characteristics that more closely identify the type and make of firearm. In addition, the firearm may impress upon the bullet individual characteristics that may identify the individual firearm.

The general characteristics of a fired bullet can help identify its type and manufacture. *Weight* in grains is characteristic but variations of several grains are within the limits of tolerance. The *material* it is composed of such as soft-nosed, lead, and other substance in useful. The *diameter* is measured to determine caliber, but may be greatly distorted in striking hard objects. *Cannelures* are knurled grooves on the curved surface. Although subject to distortion from impact, *contour* or shape is often retained after firing. The *base,* whether flat or hollow, is another useful characteristic. *Size and weight* serve to identify shotgun pellets.

When a bullet is fired, the marks imparted on the projectile are called *rifling impression. Rifling* is grooves cut into the barrel (*broach process*) or impressed into the barrel (*button process*) to cause the bullet to spin to stabilize the trajectory and improve accuracy. The cutting tools used in the rifling process produce characteristic marks. *Land impressions* are produced by the "raised ribs running in a spiral (helix) lengthwise through the bore. They slant to the left or right, corresponding to the direction of twist in the bore of the firearm. The surfaces of the lands are the original surfaces of the interior of the barrel before the rifling is cut. *Groove impressions* correspond to the grooves or indentations produced by the rifling cuts. They are equal in number to the lands and vary by manufacturer in width, depth, driven edges (whether rounded or not), and angle of spiral. The width of the lands is usually slightly less than that of the grooves except in the case of firearms using small bullets. The *number of lands and grooves* typically varies from four to sixteen.

Other characteristics of rifling include diameter and pitch. The diameter is measured in two ways. *Bore diameter* is the distance from land to land. *Groove diameter* is the distance from bottom to bottom of opposite grooves. The direction of spiral or *pitch* also indicates manufacturer. The majority of firearms are made with clockwise (right) direction to the pitch. In the United States, the Colt and several other firearms have a left (counter-clockwise) pitch.

Individual characteristics result from imperfections in the barrel from the manufacturing process, rust, wear, or abuse. They constantly change in small degrees because of fragments of lead that remain in the barrel after a discharge. Subsequent bullets push forward the particles and alter the scoring. Imperfections near the muzzle of the barrel produce the most marked effect on the bullet.

To determine if a bullet was fired from a specific firearm, test bullets are compared to evidence bullets. Test bullets are obtained by firing the weapon into either a box of cotton wadding or a water tank. The water tank is often preferred because cotton is mildly abrasive and could polish away some of the finer striations from the surface of the bullet.

The first step is to ensure test and evidence bullets have similar class characteristics and no disqualifying dissimilarities. A comparison microscope is used to see corresponding parts of the two bullets in the same field. If striations are found to match, they can be aligned to appear collinear. The entire circumference of both bullets is studied under low magnification. Rifling impressions nearer the nose of the bullet will sometimes be parallel to the longitudinal axis of the bullet. These are known as "skid marks" or

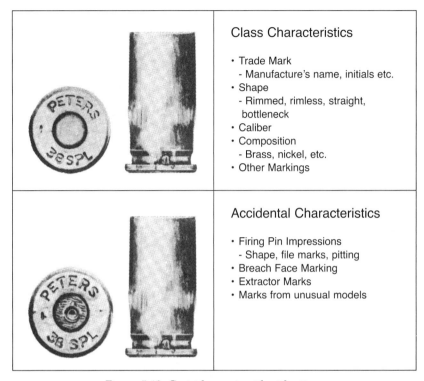

Figure 5-10. Cartridge casing identification.

"slippage." They are considered by some to be produced by worn rifling or by the action of a revolver in which the bullet travels a distance without a spinning motion (due to the absence of rifling in the cylinder).

b. **Cartridge Casings.** Casings acquire similar general characteristics when manufactured. The *manufacturer* is indicated by the name, initials, or trademark stamped on the head (although some makes are not marked). The *shape* can refer to the base as rim, rimless, semi- or auto-rim, or the wall as straight, tapered, or necked. The *caliber* is generally stamped on center fire cases. The composition may be brass, nickel-plated, copper, plated steel, paper, or plastic.

The process of firing a bullet may also impart individual characteristics to the cartridge casings. The case is ejected from auto-

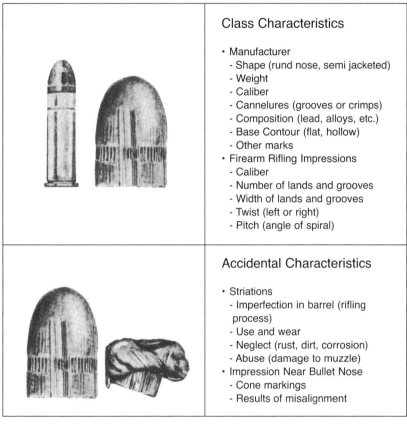

	Class Characteristics

	• Manufacturer
	  - Shape (rund nose, semi jacketed)
	  - Weight
	  - Caliber
	  - Cannelures (grooves or crimps)
	  - Composition (lead, alloys, etc.)
	  - Base Contour (flat, hollow)
	  - Other marks
	• Firearm Rifling Impressions
	  - Caliber
	  - Number of lands and grooves
	  - Width of lands and grooves
	  - Twist (left or right)
	  - Pitch (angle of spiral)

	Accidental Characteristics
	
	• Striations
	  - Imperfection in barrel (rifling process)
	  - Use and wear
	  - Neglect (rust, dirt, corrosion)
	  - Abuse (damage to muzzle)
	• Impression Near Bullet Nose
	  - Cone markings
	  - Results of misalignment

Figure 5-11. Bullet identification.

matics and semi-automatics but remains in the cylinder of revolvers and chambers of single shot firearms until discarded by a separate ejection action. Therefore, casings are more likely to be found at the crime scene when auto or semi-auto firearms are used.

There are several characteristics often found on casings. *Firing pin indentations* are produced when the firing pin strikes the primer. The tip of the pin produces its own shape and also may leave file and pitting marks. When the primer ignites the powder, the powder burns, creating gas that propels the bullet down the barrel. At the same time the casing is driven back against the breech or bolt

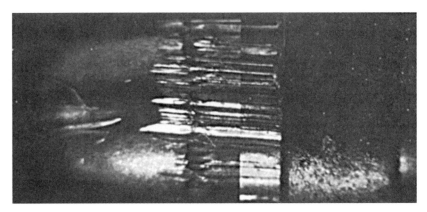

Figure 5-12. Photomicrograph made with the comparison microscope. The fatal bullet is seen on one side of the fine line near the center and the test bullet fired from the suspect's gun on the other. The striations of one bullet appear to run into those of the other, thus showing that they were discharged from the same weapon.

head of the weapon creating *breech face markings*. File marks, machining marks, or imperfections present on the breech face from the manufacturing processes or from use are impressed on the soft face of the primer. *Extractor marks* are produced on the rim of a rimmed case and the flange and sometimes on the groove of a rimless case. The cylindrical surface of the case just below the rim or groove may also be marked. The extractor, under spring tension, is forced over the rim of the case when loaded into the chamber of an auto loading firearm. *Ejector marks* are found on the base of the case, the rim, or the flange. They are usually located on the side opposite the extractor marks. When the fired case is drawn from the chamber by the extractor, the base of the shell strikes against the fixed ejector and receives characteristic marks. In addition, there are *peculiarities* associated with certain models of firearms. At one time Colt semi-automatics tended to leave a flat area on the mouth of the case as it was ejected. The Thompson submachine gun typically left a half-moon shaped mark on the head of case from striking the bolt.

26. Powders

Black powder, the traditional gunpowder, is a mixture of salt-peter (potassium nitrate), charcoal (carbon), and sulphur in the approximate proportions of 75:15:10. It is, today, used principally for replica weapons having been replaced by smokeless powder in modern ammunition. Smokeless powder consists of cellulose nitrate and may have glycerol nitrate (nitrocellulose).

27. Gunshot Primer Residue (GSR) Test

When a gun is fired, invisible primer residues are dispersed throughout the area within 10 feet of the discharge. More impor-

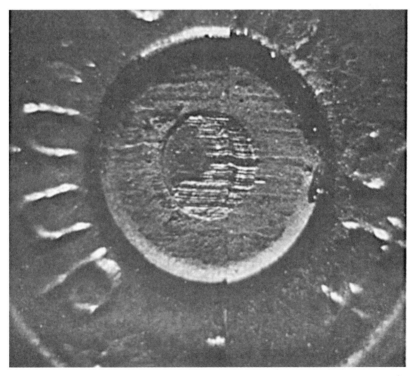

Figure 5-13. Comparison photomicrograph of firing-pin marks on two cartiridge cases. The left side of the test shell is merged with the right side of the evidence shell. The fine scratches appear to run continuously from one shell to the other.

tantly, these minute particles will be deposited on the hands of the shooter. If a suspect is identified within a couple of hours of the shooting, invisible particles of gunshot primer, particularly the elements of antimony and barium, may still be on his or her hands.

The chemical elements of antimony and barium are found at trace levels throughout our environment. If there are elevated readings from the suspect's hands, the test result will be positive. A positive finding does not verify that the suspect has fired a gun, but only that the individual was in the presence of a discharged firearm. He or she may be the shooter, happened to place his or her hand near the gun as it discharged, or is a bystander who handled a firearm after it was discharged. This information is important if the suspect denies having been in the presence of a firearm.

There can be many explanations for a negative finding and may not eliminate the suspect. Occasionally, a firearm will not leave any significant amount of residue on the hand. Gunshot residue primer will rub off easily or can be washed off the hands. Also, many brands of .22-caliber ammunition may not include antimony or barium in their primer. A failure to find GSR on the hands of the suspect means no conclusion can be drawn.

a. **Forensic Testing**. When a victim is shot from close range, GSR may be deposited on the hands of both the shooter and victim, especially if the victim was reaching for the gun. In these situations, the GSR test is not helpful in distinguishing between a suicide and a homicide. To avoid unproductive analysis, the GSR test should be performed on a suspect only if there are no witnesses to the shooting, evidence is collected within a couple of hours of the shooting, and the suspect's hands have not been washed.

Swabbing is a common method for collecting GSR evidence. Multiple cotton swabs are used to methodically swab both hands (and sometimes the cheek if a rifle was used) with a 5 percent solution of nitric acid. Wear disposable latex gloves to avoid evidence contamination. Control swabs, moistened with the nitric acid solution, should also be collected and submitted, along with any spent cartridge casings. The evidence samples are tested by atomic absorption spectrophotometry (AA) or neutron activation analysis (NAA) or to determine the concentration of antimony and barium present.

A more effective method uses scanning electron microscopy/ energy dispersive x-ray analysis (SEM/EDX). Evidence is collected using adhesive-coated aluminum disks that are pressed repeatedly over palms and back of the hands to collect any GSR particles. SEM/EDX has the advantage of providing a visual image of the residue particles showing size and shape as well as a chemical analysis of their composition.

28. Powder Residue

Grains of burned and unburned powder, smoke, and other residues are deposited on the skin or clothing of the victim if the muzzle of the firearm was held within six feet in the case of black powder and 24 inches (or even more depending on the load and other factors) in the case of smokeless powder. The pattern is useful in estimating distance of discharge, a problem often arising in suspicious suicide cases. GSR patterns are enhanced using ALS or chemical processing. High contrast photography, infrared photography, or soft x-ray radiographs should precede chemical development. The examiner test fires into paper, cardboard or linen to determine the GSR pattern at various distances. Comparing the test patterns to the crime scene pattern will provide an estimate of the distance of the muzzle from the target. To improve the accuracy of the estimate, the same weapon and ammunition should be used (or same type if original is not available) and fired into a similar fabric (receiving surface) when possible.

29. Trace Metal Detection Technique (TMDT)

Trace Metal Detection Technique is a means for determining whether a person's hand or clothing has recently been in contact with a metal object such as a tool or weapon. The surface (usually the hand) to be examined is treated with a test solution and placed under the ultraviolet light, where its fluorescence can be studied and photographed. Traces left by different metals differ in the color of their fluorescence. The pattern left by handling a metal object will be determined by its shape and the way it is used. From a study of the fluorescent pattern on a person's hand, the examiner can draw some useful conclusions as to whether or not he or she handled a weapon or tool.

In the case of a handgun, the examiner will look on those parts of the hand that came in contact with the gun: the index finger that rested on the trigger, the remaining fingers and thumb that enclosed the gun, the palm, and the back of the hand. The examiner also looks for any irregularities or distinctive marks in the pattern that may have been made by screws, protrusions, ornamentations, and other markings. A photograph is then made of the pattern produced under ultraviolet light. While not conclusive in the sense of determining if a specific tool or weapon was handled, it does provide additional useful information for the investigator.

30. Fingerprints on Firearms

Contrary to media portrayals, it is difficult to obtain fingerprints from firearms. Well maintained firearms tend to be coated in a thin layer of oil. Tightly gripping the weapon can smudge prints. Placing the weapon in a case, pocket, or holster can wipe the prints from the weapon. The investigator should always attempt to recover fingerprints from firearms, but failure to successfully develop prints is not unusual.

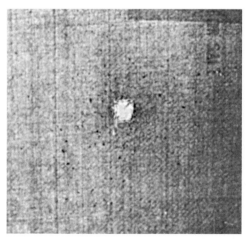

Figure 5-14. Powder residue around a bullet hole in dark clothing, revealed by means of an infrared photograph.

ADDITIONAL READING

Impressions

Abbott, J.R.: *Footwear Evidence: The Examination, Identification, and Comparison of Footwear Impressions.* Springfield, IL: Thomas, 1964.

Bodziak, W.J.: *Footwear Impression Evidence: Detection, Recovery, and Examination* (2nd ed.). Boca Raton, FL.: CRC Press, 1999.

——: Manufacturing Processes for Athletic Shoe Outsoles and Their Significance in the Examination of Footwear Impression Evidence. *Journal of Forensic Sciences, 31* (153), 1986.

——: Shoe and Tire Impression Evidence. *FBI Law Enforcement Bulletin, 53* (7), 1984.

Cassidy, M.J.: *Footwear Identification.* Ottawa: Royal Canadian Mounted Police, 1980.

Cook, C.W.: Footprint Identification. *Fingerprint and Identification Magazine, 57* (6), 1975.

Davis, R.J.: An Intelligence Approach to Footwear Marks and Toolmarks. *Journal of the Forensic Science Society, 21* (183), 1981.

Facey, O.E.: Hannah, I.D. and Rosen, D.: Shoe Wear Patterns and Pressure Distribution under Feet and Shoes, Determined by Image Analysis. *Journal of the Forensic Science Society, 32* (15), 1992.

Fawcett, A.S.: The Role of the Footmark Examiner. *Journal of the Forensic Science Society, 10* (227), 1970.

Giles, E. and Vallandigham, P.H.: Height Estimation from Foot and Shoeprint Length. *Journal of Forensic Sciences, 36* (1134), 1991.

Given, B., Nehrich, R. and Shields, J.: *Tire Tracks and Tread Marks.* Houston: Gulf Publishing, 1978.

Hueske, E.E.: A Superior Method for Obtaining Test Prints from Footwear and Tires. *Journal of Forensic Identification, 41* (165), 1991.

Laskowski, G.E.: An Improved Technique for the Visualization of Footprint Impressions in the Insoles of Athletic Shoes. *Journal of Forensic Sciences, 32* (1075), 1987.

Laskowski, G.E. and Kyle, V.L.: Barefoot Impressions–A Preliminary Study of Identification Characteristics and Population Frequency of their Morphological Features. *Journal of Forensic Sciences, 33* (378), 1988.

Lorring, M.: Bloodhound Trailing Evidence, Is It Admissible? *Law and Order, 36* (7), 1988.

Lloyd, J.B.F.: Luminescence of Tyre Marks and Other Rubber Contact Traces. *Journal of the Forensic Science Society, 16* (5), 1976.

McDonald, P.: *Tire Imprint Evidence.* New York: Elsevier, 1989.

McGonigle, C.: Tracking: An Ancient Skill Makes a Comeback. *Law and Order, 36* (2), 1988.

Ojena, S.M.: New Electrostatic Process Recovers Visible and Invisible Dust Particles at Crime Scenes. *Law and Order, 36* (7), 1988.

Ojena, S.M.: A New Improved Technique for Casting Impressions in Snow. *Journal of Forensic Sciences, 29* (322), 1984.

Petty, C.S., et al.: The Value of Shoe Sole Imprints in Automobile Crash Investigations. *Journal of Police Science and Administration, 1* (1), 1973.

Robbins, L.M.: Estimating Height and Weight from Size of Footprints. *Journal of Forensic Sciences, 31* (143), 1986.

——: *Footprints: Collection, Analysis and Interpretation.* Springfield, IL: Thomas, 1985.

Saferstein, R. Criminalistics: An Introduction to Forensic Science (10th ed.). Upper Saddle River: N.J. Pearson Prentice Hall, 2011.

Thomson, M.W.: Photographic Reproduction of Footprints. *Forensic Photography, 2* (4), 1973.

Vandiver, J.V. and Wolcott, J.H.: Identification of Suitable Plaster for Crime Scene Casting. *Journal of Forensic Sciences, 23* (607), 1978.

Vandiver, J.V: Tire Marks. *Law and Order, 25* (7), 1977.

Vandiver, J.V.: Footwear Marks. *Law and Order, 24* (9), 1976.

Van Krunkelsven, H.: Improved Photographic Method for Making Hand and Footprints. *Forensic Photography, 2* (5), 1973.

Tool Marks

Biasotti, A.A.: The Principles of Evidence Evaluation as Applied to Firearms and Tool Mark Identification. *Journal of Forensic Sciences, 9* (428), 1964.

Burd, D.Q. and Gilmore, A.E.: Individual and Class Characteristics of Tools. *Journal of Forensic Sciences, 13* (390), 1968.

Davis, J.E.: *An Introduction to Tool Marks, Firearms and the Striagraph.* Springfield, IL: Thomas, 1968.

Ojena, S.M.: A New Silicone Rubber Casting Material Designed for Forensic Science Application. *Journal of Forensic Sciences, 29* (317), 1984.

Peterson, J.L.: Utilizing the Laser for Comparing Tool Striations. *Journal of the Forensic Science Society, 14* (57), 1974.

Scott, J.D.: *Investigative Methods.* Reston, VA: Reston Publishing, 1978.

Townshend, D.G.: Photographing and Casting Toolmarks. *FBI Law Enforcement Bulletin, 45* (4), 1976.

Vandiver, J.V.: Identification and Use of Tool Mark Evidence. *Law and Order, 24* (7), 1976.

Bite Marks

Barry, R.J.: Forensic Odontology: Identification through Dental Evidence. *Police Chief, 55* (8), 1988.

Dinkel, E.H., Jr.: The Use of Bite Mark Evidence as an Investigative Aid. *Journal of Forensic Sciences, 19* (535), 1974.

MacDonald, D.G.: Bite Mark Recognition and Interpretation. *Journal of the Forensic Science Society, 14* (229), 1974.

Mittleman, R.E., Stuver, W.C. and Souviron, R.R.: Obtaining Saliva Samples from Bitemark Evidence. FBI Law Enforcement Bulletin, 49 (11), 1980.

Rao, V.J. and Souviron, R.R.: Dusting and Lifting the Bite Print: A New Technique. *Journal of Forensic Sciences, 29* (326), 1984.

Souviron, R.R., Mittleman, R.E. and Valor, J.: Obtaining the Bitemark Impression (Mold) from Skin. *FBI Law Enforcement Bulletin, 51* (1), 1982.

Sperber, N.D.: Bite Mark Evidence in Crimes Against Persons. *FBI Law Enforcement Bulletin, 50* (7), 1981.

——: Chewing Gum–An Unusual Clue in a Recent Homicide Investigation. *Journal of Forensic Sciences, 23* (792), 1978.

Swanson, C., Chamelin, N., Territo, L. and Taylor R. *Criminal Investigation.* Boston: McGraw Hill, 2009.

Vale, G.L., et al.: Unusual Three-Dimensional Bite Mark Evidence in a Homicide Case. *Journal of Forensic Sciences, 21* (642), 1976.

West, M.H. and Frair, J.: The Use of Videotape to Demonstrate the Dynamics of Bite Marks. *Journal of Forensic Sciences, 34* (88), 1989.

Palm Prints and Sole Prints

Alexander, H.L.V.: *Classifying Palmprints: A Complete System of Coding, Filing and Searching Palmprints.* Springfield, IL: Thomas, 1973.

Guide to Taking Palm Prints. Washington, D.C.: U.S. Government Printing Office, n.d.

Kolb, P.A.: *H.I.T.–A Manual for the Classification, Filing, and Retrieval of Palmprints.* Springfield, IL: Thomas, 1979.

Myers, D.A.: *Sole Prints: A Reference Guide for Law Enforcement Personnel* (2nd ed.). Beaverton, OR: S.O.L.E. Publications, 1982.

Rogers, S.L.: *The Personal Identification of Living Individuals.* Springfield, IL: Thomas, 1986.

Shimoda, S.C. and Franck, F.E.: Writer's Palmar Impressions. *Journal of Forensic Sciences, 34* (468), 1989.

Stapleton, M.E.: Infant Footprints. *FBI Law Enforcement Bulletin, 63* (11), 1994.

Wentworth, B. and Wilder, H.H.: *Personal Identification* (2nd ed.). Chicago: T.G. Cooke, The Fingerprint Publishing Association, 1932.

Earprints and Lip Prints

Alberink, I. & Ruifronk, A.: Repeatability and Reproducibility of Earprint Acquisition. *Journal of Forensic Sciences, 53* (2), 2008.

BBC News. 'Earprint' man cleared of killing, http//news.bbc.co.uk/2/hi/uk _news/England/west_yorkshire /342081.stm available 2/3/2011.

Iannarelli, A.V.: *Ear Identification* (Rev. ed.0. Freemont, CA: Paramount Publishing, 1989.

Moenssens, A.A.: Ear Identification Research. Forensic-Evidence.com, http: //forensic-evidence.com/site/ID/ID00004_4.html, available 2/3/2011.

Morgan, J.: Court holds Earprint Identification Not Generally Accepted in Scientific Community. Forensic-Evidence.com, http://forensic-evidence.com/site/ID/ID_Kunze.html available 2/3/2011.

Rogers, S.L.: *The Personal Identification of Living Individuals.* Springfield, IL: Thomas, 1986.

Schnuth, M.L.: Lip Prints. *FBI Law Enforcement Bulletin, 61* (11), 1992.

Williams, T.R.: Lip Prints—Another Means of Identification. *Journal of Forensic Identification, 41* (190), 1991.

Trace Evidence

Dutelle, A.W.: *An Introduction to Crime Scene Investigation.* Sudbury, MA: Jones and Bartlett, 2011.

Fisher, B.A.: *Techniques of Crime Scene Investigation* (7th ed.). Boca Raton: CRC Press, 2004.

Fong, W.: The Value of Glass as Evidence. *Journal of Forensic Sciences, 18* (398), 1973.

Gaensslen, R.E.; Harris, H.A. & Lee, H.: *Introduction to Forensic Science & Criminalistics.* Boston: McGraw Hill, 2008.

Gilbert, J.N.: *Criminal Investigation* (8th ed.). Upper Saddle River, N.J.: Prentice Hall, 2010.

McJunkins, S.P. and Thornton, J.I.: Glass Fracture Analysis: A Review. *Forensic Science, 2* (1), 1973.

Miller, E.T.: Glass Comparison. In Saferstein, R. (Ed.): *Forensic Science Handbook.* Englewood Cliffs, N.J.: Prentice-Hall, 1982.

Pearson, E.F., May R. W. and Dabbs, M.D.: Glass and Paint Fragments Found in Men's Outer Clothing—A Report of Survey. *Journal of Forensic Sciences, 16* (283), 1971.

Slater, D.P. and Fong, W.: Density, Refractive Index, and Dispersion in the Examination of Glass: Their Relative Worth as Proof. *Journal of Forensic Sciences, 27* (474), 1982.

Stahl, C.J., et al.: The Effect of Glass as an Intermediate Target on Bullets. *Journal of Forensic Sciences, 24 (6), 1979.*

Stoney, D.A. and Thornton, J.I.: The Forensic Significance of the Correlation of Density and Refractive Index in Glass Evidence. *Forensic Science International, 29* (147), 1985.

Swanson, C.R.; Chamelin, N.C.; Territo, L. & Taylor, R.W.: *Criminal Investigation* (10th ed.). Boston: McGraw Hill, 2009.

Woods, J.: Headlights Are Tools in Traffic Accident Investigation. *Law and Order, 25* (6), 1977.

Firearms

Aaron, R.W.: Gunshot Primer Residue: The Invisible Clue. *FBI Law Enforcement Bulletin, 60* (6), 1991.

Andrasko, J. and Maehly, A.C.: Detection of Gunshot Residues on Hands by Scanning Electron Microscopy. *Journal of Forensic Sciences, 22* (279), 1977.

Basu, S.: Formation of Gunshot Residues. *Journal of Forensic Sciences, 27* (72), 1982.

Biasotti, A.A.: Rifling Methods—A Review and Assessment of the Individual Characteristics Produced. *Association of Firearms and Too Mark Examiners Journal, 13* (34), 1981.

Bosen, S.F. and Schewing, D.R.: A Rapid Microtechnique for the Detection of Trace Metals from Gunshot Residues. *Journal of Forensic Sciences, 21* (163), 1976.

Brill, S.: *Firearms Abuse: A Research and Policy Report.* Washington, D.C.: Police Foundation, 1977.

Burrard, G.: *Identification of Firearms and Forensic Ballistics.* Prescott, AZ: Wolfe Publishing, 1990.

Copeland, A.R.: Accidental Death by Gunshot Wound. Fact or Fiction. *Forensic Science International, 26* (25), 1984.

DeGaetano, D. and Siegel, J.A.: Survey of Gunshot Residue Analysis in Forensic Science Laboratories. *Journal of Forensic Sciences, 35* (1087), 1990.

Di Maio, V.J.M.: Accidental Deaths Due to Dropping of Handguns. *Forensic Science Gazette, 3* (5), 1972.

Goleb, J.A. and Midkiff, C.R., Jr.: Firearms Discharge Residue Sample Collection Techniques. *Journal of Forensic Sciences, 20* (701), 1975.

Havekost, D.G., Peters, C.A. and Koons, R.D.: Barium and Antimony Distributions on the Hands of Nonshooters. *Journal of Forensic Sciences, 35* (1096), 1990.

Hill, T.: Firearms Tracing: A Crimefighting Weapon. *FBI Law Enforcement Bulletin, 54* (7), 1985.

Kates, D.B., Jr. (Ed.): *Firearms and Violence: Issues of Public Policy.* Cambridge, MA: Ballinger, 1984.

Kleck, G.: *Point Blank: Guns and Violence in America.* Hawthorne, NY: Aldine De Gruyter, 1991.

Krishnan, S.S.: Detection of Gunshot Residue on the Hands by Trace Element Analysis. *Journal of Forensic Sciences, 22* (304), 1977.

Krishnan, S.S., Gillespie, K.A., and Anderson, E.J.: Rapid Detection of Firearm Discharge Residues by Atomic Absorption and Neutron Activation Analysis, *Journal of Forensic Sciences, 22* (144), 1977.

Lester, D.: Gun *Control Issues and Answers.* Springfield, IL: Thomas, 1984.

Lewis, J. (Ed.): *Handguns '97.* Northbrook, IL: DBI Books, 1990.

Maiti, P.C.: Powder Patterns around Bullet Holes in Bloodstained Articles. *Journal of the Forensic Science Society, 13* (197), 1973.

Martiney, B.J.: Study of Spent Cartridge Cases. *International Criminal Police Review, 28* (270), 1973.

Mathews, J.H.: *Firearms Identification,* 3 vols. Springfield, IL: Thomas, Vols. I and I, 1962, Vol. III, 1973.

Messler, H.R. and Armstrong, W.R.: Bullet Residue as Distinguished from Powder Pattern. *Journal of Forensic Sciences, 23* (687), 1978.

Millard, J.T.: A *Handbook on the Primary Identification of Revolvers and Semiautomatic Pistols.* Springfield, IL: Thomas, 1974.

National Integrated Ballistic Information Network. www.nibin.gov.

Nennstiel, R.: The Determination of the Manufacturer of Ammunition. *Forensic Science International, 31* (1), 1986.

Pillay K. and Sagans, J.: Gunshot Residue Collection Using Film-Lift Techniques for Neutron Activation Analysis. *Journal of Police Science and Administration, 2* (388), 1974.

Rathman, G.A. and Ryland, S.G.: Use of the SEM-EDXA as an Aid to the Firearms Examiner. *Association of Firearms and Tool Mark Examiners Journal, 19* (388), 1987.

Robin, G.D.: *Violent Crime and Gun Control.* Cincinnati: Anderson, 1991.

Rowe, W.F.: Firearms Identification. In Saferstein, R. (Ed.): *Forensic Science Handbook,* vol. 2. Englewood Cliffs, N.J.: Prentice-Hall, 1988.

Schlesinger, H.L., et al.: *Special Report on Gunshot Residues Measured by Neutron Activation Analysis.* Springfield, VA: National Technical Information Service, 1970.

Schuster, Beth. (2008, July). Cold cases: Strategies explored at NIJ regional trainings, *NIJ Journal, 260:* 24-26, NCJ 222904.

Scroggie, R.J.: Firearm Silencers. *FBI Law Enforcement Bulletin, 46* (5), 1977.

Shaw, W.: The Electronic Stun Gun. *Law and Order, 24* (8), 1976.

Smith, O.C. and Harruff, R.C.: Evidentiary Value of the Contents of Hollow-Point Bullets. *Journal of Forensic Sciences, 33* (1052), 1988.

Steinberg, M., Leist, Y. and Tassa, M.: A New Field Kit for Bullet Hole Identification. *Journal of Forensic Sciences, 29* (169), 1984.

Stone, I.C.: Observations and Statistics Relating to Suicide Weapons: An Update. *Journal of Forensic Sciences, 35* (10), 1990.

Stone, I.C., Di Maio, V.J.M. and Petty, C.S.: Gunshot Wounds: Visual and Analytic Procedures. *Journal of Forensic Sciences, 23* (361), 1978.

Tassa, M., et al.: A Field Kit for Sampling Gunshot Residue Particles. *Journal of Forensic Sciences, 27* (671), 1982.

——: Characterization of Gunshot Residues by X-Ray Diffraction. *Journal of Forensic Sciences, 27* (677), 1982.

Thurman, J.V.: Interpol Computers Keep Track of Firearms, Explosives. *Police Chief, 58* (10), 1991.

Wilber, C.G.: *Ballistic Science for the Law Enforcement Officer.* Springfield, IL: Thomas, 1977.

Williams, M.: *The 9mm and Law Enforcement Today.* Springfield, IL: Thomas, 1989.

——: *Practical Handgun Ballistics.* Springfield, IL: Thomas, 1980.

Wolten, G.M., et al.: Particle Analysis for the Detection of Gunshot Residue. I: Scanning Electron Microscopy/Energy Dispersive X-Ray Characterization of Hand Deposits from Firing. *Journal of Forensic Sciences, 24* (409), 1979.

Wright, J.D. and Rossi, P.H.: *The Armed Criminal in America: A Survey of Incarcerated Felons.* Washington, D.C.: U.S. Government Printing Office, 1985.

Wright, J.D., et al.: *Under the Gun: Weapons, Crime and Violence in America.* Hawthorne, N.Y.: Aldine De Gruyter, 1986.

Chapter 6

CARE OF EVIDENCE

1. Overview

PHYSICAL EVIDENCE consists of articles and materials that aid in determining the *corpus delicti,* associating the perpetrator to the crime, identifying the perpetrator, locating the perpetrator, or revealing the circumstances of the crime. These categories are not mutually exclusive. Physical evidence must be properly handled to ensure its full forensic value will be achieved. Evidence that is not properly labeled, collected, and stored may not be suitable for forensic analysis or admitted into court proceedings. Investigators must properly handle evidence from its initial discovery at the scene of the crime until its final appearance in the court.

Corpus delicti evidence consists of objects or substances that tend to establish a crime has been committed. For example, in a homicide the body of the decedent is part of the *corpus delicti* of the offense. The narcotic found in the addict's unlawful possession is part of the *corpus delicti* of a narcotics violation.

Associative evidence links the suspect to the crime scene or to the offense. For example, traces of safe lining found in a suspect's shoe may associate him or her with a safe burglary. Headlight glass found at the scene of a hit-and-run motor vehicle homicide may associate the suspect's car to the scene. Fingerprints and shoe impressions may also associate a suspect to the crime scene.

Identifying evidence is associative evidence that establishes the identity of the perpetrator. Fingerprints, foot impressions, DNA, or the suspect's wallet found at the scene would all be identifying evidence.

Tracking evidence assists the investigator in locating the suspect. A laundry mark, sales receipt, or telephone number may assist in tracking a fugitive. Similarly, a credit card would provide another tracking clue.

2. Evaluation of Physical Evidence

Before an object can become evidence it must be recognized as being significant. Investigators should develop their ability to recognize valuable physical evidence through experience and training.

Investigators can enhance their skills by understanding legal procedures, criminal behavior, and forensic analysis. Knowledge of substantive and procedural criminal law is essential. An ability to recreate the events before, during, and after the commission of a crime, along with an ability to recognize *modus operandi,* guides investigators in finding evidence. Good investigators are continually studying their profession and advances in forensic to better interpret the information available to them.

3. Procedure

Physical evidence must be recognized, properly collected, and correctly stored until its introduction at the trial. Only competent (material and relevant) evidence that is properly identified and supported by a documented chain of custody can be introduced into a criminal trial.

Everyone who comes into contact with evidence must be able to later identify the evidence in court. Whether it is the officer that originally found the evidence or someone who later processed it, each individual must be able to distinguish it from any similar article. Without a systematic procedure for handling evidence, it is unlikely evidence can withstand the scrutiny of legal procedure.

4. Chain of Custody

The chain of custody is a record of the care and custody of evidence from the time it is discovered until its ultimate disposal. The number of persons who handle evidence should be kept to a minimum. Each transfer of the evidence should be acknowledged by a signature. It is the responsibility of everyone coming into contact with evidence to account for it during their time of possession, to protect it, and to record from whom it was received or delivered, along with the time and date of transfer. Chain of custody is a simple concept but one sometimes neglected during the pressure of an investigation. Investigators should understand that criminal defense attorneys may not fully understand investigative and forensic techniques, but they do understand chain of custody and will likely scrutinize it for errors. There is no excuse for not properly documenting the care and custody of evidence.

5. Protection

Physical evidence needs to be protected from damage and preserved in its original condition. Certain types of evidence, such as latent fingerprints, are fragile in nature. If handled in a careless manner the value of the evidence can be destroyed. Evidence also needs to be similar to its original condition when presented in court. It is necessary to show the object has not substantially changed since the time of the offense. Evidence should be protected from accidental or intentional alteration.

Special precautions are necessary for fragile evidence. Contamination, chemical change, alterations of shape, removal of a part, or addition of extraneous characteristics may occur from natural causes such as failing to protect the evidence from the weather or not refrigerating perishable items. Negligence or accident by failing to observe ordinary precautions may result in breakage, loss, or the acquisition of new characteristics. Examples of this are the careless dropping of a fragile article, accidentally marking on a document to be used in a handwriting comparison, or opening a box containing fibers in an area exposed to strong drafts. *Intentional damage or theft* may result by someone attempting to alter the outcome of an investigation or trial. Measures should be taken to protect evidence from destruction, theft, and access by unauthorized persons.

a. **Protecting Evidence**. Physical evidence at a crime scene can easily be damaged before its significance is recognized. All unnecessary persons should be excluded from the scene to prevent their handling or stepping on evidence. Entry to the crime scene should be restricted to only those needing to perform legitimate crime scene tasks. Investigators should, of course, take immediate action to protect crime scene evidence from damage from rain, snow, wind, or sun.

Physical evidence may also be obtained from informants or found among the possessions of suspects. Victims may later find additional evidence of the crime. This evidence needs to be treated in the same manner as crime scene evidence, and properly labeled, packaged, and secured as soon as possible.

b. **Transporting**. There is always some risk associated with transporting evidence. Fingerprints may be obliterated from an object due to vibration and rubbing of surfaces. Jars containing liquids and casts can be broken. Investigators must use extreme care in packaging items for transport.

c. **Standards of Comparison**. Known specimens are samples whose origins can be documented. They are compared to unknown specimens to link suspects to the crime. For example, soil found trapped in the tread of the suspect's shoe might be compared to soil from the crime scene. The samples to be collected will depend on the evidence collected and the nature of the investigation.

d. **Containers and Packaging**. Evidence that can be easily removed and packaged should be placed in clean containers such as envelopes, pill boxes, cardboard boxes, and glass containers. The choice of container will depend upon the size of the specimen, its physical state, and the likelihood of damage by transporting. Evidence that will first be transported to the investigator's office and later shipped to a forensic laboratory may need to be repackaged depending on the mode of transportation. Each time evidence is transported measures must be taken to ensure its safe arrival.

e. **Storage**. Each investigative agency needs to maintain adequate facilities for storing evidence. The evidence room should be constructed and equipped to provide physical protection against alteration or destruction of evidence from natural causes or unauthorized contacts. Removing evidence from the property room for examination or analysis should be recorded in property room records and case files through receipts or barcode scans. When evidence is received into the property room, the record should indicate the *date, file number* of case, *title* of case, *person* or *place* from whom or where it was received, *person delivering* the evidence, a *complete description* of items, the *disposition,* and the *signature* of the officer in control of the evidence room. When evidence is checked out, the signature of the person receiving the evidence, along with the date, time, and signature of the person releasing the evidence, should all be recorded.

6. Preservation

Perishable items, such as food, blood, or tissue, present special problems. Most organic matter changes in character as it decomposes. Unless measures are taken to preserve organic materials, its suitability for forensic analysis may be destroyed. Time and temperature are both factors. In warm weather there should be a minimum of delay in placing the evidence in appropriate storage. High temperatures greatly accelerate the decomposition of organic matter, and freezing can also be detrimental. Blood, for example, will lose some of its value as evidence if it is exposed to high temperatures for a long period of time or if it is permitted to freeze. Generally blood or other perishable specimens should be stored between 40° and 50°F.

7. Preservatives

Some perishable evidence may require special preservatives. For example, a blood specimen to be used to determine blood-alcohol levels can be preserved for a week at room temperature or indefinitely in a refrigerator if sodium fluoride is added. As a general rule, however, no preservative should be used without consulting an expert. If the evidence specimen must be retained for a number of days without refrigeration, consult a chemist or toxicologist about preserving the sample.

8. Collection

Improper collection can diminish the suitability of evidence for analysis. Most of the errors committed in connection with evidence take place in the collection of the samples. Insufficient evidence samples and a lack of standards of comparison or control samples are the most common errors. These issues can be overcome through better training.

a. **Adequate Sampling**. When possible, collect a generous sample of the evidence. Analysis may consume part of the evidence. The difficulties for the forensic analyst increase for small samples. It is desirable to preserve a quantity of the evidence in its original condition to present in court or for the review of other analysts. With a small sample the analyst may find it necessary to use almost all of the evidence. A larger sample also permits confirmatory tests and increases the likelihood of a representative sample. An extremely limited specimen may not represent the true nature of the material due to contaminates or extraneous material.

b. **Standard or Known Samples**. It is not uncommon for foreign material to found in an evidence sample or stain that could affect the analysis. To control for this, the foreign substance or background material should also be collected. For example, if the stain is found imbedded in wood or on linoleum, it should be collected by cutting off part of the wood or linoleum. In this way the analyst can better understand the difficulties inherent in the analysis. A sample of the unstained wood or linoleum should also be removed and submitted (a control sample) to identify any impurities that may affect the analysis. The control sample should be taken from an area near the stain.

c. **Integrity of Sample**. Evidence samples must be protected from any contaminating matter. Even well intended errors can damage a case. For example, there is a temptation for investigators to try to fit the tool possessed by the suspect into the tool impression found at the scene to determine if they might match. The result, however, will contaminate any paint traces that might be on the tool which could more strongly associate the tool to the crime than would the impression alone. Contamination can also occur when poorly packaged known and unknown samples are placed in the same container. Evidence should be separately wrapped and should not share the same container unless all danger of mingling is removed.

d. **Types of Evidence**. If the evidence is readily portable, investigators should collect the whole object. For example, a fingerprint found on a cash box should be developed, photographed, and then the box itself should be submitted as evidence. No attempt should be made to lift the print. The removal of large or bulky items will often depend on the importance of the case. For a serious crime, the investigator should not hesitate to remove a door that bears a good tool impression.

In some cases, portions of fixed or large objects can be removed. A piece of wooden floor could be removed if the importance of the evidence and the gravity of the case demand it. Such decisions will depend upon the individual case. When it is not possible or practicable to remove the evidence, photography and casting should suffice.

1) ***Fingerprints***. Articles bearing fingerprints are the most common forms of physical evidence. The nature of the article will determine how it should be handled. A document should be handled with tongs or forceps and placed into a cellophane envelope. It should not be folded unless it is very large and then only along existing fold lines. Drinking glasses and bottles should be placed over pegs imbedded in a board and protected in an appropriate container or box.

2) ***Firearms, Knives, and Tools***. Articles such as these can be tied to a peg board by strings passing through perforations and then packed securely in a cardboard or wooden box.

3) ***Hairs and Fibers***. Hair or fiber should be picked up with forceps and placed in a druggist fold or bindle. A druggist fold is formed by starting with a piece of 8 1/2 by 11 paper held in landscape orientation. Fold in half from right to left. Next fold the paper in thirds from top to bottom. Unfolding two-thirds of the paper and separating the ends will create a cone shaped cup. Place the evidence in the bottom of the cup. Refold the paper. Fold again into thirds. Tuck one end into the other. Tape may be used to seal the package.

4) ***Dirt, Soil, Particles, Filings, and Fragments***. Minute quantities of this kind of material should be placed in a druggist fold then placed in a pillbox or plastic vial. Larger quantities should be transferred directly into an appropriately sized box or plastic vial.

5) ***Bullets and Fired Cases***. These should be put in separate small boxes and surrounded with cotton.

6) ***Clothing***. Avoid unnecessary folding or folding across areas of evidentiary interest. Each article of clothing should be packed

separately in a paper bag or cardboard box. Plastic bags should not be used. Wet cloths should be air-dried before packing.

7) ***Blood.*** Latex gloves should be worn when handling blood or any other biological evidence to avoid contaminating the evidence and to protect from infectious diseases. If there is a large pool of blood, collect two samples (approximately 5cc each) with an eye-dropper or a syringe and place in a sterile test tube. If no preservatives or anticoagulants are added, it should be quickly refrigerated. Liquid blood should never be frozen. Anticoagulants, such as EDTA, or preservatives, such as sodium fluoride, will help preserve the samples if refrigeration is delayed. Blood droplets should be collected with a cotton swab or gauze pad. The swab or gauze is then air-dried at room temperature and placed in an envelope, a test tube, or some other sterile container.

When dried bloodstains are found on small objects or articles of clothing, the entire item should be collected. If the garment is dry, it is folded carefully and packaged separately in a paper bag or cardboard container. Dried stains on walls or floors can be scraped with a razor or a scalpel onto filter paper creased in a druggist fold. Bloodstains on carpet or mattress covers can be removed by cutting out the stain and a portion of unstained material as a control sample. A swab or gauze pad moistened with distilled water can be used on stains that cannot be scraped or otherwise removed.

If there are multiple bloodstains, they may come from different sources. Instruments used to collect blood, such as an eyedropper, scalpel, or swab, should be used on only one stain to avoid contaminating the evidence.

8) ***Semen.*** Semen can be found at the scene of sexual assault and other sexually motivated crimes. If the stain is moist, it can be collected with an eyedropper and placed in a sterile test tube to dry. A swab or gauze pad can be used to absorb smaller stains. When found on clothing or bedding, collect the entire item. Samples on clothing and objects must be air-dried before being packaged and sent to the laboratory. Once dry, you need to fold carefully in order to avoid creasing the stained area. As with all biological stains, the item should be packaged in a "breathable" container such as a paper bag or cardboard box to prevent the growth of mold.

If a dried semen stain is found on items that are not transportable, samples can be scraped onto filter paper and appropriately packaged. Dried stains on porous surfaces that can neither be moved nor scraped can be moistened with distilled water and absorbed with a swab. After being air-dried, swabs are placed in an envelope or a sterile test tube.

9) *Saliva*. Once it has dried, saliva is difficult to see or find at a crime scene. It is often more productive to collect items that may contain saliva, such as a cigarette butt or water bottle, than to search for saliva samples. Saliva should be collected in a test tube or with a swab and air-dried before being packaged and sent to the laboratory.

10) *DNA*. DNA analysis requires only a small quantity of evidentiary cells. Small samples can be replicated and amplified to create sufficient evidence to analyze. The sensitivity of modern techniques also means that great care must be taken to prevent extraneous DNA from contaminating evidence samples. For this reason, it is essential when collecting samples to use disposable instruments, avoid touching the evidence, and refrain from talking and sneezing over the evidence.

Blood, semen, saliva, sweat, hair, and skin cells are common sources of DNA. Clothing, bedding, hats, tissues, and wash cloths are productive sources of DNA evidence. Samples may also be recovered from bite marks, fingerprints, fingernail scrapings, cigarette butts, postage stamps, dental floss, and the rims of cups and glasses. Follow the previously described procedures for collecting hair, clothing, blood, semen, and saliva. All biological evidence should be air-dried and placed in paper bags, away from moisture and warm temperatures.

11) *Paint on Vehicles*. Paint chips on or near a vehicle are collected with tweezers, and placed in a paper bindle. Paint smears adhering to the surface of a vehicle require removing a portion of the original painted surface. Use a scalpel to cut through the paint layers until bare metal is reached. A paint chip bearing the smear, approximately one-half inch square should be removed. A similarly sized comparison sample should be collected in an undamaged adjacent area. Package samples separately.

12) *Glass*. See Chapter 5.

Table 6-1. Locating the DNA Evidence.

baseball bat or similar weapon	handle, end	sweat, skin, blood, tissue
hat, bandanna, or mask	inside	sweat, hair, dandruff
eyeglasses	nose or ear pieces, lens	sweat, skin
facial tissue, cotton swab	surface area	mucos, blood, sweat semen, ear wax
dirty laundry	surface area	blood, sweat, semen
toothpick	tips	saliva
used cigarette	cigarette butt	saliva
stamp or envelope	licked area	saliva
tape or ligature	inside/outside surface	skin, sweat
bottle, can, or glass	sides, mouthpiece	saliva, sweat
used condom	inside/outside surface	semen, vaginal or rectal cells
blanket, pillow, sheet	surface area	sweat, hair, semen, urine, saliva
"through and through" bullet	outside surface	blood, tissue
bite mark	person's skin or clothing	saliva
fingernail, partial fingernail	scrapings	blood, sweat, tissue

Source: *What Every Law Enforcement Officer Should Know About DNA Evidence,* National Institute of Justice.

13) ***Electronic Devices.*** Electronic devices can be important sources of evidence. Besides computers and their peripherals, there are cellular phones, caller ID systems, answering machines, pagers, digital cameras, and other devices too numerous to list. When collecting electronic devices, be sure to preserve any physical evidence (fingerprints, blood, hair, etc.) as well as the stored electronic data. When possible, seek advice from a forensic specialist before attempting to collect electronic devices.

Table 6-2. Recommended Methods for Handling Specific Evidence

Item	Method
Handguns	Use your fingers on knurled grips. Do not touch smooth grips or smooth metal parts. Use the tip of the grips. Do not touch the magazine base of pistols. Place in a box, bracing the weapon at the front and rear.
Paper money, documents, paper	Use tweezers. Do not place tweezers over any obvious smudge. Place each item in a clean envelope or bag.
Broken glass	Use your fingers on the edges of larger pieces. Do not touch flat surfaces. Use tweezers on pieces too small for your fingers. Do not grasp at point of any obvious smudges. Wrap pieces individually in clean tissue, place in a box, and stabilize to prevent rubbing, shifting, or breakage.
Dried stains on smooth surfaces of furniture	Collect portion of furniture bearing surfaces of furniture stain in original pattern, if possible; otherwise scrape with pocket knife or putty knife, removing as little of the finished surface as possible.
Bottles, jars, drinking glasses	Insert two or more fingers into large mouth vessels. Place the index fingers on the top and bottom of small mouth vessels. Do not contaminate or spill any substances in the vessel that may have evidence value.
Bullets	Use your fingers or use tweezers with taped ends. Avoid damage to rifling marks on the circumference. Place in a pillbox.
Dried stains on a floor	Collect portion of floor bearing stain in original pattern, if possible; otherwise, remove by gouging deeper than the stain with putty knife, wood chisel, or other tool. Place in pillbox or larger similar container.

Source: U.S. Army. Field manual 19-20.

Begin by documenting the location and connections of each component of a computer system. Note the power status (on, off, or in sleep mode) and what appears on the monitor screen. Do not change the condition of an electronic device. If it is on, leave it on. Determine if the device is connected to a network. A computer specialist should assist when a computer network is involved. Some electronic devices require continuous power to maintain the data in their memory. Information will be lost if the device is unplugged or the battery is permitted to discharge.

9. Identification

Evidence should be marked or labeled for identification as it is collected. Identification is generally accomplished by marks or labels placed on the evidence. The investigator's notebook should contain a description of the object, the position where it was found, the place where it was collected or the person from whom it was received, the names of any witnesses, any serial numbers present, and the case reference data. Many months after the crime the investigator may be called to testify, identify the object, and provide a complete chain of custody for the evidence. These demands can only be met if the evidence has been properly marked and stored.

a. **Marking**. Solid objects should be marked for identification with the initials of the investigator receiving or finding the evidence (see Figure 6-1). Avoid marking where it might disturb evidence on the object. A sharp-pointed instrument such as a metal scribe or permanent marker should be used for marking hard objects. Pen and ink can be used for absorbent articles. Use special care when marking articles of great intrinsic value (e.g., jewelry). Objects too small to mark should be placed in a container such as a pillbox and the container then sealed and labeled. Liquids and pastes should be retained in their original containers and appropriately sealed and labeled. If the evidence consists of a large number of similar items, consult the prosecuting attorney to determine how many of the items need be brought into court and how many should be marked for identification.

b. **Sealing**. Evidence should be enclosed in separate containers. Pillboxes, envelopes, test tubes, and bottles containing evidence should be sealed so that they cannot be opened without breaking the seal (see Figure 6-2).

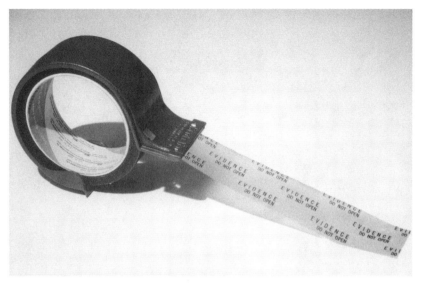

Figure 6-1. Evidence tape for sealing physical evidence properly and easily. (Courtesy of the 3M Company.)

The investigator's initials (or name) and the date of sealing should be written in ink overlapping the seal and the container.

C. **Labeling**. After sealing evidence in a container, a label bearing the case information should be affixed. An adhesive label may be placed on the container or a tag tied to the object. A bullet would be marked on the base with the investigator's initials, placed in a pillbox, sealed and initialed, and finally labeled by affixing a paper sticker to the box. A drug specimen would be placed in protective paper, inserted in a sealed envelope, an evidence seal placed across the flap of the envelope, and labeled with the case information. A rifle would be marked and then tagged. A label or tag should contain the case number, date and time, name or description of the article, location of discovery, signature of the person who found the item, and names of anyone who witnessed the discovery.

1) *Documents*. The best method of marking is to initial and date with a fine-point pen in a place that will not affect the examination. The document should then be placed in a cellophane envelope

Figure 6-2. A demonstration of how evidence tape resists tampering. (Courtesy of the 3M Company.)

and properly sealed. The envelope can be sealed with an evidence label or seal and the date and initials of the investigator placed thereon. Information identifying the document should be placed on the outside of the envelope.

2) *Firearms Evidence.* Unload firearms prior to submission to the laboratory. They should be marked with a metal scribe on some inconspicuous area of the frame to avoid unnecessarily defacing the weapon. Ordinarily, on the bottom of the frame inside the trigger guard is a good place to mark a firearm. If the firearm is rigidly assembled so that the firing pin or barrel cannot be removed without tools this marking will be sufficient. If parts that may leave imprints on bullets or cartridge casings are removable without the aid of tools, each part should be marked. For example, the barrel, slide, and receiver of a .45 caliber semiautomatic pistol should be individually marked. Similarly in a hinge-

frame type of revolver the barrel, cylinder, and frame should each be marked. In bolt-action rifles, the bolt and frame should be marked. If the barrel of a shoulder firearm is removable without tools, it should be marked.

For revolvers, a diagram should be made of the rear face of the cylinder showing the position of each cartridge with respect to the firing pin. The cartridges should be numbered to correspond to the numbering of the chambers, and a mark placed on the rear face of the cylinder to show the chamber that lay under the firing pin.

BULLETS. A bullet should be marked only on its base. Marking the sides could damage rifling marks and marking the nose could destroy other evidentiary material. The nose of the bullet might bear the impression of fabric, blood, tissue, fibers, paint or other materials. Fragmented or deformed bullets should be wrapped in cotton, placed in a pillbox, then sealed and labeled.

CARTRIDGE CASES. A fired cartridge case should be marked inside of the mouth or, if the caliber is too small, on the cylindrical outer surface at a point near the mouth. Never mark the head of a casing since this area may bear breech-face markings or firing-pin indentations. If the casing is to be processed for fingerprints, seal in a container and mark the container rather than the casing.

SHOTGUN SHELLS. If the shell is made of paper, it should be marked with ink; a plastic shell can be marked with a metal scribe. Brass shells should be treated as cartridge cases.

SHOTGUN WADS. The wad should be placed in a pillbox, sealed and labeled.

SMALL SHOT. Buckshot, birdshot and similar ammunition are too small to be marked. Hence, specimens should be placed in a pillbox, sealed and labeled.

COMPARISON STANDARDS. When submitting a firearm for examination, try to also submit a supply (about 10 cartridges) of the same type of ammunition for comparison testing. When possible, a search of the suspect's property may produce similar ammunition.

3) **Clothing**. Articles of clothing can be marked in ink on the lining of the garment. A string tag attached to a button or a button hole will serve as a label.

Table 6-3. FBI Recommendation for Evidence Collection

Was it obtained legally?	• Warrant. • Consent. • Incidental to arrest
Describe it in notes.	• Location, circumstances, how obtained. • Date, chain of custody. • How identified.
Identify it properly.	• Use initials, date, case, number. • Preferably on evidence itself. Liquids, soils, tiny fragments must be placed in suitable containers, sealed and marked on the outside.
Package it properly.	• One case to a box: • Use suitable containers such as round pillboxes, plastic vials, glass or plastic containers, strong cardboard cartons. • Seal securely against leakage. • Package each item separately. Avoid any leakage or contamination. • If wet or bearing blood, air-dry before packaging (except arson cases where hydrocarbons are present).
Maintain chain of custody.	• Keep it short: • Same person or persons that recovered the evidence should initial, seal and send evidence, if possible. • Maintain in a locked vault, cabinet or room until shipped. • Send by air express, registered mail, registered air mail or personal delivery to the laboratory or identification division (there is no way to trace parcel post, certified mail or regular mail).

Source: FBI. *Handbook of Forensic Science,* Rev. ed. Washington, D.C.: U.S. Government Printing Office, 1990.

4) *Plaster Casts.* Casts should be marked on the back before the plaster has dried. When the cast has hardened the marks will be permanent. Subsequently the cast should be placed in a wooden box of suitable size and appropriately labeled.

5) ***Photographs***. Each print should be marked on the reverse side with the date the photograph was taken, the name of the photographer, and the place where it was taken. Any information regarding special processing may also be included. Photographs should be carefully marked to avoid damage and any supplementary marks (such as measurements, arrows to indicate direction, or lines leading to characteristics of a fingerprint pattern) may require explanation by a qualified witness. Marking must not detract from the merits of the picture, and should contribute to expressing a pertinent fact. Improper marking may render a photograph inadmissible. It is generally advisable to have duplicate unmarked prints or use transparent overlays.

10. Transmission

Evidence must be carefully packaged before transporting to a forensic laboratory. If local or state laboratory facilities are not available, law enforcement agencies may seek the services of the FBI Laboratory (see Table 6-3). A letter should accompany the evidence indicating the type of examinations requested and describing the essential facts of the case, along with any information that might assist the examiner. The communication should indicate that the evidence has not been and will not be examined by an expert other than one from the FBI Laboratory. Be sure to comply with postal regulation when transmitting evidence by mail. For example, the postal service should not be used in transmitting live ammunition or flammable liquids.

ADDITIONAL READING

Care of Evidence

Cook, C.W.: *A Practical Guide to the Basics of Physical Evidence.* Springfield, IL: Thomas, 1984.

Crime Scene Investigation: A Guide for Law Enforcement. Washington, D.C.: National Institute of Justice, 2000.

Federal Bureau of Investigation. *Handbook of Forensic Science* (Rev. ed.). Washington, D.C.: U.S. Government Printing Office, 1990.

Fox, R.H. and Cunningham, C.L.: *Crime Scene Search and Physical Evidence Handbook.* Boulder, CO: Paladin Press, 1988.

Genova, J.: Automating Crime Labs and Evidence Control. *Police Chief, 56* (4), 1989.

Goddard, K.W.: *Crime Scene Investigation.* Reston, VA: Reston Publishing, 1977.

Hamilton, T.S.: Developing an Automated Evidence Tracking System. *Police Chief, 58* (4), 1991.

Hawthorne, M.R.: *First Unit Responder: A Guide to Physical Evidence Collection for Patrol Officers.* Boca Raton, FL: CRC Press, 1998.

Herig, J.A.: Computer Evidence Recovery. *Police Chief, 64* (1), 1997.

Kennedy, D.B., Homant, R.J., and Emery, G.L.: AIDS and the Crime Scene Investigator. *Police Chief, 56* (12), 1989.

Noblett, M.G.: The Computer: High-Tech Instrument of Crime. *FBI Law Enforcement Bulletin, 62* (6), 1993.

O'Brien, K.P. and Sullivan, R.C.: *Criminalistics: Theory and Practice* (3rd ed.). Boston: Allyn and Bacon, 1980.

Pilant, L.: Electronic Evidence Recovery. *Police Chief, 66* (2), 1999.

——: Property and Evidence Management. *Police Chief, 63* (7), 1996.

Samen, C.C.: The Evidence Collection Unit. *Law and Order, 19* (7), 1971.

Sauls, J.G.: Computer Searches and Seizures. *FBI Law Enforcement Bulletin, 62* (6), 1993.

Scene of the Crime: U.S. Government Forensic Handbook. Boulder, CO: Paladin Press, 1992.

Part III

OBTAINING INFORMATION

Chapter 7

OBSERVATION AND IDENTIFICATION

OBSERVATION

1. Overview

INVESTIGATORS frequently rely on indirect sources of information (witness statements, reports of other investigators, laboratory reports, photographs, and sketches). They also rely on information from their own senses. Information must be observed, recalled, and articulated before it can become part of the investigation, so investigators must be trained to recognize, remember, and describe important events and behaviors.

2. The Senses in Observation

Our perception is our reality. Misperceptions may never come to light or be acknowledged. A person's confidence in the truthfulness of a statement is related to his or her intent to be forthcoming—not in its factual accuracy. Honesty and accuracy are not synonymous. We believe what we perceive. When our perceptions or memories are incorrect, our statements and declarations may be inaccurate even though we are trying to be honest.

We employ our senses, primarily sight and secondarily hearing, smell, touch, and taste, to understand the events of our daily lives. Vision is the most fruitful source of information, but in the absence of training it is also one of the most unreliable because of our tendency to fill in the gaps of inadequate observation. Hearing is the most objective sense but inaccurate when estimating the distance of sound. The sense of touch is usually unreliable because few people are sufficiently trained in developing the skill. Smell and taste are considered relatively unreliable because of their susceptibility to suggestion. It has been estimated by psychologists that approximately 85 percent of our sensual knowledge is gained through sight; 13 percent through hearing; and the remaining 2 percent through smell, touch, and taste, but people vary in their physical abilities to use each of the senses.

3. Psychological Elements

A person cannot observe a phenomenon until he or she is aware of it. The perceptual process begins when something come to our *attention.* We often see what we expect to see. Our attentiveness may be influenced by such factors as size, change, interest, physical condition, suggestion, and repetition.

Recognition of the significance of a phenomenon is termed *perception.* In this stage the observer not only *apprehends* a phenomenon but also *understands* it. Our understanding is influenced by several factors. Experiments have shown that people tend to overestimate time and distance and generalize to preserve consistency in their environment. *Intelligence* affects our capacity to understand and interpret. *Educational background* broadens our experience and associations. More educated individuals tend to be more verbal and report more details per incident. Less educated individuals tend to report fewer details but make more inferences. A person's *experience and occupation* structure his or her frame of reference. During times of *stress or danger,* people tend to overestimate time and distance. It is common for victims to overestimate the size of their assailants and the length of time it took for police to arrive.

Once the event is perceived, it must be remembered and articulated before the information can become part of an investigation. During recollection, considerable transformation can occur. Recollection is affected by the intensity of the emotional impact on the individual, and can be affected by suggestion and social attitudes. False memories become more difficult to change with each repetition of a story. Multiple experiences can be fused into one event, and a single incident can be remembered as occurring multiple times. Translating mental images into words can introduce additional errors. Gaps in memory are filled with logical deductions to improve the quality of the narration. Bias affects both perception and recall. Written statements tend to produce more details than verbal accounts, but the quantity of details fades with the passing of time.

PHYSICAL DESCRIPTIONS

4. Describing People

People can overcome the limitations of human perception and become better observers. Before the advent of fingerprint identification, Alphonse Bertillon (1853–1914) developed a system of identification based on physical descriptions. While working at the Paris police department, he recognized the importance of standardizing physical identification based on the measurements of various physical features. This system was known as *anthropometry* or *bertilonage*. Bertillon also developed *portrait parlé,* a systematic method for verbally describing a person after only a brief observation.

5. General Information

You seldom know what information you will need to identify, locate or link perpetrators to their crimes. The verbal description or *portrait parlé* is still considered a reliable aid. As opportunities arise, it is best to collect as much information as possible. A thorough (but not exhaustive) list of identifying information can be found in Table 7-1. It is unlikely you will be able to collect all of this information, but you should strive to collect as much as possible.

Physical descriptions, not only help identify the perpetrator, but also describe suspects to others. Your purpose is to communicate information. Sometimes national origins or ethnicity can convey the traits you are trying to describe. Irish-American or Italian-American may aid in communicating more descriptively than a list of the facial characteristics, however, these stereotypes should be used with caution. People of all nationalities and ethnicities vary greatly. Your stereotypical image of an Irish-American may be significantly different from that of a witness, victim, or other investigator. National origins or ethnicity may provide a starting point for a physical description but will need additional detail and clarification to provide a useful description.

Even when people are trying to hide or disguise themselves, personal habits may emerge. For example, some people routinely wear heavy makeup or excessive cologne. Others find it difficult to change their standard of dress. Tendencies toward sport clothes or loud dress will be retained. Slovenly, neat, expensive, cheap, or conservative are a few of the adjectives that may be used to describe or elicit descriptions.

A person's habits may be useful in locating him or her. A propensity for frequenting bars, theaters, bowling alleys, and other forms of entertainment; a "weakness" for sex diversion; an addiction to drugs; or a desire to engage in sports can aid the search for a wanted person.

Table 7-1. Identifiers of People.

Name & aliases	full name (not merely initials), varied spellings of the different aliases, nicknames, user names and passwords
Identification numbers	employment Id, social security, military serial number, fingerprint classification
Address	present and former
Scars & marks	healed wounds, birthmarks, tattoos
Relatives and associates	names, addresses, and occupations of relatives, friends, associates, and acquaintances
History	education, military history, criminal record, and professional or occupational background
Age & sex	estimate
Race or color	estimate, skin tone and shade
Height	estimated within 2 inches
Weight	estimated within 5 pounds

Table 7-1 — *Continued.*

Build	thin, slender, medium, and stout
Posture	erect, slouching, round-shouldered
Voice	high/low pitch, loud/soft
Speech	Enunciation, accent, educated/uneducated
Walk	athletic, limping, shuffling, bowlegged, flatfooted, and pigeon-toed
General impression	personality; apparent social status; comparison by name with an actor, political figure, or other well known person
Head	Size (small, medium, or large), shape, (round, long, dome-shaped, flat on top, or bulging in the back)
Hair	color, style, length, sheen, part, straight/ curly, area of baldness
Face	General impression, **Forehead** (high, low, bulging, receding), **Eyebrows** (bushy or thin; shape), **Mustache** (length; color; shape), **Eyes** (small, medium, or large; color; clear, dull, bloodshot; separation; glasses), **Ear** (size; shape; size of lobe; angle of set), **Cheeks** (high, low, or prominent cheekbones; fat, sunken or medium), **Nose** (short, medium, big, or long; straight, aquiline, or flat; hooked or pug), **Mouth** (wide, small, or medium; general expression), **Lips** (shape; thickness; color), **Teeth** (shade; condition; defects; missing elements), **Chin** (size; shape; general impression), **Jaw** (length; shape; lean, heavy, or medium)
Neck	shape; thickness; length; Adam's apple
Shoulders	width and shape
Waist	size; shape of stomach
Hands	length; size; hair; condition of palms
Fingers	length; thickness; stains; shape of nails; condition of nails
Arms	long, medium, or short; muscular, normal or thin; thickness of wrist
Feet	size; deformities

6. Voice Identification

We commonly recognize the voice of others. Picking up a telephone we may recognize immediately the voice of a person we have not seen for months or even years. Voices are distinctive, and individuals can be distinguished by the sounds such as pitch, intensity, and "quality," that the human ear discerns as unique patterns.

Investigators are generally less interested in recognizing a human voice than in proving the identity of the speaker in court. Courts are often more willing to accept identification testimony from an individual familiar with the subject than from forensic experts. Continued controversy in the scientific and legal community means that voice identification remains limited, examined case by case, and accepted in some jurisdictions but not others.

Voice identification can arise in a variety of ways. For example, it may be necessary in a conspiracy case to identify the speakers in a recording of a conversation. Similarly, it may be necessary to identify the speaker in a recorded bomb threat, kidnapping ransom demand, or extortion threat.

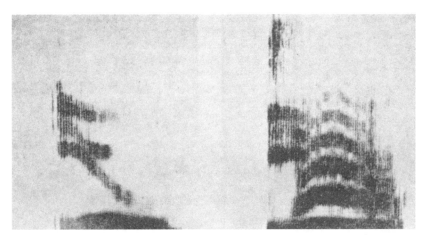

Figure 7-1. *Voiceprints* are visual representations of characteristics of the human voice that permit identification by comparison. The spoken word "you," for example, can be recorded to provide "spectrograms" such as these, in which an expert can find an adequate base of similarities and differences for a definite opinion as to the identity of the speaker.

Forensic voice identification relies, in part, on an electronic recording of the energy output of the subject's voice when speaking a specified word. A sound "spectrogram" can be used for comparison. Whenever a person says the word–"you," for example–regardless of pitch, volume, or attempt to disguise his or her voice, the "spectrogram" or "voiceprint" will be substantially the same.

The consistency is due to the physical characteristics of the vocal cavities (in the throat, the nasal system, and the mouth) and the structure and use of the lips, the jaw, and the tongue. Speaking is a randomly learned process as children try thousands of vocal combinations before coming up with their own unique voice. The attributes of voiceprint identification are not under the speaker's conscious control. Loudness, rapidity of speech, and pitch can be controlled consciously and are not part of the identification process. Even the use of a different language does not affect the identification.

An early case of voiceprint identification involved a police shooting in St. Paul. Police responded to an anonymous telephone call of a woman about to give birth. When officers arrived, a sniper killed one officer. The only clue was a taped recording of the telephone call. The investigation sought to identify the voice. Police recorded thirteen neighborhood women. As a result of voiceprint analyses, Caroline Trimble was arrested and indicted for murder.

Two earlier cases involving voiceprints came before courts in New Jersey (1967) and California (1968), and both times the appeals courts rejected the method as unreliable. In another 1967 case, erroneous voiceprint identification was made of a deputy police inspector in a grand jury investigation of police corruption. Four years later, the error was acknowledged after the police official, through his own investigative efforts, found and produced the true perpetrator.

At the present, technical uncertainties and the substantial lack of agreement among speech scientists surround voice identification. The method is ill-served by excessive claims of specificity and infallibility. Even though a method falls short of 100 percent reliability, it can still be quite useful to the courts and the police, provided that the users are aware of limitations. Investigators should not be misled by "voiceprints" and "voice spectrograms" with their implied analogies of fingerprints and DNA. There remain limitations in the method that require continuing research and standards for examiners.

7. Lost or Stolen Property

Electronic databases of articles reported lost, stolen, pawned, or sold at second hand shops are effective tools for recovering lost or stolen property. Many thieves lack the means to dispose of property. They usually dispose of property by selling to pawnbrokers, secondhand dealers, innocent friends, strangers, or fences.

No matter how the thief originally disposes of the property, the stolen object may eventually find its way to a pawn shop or a secondhand dealer. Most cities require pawn shops and secondhand dealers to daily report to the police department the pawning or purchase of certain types of property. A detective investigating a larceny can then readily check on property.

a. **Description of Property**. Property should be described in as much detail as possible. Watches, automobiles, electronic equipment, and cameras, for example, usually bear a serial number. Unfortunately, many owners (and even dealers) keep no record of these numbers. In describing property, strive to record any detail that might help to identify it. Identifying qualities include: *kind* of article (e.g., watch or camera), *physical appearance* (model, size, shape, and condition), *material* of which it's composed (plastic, wood, aluminum, gold or silver, etc.), *brand name, number* of articles or weight, and *identifying marks* (serial numbers, personal inscriptions, wear or damage).

Items differ in their identifying characteristics. Some common examples include: *automobiles* (registration plate, VIN, make, model, color), *watches* (case number, movement number, make, model, metal, inscriptions, setting), *jewelry* (kind, style, metal, setting, kind and number of stones), *rings* (type: engagement, wedding, cocktail, etc., initials or inscriptions if present, the number and kind of stones, shape and cut of the stones), *fur* (kind of fur, style, manufacture), and *cameras* (kind, manufacturer, model, kind of lens including lens focal length, f/number, and serial number).

b. **Personal Marking**. To facilitate the recovery of stolen property, a number of police departments are encouraging citizens to engrave their telephone or driver's license numbers on their valuables. By means of an electric scriber, citizens can engrave these numbers on bicycles, television sets, silverware, cameras, and jewelry. If an item is subsequently stolen and later recovered in a pawnshop or with a secondhand dealer, the department's computer can match the article with the owner. Ordinarily the police must check their lists of stolen property or go through a manufacturer's list of serial numbers in a time-consuming procedure that may require several weeks to trace the owner of recovered property. Citizens should not use Social Security numbers for this purpose. Aside from the possibility of identity theft, police are unable to access them.

IDENTIFICATION BY WITNESSES

8. Difficulties

The typical witness is not trained as an observer and knows little of investigative procedures. As a consequence, witnesses are seldom prepared to provide investigators the information they need. Investigators must skillfully assist witnesses to describe criminals while safeguarding against suggesting characteristics to impressionable witnesses.

9. Identifying Wanted Criminals

Witnesses are asked to describe suspects to provide a verbal description or to help an artist create a sketch. Depending on whether the witness knows the perpetrator, investigators may vary their approach.

When the witness knows the perpetrator, investigators begin by determining the context of the association. Does the witness recognize the suspect from his or her neighborhood, workplace, and so on? Who else may be able to provide information about the suspect? Relatives and other friends can offer a description. Police records may contain descriptions or photographs. Police may proceed as if conducting a limited background investigation. Emphasis should be placed on peculiarities and defects to better distinguish the suspect from others. Social acquaintances are more likely to stress odd characteristics and peculiarities of dress. By collecting all available photographs and a number of verbal descriptions, an excellent pictorial and verbal description can be obtained.

Identifying unknown perpetrators is more difficult, and investigators must use caution with eyewitness accounts. The fallibility of eyewitness identification is well known. Instances of mistaken identity and inaccurate reporting are common when dealing with untrained observers. Investigators' questions must not be suggestive and information must be verified.

10. Identifying Methods

There are several ways to assist witnesses to describe an unknown criminal. The process generally starts with a *verbal description* or *portrait parlé*. There are issues with this method and investigators may want to judge the witnesses' abilities by asking them to describe someone known to investigators. This description can serve as a control in judging the reliability of the description of the unknown criminal.

Photographic files (Rogues' Gallery) are maintained of known criminals. The *modus operandi* of the crime may suggest a group of photographs for viewing by the witness. Witnesses should be told that the suspect's photograph may not be contained in the file. Witnesses should also be instructed to point out any strong similarity such as a similar nose or mouth.

General photographs representing a variety of facial types may be used to help witnesses describe a suspect. These photos may not be of criminals but illustrate various facial features. Facial images should be of the same size in all the pictures. The selection of photos should include the varieties of features such as degree of baldness, length and shape of nose, shape of ear, and so forth.

a. **Computer Assisted Identifications**. Artists are sometimes used to sketch suspects from features described by eyewitnesses.

Witnesses may be asked to select features that most nearly represent the suspect from a chart of noses, eyes, and ears. The artist then draws a composite face that may approximate the criminal.

Composite sketches can also be created with computer software. The enormous data storage and graphics display capability of the computer make it ideally suited to create a composite sketch. A computer system can store thousands different facial features that can be combined to form different faces. In a matter of seconds, a new feature can be added or removed from the computer display. The computer sketch can be created from responses to questions designed to help the witness remember important facial features. Computer composite drawing software tends to be easy to use and requires little training of operators.

A good sketch or composite is the result of unbiased and accurate information. If there are a number of witnesses, they should be separated or advised not to discuss the matter. A witness who is susceptible to suggestion may readily acquiesce to the opinion of a more forceful person. To retain the value of the witness's initial impression it is necessary to obtain a description before he or she has spoken at length with others.

After listening to witnesses' *oral accounts* of the incident and descriptions of the criminal, ask them to produce *written descriptions*. After studying the written descriptions, investigators will be able to establish a *composite description* of the criminal. Weigh the description according to observations of the witness's reliability. At this point, an artist or technician can create *preliminary sketches and composites*. Several sketches are produced from the written descriptions with variants of the common features. Witnesses are separately requested to examine the sketches, select the closest approximation, and record their suggestions for improvement. A finished *sketch or composite* is prepared from the new information. Witnesses are then called in as a group and may discuss the second and the preliminary sketches with the artist or technician. Suggestions are offered, studied, and incorporated into a finished sketch.

New technology is opening new possibilities for investigators. Generally the final sketch or composite is circulated in the hope the police or public recognize the suspect. Researchers Brendan Klare and Anil Jain, at Michigan State University, are working to utilize police records and automate the search. They have developed a computer program to match sketches to mug shots. Currently, the system has a nearly 30 percent accuracy rate, but work continues. Investigators may also have an image of suspects, such as surveillance video, and need to identify them. Biometric facial recognition has an accuracy rate of over 90 percent if the image is of the quality of a mug shot or driver's license photo. Unfortunately, most surveillance images are not of that quality. Video is often of low quality, and cameras are placed to cover a large area. With improvements in video quality and better camera placement, facial recognition systems will become a more effective tool for investigators.

11. Identification of a Suspect

Eyewitness identification can be critically important to a criminal investigation. To insure that the identification is an independent and honest recollection, investigators must be familiar with some techniques and precautions. Three important methods of eyewitness identification are the "lineup," the "showup," and the photographic array. The lineup is the customary means of identifying suspects. When conducted properly, it is considered more accurate than the other methods. The showup, or single suspect confrontation, is used in emergency situations, such as when the victim is dying or when a lineup is impractical. A photographic array is employed when a lineup cannot be held because the suspect is not in custody.

a. **Lineups**. A lineup is an identification procedure where the suspect is presented with a number of similar-looking persons to determine if witnesses can identify the perpetrator. Witnesses are asked if they recognize any of the members of the lineup as participating in the crime. Nothing about the lineup should suggest who the witness should choose, and witnesses should not feel compelled to make a choice.

A lineup should only be used when necessary and may not be appropriate in some situations. When a witness knows the suspect and recognized him or her during the offense, a lineup adds little to the case. If there is a significant amount of other incriminating evidence and the eyewitness recollection is weak, a lineup is often unproductive. If the suspect's appearance is so unusual that suitable lineup participants cannot be located, a lineup is not appropriate.

To conduct a lineup, a group of at least six persons, including the suspect, should be assembled. Participants in the lineup can be presented simultaneously or sequentially. Nothing should be said or done by investigators or lineup participants to unfairly distinguish the suspect from the other participants in the lineup. The persons participating in the lineup should have the same general appearance as the suspect such as race, sex, height, hair, and clothing. The suspect should be permitted to select his or her own position in the lineup. Persons known to the witness should not be used in the lineup.

The lineup should be held in a room away from public view with little opportunity for disturbance. The room must at least be large enough to accommodate six lineup participants side-by-side while still leaving room for movement. Though not required, it is best to use a room with a screen or a two-way mirror that separates witnesses from the lineup participants.

When there are multiple witnesses, they should be separated, view the lineup individually, and not have contact with each other until after all have viewed the lineup. Witnesses should be instructed before entering the lineup room that the suspect may or may not be among the persons in the group. Suspects should not be able to determine if they have been identified. If identifications cannot be made privately, witnesses should be instructed to enter the room and study the group without indicating a decision. Identifications can be made silently by marking a card. Investigators should limit the possibility of an outburst designed to intimidate witnesses and preserve interrogation opportunities by restricting the suspect's knowledge of the details and strength of the identification.

The lineup members should not talk while in the room unless voice identification is required. Determine whether it will be necessary to have the lineup members wear specific apparel, walk, speak, etc. before bringing in witnesses. If, during the lineup, witnesses desire the lineup members to perform certain actions, it should be communicated quietly to investigators.

An incarcerated suspect does not have the right to refuse either to participate in a lineup or to perform the acts or utterances requested by investigators. A court order may be obtained to compel the suspect to participate, and disruption of the lineup or refusing to participate may be used in court.

1) **Right to Counsel**. For indicted suspects the lineup is considered a "critical stage" of the proceedings and the suspect is entitled to legal representation. Suspects may waive their right to counsel by signing a waiver form. As with a confession, a valid waiver must be informed and voluntary.

A suspect's request for legal counsel at a lineup should be honored, even if it is not necessarily required by law. Defense attorneys are limited to observing. They are not entitled to participate in conducting the lineup or converse with any of the witnesses or the participants. Defense counsel, however, should be permitted, and even encouraged, to make suggestions about the procedure of the lineup to insure fairness. Reasonable requests should be adopted. Defense counsel may even assist in selecting individuals to stand in the lineup with the suspect.

2) **Recording the Lineup**. The lineup should be photographed, front and profile, as viewed by the witnesses. Some agencies use video to record their lineups. Identification forms used by witnesses should be retained. The officer in charge of the lineup should prepare a report describing where and how the lineup was conducted along with the names and addresses of all the participants. Statements by the witnesses and any objections or suggestions from defense attorneys should be noted.

3) **Supreme Court Rulings**. In *U.S. v. Wade,* 388 U.S. 218 (1967) the Court ruled that lineups are a critical stage of the prosecution, and the Sixth Amendment guarantees the right of counsel. In *Kirby v. Illinois,* 406 U.S. 682 (1972), the Court ruled that only suspects who have been formally charged with a criminal offense are entitled to have lawyers at lineups. The Court affirmed that identifications will be barred from evidence whenever a defendant can show that a lineup was unfair.

b. **Showups**. A showup is the showing of a single suspect to a witness for the purpose of identification. If a suspect is seized shortly after the commission of a crime and in vicinity of the crime scene, he or she may be returned to the crime scene or detained to be identified by witnesses. Up to one hour after the commission of the crime is usually considered a reasonable time period, but the special circumstances of the case may justify an extension.

Because a single suspect showing is inherently suggestive, it is, in most cases, preferable to use a lineup for identification. Forming a lineup, however, is not always practical. It can cause a substantial delay and the time elapsed may affect witnesses' ability to recollect, diminish the reliability of the identification, and extend the detainment of an innocent person while a dangerous suspect remains loose. If there are a number of suspects and the crime was committed by a single individual, conducting a lineup for each of the suspects would take a long time and require the detention of innocent parties unnecessarily. If the victim has been seriously injured and may die before a lineup can be prepared, a showup may be appropriate.

1) *Procedure*. If a suspect has been arrested, he or she may be brought back to the crime scene for identification. If the suspect has not been arrested and does not voluntarily return to the crime scene, the witness should be brought to where the suspect is being temporarily detained. Unless there is a state law to the contrary, a suspect does not have the right of legal representation at a showup.

Investigators should ensure the showup is accomplished in a fair and reasonable manner. If possible, the suspect should not appear in handcuffs. The investigator should not convey details of the apprehension to witnesses. Witnesses should merely be informed that a person fitting the description of the suspect has been detained for questioning. Witnesses, when confronting the suspect, should be asked "Is this the person?" The investigator should not comment on the identification in the presence of the suspect or the witness. A written report of the procedure should be made and retained in the case file.

c. **Photographic Lineup**. A photographic lineup, or photographic identification, is a process where witnesses try to identify suspects from a series of photographs. The same consideration of fairness applies to the photographic identification as to an ordinary lineup. The photographs must be of people who have a similar general appearance, and they must be displayed in a manner that is not suggestive.

Photographic lineups are commonly used when a suspect is not in custody. Often a previous arrest photo is used, but any representative photo can be used as long as the other photos in lineup are of a similar nature. A photographic identification may also be used when a lineup is impractical. There may not be enough people available who resemble the general appearance of the suspect or a witness may live too great a distance from where the suspect is being held.

Procedure. At least six photographs, including that of the subject, should be used. Photos can be shown simultaneously or sequentially. Each photograph should resemble the general appearance of the suspect and should be of someone whose identity is known. If any of the photos have suggestive or prejudicial content, a cropping map can be constructed to cover the undesirable content (for example, booking photos containing the name of the individual). A photo lineup comprised of six booking photos might consist of a large mat with six viewing areas that display only the face and shoulders of each photo or individual mats for each photo. The revealed portion of each photo should be consistent.

If there are multiple witnesses, they should be separated and view the photo lineup individually. The investigator should instruct each witness that the person who committed the crime may or may not be among those presented. If the witness identifies the suspect, he or she should be instructed to initial the back of the photograph chosen. The investigator should also initial it and request the witness to furnish details of the identification in a signed statement. The investigator should not comment on the selection or the lack of a selection. If there are other witnesses, they should not be informed of the results of the viewing by another witness.

If a suspect is identified, all the photographs used in the display should be retained along with the identifying information of the persons in the photos. Investigators should report the details of the identification. This report will include: the date, time, location, and procedure of the identification; the identities of the investigators, witnesses, and the persons depicted in the photographs; the presentation order of the photographs; any statements made by the witnesses pertaining to the identification; and the presence or absence of any marks, scratches, writing, or other physical characteristics on the photographs.

The suspect does not have the right to have a lawyer present at a photographic identification, but whenever possible a physical lineup, rather than photos, should be used if the suspect is in custody. The suspect does not need to be informed that a photographic lineup has been conducted.

12. Self-Incrimination

The Fifth Amendment guarantees that "No person . . . shall be compelled in any criminal case to be a witness against himself." This right against self-incrimination is violated when people are required to give testimonial evidence against themselves. The interpretation of self-incrimination has been limited by the courts to compelling people to give statements against their own interests. Non-testimonial evidence is generally not protected by the Fifth Amendment.

Non-testimonial evidence is evidence taken from the person of the suspect that does not involve his or her comment on guilt (e.g. hair, identification photographs, items of clothing, etc.). In general, a suspect under lawful arrest for an offense has no constitutional right to refuse to provide non-testimonial evidence and no right to warnings such as those given under *Miranda*. Non-testimonial evidence may be forced, without a warrant, from the suspect against his or her will and used to convict. The preferred method of compelling evidence from a suspect is to obtain a court order directing the individual to surrender the evidence desired.

Compelling a suspect to give a blood sample (*Schmerber v. California*, 384 U.S. 757, 1966), handwriting sample (*Gilbert v. California*, 388 U.S. 263, 1968), fingerprints (*U.S. v. Laub Baking Co.*, 283 F. Supp. 217, 1968), to repeat the words used in a crime

(*U.S. v. Wade,* 388 U.S. 218, 1967) or appear in a lineup does not violate protection from self-incrimination. Courts have held that:

> . . . it (the privilege against self-incrimination) offers no protection against compulsion to submit to fingerprinting, photographing, or measurements, to write or speak for identification, to appear in court, to stand, to assume a stance, to walk, or to make a particular gesture. The distinction which has emerged, often expressed in different ways, is that the privilege is a bar against compelling communications or testimony, but that compulsion which makes a suspect or accused the source of real or physical evidence does not violate it. (*Schmerber v. California,* 384 U.S. 757 1966)

ADDITIONAL READING

Observations and Description

Basinger, L.F.: *The Techniques of Observation and Learning Retention: A Handbook for the Policeman and the Lawyer.* Springfield, IL: Thomas, 1988.

Coleman, S.: Biometrics: Solving Cases of Mistaken Identity and More. *FBI Law Enforcement Bulletin, 69* (6), 2000.

Davies, H.M., Ellis, H.D. and Shepherd, J.W. (Eds.): *Perceiving and Remembering Faces.* London: Academic Press, 1981.

McGuire, M.V. and Walsh, M.F.: *The Identification and Recovery of Stolen Property Using Automated Information Systems: An Investigator's Handbook.* Washington, D.C.: U.S. Government Printing Office, 1981.

Marshall, J.: *Law and Psychology in Conflict.* Indianapolis, IN: Bobbs Merrill, 1980.

Nash, D.J.: *Individual Identification and the Law Enforcement Officer.* Springfield, IL: Thomas, 1978.

Penry, J.: *Looking at Faces and Remembering Them. A Guide to Facial Identification.* London: Elek Books, 1971.

Rogers, S.I.: *The Personal Identification of Living Individuals.* Springfield, IL: Thomas, 1986.

Starrett, P. and Keegan, J.M.: *Police Identification Guide.* Palo Alto, CA: Starrett Publishing, 1983.

Zavala, A. and Paley, J.J. (Eds.): *Personal Appearance Identification.* Springfield, IL: Thomas, 1972.

Voice Identification

Albrecht, S.: Catching Crooks with Voiceprints. *Law and Order, 35* (7), 1987.

Bloch, E.: *Voiceprinting.* New York: David McKay, 1975.

The Evidentiary Value of Spectrographic Voice Identification. *Journal of Criminal Law, Criminology and Police Science, 63* (349), 1972.

Gilbert, J.: *Criminal Investigation* (7th ed.). Upper Saddle River, NJ: Pearson Prentice Hall, 2007.

Greene, H.F.: Voiceprint Identification: The Case in Favor of Admissibility. *American Criminal Law Review, 13* (171), 1975.

Hollien, H.: *The Acoustics of Crime: The New Science of Forensic Phonetics.* New York: Plenum Press, 1990.

Jones, W.R.: Evidence Vel Non: The Non Sense of Voiceprint Identification. *Kentucky Law Journal, 62* (301), 1973-1974.

Kersta, L.G.: Voiceprint Identification. *Police Law Quarterly, 3* (3), 1974.

Koenig, B.E.: Speaker Identification (Part 1) Three Methods–Listening, Machine, and Aural-Visual. (Part 2) Results of the National Academy of Sciences' Study. *FBI Law Enforcement Bulletin, 49* (1 & 2), 1980.

On the Theory and Practice of Voice Identification. Washington, D.C.: National Academy of Sciences, 1979.

Saferstein, R.: *Criminalistics: An Introduction to Forensic Science* (9th ed.). Upper Saddle River, NJ: Pearson Prentice Hall, 2007.

Tosi, O.: *Voice Identification: Theory and Legal Applications.* Baltimore: University Park Press, 1979.

Tosi, O. and Nash, E.: Voiceprint Identification Rules for Evidence. *Trial, 9* (1), 1973.

Voice Identification Research. Washington, D.C.: U.S. Government Printing Office, 1972.

Voiceprint Identification: The Trend Towards Admissibility. *New England Law Review, 9* (419), 1974.

Voiceprint Technique: How Reliable is Reliable? *Illinois Bar Journal, 63* (260), 1975.

Identification by Witness

Bocklet, R.: Suspect Sketches Computerized for Faster Identification. *Law and Order, 35* (8), 1987.

Brown, E., Deffenbacher, K. and Sturgill, W.: Memory for Faces and the Circumstances of Encounter. *Journal of Applied Social Psychology, 62* (311), 1977.

Buchanan, D.R.: Enhancing Eyewitness Identification: Applied Psychology for Law Enforcement Officers. *Journal of Police Science and Administration, 13* (303), 1985.

Clede, B.: Computerized ID Systems. *Law and Order, 36* (1) 1988.

——: The Psychology of a Composite ID. *Law and Order, 34* (11), 1986.

Clifford, B.R. and Bull, R.: *The Psychology of Person Identification.* Boston: Routledge and Kegan Paul, 1978.

Cohen, A.A.: Number of Features and Alternatives Per Feature in Reconstructing Faces with the Identi-Kit. *Journal of Police Science and Administration, 1* (349), 1973.

Ellis, H.D.: Recognizing Faces. *British Journal of Psychology, 66* (409), 1975.

Geiselman, R.E., et al.: Enhancement of Eyewitness Memory: An Empirical Evaluation of the Cognitive Interview. *Journal of Police Science and Administration, 12* (74), 1984.

Hernadez, C.: System Matches Suspect Sketches to Mug Shots. SmartPlanet. Available http://www.smartplanet.com/blog/pure-genius/system-matches-suspect-sketches-to-mug-hots/5790?tag=search-river, March 17, 2011.

Hess, E.: Why Isn't Automated Face Recognition Where Fingerprint Identification is Today? *Identification News, 41* (4), 2011.

Hinkle, D.P.: *Faces of Crime* (True crime stories from the files of a police artist). Atlanta: Peachtree Publications, 1989.

——: *Mug Shots: A Police Artist's Guide to Remembering Faces.* Port Townsend, WA: Loompanics, 1990.

Hopper, W.R.: Photo-Fit–The Penry Facial Identification Technique. *Journal of the Forensic Science Society, 13* (77), 1973.

Laughery, K.R., et al.: Time Delay and Similarity Effects in Facial Recognition. *Journal of Applied Science Psychology, 59* (490), 1974.

Loftus, E.F., Altman, D. and Geballe, R.: Effects of Questioning upon a Witness'Later Recollections. *Journal of Police Science and Administration, 3* (162), 1975.

Morton, D.W.: Composite Drawings as Evidence and Investigative Tools. *Law and Order, 35* (5), 1987.

Owens, C.: Identi-Kit Continues to Score. *Fingerprint and Identification Magazine, 55* (1), 1973.

Lineups

Adams, T.F.: *Police Field Operations* (2nd ed.). Englewood Cliffs, N.J.: Prentice-Hall, 1990.

Compelling Nontestimonial Evidence by Court Order. *FBI Law Enforcement Bulletin, 40* (2), 1971.

Doob, A.N. and Kirshenbaum, H.M.: Bias in Police Lineup–Partial Remembering. *Journal of Police Science and Administration, 1* (287), 1973.

Eywitness Evidence: A Guide for Law Enforcement, NCJ 178240, Washington D.C: U.S. Department of Justice, 1999.

Klotter, J.C. and Kanovitz, J.R.: *Constitutional Law* (6th ed.). Cincinnati: Anderson, 1991.

Levine, F.J. and Tapp, J.L.: The Psychology of Criminal Identification: The Gap From *Wade to Kirby.* 121 *University of Pennsylvania Law Review,* 1079, 1973.

Pitts, M.E.: How Sound is Your Lineup? *FBI Law Enforcement Bulletin, 40* (12), 1971.

Rifas, R.A.: *Legal Aspects of Video Tape and Motion Pictures in Law Enforcement.* Evanston, IL: Traffic Institute, Northwestern University, 1972.

Ringel, W.E.: *Identification and Police Line-ups.* Jamaica, NY: Gould Pub., 1968.

Tobias, M.W. and Petersen, R.D.: *Pre-Trial Criminal Procedure.* Springfield, IL: Thomas, 1972.

Trapp, W.H., Jr., Pretrial Identification Confrontations. *Mississippi Law Journal, 45* (489), 1974.

Eyewitness Testimony

Borchard, E.M.: *Convicting the Innocent: Errors of Criminal Justice.* New Haven, CT: Yale University Press, 1932.

Buckhout, R.: Eyewitness Testimony. *Scientific American, 231* (6), 1974.

Ceci, S.J., Toglia, M.P. and Ross, D.F. (Eds.): *Children's Eyewitness Memory.* New York: Springer-Verlag, 1987.

Hinkle, D.P. and Malawista, D.: Sudden Fear and Witness Reliability. *Law and Order, 35* (7), 1987.

Lipton, J.P.: On the Psychology of Eyewitness Testimony. *Journal of Applied Social Psychology, 62* (1), 1977.

Lloyd-Bostock, S. and Clifford, B.R. (Eds.): *Evaluating Eyewitness Evidence.* Chichester, Eng.: Wiley, 1983.

Loftus, E.F.: *Eyewitness Testimony.* Cambridge, MA: Harvard University Press, 1979.

Sagatun, I.J. and Edwards, L.P.: The Child as Witness in the Criminal Courts. *Police Chief, 56* (4), 1989.

Sobel, N. R.: *Eyewitness Identifications: Legal and Practical Problems.* New York: Clark Boardman, 1972.

Wall, P.M.: *Eyewitness Identification in Criminal Cases.* Springfield, IL: Thomas, 1966.

Wells, G.L. and Loftus, E.F. (Eds.): *Eyewitness Testimony.* Cambridge, Eng.: Cambridge University Press, 1984.

Woocher, F.D.: Did Your Eyes Deceive You? Expert Psychological Testimony on the Unreliability of Eyewitness Identification. *Stanford Law Review, 29* (969), 1977.

Chapter 8

INTERVIEW AND INTERROGATION

1. Overview

ACQUIRING AND PROCESSING INFORMATION is the essence of effective criminal investigation. Most crimes are solved through information that may come from complainants, witnesses, informants, other knowledgeable individuals, or suspects through interviews and interrogation (defined in Chapter 1). Rarely is circumstantial evidence alone sufficient to obtain a conviction. Investigators start with few facts and must develop the necessary information through patient and intelligent questioning. Skilled interrogators may elicit much of the information necessary for conviction, while inexperienced or inept investigators come away with little.

The investigator starts by trying to establish the elements of the offense. Can the victim identify the perpetrator? Can the stolen property be recognized by markings, serial numbers, or a bill of sale? Is the accused the person he or she claims to be? Are there records to identify the accused or to verify his or her location when the crime was committed? Are there witnesses?

Missing suspects must be tracked by the investigator. What information, both official and unofficial, is available? Records, service providers, police files, hotel registers, vital statistics, employers, associates, and many other sources may yield valuable information. Investigators must often rely upon strangers for information. Depending upon their interviewing skill, investigators may come away with compelling facts or worthless statements. In addition, investigators must convince the witness to testify or make a written statement.

2. Definition of Terms

a. **Witness**. A witness is a person, other than a suspect, who is questioned about an incident or individual. A witness may be a victim, complainant, accuser, source of information, observer of the incident, scientific specialist, or a custodian of official documents. A witness is usually interviewed, but may be interrogated if suspected of lying or of withholding information.

b. **Suspect**. A suspect is a person whose guilt is considered a reasonable possibility.

c. **Subject**. The term subject is commonly used to represent a person, whether witness or suspect, who is being interviewed or interrogated. It is a generic term and does not imply that the individual committed a crime. The term is also used in case reports to refer to an individual who has not been identified.

3. Canvassing for Information

The "neighborhood canvass" is the system interviewing of people living near or frequenting the vicinity of the crime scene to uncover information about the crime. Because a canvas can be time consuming and may not produce leads, some investigators may forgo it and move on to other duties. This is a mistake. Witnesses do not always report what they know to the police because they may assume police already know the information or they are unaware they possess information relevant to an investigation.

Sometimes a canvas can produce key information. The canvas may reveal a witness to the crime or even the perpetrator. While few suspects will confess because an investigator happens to come to their door, nervous or odd behavior may prompt investigators to more closely scrutinize the individual.

In a Michigan case, a neighborhood canvass brought investigators to the door of a young man who murdered his neighbor the night before. The perpetrator appeared calm and cooperative until asked about a suspicious individual that neighbors had reported in the area days before. He then rattled off a highly detailed description, including eye color, of an individual who was supposedly observed from over 100 feet away. Upon leaving, investigators commented on the odd behavior and noted they might have to investigate further. Later that evening, the perpetrator, fearing for his safety, approached police to surrender. As the day had progressed, neighbors and relatives talked about the murder and being interviewed by police. The perpetrator and his relatives (as they began to realize his involvement) felt it was safer to surrender than wait for police to arrest him. While investigators had not yet focused on the perpetrator, he assumed he would be identified because he perceived the canvas indicated an intensive police investigation.

1) *Procedure.* Ideally, the canvass should be conducted at the approximate time of day as when the crime occurred to interview people normally in the area. In addition to residents, possible witnesses include shopkeepers, delivery persons, commuters, dog-walkers, and shoppers.

The canvass can be conducted by a single investigator but is often assigned to a team of investigators. Each investigator should be familiar with all the details of the case so that they will be able to ask the appropriate questions and recognize a valuable lead. The circumstances of the crime will determine the area to be covered. The scope of the canvass will normally include houses and stores in view of the crime scene as well as those lining the probable route of the suspect's flight. People walking on the street, parking their car, or waiting for a bus may be interviewed. Investigators should record each address visited and the name and address of each person interviewed whether or not they provide information. If no one is at home, that should also be recorded. This information will be important if for some reason the canvass needs to be repeated. When a possible witness is located, a more extensive interview is scheduled.

INTERVIEWS

4. Interview Defined

An interview is the questioning of a person who may have knowledge pertinent to an investigation. The relationship between investigator and interviewee is generally amicable and information is generally freely exchanged, but the investigator may need to skillfully extract information from a reluctant witness. In most cases, the person being interviewed has little reason to withhold information. Where the information is to be used as evidence, however, such as a witness who may later refuse to testify, interrogation rather than interview techniques may be appropriate.

Interviews comprise a substantial portion of an investigation and constitute a major source of information. Because of the apparent simplicity of the typical interview, novice investigators may neglect to develop their technique. Investigators should devote great effort to developing and refining effective methods of interviewing. Each interview provides a unique opportunity to acquire information. After each interview, investigators should assess the quantity and quality of the information and the level of rapport they established with the subject.

5. Qualities of a Good Interviewer

Good interviewers share some of the qualities of successful salespeople, actors, bartenders, barbers, and psychologists. They put people at ease and induce them to talk. They can find themselves discussing a variety of sensitive subjects with strangers. They must extensively question subjects while employing discretion, perseverance, insight, and intelligence. Investigators must be able to quickly assess their subjects and be chameleon-like in their approach while appearing equally comfortable speaking with the social elite or a street person. Language and demeanor must be seamlessly adjusted so subjects are comfortably compelled to share their knowledge.

a. **Rapport**. Good interviewers must draw on a variety of personality skills. The first step in a successful interview is to develop a favorable relationship. If the relationship is strained, uncomfortable, or marked by mistrust, the subject may be reluctant to give useful information. By establishing rapport with the subject, investigators may be able to unleash the flow of information. Winning the confidence of the subject facilitates the sharing of information. Where this is not possible, a forceful personality, persistence, or other interrogation qualities may need to be employed.

b. **Personality**. Projecting confidence and strength of character can create the trust needed for subjects to confide in investigators. There should be no air of superiority, but a demeanor projecting sympathy, tolerance, and understanding. Create conditions so the subject can identify with the interviewer without clashing with any prejudices held by the subject.

c. **Breadth of Interests**. Projecting common interests helps to establish rapport. People tend to perceive that those who share common interests are likely to be sympathetic. Investigators' range of interest and practical knowledge must be broad to cover all they will encounter. Investigators must incorporate the diverse traits, habits, and behaviors of the people they meet to formulate good interview strategies and tactics.

6. The Place and Time

Investigators should ideally conduct interviews as soon as possible after the crime in a place that provides a psychological advantage. The information is then fresh in the mind of the witness. Moreover, they have little time to contemplate reasons not to cooperate. Naturally this rule must be modified to suit the exigencies and nature of the case. The order in which interviews are conducted may have strategic implications.

a. **Background Interviews**. When conducting a background interview, selecting the time and place is generally not an issue. Subjects' references, coworkers, former employers, etc, can generally be interviewed during normal business hours.

b. **Routine Criminal Cases**. Interviews in criminal cases should be arranged to obtain as much relevant information as possible. A time should be selected when the subject can devote full attention to the matter. If a subject appears distracted, the interview should be postponed. Privacy is another consideration. An open office among co-workers is not conducive to candid opinions or substantive accounts.

c. **Serious Criminal Cases**. Investigators should arrange to interview witnesses in important cases at places other than their homes or offices. Unfamiliar surroundings will help investigators maintain control of the interview by providing a psychological advantage. Interviewees must respect investigators and not withhold or color information. An interview room, free of distractions at the law enforcement agency, is generally the ideal place to conduct an interview.

7. The Approach

On first meeting, investigators should show their credentials and clearly identify themselves. This will reduce potential charges of misrepresentation later. When interviewing at a residence, try to ease the subject's concerns and be invited in rather than conducting the interview at the door.

8. Background Interviews

Pre-employment background interviews are generally uncomplicated and can be approached in a straightforward manner. The

Table 8-1. Common Background and Credit Check Information.

Background Data	Credit Check Data
• Date and time of the interview. • Recent change in address. • Name, vocation, and address of the interviewee. • Subject's full name. • Length of acquaintance in years. • Type of conduct, whether business or social. • Degree of association, whether daily, occasional, or rarely. • When last seen. • Names—parents, brothers, and sisters. • Marital status and children. • Residence, past and present. • Educational background. • Personal and financial habits. • Personality traits. • Membership in organizations. • Relatives in foreign lands. • Honesty, loyalty, and discretion. • Recommendation for a position of trust. • Evaluation of subject for position. • References.	• Other pertinent information. • Place of employment. • Name of spouse or parent. • Number of account. • Date opened. • Type of account. • Manner of payment. • Date closed. • Credit rating. • Eligibility for further credit • Other pertinent information. • Evaluation. • Cross reference.

purpose of the interview is to determine if the subject is qualified to hold a position of trust.

9. Criminal Case Inerviews

The interview technique must be adjusted for the subject matter, the relationship of the subject to the incident, and the abilities of the interviewer. Investigators may want to convey the feeling of a casual conversation, but the interview should be carefully designed to reveal information.

The interview process begins with preparation. Before interviewing witnesses, investigators should review the case facts and assess what each witness can contribute. Becoming familiar with the background of the witness will facilitate and ease conversation. The interview should be structured to avoid overlooking any important points.

The first few minutes are a "warm-up" period to set the tenor of the interview before relevant questions are asked. Being intimidating or overly aggressive early in the interview may cause the witness to become tense and reluctant to divulge information. After identifying themselves, investigators should open with friendly and nonthreatening remarks. Conversation about the weather, current events, sports, or matters of mutual interest will facilitate conversation. Although friendly, the approach should remain professional. Only after witnesses are in a communicative mood should the conversation turn to the case under investigation. Witnesses should be given every opportunity to give a complete account without interruptions. A mental note should be made of inconsistencies, and other matters requiring clarification. As witnesses tell their stories, investigators assess their personalities (prejudices, educational attainments, moral traits, intelligence, etc.), develop an interview strategy, and build rapport.

a. **Questioning**. After telling their stories, investigators should review them with witnesses to clarify or amplify important facts. At this point investigators probe for any missing details or case elements that need to be addressed.

In telling their accounts, witnesses may ramble or give lengthy and nonresponsive answers. Investigators must control the interview so that complete and accurate information is obtained. Information obtained from one witness will need to be *corroborated* with that obtained from others. Important facts should be supported with specific and detailed information. *Inaccuracies* (discrepancies, falsehoods, and inconsistencies) may become apparent during the interview. Questionable points will need to be examined by reworded and supplemental questioning. Honest mistakes should be distinguished from misrepresentations.

Questioning should not begin until the witness appears ready to provide accurate information. Asking direct questions too soon may create stress and constrain the witness and should be avoided until the witness has told his or her story and is ready to offer additional information. This can be assessed by the conversation and the subject's body language.

1) ***Ask one question at a time.*** Asking multiple questions can confuse the witness. It also makes sorting answers more difficult and provides an opportunity for the person to misdirect the interview by focusing on some questions and avoiding others.

2) ***Avoid questions with implied answers and maintain a positive attitude.*** The interview becomes futile if the answers are suggested in the questions. The objective is to find out what the person knows, not signal what the investigator believes. An interviewer who questions a witness by saying, "You couldn't remember what he said, could you?" is inviting a negative answer. The interviewer has unconsciously suggested that a negative reply will be acceptable and provides a way to avoid answering the question. A positive approach should always be employed. Investigators should convey by their tone of voice and phrasing that they do not contemplate the possibility of negative or non-informative answers. Timidity and lack of confidence are easily detected.

3) ***Simplify questions.*** Long, complicated, legalistic questions only serve to confuse and irritate. Witnesses may answer that they do not know; when in reality they simply do not understand the question. These questions can embarrass witnesses and cause resentment.

4) ***Allow the witness to save face.*** If it becomes apparent that answers contain exaggerations or errors in matters of time, distance, and description, the investigator should help the witness

avoid embarrassment. Do not ridicule but allow the witness to save face for his or her lack of common sense, poor judgment, or other deficiency. Again, the investigator should separate misrepresentation from unintentional mistakes.

5) ***Avoid asking questions that can be answered "yes or no."*** Such questions reduce the flow of information and can be unfair to the witness. Allow witnesses an opportunity to present relevant knowledge in its entirety. Witnesses should be encouraged to explain and qualify their answers.

6) ***Maintain control of the interview.*** Investigators must project confidence and authority. Hesitancy and doubt encourage evasion, while weakness fosters resistance. Small psychological gestures may help control a difficult witness. Instructing the witness to cease smoking, turn off a cell phone, or to sit in a chair other than the one he or she has selected will help establish control. The difficult witness must learn quickly that the investigator intends to direct the situation.

10. Techniques for Controlling Digression

After establishing rapport and permitting the witnesses to tell their stories, investigators are confronted with the difficult task of controlling digression. If interviewers cannot control rambling discourse, their interviews will be inefficient and ineffective. Interviewers need to keep interviews focused and on track.

a. **Precise Questioning**. Digressions and rambling interviews are often attributable to a lack of focus and direction. Questions should be constructed as precisely as possible so that answers fall within the range of the inquiry. Broadly constructed questions invite irrelevant responses. To ask, "Can you tell me something about the habits of John Doe?" is likely to encouraging a general discourse on the suspect and the values of the witness. On the other hand, asking "Have you ever seen John Doe intoxicated?" helps focus the response to information relevant to the case.

b. **Shunting**. This technique consists in asking a question related to the digression but is a step toward the focus of the interview. This maneuver is preferable to interrupting the subject since the "shunt" appears to rise out of an interest in what the subject is saying. For example, if the subject is talking about his or her employment history but dwells too long on a previous job, the interviewer could ask, "How much did they pay you for all this work?" When the subject answers, "$29,000 a year," the interviewer could ask, "And how much did your next job pay?" and the interview moves to another phase of the individual's career.

c. **Skipping by Guessing**. If the subject's narration lingers on irrelevant or obvious details, the interviewer may interject a question designed to move on to more important information. Asking "Was he hurt?" anticipates a conclusion and skips intermediary details. Other examples include "How did he finally get home?", or "Was he arrested?" A shrewd guess, made at the appropriate time in the subject's recital, will encourage the skipping of intervening details. The question, "So you met Jones at the bar the next morning, and that was how you came to meet Brown?" and similar questions will greatly reduce digressing details and advance the interview.

11. Interview Characteristics by Age of Subjects

The interview technique should be tailored to personality of the individual being interviewed. The following categories offer some suggestion to be considered, but individual differences in each category are significant. For any interview, the investigator must assess the individual and determine the correct approach.

a. **Children**. Investigators must use caution when interviewing children and adhere to statutory and court mandates. Wherever possible obtain permission from parents or guardians before interviewing children. Attempts to use children secretly as informants may create legal and public relations issues and should not be attempted without legal review.

Young children have short attention spans and will find it hard to concentrate for long periods of time. A series of short interviews may be more productive than a single session. Young children may be given to flights of imagination. They may indulge in imaginary journeys and relate a series of unreal events. The child may be unable to distinguish between fantasy and reality. A child under six years old may invent a story in reply to a question. An older child, from six to ten, may tend to distort the story. Older children, however, may observe, remember, and express themselves free from motives and prejudices.

b. **Young Adults**. Young adults may be too preoccupied with themselves and their close circle of associates to pay great heed to others. They may be inclined to be truthful, but their testimony may suffer from a lack of awareness and observation of others.

c. **Middle-aged Persons**. A middle-aged person is often the ideal witness. They may be keenly aware of others in their environment. They often have an interest in their community and safety of their families that is coupled with good perception, unimpaired faculties, and mature judgment.

d. **Older Persons**. Older adults make very effective witnesses because of a maturity of judgment and sufficient time to observe their environment. Physical impairments or regression into self-preoccupation seriously affect the value of older persons as witnesses.

12. Interview Characteristics by Attitudes of Subjects

The interviewer's approach should be tailored to the personality and attitude of the person being interviewed. As the interview begins, the interviewer should begin assessing the subject. Each individual is different and the interviewer may need to probe and assess the most effective interview tactic, but the initial strategy may benefit from common generalizations of personality types and attitudes of subjects.

a. **Know-Nothing Type**. Some people are reluctant to act as witnesses. This is particularly true of people who imagine that any contact with police means "trouble." An extensive warm-up, followed by persistent questioning, may yield results. It may be useful to ask a large number of questions that are difficult for the subject to claim to have no knowledge of, and then progress on to more relevant questions. If the subject continues to claim a lack of information, the investigator will need to determine if the subject is truly so disengaged from his or her environment or whether he or she is withholding information and will require a more persistent technique.

b. **Disinterested Type**. The uncooperative, indifferent person must be aroused. Flattery or appeals to pride may increase the flow of information. Stressing the importance of the information and the individual's cooperation to the case may be effective.

c. **Inebriated Type**. Intoxicated individuals can be very uncooperative and present difficulties in obtaining written statements. At other times, information may be freely shared that the individual would have more closely guarded when sober. Flattery is often an effective inducement to cooperation.

d. **Suspicious Type**. The interviewer must allay the fears of suspicious persons. Appealing to civic duty and good citizenship is sometimes productive. Failing this, investigators might imply a greater knowledge of the case than they actually possess to induce subjects to feel their statements are harmless or they look foolish by continuing to withhold information. Caution must be exercised when using this approach. Being caught overstating your hand may reinforce the individual's initial suspicion and end the flow of information.

e. **Talkative Type**. The garrulous witness merely requires management. Information flows but requires channeling. Subtly lead and interject remarks as needed to keep the subject on track.

f. **Honest Witness**. Honest and cooperative witnesses are a boon to an investigation. They can be developed with a little care and guidance. Start by clearly stating that the purpose of the investigation is to discover the truth, and not to punish or persecute anyone. Then, use illustrative examples to distinguish between direct and hearsay evidence, and convey the importance of accurate, relevant information.

g. **Deceitful Witness**. Investigators can obtain useful information even if witnesses are trying to deceive them. Witnesses who are obviously lying should be permitted to continue until they are well enmeshed in falsehoods and inconsistencies. Investigators can then confront the witness with the falsehoods using specific examples and imply knowledge of others. If the interview has been electronically recorded, a playback of false statements can be extremely effective. Investigators may discuss obstructing justice and the seriousness of aiding in a criminal offense. Even if attempts to deceive by witnesses are not a criminal offense, they may perceive they are in legal jeopardy and become more cooperative.

h. **Timid Witness**. Some witnesses, because of personality or background, may be overwhelmed by law enforcement procedures and become unusually timid. Investigators should work to win their confidence with a friendly approach that explains the process and confidentiality of investigative procedures.

i. **Boasting, Egotistic, or Egocentric Witness**. The self-centered witness must be treated with patience and flattery. These individuals are potentially excellent witnesses because of their drive toward self-expression, but are prone to self aggrandizement. Careful and persistent questioning is required.

j. **Refusal to Talk**. Information cannot be obtained from witnesses who will not talk. Witnesses who will say nothing are the most difficult of all types. Experienced criminals will probably remain silent. With other types investigators must persevere. Conversation may be induced by starting with neutral topics. All possible motivations should be exhausted before admitting defeat. Witnesses should be made to feel that they "owe it" to themselves, their families, and the victim, to do what is "right."

13. Approaches

A direct approach is generally effective with willing witnesses. Begin with a friendly conversational tone and develop the information naturally. With difficult witnesses, such as those who dislike law enforcement officers or who fear retaliation, an indirect approach may be necessary.

a. **Complainant**. When interviewing complainants, investigators should appear sympathetic, project an interest in the case, and show appreciation for reporting the crime. Elicit all the facts and assure the complainant of full cooperation. Determine whether the elements of an offense are present. As complainants tell their stories, investigators should assess their reliability. Later, check records to discover whether the person is a chronic complainer or has a criminal history. Determine the motivation of the complainant. Jealousy, grudges, or similar motivations may skew the complainant's point of view.

b. **Suspects**. The purpose of this interview is to determine whether the suspect committed a crime. Before questioning, review the law and elements of the crime. Determine the individual's reputation and criminal history. Preliminary questioning should be impartial and probing.

c. **Informants**. Investigators need to determine the informant's motivation for providing information. Flattery may work well with someone motivated by civic duty, while being a tough negotiator is required for people motivated by money or a reduction in criminal charges. First, allow the informant to talk freely and then question for details. Finally, assess the importance of the information.

d. **Victims**. Be sympathetic with victims. When victims perceive investigators to be indifferent, they may feel violated a second time. Listen to the complete story and permit victims to offer opinions. Gather facts and maintain an uncritical demeanor.

14. Evaluation

During interviews, investigators should use a variety of factors to assess the credibility of witnesses. *Physical mannerisms* (nervousness, evasive facial expression, embarrassment at certain questions, perspiration, and similar signs) will give some indication of the trustworthiness of the person. Test the truthfulness of the person by asking questions for which you already know the answers. Also, check for significant omission of things the witness should know. Carefully observe for any unusual reaction to questions to determine the individual's emotional state. Unwarranted indignation or excessive protests may indicate guilt. Spite, jealousy, and prejudice can be easily detected. Finally compare the content of statements with information given by other witnesses and with known facts for discrepancies and misrepresentations.

15. Recording Statements

The decision to use a notebook or electronic device to record an interview will depend on the individual and circumstances. Witnesses being interviewed on sensitive matters may become excessively cautious if a recording device is produced early in the interview. It is often best to listen to the subject's story, then request permission to record the statement.

16. Hypnosis

Hypnosis can unlock repressed memories but can also place an investigation in peril. Subjects are placed in a sleep-like state of heightened awareness and concentration. The mind continuously records images, at the subconscious level, even while the subject is sleeping, intoxicated, or otherwise inattentive. After a traumatic experience, victims may not remember details as the mind seeks protection by repressing memory. At other times, witnesses may have forgotten details or were distracted. Under hypnosis, subjects may become aware of repressed or forgotten memories, or details not fully comprehended when experienced. Hypnosis should only be conducted by a qualified psychologist or a physician skilled in medical hypnosis.

While under hypnosis, subjects become very receptive to suggestions. Placing witnesses under hypnosis may enhance their recollection or may plant false memories. Many state courts will not permit or will severely restrict the testimony of witnesses who have been hypnotized. To avoid this problem, hypnosis is often restricted to witnesses who are not expected to testify. In many circumstances, the use of the "cognitive interview" described below may be a better option.

17. The Cognitive Interview

Rarely do interviews uncover everything witnesses know about a crime. It is not that they are withholding information or were not paying attention. Some details do not flow to conscious memory. To deal with this problem, Edward Geiselman of UCLA and Ronald Fisher of Florida International University developed a method called "the cognitive interview." It consists of a series of techniques designed to enhance memory recall. These techniques are meant to be used together in the order they appear below.

a. **Avoiding Interruption**. Encourage witnesses to speak freely about the crime without interruption or direction. The goal is for witnesses to feel confident that they have all the time they need to speak and reflect about the event.

b. **Reliving the Event**. Witnesses are then asked to mentally recreate the period before, during, and after the crime. Encourage them to vividly recall the setting and circumstances. Review routine tasks, errands, and problems that led up to the crime. This will help witnesses recall their thoughts, actions, emotions, and attitudes as the crime unfolded. Through reliving the event in the context of a normal day, witnesses can concentrate more intensely on the details of the crime.

c. **Recalling Details**. Normally, witnesses recounting a story will skip over unimportant details to avoid boring the listener. Now witnesses should be instructed not to edit the progression of the event. Encourage them to provide every detail no matter how insignificant it seems even if unsure it is being remembered accurately.

d. **Changing the Order**. When first interviewed, witnesses narrate the story in chronological order. Now investigators, by a series of questions, lead witnesses to recall events in a different sequence. If a reverse order is chosen, investigators, at pauses in the interview, might ask the witness: "What did you do before that?" Step-by-step, investigators lead witnesses backwards through each stage of the event. Normally during narration, the mind, anticipating reaching the end tends to truncate experiences by skipping over detail. When the order of events is changed, the mind naturally pauses at each stage until instructed to continue. This prompts witnesses to consider each stage of an event as a separate incident and may promote recall of forgotten details.

e. **Changing Perspective**. At this stage, witnesses are encouraged to view the event from a different perspective. They may adopt the point of view of the victim, the suspect, another witness, or an imaginary video camera on the wall. By experiencing the crime through "someone else's eyes," witnesses may now recall details they neglected in previous accounts.

f. **Recollecting by Association**. The cognitive interview is concluded with a series of questions designed to elicit specific information. Witnesses are asked to associate their perceptions of the event to people, places, and things that are familiar. A typical question might be: "Does the suspect remind you of anyone you know? In what way? Did you ever see a hat like that one before?"

Cognitive interviewing will increase the amount of information obtained. It not only addresses the problem of witnesses who can't remember but also aids interviewers who may run out of questions and have difficulty continuing a interview.

INTERROGATIONS

18. Overview

The United States Supreme Court's ruling in *Miranda v. Arizona* radically changed the procedural requirements for questioning suspects in custody. To ensure that statements are voluntary, suspects in police custody should be advised of their legal rights. After identifying themselves as law enforcement officers, investigators should explain, in general terms, the nature of investigation and request to speak with the individual about the offense. Next, suspects should be informed of their right to remain silent and not answer questions. If they choose to answer questions, their responses can be used as evidence. They have a right to legal counsel and the state will provided an attorney if they are cannot afford one. Finally, suspects must acknowledge that they understand their rights.

19. Admissions

An admission is a self-incriminatory statement falling short of full acceptance of guilt. It is an acknowledgment of a fact or circumstance from which guilt may be inferred. It implicates but does not directly incriminate. A simple statement to the effect that the subject was present at the scene of the crime may be an admission. Combined with a motive, the admission may provide an inference of guilt.

20. Confessions

A confession is a direct acknowledgment of guilt or of some essential part of a criminal act. To be admissible, a confession must be *voluntary* and *trustworthy* and obtained through *civilized police practices*. The use of coercion, unlawful influence, or unlawful inducement is outside the limits of civilized police practice. Threats of bodily harm or confinement, illegal detainment, deprivation of necessities or necessary privileges, physical oppression, promises of immunity, clemency, or of substantial reward or benefit will render a confession inadmissible.

An interrogation is the questioning of a suspect or person reluctant to make a full disclosure of information. The rights under *Miranda* must be given by investigators before questioning a person in custody. The responses of the suspect will determine investigators' action.

Should suspects invoke their right remain silent, at any time, the interrogation must cease. Threats, tricks, or cajoling designed to persuade suspects to waive this right are forbidden. If legal counsel is requested, no questioning should be attempted until a lawyer is present.

If suspects waive their rights, investigators should attempt to obtain a signed waiver of rights (see Figure 8-2). The burden of proof of waiver is on the State. Suspects can withdraw a waiver at any time. If the interrogation continues without the presence of an attorney and a statement is taken, the burden falls on the Government to demonstrate that suspects knowingly and intelligently waived their rights.

Miranda Rights

You must read the suspect the following information before subjecting him or her to custodial interrogation:

- You have the right to remain silent.
- If you choose to speak, anything you say can be used against you in court.
- You have the right to consult with an attorney and have the attorney present during questioning. If you cannot afford an attorney and wish to have one, an attorney will be provided for you before any questions are asked.
- If you choose to waive your rights and answer questions now, you have the right to cut off the questioning at any time.

Figure 8-1. *Miranda* warning card.

Proof of waiver of constitutional rights may take the form of a statement that the suspect is willing to talk and does not want an attorney. A valid waiver will not be presumed from the silence of the accused. It must be shown that the accused was offered counsel but intelligently and understandingly rejected the offer (Carnley v. Cochran, 369 U.S. 506, 516 [1962]). Suspects may answer some questions or give some information and then invoke the right to remain silent. Lengthy interrogations or holding suspects incommunicado increases the burden on investigators to prove statements were voluntarily given. Waivers will be invalidated if there is any evidence of trickery or threats to acquire information.

21. Interviews Unaffected by *Miranda*

The warnings must be given when the individuals are subjected to police questioning while in custody or while otherwise deprived of their freedom. The Court's ruling does not affect information gathered from persons whose freedom is not restricted by the police.

a. **Confessions Without Warnings**. Any statement given freely and voluntarily is admissible as evidence. There is no requirement that police stop a person who enters a police station and states that he wishes to confess to a crime. Similarly, there is no requirement to stop a person who calls the police to offer a confession (or any other statement). Volunteered statements of any kind are not barred by the Fifth Amendment and their admissibility is not affected by the *Miranda* decision.

b. **Field Investigation**. Interviews can be conducted in the field without advising of *Miranda,* as long as the individual is not in custody or under restraint. General on-the-scene questioning about a crime and other general fact finding is permitted. Questioning of this nature is not affected by *Miranda,* since the compelling atmosphere of in-custody interrogation is not present.

c. **Public Safety Exception**. When there is an immediate threat to public safety such a bomb, officers may question an in-custody suspect about it without first giving *Miranda* warnings. In *New York v. Quarles* (467 U.S. 649 1984) the Supreme Court creat-

---

WAIVER OF RIGHTS FORM

My *Miranda* rights as they are set forth below have been read and explained to me, and I fully understand them.

Because I wish to respond to questions now and do not wish to have an attorney present, I hereby knowingly and voluntarily waive these rights:

- I have the right to remain silent.
- I have the right to consult with an attorney and have the attorney present during questioning. If I cannot afford an attorney, one will be provided for me before any questions are asked.
- I understand that anything I say in response to questions may be used against me in court.

_____	_____
signature	date
_____	_____
officer's signature	date
_____	_____
witness' signature	date

Figure 8-2. Waiver of rights form.

ed an exception to the *Miranda* rule in situations where the safety of the public is in jeopardy. The case involved a loaded handgun hidden prior to arrest. The unattended weapon was deemed a threat to the public safety and became the standard for the public safety exception.

d. **Summary**. The investigator must be able to show confessions are voluntary and freely given. A spontaneous utterance is freely given and not prompted by police questioning. Statements obtained without coercion while subjects are not in custody are permissible as are statements made by subjects in custody but not prompted by questions. Statements obtained during questioning after subjects have been informed of their *Miranda* rights and waive them are permissible.

22. A Brief History of the Right to Counsel

The United States Supreme Court gradually transformed criminal law and procedure from a time when individuals could be legally tried and sentenced to death without legal representation by requiring free legal counsel to anyone facing a possible jail term but unable to afford an attorney. This evolution occurred through several criminal cases.

In 1932, the Court declared, in the "Scottsboro Boys" rape case, that the Constitution guarantees the right to counsel in state court trials whenever the defendant's life is at stake (*Powell v. Alabama,* 287 U.S. 45 [1932]). By 1963, the Court extended the rule to all felony cases by requiring states to furnish free lawyers to poor defendants (*Gideon v. Wainwright,* 372 U.S. 335 [1963]). In 1966, in *Miranda v. Arizona,* the Court ruled that a person in police custody had a right to legal counsel during interrogation, and that suspects must be advised of the right to counsel before interrogation. If suspects request counsel, no interrogation must be attempted until the lawyer of their choosing or a state-appointed lawyer is present (*Miranda v. Arizona,* 384 U.S. 436 [1966]).

In the 1970s, the Court expanded the Sixth Amendment's right to counsel to whenever the "actual deprivation of a person's liberty" is at stake. Judges must now decide before the trial of an indigent defendant if imprisonment is possible. Where a jail sentence is possible, the court must offer the defendant free legal counsel. Otherwise, the defendant can be given only a fine as punishment (*Argersinger v. Hamlin,* 407 U.S. 25 [1972]). In a related development the Supreme Court decided in 1971 that a person could not be put in jail for the inability to pay a fine.

An enormous increase in drug-related crime during the 1980s placed a tremendous strain on all branches of the criminal justice system. Resources for providing legal counsel were stretched thin. In many cities, representation for even the more serious crimes is inadequate. For many defendants who cannot "make bail," it is not unusual to wait months in jail for the arraignment. In many places, legal representation of the indigent is, at best, minimal.

23. Purpose of Interrogation

The primary purpose of interrogation is to acquire information. In addition to admissions and confessions, it may be used to discover the existence and locations of physical evidence, learn the circumstance of a crime, identify accomplices, develop additional leads, and link previous or related crimes.

An interrogation may help to exonerate someone falsely suspected of a crime. Each day a great number of people will be lawfully arrested for a wide variety of reasons. Routine questioning may determine they did not perpetrate the crimes.

24. The Interrogator's Skills and Personality

Interrogators must be professional in their attitude and actions. They must project formal authority and command respect, while inspiring confidence, empathy and understanding. Investigators should appear strong and confident, for suspects will attempt to resist interrogation by exploiting any weakness they perceive. Investigators should project an interest in suspects' points of view and problems. Suspects who feel stressed may confide in investigators who they perceive to be understanding and fair.

a. **General Knowledge and Interests**. Investigators should develop a broad range of interests and general knowledge to deal with a variety of individuals. A basic knowledge of many topics is necessary to establish rapport, evaluate statements, and speak intelligently to subjects. To acquire this breadth of knowledge, investigators must be intellectually curious and observant. A genuine interest in people and their problems will help investigators to understand motives of various personalities in multiple situations. In some cases, an understanding of specific professional and technical matters is needed to intelligently question and evaluate responses. A good investigator is a life-long student and observer.

b. **Alertness**. A good observer is alert. Investigators need to stay alert to analyze subjects accurately, adapt techniques, uncover and explore leads, and alter tactics as needed. Logic alone may not reveal contradictions. Investigators must be able to detect contradictory information. Discovery of gaps in subjects' stories after interrogation is less effective because it provides them the opportunity to amend, refine, and fabricate their stories.

c. **Perseverance**. Patience is required when dealing with both uncooperative and willing subjects. Memory is a complex process. A patient approach will help strengthen recall, explain discrepancies, and obtain complete and accurate information.

d. **Integrity**. If subjects doubt the integrity of an interrogator, it will be impossible for that person to inspire confidence or trust. Never make a promise you cannot keep, and keep the promises you make.

e. **Logical Mind**. Interrogation should not be a haphazard process. Questions should follow a logical line of inquiry with their objectives clearly understood by the investigator. A plan of questioning should be constructed around establishing the elements of the offense and the circumstances of the crime.

f. **Observation and Interpretations**. Investigators must be able to "size up" individuals, and observe and interpret their reactions to questions. Subtle reaction or no reaction is often most telling.

g. **Power of Self-control**. Investigators must maintain control of their emotions at all times. Loss of temper results in the neglect of important details.

h. **Playing the Part**. Investigators sometimes need to be actors playing a role. They may need to act angry to prompt a reaction or to act sympathetic when they are repulsed. Anger, however, should never be simulated to the degree it becomes coercive.

24. Conduct of the Interrogator

Interrogators by their behavior and demeanor at the outset of questioning set the tone for the interrogation. Investigators must create an atmosphere that induces subjects to respond. Personal mannerisms that distract or antagonize must be controlled. Information cannot be obtained unless subjects are willing to respond. Investigators must structure the interview environment in a way that maximizes the flow of useful information.

a. **Control of the Interview**. Interrogators must project a strong personality and always be in control of the interview. They must be prepared and resourceful. Investigators lose control when they succumb to indignation, ill temper, are hesitant in the face of violent reactions, or fumble for questions.

b. **Distracting Mannerisms**. Investigators must impress upon subjects the seriousness of the situation. Pacing the room, checking your cell phone, "doodling," and similar forms of behavior tend to convey inattentiveness or a lack of concentration. Investigators should sit close to the subject with no intervening furniture. Distance or obstructions tend to provide subjects with comfort and psychological relief. Give full attention to the emotional responses of the subject.

c. **Language**. Choice of words matters. Adapt your language to the educational and cultural level of the subject. Profanity and vulgarity should be avoided, since they compromise the dignity of the investigator and antagonize the subject. Your approach should be straight forward and direct, neither talking over nor talking down to the subject. It is especially important in sex cases to avoid ambiguities. Slang may be used if it promotes ease of speech or fluency for the subject. Choose words to encourage a free flow of dialogue. Be sensitive to the impact of words. A suspect may shy away from words such as "assault" and "steal," but admit to "hitting" or "taking." Some individuals are more comfortable describing their conduct in euphemisms that can be clarified later by investigators.

d. **Dress**. Uniforms can be intimidating to subjects about to be interrogated. Investigators dressed in civilian clothes are more likely to inspire confidence, friendship, and status. Similarly, symbols of force should be removed from view. The sight of weapons or handcuffs may make suspects defensive and reluctant to talk.

e. **Attitude**. The purpose of interrogation is to determine the facts, discover the truth, or clarify a misunderstanding, not to punish. Interrogators are not in competition with suspects. A conviction is not a prize. The goal is justice. Investigators are inquisitors who seek the truth, and their approach and language must adjust to the task.

f. **Preliminary Conduct**. After identifying yourself, state in general terms the purpose of the investigation. Subjects who are in custody should be advised of their *Miranda* rights. Questioning should not begin unless subjects waive the right to be silent. Obtain a signed waiver, when possible, and begin building rapport.

g. **Presence of Other Persons**. The number of investigators or police officers in the room should be limited. Normally an interrogation is conducted by one or two investigators. If a confession is obtained the defense may claim duress if multiple police officers are in the room. Moreover, some courts require the prosecution to produce everyone who witnessed of a confession. A multitude of detectives parading to the witness stand creates an unfavorable impression and increases the likelihood of inconsistencies in the testimony. Other parties may be brought in for a specific purpose, such as witnessing the signing of a confession.

25. The Interrogation Room

The interrogation room should be of medium size and free of distractions. It should be simple and uncluttered to enhance the concentration of both the interrogator and the subject being questioned. Walls should be bare, without pictures or bulletin boards. There should be no glaring lights and minimal furniture.

Privacy is essential. An interruption at a key moment can ruin an interrogation. Access to the room should be restricted, with a single door. Ideally, the room should have no windows and be sound-proofed. If a telephone is present, the ringer and pager should be silenced.

The interrogator and the subject should be seated with no large furniture between them. The subject should be seated in an armless straight-back chair with his or her back to the door. The subject should not be able to easily move his or her chair. The subject's attention should be on the interrogator and not on the possibility of distraction or interruption from the door. It is preferable for the interrogator to be seated in a wheeled office chair. If a wheeled chair is used, ensure that the casters are well oiled so it does not creak or create distracting noises when moved. The interrogator may need to subtly increase or decrease the distance to the subject. If a table or desk is present, it should be positioned alongside the interrogator to facilitate writing but not as a barrier between the interrogator and the subject.

Although access to the room should be limited, others (police officers, investigators, supervisors, prosecutors) may need to monitor the interrogation. Other investigators may need to assist the interrogator, make suggestions during breaks in the interrogation, or follow-up on statements made by the subject. The ability to monitor the interrogation room through a two-way mirror and listening device or through video is useful. (Important interrogations should be recorded.) While two-way mirrors will not deceive anyone as to their purpose, the subject never knows when he or she is being observed, and experienced criminals will likely assume they are always being monitored.

A log is useful as a chronological record of the time periods and activities of the interrogation. The interrogation log may be maintained by the interrogator but is best recorded by an assistant observing the procedure. A log is useful for answering allegations of duress.

26. Information Sought

The primary purpose of an interrogation is to obtain facts or information concerning the offense, to identity the perpetrator, and to procure evidence for prosecution. The first objective is to determine if the subject is involved in the crime. If so, questioning turns to placing the subject at the scene or developing other associative or corroborative evidence. The details of the crime, along with the identity of accomplices and location of evidence, are important.

Interrogators need to be well prepared before asking any questions. Every significant detail of the case should be studied and a mental outline prepared of the elements of the offense and proof required.

27. Selection of Technique and Approach

After reviewing case information and the criminal record of the subject, interrogators begin their analysis. Learn as much as possible about the subject. Review any appropriate witness statements or interviews. Conduct an Internet search and search social network sites for information about the subject. When possible, a preliminary interview will often assist in determining the character and personality of the suspect and help investigators determine the techniques to be used. The simplest approach is often best. Avoid being overly devious or clever. You may outwit yourself by confusing and antagonizing the subject. The proper approach often requires ingenuity and intelligence.

Often, the interrogation will focus on obtaining an admission of guilt. Interrogators must adhere to legal requirements for admissible confessions. A confession must be *voluntary* and *trustworthy* and must be obtained by *civilized police practices.* The statement must result from the free and unconstrained choice of the subject and not from undue pressure. The courts will examine the *totality of circumstances* to determine admissibility. The techniques used and other relevant circumstances are examined to determine their effect on the defendant's decision to confess.

Trickery and deception are acceptable if held to reasonable levels and are not coercive. The Supreme Court in *Frazier v. Cupp* (394 U.S. 731 [1969]) gave tacit approval to the use of deception in obtaining a confession. In this case the defendant was falsely informed that an accomplice (Rawls) had confessed. "The fact that the police misrepresented the statements that Rawls had made is, while relevant, insufficient in our view to make this otherwise voluntary confession inadmissible. These cases must be decided by viewing the 'totality of the circumstances'. . . ." Trickery and deception that might lead to a false confession is unacceptable and will render a confession inadmissible. Avoid using trickery or deception when a straightforward approach can achieve the same results. Unnecessary use of trickery and deception can unduly complicate a case and may be distasteful to judges and juries.

28. Interrogation Techniques

There are many interrogation techniques. The choice depends on the nature of the crime, character of the subject, and the personality strengths of the interrogator. The technique should fit both the subject and interrogator.

a. **The Helpful Advisor**. This is a simple approach with the interrogator acting as a friend. The subject is treated kindly and the interrogator is there to help. The interrogator acts reassuring and understands that the subject is probably bewildered by the recent happenings. Between the two of them they are going to straighten things out. Once the subject explains everything, the investigator can help figure it out. The investigator understands the law, the district attorney, and police procedures and can help the subject through this problem.

b. **The Sympathetic Counselor**. This approach works best with subjects needing to clear their conscience. For the sake of their families and own self respect, they need to acknowledge their mistake. The interrogator assumes the role of friend who has helped others through similar circumstances. The interrogator knows the suspect is seeking peace of mind. It may look bleak, but the investigator can help the subject reclaim dignity. The first step is to "come clean so we can put it behind you." The investigator is there to help.

c. **Greater and Lesser Guilt**. In most crimes, there are several offenses involved. After an initial claim of innocence, the interrogator focuses on one of the minor offenses. Subjects, who primarily fear the consequences of the major offense, may see this as an opportunity to escape the more serious charge by confessing to a minor crime. Once the subject is committed to the less serious charge, the investigator pursues the serious offense. The interrogator stresses that the suspect first lied about the lesser offense, so it is obvious that he or she is lying about the more serious crime.

d. **Knowledge Bluff**. In this approach, the interrogator prepares by studying the crime and the subject's background to create the impression of knowing everything about the crime. The interrogator reveals a number of pertinent facts to the subject. (Proceed with caution. Mis-stating a fact will alert the subject to your bluff and defeat this approach.) The goal is to convince the subject that it is futile to resist since the interrogator obviously has sources of information. This approach tends to be effective if the subject is confused or unsophisticated.

e. **Bluff on a Split Pair**. This approach applies to crimes with more than one offender. The suspects are separated and informed that another has talked. A variation of this technique, that is less likely to be seen as a bluff, is to obtain individual, detailed accounts from each suspect, no matter how fanciful or erroneous they may be, and to play the discrepancies against each suspect's story. A stronger form of this technique is to pretend that an accomplice is placing all the blame on him or her. Create a need for the suspect to seek protection by telling the truth.

f. **Questioning as a Formality**. The interrogator takes the approach that the case is solved and the interview is merely a legal requirement. A series of questions are asked as if mandated. The interrogator implies knowledge of the answers but is required to give the accused the right to respond. The procedure is business-like with deliberate pauses to give the suspect *one more* chance to tell the truth. Such phrases as the following can be used; "You were in the apartment at seven o'clock." "You're sure about this fact?" "Do you want me to write your answer exactly the way you said it?" "I'm going to give you a fair chance to answer this question truthfully. Think it over for a while; then, give me your answer." When the suspect denies involvement, the investigator may skeptically put down a pen, look at the suspect, stare at a note pad and then with a shake of the head ruefully remark, "I don't know what you're trying to do to yourself," or "You would think you'd give yourself a break." Even a prolonged silence may prompt the suspect to be more forthcoming.

g. **Pretense of Physical Evidence**. Interrogators state they do not need a confession and are not interested in the suspect's reasons. There are, however, a few formalities to complete. Interrogators tell the suspect that they need to provide an opportunity to explain. Interrogators then pretend that laboratory experts have found incriminating evidence. Many people believe that forensic science can solve virtually any case. By mixing pseudoscience into their statements, investigators can often convince subjects that incriminating evidence has been found. Any scientific analysis could be employed, but fingerprint and DNA analysis are particularly effective.

29. Control

Even the best planned interrogation can go awry, but it is essential that interrogators remain in control. Unexpected answers and emotional outbursts can push the interrogation off course. Resistance, obstinacy, or forced adjustments in questioning must not provoke interrogators to anger, confusion, or a discouraging stalemate. Experience and careful preparation will help interrogators anticipate and overcome some of these challenges.

In the initial phase of an interrogation there is typically little need for control. Permit subjects to tell their stories without interruption. A few general questions will usually launch subjects into their narrative. Once started, some subjects will work themselves into confessions while interrogators need only assist with a word or phrase.

If subjects do not confess during their initial narratives, interrogators should begin their planned questions. The tone of the interrogation should be adjusted to the subject's responses. Spontaneous answers that appear to be given without much reflection tend to be more valuable and trustworthy. Try to build the pride of subjects who appear to be cooperating.

Interrogators must remain calm when confronted with uncooperative subjects. Loss of temper will likely end the conversation and anger can lead to duress. A loss of emotional control by interrogators may also help subjects feel superior. Harassing a suspect can produce false statements. It is always possible that suspects do not have the information being sought. An indifferent subject may give an answer (regardless of its truth) merely to be rid of the interrogator. Controlling feelings of contempt, impatience, sarcasm, or anger, and appealing to honor, duty, loyalty, patriotism, religion, or family commitment is generally more effective.

If interrogators sense they are losing control or their tactics are not working, it may be time for a *strategic interruption* to devise a new plan. Interrogation rooms should be equipped so interrogators can surreptitiously activate a buzzer or signal to pause. A button under a table or desk that interrogators can push with a foot or knee or even a predetermined signal to an assistant in the viewing room can be quite effective.

30. Detection of Deception

Interrogators strive to obtain accurate information, so they must learn to distinguishing truth from falsehood. Common sense, experience, and knowledge of human behavior can frequently help sort facts from misleading, false, evasive, or ignorant statements. Identifying inconsistencies and improbabilities in subjects' statements are helpful. Often, however, interrogators must be able to read the emotional reactions of subjects through their features, mannerisms, unconscious physical behavior, or body language.

a. **Physiological Indicators**. Carefully observing any physical reactions to questioning has long been a means of detecting guilty knowledge or deception. Primitive societies relied on sniffing the odor of the unusually nervous person from a group of suspects, or identifying guilt from the dryness of mouth by difficulty in chewing and swallowing a handful of dry rice.

There are many physical factors observant investigators can use to attempt to determine the truth. Some claim that sweating or changes in the color of the face are indicators of guilt. Perspiration on the brow may indicate excitement, nervousness, or simply the fact that the room is rather warm. Sweating palms, however, are indicative of tension and nervousness rather than warm surroundings. A flushed face indicates anger or embarrassment but not necessarily guilt. An unusual pallor, considered by some a likely sign of guilt, is often associated with fear or shock.

A dry mouth, frequent swallowing, wetting of the lips, and thirst are indicators of nervous tension that is sometimes associated with guilt and deception. An increase in the subject's pulse rate or breathing can be caused by an attempt to deceive.

A subject's physical positioning can be a useful indicator of stress and tension. Classic indicators include crossed legs or arms, clenched fists, furrowed brow, or narrowed stare. Subjects who are stressed or trying to deceive may also demand more personal space between themselves and interrogators. This is why it is beneficial for the subject to be seated in an unmovable chair while the interrogator remains more mobile.

Tense or deceptive subjects will tend to lean back or push back in their chair at critical points in the interrogation. Interrogators should note this reaction and adjust their questioning. Early in the questioning, nervous or deceptive subjects may require substantial personal space. As interrogators establish rapport, subjects begin to relax and require less personal space. As the questioning approaches sensitive topics, subjects may again try to expand their personal space. Interrogators need to note this reaction and access their approach. Do you push on and take a chance that the subject will stop talking, or do you move away from the topic, and allow the subject to relax, then approach the topic in another manner? The proper tactic will depend on the stage of the interrogation and interrogator's confidence that he or she can provoke the desired response. Interrogators can measure physical space to determine their progress. If the subject moves away when interrogators narrow the amount of physical space, the subject is tense and trying to resist. If the subject does not attempt to reclaim personal space, interrogators may be on the verge of a breakthrough. Subjects who lean forward when speaking are more likely to be trying to communicate, while subjects who lean back are trying to resist. Ideally, the subject about to confess has allowed the interrogator to move into a consoling position to allow for a pat on the shoulder or arm, or other gesture of understanding.

b. **The Polygraph.** The polygraph is an instrument designed to measure physiological reactions in order to uncover deception. The brain reacts to emotional disturbances by transmitting through the nervous system signals that affect and regulate bodily functions. A suspect's emotions will produce physiological changes such as increasing heartbeat, rate and volume of breathing, blushing, perspiration, and dryness of the mouth. These are autonomic changes that are difficult to control consciously. A number of these changes are measured and recorded by the polygraph.

The polygraph does not record lies as such but simply measures changes in blood pressure, pulse rate, breathing, and in the resistance of the skin to electrical current. The most important element in the process is the qualifications of the examiner. Without a suitable background in psychology, physiology, and scientific method, the examiner's interpretation of the data has little meaning. Examiners should possess extensive education, training, experience, and certification. The interpretation of the chart is critically important.

The polygraph examination consists of both neutral questions (irrelevant to the issues of the case) and relevant questions. Neutral questions enable the examiner to establish a norm or baseline for the subject's reactions to questions relatively free of emotional content. The relevant questions provide the examiner with some insight into the subject's fears–the guilty person's fears usually increase during a test and reactions usually become stronger while the fear and nervousness of the innocent person tends to decrease during the test.

Although the results of a polygraph exam are not generally accepted as direct evidence in United States courts, the test are considered a valuable investigate tool. Polygraphs are used to measure an individual's honesty, compare inconsistent statements, verify statements, and develop leads. There are many instances where suspects have confessed after failing a polygraph exam.

The polygraph is not suitable for some people. Individuals with certain heart conditions and breathing disorders are unfit to take the test. A highly nervous or excitable person may be unfit. Temporary conditions such as drunkenness, sickness, injury, pain, extreme fatigue, and certain respiratory ailments may affect a person's suitability for the test.

Permanent mental deficiency or insanity renders persons unsuitable because it may be difficult or impossible for them to distinguish the truth from a lie, or to understand the purpose of the test. Persons of very low intelligence may possess insufficient moral consciousness or fear of being caught in a crime or a lie. Temporary conditions such as emotional trauma or being under the influence of sedatives may also disqualify a person as a subject.

1) ***Procedures.*** The success of a test depends, in part, on how subjects were treated before being asked to take the test, the manner in which they were asked to take the test, and how they were treated while awaiting the test. A proper interview seldom affects the test results, provided it is not unduly long or rigorous. Investigators should not reveal details of the crime to persons who may be asked to take the test. Interviews should be straightforward, without tricks or bluffs or other ruses that may upset the subjects or make them suspicious.

When requesting subjects to take polygraph exams, investigators need to ensure they understand their rights under *Miranda*. Investigators should, in simple language, describe the test to remove any misconceptions. Emphasize it as a means to demonstrate innocence. Do not suggest that a refusal to take the test will indicate guilt. Without false claims or exaggeration, describe the test as a tool for finding the truth.

The test, however, should be scheduled promptly to avoid unnecessary delays. Subjects should be treated normally as they await the test. If the test can be quickly administered and subjects are to remain with investigators or in custody, be sure food and exercise are available at appropriate times. Suspects in the same case should not be allowed to communicate with each other.

Test procedures will vary somewhat with the person tested and the facts of the case. Two common approaches are the *general question test* and the *peak of tension test.*

The general question test consists of a series of relevant (concerning the offense) and irrelevant (not concerning the offense) questions asked in a planned order. The relevant questions are asked to obtain a specific response. The irrelevant questions are asked to give the subject relief after pertinent questions and to establish a normal reaction on the test chart. The questions are arranged so that specific reactions to relevant question can be compared with normal reactions to irrelevant questions. Usually subjects do not know beforehand what questions are to be asked. Questions are often asked multiple times during the testing procedure.

The peak of tension test depends on the building of emotional stress. Subjects usually are told questions that will be asked. The series of questions contain one question about a specific detail of the offense. The test charts of untruthful or unduly disturbed subjects usually show a rise in the stress in anticipation of lying to the relevant question (peak of tension) and a decline (due to relief) thereafter. The peak of tension works best when examiners know some unpublicized details of the crime. It is also used to probe for weaknesses in subjects' testimony. Variations of this test are used as preliminary tests to ascertain if a person is capable of giving a reliable response.

2) ***Test Questions.*** By providing detailed and verified information about the offense, investigators can greatly assist examiners in preparing test questions. Whenever possible, provide the examiner with unpublicized facts of the offense, particularly those known

only by victims and offenders. Questions should be short, simple, and easily understood by the subject. They are formulated into a yes or no format. The purpose of the question is to gain information or invoke a reaction, not to require complex thought.

A few precautions can increase the likelihood the polygraph exam will be successful. Do not wait until the last minute to ask a subject to take the test. The test should not be used as a last resort after all other methods have failed. Do not tell suspects everything you know about the offense or about them. Carefully investigate the case before asking subjects to take the test. A faulty or cursory investigation of the case or subject's background information can render the examination ineffective. Narrow the list of suspects as much as possible. Avoid using polygraphs for a mass screening of suspects.

After the polygraph exam, the examiner usually follows-up with some skillful questioning. The approach is based on the case information, subject's background, test results, and the effects it seems to be having on the subject. Investigators should be available to assist the examiner with additional information if necessary.

3) *Judicial Rejection*. In *Frye v. U.S.* (293 F. 1013 [D.C. Cir. 1923]) the Circuit Court of the District of Columbia ruled against the admissibility of polygraph results as evidence, and established the criteria for the judicial acceptance of scientific procedures. In order for expert testimony based on a scientific principle or procedure to be admissible as evidence, it must have already received general acceptance in its particular field. This is known as the "general acceptance" or the "*Frye* test" and is recognized as one of

Table 8-2. Suggested Polygraph Question Topics.

• Specific articles or exact amounts of money stolen. • Peculiar aspects of the offense, such as a strange or obscene act committed at the scene. • The exact time at which the offense occurred.	• Results of laboratory tests. • Known facts about a suspect's actions or movements • Facts indicating a connection between suspects, victims, and witnesses, especially when they deny any connection. • Exact type of firearm, weapon, or tool used.

Table 8-3. Sample Test Questions.

General Question Test	Peak of Tension Test
Is your last name Simpson? Are you over 21? Do you know who shot Rowe? Did you shoot Rowe? Were you born in Indiana? Did you take Rowe's money? Did you shoot a .45 caliber pistol last night? Is your hair brown? Have you answered my questions truthfully?	FIRST TEST. Did you stab a man? Did you poison a man? Did you drown a man? Did you shoot a man? Did you hang a man? Did you strangle a man? SECOND TEST. [The subject is a member of the military.] Did you shoot a submachine gun last night? Did you shoot a carbine last night? Did you shoot an M1 rifle last night? Did you shoot a .45 caliber pistol last night? Did you shoot a cannon last night? Did you shoot a shotgun last night? Did you shoot a .22 caliber rifle last night?

The questions above are based on a sample case. Allen Rowe was found dead, killed by a bullet from a .45 caliber weapon. Rowe's wallet, which his friends say contained about five hundred dollars, was found beside his body, empty. Investigation reveals John Simpson as a suspect.

the two standards used by courts to evaluate the admissibility of scientific techniques.

The standard is Daubert (*Daubert v. Merrel Dow Pharmaceuticals, Inc.,* No. 92-102, 113 S. Ct. 2786 [1993]), decided by the Court to clarify the "relevancy standard" of the Federal Rules of Evidence. The decision directs the courts to consider other factors in judging admissibility besides the general acceptance in a particular scientific discipline. These factors include the *relevancy of the expert's opinion, expert's qualifications, specialized literature* on the topic, *reliability of the testimony, potential for error,* and *potential for unfair prejudice* against the defendant. Although general scientific acceptance is considered an important factor in the relevancy standard, it is not the only or overriding factor taken into consideration. Trial judges serve as "gatekeepers" who access the scientific principles of procedures to determine if evidence is admissible. Federals courts and a number of states follow the Daubert standard.

31. Psychological Stress Evaluator

The Psychological Stress Evaluator (PSE), or voice stress analyzer, was designed to detect lies without attaching leads and monitors to the subject's body. Subjects speak into a microphone, or voice recordings are used, to analyze levels of stress associated with deception. By using recordings, the PSE can be used surreptitiously.

In theory, when one speaks the voice has two modulations—audible and inaudible. The audible portion is what we hear. The inaudible comes from the involuntary areas (those not directly controlled by the brain or thought processes). Internal stress is reflected in the inaudible variations of the voice. These differences cannot be heard but can be detected and recorded by instrumentation. To the human ear, a person may sound perfectly normal, free of tremors or "guilt-revealing" sound variations. The PSE senses the differences and records the changes in inaudible modulation qualities. When the chart is interpreted by an experienced examiner, it reveals the key stress areas of the person being questioned. The validity and reliability of PSE analysis is questioned by some in the scientific community.

WRITTEN STATEMENTS

32. Overview

If after intelligently waiving their rights subjects make admissions or confess to a crime, investigators should request they compose a written statement or sign a transcript of the interview. Having multiple ways to document admissions strengthens the case and demonstrates a clear and voluntary acknowledgement of guilt.

It may also be appropriate to request written statements from witnesses. Whenever important statements are made a written documentation will strengthen its evidentiary value. Investigators should seek written statements from recalcitrant or reluctant witnesses, key witnesses, witnesses who will not be available for trial, and any time there are indications that witnesses may change their minds.

Written statements serve many functions. They provide a written record for the case file. Statements can be used by the prosecution at the trial to refresh recollection, impeach witnesses, and monitor testimony. They tend to discourage a witness from wrongfully changing testimony at the trial. Written statements are used by the prosecution in planning its presentation and reducing unforeseen testimony.

While written statements are important, they should not supplant a full investigation. Statements might not be allowed into evidence, and if admitted will receive extensive scrutiny from defense counsel. Expect defense counsel to question the voluntariness of statements and make accusations of duress and coercion. Investigators should continue to investigate to develop a case independent of any written admissions or confessions.

33. Depositions

A deposition is the record of out-of-court testimony made under oath or affirmation in answer to questions and cross-examination submitted in a criminal or civil case. Normally depositions are taken as part of the discovery process or to record the testimony of a witness who may not be available to testify at trial. Ordinarily a deposition should be taken by an attorney and not an investigator.

34. Content of Statements

Lengthy interviews or interrogations will invariably develop a large volume of irrelevant or immaterial information. Investigators must carefully guide subjects in the information to include in their written statements. Subjects may not agree to produce a subsequent document, so it is important to ensure the first attempt is adequate.

Statements from witnesses should include information that supports the investigation and is likely to be covered in their court testimony. Statements of suspects should substantiate the elements of the charge, along with information pertinent to the case and details of any extenuating circumstances or explanations offered by the suspect. Finally, investigators should strive for written documentation that is clear, complete, accurate, and addresses the issues of the investigation.

35. Methods of Taking Statements

Written statements should be made as soon as possible after subjects have thoroughly discussed the incident. Do not interrupt suspects as they are freely expounding on the crime. Subjects are often willing to speak of the crime before they are psychologically prepared to put their comments in writing. If investigators appear too eager to get statements in writing, subjects may become more guarded. After a thorough discussion, subjects are more likely to feel committed to their story.

There are several ways to produce a written statement requiring varying levels of involvement by investigators. The most appro-

Table 8-4. Written Statement Methods.

• Subject writes statement without guidance. A statement of this nature, which is sufficiently comprehensive, is the most desirable form. • Subject dictates to a stenographer without guidance. • Subject is given a list of the essential points to be covered in the statement along with whatever other pertinent information subject desires. • Subject delivers statement orally to the investigator who writes it verbatim.	• Subject delivers statement orally to the investigator or a stenographer in response to questions from the investigator. The responses are recorded verbatim. • Investigator assists subject in dictating statement by suggesting wors and locutions which will express the subject's intended meaning. (Caution must be exercised to protect from a charge of influencing the subject. An electronic recording is recommended. • Investigator writes statement using information and expression of subject. Subject reviews statement and makes corrections.

priate method depends on the writing ability and temperament of the suspect, the amount and nature of the information to be recorded, and the availability of transcription services.

36. Form for Statements

Each law enforcement agency is likely to have its own format for written statements. In general, they follow a basic reporting design. The first paragraph of a statement generally contains *identifying data* such as the date, place, name of person preparing the statement, name of the investigator, and a declaration that the statement is being made voluntarily.

The *body* of the statement consists of a narrative of events. For confessions, the statement should include all of the elements of the crime and the facts associating the subject to these elements. The words of the subject should be used, but the scope of the confession should be guided by investigators. Sometimes investigators may write the statement to insure the inclusion of all the necessary details. Subjects then read the statement and sign each page at the bottom. To establish that the subject read the statement, investigators may include intentional errors, typographic or otherwise, for the subject to correct by striking the error and correcting in the margin. If subjects fail to recognize the errors, they should be identified by investigators for the subject to correct. Each page should be numbered by "Page __ of __ Pages."

The concluding paragraph should state that the subject has read and signed the document. Investigators should then request the subject to sign each page of the statement and initial corrections as described above.

37. Witnesses to a Confession

Having someone witness the signing of a statement will help to rebut any claim that investigators used duress, threats, or promises to obtain the signature. After the statement is prepared for signature, witnesses may be introduced. Witnesses should be able to verify the statement was voluntarily and intelligently provided. They should also be able to testify that the subject read and revised the entire statement; objected to certain words, phrases, or statements; corrected certain words and phrases; appeared to understand the contents of the confession and acknowledged it to be true and correct; and seemed to be acting voluntarily, and in full knowledge of his or her actions.

38. Investigation Subsequent to a Confession

The investigation does not end simply because the subject confesses to the crime. A confession needs to be critically reviewed in relation to the charge. Then it must be determined what, if any, information is needed and what questions remain to be answered. Have the elements of proof been established? Has the investigation revealed facts that corroborate the confession? If not, what else needs to be learned? Is there sufficient evidence, independent of the confession, to support the charge in court? Normally, a conviction cannot be obtained on a confession alone but must be substantiated by other evidence. If the court rules the confession to be inadmissible, is there other evidence to support a conviction?

39. Admissibility of Confessions

Confessions must be free of duress or compulsion and adhere to constitutional safeguards to be admissible in court. Failing to abide by these standards will likely render inadmissible the confession and any leads or evidence subsequently collected through the statement. Investigators must exercise great care to ensure the legality of their investigations.

A confession must be voluntary and trustworthy, and it must have been obtained by civilized police practices. The U.S. Supreme Court requires that the police methods should not be "inherently coercive" and should not have a *tendency* to compel a confession.

Police must maintain constitutional safeguards. When appropriate, suspects must receive *Miranda* warnings. Questioning cannot begin unless suspects waive their right to remain silent. No conclusion can be drawn from a suspect's silence after the warnings have been given. An express statement, preferably written and witnessed, is required. Statements must result from free and rational choice. The record of the interrogation, including the investigator's notes and the interrogation log, should reflect a continuous regard for the suspect's rights, the absence of any threats, tricks, or cajoling to obtain a waiver of rights, and the absence of duress and coercion during the interrogation.

40. Forms of Duress and Coercion

Three types of police behavior can render a confession inadmissible: coercion, duress, and psychological constraint. Investigators must safeguard against all of them.

Coercion connotes the application of physical force and other illegal physical methods. This could entail beatings or assault such as hitting with a rubber hose or newspaper, punching, using glaring lights, administering drugs, using improper restraints, torture, and so forth. Threats of such abuse are also included in this category.

Duress is the improper restriction of physical behavior. This includes prolonged (six hours, for example) detention in a dark cell, deprivation of food or sleep, imposing conditions of excessive physical discomfort, and continuous interrogation over extraordinarily long periods (such as twenty-four hours). If subjects are given appropriate intervals of rest, an interrogation may extend for a period of several days or weeks without violating this prohibition of duress, as long as subjects are able to invoke their right to remain silent and right to counsel. In determining the question of duress, the subject's age, sex, temperament, and physical condition must be considered.

Psychological Constraint is the unlawful restraint of action by threat or other means of instilling fear. Suggesting that suspects, their relatives, or property might be harmed can be interpreted as psychological abuse even if the suggestions are not explicit threats. A susceptible person could, under these circumstances, be induced to give a false confession. It is sufficient if subjects reasonably think they are in danger. Telling subjects that unless they confess they will be hanged, given over to a mob, or sent to prison for a more serious crime is sufficient to affect admissibility. However, it is permissible to tell subjects that the police will discover the truth anyway, that subjects run the risk of imprisonment, to display impatience with a subject's story, and to give the impression that investigators consider the subject guilty.

41. Limiting the Scope of a Confession

Investigators should limit each confession to a single criminal event. Including a number of separate crimes in a single confession creates problems in admitting the confession into a criminal trial. Normally it is not permissible to introduce evidence of the defendant's participation in unrelated offenses unless used to establish intent, guilty knowledge, the identity of the defendant, or use of similar M.O. in a previous crime. If the additional crime is part of the same transaction, the confession is admissible.

RECORDING INTERVIEWS AND INTERROGATIONS

42. Overview

Information obtained in an interview or interrogation is of little value unless it can be recalled later. The accurate retention of information from sensitive interviews is a recurring problem for investigations. Several methods are used depending on the circumstances of the investigation and interview.

Relying on *mental notes* has the advantage of permitting an uninterrupted flow of information. The simple act of writing notes can induce caution if the suspect is suspicious or fearful. Unless well trained in memory techniques, however, investigators retain little more than a general impression and a few phrases.

Written notes are a great improvement over mere memory but by necessity are sketchy. They can record significant data and are satisfactory for routine interviews. For interrogations that may result in a confession, a more exacting reproduction is needed. At a critical point in the interrogation, investigators may be overwhelmed if subjects suddenly unburden themselves with a flood of information.

The presence of a *stenographer* may hinder the flow of information from a hesitant subject. Moreover, investigators seldom have stenographic services at their disposal.

Audio recording is a simple and practical means of documenting interviews or interrogations. The physical and technical requirements of audio recording are modest.

Video recording is the ideal way to document an interview. In important cases where subjects confess, a video recording will provide the most convincing evidence for a jury.

43. Recording

Wherever practicable, important interviews should be recorded. The suspect's words and image combined can often reveal tone, inflection and even demeanor, i.e., the true meaning of what he or she is saying. Although recording a conversation may appear to be a simple process, producing a recording that yields a quality transcript requires good interviewing technique.

a. **Types of Recording**. There are two general types of recording: the *overt* and the *surreptitious.* The use of each is determined by the nature of the case. Overt recordings are made when there is no need to conceal that the conversation is being recorded. The suggestion to record the conversation may be made by investigators or interviewees. Some individuals in important positions make a practice of recording such interviews for their own protection. The nature of the interview will determine whether investigators should suggest that a recording be made. If witnesses are "friendly to the prosecution" and the information is complex, the most practical procedure is to request permission to record. A courtesy copy of the recording may be given to subjects on request. The advantage of overt recordings is the relative ease in producing these recordings. Recordings of telephone conversations can be useful with permission of the subject.

Surreptitious recordings are those done without the knowledge of the interviewees. Sensitive interviews and interrogations should always be recorded in important cases. Interrogation rooms should be equipped with recording capabilities, and other rooms can be quickly prepared using miniature recorders or transmitting devices.

b. **Purpose of Recording**. There are many reasons to record an interrogation. The recording may be used as *evidence for court* *presentation,* especially if the subject later recants a confession. During the interrogation the subject may deny guilt or knowledge of the crime and may offer elaborate alibis and excuses. Investigators may play back recordings of the subject's *contradictions* and inconsistencies to show the futility of deception. Subjects may provide information that *implicates associates.* The recording can later be played for the associates to induce them to confess. Recordings are also used to *assist subsequent interrogation.* After the first recital of the subject's story, the investigator interrupts the interrogation to listen to the statement, analyze it for consistency and credibility, and check certain points for trustworthiness. After determining the weak points, new strategies and tactics can be developed.

44. Techniques

There are several tactics investigators can use to effectively record interviews. One method is the *radio technique.* Investigators must manage the dialogue to satisfy the needs of future listeners. Unlike television broadcasters who are aided by visual images, radio broadcasters must insure that the dialogue does not result in a meaningless jumble of voices and unintelligible references. The performance must be managed so that listeners can understand *what* is being said, *who* is speaking, and *what object* is being referenced at any given moment. In a surreptitious recording, the investigator is restrained from giving explicit directions and must avoid obvious cues that divulge the conversation is being recorded.

Investigators need to *identify persons* when interviewing two or more people. Voices may not be readily distinguishable, but for the recording to serve as evidence the voices must be identified to specific individuals. To clarify the identity of speakers, investigators should refer to the interviewees as often as possible by name. This can be accomplished under the guise of courtesy. A statement may be associated with a definite person by tagging the conclusion with a remark addressed to the speaker such as, "Was that on Tuesday, Mr. Smith?" The statement can also be associated by a leading question such as "What did Brown say to you, Mr. Smith?"

It is important that the dialogue is clear when *identifying objects.* Statements such as "I gave him this one," or "He had that one" are not effective as evidence because the object being referenced cannot be identified by the recording alone. Investigators should follow such a statement with an identifying question, such as "You mean check number four, Mr. Smith?" or "You saw him with the blue handled knife Mr. Jones?" Although these statements may appear stilted on paper, to the interviewee they will seem to be the normal plodding methods of the investigator. Investigators may not impress interviewees with these tedious, repetitious questions, but they will rescue the recording from becoming a meaningless recital of untagged pronouns.

If the statement involves some physical act, the dialogue should be clear in *describing physical action.* For example, the victim may demonstrate an assault along with some non-descriptive sentence such as "He hit me here like this. . . ." Investigators then need to interject a few clarifying sentences, such as, "Let me get this straight, Mr. Brown. You were standing sideways, two feet from Black when Black swung his right fist and hit you on the back of the neck just below the left ear. Is that right?"

When making overt recordings, more elaborate clarifications are possible. If there are a number of persons present, speakers may be asked to identify themselves before each statement. If several speakers overlap, they can be instructed to repeat statements separately. If it becomes necessary to pause the interview, the recording should indicate this with a comment such as, "We are going to pause the recording." When reconvening, investigators should indicate the interview, "Back on the record."

As previously stated, some people may attempt to protect themselves from misquotations by secretly making their own recordings. Whenever investigators conduct interviews in the office of another, they should be aware of the possibility of a secret recording and guide their own conversation accordingly. Avoid statements or remarks that are susceptible to misinterpretation and may be detrimental to the investigation or the investigator's reputation.

a. **Video Recording Confessions**. In important felony cases, confessions should be video recorded. A video recording provides the strongest evidence that the confession was voluntarily. It is difficult for defense attorneys to claim their clients were coerced when confronted with the sight and sound of them freely recounting their deeds. Recordings protect police from false allegations and lead to more guilty pleas, saving an enormous sum in court costs. Few suspects will retract their confession knowing that the jury will be viewing the entire video record of their questioning.

Interviews should be conducted in a quiet room without distractions. A clock should be placed in view of the camera to assure that no erasures have been made. The recorder should be operated by someone other than the interrogator, who should focus on the interview.

It is important to remember that a video recording supplements but does not replace a written confession. Written confessions should be obtained before the recording. If for some reason the video is found not to be admissible, investigators may still use the written confession.

Investigators should begin by stating the date, time, and location of the interview, and identify the people present. Suspects then should be recorded waiving their rights and acknowledging they signed a waiver. Any interruptions in the recording are documented in the interrogation log. Normal refreshments and courtesies are extended and recorded to demonstrate that suspects are not under duress. An object of evidence can be properly documented by having the suspect identify it and possibly reading the serial number of the object on camera. When the recording is concluded a transcript should be prepared.

ADDITIONAL READING

Interview

Bennett, M. and Hess, J.E.: Cognitive Interviewing. *FBI Law Enforcement Bulletin, 60* (3), 1991.

Copinger, R. B., Jr.: Planning the Investigative Interview. *Security World, 9* (7), 1972.

Einspahr, O.: The Interview Challenge. *FBI Law Enforcement Bulletin, 69* (4), 2000.

Evans, D.D.: 10 Ways to Sharpen Your Interviewing Skills. *Law and Order, 38* (8), 1990.

Geiselman, R.E. and Nielsen, M.: Cognitive Memory Retrieval Techniques. *Police Chief, 53* (3), 1986.

Geiselman, R.E., et al.: Enhancing Eyewitness Memory: Refining the Cognitive Interview. *Journal of Police Science and Administration, 15* (292), 1987.

Hess, J.E.: *Interviewing and Interrogation for Law Enforcement.* Cincinnati: Anderson, 1997.

MacHovec, F.J.: *Interview and Interrogation: A Scientific Approach.* Springfield, IL: Thomas, 1989.

Olsen, L. and Wells, R.: Cognitive Interviewing and the Victim/Witness in Crisis. *Police Chief, 58* (2), 1991.

Pinizzotto, A.J. and Deshazor, G.D.: Interviewing Erratic Subjects. *FBI Law Enforcement Bulletin, 66* (11), 1997.

Royal, R.F. and Schutt, S.R.: *The Gentle Art of Interviewing and Interrogation: A Professional Manual and Guide.* Englewood Cliffs, NJ: Prentice-Hall, 1976.

Ryals, J.R.: Successful Interviewing. *FBI Law Enforcement Bulletin, 60* (3), 1991.

Wicks, R.J. and Josephs, E.H., Jr.: *Techniques in Interviewing for Law Enforcement and Corrections Personnel.* Springfield, IL: Thomas, 1972.

Yeschke, C.L.: *Interviewing: An Introduction to Interrogation.* Springfield, IL: Thomas, 1987.

Zulawski, D.E. and Wicklander, D.E.: *Practical Aspects of Interview and Interrogation.* New York: Elsevier, 1991.

Hypnosis

Arons, H.: *Hypnosis in Criminal Investigation.* South Orange, NJ: Power Publishers, 1977.

Ault, R.L., Jr.: Hypnosis: The FBI's Team Approach. *FBI Law Enforcement Bulletin, 49* (1), 1980.

Depresca, J.: Forensic Hypnosis. *FBI Law Enforcement Bulletin, 44* (9), 1996.

Hibbard, W.S. and Worring, R.W.: *Forensic Hypnosis: The Practical Application of Hypnosis in Criminal Investigations* (rev. 1st ed.). Springfield, IL: Thomas, 1996.

Howell, M.: Profile of an Investigative Hypnosis Interview. *Law and Order, 37* (3),1989.

Kingston, K.A.: Admissibility of Post-Hypnotic Testimony. *FBI Law Enforcement Bulletin, 55* (4), 1986.

Kline, M.V.: *Forensic Hypnosis: Clinical Tactics in the Courtroom.* Springfield, IL: Thomas, 1983.

Orne, M.T., Tonry, M.H., et al.: *Hypnotically Refreshed Testimony: Enhanced Memory or Tampering with Evidence?* Washington, D.C.: U.S. Government Printing Office, 1985.

Reiser, M.: *Handbook of Investigative Hypnosis.* Los Angeles: Lehi Publishing, 1980.

Timm, H.W.: The Factors Theoretically Affecting the Impact of Forensic Hypnosis Techniques on Eyewitness Recall. *Journal of Police Science and Administration, 11* (442), 1983.

Wagstaff, G.F. and Maguire, C.: An Experimental Study of Hypnosis, Guided Memory and Witness Memory. *Journal of the Forensic Science Society, 23* (73), 1983.

Interrogation

Aubry, A.S. and Caputo, R.R.: *Criminal Interrogation* (3rd ed.). Springfield, IL: Thomas, 1980.

Corr, K.: Questioning Invited Suspects at the Police Station. *Police Chief, 64* (9), 1997.

Crawford, K.A.: Intentional Violations of *Miranda. FBI Law Enforcement Bulletin, 66* (8), 1997.

——: Invoking the *Miranda* Right to Counsel: The Defendant's Burden. *FBI Law Enforcement Bulletin, 64* (3), 1995.

Hendrie, E.M.: Beyond *Miranda. FBI Law Enforcement Bulletin, 66* (3), 1997.

Hess, J.E.: *Interviewing and Interrogation for Law Enforcement.* Cincinnati: Anderson, 1997.

Higginbotham: Post-*Miranda* Refinements. Parts I and II. *FBI Law Enforcement Bulletin, 55* (2 & 3), 1986.

——: Waiver of Rights in Custodial Interrogations. *FBI Law Enforcement Bulletin, 56* (11), 1987.

Inbau, F.E.: Legally Permissible Criminal Interrogation Tactics and Techniques. *Journal of Police Science and Administration, 4* (249), 1976.

——: Over-reaction–The Mischief of *Miranda vs. Arizona. The Journal of Criminal Law and Criminology, 73* (97), 1982.

Inbau, F.E., Reid, J.E. and Buckley, J.P.: *Criminal Interrogation and Confessions* (3rd ed.). Baltimore: Williams and Wilkins, 1986.

MacHovec, F.J.: *Interview and Interrogation: A Scientific Approach.* Springfield, IL: Thomas, 1989.

Napier, M.R. and Adams, S.H.: Magic Words to Obtain Confessions, *FBI Law Enforcement Bulletin, 67* (10), 1998.

Riley, C.E. III: Fine Tuning *Miranda* Policies. *FBI Law Enforcement Bulletin, 54* (1), 1985.

——: Confessions and Interrogation: The Use of Artifice, Strategem, and Deception. *FBI Law Enforcement Bulletin, 51* (4), 1982.

——: Interrogation after Assertion of Rights. Parts I and II. *FBI Law Enforcement Bulletin, 53* (5 & 6), 1984.

Robin, G.D.: Juvenile Interrogation and Confessions. *Journal of Police Science and Administration, 10* (224), 1982.

Vessel, D.: Conducting Successful Interrogations. *FBI Law Enforcement Bulletin, 67* (10), 1998.

Yeschke, C.L.: *Interviewing: A Forensic Guide to Interrogation* (2nd ed.). Springfield, IL: Thomas, 1993.

Zulawski, D.E. and Wicklander, D.E.: *Practical Aspects of Interview and Interrogation.* New York: Elsevier, 1991.

Detection of Deception

Ansley, N. (Ed.): *Legal Admissibility of the Polygraph.* Springfield, IL: Thomas, 1975.

Desroches, F.J. and Thomas, A.S.: The Police Use of the Polygraph in Criminal Investigations. *Canadian Journal of Criminology, 27* (43), 1985.

Brenner, M., Branscomb, H. & Schwartz, G.: Psychological Stress Evaluator–Two Tests of a Vocal Measure. *Psychophysiology, 16* (4): 351-357, 1979.

Ferguson, R.J., Jr. and Miller, A.L.: *The Polygraph in Court.* Springfield, IL: Thomas, 1973.

Furgerson, R.M.: Evaluating Investigative Polygraph Results. *FBI Law Enforcement Bulletin, 58* (10), 1989.

——: Polygraph Policy Model for Law Enforcement. *FBI Law Enforcement Bulletin, 56* (6), 1987.

Hunter, F.L. and Ash, P.: The Accuracy and Consistency of Polygraph Examiners' Diagnosis. *Journal of Police Science and Administration, 1* (370), 1973.

Inbau, F.E. and Reid, J.E.: *Truth and Deception: The Polygraph (Lie Detector) Technique* (2nd ed.). Baltimore: Williams and Wilkins, 1978.

Grantham CE, Pearl MH, Manderscheid RW, Silbergeld S.: The Psychological Stress Evaluator as a clinical assessment instrument. Evaluation and implications. *Journal of Nervous and Mental Disease, 169* (5): 283-8, 1981.

Lesce, T.: SCAN: Deception Detection by Scientific Content Analysis. *Law and Order, 38* (8), 1990.

Lynch, B. & Henry, D.: A validity study of the Psychological Stress Evaluator. *Canadian Journal of Behavioural Science, 1* (1): 89-94, 1979.

Matte, J.A.: *The Art and Science of the Polygraph Technique.* Springfield, IL: Thomas, 1980.

Murphy, J.K.: The Polygraph Technique: Past and Present. *FBI Law Enforcement Bulletin, 49* (6), 1980.

Nachshon, I & Feldman, B.: Vocal Indices of Psychological Stress–A Validation Study of the Psychological Stress Evaluator. *Journal of Police Science and Administration, 8* (1): 40-53: 1980.

Nachshon, I., Elaad, E. and Amsel, T.: Validity of the Psychological Stress Evaluator: A Field Study. *Journal of Police Science and Administration, 13* (275), 1985.

Polygraph: A Critical Appraisal. *Journal of the Beverly Hills Bar Association, 8* (35), 1974.

Ronayne, John A.: Admissibility of Testing by the Psychological Stress Evaluator Commentary. *Pace Law Review, 9* (2), 1989.

Scientific V. Judicial Acceptance. *University of Miami Law Review, 27* (254), 1972.

Timm, H.W.: The Efficacy of the Psychological Stress Evaluator in Detecting Deception. *Journal of Police Science and Administration, 11* (62), 1983.

Confessions

Burke, J.J.: Confessions to Private Persons. *FBI Law Enforcement Bulletin, 42* (8), 1973.

DiPietro, A.L.: Lies, Promises, or Threats: The Voluntariness of Confessions. *FBI Law Enforcement Bulletin, 62* (7), 1993.

Inbau, F.E.: Legally Permissible Criminal Interrogation Tactics and Techniques. *Journal of Police Science and Administration, 4* (249), 1976.

Inbau, F.E., Reid, J.E. and Buckley, J.P.: *Criminal Interrogation and Confessions* (3rd ed.). Baltimore: Williams and Wilkins, 1986.

Invergo, M.: Questioning Techniques and Written Statements. *Police Law Quarterly, 5* (3), 1976.

Macdonald, J.M. and Michaud, D.L.: *The Confession: Interrogation and Criminal Profiles for Police Officers.* Denver, CO: Apache Press, 1987.

Nissman, D.M., Hagen, E. and Brooks, P.R.: *Law of Confessions.* Rochester: Lawyers Co-operative, 1985.

Riley, C.E. III: Confessions and Interrogation: The Use of Artifice, Strategem, and Deception. *FBI Law Enforcement Bulletin, 51* (4), 1982.

———: Confessions and the Sixth Amendment Right to Counsel. Parts I and II. *FBI Law Enforcement and Bulletin, 52* (8 & 9), 1983.

Robin, G.D.: Juvenile Interrogation and Confessions. *Journal of Police Science and Administration, 10* (224), 1982.

Shuy, R.W.: *The Language of Confession, Interrogation, and Deception.* Thousand Oaks, CA: Sage, 1998.

Tousignant, D.D.: Why Suspects Confess. *FBI Law Enforcement Bulletin, 60* (3), 1991.

Recording Interrogation

Crawford, K.A.: Surreptitious Recording of Suspects' Conversations. *FBI Law Enforcement Bulletin, 62* (9), 1993.

Gebhardt, R.H.: Video Tape in Criminal Cases. *FBI Law Enforcement Bulletin, 44* (5), 1975.

Geller, W.A.: Videotaping Interrogations and Confessions. *FBI Law Enforcement Bulletin, 63* (1), 1994.

Hollien, H.: *The Acoustics of Crime: The New Science of Forensic Phonetics.* New York: Plenum Press, 1990.

Koenig, B.E.: Making Effective Forensic Audio Tape Recordings. *FBI Law Enforcement Bulletin, 56* (5), 1987.

McDonald, W.H.: The Use of Videotaping in Documenting Confessions. *Police Chief, 50* (2), 1983.

Rifas, R.A.: *Legal Aspects of Video Tape and Motion Pictures in Law Enforcement.* Evanston, IL: Traffic Institute, Northwestern University, 1972.

Chapter 9

SOURCES OF INFORMATION
AND MISSING PERSONS

TRACKING AND SOURCES OF INFORMATION

1. Overview

INVESTIGATORS spend a significant amount of time and use many sources of information trying to locate missing or wanted persons. Locating a person may be as simple as making a few telephone calls, searching the Internet, or visiting a previous residence. At other times, the hunt can become a lengthy and complicated ordeal.

The hunt for individuals commonly requires a search of records and various sources of information from public and private agencies. Investigators must be versatile in their ability to uncover information. Some investigators spend weeks obtaining information from interviews and informants that could have easily been found in a public directory. Sometimes traditional training and customs can lead to information being overlooked. While newspaper reporters and private investigators are trained in developing information, the police tend to rely on their authority and inducing people to talk. Often pressed for time, they may not develop good research skills.

2. Tracking a Missing Witness, Victim, and so Forth

The first step in searching for people is to obtain information to identify them. A description, identifying data, social, business, and criminal history will all serve to identify them. Information received through informants should be verified. Start with direct and simple procedures.

A simple telephone call to the individual's home or workplace may yield valuable information. Ask simple, direct questions. Is he or she home? Where has he or she gone? What is his or her present address? Call friends and relatives and make inquiries. Obviously investigators should follow up on any leads obtained from these sources.

If telephone inquiries are fruitless, investigators should visit the address. Question the family. If the family has moved, make inquiries of the neighbors to learn the habits, hangouts, and social life of the person. Habits have a strong effect on behavior, so the individual is likely to frequent similar places in his or her new surroundings. What was the state of mind of the person? Was he or she worried or nervous? What were his or her plans or ambitions? Were home and vocational conditions satisfactory? Did he or she withdraw money from the bank? What was the condition of his or her room? Who saw him or her last? What was the conversation? How did he or she behave when last seen? The landlords or realty agents may know the name of the mover or possess a list references. The local tavern, drug store, gas station, and convenience store should be visited.

Check the Internet for leads. Search for the individual's name using several search engines. Try social networking sites. Attempt to identify the subject's interests, hobbies and associates.

Another simple place to start is to check for a *change of address*. The individual may not be hiding but just relocated. Public agencies such as the Postal Service, Board of Education, County/City Clerk, Department of Motor Vehicle, utilities, and tax assessment lists are good places to start. Private agencies such as financial institutions, movers and haulers, Internet and television providers are also possible sources of information.

A *mail cover* can be helpful in some cases. A request can be made to the postal inspector to have a mail cover placed on the homes of relatives. A copy will then be made of any external markings (mailing place, date stamp, return address, etc.) on the front and back of each piece of mail sent to the address being covered. A cover is usually placed on mail for two weeks or a month and is restricted to no more than 120 days. The mail is not opened; only the markings are recorded. Considering the work involved, a request should be made only when useful results can be reasonably expected. Investigators should cancel the mail cover once the desired information is obtained. Attention should be paid to computer printed address labels, especially if several are sent from the same location and no return address is given, for they are unlikely to be business letters. If handwriting samples are available, they can be compared with the mail covers.

Investigators can often obtain useful information from *reverse directories*. These databases cross-reference telephone numbers and addresses to names. Copies of the local directories can often be found in the public library or can be accessed on the Internet. By looking up the address of the missing person in the directory, investigators can quickly compile a list of the names, addresses, and telephone numbers of neighbors or identify individuals from telephone numbers.

A *pen register* monitors telephone use in a similar manner as the mail cover does for postal service. That is, it records the data concerning the fact that the communication was made, not the contents of the communication. Once strictly a device attached to phone lines, the term is now used to describe any device, trap, or computer software used to log calls. Every number dialed from a particular phone, as well as the date, the time, and the duration of the call is recorded by the telephone company. If the person you are trying to locate is suspected of using the telephone of a friend or a relative to contact associates, a pen register can be helpful. Federal law requires that a court order be obtained before a pen register can be used.

3. Tracking Fugitives

Techniques for tracking fugitives vary with the skills and personality of the subject. More sophisticated fugitives necessitate discreet methods. More direct approaches (such as those discussed above) are possible with inexperienced criminals.

Depending on the circumstances, investigators may issue BOLOs (Be On the Look Out) or ATLs (Attempt To Locate) in local, state, and national law enforcement databases. Where appropriate con-

Table 9-1. Routine Information.

• Full name and alias. • Physical description. • Modus operandi. • Motive. • Associates past and present. • Habits, hangouts, and places known to frequent. • Criminal record, photograph, and fingerprints. • Residence, last known and previous locations.	• Employment, last known and previous employers. • Relatives, names and addresses of all available. • Close friends, names and addresses. • Physical condition. • Motor Vehicle Bureau, check for operator's license & vehicles owned. • Social Security Number. • Military records. • Handwriting for comparison with mail covers, hotel registrations, etc.

tact or alert other law enforcement agencies, courts, probation or parole offices, former arresting officers, or private security agencies.

A search warrant will be required, but investigators can check cell phone and credit card usage to locate individuals. Either may narrow the geographic areas to search. Cell phone locations can be determined and records are maintained by most service providers for a year or more. Law enforcement tracking technology uses cell phone towers to triangulate the location of the phone.

4. Federal Bureau of Investigation Databases

a. **NCIC.** The National Crime Information Center (NCIC) is the FBI's computerized index containing information on warrants, wanted persons, criminal histories, and stolen and/or missing property. Through extensive communications networks, local, state, and federal law enforcement agencies can enter and access records.

The Wanted Persons File contains information and warrants for individuals charged with felonies or serious misdemeanors. Probation or parole violators are also entered in the NCIC. Law enforcement agencies in the federal government, the fifty states, the District of Columbia, Puerto Rico, Virgin Islands, Guam, and Canada have direct on-line access to the computer records to identify suspects and apprehend fugitives.

Table 9-2. Federal and State Sources of Information.

Federal Agencies	State Agencies
Homeland Security & Fusion Centers	Assessor's Office
Alcohol, Tobacco, Firearms, & Explosives	Attorney General's Office
Immigration & Customs Enforcement	Clerk's Office
Civil Service Commission	Department of State Records
Coast Guard	Fish and Game Warden's Office
Drug Enforcement Administration	Judges—Justices of Peace
Federal Communications Commission	Retirement/Pension Offices
Department of Labor	Penal agencies
Federal Unemployment Offices	Personal Property records
Internal Revenue Service	Commercial licensing
Federal Bureau of Investigation	Probation and Parole Bureaus
Maritime Commission	Public Welfare and Social Service Offices
Military Services	Social Services records
US Postal Service	Secretaries of Agriculture
Probation Bureaus	Tax Collectors' Offices
Provost Marshal's Offices	Treasurers' Offices
Secret Service	State Compensation Offices
Selective Service Administration	State Unemployment Office
Veterans Administration	Voting registers
Defense Department	Workers' Compensation Boards

Descriptive data includes name, sex, race, nationality, date of birth, height, weight, hair color, FBI number, NCIC fingerprint classification, miscellaneous identification numbers, social security number, driver's license data, charges and date of warrant, and data identifying license plates and automobiles associated with the wanted person.

b. **IAFIS**. The Integrated Automated Fingerprint Identification System (IAFIS) is a national clearinghouse containing over 66 million subjects in the criminal file and more than 25 million civil print cards. It is the largest biometric database in the world. The civil file is comprised of the cards of federal employees and applicants, military personnel, civilian employees in national defense industries, aliens, and persons wishing to have their fingerprints on file for identification purposes.

Fingerprint cards contain the name, signature, and physical description of the person fingerprinted; information concerning the

Table 9-3. Local and Private Sources of Information.

County/City Agencies	Private Organizations
County Sources of Information	Airlines
Assessors' Offices	American Red Cross
Boards of Supervisors	Banks
Clerks' Offices	Bonding companies
Agents' Offices	Brokerage offices
Judges—Justices of Peace	Commercial investigative agencies
Probation and Parole Bureaus	Contractors
Prosecuting officials	Credit bureaus
Tax Collectors' Offices	Fraternal organizations
Treasurers' Offices	Hotels/Motels/Lodging
Voting registers	Income records
Sheriffs' Offices	Industrial organizations
City Sources of Information	Insurance companies
Records of applications for	Loan and financial companies
Licenses: (marriage, car, etc.)	Mortgage, Debt, and Lien records
Assessor's Office	Railroad companies
Boards of Commissioners	Real estate agenices
Boards of Health	Rental agenices—real estate, cars,
Clerks' Offices	trucks
Coroners' or Medical Examiners'	Steamship companies
Court Records, Civil and Criminal	Storage companies
Election Boards	Telephone companies
Fire Marshals	Trade union records
Health, Sanitation	Transportation companies (bus,
Building Inspectors' Offices	cruise lines)
Judges - Justices of Peace	Water, electric, and gas companies
Personal Property records	
Police Departments	
Probate records	
Prosecuting officials	
Public Schools	
Tax Collectors' Office	
Title Records Offices	
Treasurers' Offices	
Truant offices	
Voting registers	

reason for fingerprinting; identity of the contributing agency; date printed; and, where applicable, the charge and disposition or sentence. Some cards contain the residential address, occupation, and employment of the person fingerprinted.

Table 9-4. Suggested Directories and Databases.

Telephone Directory	American Men and Women of
Criss-Cross or Reverse Directory	Science
Who's Who in America	Martindale-Hubbell Law Directory
Who's Who in Finance and Industry	Who's Who in Education
Who Knows What (experts in	Polk's Bank Directory (financial
various fields)	officials)
American Medical Directory	National Change of Address System
Directory of Medical Specialists	Postal Directory
Who's Who in Engineering	Insurance Directory
	Dun and Bradstreet

Identification records, compiled from fingerprint cards, contain the identity of the contributors of the cards, names and aliases of the subject of record, agency identifying numbers, dates of arrest and/or incarceration, charges, and dispositions. IAFIS receives approximately 162,000 fingerprint ten-print submissions a day, and can process electronic criminal submissions in less than 10 minutes.

5. Scope of Federal Information Gathering

Agencies of the federal government maintain records according to their function, responsibilities, and security requirements. The nature and amount of information will vary with the agency.

Civilian personnel records typically include: name, date of birth, social security number, educational background, professional qualifications, job assignments, and so forth. Ordinarily the file will include employment applications, proficiency reports, and information relating to the person's security clearance status.

Military records contain information similar to civilian personnel records for present and former members of the Armed Forces. Current duty or standby status is maintained in the active files of the Defense Department or other appropriate agency. Records of former military personnel are maintained in the files of the Veterans Administration.

Information on private individuals is maintained for criminal activity or security matters (a granted or withheld security clearance). A far larger amount of information is contained by Census Bureau, the Internal Revenue Service, and the Social Security Administration.

In recent years, advances in technology and communication have opened a new era of gathering and distributing information. High-speed data retrieval systems and the expansion of the Internet have resulted in databanks with instantly available information.

The governmental process of gathering, storing, retrieving, and disseminating data on individuals has always threatened the functioning of a free society. Today, incredible advances in technology allow for surveillance capability undreamed of in previous times. Electronic and photographic developments now permit the collection of vast amounts of data on day-to-day activities of all citizens without their knowledge. Information in electronic form is more readily accessible and usable exposing millions of people to a new level of scrutiny.

a. **The Threat to Privacy**. We need to control when and how information can be used. Several safeguards have been suggested to protect the public and preserve the sense of privacy that is essential to a democracy. Some of these safeguards may not be appropriate in some circumstances, but they do address the larger issue of the ethical use of information.

People can no longer escape their past lives by moving to another town. Our ability to collect, process, and store information places everyone under a level of scrutiny never imagined in the past. Several privacy issues pertaining to how police and other government agencies handle information need to be addressed. How long should the state be able to maintain surveillance information? Should old information be purged? Should individuals be allowed to access their files to correct or challenge inaccuracies? Should individuals be notified if someone requests information from their file? What safeguards are needed when information that was collected for one purpose is used for another? What standards are needed to ensure the information being created, maintained, used, or disseminated is reliable and being used for its intended purpose? What measures are in place to protect the security of information and to ensure secret record keeping is not taking place? All of these issues become more important as information technology continues to advance.

ANALYSING INFORMATION

6. *Modus Operandi*

Past experience affects our actions and the decisions. We tend to repeat what works as long as it is effective or until we discover something better. If we encounter a problem, we adjust and soon settle into a new pattern. Each success reinforces our habit. Our choices are shaped by knowledge, physical abilities, critical thinking skills, and opportunities. Criminals function in a similar manner. They repeat behavior that has been successful until confronted with reason to change. With each crime, they make adjustments as they refine their method. A summary of the habits, techniques, and peculiarities of behavior is the *modus operandi* or MO, a term that essentially means method of operation.

MO files provide information for investigators to determine patterns of criminal behavior, link crimes together, associate crimes to perpetrators, project future crimes and targets, and to formulate crime prevention measures. MO files are most effective in serial crimes involving personal contact, such as felonies against a person, confidence games, and forgery. Along with the manner used to commit a crime, characteristics such as physical description, mannerisms, and speech can be important components of MO analysis.

a. **Organization**. The traditional elements of the MO system, developed by Major L. W. Atcherley in the 1880s, are still an effective guide to organizing information. Important elements include *property* (nature, type, kind of property), *description of perpetrator, observations at the scene* (e.g. what was seen, heard, smelled, tasted, or felt), *motive* (in addition to theft), *time* (when the crime was committed), *peculiarities* (drinking or eating at the scene, unnecessary destruction, defecation, and theft of inconsequential items, etc.), and *observed peculiarities* (enunciation, dialect, diction, mannerisms, etc.). Together these factors help to discover patterns and connections from what may appear to be a collection of random acts.

7. Signature Behaviors

Signature behaviors are compulsive acts that are rooted in suspects' personalities. Unlike MO behavior, signature behavior is not necessary to perpetrate a crime. They are additional or extraneous acts that perpetrators perform to derive psychological satisfaction from the crime. For example, turning on the water before leaving a home after burglarizing it or posing the dead body of a victim are not acts necessary to complete the crime, but may be acts the perpetrator is compelled to perform. A signature is a psychological calling card. When recognized by investigators, signatures help investigators to link crimes together. Because it is psychologically based, signature behavior is consistent, unlike MO behavior that evolves and refines. A perpetrator's signature is a unique feature.

8. Criminal Personality Profiling

Our personality and psychological make-up is expressed in our actions. Criminal activity is no exception. By identifying and analyzing the habits and personality traits of people who have committed crimes, descriptions of a typical offender's personality and behavior can be developed. Once we understand the psychological dynamics of specific behaviors we can infer from a behavior the psychological motivators that caused it. In essence, by observing crime scene behavior we can identify the personality traits of the person who committed the crime.

If, in examining the circumstances of a crime, investigators can determine that the criminal's behavior is consistent with a typical pattern, they can evaluate the likelihood that a specific suspect committed the crime. Those who do not fit the psychological profile can be eliminated from consideration as suspects. Investigative resources can then be focused on more likely suspects. This process of studying crime scene details to identify personality and behavioral traits of the perpetrator is called criminal profiling.

a. **Factors Considered**. The crime is examined with special attention paid to the apparent level of planning and risk taken. The actions of the perpetrator, evidence present or missing, and circumstances of the immediate environments are reviewed. Witness statements, crime scene reports and photographs, background and activities of the victim, and any other pertinent information are considered.

b. **Types of Crimes**. Most crimes do not lend themselves to personality profiling. Crimes involving minimal contact with the crime scene and the victim are usually not conducive to profiling, for little of the personality of the offender can be determined. Crimes motivated by greed are too common to provide a useful profile.

Serial crimes such as bank robberies, rape, arson, pedophilia, sadistic ritual crimes, sadistic sexual assaults and murder lend themselves to profiling. Criminal profiling is suitable for crimes with abundant physical evidence or considerable interaction with the victim that displays the offenders thought process. Ritualistic crimes, torture, and murders involving post-mortem disfigurement, though extremely rare, are especially conducive to this kind of analysis because they are committed by criminals with pronounced psychological disorders. A personality profile of the offender will help to evaluate and eliminate potential suspects. The FBI's Behavioral Science Unit offers assistance in profiling to all official law enforcement agencies.

c. **Psycholinguistic Analysis**. The contents of threatening communications, anonymous letters, emails, and telephone calls can be profiled through psycholinguistic analysis. Information can be derived about the primary message, as well as the personality, background and frame of mind of the subject. Word usage can be compared to ordinary speech or writing to determine whether multiple messages are originating from the same person. Analysis also provides information about the author's personality and educational background.

d. **Organized and Disorganized Personalities**. The FBI interviewed thirty-six convicted sexual murderers and studied their crime scenes and their behavior during the crimes to better understand violent offenders. From this information, they were able to classify sexual murders into two types, "organized" and "disorganized." These characteristics reflect how individuals structure and lead their lives. The characteristics should be viewed as a continu-

Table 9-5. Crime Scene Characteristics of Organized & Disorganized Murderers.

Organized	Disorganized
Planned offense	Spontaneous offense
Victim a targeted stranger	Victim/location known
Personalizes victim	Depersonalizes victim
Controlled conversation	Minimal conversation
Crime scene reflects overall control	Crime scene random and sloppy
Demands submissive victim	Sudden violence to victim
Restraints used	Minimal use of restraints
Aggressive acts prior to death	Sexual acts after death
Body hidden	Body left in view
Weapons/evidence absent	Evidence/weapon often present
Transports victim or body	Body left at death scene

Source: FBI Law Enforcement Bulletin, 54 (8), 1985.

um with organized and disorganized on opposite ends. Few individuals will fit all the characteristics of either category, and many may display characteristics of both or mixed characteristics. If investigators can determine that the crime scene is either "organized" or "disorganized," they will have some indication of the character traits of the assailant.

Table 9-6. Characteristics of Organized and Disorganized Murderers.

Organized	Below-average intelligence
Disorganized	Socially inadequate
Average to above-average intelligence	Unskilled work
Socially competent	Sexually incompetent
Skilled work preferred	Low birth order status
Sexually competent	Father's work unstable
High birth order status	Harsh discipline as child
Father's work stable	Anxious mood during crime
Inconsistent childhood discipline	Minimal use of alcohol
Controlled mood during crime	Minimal situational stress
Use of alcohol with crime	Living alone
Situational stress	Lives/works near crime scene
Living with partner	Minimal interest in news media
Mobility with car in good condition	Significant behavior change (drug/
Follows crime in news media	alcohol abuse, religiosity, etc.)
May change jobs or leave town	

Source: FBI Law Enforcement Bulletin, 54 (8), 1985.

9. Crime Analysis

Crime analysis is a means of deciphering the massive amounts of data police collect to identify crime patterns and trends, link crimes to perpetrators, devise crime prevention strategies, better allocate resources, and plan for the future. It draws on many disciplines including psychology, statistics, geography, criminology, sociology, and crime mapping. It is a systematic and analytical means of interpreting crime data.

Crime analysis guides problem solving by systematically studying crime, disorder and other policing issues. Using sociodemographic, spatial, and temporal data, analysts evaluate police efforts, identify crime patterns, and design crime prevention strategies. Data is analyzed to identify trends or patterns both general and specific to offenders or locations. *Hot spots* (locations with significant levels of crime), *hot dots* (offenders or victims associated with unusual amounts of crime), and *hot products* (property targeted disproportionately) are identified to guide strategies and tactics. Investigators should work closely with crime analysts to ensure information is used efficiently and effectively.

10. Cold Case Units

The definition of a cold case varies but generally includes cases that have not been solved after an extended period of time and have few or no active leads. Many definitions specify that cases be at least a year old and cannot be addressed by the originally assigned investigators. In general, a case is considered cold if all leads are exhausted. Approximately one-third of homicide cases in the United States will remain unsolved after the first year.

The composition of cold case units also varies greatly. Most units are staffed by detectives with extensive investigative experience. Some units are comprised of volunteers with diverse backgrounds and expertise from outside policing. Other units consist of retired homicide detectives, auxiliary officers, or criminal justice interns. Cold case homicide investigation is one of the most frustrating assignments police encounter. Investigators assigned to cold case units should be exceptionally skilled, innovative, and persistent. Whatever the strategy, it is important to have the right mix of investigative and supervisory personnel.

a. **Reopening a Cold Case**. Cases tend to be reopened because new information develops through witnesses, suspects, or physical evidence. Spin-off cases are common, as are new leads, tips from programs like Crime Stoppers, or information from informants.

As relationships change, individuals may come forward with new information. Witnesses' fears may subside, motivations change, or they may choose to cooperate in exchange for help with their own legal problems. Sometimes new victims are identified and investigations resume.

As time passes, the identity of suspects may become known. Perpetrators may begin to brag about their crimes. Occasionally suspects just want to talk about their crimes for psychological or religious reasons.

Advances in techniques and databases in DNA, latent prints, and ballistics bring new value to old evidence. Studies have shown that over one-third of reopened cases are solved.

11. Internet as an Investigative Tool

The growth of the Internet brings new challenges to investigators. Advances in technology bring new crimes and new ways to commit old crimes. The Internet allows predators to access homes, businesses, and government offices. The perceived anonymity of electronic communications may also undermine individuals' sense of accountability. Internet activity, however, is more traceable than many people imagine. Trained specialists can uncover substantial amounts of information about electronic activity.

While the Internet has fostered new crimes difficult to investigate through conventional means, it also allows investigators to readily access information that was hard to obtain in the past. Addresses, telephone numbers, business and real estate records, professional license, and a variety of other information are available on the Internet. Aside from the ready access to data and records from government websites, individuals frequently provide access to their personal lives. The Internet is a good place to begin background searches. Suspects may reveal more information on social networking sites than a team of investigators could uncover in months of investigation. Obviously, information gained from such sites needs to be verified, but it is a good source of investigative leads.

The Internet is also useful for quickly disseminating information. Information on crime patterns, investigations, wanted persons, missing persons, or stolen property can be posted on websites or distributed through electronic mailing lists to generate tips from the public.

12. Digital Crime Scenes

While advances in digital technology have opened new possibilities and access to investigators, they have also produced new challenges. New crimes, and new means of executing crimes, are accompanied by new demands for collecting evidence. The processing and analysis of digital evidence is a specialty that should be left to trained technicians. Unless investigators are trained in recovering electronic evidence, they should limit their activities to those of a first responder.

While beyond the skills of most investigators, a basic knowledge of forensic data collection is necessary to prevent destruction of valuable evidence. Computers, cell phones, and mobile electronic devices may contain a wealth of information and potential evidence if properly collected. Simply shutting down the device and transporting to a forensic technician can result in the loss of open files, temporary files and malicious programs, and may cause the encrypting of saved data. Putting the device into hibernation or leaving it on for "live data collection" may preserve evidence that would otherwise be lost. Battery powered mobile devices can generally be more safely transported, but should be delivered to a forensic technician before the battery expires.

Electronic devices should be treated with the same regard as any other physical evidence. Document the conditions as found through notes, photographs, and sketches. If the device is on, photograph the screen and record any information displayed. If it appears that data is being deleted or it is a Microsoft Windows based operating system, pulling the power cord from the back of the device may be the safest alternative. When in doubt, always contact a trained specialist before taking action.

Once the device is off or if you discover it in the off position, document, sketch, and photograph all devices and cables attached. Label and remove all cables, power cords, USB connections, etc. Place tape across all ports, disk slots, power switch, etc. Record the make, model, and serial number. Package the evidence to prevent damage and transport it to a forensic analyst.

MISSING PERSONS

13. Overview

The investigation of missing persons is included in this chapter because it draws on many of the skills just discussed. While most missing person cases do not turn into death investigations, it is important that missing person cases are properly investigated should the disappearance be the result of foul play. Although finding and identifying missing persons is often not viewed as exciting detective work, it is an important task. *Missing persons* can be anyone reported absent from their normal activities. Most active cases include juveniles, adults unable to care for themselves due to mental or physical limitations, or anyone when there are circumstances indicating an involuntary disappearance. Missing persons should not be confused with "wanted persons" who are sought by the police in connection with a crime. In a large city, missing person cases can be a sizable portion of the case load. Missing Persons units ordinarily focus on missing juveniles, unidentified dead, and unidentified persons. Absent suspicion of a crime, missing adults who are not considered a danger to themselves or others may not receive a high priority. When missing persons are victims of violent crime, the early stages of the investigation are critical.

The FBI's NCIC Missing Person and Unidentified Person Statistics website report over 85,000 missing person cases with nearly half being juveniles. During 2010, over 690,000 cases were added to the database and over 703,000 cases removed because the individual was found, returned, or the report invalid. There are also over 7,500 unidentified persons who are either living but unidentified, deceased, or victims of catastrophes.

14. Crimes and Conditions Associated with Missing Persons

a. **Homicide**. Each year thousands of people are reported missing, and it is not surprising that some are victims of violence. Murder, the unspoken fear of the relatives and the police, must always be considered by investigators. Shrewd investigators have uncovered homicides. The two most popular motives for this type of homicide are money and love. There are many cases of a spouse or roommate filing a missing person report to cover a murder. Investigators, when taking the report, should encourage complainants to talk about their relationship with victims and speculate on what may have happened to them. Look for subtle and underlying motives. Note the speaker's context and tense they use when referring to the missing person. Keep in mind that friends and family do not speak of a missing person in the past tense unless they already know he or she is dead.

b. **Suicide**. While the possibility of suicide often comes to mind, only about one in 2,000 missing persons take their own lives. Suicides are ordinarily motivated by financial difficulties such as business failures, domestic troubles, or incurable diseases. Investigators should try to discover the motive for the disappearance. People voluntarily disappear to escape from personal, domestic, or business conflict. Those seeking to escape boredom or to change their lives rarely turn to suicide. Even failed romantic relationships seldom result in suicide.

1) *Fabricated Suicide*. Attempts to simulate a suicide are usually efforts to defraud insurance companies or to leave a failed marriage. The scene is fabricated so others will assume the individual is dead even though the body is missing. It is common to stage a suicide near water to suggest the individual drowned. Clothing and personal items are placed at the scene to ensure identification. In general, investigators should reserve judgment until a body is recovered. Drowning victims will ordinarily return to the surface within five to ten days. After twenty days (unless in very cold

water), it may be concluded that the body has been carried down river or out to sea, or that the person is still alive. Investigators should inquire about insurance policies and other motives and check credit card and cell phone usage.

c. **Extortion**. Missing person cases that generate extensive publicity may produce extortion demands. Police and relatives of the missing person may be besieged by crank calls suggesting the missing person is being held for ransom. The ransom messages usually demand large sums of money. While some incidents may be actual kidnappings, these are rare. More likely these messages are the work of disturbed individuals exploiting the emotions of relatives. Naturally, investigators should attempt to track the extortion message.

d. **Amnesia**. Loss of memory and knowledge of identity is extremely rare even among missing persons cases. Of the authentic cases, the most frequent cause is brain damage from a head injury.

e. **Mental Incapacitation**. Investigators may need to deal with mentally incapacitated individuals of unknown identity. These individuals are often brought to a local hospital for examination. They may be psychotic, suffering from dementia, or some other malady. Along with a lack of memory they are often disoriented and confused.

f. **Abandonment**. Unhappy marriages account for a large number of disappearances. The voluntary disappearance of an adult may be a case of abandonment.

g. **Runaways and Throwaways**. Many missing person reports involve juveniles who leave their homes for a variety of reasons. They may be discipline problems or victims trying to escape abuse and neglect. Some leave of their own volition while others have been forced out of their homes. Most are found or return home in a short period of time, but those remaining on the streets are vulnerable to predators.

15. Investigative Steps

a. **Unidentified Dead**. After a report is received and investigators arrive at the scene, a complete description of the deceased is compiled. The Missing Persons Unit should be notified and a search of the missing persons records begun. In addition to normal crime scene photographs, identification photographs of the face should be taken. Normally, additional evidence is collected after the body has arrived at the morgue but some of it may be collected at the scene. Fingerprints and DNA should be collected as soon as possible. Scars, tattoos, deformities, and other outstanding characteristics should be photographed. The body is examined for wounds, signs of struggle, or additional evidence. The clothing is searched for any markings and labels. Any property is recorded and documented for identification. Any appliances or devices such as artificial limbs, pacemakers, etc. are documented and traced through the manufacturer. A complete description of the body is made and x-rays taken. A forensic odontologist may be needed to document the teeth.

b. **Missing Persons**. The investigative steps in a missing person case are similar to those of tracking a wanted person. Unlike the wanted person, the missing person may be trying to establish a new life rather than hiding. Investigators should first notify other law enforcement agencies, circulate descriptions and photographs, and check hospitals and morgues.

Investigator should interview the relatives and friends of missing persons to establish motives for their disappearance. A background investigation should include the domestic situation, personal habits, work/business history, associates (social and business), medical history, education, and family history.

ADDITIONAL READING

Information

Boba, R.: Using the Internet to Disseminate Crime Information. *FBI Law Enforcement Bulletin, 68* (10), 1999.

Bowker, A.L.: Criminal History Investigations: The Key to Locking up the Repeat Offender. *FBI Law Enforcement Bulletin, 64* (10), 1995.

Bowker, A.L. and Drinkard, L.N.: Downloading: Using Computer Software as an Investigative Tool. *FBI Law Enforcement Bulletin, 65* (6), 1996.

Buhler, M.L.: The Fugitive Task Force: An Alternative Organizational Model. *FBI Law Enforcement Bulletin, 68* (4), 1999.

Diaz, T.: Computer-Enhanced Investigations. *Police Chief, 66* (9), 1999.

Dobeck, M.: Taking Advantage of the Internet. *Police Chief, 64* (1), 1997.

Grotenrath, M.J.: DOJ's Fugitive Unit: Your Partner in International Extradition. *Police Chief, 65* (3), 1998.

Harry, B.: A Diagnostic Study of the Criminal Alias. *Journal of the Forensic Sciences, 31* (1023), 1986.

McManus, E.A. and Locke, J.: Fugitive Apprehension Task Force. 64 *FBI Law Enforcement Bulletin, 6,* 1995.

Sparrow, M.K.: Information Systems: A Help or Hindrance in the Evolution of Policing? *Police Chief, 58* (6), 1995.

Privacy

Albanese, J.S.: *Justice, Privacy and Crime Control.* Lanham, MD: University Press of America, 1984.

Bulzomi, M.J.: The Workplace Privacy of Law Enforcement and Public Employees. *FBI Law Enforcement Bulletin, 67* (6), 1998.

Carroll, J.M.: *Confidential Information Sources: Public and Private* (2nd ed.). Stoneham, MA: Butterworth-Heinemann, 1991.

Dintino, J.J. and Martens, F.T.: *Police Intelligence Systems in Crime Control: Maintaining a Delicate Balance in a Liberal Democracy.* Springfield, IL: Thomas, 1983.

Eaton, J.W.: *Card Carrying Americans: Privacy, Security and the National ID Card Debate.* Totowa, NJ: Rowman, 1986.

Federal Government Information Technology: Electronic Surveillance and Civil Liberties. Washington, D.C.: U.S. Government Printing Office, 1985.

Halperin, M.H. and Hoffman, D.: *Freedom vs. National Security: Secrecy and Surveillance.* Port Townsend, WA: Loompanics, 1977.

Hendrie, E.M.: Curtilage: The Expectation of Privacy in the Yard. *FBI Law Enforcement Bulletin, 67* (4), 1998.

Marx, G.T.: *Undercover: Police Surveillance in America.* Berkeley: University of California Press, 1988.

NCIC, http://www.fbi.gov/about-us/cjis/ncic.

O'Neal, C.W.: Surreptitious Audio Surveillance: The Unknown Danger to Law Enforcement. *FBI Law Enforcement Bulletin, 67* (6), 1998.

Riggin, S.P.: U.S. Information Access Laws: Are They a Threat to Law Enforcement? *FBI Law Enforcement Bulletin, 53* (7), 1984.

Williams, D.P.: Caller ID: Maintaining Investigative Security. *FBI Law Enforcement Bulletin, 66* (10), 1997.

MO and Criminal Profiling

Adams, S.H.: Statement Analysis: What Do Suspects' Words Really Reveal? *FBI Law Enforcement Bulletin, 65* (10), 1996.

Bradway, W.C.: Crime Scene Behavioral Analysis, Law and Order, 38 (9), 1990.

Crime Scene and Profile Characteristics of Organized and Disorganized Murderers. *FBI Law Enforcement Bulletin, 54* (8), 1985.

Douglas, J.E. and Burgess, A.E.: Criminal Profiling: A Viable Investigative Tool Against Violent Crime. *FBI Law Enforcement Bulletin, 55* (12), 1986.

Douglas, J.E. and Munn, C.: Violent Crime Scene Analysis: *Modus Operandi,* Signature, and Staging. *FBI Law Enforcement Bulletin, 61* (2), 1992.

Geberth, V.J.: Criminal Personality Profiling. *Law and Order, 43* (11), 1995.

Holmes, R.M.: *Profiling Violent Crimes: An Investigative Tool.* Newbury Park, CA: Sage, 1989.

Lesce, T.: Computer-Aided Profiling: Help for Small Departments. *Law and Order, 37* (7), 1989.

MacKay, R.: Geographic Profiling: A New Tool for Law Enforcement. *Police Chief, 66* (12), 1999.

Pickett, P.O.: Linguistics in the Courtroom. *FBI Law Enforcement Bulletin, 62* (10), 1993.

Pinizotto, A.J.: Forensic Psychology: Criminal Personality Profiling. *Journal of Police Science and Administration, 12* (32), 1984.

Turvey, B.E., Tamlyn, D., and Chisum, W.J.: *Criminal Profiling: An Introduction to Behavioral Evidence Analysis.* San Diego: Academic Press, 1999.

Vollmer, A.: *Journal of the American Institute of Criminal Law and Criminology, 10* (2), Aug., 1919.

Artificial Intelligence and Expert Systems

Bayse, W.A. and Morris, C.G.: Automated Systems' Reasoning Capabilities: A Boon to Law Enforcement. *Police Chief, 57* (6), 1990.

Cameron, J.: Artificial Intelligence: Expert Systems, Microcomputers and Law Enforcement. *Law and Order, 36,* 1988.

Kingston, C.: Expert Systems in Forensic Science. *Journal of Forensic Sciences, 35* (1404), 1990.

Ratledge, E.C. and Jacoby, J.E.: *Handbook on Artificial Intelligence and Expert Systems in Law Enforcement.* Westport, CT: Greenwood Press, 1989.

Reboussin, R. and Cameron, J.: Expert Systems for Law Enforcement. *FBI Law Enforcement Bulletin, 58* (8), 1989.

Crime Mapping, Analysis, Internet, and Electronic Evidence

Angwin, J. & Thurm, S.: Judges Weigh Phone Tracking. *The Wall Street Journal, 263* (111): A1, A12. Nov. 9, 2011.

Baker, T.: *Introductory Criminal Analysis: Crime Prevention and Intervention Strategies.* Upper Saddle River, NJ: Pearson Prentice Hall, 2005.

Black Book Online: Available at http://www.blackbookonline.info/.

Bennett, W. & Hess, K.: *Criminal Investigation.* Belmont, CA: Wadsworth, 2007.

Boba, R.: *Crime Analysis with Crime Mapping* (2nd ed.). Los Angeles: Sage, 2009.

Lutz, W.E.: Computer Mapping Helps Identify Arson Targets. *Police Chief, 65* (5), 1998.

National Institute of Justice: *Electronic Crime Scene Investigation: A Guide for First Responders,* NCJ227050, U.S. Department of Justice, 2009.

NetSecurity: http://www.netsecurity.com/marketing/NetSecurity-RespondingTo TheDigitalCrimeScene-GatheringVolatileData-TechnoForensics-Keynote.pdf

Pilant, L.: Crime Mapping and Analysis. *Police Chief, 66* (12), 1999.

——: Computerized Crime Mapping. *Police Chief, 65* (12), 1997.

Balentino-DeVries, J.: 'Stingray' Phone Tracker Fuels Constitutional Clash, *The Wall Street Journal, 263* (70): A1, A 16, Sept. 22, 2011.

Balentino-DeVries, J.: Feds Shift Tracking Defense, *The Wall Street Journal, 263* (106): A3, Nov. 3, 2011.

Wenicke, S.C. and Stallo, M.A.: Steps Toward Integrating Crime Analysis into Law Enforcement. *Police Chief, 67* (7), 2000.

Wideman, D.A.: Multifunctional Aspects of Crime Analysis in the Investigation of Violent and Sexual Crimes. *Police Chief, 67* (7), 2000.

Woods, M.: Crime Analysis: A Key Tool in Any Crime Reduction Strategy. *Police Chief, 66* (4), 1999.

Cold Case Inestigation

Adcock, J.: Police need help to solve cold cases. Available 10/12/2010 at http: //www.ajc.com/opinion/police-need-help-to-620261.html, 2009.

Heurich, C.: Cold cases: resources for agencies, resolution for families. *NIJ Journal, 260:* 20-23, NCJ 222903. 2008.

Johns, L., Downes, G., & Bibles, C.: Resurrecting cold case serial homicide investigations. *FBI Law Enforcement Bulletin, 74* (8): 1-6, 2005.

Kirsch, L.: Heating up cold cases. *Forensic Examiner, 15* (2): 34-35, 2006

Lord, V.: Implementing a cold case homicide unit. *FBI Law Enforcement Bulletin, 74* (2): 1-6, 2005.

Nyberg, R.: Cold case squads re-activate old investigations. *Law & Order, 47* (10): 127-130, 1999.

Regini, C.: The cold case concept. *FBI Law Enforcement Bulletin, 66* (8): 1-6, 1997

Reyes, N.: Cold case investigation units. *Telemasp Bulletin: Texas Law Enforcement Management and Administrative Statistics Program, 16* (1): 1-10, 2009.

Smith, C.: Tulsa's gray squad: Solves cold cases. *FBI Law Enforcement Bulletin, 47* (11): 48-49, 1999.

Turner, R. & Kosa, R.: Cold case squads: Leaving no stone unturned. *Bureau of Justice Assistance Bulletin.* NCJ 199781, 2003.

Missing Persons

Bishop, D.R.: and Scheusseler, T.J.: The National Crime Information Center's Missing Person File. *FBI Law Enforcement Bulletin, 51* (8), 1982.

Crnkovic, G.: I SEARCH for Missing Children. *Law and Order, 35* (7), 1987.

Erickson, R.G. II: *How to Find Missing Persons: A Handbook for Investigators* (rev. ed.). Port Townsend, WA: Loompanics, 1984.

Fallis, G. and Greenberg, R.: *Be Your Own Detective.* New York: M. Evans and Co., 1989.

Ferguson, A. and Mascaro, D.G,.: I-SEARCH for Missing and Exploited Children. *FBI Law Enforcement Bulletin, 55* (4), 1986.

Ferraro, E.: *You Can Find Anyone: A Complete Guide on How to Locate Missing Persons* (rev. ed.). Santa Ana, CA: Marathon Press, 1989.

Forst, M.I.: Law Enforcement Policies on Missing Children. *Law and Order, 38* (6), 1990.

——: Missing Children: *The Law Enforcement Response.* Springfield, IL: Thomas, 1990.

Gallagher, R.S.: *"If I Only Had It To Do Over Again. . . ."* New York: Dutton, 1969.

Goldfader, E.: *Tracer: The Search for Missing Persons.* Los Angeles: Nash, 1970.

Hirschel, J.D. and Lab, S.P.: Who Is Missing? The Realities of the Missing Persons Problem. *Journal of Criminal Justice, 16* (35), 1988.

Hotaling, G. T. and Finkelhor, D.: Estimating the Number of Stranger-Abduction Homicides of Children: A Review of Available Evidence. *Journal of Criminal Justice, 18* (385), 1990.

Hyde, M. and Hyde, L.: *Missing Children.* Danbury, CT: Watts, 1985.

Identifying the Unidentified. *FBI Law Enforcement Bulletin, 59* (8), 1990.

Investigator's Guide to Missing Child Cases: For Law Enforcement Officers Locating Missing Children. Washington, D.C.: National Center for Missing and Exploited Children, 1985.

Johnson, R.S., Lt.Col.: *How to Locate Anyone Who Is or Has Been in the Military.* Port Townsend, WA: Loompanics, 1990.

Krauss, T. C.: Forensic Odontology in Missing Persons Cases. *Journal of Forensic Sciences, 21* (959), 1976.

Morrison, R.D.: Finding Missing Children. *Law and Order, 44* (9), 1996.

Naumann, R.: *How to Locate (Almost) Anyone.* Hayward, CA: PI Publications, 1985.

NCIC Missing Persons and Unidentified Person Statistics for 2010. Available at http://www.fbi.gov/about-us/cjis/ncic/ncic-missing-person-and-unidentified-person-statistics-for-2010

Parker, S.: Missing People: How to Find Them. *Law and Order, 36* (5), 1988.

Thomas, R.D.: *How to Find Anyone Anywhere* (2nd rev. ed.). Austin, Texas: Thomas Publications, 1986.

Zoglio, M.: *Tracing Missing Persons: A Professional's Guide to Techniques and Resources.* Doylestown, PA: Tower Hill Press, 1982.

Chapter 10

INFORMANTS, SURVEILLANCE AND UNDERCOVER ASSIGNMENTS

INFORMANTS

1. Overview

THE ABILITY TO DEVELOP sources of information is a key factor to the effectiveness of investigators. Informants play a role in both the practice and perception of investigation. Informants can often access information and interact with individuals unavailable to investigators. Many important cases are solved by information from informants. Some informants provide information in one specific case, while other informants become an ongoing source of information.

Investigators need to continually seek new sources of information while maintaining active sources. The social status of informants will vary with the nature of the offense or inquiry. Investigators should be able to interact with all levels of society, but many street crime investigations require infiltrating social groups that are difficult for outsiders to breach. When investigating street predators, investigators must be able to navigate their social environment to cultivate information from service workers and others. The media often portrays informants as colorful individuals living on the edge of society, but anyone can be an informant. Many times information is offered by someone wanting to be a good citizen. Sometimes informants are paid by favors or cash. In all case, investigators need to be guided by professional ethics.

Informants may give information to investigators openly and even offer to testify in court, or they may inform surreptitiously and request to remain anonymous. *Confidential* informants provide investigators with secret information concerning past or future crimes and do not wish to be identified as the source of the information (generally there is an expectation of a continuing relationship). Investigators must take special precautions to protect the identity of such informants since their value as a source of information is lost if they are identified.

2. Motives

Investigators need to understand the motives of their informants. Informants reveal their information for numerous reasons. Misunderstanding the motivation of informants may invite serious problems. Investigators must always maintain a professional relationship. Aside from occasional incidences where a social acquaintance provides useful information, informants are not your friends and cannot become your friends. Investigators can be personable and friendly but not overly trusting. As with interrogations, investigators must play many roles to cultivate information. Informants are sources and tools of investigation that must be managed. Relying on the friendship of informants has been the ruin of many investigators.

The motivations of informants are limitless, but most fall into some common categories. Like investigators, informants are trying to achieve something, but they do not share the same goals as investigators. If investigators do not understand the motivation of informants, they may be manipulated into embarrassing or dangerous situations.

Some informants are motivated by *vanity or ego*. They tend to be self-aggrandizing people who delight in giving information to gain favorable attention from police authorities. They seek attention but their desire for control makes them difficult to handle. Investigators should appeal to their ego.

Civic-minded informants are public-spirited individuals of good standing in the community who are interested in justice. These individuals act from a sense of duty. They want to help, but may not have useful information. Investigators must be careful not to dismiss these individuals too quickly, for they may possess important information. If they feel unappreciated, they may not offer information in the future.

Fear can also be a motivator. Some people want protection from real or perceived enemies. They may seek the arrest of their adversaries, police protection, relocation, or isolation (if incarcerated). Investigators actions will depend on the value of the information.

Repentant informants are usually accomplices, who had a change of heart and wish to relieve their conscience. They accept their need for punishment but want to be understood. Investigators should project their desire to help these people straighten out their lives and regain self-respect.

Some informants provide information to *avoid punishment.* These people have been apprehended for a minor offense and hope to avoid prosecution by revealing information about a major crime. Investigators help negotiate a settlement.

Informants may come forward out of *gratitude or appreciation.* These people feel they were previously helped or treated fairly by investigators. They may feel investigators looked after their welfare or that of their family. Like the repentant informant, these individuals want to repay a debt.

Informants may be providing information to *eliminate the competition.* Their purpose is to further their own criminal activity. They can often provide valuable information but investigators must recognize the circumstances.

Revenge and jealousy motivate some informants. They seek to settle a grudge or humiliate another. These informants may be obsessed with punishing their target. Their obsession may lead them to fabricate information if they feel it necessary to get investigators to take action. These individuals can suddenly become uncooperative if the relationship changes.

Remuneration is the motivation of paid informants. They are mercenaries acting solely for material gain. They betray others for money, and will betray investigators for the right price. They may shop their services to other police agencies to determine where they can get the most money. Some of these individuals become skilled in manipulating investigators. By connecting stray conversation of officers, notes lying on a desk, and investigators' questions, these informants may sometimes be able to deduce what will pique investigators' interests and provide ready cash. On occasion, some naïve investigators have wasted resources buying useless information from these manipulators.

Other informants are *wannabes.* They would like to be detectives or lead a more exciting life. They seek excitement and want to be "part of the action." They often want to develop a relationship with investigators. Many of these people are prone to exaggeration and seldom possess good information. Others may be respectable professionals in other fields, with an interest in criminal investigation, who can contribute useful information.

Some informants are *mentally ill.* They may come forward with information about a crime or confess to a crime themselves. Depending on their affliction, their stories may sound credible or bizarre. Their information may be worthless but require many investigative hours to evaluate. They cannot simply be dismissed, however, because occasionally their information is accurate.

3. Obtaining Confidential Informants

Investigators whose geographic assignment remains consistent will have opportunities to acquire informants both through skill and chance. Effective investigators are continually looking for new sources of information. Some come forward of their own volition, others need to be cultivated. Investigators can skillfully use their motivation to gain cooperation. Through persuasion or negotiation investigators provide opportunities for informers to fulfill their motivations.

Investigators who work to develop information will find many potential sources. Service workers (e.g., utility workers, delivery persons, postal clerks and carriers), sales associates at places such as grocery and convenience stores, pharmacies, coffee shops, taverns, and newsstands, or even disgruntled employees, unfriendly neighbors, business competitors, and many others may respond if approached correctly.

4. Protecting the Informant

In general, investigators should compromise neither themselves nor informants in the pursuit of information. They should make no unethical promises, "deals," or commitments they cannot fulfill. When appropriate, try to accept the information on the terms of the informant.

There is a mythology surrounding the protection of informants that reflects practice and a romanticized view of investigation. Investigators must behave ethically but should not be guided by folklore. For example, the adage that "if you 'burn a snitch,' you will have no informants" is only partially true. It may be true that if you develop a reputation for treating your informants poorly then rational informers may no longer come forward or may take their information elsewhere. Many informers, however, do not act rationally or have few options. They will not necessarily know the investigators' past practices or view themselves susceptible to the same treatment. Informers seeking a reduction in criminal charges or sentencing often have few options. Investigators need to deal with informants in an ethical and business-like manner.

The identity of informants should not be disclosed unless necessary and then only to the proper authorities. To preserve secrecy, each confidential informant may be assigned a number, symbol, or fictitious name, and should be referred to by such designation in reports. Care must be exercised when meeting or communicating with informants.

Confidential informants are not generally called to testify in court. Such action reveals the informers' relationship with law enforcement, terminates their ability to acquire information, and in a few cases may expose them to danger. Nevertheless, in extraordinary circumstances it may be practical and desirable to summon a confidential informant as a witness in court.

5. Treatment of Informants

In all circumstances, informers should be treated fairly. While investigators use the motivation of informers to manipulate them, this must be done in a professional and ethical manner. Informers are valuable only if they are able to obtain information and are willing to divulge it. Investigators need to be able to motivate informers within justifiable parameters.

Investigators are obligated to maintain *reliability.* They need to fulfill all ethical promises they make and avoid promising what they cannot deliver, or risk losing trust and their informants. Investigators are also obligated to validate the continued reliability of confidential information. Measures used to protect the identities of confidential informants should not be used to shield unreliability. For example, a confidential informant who has provided some reliable information along with much unreliable information should not be presented or reported as a person who provides reliable information with no mention of frequently being unreliable. Such actions misrepresent the value of the informant and the privilege of confidentiality.

Investigators must also always remain in *control.* Informants should not be permitted to take charge of any phase of the investigation. Even if informers have a long-term relationship with investigators, they must be controlled. Investigators remain responsible for the actions and consequences of the investigation.

6. Communicating with the Informant

To protect the identity of informants, caution must be used when communicating with them. Meetings should not be held at the investigator's office. Contacts times and locations should not be repeated so as to create a recognizable pattern. Informants' names should not be used when telephoning. Codes or aliases are advisable for obvious reasons. The investigator's agency should not be identified in any correspondence with the informant.

Investigators must also be wary of false accusations by informants. A disgruntled informant may attempt to blackmail an investigator. Measures taken to ensure private meetings can also make it difficult for investigators to defend themselves against accusations of misconduct.

7 Evaluating Informants

Informants should be continually evaluated to determine their reliability. Information received should be tested for consistency by checking against information obtained from other persons. The motives and interests of the informer should be part of the evaluation. The reports or leads from informers (either known or unknown) should be considered potentially valuable and should be developed by the investigation until their true value is determined. Many tips will prove to be untrue but investigators cannot become discouraged and should remain receptive to future information. Finally, informers who call in anonymous telephone tips ordinarily do not call again. Investigators should endeavor to draw out all relevant information before the anonymous caller ends the conversation.

8. Informant's Status

The informant belongs to the organization and not to individual investigators. This can be a sensitive issue for investigators who have worked hard to develop their sources of information. In addition, informants may insist on only talking to specific investigators. Regardless of preferences or egos, investigators develop informants through their association with their law enforcement agency, and the organization must maintain control.

The identity of the informant should be maintained in a central file. Unit supervisors should personally maintain the file, and they should be kept confidential. Each informant should be assigned a designation that identifies the investigative unit and the informant. The assigned codes or aliases should be used in reports, not names.

9. Dismissal of Informants

If an informant becomes undesirable, investigators should advise their supervisor and arrange for a debriefing of the informant. During the debriefing, investigators should avoid antagonizing the informant or creating animosity. The reasons for dismissal should be recorded to guide any future decision to use the informant. Among the more common reasons for dismissal are ineptitude, compromise of identity, security risk, criminal record or act, and submitting false information. Informants should be dismissed without prejudice if they request to be released from the program or their service is no longer required.

SURVEILLANCE

10. Overview

If a case is not solved after obtaining and developing all the information available from complainants, victims, and witnesses, it may then be time to locate known criminals, study their habits, or identify new sources of information. This begins the tedious task of observing the activities of subjects in the case. It may require following persons or maintaining a fixed surveillance of a place. This task may appear simple, but requires systematic procedures and methodical precautions. There are techniques of observation that have been developed through experiment and practice to avoid pitfalls and errors that lead to failure. A failed surveillance not only wastes resources, but may alert the subjects to take increased precautions.

Surveillance should be a last resort, not a first step. While a novice may view surveillance as an exciting aspect of investigation, a proper surveillance is tedious and labor intensive. It should not be commenced unless more efficient methods have been exhausted.

11. Definitions

Surveillance is covert observation to obtain information on the identities or activities of subjects. The surveillant is a person who maintains the surveillance or performs the observation. The subject is a person or place being watched. Surveillance may involve observing places, people (tailing or shadowing), and undercover investigation (roping). The objectives and methods will vary for each type of observation.

a. **Surveillance of Places**. Surveillance of a place is common in investigations of gambling, prostitution, fencing stolen property, and the sale of contraband. In general, the objective is to detect criminal activities, identify persons who frequent an establishment and determine their relationships, discern the habits of persons who live in or frequent a place, obtain evidence of a crime or prevent the commission of a crime, or procure information for obtaining a search warrant.

A *preliminary survey,* or assessment of the surrounding area, should precede any surveillance of a place. The character of the neighborhood and people (both residents and transients) should be noted. After careful study an observation point should be selected. This may be a room in a nearby house or business (where the surveillant can observe without being detected) or an outdoor post where the surveillant poses as someone who would not raise suspicion (such as a laborer, utility worker, street vendor, or an employee of the building under observation).

Prior to starting surveillance, it should be determined what equipment will be needed. The list of equipment will vary with the situation. Video and high quality still cameras with telephoto lenses are desirable. A small telescope, binoculars, and night vision equipment are especially useful. If authorized, wiretaps and recording apparatus can be employed.

A complete log of the activities and observations will form the basis of the report. The time of arrival and departure of each person should be carefully noted. Photographs and video should be numbered with reference to time and date. In addition to, or in lieu of, photographs, descriptive notes of people and activities should be made.

The process of setting up the observation post, moving in equipment, relieving surveillants, and terminating surveillance should be as unobtrusive as possible. Surveillants should enter and leave separately. Sometimes it is necessary to interact with people at or around the observation point. Keep the number of confidants to a minimum and do not reveal your purpose.

12. Surveillance of People

The first rule in the surveillance of people, or shadowing, is to avoid drawing attention. Surveillants need to fit into the environment and appear appropriate to the scene. The surveillant should be of average size, and build, without noticeable peculiarities in appearance or mannerism. Avoid wearing conspicuous jewelry or clothing.

Good surveillants are resourceful, versatile, and quick witted, and can readily conceive of reasons or excuses for being in any given place. They appear to be attending their own business without interest in what others are doing. They have perseverance and can wait for hours at a time without showing any signs of impatience or irritation that would attract attention. They should be fluent speakers, who can talk their way out of embarrassing situations without arousing suspicion. Surveillants should prepare one or two good covers (such as canvassing for the city directory or selling common items) and possess necessary support items (such as forms, identification, or equipment) to appear authentic.

a. **Shadowing**. Shadowing or tailing is simply the act of following a person. The purpose of shadowing will depend upon the nature of the investigation. It may be to detect criminal activities, identify the associates of a suspect, find a wanted person, or protect a witness.

The objective of the surveillance will determine the technique to use. The surveillance may be very loose (*loose tail*) if a general impression of the subject's habits and associates is required. Surveillance may be obvious (*rough shadowing*) if suspects are aware they are being followed or when subjects are witnesses who must be protected.

Subjects may also be followed covertly with extreme precautions to prevent losing the subject or being detected (*close tail*). A close tail may be used when subjects are believed to be engaged in impending criminal activities or will lead investigators to evidence or the hideout of criminals.

b. **Preparation**. Preparation is essential before beginning the surveillance of people. Obtain a complete description of the subjects and, if possible, arrange to have someone familiar with them point them out to the surveillants. Descriptions should include details of the back of the subject, since that is the vantage point of the surveillant. How does the subject generally dress (hat, coat, suit, and shoes)? Describe the subject's general carriage (head and shoulders) and movements (walks fast or slow, short or long steps, walks purposefully or tends to be hesitant and erratic). Investigators should learn as much as possible about the subject's habits, preferences, hangouts, and social life.

From the information acquired, investigators should dress and act to fit into the environment where they expect to find the subject. Create a plausible story, supported with documents and knowledge, for being in the area. Act the part of one who belongs to the neighborhood, casual and interested in matters other than the subject. Nervousness and haste will undermine your cover. Study the neighborhood carefully to identify transportation lines and the likely pedestrian routes between appropriate points so if you lose a subject, you are better prepared to locate them again.

c. **Shadowing by Foot**. The technique of a walking surveillance will vary with the number of surveillants available. Surveillance by one person is risky and as many as six surveillants may be necessary to tail effectively. The purpose of using multiple persons is to minimize the risk of detection by being viewed too often or by being forced to make abrupt changes of direction.

A three-person tail is described here as typical of shadowing technique. The three surveillants will be referred to as *A*, *B*, and *C* (see the ABC Method in Figure 10-1). *A* is closest to the subject *S*, and follows *S* at a distance determined by the conditions of pedestrian traffic. *B* follows *A*, at about the same distance from *A* as *A* is from *S*. *C* may precede *S* or, if vehicular traffic is moderate, may be approximately opposite *S* on the other side of the street. *B* and *C* take turns in occupying position *A* to reduce the chance that S will notice a tail.

If the subject becomes suspicious, any of the surveillants can quickly drop out of the tail. If *S* suddenly turns a corner, *A* may continue straight ahead, instead of hurrying to the corner and anxiously looking for the subject, *C* may then cross the street and follow *B*, taking up the *B* position. *C*, moreover, is in a position to view any sudden disappearance into a building. Prearranged signals should be employed. For example, if *A* feels that he or she has been "made," an adjustment of a hat can signal another surveillant to take over the *A* position.

1) *Tactics*. Surveillants should be inconspicuous to prevent subjects from realizing they are being followed. Avoid looking directly at subjects. Shift from left to right, never remaining for long directly behind a subject. Both sides of the street should be used. If it appears a subject has become alerted to the tail, surveillants should request immediate removal from the assignment.

A number of situations may arise to test the resourcefulness of investigators. If the subject turns a corner, the surveillant should

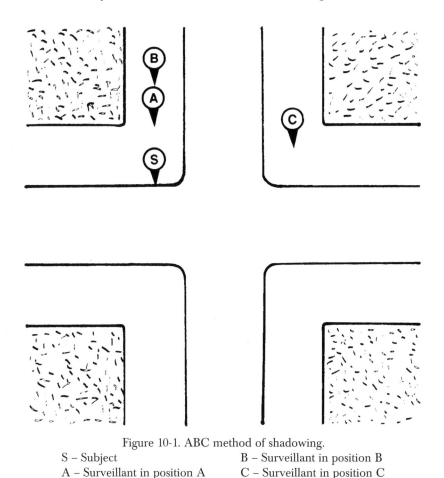

Figure 10-1. ABC method of shadowing.

S – Subject   B – Surveillant in position B
A – Surveillant in position A   C – Surveillant in position C

not hurry. If the subject is lost, the nature of the neighborhood will determine the subsequent procedure. In most cases it is preferable to lose subjects than to alert them of the tail.

Subjects entering a building create another challenge. If the subject enters a small store or office building, surveillants should wait until the subject comes out. If the subject enters a large store or an establishment with a number of exits, it will be necessary to follow. If the subject enters the elevator of a building, the surveillant should board the same elevator and request the same floor if asked. If two surveillants are present, one should exit at the subject's floor but

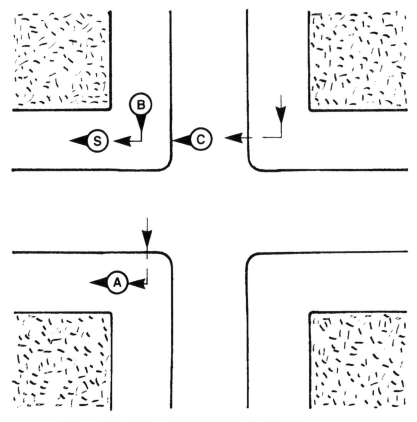

Figure 10-2. ABC method of shadowing: Turning a corner.
S – Subject   B – Surveillant in position A
A – Surveillant in position C   C – Surveillant in position B

proceed in a different direction. The other should return to the first floor and wait for the subject.

A third challenge is presented if the subject boards public transportation. If the subject boards a bus, a surveillant should board the same bus and sit behind the subject and on the same side. If surveillants cannot board, attempt to arrange transportation to board the bus at a point ahead. When the subject takes a cab, the surveillant should record the time, place, name of the taxi company, and license. Follow in another vehicle or taxi, if possible, or contact the taxi company and determine the destination. If the subject buys a train ticket, attempt to board the same train or determine the destination of the train.

Finally, there are other challenges involving public places. If the subject enters a restaurant, wait a few minutes before entering, take an obscure seat and try to pace your meal with the subject. At a hotel, the subject's room number can be learned from the registration desk and, if necessary, rent an adjacent room. In a theater, sit behind the subject and note the exits.

2) ***Recognition of Surveillant.*** There are two constant risks in a mobile surveillance–being "made," (recognized as following by the subject) and losing the subject. This can happen to even the most experienced surveillant, so plan to take intelligent counter-measures.

It is common for inexperienced surveillants to be oversensitive to being made by the suspect. This perception arises from the self-consciousness of the inexperienced surveillant and is not necessarily true. When suspects do make the surveillant, their actions often leave little doubt. If surveillants are certain they have been made, the surveillance should be dropped and caution exercised in subsequent actions. Although suspects may discover they are being followed, they do not necessarily know the identity of surveillants. Subjects may decide to follow the surveillant to determine their identity. Returning to home or to the office will provide the subject with valuable information. Surveillants must be certain they are not being followed, either by the suspect or by someone else, before going any place that might reveal their identity.

3) ***Testing a Tail.*** Cautious subjects may "test for a tail" to determine if they are being followed. A common ploy is to board public transportation, wait until just before the door closes, and then jump off the vehicle. The subject then looks about quickly to determine if any other person jumped off. In such situations, the surveillant's best tactic is to remain on the vehicle until the next stop. To avoid being caught in this manner, the experienced surveillant will arrange to be the last passenger to board the vehicle, and will remain just inside the door until it is closed. If the suspect starts toward the door, the surveillant can immediately step off and appear to be waiting for another car or train.

Another ploy is the "convoy." Subjects may guard against being followed by having an associate follow a reasonable distance to observe a tail. Surveillants must guard against this. If it is determined that the subject does have a follower or convoy, the surveillant must get behind the convoy and follow him or her instead of the subject.

d. **Shadowing by Automobile**. Many of the procedures for shadowing by foot are applicable to surveillance by automobile. The number of persons and cars assigned to the task will depend on the importance and difficulty of the assignment. Using multiple cars and steadily interchanging positions greatly reduces the risk of detection. The following distance must be adjusted to accommodate traffic conditions. Surveillants should coordinate their action using coded messages or secure communications.

Tailing at night poses additional challenges. While it is more difficult for the subject to identify a trailing vehicle, it is also more difficult for the surveillant to identify the subject's vehicle in traffic. Some investigators have marked the subject's vehicle with a spot of reflective tape to help identify it in traffic. Radio transmitters (homing devices) and GPS locators are very effective but require a court order to attach to the suspect's vehicle. In *United States v. Antoine Jones*, the Supreme Court ruled police must obtain a search warrant before placing a GPS locator on a suspect's vehicle.

1) *Disguising the Car*. Surveillance vehicles should not draw attention. A car of popular type and color should be used. If possible, vehicles should be changed each day. Registration plates should not be traceable to the investigative agency. The fleet of surveillance vehicles can be supplemented with rental or leased vehicles to add variety.

It is possible to alter the appearance of a car by various devices such as the use of removable stickers or other windshield adornments, changing license plates, shifting the headlights from dim to bright, using a multiple contact switch to eliminate one of the headlights, rearranging the seating of the occupants, changing the occupant's clothes (jackets or hats), or changing the number of the occupants.

2) *Techniques*. Surveillants should frequently vary their manner of driving. On multi-lane streets, surveillants should alternate between lanes. A suspicious subject may suddenly stop to observe whether the surveillance car passes by. The surveillance car should

proceed at the same speed until able to halt unobtrusively and permit the subject to pass. Where two tail cars are employed, the second car continues the tail. If the subject parks and enters a building, surveillants should park as far away as practical and still be able to observe. A car parked in the same block in which the subject resides will usually cause suspicion. The surveillant car should be parked in the next block, if possible. The building exits and the subject's car can be observed using binoculars. Surveillants should avoid sitting in the same position for long period of time. Change positions by moving to the passenger seat or back seat. When possible if you must wait a considerable time, leave the car and continue the surveillance from a nearby store or coffee shop to lessen suspicion.

Some errors are commonly made by inexperienced surveillants. These include staying parked in the same spot too long, using a conspicuous car, having both surveillants in the front seat for an extended period of time, furtively approaching the parking space, parking in a prohibited zone, operating a police radio with excessive volume, and conspicuously changing personnel with the relieving team.

13. Documenting Surveillance

Observations by investigators during surveillance may later become evidence in a trial or the basis of an interrogation. The activities of both surveillants and subjects should be recorded in a log. The log will also help investigators prepare to testify in court. During an interrogation the record of the subject's activities, along with some intelligent guesses, can often lead subjects to perceive investigators have more knowledge than they actually possess. This may more easily persuade the subject to confess. In addition, good documentation can help evaluate the results of the surveillance and the operating theory of the investigation.

14. Other Surveillance Methods

So far the discussion has focused on visually observing the subject of surveillance. Advances in technology, as in other areas of investigation, provide new investigative techniques. At one time, investigators might make a small puncture to the bottom of a can of paint and tie it to the undercarriage of a vehicle. They could then follow the droplets of paint to the destination. This crude method was replaced by battery powered radio transmitters (homing devices) and today by global positioning devices. Gamma-ray technology is used to view the contents of packages and cargo at transportation ports. Wall penetrating radar can see through concrete walls to provide images of people and objects. Aerial surveillance platforms (piloted and remote control aircraft, satellites, etc.) equipped with cameras, thermal imaging, and night vision optics can locate and follow subjects from great distances. Drone technology, refined in combat by the military, now provides new surveillance opportunities to police. In many cities, large areas of public space are covered by surveillance cameras. Surveillance images can be analyzed by facial recognition software to identify missing and wanted persons.

a. **Wiretaps and Bugs**. While advances in technology and digital communications have often made it easier to intercept and monitor conversations, state and federal courts regulate this activity more closely than in previous eras. Intercepting transmitted communications or conversations where there is a reasonable expectation of privacy require court approval. Officers should consult with prosecutors before initiating an electronic surveillance. A *wiretap* is the interception of a telephone signal. In the past, wiretapping required the connection of a physical device to capture the signal. Today, digital telephone signals can be captured using a computer. A bug detects voices in a defined space. Protection from wiretapping is based on the Wire and Electronic Communications Interception and Interception of Oral Communications Act (formally known as the "Title III" Wiretap Act, 18 U.S.C §§ 2510-2520), while protection from bugging relies on the Fourth and Fifth Amendments. Closed circuit television and high-definition video cameras, improved audio transmission and recording, along with computer software (such as key stroke recorders) have greatly expanded the tools available to investigators.

15. Surveillance and Society

The technology that vastly increases the potential scope and effectiveness of surveillance also poses a threat to individual privacy. Each individual acquires innumerable records such as birth certificates, church records, school records, records of offenses, credit records, employment records, military service records, and so forth. Computerization exacerbates privacy concerns.

Business has now supplanted government as the chief data collector in the United States. The corporate computer has become a repository of both the mundane and the intimate details of our lives. The nature and the extent of this personal information raise concern. Telephone companies have a record of every call we make. Internet services provide record our digital activities. Banks have a copy of every check we write and a record of every credit card purchase. Insurance companies know our complete medical history while the pharmacies have a computerized list of all the medicines we take. Airline and car rental companies know where we have been and where we plan to go. Video stores have a list of every movie we have rented and the cable television company has a record of every pay-per-view show that we have ordered from the "privacy" of our own homes. Many of these applications are well intended, but most of them can be adapted to questionable purposes or abuse.

Investigators have a key role to play as representatives of the community and must assume major responsibility for properly conducting surveillances and lawfully using the resources of surveillance. The ultimate determinant must be the ethical judgment of the individual investigator, guided by the spirit of the law as interpreted through court decisions and agency policy. In this spirit, we can understand Justice Oliver Wendell Holmes's observation that the law of the land may be the United States Constitution but to most of us it's whatever the policeman on the beat says it is.

UNDERCOVER ASSIGNMENTS

16. Overview

Undercover work is encumbered in occupational and media mythology. Undercover investigators are often portrayed as living exciting lives that entail infiltrating criminal enterprises while battling inept police administrators. In reality, successful undercover operations are closely monitored and regulated team efforts. Once called "roping," the investigator assumes a different and unofficial identity in order to obtain information. In many ways it is a type of surveillance, and like surveillance can be inefficient. It may be appropriate if traditional investigative methods have failed to solve a case. Investigators adopt identities compatible with the environment, and position themselves to observe and gain the confidence of their target. When successful, investigators induce subjects to reveal useful information.

Undercover work is most useful when investigating crimes that require organization. "Selling crimes" involving drugs, alcohol, pornography, stolen goods, contraband, or black market operations, along with fraud, extortion, and blackmail constitute a large part of undercover work. It is often a critical tool in the investigation of terrorism, subversive activities, and systematic thefts. Undercover work is most successful when there is information that specific persons are engaged in criminal activity but insufficient evidence to prove a case in court.

Investigators are sometimes placed in a cell with an incarcerated criminal to gather information about particular crimes or the activities of organized criminal enterprises. The undercover agent who has infiltrated a criminal gang is in a position to learn the operations, identify members, and gather evidence of past and future activities. This information coupled with information acquired through electronic surveillance of gang members can lead to successful cases against the gang or any individual member.

17. Objectives

The objective of most undercover investigations is to obtain evidence for criminal prosecution. The operative may uncover evidence by observing criminal activities or listening to conversations among criminals. He or she may learn from the criminals themselves the intimate details of the crime.

There are, however, other reasons to conduct an undercover investigation, such as evaluating information, determining the extent of criminal activity, or building a foundation for a future investigation. Investigators may check the validity of information received from informants through undercover operations. Undercover operatives, through their association with suspects, can monitor their activity, develop information for search warrants, or possibly install or maintain surveillance equipment.

18. Selection of the Undercover Investigators

Undercover assignments require special skills and personality traits. Ideally, undercover agents are both good actors and investigators. Many investigators do not have the temperament for undercover work and do not find it fulfilling.

Investigators must have the proper background for the assignment. They should not stand out by physical or racial characteristics. Their speech and demeanor must be compatible to the environment. Educational and technical background must be appropriate for the cover, as well as hobbies, sports interests, and topics of general conversations.

Undercover operatives need to be calm, affable, yet persistent. They should be self-confident and resourceful enough to adjust to a change. Undercover agents should be intelligent and possess a clear view of the objective of the mission and the overall strategy to accomplish it. A retentive memory, keen imagination, good powers of observation, and sound judgment are necessary to make decisions that will not jeopardize the investigation.

19. Types of Assignments

Undercover work varies widely, and an assignment may place an investigator in several different social settings, while testing resourcefulness, adaptability, and endurance. More complex assignments require more complete and flawless cover stories.

For a *neighborhood assignment,* the investigator moves into the neighborhood, or possibly the same building, as the subjects. The assimilation into the neighborhood must be gradual and natural. A long period of time is required before the agent is accepted.

In a *social assignment,* the investigator frequents clubs, taverns, or other social meeting places visited by the subject or known to be centers of illegal activity. Once again, agents must "fit in" and gradually allay any suspicions.

In the investigation of systematic thefts in a place of business it may be necessary for investigators to assume the role of employees. This can be a simple role to establish because operatives do not have to explain or justify their presence. If the job is complex, such as a skilled trade or profession, some experience or training may be needed prior to the assignment. The *work assignment* may also replace a neighborhood assignment.

20. Preparing for an Undercover Assignment

The cover story and role investigators assume depends on the nature of the investigation. Investigators should not begin an undercover assignment without the authorization of their supervisor.

The first step in preparing for an undercover assignment is to study your subject. Preparing a list of essential information will help organize your efforts (see Table 10-1).

In addition to understanding their subjects, investigators should thoroughly study the environment of their assignment. If investigators are to pretend previous residence in the area, they should possess an intimate knowledge of neighborhood details. Study *maps* for general layout and features of the immediate and bordering areas. Determine the *national and religious background, and racial composition* of inhabitants of the area. Routes and schedules of public *transportation* should be known. Investigators should have a general familiarity with the public services schedule such as mail delivery, trash pickup, utility meter reading, and other *public services.* It is important to know the location of popular neighborhood *restaurants, bars,* and *stores* in the area.

a. **Cover Story**. The fictitious background and history for an investigator should include names, addresses, and descriptions of places of education, employment, associates, neighborhoods, and travels. The cover story should seldom, if ever, be wholly fictitious. It is best if investigators use cities in which they actually lived and with which they are acquainted. Try to avoid the home town of one of the subjects. When possible, arrange to have principals in the fictitious history ready to corroborate details should the subject check the story. It is good practice to select corroborating principals who are engaged in occupations which will not cause suspicion or arouse too much interest on the part of the subjects. A suc-

Table 10-1. Subject Background Information.

Name	Full name, aliases, nicknames, titles
Addresses	Past and present, residential and business
Description	A portrait parlé as given in Chapter 7
Family & Relatives	Knowing family relationships may suggest other sources of information
Associates	Essential to an understanding of the subject's activities.
Character & Temperament	Strengths and weaknesses, likes, dislikes, prejudices, etc.
Vices	Drug addiction, alcohol, gambling, etc.
Hobbies	May suggest a way to meet subjects or create a bond
Education	Suggests the limitations of the subject and will indicate the needed level of education for the investigator
Occupation & Specialty	May suggest a way to meet a subject, and his/her character

cessful undercover investigator must possess all of the requirements of the assignment, such as appropriate personality, ability, background story, and attention to details.

The cover story should provide a rationale for frequent contact with the subject and some mutual interests. The background should enable the investigator to maintain a similar financial and social status as the subject. Freedom of movement, justification for actions, and a means of communicating with police supervisors should be built into the cover. It is advisable to have an alternate cover story in the event that the original cover story is compromised. Once the operation is completed, investigators need to leave the area quietly without drawing suspicion. Undercover investigators should not vanish. A plausible reason for departure should be invented. Discharge from employment, family illness, and fear of local police are among the many reasons that can be offered. Investigators should leave open the avenue of return so the investigation can resume if necessary.

b. **Personal Possessions**. Personal possessions carried by undercover investigators should be appropriate (quality, price, age, fit, cleanliness, and manufacturer's design) to support the cover story. Personal possessions may include clothes, a wallet, a ring, a token, a suitcase, movie or transportation ticket stubs, cigarettes, matches, photographs, letters, certificates, or amounts of money. Undercover investigators must not possess any articles which will suggest their true identity. Badges or credentials should not be carried, and a firearm or other weapon may be carried only where compatible with the background story.

c. **Testing**. Investigators should memorize all details of their cover stories and the fictitious biographies. Preparation should include prolonged questioning and surprise inquiries.

d. **Disclosure of Identity**. In preparing for the assignment, it should be decided whether investigators should disclose their identity or remain undercover if arrested by other authorities. A plan should also be formulated for the accidental disclosure of identity.

21. Conduct of the Assignment

The demeanor of the undercover agent must be consistent with the part being played. Appearance, language, attitude, opinions, interests, and recreations must support the assumed role. Speak little, but act with conviction. When required, speak and act with confidence regarding past actions and trade. Do not ask questions except as part of the assumed identity. Inquiries, as well as bragging or showing too much knowledge, invite unwanted attention.

The initial approach is often the first obstacle of the undercover investigation. Making contact with subjects must appear natural. It is best if the investigators can create situations where subjects become interested in approaching them. Subjects may become interested in the new person living in the building, or in someone they frequently encounter in the neighborhood, club, business, hobby, recreational activity, etc.

a. **Entrapment**. Investigators cannot incite or participate in the commission of a crime. Undercover officers must, therefore, ensure they do not become accessories to crimes. They may pretend to help in planning a crime but should never make any suggestions or promises, or render any real assistance with regard to the perpetration of crime. Investigators cannot plant the criminal idea into the mind of the subject. At the trial, defendants may plead entrapment and blame investigators for their actions.

Illegal drug undercover work is particularly susceptible to charges of entrapment. The accused may assert that police provided the money, motivation, and connections to make the deal or that police forced them to supply drugs. Undercover investigators can protect themselves from these charges by making several buys from the same dealer and by obtaining testimony of the dealer's character and reputation. As a general rule undercover investigators can avoid charges of entrapment by taking a restrained and passive role and not engaging in "creative activity" to further the offense.

22. Taking Notes

Undercover operatives are confronted with a dilemma in recording their findings. To be used in court, notes should be contemporaneous to the events they record, but writing or maintaining notes can jeopardize the investigator's cover. Writing notes is often limited to events of unusual importance and to information that cannot otherwise be remembered. Notes often need to be cryptic and unintelligible to anyone else. Numbers may be written as parts of a mathematical problem or as a telephone number. They may be written on inconspicuous materials such as chewing gum or cigarette wrappers, toilet paper, paper napkins, match books, magazines, or on wallpaper. Digital photographs should be immediately sent or transferred and removed from the investigator's camera or cell phone.

23. Communication with Headquarters

Undercover operatives need to communicate with their supervisors without drawing attention or jeopardizing their cover. When contacting headquarters by telephone, it is best to call from a public telephone or to a number not identified with the police department. The call history on your phone should not include numbers traceable to the police. In an emergency, calling a number not identified with the police and using prearranged code words can deliver a message or initiate action.

Written reports may be addressed to a fictitious individual (at a post office box, address, or email address) that is not traceable to the police agency. It is best not to include a return address on an envelope to prevent it being returned and falling into improper hands. Beware of becoming conspicuous by mailing numerous letters. If reports are emailed, be sure to take steps to purge them from the memory of the sending device. Coded messages can be posted on social networking sites. Prior to starting the assignment, confer with a forensic computer specialist about taking steps to reduce the likelihood your reports and messages will fall into the wrong hands.

Clandestine meetings with supervisors or other police officers can be prearranged but also come with risks. Investigators may be followed to the meeting, or police officials may be recognized going to or coming from the rendezvous. Even if the undercover investigator is not seen with police officials, being at the same location will raise suspicion. If investigators discover they are being followed to a meeting with police officials, attempt to lose the tail without appearing to be elusive or forgo the rendezvous for an activity that would appear natural to the shadow.

24. Large-Scale Operations

Undercover work varies widely in the length of the operation and the complexity of the cover. A simple *buy and bust* operation may consist of finding an unwary drug dealer, making a buy and making an arrest. A more sustained and elaborate *fencing or sting operation* may require renting a warehouse and setting up several undercover investigators as criminals. Investigators then begin buying stolen merchandise while electronically recording each transaction to recover stolen property and to identify and arrest the thieves and fences responsible. While most of these operations result in arrests related to stolen property, some have led to arrests for murder, rape, bank robbery, arson, and other offenses. The buying and selling of stolen property often results in close relationships with suspects who think they are dealing with fellow criminals.

ADDITIONAL READING

Informants

Brown, M.F.: Criminal Informants: Some Observations on Use, Abuse, and Control. *Journal of Police Science and Administration, 13* (3), 1985.

Crawford, K.K.: Cellmate Informants: A Constitutional Guide to Their Use. *FBI Law Enforcement Bulletin, 59* (12), 1990.

Earhart, R.S.: *A Critical Analysis of Investigator–Criminal Informant Relationship in Law Enforcement.* Washington, D.C.: International Association of Chiefs of Police, 1964.

Gutterman, M.: The Informer Privilege. *Journal of Criminal Law, Criminology and Police Science, 58* (32), 1967.

Harney, M.L. and Cross, J.C.: *The Informer in Law Enforcement* (2nd ed.). Springfield, IL: Thomas, 1968.

Hight, J.E.: Avoiding the Informant Trap: A Blueprint for Control. *FBI Law Enforcement Bulletin, 67* (11), 1998.

——: Working with Informants: Operational Recommendations. *FBI Law Enforcement Bulletin, 69* (5), 2000.

Lee, G.D.: Drug Informants: Motives, Methods, and Management. *FBI Law Enforcement Bulletin, 62* (9), 1993.

Luger, J.: Snitch: *A Handbook for Informers.* Port Townsend, WA: Loompanics, 1991.

McCann, M.G.: *Police and the Confidential Informant.* Bloomington: Indiana University Press, 1957.

McClean, J.D.: Informers and Agents Provocateurs. *Criminal Law Review, 527,* 1969.

McGuiness, R.L.: Probable Cause: Informant Information. Parts I and II. *FBI Law Enforcement Bulletin, 51* (11 & 12), 1982.

Miller, J. M.: Becoming an Informant. *Justice Quarterly, 28* (2): 203-220. 2011.

Morris, J.: *Police Informant Management.* Orangeville, CA: Palmer Enterprises, 1983.

Mount, H.A., Jr.: Criminal Informants: An Administrator's Dream or Nightmare. *FBI Law Enforcement Bulletin, 59* (12), 1990.

Pena, M.S.: Practical Criminal Investigation. Fifth edition. Incline Village, NV. Copperhouse Publishing, 2000.

Reese, J.T.: Motivations of Criminal Informants. *FBI Law Enforcement Bulletin, 49* (5), 1980.

Rissler, L.E.: The Informer-Witness. *FBI Law Enforcement Bulletin, 46* (5), 1977.

Swanson, C., Chamelin, N., Territo, L., & Taylor, R.: *Criminal Investigation* (10th ed.). Boston, McGraw-Hill, 2009.

Physical Surveillance

Buckwalter, A.: *Surveillance and Undercover Investigation.* Stoneham, MA: Butterworth, 1984.

Degarmo, J.W., Jr.: The Nature of Physical Surveillances. *Police Chief, 42* (2), 1975.

DiPietro, A.L.: Aerial Surveillance: Fourth Amendment Considerations. *FBI Law Enforcement Bulletin, 58* (12), 1989.

Hanna, M.J. and Mattioli, R.P.: Tactical Surveillance with a Twist. *FBI Law Enforcement Bulletin, 64* (8), 1995.

Hendrie, E.M.: Curtilage: The Expectation of Privacy in the Yard. *FBI Law Enforcement Bulletin, 67* (4), 1998.

Hough, H.: *A Practical Guide to Photographic Intelligence.* Port Townsend, WA: Loompanics, 1990.

Kingston, K.A.: Reasonable Expectation of Privacy Cases Revive Traditional Investigative Techniques. *FBI Law Enforcement Bulletin, 57* (11), 1988.

Lapin, L.: *How to Get Anything on Anybody–Book I: The Encyclopedia of Personal Surveillance.* Port Townsend, WA: Loompanics, 1991.

Lesce, T.: Low-Light and Night-Vision Equipment. *Police Chief, 64* (11), 1997

McEvoy, R.T., Jr.,: Surveillance Photography: What You Need to Know. *Law Enforcement Technology,* February/March, 1986.

McGuiness, R.I.: In the Katz Eye: Use of Binoculars and Telescopes. Parts I and II. *FBI Law Enforcement Bulletin, 50* (6 & 7), 1981.

Rapp, B.: *Shadowing and Surveillance: A Complete Guide Book.* Port Townsend, WA: Loompanics, 1985.

Sighting in the Dark. Law and Order, 34 (6), 1986.

Siljander, R.P.: *Applied Surveillance Photography.* Springfield, IL: Thomas, 1975.

——: *Fundamentals of Physical Surveillance.* Springfield, IL: Thomas, 1978.

Siuru, W.D., Jr.: Turning Night into Day. *Law and Order, 37* (7), 1989.

Vandiver, J.V.: Electronic Visual Surveillance. *Law and Order, 36* (10), 1988.

Electronic Surveillance

Bourniquel, P.M.: Visiophone: French High-Tech Security. *FBI Law Enforcement Bulletin, 60* (7), 1991.

Church, G.J.: The Art of High-Tech Snooping. *Time, 129* (16), April 20, 1987.

Colbridge, T.D.: Electronic Surveillance: A Matter of Necessity. *FBI Law Enforcement Bulletin, 69* (2), 2000.

Compoy, A.: The Law's Eye in the Sky. *The Wall Street Journal, 68* (139), A3, 12/13/2001.

French, S. and Lapin, L.: *Spy Game: Winning Through Super Technology.* Port Townsend, WA: Loompanics, 1985.

Hollien, H.: *The Acoustics of Crime: The New Science of Forensic Phonetics.* New York, Plenum Press, 1990.

Jones, R.N.: *Electronic Eavesdropping Techniques and Equipment.* Washington, D.C.: National Institute of Law Enforcement and Criminal Justice, 1975.

Moran, W.B. (Ed.): *Covert Surveillance and Electronic Penetration.* Port Townsend, WA: Loompanics, 1983.

National Conference of State Legislatures: Electronic Surveillance Laws. http://www.ncsl.org/default.aspx?tabid= 13492. Available 8/5/2011.

Pollock, D.A.: *Methods of Electronic Audio Surveillance.* Springfield, IL: Thomas, 1984.

Privacy Rights Clearinghouse: https://www.privacyrights.org/fs/fs9-wrtp.htm, Available 8/5/2011.

Swanson, C., Chamelin, N., Territo, L, & Taylor, R.: *Criminal Investigation* (10th ed.). Boston, McGraw Hill, 2009.

Surette, R.: Video Street Patrol: Media Technology and Street Crime. *Journal of Police Science and Administration, 13 (78), 1985.*

Vandiver, J.V.: Surveillance: Eavesdropping and Wiretapping: Equipment and Techniques. *Law and Order, 36* (9), 1988.

Electronic Surveillance and the Law

Bravin, J.: Justices Rein in Police on GPS Trackers. *The Wall Street Journal,* A 1–2, 259 (18), 1/24/2012.

Carr, J.C.: *The Law of Electronic Surveillance* (2nd ed.). New York: Boardman, 1986.

Courtney, J.: Electronic Eavesdropping - Wiretapping and Your Right to Privacy. *Federal Communication Bar Journal, 26* (1), 1973.

Federal Government Information Technology: Electronic Surveillance and Civil Liberties. Washington, D.C.: U.S. Government Printing Office, 1985.

Fiatal, R.A.: The Electronic Communications Privacy Act: Addressing Today's Technology. Parts I, II and III. *FBI Law Enforcement Bulletin, 57* (2, 3 & 4), 1988.

——: Lights, Camera, Action: Video Surveillance and the Fourth Amendment. Parts I and II. *FBI Law Enforcement Bulletin, 58* (1 & 2), 1989.

——: Minimization Requirements in Electronic Surveillance. Parts I and II. *FBI Law Enforcement Bulletin, 58* (5 & 6), 1987.

Hall, J.C.: Electronic Tracking Devices: Following the Fourth Amendment. Parts I and II. *FBI Law Enforcement Bulletin, 54* (2 & 3), 1985.

Paulsen, M.G.: *The Problems of Electronic Eavesdropping.* Philadelphia: American Law Institute, 1977.

Saunders, E.F.: Electronic Eavesdropping and the Right to Privacy. *Boston University Law Review, 52* (831), 1972.

Sharp, A.G.: The Rights and Wrongs of Taping Phone Calls. *Law and Order, 38* (2), 1990.

U.S. Attorney's Manual on Electronic Surveillance. Port Townsend, WA: Loompanics, 1988.

Undercover Assignments

Anderson, K.P.: *Undercover Operations: A Manual for the Private Investigator.* Boulder, CO: Paladin Press, 1988.

Band, S.R. and Sheehan, D.C.: Managing Undercover Stress. *FBI Law Enforcement Bulletin, 68* (2), 1999.

Barefoot, J.K.: *Undercover Investigation* (2nd ed.). Stoneham, MA: Butterworth, 1983.

Buckwalter, A.: *Surveillance and Undercover Investigation.* Stoneham, MA: Butterworth, 1984.

Hicks, R.D. II: *Undercover Operations and Persuasion.* Springfield, IL: Thomas, 1973.

Kukura, T.V.: Undercover Investigations and the Entrapment Defense. *FBI Law Enforcement Bulletin, 62* (4), 1993.

MacInaugh, E.A.: *Disguise Techniques.* Port Townsend, WA: Loompanics, 1984.

Marx, G.T.: *Undercover: Police Surveillance in America.* Berkeley: University of California Press, 1988.

Pilant, L.: Undercover Operations. *Police Chief, 64* (5), 1997.

Pistone, J.D. and Woodley, R.: *Donnie Brasco: My Undercover Life in the Mafia.* New York: NAL-Dutton, 1989.

Rapp, B.: *Undercover Work: A Complete Handbook.* Port Townsend, WA: Loompanics, 1985.

Sample, J.: *Methods of Disguise.* Port Townsend, WA: Loompanics, 1984.

Schiano, A. and Burton, A.: *Self-Portrait of an Undercover Cop.* New York: Dodd Mead, 1973.

Vasquez, I.J. and Kelley, S.A.: Management's Commitment to the Undercover Operative: A Contemporary View. *FBI Law Enforcement Bulletin, 58* (2), 1989.

Wade, G.E.: Undercover Violence. *FBI Law Enforcement Bulletin, 59* (4), 1990.

Part IV

SELECTED PROPERTY OFFENSES

Chapter 11

ARSON AND CRIMINAL EXPLOSIONS

ARSON

ARSON and criminal explosions that target people are clearly violent crimes, but they are presented here in the property crimes section because they are most often committed to target property. The role of investigators studying the property damage is the same regardless of the intended target.

A suspicious fire requires a thorough investigation by competently trained arson investigators. Each year, there may be hundreds of suspicious fires in major cities. During times of economic hardship, the number of arsons may rise (as individuals burn their unprofitable businesses or homes to collect insurance money) while cities are attempting to conserve money by laying-off fire investigators. Paradoxically, there may be an increase in arson activity at the same time that arson prosecutions decline.

Arson is often difficult to prove. It is usually a crime of stealth, often taking place at night under the cover of darkness, with no witnesses. Moreover, the physical evidence that would connect offenders to the offense is often consumed in the blaze. The true number of arsons in a given year is unknown because of the difficulty determining which fires, classified as starting from "unknown causes," were actually intentionally set.

Arson is committed primarily by young, white men. Most arsonists live within two miles of their fires. About 50 percent will return to the scene, and of those, 97 percent will return within 24 hours. Arson is not always a solo activity and may be part of an organized conspiracy. While large scale arson rings have been uncovered, small-scale operations are more common. For some landlords, arson is seen as a way to profitably liquidate otherwise unprofitable assets.

The traditional problem in investigating arson is finding proof. The fire too often consumes the evidence and masks the arsonist's activity. Many arsonists rely on simple methods such as matches, fuses, and gasoline. There are, however, expert firesetters who build clever ignition devices that are consumed in the fire.

Because the arsonist may be part of a conspiracy, investigators may have to look beyond the immediate crime scene. For example, federal mail fraud statutes (the mails are used for false insurance claims) have been used because it is often easier to prove mail fraud than to connect perpetrators to arsons. The formidable difficulties in proving arson can be seen in attempts by insurance companies to prevent fraud. Although the companies bring only 10 percent of questionable fire cases to civil court, they still lose eight out of ten such suits.

BURNING OF BUILDINGS

1. Arson Defined

Under common law, arson is the malicious burning of another's house. States have revised their criminal codes to expand the definition to include most other structures. The gravity of the offense lies in the danger to the lives of persons who may be dwelling or occupying the structure at the time of the fire. The elements of proof generally include "burning," "malice" and "dwelling" aspects of the offense.

Burning involves heating to the point of ignition. Any appreciable burning is sufficient. It is not necessary that there be a flame or that the structure be consumed or materially injured. The ignition satisfies the requirement of burning.

Malice is the intent to injure another. There must be a malicious intent to burn to constitute the crime of arson. Negligent or accidental fires are not arson. The intent is to be inferred from the facts. Threats, quarrels, expressions of dislike, application of fire insurance, and so forth, may supply a basis for inferring intent. The prosecution, to overcome the legal presumption that fires are accidental in origin, must show that the burning resulted from a criminal design.

If the structure is used exclusively or in part for a residence, it is classified as an *inhabited dwelling*. It is not essential that a person is actually present. A trailer, tent, church, or theater could qualify. The value and ownership of the structure are relevant elements of the crime.

a. **Attempted Arson**. Attempted arson is an act done with specific intent to commit arson that would have resulted in the offense except for the intervention of some preventing cause. An attempt must include intent and an overt act. Merely gathering incendiary materials with malicious intent to burn a structure is not sufficient. Lighting a match and applying it to a structure or property, however, fulfills the requirements, even if the match may be immediately extinguished by the elements or other conditions.

2. Methods of Proof

The great variety of methods and practices employed by arsonists, and the destruction of physical evidence by the fire can make the investigation of arson very complex. The legal presumption, that every fire is of accidental origin until proven otherwise, must be overcome. Evidence must establish the *corpus delicti* and the essential facts of the offense. An unsupported confession of an alleged perpetrator is insufficient and inadmissible without an independent showing of the *corpus delicti.*

The *corpus delicti* of arson consists of burning and criminal design. To establish *burning,* it must be shown that there was a fire (burning or charring as distinguished from a mere scorching). The complainant, fire department personnel, or other eyewitnesses can testify to the burning of the property and its location. Physical evidence, such as burned parts of the building, may also be offered as proof. *Criminal design* may be established directly by the discovery of an incendiary device or plant (such as a candle or mechanical device), by the unexplained presence of accelerants (such as kerosene or gasoline), or by eyewitness testimony. The incendiary nature of the fire can also be shown by eliminating accidental and natural causes. Experts can testify that the fire was not of an accidental or natural origin. Properly qualified electrical, heating, or structural engineers can testify to the absence of wiring deficiencies, structural defects, or other conditions that could cause a fire. Evidence must sufficiently exclude all other reasonable explanations.

a. **Other Evidence**. After establishing the *corpus delicti,* evidence must identify the perpetrators and show they acted with criminal intent. There is often little direct evidence, so investigators generally rely on circumstantial evidence to build their case. Evidence associating the suspect with the scene may include tools, matches, and clothing found at the scene that can be linked to suspects. Similarly, suspects may carry on their person or clothing trace evidence linking them to the scene. Evidence of intent can include prior action of suspects. For example, removing valuable articles or substituting inferior articles implies knowledge of the impending fire. Conflict between perpetrators and occupants of the burned building may show motive. Other incriminating behavior may include making no legitimate attempt to extinguish the fire, not reporting the fire in a timely manner, or fleeing the scene.

3. Motives

Although it is not required to establish motive, determining motive can help guide the investigation and presents a more compelling case to a jury. This is especially true in cases built principally on circumstantial evidence. Some common motives for arson include economic gain, concealment of a crime, revenge, intimidation, and pyromania. For many arson cases, motive may not be apparent or clearly defined. For example, during a riot there may be several random fires. Some juveniles purposely set fires out of mischief.

a. **Economic Gain.** A property owner may benefit from a fire directly through an insurance claim or indirectly for other reasons (e.g., improvements required by building codes, future taxes, etc.). Since government property is not insured, economic gain is not generally a motive in fires on government-owned property.

The motives in defrauding an insurance company are often complex and not readily apparent. (Although this discussion centers on business establishments, the motives described are applicable to many other property owners.) The more common motives involve the location of the business or dispositions of merchandise. There may be a desire to move the business because of a deteriorating building, the location is no longer profitable, or the business has outgrown the size of the structure. A fire may be set to dispose of merchandise that has lost value (obsolescence, seasonal items, overstock, change in the market, etc.). Arson may be attractive for a business facing impending liquidation, settlement of an estate, a need for cash, prospective failure, increasing land values, or being over insured.

Sometimes arson benefits a perpetrator who is not the property owner or beneficiary of an insurance claim. Unscrupulous insurance agents, adjusters contractors, salvagers, or even security personnel may try to increase their business through arson. Other business owners may try to eliminate competitors. Residents or sublessors may try to break a lease. The benefits of arson may not be apparent or direct.

b. **Concealment of a Crime**. Arsonists may burn a building to conceal a crime, destroy evidence of a crime, or to divert attention while a crime is committed at another location. The most common of these motives, however, is to destroy evidence. A person whose office records would not pass inspection may conceal mismanagement by burning the documents. Inventory shortages can be concealed by arranging a fire in the supply room. Finally, it is not uncommon for criminals to attempt to conceal crimes such as larceny or murder by burning the building where the crime occurred.

c. **Punitive Measure**. Arsonists may use fire to punish others for reasons of jealousy, hatred, or revenge. For example, a disgruntled employee might set fire to his or her employer's property.

d. **Intimidation and Economic Disabling**. Fire may be used as a weapon for personal or political motives. It may be used by saboteurs, unscrupulous strikers, or extortionists to force submission to certain demands.

e. **Pyromania**. Pyromania is an uncontrollable impulse to set fires. It is a mental affliction and not a rational motive. Pyromaniacs have a passion for fire that can be satisfied only by watching flames. Pyromaniacs generally work alone. They may not run from the scene, turn in an alarm, or do anything to associate them with the fire. Within this group are several subcategories.

The *abnormal youth* are mentally deficient persons of both sexes who set fires but do not realize the seriousness of their acts. Their enthusiasm and rapture at the sight of the blaze, together with their general conduct, will often make them noticeable even in a crowd at the scene of a fire.

The *hero type* sets fires, pretends to discover them, and turns in the alarm. Persons of this type seek attention and notoriety. They may desire to be firefighters or security personnel and set fires to get attention and accolades by rescuing others from danger.

Some *alcoholics and drug addicts* develop strong urges to set fires. When not under the influence, these persons do not show any sign of pyromania. When impaired, though, they succumb to uncontrollable desires to see a fire.

Sexual deviates are usually males who derive sexual stimulation from setting fires and watching flames. Their sexual gratification is enhanced by acts of arson.

4. Factors Influencing Burning

Fire is a form of *oxidation;* it is a chemical reaction of combining oxygen with another substance to produce a new substance. A fire is a form of oxidation that produces *combustion,* the release of heat and light along with other byproducts. Oxygen is a key component of any fire. Liquids must be sufficiently heated to release vapors (the *flashpoint*) before they can burn. The process of heating a solid to the point where it begins to decompose and can burn is *pyrolysis.* Once the *ignition temperature* of the fuel is reached, combustion begins.

Several factors affect the rate and extent of the spread of fire. The wind, including velocity and direction, can affect the intensity and movement of fire. The relative humidity and dryness of the materials influences how quickly they burn. The air temperature and nature and condition of any vegetation surrounding a building may play a role in how readily it will burn. The nature of the building construction (the presence of wood or other combustible materials and the possibility for drafts) influence the spread. Partitions, laths, eaves, roofs, and shingles which are constructed of wood will aid the spread. Drafts created by stairwells, elevator shafts, and open doors and windows will hasten the conflagration.

5. Causes of Fire

Fires may occur accidentally, but to be arson they must result from an intentional act. One method of proving that a fire was intentionally set is to systematically eliminate the possibility of accident. An accidental fire may arise from forces of nature, negligence, or defects in equipment or materials. These causes are accidental, in that the resulting fire was not intentionally set, but they may be crimes under other statutes.

There are many common causes of accidental fires. Carelessly discarding cigarettes and matches or improperly disposing of or storing combustible materials such as oily waste and painting equipment can produce an unintentional fire. Spontaneous combustion can result from the storing oily or chemically saturated materials such as cloth, paper, or cotton waste in poorly ventilated places. The improper storage of petroleum products and other flammable substances may result in an explosion.

Fire may be caused by poorly managed or defective heating systems. This includes overheated and overturned stoves, clothes dried too close to a fireplace, lint from fabrics coming in contact with open fires or radiant heaters, faulty chimneys and flues, explosions resulting from kerosene stoves, and leaks in pipes of gas stoves.

Naturally occurring events, such as sun rays focused by bubbles in window panes or by some other peculiarly shaped glass article may create an ignition source. Lightning strikes may ignite a fire. If a thunderstorm occurred at the time of a fire, an examination should be made for evidence of a lightning strike. Melted metal parts, paint streaked with burned areas, cracks in the walls, broken bricks, and soot driven into the rooms from the chimney are some signs. Lightning usually strikes a high point of the building and may be traced in its path to the ground.

Fires due to electrical mishaps are common. Our increasing demand for electricity to run appliances, air-conditioning and heating, tools, and recreation devices can surpass the designed capacity of the electrical system in structures where we work and live. Defects in any part of the system can cause a spark, excessive heat, or both.

The flow of electrical circuit may be broken by a loose contact or by flipping a switch. When an inductive circuit is suddenly broken, the electrical current may jump across the opening contact points in the form of a *spark.* If an electric circuit is carrying a current greater than the capacity of the switch, the resulting spark may vaporize sufficient metal to cause an *arc* (a sustained spark). Any combustible material in the area surrounding the arc may provide fuel for a fire.

Electrical current flowing through a wire produces heat. If the current exceeds design capacities, *overheating* occurs. The smaller the diameter of the wire, the greater the heat produced. A short circuit may lead to more current flowing through the circuit than the wire can maintain. The result is the melting of insulation and the ignition of nearby combustible materials. Some causes of overheating include faulty wiring, improper voltage, low line capacity, and neglected electric motors. Some tools and appliances, such as soldering irons, curling iron, flat irons, vacuum cleaners, refrigerators, and microwave ovens, or a combination of too many devices operating simultaneously can overload a circuit or overheat.

6. Methods of Arsonists

The techniques, devices, and materials employed by arsonists vary. Those who plan fires for insurance fraud or to conceal embezzlement will ordinarily plan their crime carefully and execute it with ingenuity. Excessive ingenuity may betray the arsonist if the fire is extinguished before the incendiary device is destroyed. A mentally deficient pyromaniac or someone concealing a spontaneous crime, on the other hand, usually acts in haste with little deception.

a. **Incendiary Materials.** Combustible material (fuel) must be present to create a fire. The fuel (solid, liquid or gas) may already be at the scene or brought to the scene by the arsonist. Strictly speaking, only gases burn. Solids and liquids must be heated to produce flammable gases. The gases in turn must be raised to the proper temperature before ignition occurs. There must be material to burn and a source of heat to ignite the fuel. Finally, there must be a supply of oxygen, since burning is an oxidation process. If the oxygen level falls to 17 percent or less, the flame is extinguished and the fire cannot be supported. Oxygen may be supplied from the air or from oxidizing agents.

1) ***Liquids***. Liquids with low flash points, such as gasoline or ether, do not require open flame for ignition. A spark can cause rapid and explosive fires when their vapors mix with air.

2) ***Gases***. Gases with low flashpoints can readily explode when mixed with air in an enclosed area. A slow, poorly-vented fire will often provide its own explosive gases.

3) ***Solids***. When solids are finely ground or in powdered form, they may be very combustible. Coal dust, grain, metals, and other

Table 11-1. Common Accelerants.

Liquid	Flash Point (Fahrenheit)
Alcohol (grain)	60°
Benzol	40°
Petroleum ether	24°
Gasoline	45°
Kerosene	100°
Naphtha (safety)	100°
Turpentine	95°

Table 11-2. Common Gases Resulting in Explosions.

Gas	Explosive Limits
Acetylen	12.6%–55.0%
Butane	1.6%–6.5%
Carbon Monoxide	12.5%–74.0%
Ethylen	13.0%–35.0%
Hydrogen	14.1%–75.0%
Natural Gas	14.8%–13.5%
Propane	2.3%–7.3%

materials will burn rapidly when combined with air and ignited. Some substances generate intense heat on contact with water. Notable among these are sodium, sodium peroxide, potassium, and calcium carbide. Certain solids, called oxidizing agents, give off oxygen as they decompose and will aid combustion. Incendiary pencils, for example, can be made with potassium chlorate (an oxidizing agent) and sugar separated from a capsule of concentrated sulfuric acid. When the capsule is broken, the acid extracts water from the sugar, leaving charcoal and giving a sufficient heat reaction to produce oxygen from the chlorate and ignite the charcoal. Typical oxidizing agents include chlorates, perchlorates (including perchloric acid), chromates (including chromic acid), bichromates, nitrates (including nitric acid), and permanganates.

b. **"Plants" and Other Contrivances**. A clever arsonist might use a remote control ignition device to avoid being at the scene when the fire starts. A "plant" is a device (like a timer) designed to ignite combustible material after an initiating action. The delay gives the arsonist an opportunity to escape and possibly establish an alibi. There are many devices used to initiate a fire.

Gas and electrical *heating appliances* can be used to ignite combustible materials. *Heaters* (flat irons, toasters, soldering irons, hot plates, and lamps) may be placed in contact with a combustible material, switched on, and abandoned giving the arsonist sufficient time to leave the scene. *Sparkers* (electrical switches, door bells, short circuits, and telephone boxes) may be used to ignite the vapor of a volatile fluid. For example, a spark may be sufficient to set off an explosive flash in the presence of a high concentration of gasoline. A plant may be designed so that an innocent person initiates the fire while the arsonist is in another place.

Mechanical devices are time triggers to ignite a fire. Clock mechanisms can be arranged to initiate the fire. Sometimes arsonists will alter equipment such as loosening gas pipes or disabling sprinkler systems to spread combustible fluids. A magnifying glass might be used to focus sunlight on a combustible material.

A common device used by arsonists is a slow burning fuse-like arrangement called a *trailer*. Streamers may be made out of candlewick, rope, or cloth and are saturated with a flammable liquid such as kerosene. They are strung from room to room to provide a path for the fire. Cigarettes can be lit and placed in a book of matches. Candles can be placed in straw, paper, or similar materials. Sometimes a piece of the candle may be recovered from the neck of a bottle used to hold it.

The combination of a plant and a *flammable gas* is a particularly dangerous arson technique. The result is usually an explosion followed by a fire. Natural gas may be allowed to fill the interior of a building by sawing off a low-lying pipe or by simply turning on a jet. A spark or pilot light will ignite the gas. Sewer gas may also be released into a structure by removing the water from a toilet, sink drain, or trap.

Chemical devices became more common after World War II. Thermite bombs, consisting of powdered aluminum and titanium oxide, are exceedingly difficult to control. Phosphorous can be used to impregnate cards, so that, on drying, the cards burst into flame. Molotov cocktails, crude incendiary devices favored by rioters, are bottles of gasoline with cloth or paper streamers that are ignited and thrown.

Explosives are sometimes used to damage machinery or injure people. While fire may not be intended, it commonly results from the explosion. Nitroglycerin, TNT, mercury fulminate, gunpowder, and gun cotton are the common explosives employed for this purpose.

7. Investigation During a Fire

There is valuable evidence and information to be gathered during a fire. Investigators may want to coordinate with area fire departments and respond to any structure fires in their area.

1) *Observations During the Fire.* The investigation during a fire will depend on the nature and severity of the fire. General observations can be made from an appropriate distance and the peripheral area can be examined. Sometimes the arsonist remains among the bystanders, so general photographs of spectators may be useful. Later, information can later be gathered from eyewitnesses.

The smoke, steam, or other vapors that emanate from the fire are useful indicators of the burning substances and any accelerants used. The presence of *steam* indicates that humid substances have come in contact with the hot combustible substances. The water present in the humid substance is evaporated before the substance begins to burn. *White smoke* emanates from the burning of phosphorus, a substance that is sometimes used as an incendiary agent. *Grayish smoke* is caused by the emission of flying ash and soot in loosely packed substances such as straw and hay. *Black smoke* is produced by either incomplete combustion or from petroleum based materials such as rubber, tar, coal, turpentine, or gasoline. *Reddish-brown or yellow smoke* indicates the presence of nitrates or substances with a nitrocellulose base (nitric acid, nitrated plastics, film, or smokeless gun powder). A number of these substances are suitable as accelerants.

The *color of the flame* is indicative of the intensity of the fire and sometimes of the combustible substances present. The temperature of the fire may vary from 500 to 1500 degrees Centigrade with the color of the flame ranging from red, through yellow, to a blinding white. Some accelerants may give a characteristically colored flame. For example, burning alcohol is characterized by a blue flame. Red flames may indicate the presence of petroleum products.

The *size of the fire* should be noted at the time of arrival and at subsequent intervals thereafter. This information may be significant in relation to the time of the alarm. An unusually rapid expansion of the fire is indicative of the use of accelerants or some other preparation. Experienced firefighters at the scene may be able to render useful opinions as to the progression of the fire. The type of construction, available ventilation, and the contents of the building are factors in determining if the fire traveled abnormally fast.

Hot gases will normally rise and sweep upward making the *direction of travel* of a fire predictable from knowledge of the construction of the building. The flames will tend to rise until meeting obstacles, and then will project horizontally to seek other vertical outlets. The extent and rate of travel in a horizontal direction will depend primarily on the direction of the wind and on ventilation such as open doors and windows. The spread of fire in an unusual direction or at an exceptional rate raises suspicion of the presence of accelerants or attempts to vent the fire.

The investigator should carefully note the *location of flames* and whether there is more than one apparent point of origin. Unrelated fires in different places indicate arson. The placing of timing devices in different places would result in separate outbreaks.

Many accelerants emit characteristic *odors.* Detectable odors at the scene of a fire will mainly be of substances stored, manufactured, or used on the premises. The smell of a highly flammable substance in an area where it is not normally used should arouse suspicion. Turpentine, alcohol, kerosene, and gasoline are among the accelerants which emit characteristic odors.

2) ***Examinations During the Fire.*** In addition to observing the flame and smoke, investigators should make other important observations of the building and the scene while the fire is still burning.

Investigators should note the condition of *exterior openings,* windows, doors, or other openings. Locked doors and obstructed entrances may indicate intent to impede the firefighters in their efforts to extinguish the fire. Open windows and interior passageway doors may suggest efforts to vent the fire and promote its rapid progress. Drawn shades or windows covered with blankets may indicate an effort to conceal the arsonist while preparing the fire.

A limited *preliminary examination of the scene* and area surrounding the fire may be made at this time. In particular, search for equipment that may have been used by the arsonist (containers, matchbooks, and tools) and evidence that may lead to the perpetrator (shoe and tire impressions).

The scene should be *photographed* while the fire is still burning. The progressive stages of the burning should be photographed from various angles. Photographs and *observations of the spectators* are useful as arsonist sometimes return to watch their work. In a series of criminal fires, the arsonist may appear repeatedly in the photographs of the spectators. Video photography is useful for recording the progression of the fire as well as the presence and behaviors of spectators. Pyromaniacs may demonstrate an exceptional personal satisfaction or excitement. If the fire takes place during normal sleeping hours, arsonists are sometimes distinguishable by being one of the few fully clothed persons among the spectators.

8. Investigation of Scene after a Fire

The challenges of finding evidence of arson are related to the extent of burning. If the fire was promptly reported and quickly extinguished, the discovery of incriminating evidence may be a relatively simple matter. On the other hand, an extensive and long-burning fire may leave behind little evidence. Regardless of the condition of the scene, a patient, methodical study of the area will often reveal indications of criminal design and sometimes will permit a reconstruction of the method of operation.

a. **Safeguarding the Scene**. As with any crime scene, it is important to preserve and safeguard the evidence by preventing unnecessary disturbance of the debris and intrusions of unauthorized persons. In this task, police officers, investigators, and firefighters must work together. In the case of suspected arson, firefighters should postpone clean-up operations until investigators complete their examination of the scene. Firefighters may need to perform a certain amount of washing down and overhauling (opening walls, ceilings, and furniture to insure the fire is out), but extreme care should be exercised to prevent excessive disturbance of potential evidence. Anyone not officially involved with extinguishing or investigating the fire should be excluded from the scene.

b. **Order of Searching**. The area immediately surrounding the burned property should be more thoroughly searched for evidence. The doors and windows of the building should be examined (closed, locked, or evidence of forced entry). Next, investigators should search the interior for evidence of accelerants or other incendiary devices. If the burning has been extensive, the search should begin with the outer shell, progress to the first open area of floor from the point of entry, then the first inner shell or wall of an inside room, and finally the general area of the suspected point of origin.

c. **Locating the Point of Origin**. A major objective of the search is to locate the point of origin of the fire. It is here that the physical evidence of the crime is most likely to be discovered. Multiple points of origin are usually an indication of arson. The area the fire originated in may be determined by information obtained from witnesses and by an examination of the debris.

1) **Depth of Charring**. The point of origin can often be found by observing the intensity of the destruction. Because heat builds up under the ceiling and enters adjacent rooms through the space underneath the door jamb, heavy charring on the ceilings and walls will be apparent directly above the doorway where the fire entered a room. An examination of the charred uprights will indicate the direction of the flames. Fire that envelops a wooden beam tends to round the edges on the side away from the source of the flames. Charring becomes deeper as you approach the point of origin. A metal probe or depth gauge can be used to compare the relative depths of charring. The charring will be the deepest at the point of origin, the place where the fire usually has its greatest intensity and duration.

2) **The "V" Pattern**. Fire characteristically burns upward and outward in a "V"-shaped pattern from the point of origin. As the fire climbs vertically, it will spread out slightly horizontally. Flames will rise in a "V" pattern until blocked by the ceiling. The fire will then travel across the ceiling and if unable to burn upward will begin burning in a downward direction on the walls. Once the room of origin has been determined (by the extent of the destruction of the ceilings and walls or by the depth of charring) locating the bottom of the "V" pattern will indicate the point of origin.

3) **Other Indicators**. Recognizing the effects of high temperatures on common materials can help locate the point of origin. *Alligatoring* is a pattern on the surface of of charred wood that is similar in appearance to the skin of an alligator. *Spalling* is the chipping, flaking, and discoloration of concrete or brick due to intense heat. Brown stains may indicate the use of an accelerant. *Craze lines* are a pattern of thin irregular lines found in glass that has been exposed to high temperatures. Crazing suggests the possible use of an accelerant. When light bulbs are subjected to high temperatures the glass will expand and become deformed (see Figure 11-1). A bulge will sometimes form on the side of the bulb closest to the source of the heat and the point of origin. Furniture springs will sag when subjected to intense heat indicating either that the fire originated in the cushions or that an accelerant was used to cause the high temperatures.

Figure 11-1. A light bulb can be a good indicator of the point of origin; it will often begin melting and bulge in the direction of the greatest source of heat. (Courtesy of Raymond P. Siljander and Darin D. Fredrickson from *Applied Police and Fire Photography*, 2nd ed.)

d. **Examining the Point of Origin**. Carefully studying the debris at the point of origin can help determine if the cause of the fire was accidental or intentional. Search for traces of combustible materials. Peculiarly colored ashes, soot, unusually formed clinkers (incombustible residue), and impregnated materials should be collected for laboratory examination. Determine what materials are ordinarily stored in the area to identify unusual items (fuel and oil cans, etc.). Peculiar odors should be noted. The remains of streamers or plants should be recorded and protected. Note the degree of burning, general appearance, carbonization, and oil content of burned objects.

e. **Traces of Accelerants**. Investigators should give special attention to any evidence of liquid accelerants such as gasoline, kerosene, or turpentine. Often the point of origin may be located by following the burn patterns of such substances. Since a fluid will flow downward to lower levels, the area underneath the level of fire should be searched for accelerants. Some of the accelerant may still remain there in an unburned state. A study of wood charring can sometimes reveal indications of an accelerant. Wood that is soaked with a petroleum product prior to burning will acquire a distinctive appearance in charring. The "alligator effect" is more easily observed. The char marks are deeper where the liquid has seeped into the wood. The charring will follow the pattern of the spilled liquid. If a soaked trailer was used, the charring will outline, by deeper burning, the area impregnated by the accelerant. The burn pattern may indicate the removal of certain objects (files, strongbox, etc.) after the fire had begun.

f. **Detection of Hydrocarbons and Accelerants**. A portable hydrocarbon vapor detector or *sniffer* is often used to determine the presence of hydrocarbons at fires of suspicious origin. This device draws surrounding air over a heated filament. Any flammable vapor will cause a rise in temperature and is record by the instrument. It is very useful in screening burnt material at a fire scene to detect unconsumed hydrocarbons that may have been used as an accelerant. Impressive results have been achieved using *arson dogs* specially trained to detect accelerants. A dog's nose is more sensitive than the hydrocarbon vapor detector and can reduce the number of samples sent to the lab for analysis. The vapor detector cannot differentiate between the hydrocarbons from burned plastics and those from unburned accelerants. This may result in a number of samples that are not accelerants being sent to the laboratory for costly analysis. Furthermore, dogs do not labor under preconceived notions of where accelerants should be located so they find them in places investigators might overlook.

g. **Altered Protective Devices**. To insure destruction, arsonists sometimes tamper with the sprinkler system or alarm devices. Investigators should have the fire protection system inspected. Water supply valves should be carefully checked. The water flow should be examined for signs of tampering. Abnormal conditions of fire doors, transoms, and windows should be reported.

9. Collecting Physical Evidence

The physical evidence found at an arson scene is often fragile. All evidence should be photographed and located on a sketch before moving. While evidence of arson can be wide ranging, some items are typical.

a. **Containers**. Arsonists may use a variety of bottles, cans, barrels, pails, or boxes to hold the combustible liquid. Any residual accelerants should be sealed in a glass container so it does not evaporate. The original container should be collected and preserved in air tight containers when possible. Wrapping paper, cardboard boxes, string or cord, or similar articles that may have held substances during transit, should also be collected. These articles may bear trace evidence, fingerprints, DNA, etc.

b. **Ashes and Debris**. If it is believed that ashes or debris contain traces of accelerant, they should be sealed in an air tight container and transported to a forensic laboratory. If straw or packing material (such as excelsior) has been used to set the fire, the ashes may retain their characteristic shape. Cloth normally will not be completely destroyed by fire, and the burned remains of clothing are sometimes significant. Wool, for example, is ordinarily not completely consumed unless it is soaked with a flammable liquid. Materials may fall to lower floors as the fire progresses, so these areas should be searched for evidence or the remains of a "plant."

c. **Fingerprints and Impressions**. A search for fingerprints should be made in the usual manner, giving special attention to objects that may have contained accelerants. Soot from the fire may develop fingerprints on objects. Brushing away the soot may reveal fully developed fingerprints underneath. Fingerprint should be developed, if necessary, and photographed. Transportable objects bearing prints should be collected as evidence. Impressions made by tools, shoes, or tires should be photographed and cast.

d. **Incendiary Devices**. Articles such as wires, fuses, straw, or candles could be part of an incendiary device. Since arsonists may create several ignition points, the search for such devices should be extensive. Closets and obscure corners should be searched for heating appliances.

e. **Stoves and Fireplaces**. Arsonists sometime insure that evidence, records, and papers are destroyed by first burning them in a stove or fireplace. Ashes remaining in stoves and fireplaces should be examined.

f. **Tools**. Tools found at the scene may have been left behind or used by the arsonist and may contain important evidence. Wax on knife blades, sawdust and chips on saws or drill bits, and metal particles on axes may be important, depending on the materials used to set the fire. Tools may contain paint particles or defects that match marks on door jambs or window sills made while breaking into the building.

10. Preparation to Burn

The condition and contents of the building should be carefully examined. Someone planning a fire may remove items of sentimental or monetary value. Fur coats and jewelry, for example, may have been removed before setting fire to a residence. Some articles may be positioned to be more exposed to the fire in an attempt to ensure their destruction. A door may be purposely left open to insure the burning of clothing in a closet where a fur coat is normally stored.

In fires designed to conceal evidence of embezzlement or other irregularities of records, arsonists may place the incriminating documents so that they will be exposed to the flames. For example, arsonists may arrange ledgers in a tented fashion on a table to aid the burning. Masses of paper, however, do not burn as well as novice arsonists imagine. Often incriminating documents are left behind in salvageable condition. The absence of certain documents from the fire scene may need further investigation. For example, missing insurance policies that are normally kept in the area of the fire may indicate knowledge of the impending fire and intent to file an insurance claim.

11. Witnesses

The search for physical evidence often focuses on establishing the *corpus delicti* and identifying the perpetrator. Additional evidence can often be obtained by carefully questioning persons associated with the discovery and control of the fire (security personnel, occupants, and the owner).

a. **Persons First Arriving at the Fire**. Every effort should be made to locate and question the person who first saw the fire. Passersby, security personnel, and police officers are among those who may have made important observations. Try to determine the identity of the person who turned in the alarm. Investigators should attempt to learn where the fire began, the number of places where flames were observed, and how the fire spread. Solicit opinions on the origin of the fire, the color of the smoke, the general appearance of the conflagration, and the presence of any suspicious activity, such as anyone hastily leaving the scene on foot or by automobile.

b. **Firefighters**. The most reliable information concerning the fire can be obtained from firefighters, who are professionally trained observers. They should be questioned concerning the nature of the fire, the color of the flames and smoke, and any perceptible odors. Information can also be obtained concerning the condition of doors, windows, and shades. Firefighters may have observed the arrangements of stock, packing cases, and furniture.

c. **Security Personnel**. If security personnel are employed in the building, they should be able to provide detailed information on the condition of the building prior to the fire. They should be thoroughly questioned about the building, the fire, recent behavior of any occupants of the building, and recent movements of stock or furniture. Inquire about any suspicions and theories of the origin of the fire. Finally, try to identify the last person to leave the building.

d. **Occupants**. The occupants and employees of the building should be interviewed separately. They should be encouraged to give their own accounts, theories, and suspicions of the fire. Try to identify the last person to leave the building and whether it was unusual for him or her to be the last to leave. Determine who ordinarily locked the premises.

e. **Owner**. The owners of the property should be questioned concerning their activities at the time of the fire. Determine if any of them use aliases. Owners should be questioned regarding prior arrests, convictions, previous fires, financial standing, businesses, domestic problems, and hobbies or amusements that could have caused reverses in their financial situation.

12. Photographing and Sketching

A photographic record should be made of the destruction and any physical evidence. Photographs should be taken of each area of significance prior to the search. Location and close-up photographs should be made of each item of evidence. As each important piece of evidence is discovered, it should be photographed in its original condition and position. Additional photographs can then be taken if debris needs to be cleared to view the details of the evidence. The point of origin should be thoroughly photographed to show the type and extent of alligatoring, charring, and the remains of any incendiary device. Sketches should be made showing the location of the various articles of evidence. Blueprints of buildings may be useful in determining the dimensions and other details of the structure.

13. Packaging and Forwarding of Evidence

After collecting and sealing in airtight containers physical evidence that may contain traces of accelerants, it should be transported to the laboratory as soon as possible. Containers should be packaged to provide adequate protection and forwarded or hand-carried to the laboratory. Flammable evidence should not be shipped through the mail. Couriers or other means of delivery should be employed in such instances. Along with the evidence the investigator should provide the following information to assist the analysis:

- An itemized list of the evidence being submitted and how it was transported to the laboratory.
- The date and time of the fire.
- A brief description of the type and construction of the burned building or object and the extent of damage or destruction caused by the fire.
- A list of the chemical agents used in extinguishing the fire.
- Photographs and scaled sketches of where the various articles of evidence were collected.

14. Sources of Information

Background investigations should be conducted on anyone associated with the building or the fire. The local fire department may be consulted for records of previous fires. Depending on the seriousness and nature of the fire, investigators should consult police records of known arsonists; records of recent repairs or alterations in the building; inventories, financial statements, and bills of sale where embezzlement or theft is suspected; and rosters of current and recently discharged personnel.

In addition, forensic databases may be useful in tracking physical evidence from its manufacturer to its point of sale or distribution. The databases of insurance companies and associations can be a valuable resource in detecting patterns of arson fraud and tracking firesetters who change insurance companies or geographic locations. Because of the tremendous financial loss that results from arson, insurance companies actively cooperate with law enforcement agencies in their investigation. Their information is particularly useful where a *modus operandi* has been repeatedly observed.

Table 11-3. Examination of the Fire Scene.

Point of Origin	• **Exterior of structure**—note fire-damaged areas. • Charring and/or smoke deposits over doorways, windows, attic vents, eaves or soffits. • Determine whether doors and windows were open or closed during fire. • Check for forced entry. • Determine if fire originated at the building's exterior. **Interior of structure.** • Locate the area or room of most severe damage. • Check the ceiling to find the worst area of damage. • Find the lowest point of burning within the area of origin or "V" patterns. • Look for directions of heat flow. Observe effects on light bulbs, window glass, metal objects, interior doors and other furnishings. • Look for multiple or non-communicating fires. • Observe alligatoring/depth of char, to determine speed and duration of fire. • Look for spalling - indicates intensity of fire on masonry material.

Cause of Fire	**Elimination of all accidental and natural causes.**
	• Electrical malfunctions.
	• Heating or cooking equipment.
	• Smoking materials.
	• Accidental explosions.
	• Spontaneous combustion.
	• Lightning.
	Identify and document evidence of incendiary fires.
	• Trailers.
	• Devices.
	• Chemicals or flammables.
	• Special burn patterns.
	• Altered or misused electrical equipment or appliances.
	• Multiple fire sets.
	• Preparations of premises for fire.
	  - Blocked windows/obscured view.
	  - Ventilation holes in interior.
	  - Missing furnishings, equipment or stock.
	• Evidence of fire to conceal other crime.

Source: Bureau of Alcohol, Tobacco and Firearms. ATF Arson Investigative Guide.

Table 11-4. Arson Checklist.

Official Data	• Address, location, and description of the building. • Date and time of fire. • Time of receipt of alarm by the fire station. • Fire station receiving the alarm. • Fire units responding. • Time of arrival and departure of fire units. • Designation of the building in terms of construction, material, size, age, and materials stored there. • Designation of type of fire by the fire department records.
Date of Ownership, Occupancy, and Property Value	• Owner of the building. • Tenants of the building. • Occupants. • Value of the property. • Insurance coverage. • Name of insured. • Name of insurer. • Loss of property through fire.
Discovery of the Fire	• Who reported the fire? • When was the fire reported? • How was the fire reported? • Did the person who reported the fire have any motive for doing so? • Who discovered the fire? • When was the fire discovered? • Under what circumstances was the fire discovered? • What was the time interval between discovery and report? How was the time interval accounted for?
Conditions Surrounding the Fire	• Initial observations of the fire. • Point of origin of fire. In what building? In what room? • Direction of winds; weather conditions such as temperature and humidity; electrical storms. • Type of fire - flash or otherwise. • Explosion. • Speed of travel. • Odors - gasoline, kerosene, etc. • Appearance of smoke—shape and color. • Appearance of flames—size, intensity, color, and area of spread. • Hissing or crackling noises.

Table 11-4—*Continued.*

	• Direction of spread. • Were any windows or doors left open that were normally closed and locked? • Evidence of forced entry. • Chemical agents used to extinguish fire—water, foam, CO_2.
Condition of the Building	• How was the room or building furnished? Was there a stove of any kind? Was there a fire in the stove? What fuel was used? Was the stove well insulated? When was it last cleaned? Where were ashes placed? • Check for changes in building while occupied by present tenant, such as partitions, electric wiring, stoves, etc. • Was any electric wiring exposed? What was its condition? Were they ever repaired? When? By whom? What was the load carried by these wires? Was there ever any heat observed in the wires or terminals? • Number and kind of electric motors in the room or building. Provisions for safeguarding against dust. • Were there any machines in the room or building? What type? When were they last used? What power did they consume? When were they were last tested and lubricated? • Location and condition of pipes, particularly gas pipes. • Location and condition of all electric lights, appliances, and wiring, including the condition of fuses, circuit breakers and electrical panels. • Existence of devices for focusing sun's rays. • Degree of care exercised in storing flammable materials. • Condition of fire-fighting equipment.
Persons Associated	• Persons present in building at time of fire. Last person in the building. Persons in and around in the last 24 hours. Loiterers in the area. • Possessors of keys to the building. • Persons responsible for the security of the building. • Names and addresses of all occupants, tenants, employees, and all persons frequently around premises.

continued

Table 11-4—*Continued.*

	• Last person to leave the building—were actions customary?
Motive	• Description of all property on premises; whe it arrived, value, and amount of insurance. • Recent movements of property. • Possible substitutions of less valuable property. • Financial condition of owners of the property. • Impending inspections, investigations, inventories, and audits. • Relations between property owners—friendly or inimical. Recent defections from partner-ships or severance of employment. • Possibility of concealment of a crime. • Existence of previous criminal record on the part of any of the occupants. • Existence of a record of confinement to a mental institution. • Possible association of any persons with other mysterious fires.
Evidence of Intent	• Failure to summon the fire unit within a reasonable time. • Tampering with warning devices or commun-ications systems. • Doors, windows, transoms, and ventilating systems left in other than normal position. • Placement of incendiary materials, such as gasoline, oil, candles, matches, timing devices, and cans containing residual flammable material in the building. • Tampering with fire-fighting equipment or fire-control systems. • Removal of property of value prior to the fire. • Bringing personal property into the building.

VEHICLE FIRES

15. Motive

Many times vehicles are stolen, stripped of their parts then set afire. Vehicles are also burned in acts of revenge, rioting, or vandalism. Sometimes vehicles are set on fire to conceal a crime. Vehicles may be deliberately set on fire to defraud an insurance company.

Common motives for this offense vary. The fire may be a result of financial difficulties where payments cannot be made and finance companies are demanding payment or repossession, or the vehicle is worth less than the amount still owed. Domestic problems may spur a person to get rid of the vehicle to prevent a spouse or partner from acquiring it. The owner of a vehicle with mechanical trouble, whose value is excessively depreciated, or a vehicle that no longer suits the owner's needs may be tempted to commit arson.

16. The Burning of Vehicles

It is difficult to totally destroy vehicles through fire because they are mainly composed of nonflammable materials. With the exception of the upholstery, wires, and tires, there is very little that can be burned. Experiments have shown that a short in the wiring will almost always burn itself out without setting fire to the vehicle. When the upholstery is set on fire it will smolder for hours without breaking into open flame.

17. Examination of Burned Vehicles

Examine the burned vehicle before interviewing the owner. The investigation should attempt to locate the point of origin and determine how the fire spread.

a. **The Electrical System**. The owner may claim that the fire started because of a short but a total fire loss from this cause is extremely rare. Locate the wiring area where the short was suspected. Look for melted strands of wire with beaded ends at the broken points. Burned out head lamps indicate a battery short. Check the battery charge. A short will usually result in a rundown battery.

b. **Fuel Tank and Fuel Line**. Fuel from the fuel tank, fuel line, or fuel pump may have contributed to the fire. Examine the fuel line for breaks, tampering, or disconnection. Examine the fuel cap for signs of fire. If there is no damage, it may have been placed on after the fire. If an explosion took place the cap will bear signs of explosive damage. The fuel pump should be examined for tampering. Determine whether the line from the fuel pump was disconnected to obtain fuel.

c. **Engine Compartment**. The possible points of origin in the engine compartment are the fuel pump, carburetor or fuel injectors, and wiring. The use of incendiary substances is indicated by lead melted from the lower or outside seams of the motor, burned fan belts, and burned rubber cushions in the front of the motor. Another indication is the presence of burned spots on the paint. When gasoline is poured over the engine, sometimes it spills on the front fender. These areas will burn even though they are not in the direct line of the fire.

d. **Body**. When an excessive amount of flammable fluid is used to burn a vehicle, some of the fluid seeps through the floor of the vehicle and the fire produces oil or gasoline soot on the underside of the vehicle. Similarly, soot deposits on the underside of the frame and springs indicate the use of flammables.

e. **Other Indicators**. Sometimes the perpetrator will remove items of real or sentimental value before starting the fire. Investigators should try to determine if items were removed from the vehicle or if inferior equipment was substituted before the fire.

18. Interviewing the Insured Owner

After examining the vehicle, investigators should interview owners. Permit them to give their account without interrupting. After owners give their statements, questioning should cover a variety of areas.

The interview should begin with background information. Request details of the purchase of the vehicle and its financing, including such details as the name of the salesperson (for possible interview). What was the condition of the vehicle? Was there extra equipment in or installed on the car at the time of fire? Determine the mileage, any defects, and where the vehicle was normally serviced.

Next focus on the activities of owners. Where were they prior to the fire? Look for motive or deception. What were their observations? Their version of the discovery and progress of the fire are often revealing. Most persons have never observed the accidental burning of a car. They may describe details that are characteristic of a fire started with flammable material. Investigators should pursue the owner's theory of the cause of the fire and opinion on the point of origin. These statements should be compared with the results of the physical examination. Finally, what did they do after the fire? How did the owner leave the scene? When perpetrators arrange for a fire to take place in an isolated location, they likely make arrangements for transportation from the scene.

The investigation now turns to remaining evidence. Witnesses should be interviewed separately. The nature of the fire and statements of the owners will dictate the approach and content of interviews. Investigators should check the vehicle's history. Check with the dealer for records of reconditioning before the sale and the prior owner's reason for sale. Also check the vehicle title to determine who has an insurable interest.

19. Law

In common law and in most jurisdictions the malicious and willful burning of an automobile is not considered arson but is prohibited under statutes relating to the malicious destruction of property. In some jurisdictions, however, the term *simple arson* is used to describe the criminal burning of property other than a dwelling and the term *aggravated arson* is used for the burning of an inhabited structure.

CRIMINAL EXPLOSIONS

20. Overview

Explosions produce wreckage, scattered and difficult to recognize physical evidence, and possibly mutilated victims. Frequently explosions are followed by fire that further complicates the investigation.

21. Initial Action

The initial police response to criminal explosions is similar to other crime scenes: make the scene safe, treat the injured, and secure the area. Explosion scenes may encompass a larger area as evidence and debris can be thrown a considerable distance. In addition, fires may need to be extinguished and measures taken to protect against further accidents or explosions from utility hazards or other dangers. The search for additional explosive devices should begin immediately. Some bombers attempt to increase their "body count" by planting secondary devices to be triggered after first responders arrive. Investigators must determine the nature and cause of the explosion, and whether its origin was accidental or criminal.

All witness should be detained, identified, and interviewed. Observations concerning the number and nature of the explosions, the color of smoke, the presence of peculiar odors, and any other sensory-based information may be important. Try to determine the movements of people before and after the explosion while these details are fresh in witnesses' memories.

22. Types of Explosions

There are two basic types of explosions. A *low explosive* event results in a push effect, leaving a diffused pattern with little apparent change in intensity from a point source. The *high explosive* incident is marked by a definite seat of origin. Movable objects are blown outward from this point, with the force of the blast diminishing in intensity with distance.

Low explosives are characterized by the relatively low velocity of the energy wave (a few thousand feet per second). Gunpowder, gasoline, and carbon monoxide are examples of low-explosive substances. The explosion is identifiable by a *low-frequency sound* (described as a puff, boom, or pop) and the *absence of severe damage* in the area of the explosion.

High explosives on the other hand, such as dynamite and nitroglycerine, have velocities as high as 25,000 feet per second, are accompanied by a shattering *high-frequency sound,* and reveal a definite crater of explosion. On the basis of these differences it is often possible to identify the character of the explosion even though no traces of the explosives remain.

23. Crime Scene Action

Crimes involving explosions present unusual problems because evidence used to establish *corpus delicti* may be damaged or destroyed in the explosion or ensuing fire. While the fundamental procedures of crime scene investigation apply, explosions require great care in handling and interpreting evidence.

a. **Defining the Scene**. Depending on the location and severity of the explosion, the crime scene may be restricted to a room or may extend over several acres. Investigators need to determine the outer limits of the crime scene and secure the area to protect the evidence. The nature of the blast may present special problems. For example, an explosion on a plane in flight may result in the distribution of wreckage over many miles.

b. **Documenting the Scene**. The pattern of debris dispersal is important in locating the point of origin. Documentation can be a painstaking process in the investigation of explosions.

Overall photographs of the scene and sectional views of important areas should be taken before anything is disturbed. During the search, close-up photographs of evidence should be taken as it is discovered. If markers or signs are used, two sets of photographs, one with and one without the markers should be taken.

The scene should also be documented with sketches—an overall sketch for the whole scene and individual sketches for separated areas such as rooms. Significant evidence should be located by symbol and accurate measurements. Rectangular coordinates are preferable for indoor scenes, while polar coordinates are more suited to outdoor explosion scenes extending over large areas. Compass directions, legends, and other essentials should be included in each sketch.

Although photographs and sketches can be invaluable supplements to the investigative report, they should not take the place of the investigator's notes. Notes should contain detailed descriptions of the scene and all important objects. Each item of evidence should be identified in the investigator's notes.

c. **Searching the Scene**. Investigators should enlist the aid of technical specialists (explosives experts, forensic laboratory experts, arson investigators) before searching the crime scene. If a point of origin can be located, a spiral method of search often works well with searchers moving outward in increasingly larger circles. The search procedure is, of course, limited by the nature of the scene.

The search should attempt to establish the *corpus delicti,* i.e., that an explosive device was used with intent to injure some object or person. It should also focus on clues to the identity of the perpetrator. Evidence may include pieces of the bomb casing (metal, pipe fragments, etc.), parts of a timing device (wire, clockworks, etc) materials used to package the bomb (string, paper, leather, wood, etc.), and unexploded materials (pieces of paper that may have been part of the explosive's wrapping, explosive tagging materials, etc.). Any trace evidence that may have been part of an explosive device or its container should be carefully collected after its location and initial appearance have been documented. Preserve bomb components and remnants of any carrying devices (brief case, backpack, etc.) for possible fingerprint and DNA analysis.

The value of trace evidence was illustrated in an early forensic investigation. A dynamite bomb was exploded near the home of a prominent citizen in California. Evidence of the bomb and packaging (burlap, paper wrappings, the dynamite sticks, caps, fuses, and a piece of string) were analyzed. After microscopic examination, the analyst drew detailed conclusions from particles adhering to the string. "This twine came from a farm upon which will be found a fast-running stream of water, pine trees, black and white rabbits, a bay horse, a light cream colored cow, and Rhode Island red chickens." Skeptical investigators traced the dynamite to its point of sale. They investigated recent sales and found a farm that matched the description. The dynamite had been stolen from the farmer by two farm hands that were later proved to have committed the crime.

d. **Examination of Victims**. Deceased persons should not be moved until released by the medical examiner/coroner. The medicolegal examination should attempt to determine the cause and manner of death, the time of death, and whether death occurred before or after the explosion. Mutilated or extensively burned victims may need to be identified by fingerprints, dental work, x-ray, or DNA analysis. Forensic experts may be able to determine age, height, and weight, even though only part of the body is available. Forensic examination may also reveal any physical ailments or previous medical treatment the victim received. Further information can be obtained through the laboratory examination of clothing, documents, and personal items, particularly metal articles such as watches, rings, or cigarette lighters. Since the position of all such articles in relation to the body is important to identifying victims, the exact location of each item should be recorded before it is collected.

e. **Utilities**. Initiating the detonation of a bomb requires very little power. Virtually any electrical device could supply the necessary power. Check telephones, electric clocks, heaters, coffee pots, and lamps for breaks or additions in the wiring. The wiring systems of the engines of lawn mowers, compressors, and pumps should also be examined for the presence of extraneous wires or fragments of fuses, caps, or detonators. In certain cases, the entire electrical system including motors, appliances, and other apparatus should be examined for defects such as exposed wires, incorrectly installed wiring or fuses that could result in overheating or sparking. Investigators should enlist the aid of a safety expert or an electrician in this phase of the search for evidence.

24. Nature of the Criminal

Investigating explosions can be unusually difficult. Quite often perpetrators are not perceived as likely bombers and do not have criminal records. The bombers' grievances may have grown out of proportion to the perceived offenses. Others act out of political motives. Through protracted anguish and prolonged contemplation, jealous suitors and deceived spouses or partners may resort to drastic measures.

In many cases, investigators may have difficulty finding logical leads. Informants are more effective in cases involving professional criminals or those who associate with criminals. The previously non-criminal bomber may not come to the attention of informants or other information sources. For these, investigators must focus on the circumstances of the case, particularly the existence of personal grievances.

There are many useful factors to guide the investigator. Who is the target? What person, property, or activity did the bomber attack? Who had opportunity to commit the crime? Who had the capability, means, knowledge, and access? What explosive materials, mechanism, and camouflage were used in the bomb?

What was the *modus operandi*? This often forms the basis of the investigation. What techniques or tactics did the perpetrator use? Why was the crime committed? In the absence of an arrest at the scene, these answers must come from eyewitnesses, physical evidence, and from the suspect's possessions. Was there a bomb threat? Any communication by the perpetrator can provide useful clues. The person who received a threat should be instructed to recall the exact words of the caller. When is the bomb to explode? Where is the bomb right now? What kind of a bomb is it? What does it look like? Was any motive given? Could gender, accent or age be determined from the caller's voice? Was the voice familiar? Were there any background noises?

25. Determining the Target

A study of the circumstances surrounding the explosion, the nature of the explosive device, the type of target, and evidence of design or intent can help identify the target. It must be shown that the explosion took place through criminal intent or through criminal negligence.

Explosions directed against a person often require an act by the intended victim to detonate. Examples include bombs placed in vehicles wired to the ignition, packages sent to the victim, or a bomb connected to a light switch in the victim's home. Bombs placed in public transportation and in buildings can be timed to insure victims' are present when explosions occur.

Ordinarily, homicide statutes will cover criminal deaths by explosion, but many states have special statutes for using an explosive to injure or kill a person. Deaths resulting from simple or criminal negligence present special problems, and relate to the statutes dealing with death caused by negligence. In bombings designed to kill but that lack apparent motive, consider the possibility of mistaken identity or an error in locating the bomb.

25. Evidence Connecting a Suspect

Constructing an explosive device requires considerable preparation and handling of materials. Trace evidence may be able to link a suspect to the crime. Guided by the evidence found at the crime scene, investigators should thoroughly search any suspects and their possessions, along with their residence, workplace, and vehicle.

a. **Search of the Suspects**. Examine the suspects' hands and clothing for traces of bomb making materials. Burns or discolorations may be present if acids were used. If suspects were near the explosion, traces of debris may be found on their person. Fingernail scrapings and even ear wax have been found to contain significant microscopic evidence.

b. **Search of Residence or Workplace**. The search should concentrate on bomb making instructions and materials, along with evidence to link suspects with physical evidence gathered at the scene. If professional explosives were used, look for dynamite, nitroglycerine, gun cotton, black powder, smokeless powder, and similar substances. In addition to professional materials such as blasting caps, fuses, and primacord, search for improvised devices such as filaments, handmade squibs, and fuses. Homemade low-explosive bombs may employ a number of common chemicals or substances.

Military explosives may be encountered, though they are more common in countries where terrorists have access to military supplies. Common military explosives consist of sheet explosives and plastic explosives. Sheet explosives are manufactured in thin rub-

Table 11-5. Common Bomb Making Chemicals and Substances.

Ammonium nitrate	Potassium nitrate
Ammonium dichromate	Potassium permanganate
Chromic acid, chromates	Powdered aluminum
Metallic peroxides	Powdered iron
Metallic potassium	Powdered magnesium
Metallic sodium	Powdered zinc
Nitric acid	Sulphur
Potassium chlorate	Sulphuric acid

bery sheets that can be cut with a knife. They contain a high explosive, either RDX or PETN, and have military and commercial uses. Plastic explosives are a group of explosives that use plasticizers in their composition to make them pliable at warm temperatures and give them a doughy appearance. RDX, the most powerful of the military explosives as well as the most common, is used in C-4 and other the explosives.

Suspects' dwelling places or workshops should be searched for tools and construction materials. Possible work areas should be swabbed for traces of explosive materials. The type of bomb will determine the tools and materials to be included in the search. For example, an explosive device with a sophisticated or complex construction will suggest the specific tools used to create it. All tools of possible evidential value should be collected and placed in separate containers. Paint, wood, fibers, metal pieces, and other materials clinging to the faces of the tools can sometimes be linked to the materials used in constructing the bomb.

c. **Search of Vehicle**. Suspects may use their vehicles to transport an explosive device or materials used in its construction. The interior and trunk should be swabbed for traces of explosives. Tools found in the vehicle should be examined for evidence that they were used to assemble the bomb or for forcing entry. Traces of materials used to construct the bomb, blasting caps, special matches, batteries, and wires are among the articles that may be uncovered. Vehicles should be examined for soil or other evidence that could link it to the explosion scene.

d. **Sources of Explosives**. Although it is possible to obtain the explosive material under the guise of legitimate uses, it is common for perpetrators to acquire dynamite and blasting caps by theft or other illegal means. In determining the source of the explosives, consider the possibility of a local theft. Carelessness in the safeguarding of explosives results in frequent thefts from local contractors and persons engaged in large-scale construction work. Though broad implementation is still controversial, taggants or chemically coded additives mixed with explosives by manufacturers can help identify the origins of explosives.

26. Motive

Motive may not be obvious in some explosion cases. Bombings associated with labor unrest are likely motivated by revenge, while bombings at public buildings or the residence of elected officials are likely political in nature. Often the motive is unclear and investigators must explore every lead and systematically eliminate unlikely motives before a motive can be discerned. During this process, investigators should consider several factors.

- Who stood to *profit* from the explosion? If the victim was a person, did someone stand to gain by that person's death? If property was destroyed, what was the financial situation of the owner? Were there any recent movements of property, such as substitutions of less valuable property?
- Was it an act of *sabotage*? Was the target special machinery, materials, or activity that could disrupt business or labor relations?
- Was the explosion an *attempt to conceal a crime*? An explosion can be used to disguise another crime, such as a homicide, larceny, or financial irregularities.
- Was it an act of *hatred or revenge*? Jealousy, family quarrels, and other personal reasons may turn someone to violence. Labor disputes, racial enmities, and religious hatreds may lead to the malicious destruction of property.

To determine the motive, investigators should gather background information on victims and other persons who are normally in the area, scheduled to be in the area, or suspected of being in the area before and after the time of the explosion. Interviews should focus on determining any relationships between these individuals.

The motive may be inferred from the nature of the explosion. Terrorists, for example, hope to intimidate, receive publicity, and create fear. They have little reason to disguise their efforts. Saboteurs and bombers with more personal motives, on the other hand, often employ camouflage to conceal their identity. Sabotage is an attempt to diminish an opponent, and saboteurs need to conceal their actions to remain effective. Those motivated by fraudulent insurance gain, the desire to conceal a crime, or the achievement of some psychological satisfaction seek to disguise their efforts.

27. Delivery of Explosive Device

If the perpetrator had to break in to plant the explosive device, investigators should proceed as they would for a burglary. Check for signs of a break in, direction from which window panes were broken, and the presence of tool marks. Points of entry or exit should be examined for tire marks, foot impressions, fingerprints, and similar clues. Were doors and windows closed and locked? Is there evidence of tampering? Any trace evidence relating to the perpetrator's movements should be photographed and collected.

Determine if security measures were in place. Conduct interviews, observe, and study directives that restrict access and determine how closely they are followed. What are the procedures for deliveries (personnel, incoming shipments, receipt systems, and protection in transit and during storage)? Check on materials recently delivered. In some cases, the materials for the construction of the bomb may be sent separately and the bomb assembled within the facility.

If the explosive device was disguised in a package and shipped to the target, fragments of the packing, wrapping, and binding materials are useful in identifying the perpetrators. Special attention should be given to pieces of paper bearing writings. In addition, the edges of such items as stamps, tape, paper, and cardboard may linked to similar materials found in the lodgings or workplaces of suspects.

Finally, investigators should search files and databases for similar bombings. Previous crimes against similar targets or with similar *modus operandi* should receive special attention.

28. Determining the Crime

The explosion may be the result of carelessness or negligence and not an attempt to injure or damage property. Misuse or mishandling of explosives is generally a violation of state statues reg-

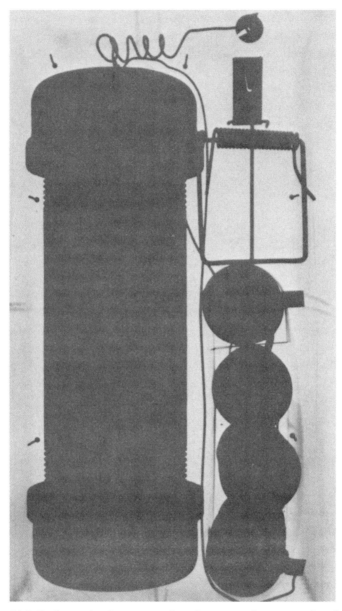

Figure 11-2. Radiograph of a suspected package, revealing a pipe bomb and a trigger mechanism.

ulating the transportation, manufacture, sale, storage, and handling of explosives.

Though state statutes regarding explosive material vary greatly, they commonly regulate four common areas. Places that *manufacture* explosives will be licensed with respect to location, construction, qualifications of specialized personnel, and the labeling of their products for shipment. Restrictions are placed on *transportation* and the type of carrier. Shipment on common carriers with passengers is forbidden. In some states the controls extend even to the type of motor used in the carrier. The places used for *storing* explosives are subject to laws that describe their size, construction, and location. Safety regulations regarding *sale and use* usually restrict the sale of explosives to legitimate users such as owners of construction companies, mines, quarries, and farm lands for clearing stumps or performing other clearance operations. Ordinarily, it is required that documentation and records be maintained.

ADDITIONAL READING

Arson

ATF Arson Investigative Guide. Washington, D.C.: U.S. Government Printing Office, 1986.

Baker, T.: *Introductory Criminal Analysis: Crime Prevention and Intervention Strategies.* Englewood Cliffs, NJ: Pearson Prentice-Hall, 2005.

Clede, B.: Arson Dog. *Law and Order, 36* (7), 1988.

DeArmond, H.T.: Automobile Arson Investigation. *Fire and Arson Investigator, 25* (3), 1975.

DeHaan, J.D.: *Kirk's Fire Investigation* (3rd ed.). Englewood Cliffs, NJ: Prentice-Hall, 1990.

Ferrall, R.T.: Arson Information: Who–What–Where? *FBI Law Enforcement Bulletin, 50* (5), 1981.

Goodnight, K.M.: Arson for Profit: The Insurance Investigation. *Police Chief, 57* (12), 1990.

Hart, F.: The Arson Equation: Arson + Circumstantial Evidence = Conviction. *Police Chief, 57* (12), 1990.

Hartnett, D.M.: Bombing and Arson Investigations Enhanced by Advances in ATF Labs. *Police Chief, 57* (4), 1990.

Henrikson, K.M.: K-9s Assist Investigators. *Law and Order, 44* (9), 1996.

Hobson, C.B.: *Fire Investigation: A New Concept.* Springfield, IL: Thomas, 1992.

Icove, D.J.: Serial Arsonists: An Introduction. *Police Chief, 57* (12), 1990.

Icove, D.J. and Estepp, M.H.: Motive-Based Offender Profiles of Arson and Fire-Related Crimes. *FBI Law Enforcement Bulletin, 56* (4), 1987.

Inciardi, J.A.: The Adult Firesetter: A Typology. *Criminology, 8* (145), 1970.

Kennedy, J. and Kennedy, P.: *Fires and Explosions: Determining Cause and Origin.* Chicago, Investigations Institute, 1985.

Levin, B.: Psychological Characteristics of Firesetters. *Fire and Arson Investigator 27* (3), 1977.

Lutz, W.E.: Computer Mapping Helps Identify Arson Targets. *Police Chief, 65* (5), 1998.

Molnar, G., Keitner, L. and Harwood, B.T.: A Comparison of Partner and Solo Arsonists. *Journal of Forensic Sciences, 29* (574), 1984.

O'Connor, J.J.: *Practical Fire and Arson Investigation.* New York: Elsevier, 1986.

Pilant, L.: Investigating Arson. *Police Chief, 64* (3), 1997.

Rider, A.O.: The Firesetter: A Psychological Profile. Parts I and II. *FBI Law Enforcement Bulletin, 49* (6 & 7), 1980.

Roblee, C.L., Mckechnie, A.J. and Lundy, W.: *The Investigation of Fires* (2nd ed.). Englewood Cliffs, NJ: Prentice Hall, 1988.

Thomas, R.B., Jr.: The Use of Canines in Arson Detection. *FBI Law Enforcement Bulletin, 58* (4), 1989.

Yereance, R.A.: *Electrical Fire Analysis.* Springfield, IL: Thomas, 1987.

Criminal Explosion

Berluti, A.F.: Connecticut's Explosive-Detecting Canines. *Police Chief, 58* (10), 1991.

Brodie, T.G.: *Bombs and Bombing.* Springfield, IL: Thomas, 1973.

Chisholm, J.J. and Icove, D.J.: Targeting Bombers. *Police Chief, 58* (10), 1991.

Fuller, T.C.: Bomb Threat: A Primer for the First Responder. *FBI Law Enforcement Bulletin, 68* (3), 1999.

Hartnett, D.M.: Bombing and Arson Investigation Enhanced by Advances in ATF Labs. *Police Chief, 57* (4), 1990.

Hiller, T.: Bomb Attacks in City Centers. *FBI Law Enforcement Bulletin, 63* (9), 1994.

Jernigan, D.K. and LaBrusciano, M.S.: Bomb Squads, Developing Mutual Aid Agreement. *FBI Law Enforcement Bulletin, 63* (10), 1994.

Kennedy, J. and Kennedy, P.: *Fires and Explosions: Determining Cause and Origin.* Chicago: Investigations Institute, 1985.

Laposata, E.A.: Collection of Trace Evidence from Bombing Victims at Autopsy. *Journal of Forensic Sciences, 30* (789), 1985.

Macdonald, J.M.: *Bombers and Firesetters.* Springfield, IL: Thomas, 1977.

Pilant, L.: Building a Better Bomb Squad. *Police Chief, 64* (9), 1997.

Stoffel, J.: *Explosives and Homemade Bombs* (2nd ed.). Springfield, IL: Thomas, 1972.

Styles, S.G.: The Car Bomb. *Journal of the Forensic Science Society, 15* (93), 1975.

Thurman, J.V.: Interpol Computers Keep Track of Firearms, Explosives. *Police Chief, 58* (10), 1991.

Twibell, J.D., et al.: The Persistence of Military Explosives on Hands. *Journal of Forensic Sciences, 29* (284), 1984.

——: Transfer of Nitroglycerine to Hands During Contact with Commercial Explosives. *Journal of Forensic Sciences, 27* (783), 1982.

Yallop, H.J.: *Explosion Investigation.* Harrogate, Eng.: Forensic Science Society Press, 1980.

Chapter 12

LARCENY AND BURGLARY

LARCENY

Larceny in General

1. Overview

LARCENY is one of the most common crimes. It is generally defined as the taking, obtaining, or withholding of money, personal property, or articles of value from the possession of the true owner or other party with legal possession, with the intent to permanently deprive or defraud another person of the use and benefit of the property. The elements of larceny customarily include the wrongfully *taking, obtaining,* or *withholding* of property with real value *of another* with the *intent to deprive.* If the intent is simply to temporarily deprive another person of the use or benefit, the offense is usually covered by *wrongful appropriation* statutes.

2. Taking, Obtaining, or Witholding

Generally, the perpetrator literally takes possession of the property, however, a perpetrator may also constructively possess the property by employing an agent or by other means. Examples of constructive possession include individuals who steal electrical energy by fraudulently bypassing the electric meter or have funds of another transferred to their own bank account. Examples of withholding include failure to return, account for, or deliver property to its owner when a return, account, or delivery is due. Individuals may commit larceny by using property for a purpose not authorized by its owner. For example, using company office supplies or tools for personal business might constitute larceny.

3. Ownership

The taking must be from the possession of the owner or someone with legitimate care, custody, management, or control. Unless an owner can be found, the charge of larceny cannot be supported. Ownership is commonly shown by a bill of sale or a record of continued possession. The owner might include an organization, government, corporation, estate, as well as an individual.

4. False Pretense

Larceny may be committed by false pretense or misrepresentation of fact (in some states this is a separate offense). For example, perpetrators may collect money by representing themselves as agents of a creditor or charity.

5. Intent

The perpetrator must have the intent to steal. This intent may exist at the time of the taking or may be formed afterward. Taking a car for a joy ride, intending to ride a short distance and return it, but then deciding to keep the car changes wrongful appropriation to larceny.

Intent in most cases can be inferred from the circumstances. If perpetrators take property, hide it, and deny knowledge of the property, the intent to steal can be inferred. Conversely, taking property openly and returning it would tend to disprove intent. A proof of subsequent sale of the property is strong evidence of intent to steal. Individuals may be guilty of larceny even though they intend to eventually return the property after collecting a reward for "finding" it. A person who pawns the property of another, intending to redeem it at a future date and return it to its owner, may be guilty of larceny. Once a larceny is committed, a return of the property or a payment is no defense.

6. Value

Investigators must establish the approximate value of the item. This element is important also in establishing the degree of larceny and in fixing punishment. The general rule is that value is the local, legitimate market value on the date of the theft.

There are many ways to determine value. In thefts of government property serviceable items are deemed to have values equivalent to the prices listed in official publications. Market value may be established by proof of the recent purchase price paid for the article on the legitimate market. Dealers, collectors, or assessors may be consulted to determine the value of an item. Owner may testify to value if they are familiar with the market value for items of similar quality and condition.

7. Miscellaneous Factors

Since larceny encompasses a variety of thefts, investigators will encounter a multitude of circumstances. Some common issues are included in this section.

A person *finding property* has an obligation to locate the owner. Taking it with intent to keep it is larceny, if there is a clue to the identity of the owner or if the owner may be found by the character, location, or marking of the property.

The *theft of several articles* at substantially the same time and place constitutes a single charge of larceny even though the articles may belong to different persons. When several articles are stolen at one time and the accused is found in possession of some of the articles, it can be presumed the individual stole them all.

The *total value of separate thefts* cannot be tabulated in a charge of larceny. If several larcenies are committed at different times from different owners, the value of the stolen items cannot be tallied to support a more serious charge.

Unexplained *possession of stolen property* is not sufficient. Though possession of stolen property normally raises a presumption that the accused stole it, investigators must acquire additional evidence linking the individual to the theft to support a charge of larceny. In most states possessing, receiving, and concealing stolen property is a separate offense.

Flight or absconding at the time of the larceny is a factor tending to establish guilt, but by itself, is not sufficient to support a conviction. As with mere possession of stolen property, investigators need to link the suspect to the theft to support a charge of larceny.

8. Motives

The most common motive for larceny is economic gain, but there may be other motives. Kleptomania is an obsessive impulse to steal. Persons suffering from this mental derangement will usually have a history of similar thefts and lack a definite plan for converting the property to their own use. Revenge and malicious mischief are other motives of larceny. People will sometimes steal solely to inconvenience others.

9. Investigative Procedure

The nature of the theft will determine the most appropriate investigative technique. Investigators should be familiar with various types of thieves, common *modus operandi,* and the specific factors of the case they are investigating. Table 12-1 lists some information useful in larceny investigations.

AUTOMOBILE LARCENY

10. Overview of Automobile Thefts

Nearly eight hundred thousand automobiles are stolen in the United States each year. Most automobile thieves are young white males. Many stolen vehicles are recovered because they were taken for temporary use rather than for resale. In areas where professional car thieves operate, fewer than half are recovered. Large municipal police departments commonly have special units consisting of detectives specifically training in the methods and practices of automobile thieves. Every state has laws relating to larceny of automobiles, but these laws are not uniform. The U.S. Code covers transporting stolen vehicles through interstate or foreign commerce. In addition, this law relates to the receiving, storing, selling, or disposing of a motor vehicle when it was known to have been stolen. While the following discussion focuses on automobile theft, much of it applies to the theft of other forms of motorized

Table 12-1. Larceny Information.

Date and time of the theft.	Precise time or range of time between when the property was last seen and the discovery of the theft.
List of property.	A complete list and description. If there are several witnesses who can offer this information, it should be obtained independently from each to verify.
Location	The location of the property immediately prior to the larceny; other places in which the property had been previously located; places searched for the property.
Reasons for placing the property in the location described above.	Is placing property in this location logical? Were there appropriate safeguards?
Identity of person who first discovered the loss.	How was the theft discovered? Was it logical for this person to make the discovery? Who should have ordinarily made the discovery? Other witnesses to the discovery.
List of those with opportunity.	A list of persons who knew the location of the property. A list of persons who knew of the existence of the property. A list of persons who had access to the property. Movements of persons having access prior. List of absentees in business establishments.
Ownership of the property.	Owner, person having possession at the time of theft, person responsible for the property. Proof of ownership, custody, or responsibility.
Estimated value of the property.	Bills of sale if possible or the approximate date of purchase and the identity of the vendor.
Suspects named by the owner or others.	Reasons for their suspicions. Employees exhibiting unusual behavior within the last month.

continued

Table 12-1—*Continued.*

Financial status	Suspects with financial problems or future money problems, or maintaining a standard of living inconsistent with their incomes.
Reconstruction of the larceny	Modus operandi; means of access; selection of time; attempts to conceal; false pretenses, the conversations and transactions between the perpetrator and victim or other parties.
Character of property	Saleability; uses; convertibility. List of possible markets for the property.
Interrogation of each suspect	Activities prior and subsequent to crime; last time he or she saw the property; last time he or she was last near the location of the property; any alibi witness; financial circumstances; present indebtedness; contemplated investments or purchases; relations with the owner.
Records	Previous larceny complaints made by the victim; history of thefts; employees with police records; background of suspects.
Interview	Interviews of neighbors, building employees, and others who may have observed persons approaching the area containing the property at unusual times or in a peculiar manner. Complete physical descriptions of any suspects developed in this manner.
Physical evidence	Latent fingerprints, shoe prints, articles of clothing, or similar traces left at the scene.

transportation and equipment.

a. **Temporary Appropriation**. Many cases of automobile larceny fall into this category. The motive is temporary use. The car is stolen, remains missing for a few days, is abandoned, then recovered and returned to the owner.

1) *Juveniles and Joy Rides*. The most common offenders are juveniles and young adults (under 25 years old) who steal vehicles

for temporary use. These are crimes of opportunity resulting when keys are left in an unattended vehicle. Many juveniles who steal vehicles in this manner have no previous arrest record.

2) ***Professional Criminals.*** Professional criminals sometimes steal a car to reduce their chances of being linked to a crime. A vehicle is often stolen from a location near the principle crime and quickly abandoned to limit the chance of being stopped by police for driving a stolen vehicle. After fleeing the crime scene they often drive to a secluded spot and then switch to their own vehicle. Since the stolen car is readily recovered, investigators are concerned with the major crime rather than the car theft.

3) ***False Report by Owner.*** Occasionally owners falsely report the theft of their vehicles to cover up serious accidents. Typically, they have injured a pedestrian and left the scene without stopping. On reflection, the seriousness of a hit-and-run charge and of the possibility or being recognized prompts them to report their vehicle as stolen. They may damage the car door or side window in order to give the appearance of a forced entry. They then abandon the vehicle and report the "theft" to police. Investigators should be suspicious of any "theft" where the recovered car shows signs of an accident. Check into all hit-and-run cases that occurred during the pertinent period to determine if the vehicle was involved.

b. **Professional Automobile Thieves**. Professional automobile thieves steal vehicles to resell or to strip for their parts. Some theft rings are well-organized groups that steal cars, disguise them, obtain fraudulent registrations, and sell them.

1) ***Stealing the Vehicle.*** The actual work of stealing a vehicle can be carried out by a professional within a few minutes. Typically, thieves target vehicles they think they can quickly steal without drawing attention. Anti-theft devices on modern passenger vehicles make it more difficult to steal vehicles. For most vehicles, the days of crossing two wires under the dash and driving off have long passed. Auto manufacturers have developed and installed devices that significantly increase the difficulty of car theft. These include: advances in alarm systems, fuel shut-offs, smart keys, GPS tracking systems, less accessible ignition system, increased number of ignition key combinations, and ignition system connector cables that are more difficult to remove from the ignition lock. In addi-

tion, combination ignition, transmission, and steering column locks are installed on all new cars.

While some of the following techniques will not work on newer vehicles, they are still effective when used on older vehicles and other forms of motorized transportation and equipment.

In older vehicles, locked doors are unlocked by inserting a "slim jim," (a thin, notched-bladed tool) to catch the lock button and raise it. Once in the vehicle, the ignition lock is defeated by jumping wires under the dash, using master keys (assortment of key combinations used by manufacturers), code cutter (device for cutting blank keys according to a car's ignition code number), or using a "slam-hammer" (tool designed to pull dents out of auto bodies) to remove the ignition lock. Auto thieves now use long, thin saws that can be inserted into the steering column to break the lock.

Some thieves simply use a tow truck to take the car away. Still others find means to copy the key to the vehicle. Thieves establish connections at a car wash, parking garage, or restaurant with a parking service and then make copies of the keys of selected cars. They can easily find the address of the registered owner of the vehicle from documents in the vehicle or barcode tags attached to key chains. Later, after locating the vehicle, thieves use the copy of the key to drive off.

Alarm systems can be neutralized by cutting or bypassing the correct wire. Malfunctioning car alarms are so common they frequently draw little attention. Thieves using a tow truck can defeat most alarm systems and locks while appearing to be legitimate workers.

2) *Identifying the Vehicle.* Passenger vehicles can be identified by means of the Vehicle Identification Number (VIN). A visible VIN will be found on a plate on top of the dash and driver's door or door frame. Hidden VIN numbers are stamped on various parts of the vehicle and locations are changed each year. The database of hidden VIN locations is maintained by the National Insurance Crime Bureau (NICB) to assist law enforcement in identifying stolen vehicles. Formed in 1992 with the merger of the National Automobile Theft Bureau (NATB) and the Insurance Crime Prevention Institute (ICPI), the NCIB is a nonprofit organization

and clearinghouse for information on vehicle theft. Along with maintaining databases on vehicle theft and insurance claims, the organization provides training for law enforcement and the insurance industry.

Professional car thieves may attempt to disguise a stolen vehicle by swapping its identity with a salvaged vehicle. Thieves will locate VIN stampings on a new car by removing the body to examine the chassis and auto frame. Knowing the locations, the car thieves remove the VIN of the stolen vehicle and replace them with those of a salvaged vehicle. The stolen vehicle is then sold and registered as the previously salvaged vehicle.

3) **Market**. The outlets thieves use to dispose of vehicles will depend on their *modus operandi*. Some focus on stealing parts, property, and electronics from vehicles to sell to fences or second-hand dealers. Others run "chop shops" that can disassemble a vehicle into parts for sale within a few hours after it is stolen. A team of specialists or "cutters" cut off the saleable parts and destroy the remainder. Some highly organized thieves may "sell to order" by first locating a buyer before stealing the vehicle. Theft rings may buy identification plates and registration papers of late-model wrecks. They then transform the identity of the stolen vehicle. In recent years an export market for stolen cars has been developed in places such as Mexico, Latin America, South America, and the Middle East.

11. Vehicle Fraud

A variety of frauds, many connected to insurance, are practiced by vehicle thieves. A number of these schemes require an elaborate organization, sometimes extending over several states. Rigorous salvage vehicle inspection programs requiring examination by trained vehicle inspectors before sale of a salvaged vehicle greatly reduce these types of fraud.

a. **Insuring a Wreck**. This is sometimes called the phantom car fraud. The perpetrator first buys a title and the vehicle registration number of a late model vehicle from a salvage yard. The transaction makes it appear as if the vehicle has been repaired to drivable condition. The vehicle information is used to register and insure it without taking possession of the vehicle. Several months later, the vehicle is reported stolen. By this time what was left of the car will have disappeared as scrap. The vehicle is never found and the owner is paid the replacement value of the vehicle.

b. **Duplicating from Salvage**. In this operation the thieves buy a wrecked car to obtain its identification papers. Subsequently they steal an identical car in good condition. The stolen car is then taken apart and the parts put back together again on the frame of the wrecked car. They have now duplicated the car for which they have legal papers and can sell it.

c. **Stripping the Car**. Perpetrators of this fraud strip their own vehicle to the frame, store the parts, and dump the skeleton in a lot. After reporting the car to the police as stolen, they anonymously report the location of the frame. The insurance company pays for the loss of the car, and the thieves sell the parts.

d. **The "Erector Set" Fraud**. As a continuation of the previous fraud, the owner will buy the frame from the insurance company for a few hundred dollars and take it to the garage for reassembly with the dismantled parts. These types of thefts declined when unibody construction became common for automobiles.

e. **Changing the VIN**. After stealing a vehicle, the VIN is removed and replaced with a new number. The numbers are changed also on other parts commonly stamped with identification numbers. Ostensibly, the vehicle is now a new car. Papers are obtained for it, often from another state. After a series of fabricated transactions, the car is put up for sale with an apparently genuine pedigree.

f. **Odometer Rollback Scheme**. The object of this fraud is to disguise a heavily used automobile so that it can be sold at the higher price as an almost-new vehicle. Perpetrators may replace worn parts such as floor mats, brake pedals, and tires. A mechanic called a "clocker" can readjust the odometer gauge in a matter of minutes.

12. Indications of a Stolen Automobile

Investigators and police officers sometimes encounter vehicles that are not yet reported as stolen. Clean registration tags on a dirty car or dirty tags on a clean car should prompt further investigation. New bolts with an old tag suggest that the tag was stolen. Bolts will usually show signs of rust after a month's exposure. A duplicate key, rather than a factory original, is suspicious. Broken or recently replaced windows may indicate a stolen vehicle. Original equipment windows will ordinarily have a trademark in the lower corner. Indications of tampering with the ignition switch, wiring, or any extraneous wires may warrant investigation.

13. Bicycle Theft

The popularity of bicycling in many parts of the country has produced both a market and a supply for the thieves. The value of bicycles has increased greatly. What was once a problem of "a few kids stealing bikes" can now be one of organized groups sweeping through a city. They fill a truck with stolen bikes and take them to a factory where they receive new paint and serial numbers, and then are sold as new bikes.

Some cities have responded by instituting mandatory bicycle registration programs. Registration aids in rapidly checking ownership and the recording of serial numbers of stolen bicycles in computerized databases.

When it becomes apparent that a theft-ring is operating, a full-scale investigation is required. Investigators should obtain the necessary information on the make, model, year of purchase, cost of the bicycle, and the serial number. The color of the paint, accessories, any marks of personal identification, defects, and damage are additional data to be recorded.

Where remanufacturing is occurring, investigators should attempt to locate the factory where the processing takes place. Depending on the size of the operation, this can require significant space. Automobile body shops can be diverted to bicycle conversion work. Sources of materials such as paints should be explored. Consultation with bicycle manufacturers may prove useful in ascertaining the nature of the equipment and the types of paint that would be used on the bicycles.

The patrol force is best suited to the field investigation of smaller operations. Bicycle riders should be questioned concerning ownership. Places where bicycles are sold should receive police attention. Sometimes stolen bicycles show up in bicycle stores. More commonly they are sold to bargain hunters on the street, in parks, in flea markets, or on the Internet.

PICKPOCKETS

14. Overview

Pickpockets are more likely found in large cities. Urban life with congested places and crowded transportation systems provides unending opportunity for the pickpocket. This type of criminal is, however, restricted by the great skill required to be successful. This skill can be a handicap in that success brings attention by police. In the age of the checkbook and the credit card the pickpocket is becoming less common. Fewer criminals have either the patience or the professional pride to devote years to their apprenticeship.

a. **Operational Techniques**. Pickpockets may work alone or with one or more associates. The purpose of the associate is to distract the victim. The *modus operandi* is of great importance in detecting pickpockets. Most pickpockets employ the same technique throughout their criminal careers. Pickpockets employ some of the techniques of professional magicians. Distracting the victim and acting swiftly are important to the pickpocket's success. Pickpockets are known by their style. Their designation is derived from the clothing area they target.

1) *Fob Worker*. Once the name used for lower skilled pickpockets who stole coins from the victim's fob pocket, today the term is used to describe operators who work from the front of the victim. They lift valuables from the most accessible places–front and side jacket pockets. They may be older pickpockets who have lost their nerve or touch. They sometimes use a handkerchief or "wipe" to cover their actions and to hide the theft.

2) *Inside Worker*. This is a more advanced operator with the skill necessary to remove a wallet from the inside pocket of a coat. To cover their operations, an inside worker usually employs a

"stiff," i.e., a newspaper that is placed against the victim. Very few pickpockets resort to inside work.

3) ***Pants Pocket Workers***. Pickpockets who steal from trouser pockets are considered the cleverest of thieves. A highly developed skill is necessary to take a wallet from a pocket without alerting the victim. The pants pocket worker uses only two fingers–the index and middle finger–to perform this operation. Sometimes they employ as many as two assistants. One of the assistants (the "stall") distracts by jostling the victim and then excusing him or herself. A newspaper may be employed in these motions. The other assistant receives the wallet in a quick pass from the operator. The "mechanic" or "tool" performs the actual picking of the pocket. The whole operation is accomplished quickly and precisely. While boarding a subway train or other vehicle, the "stall" will fall or push against the victim from the front and mutter regrets or muffled curses. Simultaneously, the "mechanic" will have lifted the wallet from the victim and passed it to an assistant. If the victim feels the theft and turns suspiciously, the pickpocket will run away. No longer having possession of the wallet, apprehension produces no evidence of the crime. The person who receives the wallet remains in the same position to avoid arousing suspicion. This person is usually someone without a previous conviction and would likely receive a suspended sentence if apprehended.

4) ***The Lush Worker***. This is the lowest form of pickpocket who steals from a drunk or a sleeping victim. Lush workers operate in trains, buses, street cars, waiting rooms, and parks. They select a prospective victim who is apparently sleeping or unconscious. Sometimes they test their victim by gently kicking or tapping them as they pass by. If the victim does not react, the lush worker proceeds to take the victim's money and other valuables.

5) ***Bag Stealers***. A bag or purse suspended from a victim's arm is an inviting target for the petty thief. In crowded areas such as department stores or trains, the thief may remove the bag or its contents without attracting attention. There are several forms of this theft. The *bag opener* surreptitiously opens the bag and then removes the valuables. The *bag clipper* cuts the strap, removes the wallet, and throws the bag away. The *bag snatcher* jerks the bag away from the victim's grasp.

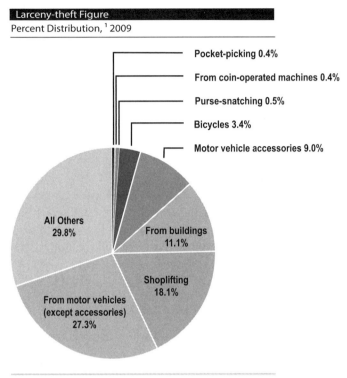

Figure 12-1. Source: FBI. *Uniform Crime Reports–2009.*

b. **Apprehending the Pickpocket**. Professional pickpockets will undoubtedly have a criminal record. The crime can frequently be solved by means of the *modus operandi*. The techniques of pickpockets are well known. Investigators can narrow the number of suspects by carefully listening to the victim's story, consulting the known pickpocket file, and showing photographs to the victim. The lush worker may be more difficult to find. If they confine their activities to a certain neighborhood or a particular transportation line, apprehension is more likely. Their weakness is a tendency to retain valuables that can be traced to their victims.

MISCELLANEOUS THIEVES

15. Baggage and Package Thieves

There is a wide variety of baggage and package thieves who plan or respond to opportunities to steal property. Baggage thieves target visitors to a city who park their vehicles near hotels, theaters and restaurants. Often working in teams, one person serves as a lookout and shield while the other breaks into the vehicle to steal luggage. Other baggage thieves will work public transportation sites to steal unattended luggage.

There are numerous forms of package theft. All of them rely upon careless practices of victims and delivery persons. One form of this crime is fraudulent receiving. The thief waits outside a business or residence for a delivery person. The thief chides the delivery person for being tardy, takes the package, and signs the receipt. Other package thieves steal from delivery vehicles when the driver enters a building or simply steal the vehicle if the keys are left in the ignition. Others steal packages left on top of mailboxes, door steps, or unattended property outside of businesses.

a. **Dishonest Employees**. The theft of merchandise, supplies, and equipment by dishonest employees can result in serious losses. Preventing employee theft requires careful background investigations of applicants prior to employment along with accountability measures and prudent monitoring of workers. On occasion, undercover work by an investigator posing as an employee may be appropriate.

b. *Shoplifters*. Department stores annually suffer considerable losses from shoplifting. The techniques of shoplifters are many and varied. Sometimes shoplifters work in collusion with a dishonest employee. Many retail stores have their own security personnel who are often equipped with extensive video monitoring capability to deal with this problem. Kleptomaniacs often target these stores. One form of shoplifting, once called pennyweighting, involves substituting merchandise. The thief, sometimes working with an accomplice, examines a piece of jewelry. When the salesperson is distracted, the thief substitutes imitation jewelry for the real piece. The operation must be "cased" and planned so that a reasonably similar substitute can be acquired.

c. **Hotel Thieves**. This type of thief steals jewelry, furs, or money from hotel rooms, sometimes working in collusion with a hotel employee. Property is stolen when guests are away from their rooms. Computerized keycard systems, that use individually programmed electronic combination cards to unlock doors and are changed when a guest checks out, have improved hotel security.

e. **Credit Card Fraud**. Credit and debit card theft and fraud remain an ongoing technological battle as our financial histories are reduced to magnetic strips and bar codes. Once only an issue of thieves making purchases with a stolen credit card until the card was reported stolen, today this fraud is widespread and practiced by organized crime and terrorist organizations.

Each advance in security is met by improvements in the technology used by criminals.

The adoption of countertop data processing units by merchants to verify the current status of an account has reduced some fraudulent transactions, but criminals respond with technological advances of their own. Some thieves are now capable of producing counterfeit cards that are exact replicas of bona-fide cards complete with the "hidden" security features.

RECEIVING STOLEN PROPERTY

Larceny investigations often evolve into cases of receiving stolen property. When locating stolen property, investigators should extensively search for physical evidence and thoroughly interview all suspects and witnesses to show involvement in a crime. These cases are difficult to prove and all avenues should be explored. Generally, the evidence is largely circumstantial. The accused often hides behind a legitimate business front leaving investigators to rely on the testimony of the thieves, who may testify against the fences in exchange for a lighter sentence. Suspects' activities should be investigated in minute detail. They should be extensively questioned and their responses checked carefully for discrepancies.

16. Investigative Questions

1) *Was the property stolen?* This is generally proven by testimony from the victim. The testimony of the thieves can also prove this element. Since the thieves are not accomplices to receiving stolen property, they may be persuaded to corroborate that the property was stolen. Sometimes, the thieves may agree to testify because they have already been convicted and have nothing to lose, or because they hope for some future leniency or consideration.

2) *Was the property received by the accused?* Again, the thieves can testify to this along with the property being found in the possession of the accused. If the stolen property was found in a location that could be accessed only by the accused, no difficulty exists. If others have access, they must be interviewed to eliminate all but the guilty. Investigators should try to show that stolen goods were located with other property of the accused or the accused was observed in possession of the property.

3) *Did the accused know the property was stolen?* This may be shown if the thieves testify that they told the accused it was stolen. It can also be shown indirectly if the purchase price was absurdly low; it was purchased from a person who could not have been the legitimate owner; or it was not purchased from an established business.

4) *Did the accused conceal or intend to convert the property to personal use?* During the search, note any attempt to conceal the stolen goods. Was there any evidence of efforts to dispose of the property?

17. Sting Operations

In a sting operation, police may pose as fences to buy stolen property from criminals. Typically, undercover detectives rent stores and warehouses in neighborhoods where burglaries and street thefts are common and begin the business of buying stolen goods. The building is equipped for surveillance, communications, and safety. An appropriate "front" is devised such as a small cleaning business or trucking operation. While one officer deals with the sellers of stolen property, another secretly operates surveillance equipment. Other surveillance officers may be positioned in buildings across the street from the store to record license plates, make other observations, and provide additional protection.

The site of the fencing operation should be readily observable, have accessible parking, and be away from public transportation to induce the sellers to use their own vehicles. Transactions are video recorded and interesting, clean-surfaced objects that can retain fingerprints should be out and available for handling by suspects. Negotiations should include attempts to learn phone numbers or locations where suspects may be reached. Casual conversations might also reveal the identity of other fences or the general nature and approximate date of the theft.

Sting operations can result in large numbers of arrests supported by recordings of criminals selling stolen property to police. These operations are expensive, however, and may even increase the number of thefts because they provide criminals with a ready outlet to dispose of stolen property.

A variation on the traditional sting to buy stolen property is the fugitive roundup sting. The purpose is to lure wanted persons to a place to be arrested. For example, an Illinois sheriff sent letters to the last known addresses of people with outstanding warrants. The letters, purported to be from an electronics company, sought to hire people to test new video games and electronic devices. The sting netted 102 fugitives who arrived at the designated time and place.

BURGLARY

18. Overview

Many burglary victims experience not only a loss of property but intense feelings of violation due to the invasion of their private spaces. Burglaries can be very traumatic and threatening for victims.

Most burglaries are committed by amateurs who strike close to home and choose targets of opportunity. Amateurs often commit many burglaries but generally do not profit significantly from them. If confronted during a burglary, they may panic and react violently. Professional burglars tend to commit fewer burglaries but profit more from each one. They carefully study their targets and plan their crimes to minimize both risk and evidence linking them to their crimes. Typically, a few individuals will be responsible for the majority of burglaries in an area. The use of surveillance, information, *modus operandi* files, and physical evidence can be effective when combined with crime analysis and computer mapping.

19. Definition

The definition of burglary varies in different states. In some jurisdictions degrees of burglary are distinguished in the law by the time of day and type of structures. Under common law, burglary is the breaking and entering in the nighttime of the dwelling house of another, with intent to commit a crime therein. The "crime therein" is usually taken to mean larceny but could be another offense.

20. Elements of the Offense

The elements of proof for the offense of burglary often include *breaking and entering,* the *dwelling house of another,* during *nighttime,* with the *intent to commit a crime* therein.

a. **Breaking and Entering**. There must be a breaking either actual (physical force) or constructive (trick or ruse). Entering a hole in the wall or a doorway where the door is standing open does not constitute breaking, while opening an unlocked door would. Entering through an open skylight, window, or other passage not intended for entry may constitute breaking in some states.

The essence of the break is the removal or putting aside of some material part of the house on which the dweller relies for security against intrusion. *Actual breaking* involves physical force to gain entry. Opening a closed door or window, unlocking or unlatching a door, lifting a fastening hook, pushing open a closed transom or trapdoor, removing a fastened screen, breaking a pane of glass, or cutting a screen are all examples of physical force. If a guest, lodger, or employee, already lawfully in the building, forces an inner door, a break has occurred. *Constructive breaking* involves the use of collusion, trick, ruse, intimidation, or impersonation to gain entry. A person who gains entry by impersonating a repairman has committed a break.

b. **Entry**. Crossing the threshold of a building with a long pole, hook, or any part of the body constitutes entry. If two people participate in a burglary, it is not necessary that both enter. If one enters, the other also commits burglary by being present and aiding in the entry.

c. **Dwelling House of Another**. The term *building* refers to a structure having four sides and a roof that is used to shelter people or property. A building could include freight cars, booths, tents, warehouses, garages, or sheds. The term *dwelling house* means a building used as a residence. Temporary absence of the occupant does not change the character of a dwelling house. If the occupants leave it temporarily with the intention of returning, though they may remain away for some time, the house remains a dwelling house. Dwellings used only during vacation periods and over weekends remain dwelling houses. The test lies in the occupant's or owner's intention to return.

b. **Nighttime**. Under common law, both the breaking and the entering must occur during the nighttime, but not necessarily the same night. Nighttime is defined as the period between sunset and sunrise, when there is not sufficient daylight to discern a person's face.

c. **Intent**. To constitute burglary, there must be intent to commit a specific offense within. The fact that the actual commission of the crime was impossible is immaterial. The breaking and entering is, ordinarily, presumptive evidence of intent to commit a crime therein. The crime intended by the burglar is in most cases larceny.

Investigators conducting burglary surveillances of suspects or places must not make arrests until the elements of proof are established. There is great temptation to arrest suspects as they make forced entry. An arrest at this time permits the criminals to escape the full crime, since they can be charged only with attempted burglary or illegal entry. A patient investigator will permit the burglars to enter and apprehend them after they have shown their intent to commit a crime therein.

21. Safe-Breaking

Criminals who attack safes have a wide variety of skills and characteristics. They may be highly skilled or bunglers, loners or part of a criminal team. Amateurs may spend hours employing crude methods without breaching the safe, while skilled safecrackers may open a safe relatively quickly and quietly.

Successful safe burglars tend to possess knowledge of safe construction, experience with power tools, patience, and tenacity. Safes vary in the degree of security they offer. Some are simply fire resistant boxes, while others are designed to be burglar resistant. Safe manufacturers are faced with contradictory purposes. They must design a safe to prevent entry by a burglar, yet allow locksmiths to gain access without destroying the contents should the mechanism malfunction or the customer lose the combination. Locksmiths rely on "drilling," "combination deduction," and "manipulation" as the preferred methods of opening a customer's safe.

a. **Safe-Breaking Methods**. An examination of the crime scene may reveal the extent of the burglar's expertise. Choice of method, ease of entry, quality of equipment, and precision of toolmarks are all indicative of level of proficiency.

1) ***Punch***. The "punch job" is a common method of opening safes. When performed by an expert, this operation is clean, quick, and reasonably quiet. Success depends on a moderate degree of skill and experience, an element of luck, selection of an appropriate safe, and the use of simple tools (sledge hammer and drift pin or center punch). The technique is relatively simple and is most effective on inexpensive or older safes. The dial is knocked off to expose the spindle. The spindle is the axle on which the tumblers or locking wheels rotate. A punch is then held against the spindle and hit sharply with the hammer. The spindle is driven back into the safe, knocking the locking mechanism out of position, releasing the lock, and allowing the handle to turn. Some safes are equipped with a relocking device that activates when the spindle is punched. Others will have a drive-proof spindle made out of a malleable metal which will flatten on impact and cannot be driven back against the lock. Investigator should look for toolmarks on the dial and the spindle.

2) **Peel.** While the punch takes only a few minutes when performed by a professional, the "peel" is physically demanding and may require several hours of strenuous work. It is commonly used after an unsuccessful punch. The objective is to separate the metal layers on the door (often riveted or spot-welded) to curl back the top layer to expose the lock or bolt. First, a hole is made in the corner of the door to insert a pry bar. The initial opening is commonly made by hammering the corner of the safe door to buckle the metal and then cutting it with a hacksaw, using a hammer and chisel to pop the spot welds or rivets, drilling it, or using an acetylene torch. A pry bar is then inserted into the opening and the top layer is curled back. This technique will not work on newer, seam-welded, burglar-resistant safes.

3) **Chopping.** A "chop job" involves cutting through the metal layers either to expose the locking mechanism or to make a hole in the safe large enough to remove the contents by hand (see Figure 12-2). Commonly a hammer and chisel or ax is used. The safe can be attacked on any surface, but generally the bottom is the weakest. One of the drawbacks of this method is that safes are often quite heavy and can be difficult to overturn. Chopping is not effective on the reinforced steel of a modern burglar-resistant safe.

4) **Carry out.** Sometimes the safe is physically removed and taken to another location to be worked on. This is more common with smaller safes.

5) **Blasting.** Blowing the safe with nitroglycerine is picturesque but not common. The noise and the danger are serious drawbacks. Measuring the correct amount of explosive requires both knowledge and experience. Too little and the safe won't open; too much and the contents of the safe will be destroyed or the burglar severely injured. In "the jamb shot," the nitroglycerine is permitted to drip slowly into the space between the safe door and the door jamb. If done correctly, when the charge is detonated the door will be blown open. In the "spindle" or "gut" shot, the dial of the safe is knocked off, the spindle is punched, and the nitroglycerine is poured through the locking mechanism and detonated, allowing the door to be opened. Other explosives, such as dynamite or military explosives, are also used.

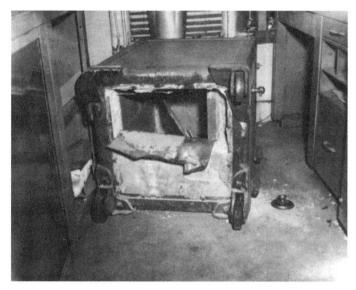

Figure 12-2. A "chop job." After overturning the safe, the burglar "ripped" through the bottom and bent the metal back. The dial on the right indicates the attack was preceded by an unsuccessful "punch." (Courtesy of Paschal Ungarino.)

6. ***Burning***. The "burn" or "torch" technique is one of the more effective methods of penetrating the burglar-resistant safe. Safe burglars often use either an oxyacetylene torch that can operate at temperatures over 4000 degrees, or the "thermal lance" or "burning bar," that can produce heat in excess of 7000 degrees. Such temperatures will burn a hole through almost any metal.

Oxyacetylene torches have many industrial uses but can be quite dangerous in the hands of the amateur. The operator of the torch must be reasonably skilled. A common method is to burn a circular hole around the dial to permit access to the lock. Cuts that are even and in appropriate areas are evidence of an experienced worker. An excess of black soot around the burn indicates an incorrect proportion of oxygen to acetylene. Any tanks, torches, and gauges left at the scene may have serial numbers that are often traceable.

The thermal lance or burning bar is a tool used for cutting steel and other metals for construction, demolition, shipbuilding, and

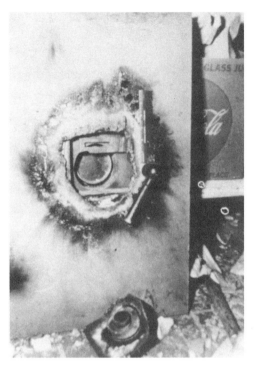

Figure 12-3. The use of an oxyacetylene torch around the dial. The rough cuts and black soot are indicative of a lack of skill. (Courtesy of Paschal Ungarino.)

other industrial purposes. Capable of reaching temperatures in excess of 7000 degrees, the thermal lance can penetrate any metal surface but consumes oxygen at a rapid rate and produces a great amount of smoke, gases, and slag making it difficult just to see and breathe, let alone operate a torch in a confined area. Moreover, some safe manufacturers insert into the wall of the safe a layer of metal that conducts heat, such as copper. This layer disperses the heat over a wider area protecting temporarily the steel underneath and slows the progress of the torch.

7) *Drilling*. In skilled hands, the drill can be effective in overcoming the defenses of a burglar-resistant safe. A high-torque drill equipped with a carbide or diamond-tipped bit is held in place by a "jig" bolted to the safe to pierce drill-resistant metals. Success with this method requires a degree of skill because the drill bits

have a tendency to bind and break with any movement of the drill or when the drill passes through metals of different temper and thickness. Locksmiths who specialize in safes have access to "drill-ing instructions" provided by the manufacturer for the simplest and least destructive method of opening any safe model. Another helpful instrument for both the locksmith and the burglar is the "borescope." This is a lighted fiber-optic instrument designed to be inserted into small holes to look into and around darkened cavi-ties. After a hole has been drilled in the safe, a borescope can be used to peer inside in order to examine its contents or to align the wheels so that the combination can be deduced.

Instead of using a solid drill bit, sometimes a core drill with a hollow cylindrical bit is used (see Figure 12-4). The core drill will create a circular hole in the safe large enough to reach in and remove its contents. It is bolt-mounted onto the safe because any movement will result in a binding and breaking of the bit. Broken drill bits and the marks of the drill mounts should be photo-

Figure 12-4. A core drill was used to expose the locking mechanism. The stains on the front of the safe are from a lubricant for the drill. (Courtesy of Paschal Ungarino.)

graphed and preserved for a possible comparison with tools found in the possession of a suspect.

8) **Combination Deduction**. This is a general phrase for determining the combination from information in the environment. *Manipulation* is the art of opening a safe using only the senses of sight, hearing, and touch. The few who are adept at this skill are usually employed as locksmiths or safe manufacturing and are not criminals. Most burglaries that appear to be cases of manipulation are really the result of careless employees who neglect to close the safe properly or who leave the combination hidden in some obvious place. Experienced burglars are familiar with the habits of workers trying to simplify their jobs. For example, an employee at closing time may give the dial only a half turn to open the safe more quickly the next morning. The safe is not actually locked, and the burglar has merely to reverse the half turn to open the safe. This practice is called putting the safe on "day-lock." It derives its name from the habit of business operators leaving the safe in this condition during the day so that they do not have to redial the entire combination every time they need to open it.

Some employees leave the combination "hidden" in some fairly obvious place to make sure they won't forget it. It may be written on the inside cover of a record book, on the side of a desk drawer, or on a door or window frame. It will be somewhere near the safe "where they won't lose it."

Safe owners may use their birthday, their wedding anniversary, their Social Security number, or some other significant number in their lives to supply the digits for their combination number. Others may not change the trial combination. New safes will already be equipped with a combination set by the manufacturer. This is called a "trial" or "try-out" combination. Each manufacturer has a set of trial combinations so that they will be able to open any safe coming from their factory. It is up to the purchaser of the safe to install a new combination. Neglecting to change the trial combination makes the owner vulnerable to a safecracker who has access to these numbers.

Burglars may employ surveillance methods to discern the combination to a safe. A "bug" placed near the safe door may pick up a conversation concerning the combination. A hidden video camera timed to photograph the opening of the safe each day, or just observing the dial regularly, may reveal the final number after each opening. With a three-digit lock, it is feasible over time to try out all of the possible combinations in order to determine the other two numbers.

True manipulation of the combination is based on the characteristics of the locking mechanisms of the safe. Each wheel of the lock is notched. When the notches of all three wheels are aligned, a lever will drop into the notched area releasing the bolt. When the wheels are not aligned, the lever will make a noise as it drops slightly as it passes over the notch. The points at which the lever enters and leaves the notched area are called the "contact points." Recording the numbers that are on the dial as the lever passes over the contact points on each wheel will provide the information needed to determine the combination. Manipulation is a challenging but by no means impossible skill to acquire. A stethoscope or electronic listening aids are very helpful. Safe manufacturers, however, make the task more difficult with the use of quieter wheels, false wheel notches, and the addition of extraneous sounds, all introduced to foil the would-be manipulator.

b. **How Safe Is a Safe?** Frequently, investigators are summoned to the scene of a safe burglary to find a dazed proprietor exclaiming, "Look what they did to my safe! How is it possible?" There the safe lies on its back, the door pried open, and the carefully maintained records scattered about the room. A thin coat of white powder (safe insulation) covers everything. Tools and miscellaneous debris are strewn about the area. The proprietor may have owned the safe for years with an unrealistic sense of security. A safe (a metal container with a combination lock) means to the proprietor an impregnable, burglarproof iron box.

Safe manufacturers, however, take a different view. They do not think (nor should safe owners) the average safe to be burglarproof. To them, it is a strongbox, a deterrent to casual larceny and a protection in the event of fire. The heavy doors that appear as an eight-inch wall of steel are in reality relatively thin metal layers containing fireproofing material. No safe is completely "burglarproof," since time and equipment will eventually prevail over the strongest construction. However, safe companies do produce burglar-resistant safes that are constructed to offer more security than a fireproof strongbox.

c. *Safe Construction*. The ordinary safe is simply fire resistant. It is constructed of sheet-steel boxes separated by several inches of insulation to protect documents from fire. It serves also as a deterrent to the thief, and may be equipped with relocking devices and burglar-resistant locks. The burglar-resistant safe, on the other hand, is built to withstand the efforts of an experienced burglar for a number of hours. It will be seam-welded with laminated steel and designed to repel any attempt at "peeling" or "chopping" of the safe walls. The walls will be layered with drill-resistant and torch-resistant metals. The more advanced models may have features to guard the safe against explosion or manipulation. As a protection from fire, the safe will be imbedded in concrete or placed within a larger fire-resistant box.

22. Commercial Burglaries

Most burglars are unskilled, while a few are highly skilled. For the most part, the selection of the point of entry and the method of breaking are determined by the opportunities and weaknesses of the building and its condition. Burglars may enter through unlocked doors or windows, but more often break windows or force locks to gain entry. Most commercial establishment are targeted via the first floor.

23. Loft Burglars

Loft burglars specialize in stealing merchandise from lofts and are often highly skilled. They may burglarize safes and carry practically the same tools as a safe burglar. They frequently possess some knowledge of the worth of merchandise and the ability to distinguish between cheap and high quality items. In addition, the loft burglars must be acquainted with fences who will dispose of the goods.

a. *Planning*. A loft job is usually elaborately "cased." The leader has accurate knowledge of the layout, protection system, merchandise on hand, and the habits of the personnel. This information may sometimes be obtained through a dishonest employee, but more often through ruse, observation, and personal inspection.

b. *Gaining Entry*. The entry usually takes place at night, preferably over the weekend when the area is relatively quiet. A common point of entrance is the skylight. Burglars may have access to a nearby building which they use to reach the roof of their target building. They may break the glass of a skylight, break in through a window (if not wired or barred), use the fire escape ladder force a door or window, or enter through a delivery chute. Some burglars enter the establishment while it is open and then hide until personnel depart at the close of business.

c. *Removing the Goods*. Loft burglars often use a truck to remove the merchandise. Since the burglary takes place in a business section of the city, the presence of a truck is unnoticed. The goods are later brought to a "drop-off" to be inspected by the receiver.

24. Apartment House Burglars

Large multiple dwelling buildings offer many advantages to burglars. Ordinarily, most tenants do not know each other and the appearance of a new face will not arouse suspicion. Once burglars gain entrance, their activities will seldom attract the attention of the neighbors. Even the appearance of a moving truck and strangers cleaning out an apartment may not arouse suspicion.

a. *Gaining Entry*. Burglars may select their target by observing the lights from the street and noting apartments with darkened windows. If the building has a common security door, burglars may use a ruse to get other residents to open the door. Entry into the apartment may be accomplished by slipping the lock or jimmying a window. If the building is protected by a doorman or guard, the burglar may enter an unguarded entrance or from the roof. If using the roof, burglars may "hit" four or five apartments in one night. Entry may also be facilitated by the lack of security of residents. Many apartment dwellers are careless about locking their doors. The "door shaker," burglar simply goes through a big apartment building or a hotel trying doors until one is found unlocked or ajar.

b. ***Procedure***. Once inside, burglars search closets and dressers for valuables such as jewelry, furs, electronic devices, and money. Sometimes they empty the drawers of dressers and cabinets on the bed or floor to facilitate the search.

c. ***Leaving the Building***. On departing, burglar may leave the stolen property in the hallway and emerge empty-handed to see if they are being watched. If it appears clear, they return to pick up the items and depart.

25. Suburban Burglars

Some burglars exploit the perception that suburban middle-class communities are safe and crime-free. These burglars take advantage of modern lifestyles with adults away at work and children in school leaving the home vulnerable to daytime burglary. Homes are sufficiently detached to enable burglars to work unnoticed. Targets are often selected by the absence of lights in the early evening and open doors revealing empty garages. Burglars may approach from the rear and try the bell to assure no one is home. Failing any response or signs of activity, breaking a window provides easy access. Even if they do not break in, bicycles, lawn mowers, and power tools are readily accessible from the open garage. The success of such burglaries is attributable to the carelessness of the homeowner rather than to skills of the burglars.

a. ***The Commuter Burglar***. Commuter burglars tend to be city dwellers that travel many miles to find their victims. They spend little time selecting their targets, and are a difficult problem for police. They operate across jurisdictions and are rarely seen twice in the same neighborhood. Typically, they drive to a residential area and cruise about until they find a house that appears to·be unoccupied. Burglars then ring the doorbell. If the homeowner answers, directions are requested to another address. If no one answers, they break into the house.

b. ***Delivery Trucks***. Some of these burglars use delivery vans to cart away items such as electronic and entertainment equipment or other valuables. Delivery trucks are common and rarely attract attention. Another ruse is to pose as a repair service using an appropriately marked truck. Sometimes genuine repair and service workers are also burglars who find targets of opportunity to break into when not on legitimate service calls.

c. ***Dinner/Party Burglars***. These burglars target wealthy suburban neighborhoods for social gatherings at large houses. While the family and guests are preoccupied with dinner in one area of a large house, burglars are busy in the relatively remote bedroom area searching the rooms for jewelry and cash. The early evening hours are promising for this sort of activity, since it is too early for the burglar alarms to be switched on. (An intelligent dog provides effective protection against this type of intruder.)

26. Vacation Home Burglary

The off-season breaking and entering of vacation houses is a relatively common offense in rural and resort areas. Thousands of vacation homeowners throughout the country are finding that their rural havens are targets for off-season burglars and vandals. Each year more vacation homes are built with more elaborate furnishings and equipment. With the burgeoning population these homes are scattered over a much wider area, presenting a serious problem to a police force. Many of these houses are hidden away or located in remote locations on roads that are little used in the summer and are impassable in the winter. The normal patrol of the sheriff's department or state troopers provides little protection in these areas.

27. Physical Evidence

Because of the frequency of burglaries and the variety of evidence associated with burglary scenes, they offer an excellent opportunity for crime scene investigators to maintain and hone their skills. Investigators often find trace evidence (hair, fibers, glass, etc.), tool marks, fingerprints, footwear prints, and DNA.

On arriving at the scene, investigators should first search the building for the burglar. Experience has shown that burglars are sometimes interrupted and find their path of escape blocked. This is particularly true of large buildings where burglars may deem it safer to conceal themselves than to risk fleeing the building. Police

Table 12-2. Common Burglary Evidence.

Footwear	Impressions around point of entry. Prints on smooth floors, furniture stepped upon, and papers discarded on floors. Prints are especially likely if a safe was attacked and safe insulation exposed.
Fingerprints	Most likely on smooth, nonporous surfaces or painted surfaces including some doors and trim, countertops, switch plates and high gloss walls, bottles, and glasses. (Perpetrators sometimes drink the victim's alcoholic beverages.) Focus on objects that have been moved and areas where items have been taken or force used. Prints may be found, but are less likely, on unfinished wood surfaces, door knobs, dressers, furniture, cartons and crates, textured surfaces on appliances and safes, plaster/plaster board walls, tools, and papers.
DNA	DNA may be found from hair, clothes left or discarded at the scene, bottles and glasses, blood droplets and smears around broken windows.
Trace Evidence	Hair and fibers; glass fragments, safe insulation, soil in suspects shoes or clothing, paint from doors and windows on tools used to force entry.
Tool Marks	Doors/windows at point of entry, doors that secure valuables.
Signature Habits	Some burglars drink the victims' alcohol or eat their food, urinate or defecate on the floor, or do other odd activities that along with providing physical evidence can help link crimes together or produce leads from M.O. files.

officers responding to the call should search the building and neighborhood for the burglar.

The point of entry is often a productive source of evidence. Hair, fiber, fingerprints, and even blood are frequently found on or adhering to broken glass. Tool impressions may be found on doors or windows. DNA may be found on discarded cigarettes or clothing left behind. Footwear impression and prints are also common around the point of entry.

TRACING MATERIALS AND DETECTIVE DYES

28. Overview

Some thefts or drug cases lend themselves to the use of tracing materials. Property treated with a tracing material will temporarily mark anyone who touches it. After coming into contact with the tracing material, it may also be possible to reconstruct perpetrators' movements through the items they touch. Money may be treated so a thief or drug dealer can be identified once he or she handles the money.

29. Methods

There are three basic types of tracing material: staining, fluorescence, and chemical detectors.

a. **Staining**. A powder is used that reacts to the moisture in the skin to become a dye. The powder is selected for the permanence of its stain and for its color. If a brown wallet, for example, is to be treated, a powder of similar color is selected.

b. **Fluorescent**. A disadvantage of using staining powders is that it might immediately alert the suspect and the stain can be removed by persistent washing. To avoid alerting the suspect to the tracing material, a powder that fluoresces under ultraviolet radiation can be used. The powder is used in small quantities and is invisible to the suspect. Under the ultraviolet lamp it fluoresces brightly.

Table 12-3. Common Staining Powders.

Name	Color-Dry	Color-Wet
Crystal Violet	Green	Violet
Chrysoidine	Maroon	Orange
Malachite Green	Green	Green
Methylene Blue	Dark Green	Blue
Rhodamine B	Brown	Cherry

Table 12-4. Common Fluorescent Powders.

Name	Visible Color	Color in Ultraviolet
Fluorescein	Maroon	Yellow
Rhodamine B	Brown	Orange
Uranyl Nitrate	Yellow	Yellow

c. **Chemical Detectors**. These are mixed into liquids that are subject to theft or illicit use. Later a chemical indicator or a fluorescent material can be detected.

30. Applications

Tracing materials can be used in a wide variety of situations, and investigators are limited only by their imaginations in finding applications.

d. **Thefts**. Systematic larcenies in common areas such as dormitories or locker rooms may provide uses for tracing materials. If wallets or pocketbooks are being stolen, a "plant" can be treated with tracing substances of a similar color. A close surveillance should be maintained to note any effort to wash off a stain. The suspect may wipe off the stain with a handkerchief or may wear gloves, and they should be seized if suspected. On apprehension the subject's hands should be examined. Traces of the stain will usually be visible in the borders of the fingernails. If a fluorescent powder is used, traces may remain on the hands or cling to the clothes of the subject after many hours.

e. **Burglaries**. Systematic burglaries can be detected by tracing materials if there is a known and limited group of suspects. Fluorescent powders can be used around likely points of entry. Doorknobs, locks, latches, and sills should be dusted with the powder. Care should be exercised so that other persons do not innocently touch these areas without the knowledge of the investigator. A line-up of suspects or personnel having access to the area should be conducted after a burglary.

f. **False Alarms**. An excellent means of detecting persons who pull fire alarms is the use of a dye which will withstand varying

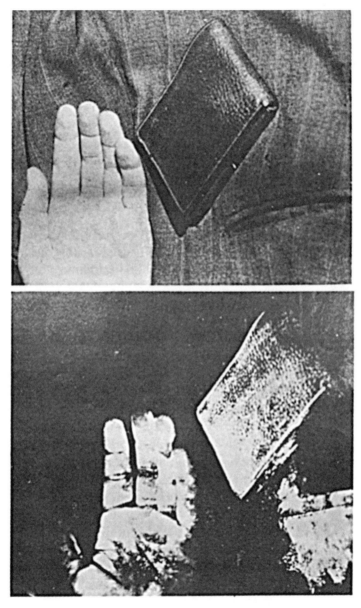

Figure 12-5. Fluorescent powder can be used to detect the perpetrator of a theft. At the top, objects labeled with this powder are seen under ordinary light. At the bottom, the same objects are photographed under ultraviolet light.

weather conditions. A saturated solution is painted on a part of the handle that is not in the line of view.

g. **Fuel Thefts**. By adding a chemical indicator to the gasoline supply, theft of the fuel can be detected in samples taken from the cars of suspects. A chemical marker, such as phenolphthalein or a florescent agent may be used.

h. **Explosives**. Some countries add taggants to explosives to provide immediate investigative leads and to trace the explosive. This process still remains controversial in the United States.

31. Radioactive Tracers

With the widespread availability of radioactive substances it is practicable for the investigator to use these materials as tracing substances. Their presence can be detected with a survey meter.

ADDITIONAL READING

Larceny

Associated Press: Illinois Sheriff: 102 Fugitives Duped by Electronics Sting. *Tribune Star,* A4, October 5, 2011.

Bailey, L.L.: Medicaid Fraud. *FBI Law Enforcement Bulletin, 60* (7), 1991.

Baker, T.J.: Combating Art Theft: International Cooperation in Action. *Police Chief, 63* (10), 1996.

Beseler, P.R.: Operation Cellmate. *FBI Law Enforcement Bulletin, 66* (4), 1997.

Chadd, G.L.: Retail Theft Investigation: Embezzlement, Falsely Reported as an Armed Robbery. *Law and Order, 39* (4), 1991.

Dubé, D.M.: Bank Employee Embezzlement. *FBI Law Enforcement Bulletin, 60* (4), 1991.

Gates, D.F. and Martin, W.E.: Art Theft - A Need for Specialization. *Police Chief, 57* (3), 1990.

Glick, R.G. and Newsom, R.S.: *Fraud Investigation.* Springfield, IL: Thomas, 1974.

Hollinger, R.C. and Clark, J.P.: *Theft by Employees.* Lexington, MA: Lexington Books, 1983.

Keeley, M.P. and Gannon, J.J.: Sneak Thefts. *FBI Law Enforcement Bulletin, 58* (12), 1989.

Kitchens, T.L.: The Cash Flow Analysis Method: Following the Paper Trail in Ponzi Schemes. *FBI Law Enforcement Bulletin, 62* (8), 1993.

Mazzone, G.L.: Travelling Criminals: Take the Money and Run. *FBI Law Enforcement Bulletin, 63* (7), 1994.

O'Brien, J.T.: Telecommunications Fraud: Opportunities for Techno-Criminals. *FBI Law Enforcement Bulletin, 67* (5), 1998.

Slotter, K.: Hidden Faces: Combating Telemarketing Fraud. *FBI Law Enforcement Bulletin, 67* (3), 1998.

——: Plastic Payments: Trends in Credit Card Fraud. *FBI Law Enforcement Bulletin, 66* (6), 1997.

Thrasher, R.R.: Voice-Mail Fraud. *FBI Law Enforcement Bulletin, 63* (7), 1994.

Uniform Crime Report. Available at http://www2.fbi.gov/ucr/cius2009/offenses/index.html.

Weber, T.L.: *Alarm Systems and Theft Prevention.* Stoneham, MA: Butterworth, 1985.

Windsor, D.L.: Timber Theft: A Solvable Crime. *FBI Law Enforcement Bulletin, 68* (9), 1999.

Yeager, W.B.: *Techniques of the Professional Pickpocket.* Port Townsend, WA: Loompanics, 1990.

Automobile Theft

Beekman, M.E.: Automobile Insurance Fraud Pays . . . and Pays Well. *FBI Law Enforcement Bulletin, 55* (3), 1986.

——: Auto Theft: Countering Violent Trends. *FBI Law Enforcement Bulletin, 62* (10), 1993.

Beekman, M.E. and Daly, M.R.: Motor Vehicle Theft Investigations: Emerging International Trends. *FBI Law Enforcement Bulletin, 59* (9), 1990.

Brickell, D. and Cole, L.S.: *Vehicle Theft Investigation.* Santa Cruz, CA: Davis Pub., 1975.

Casey, S.J.: Car Thieves Smell a RATT. *FBI Law Enforcement Bulletin, 64* (11), 1995.

Chilimedos, R.S.: *Auto Theft Investigation.* Los Angeles: Legal Book Corp., 1971.

Clede, B.: Lo-Jack. Law and Order, 36 (10), 1988.

Colombell, W.E.: Examination of Vehicle Identification Numbers. *FBI Law Enforcement Bulletin, 46* (6), 1977.

Cook, C.W.: *The Automobile Theft Investigator.* Springfield, IL: Thomas, 1986.

Finn, P.: Labeling Automobile Parts to Combat Theft. *FBI Law Enforcement Bulletin, 69* (4), 2000.

Frazier, S.F.: A Comprehensive Approach to Auto Theft. *Law and Order, 35* (2), 1987.

National Insurance Crime Bureau. Available at https://www.nicb.org//.

Nilson, D.W.: Vehicle Recovery: New Technology Captures Chicago's Attention. *Law and Order, 38* (2), 1990.

Poplinger, C.A.: VINSLEUTH: Outsmarting the VIN Changers. *Police Chief, 53* (5), 1986.

Rapp, B.: *Vehicle Theft Investigation: A Complete Handbook.* Port Townsend, WA: Loompanics, 1989.

Scripture, J.E., Jr.: Odometer Rollback Schemes. *FBI Law Enforcement Bulletin, 59* (8), 1990.

Stern, G.M.: Effective Strategies to Minimize Auto Thefts and Break-Ins. *Law and Order, 38* (7), 1990.

Shoplifting

Baumer, T.L. and Rosenbaum, D.P.: *Combating Retail Theft: Programs and Strategies.* Stoneham, MA: Butterworth, 1984.

Brindy, J.: *Shoplifting: A Manual for Store Detectives* (rev. ed.). Matteson, IL: Cavalier, 1975.

Curtis, B.: Retail Security: *Controlling Loss for Profit.* Stoneham, MA: Butterworth, 1983.

Farrell, K.L. and Ferrara, J.A.: *Shoplifting: The Antishoplifting Guidebook.* Westport, CT: Praeger, 1985.

Murphy, D.J.I.: *Customers and Thieves.* Brookfield, VT: Gower, 1986.

Rapp, B.: *Shoplifting and Employee Theft Investigation.* Port Townsend, WA: Loompanics, 1989.

Sklar, S.L.: *Shoplifting: What You Need to Know about the Law.* New York: Fairchild, 1981.

Criminal Receiving

Frazier, S.K.: *The Sting Book: A Guide to Setting Up and Running a Clandestine Storefront Sting Operation.* Springfield, IL: Thomas, 1994.

French, M.P.: Is a Sting Feasible for Your Agency? *Police Chief, 57* (4), 1990.

Klockers, C.B.: *The Professional Fence.* New York: Free Press, 1975.

Klose, K., Lewis, A.B. and Shaffer, R.: *Surprise! Surprise! How the Lawmen Conned the Thieves.* New York: Viking, 1978.

Langworthy, R.H. and LeBeau, J.L.: Spatial Evolution of a Sting Clientele. *Journal of Criminal Justice, 20* (2), 1992.

Law Enforcement Assistance Administration. *Strategies of Combatting the Criminal Receiver.* Washington, D.C.: U.S. Government Printing Office, 1976.

McGuire, M.V. and Walsh, M.E.: *The Identification and Recovery of Stolen Property Using Automated Information Systems: An Investigator's Handbook.* Washington, D.C.: U.S. Government Printing Office, 1981.

Nielsen, S.C.: The Small Agency and Sting Operations. *Law and Order, 35* (6), 1987.

Raub, R.A.: Effects of Antifencing Operations on Encouraging Crime. *Criminal Justice Review, 9* (78), 1984.

Sharp, A.G.: Stings Are Not Just for Large Departments. *Law and Order, 38* (5), 1990.

Steffensmeier, D.J.: *The Fence: In the Shadow of Two Worlds.* Totowa, NJ: Rowman and Littlefield, 1986.

Trainum, J., Brown, N. and Smith, R., Jr.: ROP-ing in Fences. *FBI Law Enforcement Bulletin, 60* (6), 1991.

Walsh, M.E.: *The Fence: A New Look at the World of Property Theft.* Westport, CT: Greenwood Press, 1976.

Weiner, K.A., Stephens, C.K. and Besachuk, D.L.: Making Inroads Into Property Crime: An Analysis of the Detroit Anti-Fencing Program. *Journal of Police Science and Administration, 11* (311), 1983.

Computer Crime

Barret, S. and Joyce, M.: Computers and Crime. *Police Chief, 65* (5), 1998.

Carter, D.L. and Katz, A.J.: Computer Crime: An Emerging Challenge for Law Enforcement. *FBI Law Enforcement Bulletin, 65* (12), 1996.

Herig, J.A.: Computer Evidence Recovery. *Police Chief, 65* (1), 1997.

Meyer, J.F. and Short, C.: Investigating Computer Crime. *Police Chief, 65* (5), 1998.

Noblett, M.G.: The Computer: High-Tech Instrument of Crime. *FBI Law Enforcement Bulletin, 62* (6), 1993.

Pilant, L.: Electronic Evidence Recovery. *Police Chief, 66* (2), 1999.

Sauls, J.G.: Computer Searches and Seizures. *FBI Law Enforcement Bulletin, 62* (6), 1993.

Schmidt, H.: The Changing Face of Computer Crime. *Police Chief, 65* (5), 1998.

Burglary

Baker, T.: *Introductory Criminal Analysis: Crime Prevention and Intervention Strategies.* Upper Saddle River, NJ: Pearson Prentice Hall, 2005.

Barnard, R.L.: *Intrusion Detection Systems: Principles of Operation and Applications.* Stoneham, MA: Butterworth, 1981.

Bennet, T. and Wright, R.: *Burglars on Burglary: Prevention and the Offender.* Brookfield, VT: Gower, 1984.

Bopp, W.J.: A Profile of Household Burglary in America. *Police Journal, 59* (168), 1986.

Conklin, J.E. and Bittner, E.: Burglary in a Suburb. *Criminology, 11* (206), 1973.

Cromwell, P.F., Olsen, J.N. and Avary, D.W.: *Breaking and Entering: An Ethnographic Analysis of Burglary.* Newbury Park, CA: Sage, 1991.

Davis, M.: *Prevent Burglary: An Aggressive Approach to Total Home Security.* Englewood Cliffs, NJ: Prentice-Hall, 1986.

Dunckel, K.: Unsafe Safes. *Law and Order, 36* (9), 1988.

Dussia, J.: Safe Burglary Investigation. *FBI Law Enforcement Bulletin, 36* (11), 1967.

Green, E.J. and Booth, C.E.: Cluster Analyses of Burglary M/Os. *Journal of Police Science and Administration, 4* (382), 1976.

Hackl, F.-X.: Trap Substances. *International Criminal Police Review, 27* (108), 1972.

Macdonald, J.M.: *Burglary and Theft.* Springfield, IL: Thomas, 1980.

Maguire, M. and Bennet, T.: *Burglary in a Dwelling: The Offense, the Offender and the Victim.* Brookfield, VT: Gower, 1982

Meiners, R.P.: Store Diversion Burglaries. *FBI Law Enforcement Bulletin, 59* (3), 1990.

Murphy, R.B. and Horton, S.: Focus on Burglary: A Management Approach to Prevention of Crime, *Police Chief, 42* (11), 1975.

Pope, C.E.: *Crime Specific Analysis: An Empirical Examination of Burglary Offender Characteristics.* Washington, D.C.: U.S. Government Printing Office, 1977.

——: *Crime Specific Analysis: The Characteristics of Burglary Incidents.* Washington, D.C.: U.S. Government Printing Office, 1977.

Rapp, B.: *The B & E Book: Burglary Techniques and Investigation.* Port Townsend, WA: Loompanics, 1989.

Rengert, G. and Wasilchick, J.: *Suburban Burglary* (2nd ed.). Springfield, IL: Thomas, 2000.

Safe Insulation and Its Value in Crime Detection. *FBI Law Enforcement Bulletin, 43* (11), 1974.

Scarr, H.A.: *Patterns of Burglary* (2nd ed.). Washington, D.C.: U.S. Government Printing Office, 1973.

Seamon, T.M.: The Philadelphia Scene Team Experiment. *Police Chief, 57* (1), 1990.

Shover, N.: Structures and Careers in Burglary. *Journal of Criminal Law, Criminology and Police Science, 63* (540), 1972.

Waegel, W.B.: Patterns of Police Investigation of Urban Crimes. *Journal of Police Science and Administration, 10* (452), 1982.

Walsh, D.: *Heavy Business: Commercial Burglary and Robbery.* New York: Methuen, 1986.

Webb, D.B.: *Investigation of Safe and Money Chest Burglary.* Springfield, IL: Thomas, 1975.

Weber, T.I.: *Alarm System and Theft Prevention.* Stoneham, MA: Butterworth, 1985.

Weiss, J.: Residential Burglaries: Nuts, Bolts and Demographics. *Law and Order, 36* (11), 1988.

Yeager, W.B.: *Techniques of Safecracking.* Port Townsend, WA: Loompanincs, 1990.

Chapter 13

ECONOMIC ENTERPRISE CRIME

1. Overview

E CONOMIC enterprise crime is what has traditionally been called white collar and organized crime. It includes business associations designed to commit crimes for profit. Street gangs that engage in illegal activity for profit are included in this definition. Embezzlement, while commonly an individual crime, is included in this section because of its traditional association with white-collar crime. Other crimes could be included in this category but are discussed in other areas because of traditional associations.

Criminal enterprises may be relatively small, local operations or large, complex, and international. They have the potential to subvert social, political, and financial institutions and are a growing problem in both mature and developing countries.

The term "white-collar crime" was first given substantial recognition in 1949 by Edwin H. Sutherland when he defined white-collar crime as, "a crime committed by a person of respectability and high social status in the course of his occupation." The definition was considerably broadened in 1970 by Herbert Edelhertz when he expanded the idea of white-collar crime beyond restrictions of class and occupation by defining it as: "an illegal act or series of acts committed by nonphysical means and by concealment or guile, to obtain money or property, to avoid the payment or loss of money or property, or to obtain business or personal advantage."

2. Categories of Economic Enterprise Crimes

In the list given below, white-collar crimes have been classified by the general environment and motivation of the perpetrator. Comprehensive and distinctive, these categories are intended to provide the following benefits: (1) to assist the study of motivation and formulate preventative programs; (2) to suggest altering environments that may give rise to criminal violations; and (3) to give insight into the psychology, susceptibility, and weaknesses of victims.

There is a vast array of economic enterprise crime and they are difficult to categorize. The following categories are suggested to assist in studying and understanding the nature of these crimes. The categories are not exclusive but provide a place to start.

The five categories presented in Table 13-1 are based on environmental factors associated with types of crimes. *Personal crimes* are committed by individuals operating *ad hoc* for personal gain in a non-business context. *Embezzlement* and abuse of trust crimes are committed by persons in the course of their occupations in business, government, or other establishments in violation of their duty of loyalty and fidelity to employer or client. *Business crimes* are offenses incidental to and in furtherance of business operations but not the central purpose of the business. *Confidence games* are crimes considered as a business or as the central activity of a business including systematic frauds known "con games." *Organized crimes* are crime organizations and businesses whose principle functions are to engage in criminal enterprises.

Table 13-1. Various Economic Enterprise Crimes.

Personal Crimes	• Purchases on credit with no intention to pay; purchases by mail or on-line in the name of another.
	• Individual income tax violations.
	• Credit card frauds.
	• Bankruptcy frauds.
	• Home improvement loan frauds.
	• Frauds with respect to social security, unemployment insurance, and welfare.
	• Unorganized or occasional frauds on insurance companies (theft, casualty, health, etc.).
	• Violations of Federal Reserve regulations by pledging stock for further purchases, flouting margin requirements.
	• Unorganized mail or Internet scams.

Table 13-1—*Continued.*

Embezzlement & Abuse of Trust	• Commercial bribery and kickbacks, e.g., by and to buyers, insurance adjusters, contracting officers, quality inspectors, government inspectors and auditors, etc. • Bank violations by bank officers, employees, and directors. • Embezzlement or self-dealing by business or union officers and employees. • Securities fraud by insiders trading to their advantage by the use of special knowledge or causing their firms to take positions in the market to benefit themselves. • Employee petty larceny and expense account frauds. • Frauds by computer causing unauthorized payouts. • "Sweetheart contracts" entered into by union officers. • Embezzlement or self-dealing by attorneys, trustees, and fiduciaries. • Fraud against the government • Padding payrolls. • Conflicts of interest. • False travel, expense, or per diem claims.
Business Crimes	• Tax violations. • Antitrust violations. • Commercial bribery of another's employee, officer, or fiduciary. • Food and drug violations. • False weights and measures by retailers. • Violations of Truth-in-Lending Act by misrepresentation of credit terms and prices. • Submission or publication of false financial statements to obtain credit. • Use of fictitious or over-valued collateral. • Check-kiting to obtain operating capital or short-term financing. • Securities Act violations, e.g., sale of non-registered securities to obtain operating capital, false proxy statements, manipulation of market to support corporate credit or access to capital markets, etc. • Collusion between physicians and pharmacists to cause the writing of unnecessary prescriptions. • Dispensing by pharmacists in violation of law, excluding narcotics traffic.

continued

Table 13-1—*Continued.*

	• Immigration fraud in support of employment agency operations to provide domestics. • Housing code violations by landlords. • Deceptive advertising. • Fraud against the government, e.g. false claims, statements, frauds. • Labor violations. • Commercial espionage.
Confidence Games	• Medical or health frauds. • Advance fee swindles. • Phony contests. • Bankruptcy fraud, including schemes devised as salvage operation after insolvency or otherwise legitimate business. • Securities fraud and commodities fraud. • Chain referral schemes. • Home improvement schemes. • Debt consolidation schemes. • Mortgage milking. • Merchandise swindles. • Land frauds. • Directory advertising schemes. • Charity and religious frauds. • Personal improvement schemes, e.g. diploma mills, etc. • Fraudulent application for use and/or sale of credit cards, airline tickets, etc. • Insurance frauds, e.g. phony accident rings; looting of companies by purchase of over-valued sets, phony management contracts, self-dealing with agents, inter-company transfers, etc.; frauds by agents writing false policies to obtain advance commissions; issuance of annuities or paid-up life insurance, with no consideration, so that they can be used as collateral for loans; sales by misrepresentation to military personnel or those otherwise uninsurable. • Vanity press and song publishing schemes. • Ponzi schemes. • False security frauds. • Purchase of banks or control thereof with deliberate intention to loot them. • Fraudulent establishing and operation of banks or savings and loan associations.

Table 13-1—*Continued*.

	• Fraud against the government:
	  - Organized income tax refund swindles, home
	    improvement, loans and mortgage frauds.
	• Executive placement and employment agency
	  frauds.
	• Coupon redemption frauds.
	• Money order swindles.

Organized Crimes	• Illegal sale/distribution/production/tax avoidance of regulated items • Extortion • Gambling • Prostitution • Money laundering

CONFIDENCE GAMES

3. Swindles

Though only a small number of people are accomplished professional swindlers, it is a topic of great interest to the public and media. Swindling is defined as the act of obtaining money or property from another by fraud or deceit. While this definition could include embezzlement, stock manipulation, and other high level commercial operations, this discussion will focus on confidence games and similar short-term frauds. In most confidence games, victims are knowingly engaging in a dishonest act. By attempting to perpetrate a larger fraud, victims are themselves defrauded. While the details and methods continue to evolve, most swindles are rooted in some classic structures.

a. **The Spanish Prisoner**. The Spanish prisoner is a fraud that exploits the victim's sense of compassion, adventure, or justice. The victim receives a request for money to free the sender, who claims to be falsely imprisoned. In return, the sender promises to share a hidden treasure with the victim. After sending the money the victim hears no more from the prisoner.

In a more modern version of this swindle, perpetrators search social networking sites to find young adults with elderly grandparents. The victim receives a telephone call from a hysterical caller pretending to be his or her grandchild. The caller claims to have been falsely arrested and needs money for bail. When the victim agrees to help, arrangements are made for a "friend" to pick up the money.

b. **The Sir Francis Drake Swindle**. The victims receive a message or a visitor informing them that they are descendants of a famous person (e.g., Sir Francis Drake) and entitled to a share in the fortune. Since the estate is not completely settled, a fee is required for litigation. The victims agree to put up the money. A few months later, they are informed that the court proceedings will be more protracted than first estimated. An additional sum is requested. This continues until the victims exhaust either finances or hope of receiving an inheritance. In the 1910s this swindle was practiced throughout the Midwest with extraordinary success. A variation of this con is the Nigerian bank fraud. The perpetrator offers to share a large sum of money if the victim can help to prevent corrupt officials from seizing it. All the victim needs to do is pay a fee for the money's release or provide bank account information so the funds can be transferred. The perpetrator either keeps the fee or depletes funds from the victim's bank account.

c. **The Money-Making Machine**. Victims are shown a machine or device that will literally make money. The perpetrator demonstrates its efficiency by showing the production of several bills. The machine is then sold to the victim at an appropriate price. Money-making machines have appeared in many different forms.

d. **Stock Swindles**. Worthless stock is sold in oil wells, resort property, or some other commodity. Millions of dollars is lost through fraud of this kind.

e. **Wallet Dropper**. This is another "short con" played by two perpetrators, *A* and *B*. The victim is walking along the street when *A* walks past rapidly and drops a wallet. Before the victim can reach down to pick it up, *B* comes from behind and seizes it. Since the wallet contains no means of identification, *B* pretends to recognize the victim's claim to a share and agrees to divide the contents. *A* is now well out of calling distance. The wallet contains a few small bills and a counterfeit large bill. If the victim can change the bill, *B* will walk away with half the money leaving the wallet to the victim. If the victim cannot produce the change, *B* consents to settle for security in the form of money or jewelry. He or she leaves the wallet in victim's possession and agrees to meet later to divide the money.

f. **The Smack Game**. This is a small con game that is worked by two people, the roper and the insider. The roper finds the victim though what appears to be casual conversation. The insider joins them under some pretext. The roper suggests that they match coins for drinks. Money bets are finally suggested. The game is played by tossing coins with the odd coin winning. While the insider is absent for a few moments, the roper feigns dislike and suggests that they fleece the insider. They scheme that the roper will always call opposite to the victim. Thus, if the victim calls "heads" the roper will call "tails." In this way they continue to always have one or the other winning the play. They agree to divide the spoils later. As the bets mount and a substantial sum changes hands, the roper acquires a considerable amount of the victim's money. When the insider finally concedes defeat, the roper and the victim walk off together. The insider then vehemently expresses the suspicion of having been fleeced by professional con artists and threatens to call the police. The roper suggests meeting the victim later to divide the money then departs in a different direction, never to be seen again.

EMBEZZLEMENT

4. Overview

Criminals show great ingenuity in devising schemes to illegally obtain money. The legal distinction between the various forms of larceny lies in the nature of the perpetrator's ownership or custody of the property. A lucrative and popular white-collar crime is embezzlement, the fraudulent appropriation of money or goods by someone entrusted with them. The perpetrator has a combination of opportunity and temptation. The motivation is primarily profit, but may include financial difficulties and a desire for power. It is a crime by an unfaithful steward, a larceny by someone in a position of trust.

Since embezzlement involves no violence, does not confront the victim, and is often committed at the expense of a fairly wealthy organization, embezzlers are seldom considered as disreputable as street criminals. While dishonest, they may also be described as "clever" and "master mind" by the media. The embezzler's deeds are sometimes recounted with ill-concealed admiration as though they are modern Robin Hoods. Each year thousands of embezzlers are arrested accounting for the loss of millions of dollars. Financial losses to embezzlement far exceed those of bank robbery.

a. *Modus Operandi.* The methods used by embezzlers vary with the nature of their control over the property in their trust. In a financial role, they may have control of the recording of accounts and the ability to manipulate them so their theft is not detectable without a complete audit. Many embezzlers have a thorough understanding of the financial operations of the organization and may be the only person with a comprehensive knowledge of the organization's finances. The theft may continue over a period of months or years.

5. Investigation

Embezzlement investigations often require the services of an accountant. Investigators should seek assistance from an experienced accountant who is not associated with the victimized organization. Before proceeding, determine the organization's policy in these matters. Many organizations prefer to avoid unfavorable publicity by simply discharging a dishonest person. Investigators need to establish the goal of their efforts or risk the investigation being derailed later.

It is often useful to begin with how the crime was discovered. The embezzler may suddenly disappear. The disappearance of an employee entrusted with large sums of money gives rise to natural suspicion. A routine audit of records may reveal the loss. Some cases are so complex that they may withstand the scrutiny of normal auditing procedures. Naïve embezzlers may draw attention to themselves by a sudden display of prosperity that arouses the suspicions of neighbors, friends, or coworkers. Rival employees, an abandoned spouse, a trusted companion, or disgruntled accomplices are other likely sources of information. In some situations, another employee may stumble upon a financial irregularity. This may trigger a review of certain accounts. Before taking any serious action with respect to any suspect, investigators should first ensure a crime has been committed. An accountant should examine the records and make a record of the financial irregularities.

a. **Suspects**. The number of suspects to embezzlement is usually quite small. The guilty person must first have access to the funds, accounts, or property. Often there is only one logical suspect.

In more complicated cases investigators may need to conduct background investigations. Investigators should focus on changes in suspects' behavior. Was there anything unusual about the suspects' office behavior? Did they appear nervous or worried? Did they take their annual vacation at the regular time? In some forms of embezzlement criminals may not risk a day's absence for fear of detection.

Are there any changes in suspects' living habits? Do the suspects live within their means? Who are their associates? Do they drink, use drugs, or gamble? Are their social aspirations consistent with their income? A discreet neighborhood check may reveal this information.

Table 13.2. Embezzlement Checklist.

Possession	The property was received by the accused.
Property Description	The property is accurately described.
Intent	A fraudulent intent was formed.
Misappropriation of Property	Appropriation and fraudulent intent is often proven by: • The disposition made of the property or money, such as deposits in a bank. • Failure to perform the assigned duty relating to the property. • Failing to return the property after a demand for the return was made subsequent to the dereliction of duty. • Denial of having received the property. • False entries in documents or ledgers recording the transaction.

What is their financial status? Are suspects solvent? What is the extent of their debts? What is the state of their bank accounts? Do these accounts show great activity even though the total value is not large? Are there accounts in other states or countries? Do they have safe deposit boxes? Credit investigating agencies can assist in this phase of the investigation. Table 13-2 documents issues and elements of proof in embezzlement cases.

LOAN SHARKING

6. Overview

Loan sharking is the lending of money at exorbitant rates of interest accompanied with the threat of violence for default in payments. Victims are generally in serious financial straits, with few other options. Loan sharking can be a significant source of revenue for organized crime.

Loan sharking is ordinarily a violation of the laws relating to usury and extortion. It is often associated with gambling, confidence games, and risky business practices. Typically, victims short on credit and collateral are attempting to relieve a heavy, short-term financial obligation by taking on a more formidable financial burden.

7. Offenders

Well-organized loan sharking can be highly lucrative for organized crime. The "boss" may be a high-ranking individual in a well-organized crime group who may also run a legitimate business.

The organizational structure of a loan sharking business is often a hierarchy designed to insulate the boss from operational activities. At the top level, the boss provides the financing, the overall supervision, and sets an interest rate. The tier below may consist of lieutenants who distribute funds to subordinates at a slightly higher interest rate. These subordinates may make loans themselves or have their own workers to make loans, again at a slightly higher interest rate. Most of the actual operations are conducted at the street level, and may consist of working bookmakers and street criminals.

Operating as a pyramid of lenders who at each (descending) level charge a higher rate of interest, the objectives is to acquire money and takeover legitimate businesses. The borrower's inability to repay the loan is met with "enforcement," a term covering the truly criminal aspect of loan sharking, namely, extortion.

8. Enforcement of Loans

The key to successful loan sharking is the borrower's fear of enforcement. Severe sanctions follow any defaults on payment. The lender makes the rules and can arbitrarily change the terms of the loan if a payment is missed.

a. **Sanctions**. Failure to meet payments is met with stern warnings and followed by severe sanctions. Depending on the circumstances and the victim's assets, a penalty is imposed. Victims may be assaulted or even murdered. If victims still possess business assets, the loan shark may become an invisible partner, if not the outright owner, of a legitimate business. Victims may be forced to provide "insider" information or steer new clients to the loan shark.

For example, a business owner takes a $100,000 loan and makes three payments before missing two. As a penalty, the loan shark declares the debt is now $200,000 with five percent interest per week. When the business owner again misses a payment, the principal is increased to $250,000. Finally, the debt grows to $300,000 and the debtor is called to account. The loan shark may then seize half ownership in the victim's business, collect half of the business profits, and still require the weekly payments on the old loan. Eventually the situation becomes hopeless and the loan shark forgives the debt by taking over the business. The loan shark may continue to run the business or raid its assets, eventually forcing it into bankruptcy.

9. Victims

It is difficult to imagine a capable business person willingly engaging the services of a loan shark, but victims are typically persons with common sense, experience and frequently well educated. In fact, successful business and professional people appear to be the preferred victims of loan sharks. In a typical case, victims are intelligent, experienced persons who find themselves in financial difficulties. They turn to a loan shark as a short-term remedy. A few months later, they find themselves in deeper financial trouble, and often discover they are now in trouble with organized crime as well. Overcome by the pressures and irresolvable demands, they are committed to a spiraling financial abyss.

10. Investigation

Loan sharking is often a personal transaction without witnesses so is difficult to investigate. Some loans are negotiated under circumstances the victim is reluctant to reveal. For example, loan sharks may exploit the financial difficulty caused by gambling losses. In fact, the people who run illegal gaming may be more interested in loan sharking than in gambling. Gamblers running short of money may try to recoup their losses with a quick loan from a loan shark. If a gambler borrows $500 and wins, $600 may need to be paid for the $500 just borrowed. If the gambler loses, the $600 is likely due within twenty-four hours. Due to the circumstances, the gambler may be reluctant to talk to the police.

Even if victims go to the police, there is little evidence beyond their uncorroborated statements. Occasionally, it is possible to record conversations of enforcers making threats (in person or by telephone). Even when the loan shark's records are seized, they are usually found to be too meager or too cryptic to serve as evidence. Sometimes mnemonic devices or substitute names are used, but even if the real names are used, the records may not constitute adequate supporting evidence.

Sometimes an undercover operation may be the only way to obtain evidence of loan sharking or other organized crime activities. Well placed informers and undercover officers have successfully unraveled complex organized crime rings.

FORGERY

11. Overview

Forgery dates from the days when merchants first transferred money by paper to thwart robbers who preyed on shipments of gold and silver. This innovation in financial transaction introduced a new and even greater evil. Armed thugs were replaced by educated, talented, and imaginative thieves, whose crime affected only property and drew less public ire.

Since forgery attacked the moneyed classes it raised less social concern. Financial transactions in business depend on paper that represents credit. Negotiable instruments, bills of lading, invoices, and similar documents are the tools of commerce. Destroy their trustworthiness and the transactions of finance suffer accordingly. The crime of forgery became so serious that the English instituted the death penalty and from 1819 to 1826 death sentences were imposed on 7,700 forgers.

12. Forger

Forgery has become a complicated procedure with a variety of instruments such as bank notes, drafts, bills of exchange, letters of credit, registered bonds, money orders, and checks being targeted. A knowledge of chemicals, papers, inks, engraving, etching, lithography, and penmanship as well as detailed knowledge of bank operations are requisites for success. Large amounts of money can be obtained through complex monetary transactions requiring planning, specialization, and organization. Large scale operations may require extensive financing to prepare for the crime, while lone forgers often operate inexpensively. Professional forgery reflects the technology of the period, with pen and ink largely being replaced by electronics and software.

a. **General Types**. Forgery is practiced by a wide variety of people, both male and female, young and old. Forgers may be elderly, incarcerated prisoners, or high school students with a new printer. They have wide-ranging levels of skill, knowledge, and a degree of risk taking. One of the most useful investigative approaches is to study the forger's *modus operandi*.

One of the most common forgers is the check passer. Some habitual forgers spend many years passing forged checks. They often spend short periods of freedom, between periods of incarceration, using mediocre skills to pass small checks. Successful check passers tend to be professional in their activities and may even band into small groups. Their manner, story, dress, appearance, and forged checks are calculated to avoid raising suspicion. Roving check passers go from one jurisdiction to another often leave the state before their checks have been found to be fraudulent. Some disguise their appearance. Electronic fund transfers have changed the environment for check passers. Merchants who scan checks can immediately determine if the account is valid and if there are sufficient funds. The criminal, however, who steals a supply of valid checks, can trade merchandise for blank checks until funds are depleted or the missing checks are reported. The merchant's scanner electronically transfers funds and prints the amount on the check. The check is returned to the perpetrator who commits the fraud without ever writing on the check itself.

13. Techniques of the Forger

a. **Check Passers**. To pass a forged check, criminals must obtain blank checks or obtain checks meant for another person and merely add the endorsement. Some forgeries begin with the theft of blank checks from homes, offices, or pilfered mail. Others print their own checks often using a stolen check as a model. Forgers must also create false identification documents, such as Social Security cards, automobile registration, driver's license, ID cards, and military discharge papers.

b. **Fraudulent Identification**. The business of selling fraudulent identification documents range from sophisticated smuggling schemes to phony identification for underage drinkers. Driver's licenses, for example, are bought by non-English-speaking persons who are not able to pass the written parts of license examinations. Others buy blank or fraudulent diplomas and degree certificates. Birth certificates, licenses, car registrations, diplomas, armed forces discharges, Social Security cards, and even passports are purchased for identity theft or other crimes. Some of these documents are counterfeit, while others are genuine document blanks stolen from government offices and printing houses.

14. Forgery Laws

Forgery laws vary from state to state. Generally, forgery is committed by a person who, with intent to defraud, knowingly makes or utters (passes, offers, or puts in circulation) a false writing that imposes a legal liability on another or affects the legal right or liability of another. Technically, signing your own name to a check with intent to defraud is not forgery while signing the name of someone else is forgery. Both incidents are fraud and in some states may be covered by the same statute.

a. **Elements of Proof**. To support a charge of forgery the following elements must be established.

1) *False Making*. The documents must be shown to be falsely made or a misrepresentation. It may involve a false signature or alteration. Alterations may be shown by physical methods, while false signatures can be established by a comparison with a true signature. Statements from victims should confirm they did not sign or produce the document or authorize the accused to sign or produce the instrument for them. If the name is fictitious, it should be shown the person did not have an account or business relationship with the victim. The forged instrument itself should be processed for physical evidence.

2) *Legal Liability*. The signature or writing must impose a legal or financial liability or affect the legal rights of another. For an alteration to constitute forgery, it must involve a material change.

3) *Identity of the Forger*. It must be shown that the accused falsely made, altered, or knowingly uttered, offered, or issued the false instrument. This may be established by a confession, statements of witnesses, or by the testimony of a document examiner.

4) *Intent to Defraud*. The intent to defraud must be shown. It need not be directed toward a particular person or directly benefit the offender. It is immaterial whether anyone was actually defrauded. The intent can often be inferred from the act. Evidence of other forgeries may be admissible to prove intent to defraud. It must also be shown that the suspect knew that the instrument was

a forgery. This is not difficult if the forger is passing the instrument, but may be a problem when the utterer and the forger are different persons. A common defense to a charge of uttering a forgery is that the accused had honestly received the forged instrument and believed it to be genuine. Investigators should develop all possible evidence to show guilty knowledge, such as similar checks or other attempts to pass forgeries.

15. Investigating Forgery

Generally, forgeries are not discovered until after the forgers have departed. Clearly the most effective method would be to catch them in the act. Alert cashiers and clerks can sometimes spot forged documents when they are presented. Other times suspicion is raised by perpetrators attempting to steal checks. Likely victims can be trained in detecting forgeries, alerted to the *modus operandi* of active forgers, and asked to immediately inform police of suspicious behavior.

a. **Interviewing Victims and Witnesses**. Victims and witnesses will need to be interviewed and may include the person who received the document, a person whose signature was on the document and an organization or institution that suffered a loss.

The person receiving the document might be a cashier or a sales person. Carelessness in not checking identification may contribute to the problem. Businesses that cash checks may be targeted, but the added business from the check cashing service may more than compensate for the losses. Interviews should focus on a detailed physical description of the perpetrator, the circumstances of the transaction (the story given by the passer; the exact words used; credentials offered; conversation and behavior), the date and time of the incident, the number of people present, any previous encounters with the suspect or other forgeries, and whether any handwriting occurred in the presence of the victim.

It is important to interview, early in the investigation, anyone whose signature has been forged. After victims examine the document, they should initial it (in a place that will not interfere with evidence processing) so they can identify it later. Several questions need to be addressed. Is it the victim's signature or writing? Has the victim given anyone permission to sign for him or her? (Investigators should request handwriting samples similar to the forged writings.) Does the victim make such documents or checks? Where are the document forms or checks kept? Who has access to them? Does the victim have employees or associates who had opportunity to forge the documents? Does the victim suspect anyone? What is the victim's financial situation? Is there a credit problem or a history of poor credit or other forgeries?

If the victim is an organization or business, information related to the account must be obtained. Is the document or check invalid? Does the person whose name appears on the document have an account? Has the person ever had an account? Has the organization or business received any similar forgeries?

16. False Identity Papers

Fraudulent identity papers comprise a significant problem for institutions and individuals. Identity theft is a rapidly growing crime that can severely damage the credit rating of its victims. Advances in printing and photocopying techniques make it more difficult to detect bogus or altered birth certificates, resident alien or "green cards," driver's licenses, and Social Security cards.

Prior to the terrorist attacks of September 11, 2001, many state and local agencies were rather lax in issuing authenticated copies of documents such as birth certificates and driver's licenses. Since then, measures have been taken to better control these documents but problems remain. With a birth certificate, an impressive array of other genuine identification can easily be acquired. Birth certificates are the most common means of establishing identity, and birth certificate frauds are among the easiest to perpetrate, according to the Federal Advisory Committee on False Identification. Because so many different forms are used and because they are generally made by photocopy, birth certificates are among the easiest documents to counterfeit or alter.

17. Physical Evidence in Forgery

The forged document is part of the *corpus delicti* and should be safeguarded as a valuable piece of evidence. When not under examination the document should be protected by a transparent envelope and kept in a secure place. For identification, the investigator's initials and the date should be placed on the back.

The examination for physical evidence should be performed by a competent document expert. Photographs and photocopies of the front and back of the document should first be made. Latent prints may present, so documents should be carefully handled. Documents should not be processed for latent prints before review by a documents examiner. Law enforcement agencies should submit the evidence to the laboratory without tampering with it in any way.

a. **Forging Methods**. The techniques used by forgers depend upon their skill, the nature of the document, and their access to technology and equipment. Obviously the techniques for making fraudulent credit cards differ from that of printing counterfeit currency or forging checks. As technology changes, so do the methods of forgers. Advances in printing and computer technologies create new opportunities for forgers and new challenges for investigators who must continue to update their knowledge.

Handwritten forgeries are far less influenced by changes in technology. Forgers may create a free hand signature or writing using the victim's previous writings as a model. This is a difficult process. If the forger's work is slow and painstaking, an examination under a low-power microscope will reveal the hesitation and the interruptions at points where the pen was lifted.

A traced signature or writing can be shown to be fraudulent by its exacting duplication of an authentic signature or writing. It is practically impossible to write twice in exactly the same way, and the forgery can be exposed by superimposing it over the model to reveal the duplication.

Once a common office tool, carbon paper can be placed over the document and the writing or signature lightly trace onto the document. Forgers then write over the tracing. When examined under a low-power microscope, traces of the carbon will be visible.

Another method to forge writing is to place a genuine writing under the forgery and illuminated from below by a strong light. The forger now traces the writing or signature which is visible over the light. This type of trace can sometimes be detected by the abnormal shading and the signs of slow, painstaking movement. Nervousness, retraced lines, varying density, interruptions caused by pen lifts, and tremor may be apparent.

b. **Alterations**. Documents may be altered to change the amount, the name, or some other feature. These changes can frequently be revealed under low power magnification, an ultraviolet lamp, or infrared photography.

If something has been added to the document, the difference in the inks may be apparent to the unaided eye or under the ultraviolet lamp. The use of filter photography or of infrared film will often reveal the difference in the inks.

When an eraser is used on paper, the sizing and the fibers are disturbed. Writing with ink placed on the erased area will have a tendency to spread or "feather." If chemical eradicators are used, a bleaching stain usually is apparent. Ultraviolet examination or merely holding the check in front of a light will usually reveal the erasure.

Other factors are useful in tracing or linking fraudulent documents to the forger. The watermark can be used to trace the source of the check paper. Watermarks can be photographed by illuminating the document from the back so as to emphasize the mark. Perforations, such as on checks, may be matched to the book from which it was extracted.

18. Obtaining Handwriting Exemplars

Exemplars should be obtained from each person whose signature or writing appears on the document as well as from any suspects. Writing samples should be made using similar materials and under similar circumstances. Duplicate as closely as possible the document and writing instrument. If the forged document is a check, blank checks should be used to collect exemplars. If a felt-tipped pen was used to produce the forgery, exemplars should be made with a similar pen. If the suspect was observed standing at a

Figure 13-1. The stock certificate, of which the upper left corner is shown in (a), appears to bear the number F 109506. Microscopic examination however revealed that the second "0" has been changed from a "9." The photomicrograph (b) shows the disturbance of the fibers. (Note the image is inverted because it is viewed through a microscope.) Courtesy of Edward Palmer.

counter when the document was made, have the exemplars made under similar conditions.

If a signature was forged, have the suspect produce about twenty-five signatures. Do not show the writer the suspected signature. After each signature is produced, remove the document so the individual cannot compare one signature with another. After several signatures have been produced, ask the subject to write with the opposite hand. Some individuals are ambidextrous, so you may not know which hand they used. After two or three signatures, return to the original hand.

If the questioned document contains several sentences or paragraphs, three to six exemplars should be sufficient. Dictate the questioned document to the subject, removing the exemplar as soon as it is completed. Do not allow subjects to copy from the original document and do not help subjects spell words. If suspects ask for help spelling a word, instruct them to do the best they can. The same spelling error in both the questioned document and exemplar may help link the documents.

ADDITIONAL READING

White-Collar Crime

Albrecht, W.S., et al.: *How to Detect and Prevent Business Fraud.* Englewood Cliffs, NJ: Prentice-Hall, 1982.

Arlidge, A. and Parry, J.: *Fraud.* Elmsford, NY: Pergamon, 1985.

Baker, T.E.: *Introductory Criminal Analysis: Crime Prevention and Intervention Strategies.* Upper Saddle River, NJ.: Pearson Prentice Hall, 2005.

Bailey, L.L.: Medicaid Fraud. *FBI Law Enforcement Bulletin, 60* (7), 1991.

Edelhertz, H.: *The Nature, Impact and Prosecution of White-Collar Crime.* Washington, D.C.: U.S. Government Printing Office, 1970.

George, B.J., Jr.: *White-Collar Crime: Defense and Prosecution.* New York: Practicing Law Institute, 1971.

Green, G.: *Occupational Crime.* Chicago: Nelson-Hall, 1990.

Hutton, G.W.: *Welfare Fraud Investigation.* Springfield, IL: Thomas, 1985.

Investigation of White-Collar Crime. Washington, D.C.: U.S. Government Printing Office, 1977.

Kramer, W.M.: *Investigative Techniques in Complex Financial Crimes: Fraud and Corruption, Racketeering, Money Laundering.* Washington, D.C.: National Institute on Economic Crime, 1988.

Mann, K.: *Defending White-Collar Crime: A Portrait of Attorneys at Work.* New Haven, CT: Yale University Press, 1985.

Ogren, R.W.: The Ineffectiveness of the Criminal Sanction in Fraud and Corruption Cases. *American Criminal Law Review, 11* (959), 1973.

Oughton, F.: *Fraud and White-Collar Crime.* London: Elek Books, 1971.

Villa, J.K.: *Banking Crimes: Fraud, Money Laundering, and Embezzlement.* New York: Clark Boardman, 1988.

Weisburd, D., Wheeler, S., Waring, E. and Bode, N.: *Crimes of the Middle Class: White-Collar Offenders in the Federal Courts.* New Haven, CT: Yale University Press, 1991.

Weiss, J.P.: Policing White Collar Crime. *Law and Order, 37* (3), 1989.

Welling, S.N.: Smurfs, Money Laundering, and the Federal Criminal Law: The Crime of Structuring Transactions. *Florida Law Review, 41* (2), 1989.

Confidence Games

Bell, J.B. and Barton, W.: *Cheating and Deception.* New Brunswick, NJ: Transaction Publishers, 1991.

Blum, R.H.: *Deceivers and Deceived.* Springfield, IL: Thomas, 1972.

Hancock, R. with Chetz, H.: *The Compleat Swindler.* New York: Macmillan, 1968.

Heintzman, R.J.: Confidence Schemes and Con Games: Old Games with New Players. *FBI Law Enforcement Bulletin, 55* (6), 1986.

Henderson, M.A.: *How Con Games Work.* Secaucus, NJ: Citadel Press, 1986.

Maurer, D.W.: *The American Confidence Man.* Springfield, IL: Thomas, 1974.

Rosefsky, R.S.: *Frauds, Swindles and Rackets.* Chicago: Follett, 1973.

Santoro, V.: *Frauds, Rip-Offs and Con Games.* Port Townsend, WA: Loompanics, 1988.

——: *The Rip-Off Book: The Complete Guide to Frauds, Con Games, Swindles, and Rackets.* Port Townsend, WA: Loompanics, 1984.

Smith, L.E. and Walstad, B.A.: *STING SHIFT: The Street-Smart Cop's Handbook of Cons and Swindles.* Littleton, CO: Street-Smart Communications, 1989.

Organized Crime

Abadinsky, H.: *Organized Crime* (5th ed.). Chicago: Nelson-Hall, 1997.

Albanese, J.: *Organized Crime in America* (3rd ed.). Cincinnati: Anderson, 1995.

Herbert, D.L. and Tritt, H.: *Corporations of Corruption: A Systematic Study of Organized Crime.* Springfield, IL: Thomas, 1984.

Keene, L.L.: Asian Organized Crime. *FBI Law Enforcement Bulletin, 58* (10), 1989.

North, D.V.: RICO: A Theory of Investigations. *Police Chief, 55* (1), 1988.

Pace, D.F. and Styles, J.C.: *Organized Crime: Concepts and Control* (2nd ed.). Englewood Cliffs, NJ: Prentice-Hall, 1983.

Forgery

Beasley, J.O., II: Forensic Examination of Money Laundering Records. *FBI Law Enforcement Bulletin, 62* (3), 1993.

Davis, J.M.: Passport Fraud: Protecting U.S. Passport Integrity. *FBI Law Enforcement Bulletin, 67* (7), 1998.

Dusak, R.A.: Automated Handwriting Technology. *Police Chief, 65* (1), 1997.

False Identification: The Problem and Technological Options. Port Townsend, WA: Loompanics, 1988.

Fraudulent *Credentials.* Port Townsend, WA: Loompanics, 1985.

Gilliam, V.J.: Taking the Bounce Out of Bad Checks. *FBI Law Enforcement Bulletin, 60* (10), 1991.

Hansen, W.N.: Combating Check Fraud. *FBI Law Enforcement Bulletin, 68* (5), 1999.

Hargett, J.W. and Dusch, R.A.: Classification and Identification of Checkwriters. *Journal of Police Science and Administration, 4* (404), 1976.

Herkt, A.: Signature Disguise or Signature Forgery? *Journal of Forensic Science Society, 26* (257), 1986.

Lemert, E.M.: The Behavior of the Systematic Check Forger. *Social Problems, 6* (141), 1958.

Levinson, J.: Passport Examination. *Journal of Forensic Sciences, 29* (628), 1984.

Rapp, B.: *Check Fraud Investigation.* Port Townsend, WA: Loompanics, 1991.

Riley, P.: Passport Examination Techniques. *Police Chief, 61* (6), 1994.

Seleno, J.: Check Print. *FBI Law Enforcement Bulletin, 58* (2), 1989.

Slotter, K.: Check Fraud: A Sophisticated Criminal Enterprise. *FBI Law Enforcement Bulletin, 65* (8), 1996.

——: The CPA's Role in Detecting and Preventing Fraud. *FBI Law Enforcement Bulletin, 68* (7), 1999.

Slyter, S.A.: *Forensic Signature Examination.* Springfield, IL: Thomas, 1995.

They Write Their Own Sentences: The FBI Handwriting Analysis Manual. Boulder, CO: Paladin Press, 1987.

Throckmorton, G.J.: Disappearing Ink: Its Use, Abuse, & Detection. *Journal of Forensic Sciences, 35* (199), 1990.

Traini, R.: Beating the Forger. *Security Gazette, 15* (10), 1973.

Turner, J.S. and Albrecht, W.S.: Check Kiting: Detection, Prosecution, and Prevention. *FBI Law Enforcement Bulletin, 62* (11), 1993.

Vastrick, T.W. and Smith, E.J.: Checkwriter Identification–Individuality. *Journal of Forensic Sciences, 27* (161), 1982.

Williams, G.: Forgery and Falsity. *Criminal Law Review, 71,* 1974.

Williamson, D.M. and Meenach, A.E.: *Cross-Check System for Forgery and Questioned Document Examination.* Chicago: Nelson-Hall, 1981.

Chapter 14

ASSAULT AND ROBBERY

1. Overview

WHETHER on the street, in the workplace or in the home, the threat of violence significantly affects our quality of life and productivity. Rather than sit on their porches, fearful citizens stay inside, reducing the natural monitoring of neighborhoods. Honest citizens stay home rather than venture onto dangerous streets causing local businesses to suffer or fail. As public spaces are relinquished to the lawless, young people experience increased pressure to join gangs to protect themselves.

Workplace violence lowers productivity and increases operating costs. Hostile or fearful employees are less creative and more distracted. Security and monitoring costs increase. Productive employees move on to safer jobs, while recruiting and training new employees become more difficult.

At one time police viewed domestic disputes as an unpleasant intrusion into a private matter. When violence occurred, victims were likely to drop charges and refuse to cooperate the next day. The traditional police response to a violent family quarrel was to placate both parties followed with a stern warning. The underlying problem was never addressed and little was done to prevent or even slow the gradual escalation of violence.

Academic studies and a fear of law suits prompted many jurisdictions to try to break the cycle of domestic violence by instructing the police to follow what is called a "pro-arrest" policy. When called to a domestic dispute with evidence of an assault, police were required to make an arrest. Prosecution will pursue the case even if the victim opposes it.

Studies of "pro-arrest" policies have shown mixed results. Researchers have concluded that these policies are instrumental in reducing the number of repeat offenses in families where the assaulter is regularly employed and does not have an extensive arrest record. In less stable families, where unemployment is the norm and an arrest is not especially frightening or demeaning, the policy is not as effective.

2. Assault and Battery Defined

The words "assault and battery" are commonly used together as if one must follow the other. In reality, they are two separate acts. An assault is a willful attempt or immediate threat to do physical harm to another with unlawful force or violence. The victim is placed in fear of imminent physical harm. The actual infliction of injury is a battery. In ordinary conversation, and many modern statutes, the term "assault" generally includes the battery. The crime of battery includes not only intentional bodily injury but also offensive touching. The injury must be done intentionally or by culpable negligence. The act must also be unlawful. It is not a battery to touch others to attract their attention or to seize others to prevent them from falling. Likewise, there is no battery if the act was done in lawful self-defense.

3. Types of Assault

Assaults are often classified by their severity as either simple assault or aggravated assault. A simple assault has no aggravating factors and less injury. A simple assault is a misdemeanor, while an aggravated assault is a felony. An aggravated assault has more serious circumstances or injuries. These aggravated factors include the causing of severe bodily harm, the use of a dangerous weapon, or the intent to commit a serious crime. The status of the victim may also be an aggravating factor. For example, assaulting a police officer or prison guard while they are performing their duties is an aggravated assault in some jurisdictions. In other jurisdictions, the categories of simple and aggravated assault are replaced by degrees of assault according to the severity of the circumstances.

4. Elements of Proof of Simple Assault

It must be shown that the accused attempted or threatened to do bodily harm to the victim by using unlawful force or violence. A threat to do bodily harm to another is placing someone in reasonable fear of violence. An attempt, however, could be made without the victim's knowledge and, consequently, would not create fear of bodily injury.

Preparation without an overt act, such as picking up a stone without any attempt or threat to throw it, does not constitute an assault nor does the mere use of threatening words. An apparent preparation to assault that is accompanied by an announcement not to consummate the assault is not an assault. However, a threat to inflict immediate bodily injury if another does not comply with a unlawful demand is an assault.

A negligent act or omission that foreseeably causes another reasonable fear of violence is an assault. A person who places another in fear by failing to restrain an attack dog may be charged with assault.

To constitute an assault, there must be an apparent ability to inflict the injury. Threats of physical violence over a telephone, for example, do not constitute an assault without additional intervening factors to make the threat imminent. An act may be an assault even if it fails for some reason unknown. If a person attempts to shoot another but a defective cartridge failed to fire, an assault has been committed.

Table 14-1. Aggravated Assault,[1] Type of Weapon Used, 2010.

Firearms	20.6%
Knives or Cutting Instruments	19.0%
Other Weapons (Clubs, Blunt Objects, Etc.)	33.1%
Personal Weapons (Hands, Fists, Feet, Etc.)	27.4%

1. In the Uniform Crime Reporting Program, aggravated assault is defined as an unlawful attack by one person upon another for the purpose of inflicting severe or aggravated bodily injury. Source: FBI. *Uniform Crime Reports—2010.*

a. **Assault with a Dangerous Weapon**. Many things can be considered a dangerous weapon. The test is whether it is used in a manner that it is likely to produce death or serious bodily injury. A bottle, glass, rock, bowl, piece of wood, a pipe, boiling water, or a number of other items may be considered a dangerous weapon, depending upon how they were used in committing the assault. It is not necessary that death or grievous bodily harm actually be inflicted. It is necessary to show that the weapon, means, or force was used in a manner likely to produce death or grievous bodily harm.

b. **Assault in With Intent to Cause Great Bodily Harm**. Great or grievous bodily harm includes fractured or dislocated bones, deep cuts, severe lacerations, serious damage to internal organs, and other serious bodily injuries. It does not include minor injuries such as a black eye or a bloody nose. When force was used in a manner likely to cause great bodily harm, it may be inferred that any resulting grievous injuries were intended. For example, breaking someone's leg by intentionally pushing him or her from a balcony is an aggravated assault. To prove this offense it is necessary to show that the accused assaulted the victim, grievous bodily harm was inflicted, and the injury was intended.

c. **Assaults with Intent to Commit Other Offenses**. This type of aggravated assault includes assaults with intent to commit murder, voluntary manslaughter, rape, robbery, sodomy, arson, burglary, or housebreaking. An assault to commit an offense is not necessarily the equivalent of an attempt to commit the offense. These acts include assaults with intent to commit another crime but fall short of a necessary stage or step in the legal definition of an attempt to commit that crime. For example, if the suspect assaults the victim with intent to rob but is interrupted before taking or demanding any property, the offense lacks an essential element of an attempted robbery charge. To prove assault with intent, it is necessary to show the accused assaulted the victim with the intent to commit another crime (usually a specified crime by statute).

5. Investigative Procedure

Many of the same techniques used to investigate homicide are used to investigate serious assaults. Investigators should take extensive notes and proceed as they would if investigating a homicide.

The crime scene and any evidence should be photographed in the same manner as any other important investigation. Sketches should be made when warranted, and weapons and other evidence that could identify the assailant or establish the elements of the crime should be collected and processed.

Victims should be interviewed as early as possible. If they know the identity of the assailant, the investigation is greatly simplified. A complete account of the incident should be obtained including actions immediately preceding the assault, possible motives, the names of witnesses, and other important details. Wounds should be photographed to show the full extent of the injuries, with another set of photographs taken approximately three days later. In cases of violent physical contact, victims' clothing should be obtained and forwarded to the laboratory for examination. If there is suspicion of victims' intoxication or use of illegal drugs, appropriate tests should be requested.

All witnesses should be interviewed about the circumstances of the crime, any motive for the assault, and the identity of the assailant. Medical reports on the victims' examination should be obtained from the attending physicians, along with an opinion whether injuries are consistent with accounts of the assault.

Suspects taken into custody at the scene or shortly thereafter should be questioned in detail about the offense and motives. If suspects are intoxicated or under the influence of drugs, appropriate tests should be conducted. An attempt should be made to recover any objects or weapons used in the assault. When appropriate, suspects' clothing should be seized and examined for incriminating evidence. Any justification, excuse, or alibi offered by suspects should be fully explored.

STALKING

6. Overview

Stalking was not viewed as a crime until the 1990s when California enacted the first statute prohibiting it. Studies have shown that eight percent of women and two percent of men have reported being stalked at one time in their lives. It may appear innocent in the beginning but often evolves into frightening behavior. A former friend, date, partner or spouse begins calling or leaving notes. Suspects do not accept that their attention is unwanted and the relationship is over. They will not go away. Victims may be followed or openly threatened. The workplace, school, or home no longer feels safe. Unwanted notes, cards, and presents may be replaced by annoying or frightening behavior. Victims' may find their credit cards canceled, jobs sabotaged, vehicles damaged, or pets stolen or killed. Suspects may become out-of-control emotional terrorists who threaten, act violently, and defy restraining orders.

Stalking represents a major law enforcement problem because of its pervasiveness, difficulty to control, and, the possibility of tragic consequences. Although stalking can be directed at anyone, most victims are women. What is also disturbing is the number of women killed annually by ex-boyfriends and ex-husbands. The FBI claims that one-third of women who are slain are killed by male offenders with a prior intimate relationship with the victim.

Stalking is a serious problem because it creates a climate of fear around victims and their families. It is often difficult to recognize because it involves a series of events that, in the initial stages, may appear to be innocuous. For example, standing on a street corner or walking down the sidewalk are both non-threatening and legal activities. When they occur in the context of a stalking case, these activities become dangerous and illegal. If the police treat incidents in isolation, little can be done. It is a pattern of incidents that cross the threshold from innocent behavior to stalking. In jurisdictions where each police call is handled by a different officer, there may not be a mechanism for recognizing stalking behavior.

There are many types of stalkers. The *love-scorn* stalkers intend to use non-fatal violence to demonstrate their love for the victim. Their principle motivation is not sexual. *Domestic* stalkers prey upon former intimate partners in an effort to get even. *Political* stalkers carefully select a stranger and engage in carefully planned activities motivated by a political ideology. *Hit* stalkers have no personal relationship with their victims and are motivated by the money of a contract killing. The *celebrity* stalker typically targets a movie star, television personality, or sports figure. They are strangers to their victim and the principle motivation is not sexual. The *lust* stalkers do not know their victim but are sexually attracted to them. Some stalkers suffer from a psychological condition known as *erotomania* where stalkers falsely believe their victims are in love with them.

7. Definition of Stalking

Stalking is the following or harassing of another accompanied with a credible threat of violence. Stalking behavior consists of repetitive acts, such as following or spying on the victim, laying-in-wait, attempting to communicate by telephone, mail or messaging, acting in a threatening manner toward the victim and victim's friends, vandalism, sending bizarre letters, and making death threats. It is against the law in all fifty states. Although the laws have varying definitions of the crime, they usually include a list of prohibited acts, a course of conduct (usually two or more acts) and a stated or implied credible threat of violence. Prohibited activity generally includes repeated occurrences of close physical or visual proximity, nonconsensual communication, overt or implied threats, or other acts that cause fear.

8. Legal Issues

Stalking legislation is unusual because it prohibits the repetition of what may be considered ordinary behavior. Many otherwise legal activities can constitute stalking behavior. Critics claim stalking laws are overly vague and ambiguous. The American Civil Liberties Union (ACLU) believes that anti-stalking laws leave citizens confused over what is illegal conduct. For instance, a legal activity, such as walking in your own neighborhood, may become stalking activity if your ex-partner or your ex-spouse also lives there. Because anti-stalking laws do not clearly define prohibited conduct, it leaves wide discretion to the police, the prosecutor, and the courts. Marital disputes may produce false accusations and criminal charges being brought. Critics maintain that stalking behavior is already handled adequately by laws prohibiting harassment, assault, battery, trespass, violation of orders of protection, and forcible entry. In this view, stalking legislation is an unnecessary response to a problem already handled adequately by existing laws. Careful stalkers, though, might be able to confine their activities to legal acts and continue to harass their victims for years if not for anti-stalking legislation.

9. The Dynamics of Stalking

The victim and the offender see their situation from very different perspectives. Victims simply want to be free of a person who wants to control and emotionally abuse them. Victims see offenders wanting to maintain power over them. Ex-husbands who stalked were significantly more likely to have engaged in abusive or controlling behavior while married than men who did not stalk. A portrait emerges of a manipulative, possessive, controlling person who is desperately trying to maintain power over a former partner after the relationship has ended. When stalkers realize they cannot recapture victims, they seek revenge, escalate emotional violence (unwanted phone calls), damage property (vandalism, harming a pet), and then move to physical violence against the victim.

Offenders may be emotionally distraught and mean no harm. Their goal is often to reconcile, and they are willing to do whatever is necessary to achieve that goal. Stalkers tend to be insecure and are unable to tolerate rejection. They may drink heavily and abuse drugs. They may progress from the desire for reconciliation, to feeling victimized, and finally turning to revenge. They want the world to understand their feelings and seek sympathy. They want their victims to suffer and to feel what they feel. They may sabotage the victims' job or credit rating, vandalize their car or home, before turning to violence. After a while, they will realize their actions are futile and believe that victims have destroyed their lives. They feel they are the true victims. Not all offenders go through these stages. Stalkers may be diverted by such things as the victim or offender relocating, the offender developing a new love interest, or the police intervening.

Table 14-2. Victim's Perception of Why Stalking Stopped.

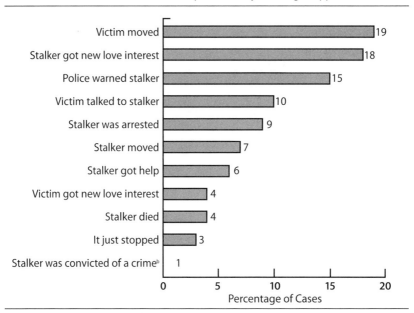

a. N=665 cases.
b. Based on 5 or fewer cases.

Source: Tajden, P. and Thoennes, N.: *Stalking in America: Findings from the National Survey,* National Institute of Justice.*Violence Against Women Survey, National Institute of Justice.*

10. Managing Threats and Interventions

Threat management may involve intervention with both victims and offenders to control or eliminate inappropriate behavior. Victim interventions may include education, behavior modification, and therapeutic counseling. Education will consist of informing victims of the nature of the crime, personal protection measures, what the police are legally able to do, and how to document the case for a possible trial. Behavior modification consists of suggesting lifestyle changes including protecting privacy, changing locks and phone numbers, changing social habits, informing employers, and, in extreme cases, moving. Therapeutic intervention involves offering emotional support to the victim and recommending support groups.

Table 14-3. Distribution of Cases by Number of Years Stalking Lasted.

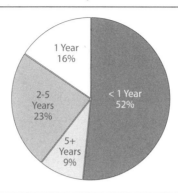

a. N=759 cases.

Source: Tajden, P. and Thoennes, N.: *Stalking in America: Findings from the National Violence Against Women Survey,* National Institute of Justice.

Table 14-4. Victim's Perceptions of Why They Were Stalked.

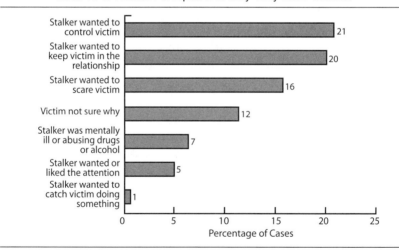

N=624 male and female victims.

Source: Tajden, P. and Thoennes, N.: *Stalking in America: Findings from the National Violence Against Women Survey,* National Institute of Justice.

Because the charge of stalking involves a series of incidents, victims should be encouraged to document their cases by keeping records of any contact with offenders, such as telephone calls, e-mails, letters, packages, or faxes. Inform victims not to respond to any communication from the stalker. Letters, e-mails, packages, and faxes should be preserved as evidence. Victims should keep journals describing how their stalkers have affected their lifestyles. Include days missed from work, sleepless nights, visits to counselors and any other information that could inform a jury of the victims' fear and trauma. Journals are also helpful in refreshing victims' memories if the case goes to trial.

a. **Offender Intervention**. After interviewing the victim, investigators should have a basis to assess the type of case and offender. The next step is to determine an appropriate strategy for dealing with the offender. The options include contacts through telephone, mail, face-to-face, protective restraining orders, arrest, mental health diversions, or incarceration. Depending on the severity of the case, one or more of these options are employed. In less serious cases, offenders may be contacted by mail or telephone to inform them of laws against stalking and the consequences of their behavior. In more serious cases, it may be necessary to conduct interviews that may provide an opportunity for incriminating admissions.

If the stalking continues, victims should be encouraged to obtain a protective restraining order against offenders. These should be strictly enforced by the police. Making arrests for trespassing, harassment or a violation of a restraining order can be a useful tactic. These charges are easier to prove than stalking and a conviction could be helpful in eventually establishing a stalking case. Surveillance cameras can be installed at victims' homes to gather evidence. Search warrants may uncover spying equipment or the presence of victims' belongings at offenders' homes.

If investigators "up the ante" after each incident with a program of warnings, interviews, restraining orders, search warrants, surveillance, and finally arrest, they can turn the table on stalkers. In many cases, stalkers are self-centered, manipulative people who take satisfaction in instilling fear but find it difficult to deal with the pressure of an investigation.

ROBBERY

11. Overview

Robbery, like assault, is a crime requiring a confrontation with the threat of violence between the perpetrator and victim. Though most robberies are completed in minutes, the event is traumatic and intensely stressful for victims. It is also a good indicator of the overall level of crime as many other crimes rise and fall along with the robbery rate. Robbery rates are higher in the United States than other industrialized nation. In 2010, it constituted nearly 30 percent of violent crimes reported to police and resulted in $456 million in losses. Many robberies require high risk but yield little for the perpetrator.

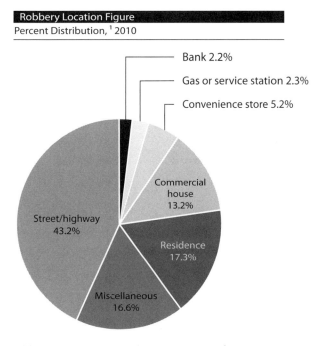

Figure 14-1. Robbery Location, 2010. Source: FBI. *Uniform Crime Reports–2010.*

Table 14-5. Robbery, Type of Weapons Used, 2010.

Firearms	41.4%
Knives or Cutting Instruments	7.9%
Other Weapons	8.8%
Strong-Armed	42.0%

Source: FBI. *Uniform Crime Reports—2010.*

Highly professional robberies, skillfully and precisely executed, may occur but are very rare. Most robberies are common mugging with little subtlety or skill.

The average citizen often uses the term robbery as a generic label for theft. To them, robbery is synonymous with burglary and larceny. There is, however, a fundamental difference between these crimes and the severity of their sentences. Robbery is the taking of a person's property, in their presence and against their will, and usually requires an element of fear. Larceny and burglary is the taking of someone else's property but it is generally not committed in the presence of the victim or by placing them in fear.

12. The Law

Robbery is similar to larceny but has the addition element of violence, actual or threatened. It involves the *taking of the property.* Some form of personal property must be taken from the victim. The theft must be *from the person or in the presence of the victim.* It is not necessary that the owner be within a certain distance of the property, though. If the victim is left tied up in one room, while the robbers take money in another room, the taking is considered to have been done in the presence of the victim.

The taking must be *against the will of the victim, by force, violence, or putting in fear.* If force is used, the amount of force is immaterial. Violence is sufficient if it overcomes the resistance of victims, or prevents them from mounting resistance. Overcoming resistance by snatching an article is sufficient. If an article is merely snatched from the hand of another or if a pocket is picked by stealth, the offense is not robbery. Putting the victim in fear of bodily injury is sufficient. The fear may be aroused by word or gesture.

13. Profiling Robbers

Most robberies are committed by young, black males. When females rob, they tend to rob other females. Robbers are more likely to target victims of their own race, except for teams of white robbers who may target black victims. Though relative depravation explains many robberies, lifestyle also plays a role. Many robbers steal to support lifestyles of conspicuous consumption and to maintain street credibility as fearless risk-takers whose lives revolve around money, drugs, and partying. Many robberies are not planned. When robberies are planned, the planning is seldom extensive or sophisticated. Robbers tend to be opportunists who also commit other crimes and have extensive criminal involvement.

14. Bank Robbery

Just as the time-lock safe reduces the number of bank burglaries, technology has helped reduce the number of bank robberies. Video surveillance, dye packs, sequentially serial-numbered currency, tracking devices inserted in the money, increased use of security guards, limiting cash access at teller stations, improved alarm systems, better physical design, and better organized police response has greatly reduced the profitability of bank robbery. Many bank robberies are rather spontaneous events committed by amateurs. Most of these robbers can be apprehended using standard investigative procedures.

The highly skilled professional bank robber is rare. Most businesses operate on checks and credit cards leaving little cash on hand. The thief who steals jewelry realizes less than 20 percent of its true value. For many criminals, bank robbery is the only source of a substantial cash "score."

a. **Profiling Bank Robbers**. Bank robbers come from all walks of life. They are diverse in age, race, ethnicity, and gender. They may work alone or in groups.

Robbers who operate alone may be motivated by greed, the desire for a thrill, or the desire for a challenge. Most commonly they pass a note to a teller demanding a large amount of cash and claim to be armed with a pistol or an explosive device. Since weapons are usually concealed, it may be difficult to determine if they are actually armed. Tellers are generally trained to assume robbers are armed and surrender conveniently available cash. This policy is known to most robbers and may encourage them to rob banks. Some robbers may return to same bank if their technique has been successful in the past.

Robbers who work in groups often have criminal records that include several serious offenses. Generally the group will consist of three or four persons. They are serious-minded, fairly competent, and often dangerous. The methods described in the succeeding paragraphs will give additional insight into the character of the professional bank robber.

b. **Patterns**. The methods of bank robbers vary widely. Banks that are targeted may be located in highly populated areas and well protected by safety devices and measures, or they may be isolated and far from the nearest police officer. Some banks have never been robbed while others may be robbed several times within a couple of years. Robberies may be planned for several months or may have been conceived on the spur of the moment. Despite these wide variations, a number of trends are common and provide a rough picture of the typical robber.

1) *Selection of Target*. Small branch banks or credit unions are preferred. Larger institutions, with more employees and customers, entail more risk for robbers.

2) *Time*. Wednesday and Friday are favored slightly, along with days when large payroll deliveries are expected. Opening time, lunch hour, and closing are preferred because fewer people are present. Robbers who have extensively planned and cased their target may know daily bank procedures, when there will be less activity, when the bank has more cash on hand, the number and identity of employees, and estimates of police response times.

3) *Disguises*. Most robbers wear hats or caps to help conceal their identity. Sunglasses are a common disguise, along with hoods and masks.

4) **Weapons**. In the majority of cases firearms are carried or simulated. Toy guns are used in about 10 percent of cases. Robbers frequently dispose of weapons by throwing them from the window of the getaway car, burying, or hurling them into a body of water. The weapons are seldom discharged, but each year fatalities occur.

5) **Escape Methods**. Bank robber may use rented or stolen cars to get away from the scene, and then transfer to their own vehicle. A popular make and model vehicle is chosen to avoid attracting attention. If robbers use their own vehicle, it often has stolen license plates that are discarded later. If a getaway vehicle is found, any articles left behind may be useful in finding the criminals.

6) **Criminal Teams**. The typical team consists of two robbers. Approximately 75 percent of these robbers have previous arrest records for robbery, burglary, or larceny. In the majority of cases, robberies are perpetrated by persons from the local area and 78 percent lived within a radius of 100 miles.

c. **Modus Operandi of Professional Robbers**. This section focuses on small groups of skilled, professional bank robbers, but is applicable to other crimes as well. These methods represent the best practices of experience and mature planning.

1) **Target Selection**. Professional thieves do not select their target by chance. Some targets are identified through experience, observation, and surveillance. Sometimes opportunities are brought to them. Petty criminals may "tip off a heist" for a small percentage of the proceeds. Legitimate business people may also identify an opportunity. A truck driver or parking lot attendant may identify a truck to hijack for a share in the proceeds. A bank manager may supply information for the safe and cash on hand to cover up an embezzlement. An unscrupulous jeweler may encourage a robbery as part of an excessive insurance claim.

2) **Casing the Job**. Professional robbers thoroughly plan their crimes. They begin with reconnaissance or "casing" their target. They obtain information on the layout of the bank building, the surrounding terrain, avenues of approach, location and movements of bank personnel, police presence and response time, and the location of bank guards. They may study the bank officers, personnel, and operating procedures.

Robbers may employ ruses to gather information about the interior of the bank, its operations, and its personnel. They may obtain information by loitering about a bank and appearing to be waiting for someone or by standing outside to observe at a distance. This form of casing is, however, likely to draw suspicion. They may enter the bank on the pretext of cashing a check, changing larger bills, opening an account, or making a small deposit. They may pose as a salesperson on legitimate business. A creative sales person pretext may allow considerable access and time in the bank to observe and collect information.

3) ***Robbery Teams.*** Robbery teams usually consist of two to four experienced criminals. The members of the group usually act as equals with an authority over their areas of experience or specialty. Every member has a special activity or assignment based on their experience through previous "jobs."

Assignments include activities prior to, during, and after the crime. Colorful names for these assignments come from robbery lore. Assignments will vary with the requirements of the job. The driver (wheelman) handles transportation from the scene of the robbery. The driver may steal a car and switch the license plates. The car selected is fairly new, inconspicuous, and capable of rapid acceleration. At a distance from the scene, the criminals will shift from the stolen or getaway car to the "front" car, which may be owned by one of the team. Another team member may be assigned to procure weapons (rodman). This person is usually a good marksman and combat tactician who is expected to protect the team if firearms are used. The inside crew are the members who perform the actual robbery, or may consist of the whole team, including the weapons specialist and driver.

4) ***Planning.*** A principle difference between an amateur and professional robbery is the level of planning. The professional plans with scrupulous attention even to seemingly trivial matters. The driver studies the geography of the area, together with its streets and traffic conditions. The getaway route is carefully laid out. The team assembles shortly before the job for a general briefing and to once again to study the layout. Team members may change their clothing to fit into the environment. They may leave separately and go to the target by separate routes. They may gather again

within a few blocks of the target to get their weapons. Team members may walk to the target while the driver parks near the entrance. The inside crew may wear masks, and usually one person is assigned to do the talking. This person often speaks evenly and avoids dramatics, since he or she is the center of attention and most likely to be identified. After obtaining the money, the robbers depart in the getaway car and drive to the second vehicle. If they are not being pursued, they change cars. During the journey, they may change clothes and transfer the money to other containers. Some of the team may take the money and guns in the second car to the place selected for the "meet." The driver often disposes of the getaway car in another part of the city. Sometimes, they will change to a third car before going to the meet.

d. **Preparing For Bank Robberies**. A bank robbery is a traumatic event for many people. Bank executives may have a strong sense of responsibility for the funds in their care. Bank employees may have mixed emotions. They may feel loyalty to their employer and want to thwart the crime, they may see the robbery as a means to appear heroic, or they may be paralyzed by fear. Bank security guards, depending on their training, may be traumatically immobilized, panicky, self-sacrificing, or professionally observant. Customers are unpredictable and are likely concerned with their own safety but may be panic-stricken and have an unrealistic perception of danger. First responding police officers, depending on their experience, may be steady and competent, panicked by the seriousness of the offense, or compelled to take action even if it is wrong. The investigation benefits when bank employees are well trained before the robbery.

1) *Role of Employees During the Robbery*. The safety of employees and customers during the robbery is the principle concern. Robbers are likely to be nervous and unexpected actions may precipitate violence. Employees should follow the instructions of robbers. Employees instructed to hand over money should obey and hand over money but should not volunteer to reach for money not visible to the robbers.

Employees should observe the robbers carefully. Physical descriptions, peculiarities of behavior, method of operation, voice, and exact words are invaluable aids to the investigators. If employees have a view of the street, they should note any accomplices outside or details of the getaway car. When the robbers leave, employees should remain until they are no longer in danger. They should be conscious of possible physical evidence and avoid obliterating evidence such as fingerprints.

2) ***Employees' Role After the Robbery***. Once the robbers have gone, employees should implement the "robbery plan" and immediately lock the doors. Even if an alarm was activated during the robbery, employees should telephone the police and keep the telephone line open. Report that a robbery has occurred, the time the robbers departed, the number of robbers, a description of each robber, a description of the getaway vehicle (make, year, color, style and license plate) and direction it departed.

Another employee should request that customers remain until the police arrive. If the customers are sufficiently composed, someone should record their names and addresses. Cooperative customers should be asked to write down descriptions of the robbers and their behavior. Customers should be discouraged from comparing notes or discussing the robbery. When police arrive they should attempt to find witnesses on the street.

e. **Investigating Robberies**. In general, robbery investigations confront many obstacles. First, if there was little physical confrontation between robbers and victims, there may be little physical evidence left behind. When compared to crimes like burglary, robbers may have little interaction with the crime scene. Second, robberies may occur very quickly giving victims little time to compose themselves and make useful observations. In addition, the short duration of the crime limits the opportunities for it to be interrupted by potential witnesses. Finally, violent encounters with robbers may dissuade victims and witnesses from cooperating with police.

Robberies are generally crimes between strangers. Ordinarily, there are no suspects remaining at the scene, and seldom is there an inside accomplice to the crime. The motive of robbery is simple and uncomplicated and yields few clues.

Physical evidence may provide little assistance in identifying perpetrators but should not be overlooked. Its value often comes in linking suspects to the crime after they have been identified. Many robberies are solved using informants, so investigators should develop a good network of informants. Suspects arrested in other crimes should be carefully interviewed concerning their activities at the times of the robberies. Daily arrests should be scrutinized for persons with past arrests or convictions for robbery. These persons should be checked against descriptions of robbery suspects. Those matching descriptions or raising suspicion during interviews should have their alibis investigated.

1) ***Interrogation***. Suspects who are willing to speak with investigators should be interrogated by someone familiar with bank robbery practices. Special techniques may be required if suspects are professional bank robbers. It may be useful to use the ruse of investigating a different crime. For example, investigators might purport to be interested in a burglary or homicide (fictitious or factual) that took place in a distant town at the same time as the robbery. Suspects may then feel free to establish alibis that place them near the scene of the robbery. Naïve suspects may even name their confederates to substantiate their alibis. Investigators should not reveal their true intent until exhausting this line of inquiry. Later, a direct accusation of the true crime with the full impact of the existing evidence (eyewitnesses, knowledge of subsequent activities, and other identifying evidence) can bring a sudden psychological disruption that confuses suspects. They were picked up for one crime, presented an alibi for a second, and then find themselves maneuvered into a third. It is now more likely investigators can induce a confession.

2) ***Interviewing Witnesses***. When proprietors report a robbery, they should be instructed to try to detain all witnesses. When the police arrive, the witnesses should be quietly separated and instructed not to discuss the crime with anyone until they have been interviewed. Each witness should then be individually interviewed concerning the event and the appearance of the perpetrators. Separating witnesses will limit them from influencing each others' accounts and descriptions. Witnesses should subsequently be taken to the local police station to view photographs of known robbers or suspects.

15. Evidence and Investigative Techniques

a. **Vehicles**. The getaway vehicle can offer important clues to the identity of robbers. Sometimes amateurs use their own vehicles. Professionals will usually steal a car and switch later to their own car. Robbers may use their own vehicle with a stolen license plate or with no license plates. At other times, a rental car is used. Investigators should obtain detailed descriptions of the vehicle from as many witnesses as possible. Obviously, if a witness noted the license plate number, investigator should determine the owner.

The description of the getaway vehicle should immediately be transmitted to patrol officers. The description should be checked against lists of stolen vehicles. Local car rental agencies should be canvassed to determine if they recently rented a similar vehicle. Investigators should account for possible errors by witnesses in the vehicle description and also check vehicles of similar make, model, and color. Rental agency personnel can often give good descriptions of their clients.

b. **Latent Prints**. The counters, furniture, and other items touched by the robbers should be processed for latent prints. Occasionally, the robber may handle papers, checks, or currency. In one case, a robber observed a bank employee watching him, picked up some advertising circulars, threw them to the employee, and ordered him to write his name on one of them. The robber placed the signed paper in his pocket. Subsequently, the circulars were processed for latent prints. On one of the circulars a print was developed and matched to the suspect.

The getaway car, which is usually recovered shortly after the crime, is an excellent source of fingerprints. The rearview mirror, front doors, and side windows are fruitful areas for processing.

c. **Restraining Devices**. Robbers frequently tie up victims with rope, towels, sheeting, or adhesive tape. Robbers may bring the ligatures with them or may use materials at the scene. When victims are found tied, use care in removing the restraints. A characteristic type of knot may help identify a perpetrator. Similarly, in removing adhesive tape, care should be taken to avoid obliterating fingerprints on either side of the tape. In addition, the restraining material may sometimes be linked to its source. A cord, for example, may be similar to cord found at the suspect's home or the edge of adhesive tape may match the end of a roll of tape found on the suspect.

d. **Stolen Property**. Robbers may not be careful in what they take. Money bags, paper bags, and small traveling bags may be used to transport the loot. If these bags are found later in the possession of suspects, they may link them to the crime. In addition to cash, they may take securities and traveler's checks that are traceable.

e. **Other Physical Evidence**. Footprints may be left on the floor by the robbers if the streets are wet or snowy. Discarded newspapers are easily stepped on and may contain footprints. Newspaper should also be processed for latent fingerprints. Discarded garments such as gloves, hats, or jackets may bear identifying marks or DNA. A firearm or other abandoned weapon may be tracked to its owner after it has been processed for prints.

f. **Robbers' Statements**. The manner of speech of robbers may be an important part of the *modus operandi*. The opening and closing statements of robbers are highly characteristic. Criminals, as they plan their crime, may determine a set of orders they will give the victims, e.g., "This is a stick-up, keep your hands down and walk to the back." Some criminals will repeat this without modification at each robbery. While fantasizing about the crime, robbers may develop violent and vulgar words to intimidate victims that become part of their character. Investigators need to obtain verbatim statements of the words used by robbers to link or profile crimes.

g. ***Modus Operandi***. *Modus operandi* can be a useful tool in the investigation of robbery. In crimes lacking physical evidence, the techniques and mannerisms of robbers are often the most valuable clues to their identity.

16. Other Robberies

a. **Loan Companies, Savings Associations and Credit Unions**. These organizations are similar to banks but may be located in buildings that are less fortified and more susceptible to forced entry. Robbers may break in at night, await the arrival of employees in the morning, and force them to open the safe.

Table 14-7. Suggested Robbery M.O. Factors.

Type of Robbery	Bank Messenger Payroll at premises Payroll messenger Armored car Transportation (cab, bus, train) Store (type of store) Theater Gasoline station Warehouse Hotels Dentists and doctors Gambling games Residences Mugging Private cars
Method of Attack	Threatening Assault Binding Drugging
Weapon/Force Used	Bare hands, kicking, etc. Blackjack Brass knuckles Firearm (Specify size and type)
Object	Money Clothing Jewelry Goods
Vehicle Is vehicle used?	Yes/no Type of vehicle
Voice and Speech	Characteristic orders, threats, or phrases
Peculiarities	Takes clothes of victim Slashes tires Cuts telephone wires

b. **Jewelry Stores**. Robberies of jewelry stores are more common in large metropolitan shops with large and valuable inventories. Robbers use various ruses. One may pose as a wealthy customer (dressed appropriately) with fastidious tastes who requests to be shown expensive jewelry. At an opportune moment, the robber (and possibly accomplices) takes the jewels. Other robbers may use a more direct approach but still rely on initially gaining the confidence of a sales associate. If the showroom is not visible from the street, robbers conduct the theft as any other robbery. Robbers who take jewelry are dependent on using a fence and may obtain only 20 percent of the value of the jewelry. Tips from jewelers and pawn brokers who recognize the high quality of merchandise presented to them are essential to solving these robberies.

c. **Closing-Time Robberies**. It is not uncommon for chain stores, fast food outlets, druggists, restaurants, and many other businesses to have large sums of money on hand in the evening, especially on Saturday nights. They can become tempting targets for robbery teams. Often a driver remains in the getaway car while a couple of robbers herd employees into a back room, take the money from the cash register, and then disappear. Since the employees often have an opportunity to observe the robbers and listen to their voices, physical descriptions and the *modus operandi* are useful in solving these robberies.

d. **Liquor Stores, Gasoline Stations, and Convenience Stores**. These are very popular targets for robbers. They may have large sums on hand and be attended by only one or two persons (but often much of the cash has been dropped into a safe they cannot open). Some are obvious targets because of their isolation and all-night service. Robbers may specialize in liquor stores, for example, and rob two or three in one evening. The type of business may be part of the *modus operandi* of the robber. Many perpetrators continue to rob the same kind of businesses until apprehended. A "plant" or "stake-out" is sometimes used by the police.

e. **Robbery of Individuals**. This crime is often opportunistic and lacks the planning of the robbery of a place of business. (Obviously all robberies involve individuals, but the term is used here to mean persons not representing a business.) Although these perpetrators may not be well armed, they can be vicious and exceedingly dangerous.

1) *Mugging*. Mugging is the robbery of an individual accompanied by an assault. The term *mugging* is derived from the practice of seizing victims from behind with one arm locked around their

neck or head and the other being used to frisk valuables from them. Muggers may act alone or with an accomplice. They attack both men and women, preferably someone who is intoxicated. Male muggers may use a female accomplice to entice victims to a secluded place.

The offense usually takes place indoors (hallways, elevators, stairways, and apartments), with more than half occurring outside of the purview of police patrols. Common targets include intoxicated victims and those seeking illicit sex whose actions make them vulnerable. Many muggers strike many times before being apprehended, and then generally return quickly to the streets. Many are allowed to plead guilty to a lesser offense (than the armed robbery and assault), because trials are expensive and jails overcrowded. Parole further reduces the time served in prison, and many juvenile muggers are treated leniently. Sentences tend to be minimal which contributes to the large number of repeat offenders.

f. **Lovers' Lane Robbers**. Robbers who target couples sitting in parked cars in secluded spots can be particularly vicious. They may take money and sexually assault victims. These robberies are difficult to solve because victims may withhold information trying to avoid publicity.

g. **Hitchhiking Robbers**. Some robbers target those generous enough to give them a ride. Female hitchhikers and males disguised in a military uniform are quite likely to find a victim willing to assist them. Once in the vehicle, the robber pulls out a weapon, takes any valuables, and then alights to be picked up by a confederate. Alternatively, they may order the driver out of the car and drive to where their own vehicle is parked.

h. **Doctors and Dentists**. Professionals, such as dentists and doctors, are targeted for robbery because their offices are open to prospective patients. Robbers often arrange to be the last appointment of the day and take whatever money is available. The victims are usually intelligent enough not to offer resistance and can be excellent witnesses. Robbers may net thousands of dollars (in money and jewelry) and commit multiple robberies before being apprehended.

i. **Elderly**. Some places have experienced a rise in the number of assaults and robberies by young men and women preying on the elderly. Various ruses are used. One method is to induce elderly victims to open their doors and then rush in to rob them. Some teams use a young woman to get victims to open their doors (often with the excuse of mistakenly receiving the victim's mail or needing help). When the door is opened, the male companions rush into the residence and overpower the victim.

j. **The Hooker's Knockout Scam**. This team of robbers target men away from home for business, conventions, or major sporting events. A sophisticated, well-dressed prostitute posing as a business representative, a health technician, or a school teacher strikes up a conversation with a man in a hotel bar or lobby. The target is selected for his professional dress and demeanor. After casual conversation, she will arrange to be invited to his room. At the first opportunity she will "spike" his drink with a sedative such as diazepam (Valium) in sufficient quantity to insure that the victim will pass out for a period of time. After removing his wallet, watch and other valuables, the perpetrator moves on to another resort or convention center. When the victim recovers he is often too disoriented to remember what happened to him or too embarrassed to report the crime to the police.

k. **Home Invasion Robbery**. With advances in security technology, it has become more difficult to rob businesses. Target hardening, such as more secure store design, improved lighting, surveillance cameras, bullet-proof booths, tracking devices, and police alarms, have help thwart the opportunistic robber. Similarly, the growing popularity of alarm systems and anti-theft devices for homes and vehicles has made theft more difficult. Some criminals have responded by escalating the level of violence. It is now easier to use overwhelming force to rob an individual than to defeat intricate anti-crime devices.

A home invasion robbery is the breaking and entering of a home for the purpose of confronting the owner and demanding the surrender of cash and valuables. These crimes often involve beatings, sexual assault, and threats of immediate harm to members of the family. Faced with this threat, owners generally open their safes and hand over all their valuables. Victims are generally bound and gagged to give the robbers ample time to get away.

Home invasion robberies are also popular with drug dealers who steal from other drug dealers. A drug dealer's house is a tempting target because there is plenty of cash belonging to someone reluctant to report the loss to the police. Other victims have been foreign business people who distrust banks, keep large sums at home, and may fear dealing with police. Members of organized crime, people with undeclared income, shop owners who bring their day's receipts home with them, and older people who keep money under their mattress are also potential victims.

The typical home invasion team is comprised of two to four members, usually males in their early twenties. Often the victim and robbers are of the same ethnic group. Each team member will have a different role. One will bind and guard the victims while another will collect the valuables. A third might drive the getaway vehicle and act as a lookout.

Robbers commonly use a simple approach to entering the home. One of the gang members may ring the doorbell then overpower the resident. Alternatively, they may pose as delivery persons or utility workers. Robbers generally strike in the evening when victims are home but have not yet activated the alarms system.

When investigating a home invasion, carefully interview victims to develop a detailed M.O. to compare with other incidents. Maintain photographs and background files on previous offenders. Check entry and exit points for fingerprints and palm prints. Examine knots on blindfolds, gags, and ligatures for similarities with knots from other incidents. If duct tape was used to bind or gag the victim, it may have hair, fibers, or fingerprints from the criminals adhering to it.

1. **Carjacking**. Carjacking is essentially a robbery where the personal property taken is an automobile. The FBI defines the crime as the taking of a motor vehicle from the person or presence of another by force, violence, or intimidation. A firearm is used in about half of the incidents and 16 percent of carjackings result in injury to the victims.

The sophistication of electronic vehicle security systems has contributed to the frequency of carjacking. Ignition keys embedded with a computer chip that can be duplicated only by the manufacturer virtually immobilize vehicles when they are removed from the ignition. Without a tow truck, stealing a vehicle with this type of protection becomes exceedingly difficult. If criminals rob owners of their keys and vehicle, they can merely drive away.

The majority of carjacking cases involve temporary use and the vehicles are eventually recovered, though not always intact. Carjackers often rob victims of their wallets and valuables, and then make their getaway in the victim's car. Often after stripping the vehicle of valuable parts, such as the radio, air bags, and wheels, the vehicle is abandoned.

Sometimes stolen vehicles are used in other crimes, such as for another robbery or selling drugs. Having an automobile whose license plates cannot be linked to the criminal is essential for convenience store or gas station robberies, as well as for drug dealing. Not only is the vehicle not associated with the dealer, but they do not risk their own car being seized by police.

Most carjackers are young males with 60 percent under the age of 21. They frequently work with one or several accomplices who drive them to the scene, provide escape if they fail, and help overwhelm victims.

Because carjackers rely on catching the victim off guard, someone vulnerable is chosen. Victims, either male or female, are usually surprised and accosted alone at night. Occasionally, a parent with small children will be the target, because an immediate threat to harm the children will overcome any resistance.

Typically victims are confronted during a temporarily stop (driveway, convenience store, self-serve gas station, or telephone). Attacks may also occur at red lights or stop signs in deserted or high-crime areas. Sometimes carjackers deliberately bump the victims' vehicle ("bump and rob" technique), so that they pull over and get out of the car to assess the damage and to exchange insurance information.

Solving these crimes depends on obtaining detailed statements from victims describing assailants, the technique used, the exact words of threats, and the type of weapons involved. Comparing *modus operandi* will help link crimes to suspects and reveal patterns for police to study. Upon recovering a stolen vehicle, investigators should look for personal articles left in the car along with fingerprints and DNA in the vehicle.

ADDITIONAL READING

Assault

Besharov, D.J.: *Child Abuse: A Police Guide.* Washington, D.C.: American Bar Association, 1987.

Bopp, W.J. and Vardalis, J.J.: *Crimes Against Women.* Springfield, IL: Thomas, 1987.

Defina, M.P. and Wetherbee, L.: Advocacy and Law Enforcement: Partners Against Domestic Violence. *FBI Law Enforcement Bulletin, 66* (10), 1997.

Harries, K.D.: *Serious Violence: Patterns of Homicide and Assault in America.* Springfield, IL: Thomas, 1990.

Kramer, L.C. and Black, H.: DVERTing Domestic Violence: The Domestic Violence Enhanced Response Team. *FBI Law Enforcement Bulletin, 67* (6), 1998.

Marvin, D.R.: The Dynamics of Domestic Abuse. *FBI Law Enforcement Bulletin, 66* (7), 1977.

Meier, J.H. (Ed.). *Assault Against Children.* San Diego, CA: College Hill Press, 1985.

Nylen, L. and Heimer, G.: Sweden's Response to Domestic Violence. *FBI Law Enforcement Bulletin, 68* (11), 1999.

Tajden, P. and Thoennes N.: *Extent, Nature, and Consequences of Intimate Partner Violence.* Washington, D.C.: National Institute of Justice, 2000.

Wattendorf, G.: Focus on Domestic Violence: Prosecuting Cases Without Victim Cooperation. *FBI Law Enforcement Bulletin, 65* (4), 1996.

Stalking

Hendricks, J. and Spillane, L.: Stalking: What We Can Do to Forestall Tragedy. *Police Chief, 60* (12), 1993.

Holmes, R.: Stalking in America: Types and Methods of Criminal Stalkers. *Journal of Contemporary Criminal Justice, 9* (4), 1993.

Tajden, P. and Thoennes, N.: *Stalking in America: Findings from the National Violence Against Women Survey.* Washington, D.C.: National Institute of Justice, 1998.

Wattendorf, G.: Stalking–Investigation Strategies. *FBI Law Enforcement Bulletin, 69* (3), 2000.

Williams, W.L., Lane, J., and Zona, M.A.: Stalking: Successful Intervention Strategies. *Police Chief, 63* (2), 1996.

Robbery

Banton, M.P.: *Investigating Robbery.* Brookfield, VT: Gower, 1985.

Burke, T.W. and O'Rear, C.E.: Armed Carjacking: A Violent Problem in Need of a Solution. *Police Chief, 60* (1), 1994.

Carroll, P. and Loch, J.R.: The Chicago Bank Robbery Initiative. *FBI Law Enforcement Bulletin, 66* (4), 1997.

Dunn, C.S.: *The Patterns of Robbery Characteristics and their Occurrence among Social Areas.* Washington, D.C.: U.S. Government Printing Office, 1976.

Einstadter, W.J.: The Social Organization of Armed Robbery. *Social Problems, 17* (64), 1969.

Feeney, F. (Ed.): *Prevention and Control of Robbery,* 5 vols. Davis: University of California Center on Administration of Criminal Justice, 1973.

Gabor, T., et al.: *Armed Robbery: Cops, Robbers, and Victims.* Springfield, IL: Thomas, 1987.

Gates, D.F. and Roberge, N.N.: Updated Solutions for Armored Car Robberies. *Police Chief, 58* (10), 1991.

Harry, B.: A Diagnostic Study of Robbers. *Journal of Forensic Sciences, 30* (50), 1985.

Hurley, J.T.: Violent Crime Hits Home: Home Invasion Robbery. *FBI Law Enforcement Bulletin, 64* (6), 1995.

Lamson, P.A.: A Concentrated Robbery Program. *FBI Law Enforcement Bulletin, 40* (12), 1971.

Macdonald, J.M.: *Armed Robbery: Offenders and Their Victims.* Springfield, IL: Thomas, 1975.

Macdonald, J.M. and Brannan, C.D.: The Investigation of Robbery. *Police Chief, 4* (1), 1974.

McCormick, M.: *Robbery Prevention: What the Literature Reveals.* La Jolla, CA: Western Behavioral Science Institute, 1974.

McDonald, W.F.: *Plea Bargaining: Critical Issues and Common Practices.* Washington, D.C.: U.S. Government Printing Office, 1985.

Ozenne, T.: The Economics of Bank Robbery. *Journal of Legal Studies, 3* (19), 1974.

Rapp, B.: *The 211 Book: Armed Robbery Investigation.* Port Townsend, WA: Loompanics, 1989.

Rehder, W.J.: Reducing Violent Bank Robberies in Los Angeles. *FBI Law Enforcement Bulletin, 69* (1), 2000.

Ronczkowski, M. and Jose, M.: The Robbery Clearinghouse: Successful Real-Time Intelligence Analysis. *Police Chief, 66* (9), 1999.

Uniform Crime Reports, 2010. Available at http://www.fbi.gov/about-us/cjis/ucr/crime-in-the-u.s/2010/crime-in-the-u.s.-2010/violent-crime/violent-crime.

Walsh, D.: *Heavy Business: Commercial Burglary and Robbery.* New York: Methuen, 1986.

Ward, R.H. and Ward, T.J.: *Police Robbery Control Manual.* Washington, D.C.: Law Enforcement Assistance Administration, 1975.

Woods, D.: Robbery: Offenders, Victims, and Places. *Law Enforcement Executive Forum Journal, 7* (2), 2007.

Hostage Situations

Carlson, E.R.: Hostage Negotiation Situations. *Law and Order, 25* (7), 1977.

Hammer, M.R., Van Zandt, C.R., and Rogan, R.G.: Crisis/Hostage Negotiation Team Profile. *FBI Law Enforcement Bulletin, 63* (2), 1994.

Maher, G.F.: *Hostage: A Police Approach to a Contemporary Crisis.* Springfield, IL: Thomas, 1977.

Marlow, J.R.: The Sacramento Situation: A Case History of Managing a Hostage-Terrorist Situation. *Law and Order, 39* (9), 1991.

Strentz, T.: 13 Indicators of Volatile Negotiations. *Law and Order, 39* (9), 1991.

Chapter 15

VIOLENT DEATH INVESTIGATION

HOMICIDE

1. Overview

THE INVESTIGATION of the unlawful killing of a human being is the classic test of the abilities of criminal investigators. Drawing on ingenuity, experience, and the available evidence, investigators construct a theory of the crime. Motives can include love, revenge, financial gain, robbery, but occasionally there may be little or no motive. Investigators need to be prepared to use all their knowledge of human behavior and the resources of forensic science to solve these crimes. The varieties of physical evidence, motives, and efforts by perpetrators to evade detection give this crime an interest and mystic found nowhere else.

THE LAW

2. Definitions

Homicide is the killing of a human being. It may be criminal or allowable, depending on the circumstances.

a. **Criminal Homicide**. A criminal homicide is the killing of a human being that is not excusable or justifiable. The crime occurs where the act or omission takes place, not where the victim dies. Death must be the result of the act or omission and occur within a year and a day. *Murder* is killing with malice aforethought (premeditation). The law presumes all homicides to be committed with malice aforethought, and the burden is on the defendant to show otherwise (that there was an excuse, justification, or alleviation).

413

Manslaughter is an unlawful and felonious killing without malice aforethought (premeditation).

b. **Nonfelonious Homicide**. Some killings are homicide, but not punishable by criminal law. *Excusable homicides* are killings resulting from an accident or self defense. A homicide resulting from an accident while doing a lawful act in a lawful manner and without negligence is excusable. For example, while lawfully operating your vehicle with due care and caution, the victim runs into your path and is killed. Other excusable homicides occur during self defense. To be excusable, individuals must reasonably believe they are preserving their lives or the lives of others. The key is the person's reasonable belief, not the actual threat. For example, if a man threatens you with a nonfunctioning pistol but you believe the weapon to be lethal and you kill him, the killing, although not authorized by law, is excusable because of the reasonable mistake of fact.

Justifiable homicides are killings authorized or commanded by the law. Killing to prevent the commission of a violent felony, such as rape or robbery, is authorized by the law. Other examples are the killing of an enemy within the rules of war or carrying out a legal death sentence.

3. Murder

A homicide is murder if there is a premeditated design to kill, an intent to kill or commit great bodily harm, if any act is inherently dangerous to others and shows a wanton disregard of human life, or a death during the perpetration (or attempt) of a felony against a person (such as robbery, burglary, sexual assault, or arson).

Premeditated design to kill, or malice aforethought, is the taking of a human life with conscious intent. It is a planned killing. It does not need to be well conceived and may be formulated briefly before the fatal act.

The *intent to kill or inflict great bodily harm* is demonstrated if the act is likely to cause serious injury. The law presumes that people intended the natural and probable consequences of their actions. Premeditation is not required.

Acts *inherently dangerous to others* show a wanton disregard of human life. Examples include shooting into a room or vehicle full of people or dropping a brick from an overpass onto traffic below.

Some *felonies against persons* have such a high probability of death or great bodily harm, even when not intended, that they are classified as dangerous (also known as felony murder). A homicide committed during the perpetration (or attempt) of burglary, sexual assault, maiming, robbery, and arson is considered to constitute murder, even though the killing was unintentional or even accidental. For example, a victim struggling to disarm a robber is killed by the accidental discharge of the assailant's firearm. Or, a robber orders victims at gunpoint to throw up their hands. One victim staggers back, falls, and dies of a fractured skull. In both examples the robber is guilty of murder.

4. Manslaughter

Manslaughter is the unlawful killing of another without malice aforethought. Manslaughter may be voluntary or involuntary depending upon whether there was intent to kill.

a. **Voluntary Manslaughter**. Voluntary manslaughter is an unlawful killing committed in the heat of sudden passion with adequate provocation. It is not murder even though there was intent to kill or cause great bodily harm. (Individuals may be so overcome by sudden passion that they strike a fatal blow before bringing themselves under control. The law recognizes that in the light of the provocation such homicides do not amount to murder.) The provocation, however, must be adequate to arouse uncontrollable passion in a *reasonable* person. There must be a causal connection between the provocation, sudden passion, and the fatal act.

1) *Heat of Passion*. The killing must be done in the heat of passion. It is not necessary that the passion be so great that killers do not know what they are doing, as long as the actions are directed by passion rather than by reason. Was the killing in the actual heat of passion? Both adequate provocation and heat of passion must be present to reduce the homicide to manslaughter. Either alone is insufficient.

The heat of passion must be *sudden*. Was the time between the provocation and the killing sufficient for a reasonable person to cool off? Did enough time pass so that actions were directed by reason rather than passion? The length of the cooling time will vary with the circumstances and is considered along with the severity of the provocation and the occurrence of intervening acts.

There must be a *causal relation between provocation, passion, and the fatal act.* It is not sufficient that the provocation, passion, and the fatal act occurred in rapid sequence. It must be shown that *adequate provocation* aroused the passion that immediately led to the fatal act. If the intent to kill existed before the provocation, the fatal act would be a murder.

2) *Adequate Provocation.* Provocation is judged by its probable effect on an average, reasonable person. If the nature of the provocation is likely to inflame the passions of an ordinarily reasonable person, it is considered adequate. A *battery,* such as an unlawful, hard blow inflicting great pain or injury, may be sufficient. An *assault* from an attempt to commit serious personal injury, although not accompanied by a battery, may excite sudden and uncontrollable passion and constitute adequate provocation. For example, an assailant shoots at you but misses and you shoot him in the back as he flees. This is not considered self-defense, but sufficient provocation may exist to reduce the homicide to manslaughter.

Mutual combat can provide adequate provocation under certain circumstances. Who was the original assailant? Was the fight truly mutual or was one person clearly the attacker? Did the original assailant have intent to kill? Did the counter-attack exceed the requirements of self-defense? If both parties engage in an altercation with unlawful intent to kill, there is no mitigation for either party.

Words are insufficient to cause adequate provocation. No matter how insulting, words alone are not sufficient.

A *trespass* into a dwelling house with implied personal danger may be sufficient. If deadly force is permitted by law under the circumstances, no question of provocation arises because no crime is committed in the slaying. A purely technical trespass, even in a dwelling house, is not recognized as sufficient (for example, if a seriously injured person enters your home is search of medical assistance).

It is generally recognized by law that certain *outrageous acts* constitute provocations. Examples include adultery, sexual abuse of a child, rape of a close relative and felonious injury to a close relative.

b. **Involuntary Manslaughter**. Involuntary manslaughter is an unlawful homicide committed without intent to kill or inflict great bodily harm. It is an unintentional killing that is neither justifiable nor excusable. It is an unlawful killing by culpable negligence, or while committing or attempting to commit a crime, other than those covered by felony murder.

Culpable negligence is a level of carelessness greater than simple negligence. It is a negligent act or omission with a disregard for the foreseeable consequences to others. A negligent act or omission may be involuntary manslaughter, even though death is not an expected (natural and probable) consequence of the act or omission. For example, target practicing so that the bullets go in the direction of an inhabited house within range; simulating shooting someone with a firearm you believe, but have not carefully checked, to be unloaded; or carelessly leaving poisons or dangerous drugs where they may endanger life.

When there is no *legal duty* to act, there can be no neglect. When a stranger makes no effort to save a drowning person, or prevent a homeless person from freezing or starving to death, no crime is committed.

IDENTIFYING THE DECEASED

5. Overview

To prove criminal homicide, investigators must show that someone is dead. Every effort should be made to identify the victim. It is not, however, a legal requirement to establish identification. Convictions have been obtained for causing the death of an unknown person.

6. Establishing Death

One of the first actions is to verify death. The pronouncement of death must come from a competent person (licensed physician, medical examiner, or coroner).

An individual is medically dead when one of the three vital functions (respiration, cardiac activity, and central nervous system activity) has ceased. In a legal sense, death occurs when all three of these vital functions have irrevocably ceased. Some *presumptive signs and tests for death* are a cessation of breathing and respiratory movements, the absence of heart sound, and the loss of flushing of nail beds when pressure on nail is released.

Cardiac activity, breathing, and the functioning of the nervous system may reach such a low level of activity that the victim appears to be dead. First responders should make every effort to resuscitate victims until death is certain. Appropriate first aid may save a life. Some conditions that produce the appearance of death include: *electrical shock, prolonged immersion, poisoning from narcotic or barbiturate drugs, prolonged exhausting diseases such a typhoid fever, and certain rare mental diseases.*

Advances in heart transplantation have increased the importance of *brain death,* or the cessation of brain activity, as an indicator of death. In ordinary cases, brain death usually coincides with the stoppage of heart and breathing. Since the early 1950s, however, medical technology can artificially maintain heart and respiratory functions even though the brain is dead. In 1972, a court in Richmond, Virginia, accepted the concept of brain death as an adequate definition of death.

7. Identification Procedure

Identifying the victim is critically important. The identification is essential to determining the victim's associates and activities and may reveal evidence of threats or criminal victimization. The victim may be a missing or wanted person, or connected to another investigation. The condition of the body may hamper identification. The identification of burned, mutilated, or decomposed bodies requires forensic assistance.

a. **Clothes and Personal Possessions**. In the absence of other evidence, investigators may need to start with the victim's clothing and personal possessions. Drivers license, Social Security card, identification cards, letters, and similar articles are helpful but should not be the sole means of identification. Identity documentation can be forged or stolen. In the absence of such items, investigators may need to try to identify the victim through physical descriptions and clothing. Occasionally a name or initials may be found on a jacket or hat, and more rarely investigators can track a purchase or laundry or dry cleaner's marks.

b. **Identifying a Body**. The procedure to be followed in identifying a body is similar to that for identifying living persons.

1) *Physical Description*. Describing a deceased person is complicated by postmortem changes. The skin with time will darken (assuming such colors as blue, blue-black, and brown), making it impossible to determine race by skin color. The hair color also changes; brown and red hair becomes lighter and gray and blonde hair darker. Also keep in mind that hair color can be altered. If the color of the head hair is patchy or if it varies close to the scalp, a dye should be suspected. Microscopic and chemical examination of samples of the head hair can determine the presence of coloring agents. Postmortem swelling can significantly change the shape and size of the body, as the features broaden and run together. The weight of the victim may be grossly overestimated. The fit of the clothing, however, will give an indication of the degree of swelling.

2) *Fingerprints and DNA*. Fingerprints and DNA are the best means of identification. Special techniques must be employed if the fingers have deteriorated from putrefaction, drowning, mutilation, or burning. Advances in fingerprints and DNA mean most bodies can be identified if the individual is in the database. For those not in fingerprint or DNA databases, identity may be confirmed if their residence or family can be located for comparison samples.

3) *Photographs*. Photographs should be taken of the whole body and the head alone, full face and profile. Significant features such as scars, deformities, and amputations should be photographed. These photographs can be shown to persons who may have known the deceased. They can also be checked against files of photographs using biometric systems.

4) *Age*. The apparent age of the deceased can be estimated only roughly from the teeth and the joining of the bones. Medical examiners using x-ray examination can estimate the age from a study of the epiphyses of the bones (the stage of uniting of bones, a con-

dition varying with age). This procedure is helpful only in persons below the age of about twenty-five years. Histological examinations (examination of tissues) may be useful.

5) ***Teeth***. Dental structure and dental work provide an excellent means of identification. Advances in dentistry, more sophisticated dental restoration, and greater use of x-rays and digital records provide more opportunities to identify victims. A forensic dentist is especially helpful in identifying burned or dismembered victims. Age can be estimated by wear on the teeth and the amount of tooth blood left in the jawbone (for preadolescents). The amount of abrasive wear indicates the socioeconomic status and diet of the victim. Jawbone construction provides anatomical landmarks that do not change, no matter how much dental work is performed. Fillings and caps are helpful, since they are highly individual.

6) ***Fractures***. The existence of old fractures may serve to identify the victim. A series of x-rays of the victim can be compared to x-rays in hospital records.

c. **Mutilated Remains**. By criminal design or traumatic event, identification can be complicated by severed or disfigured body parts. Clearly DNA analysis is simplified when the victim is in the database. At other times, investigators must rely on medical examiners, anatomists, dentists, and radiologists for assistance.

Several questions must be addressed. Are the remains *human or animal?* This determination is generally not difficult. How much *time has elapsed since burial or death?* It takes a considerable number of years for all tissue to disappear from a buried body. If only bones are discovered, it may be said that they have been buried for a long time. If the organic matter is present, some conclusions can be drawn from the state of decomposition. What *means, if any, were used to cut up the body?* A study of the body will determine the level of skill used in its dissection. Is there *more than one body?* The medical examiner can usually determine whether the parts belong to one body or several bodies. What is the victim's *sex?* Differences in the weight and structure of the skeleton will indicate the sex. What was the victim's *body structure?* To form an accurate estimate of the height, it is usually necessary to have at least half the skeleton, but a rough estimate can be made from a single bone.

THE INVESTIGATION AT THE SCENE

8. Overview

The investigation of a homicide can be one of the most exciting and rewarding experiences of an investigator's career. Homicide investigation is important and comes with serious responsibilities and pressures. Merely being assigned to direct a homicide investigation demonstrates organizational confidence in the investigator's abilities.

Criminal homicide investigation is complicated by the varied and devious motives of perpetrators and diverse methods they use to commit their crimes. Equally diverse is the variety and amount of physical evidence that can overburden the forensic laboratory and overwhelm the investigative team. Homicides are investigated by a team consisting of investigators, medical examiners/coroners, laboratory technicians, other officers, district attorneys, and other investigating agencies. Investigators must be aware of what services are available and how they can be utilized to further the investigation.

A properly secured and processed crime scene assists the medical examiner to determine the probable cause of death. Physical evidence helps recreate how the crime was committed and the actions of individuals involved in the crime. Common sense (based on training and experience) guides investigators in discovering links and relationships. Imagination aids investigators to reconstruct crimes from the physical evidence and information of witnesses.

a. **Preliminary Procedures**. The key to successful homicide investigation is to carefully adhere to well constructed and methodical procedures. Investigators must resist acting impulsively though curiosity, false urgency, or a desire for immediate action. Investigators' initial activities can determine the success or failure of investigations. If investigators remain calm and act deliberately, they will avoid making mistakes and reduce the anxiety level of others at the scene.

When notified of a possible homicide, investigators should record the date and exact time they received the information.

Document how the information was received and who provided the information. Then record completely the information provided.

b. **Action on Arrival**. The initial phase of an investigation comes with great pressure to do something. Investigators should expect to find poorly organized chaos. Their first priority is to establish order and begin investigative procedures. Ensure the scene is secure and proper crime scene procedures are in place. Note conditions and procedures already taking place upon your arrival.

9. Blood and Other Bodily Fluids

Blood and bloodstains are commonly found at homicide scenes. Blood evidence is useful for identifying individuals, linking them to crime scenes, and recreating the crime (pattern analysis).

a. **The Victim's Blood**. Samples of the victim's blood are generally taken during an autopsy for a variety of purposes. Blood is sent for toxicology analysis to determine the presence of alcohol, drugs, or poisons. This blood can also be used to identify the source of spatter and stains found at the scene and used to recreate the actions of individuals during the crime. The victim's blood can link suspects to the crime if found on their clothing or items in their possession.

b. **Bloodstains**. Blood can be linked to an individual using DNA analysis. Advancements in DNA analysis make it possible to analyze smaller and more deteriorated samples. Blood analysis answers a number of questions, such as is the stain indeed blood, is it human blood, or is it blood from a specific individual?

1) *Preliminary Field Tests*. A preliminary field test is used to determine if a stain could be blood. In the investigation of a homicide, numerous stains may be brought to the attention of investigators. Some are blood and others may be lipstick, rust, food, or other substances. Determining possible blood stains can save time and guide the investigation.

There are several preliminary tests for blood. Some common color-change reagents include phenolphthalein (pink), leucomalachite (green), and orthotolidine (blue). Luminol is useful for detecting minute traces of blood when searching large areas such as walls or carpeting. It is sensitive enough to locate blood even after the crime scene has been cleaned up. Luminol is sprayed on a surface and reacts with blood by producing a blue-white luminescence (a darkened room is necessary for the luminescence to be visible).

2) **Confirmatory Tests**. The preliminary field tests are screening tests. If the appropriate color does not appear, then you know the specimen is not blood. A positive result means that the specimen could be blood. Because there are other substances that could cause positive reactions (such as many kinds of fruits and vegetables), a confirmatory test that is specific for blood is necessary.

Two of the most popular confirmation tests are the crystal test and the precipitin test. The crystal test examines crystals in the sample after specific chemicals are added. The precipitin test determines whether the sample is human or animal blood. Antihuman serum is produced by injecting a test animal with human blood. If the suspect blood reacts to the antihuman serum, it is human blood.

10. DNA Analysis

In 1985, Dr. Alec Jeffreys with a research team from the University of Leicester produced a technique for the positive identification of genetic material: *deoxyribonucleic acid,* or DNA. Biological evidence left at the scene of the crime could now be compared with a specimen obtained from a suspect. Using DNA analysis, it could be stated with certainty whether evidence came from the suspect. DNA is the complex genetic material found in the cells of an organism. The DNA is identical in all of the cells throughout the body and is unique to the individual. Only identical twins share the same genetic material.

DNA is comprised of *nucleotides,* molecules consisting of sugar, phosphates, and a nitrogenous base. There are only four kinds of nucleotides: adenine (A), guanine (G), cytosine (C), and thymine (T). Nucleotides combine with each other in a specific manner called complimentary base pairing. Adenine pairs with thymine and guanine pairs with cystosine. These pairs form long chains that contain millions of nucleotides. There are an almost incalculable number of combinations of pairs possible.

Through DNA analysis, biological evidence (such as blood, semen, saliva, perspiration, urine, tissue, skin cells, bone, teeth, fingernails, hair, etc.) became more significant and useful. Minute quantities of human cells, invisible or barely visible, can be amplified and analyzed to identify an individual. Through polymerase chain reaction (PCR), a small sample can replicated to provide sufficient material for DNA analysis. The short tandem repeat (STR) process examines short segments of the DNA making it more effective when samples are degraded. Mitochondrial DNA (mtDNA) allows the analysis of DNA found outside the nucleus of a cell. In addition, advancements are reducing processing time so that soon results may be available in about one hour.

a. **Advantages**. DNA analysis is often referred to as DNA typing or DNA profiling, and provides a visual image that will distinguish each DNA sample. These DNA band patterns can be computerized and compared to other samples.

There are many advantages in using this method of identifying biological evidence. DNA analysis can differentiate sources of mixed stains that are common in sexual assault cases. When semen is combined with vaginal secretions or blood, the DNA from each individual can be identified. Dried or old stains can also be analyzed.

A visual image, resembling bar codes, is made of the genetic markers. These patterns can then be examined visually or by computer assisted analysis. A match is made when the pattern of bands from the evidence sample is the same as the pattern from the suspect sample. An estimate can then be made of how often one would expect to find this pattern or DNA profile in the general population.

b. **CODIS (COmbined DNA Index System)**. CODIS is a nationwide electronic database of DNA profiles organized under two types of indexes. The *offender index* contains DNA profiles of convicted felons. Each state has a law defining the types of crimes a person has to commit in order to be entered into CODIS. The *forensic index* contains DNA profiles of unknown sources from crime scenes. As records of convicted offenders are entered into the database, profiles from unsolved crimes may be identified. If the same

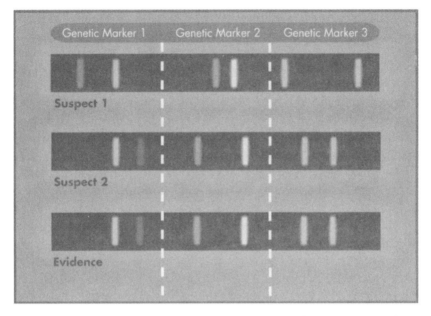

Figure 15-1. DNA band patterns from three genetic markers. The pattern from suspect 2 matches the pattern of the evidence sample. (Source: Weed, V. W. and Hicks, J. W.: *The Unrealized Potential of DNA Testing.* Washington, D.C.: National Institute of Justice, 1998.)

DNA profiles are found at different crime scenes, it indicates authorities should be looking for a serial offender.

The most powerful feature of CODIS is its capacity to compare DNA profiles from unsolved crimes to offenders in its database. CODIS allows federal, state, and local law enforcement units to work together to solve crimes. No longer can offenders escape detection by moving to other parts of the country.

DNA can be used to both identify and eliminate individuals as suspects. In a case from New York, a homeless man was eliminated as a suspect to six murders after providing a DNA sample. He then conveyed his suspicions about another homeless man who might have been involved. The new suspect was brought in for questioning and refused to supply a DNA sample. Fortunately, one of the detectives remembered that the suspect had spit on the sidewalk before entering the police station. When the saliva sample was collected, the laboratory determined that the DNA in the sample matched that found on four of the victims.

11. Location of Stains

Prior to a general search of the crime scene, floors should be examined carefully to identify possible evidence before it is stepped on. Biological stains are often very perishable and undergo rapid changes as they dry. They decompose quickly, especially when exposed to oxygen and heat. Even as forensic technology becomes more capable of analyzing decomposed samples, it is best to send samples to the laboratory as soon as possible after their discovery.

a. **Clothing**. All clothing of victims and suspects should be collected and examined. Shoes should be given special attention. No article of clothing should be discarded simply because a superficial examination fails to reveal suspicious stains. Garments that have been washed may still retain sufficient evidence for analysis.

b. **Fingernails**. It is not unusual to find the victim's blood or tissue under the fingernails or cuticles of suspects. Similar evidence from suspects may be found on victims who struggled during the attack. Moreover, victims are less likely, and sometimes unable, to wash their hands after the offense to remove evidence.

c. **Furniture**. The search for biological stains on furniture should include the underside and tops of tables, chairs, desks, and other objects. This also applies to the bottoms of all drawers in dressers, vanities, desks, and similar items. It is not uncommon to find fingerprints in blood in these places. Special effort should be directed toward pieces of furniture that appear to have been moved.

d. **Motor Vehicles**. The location and amount of blood on the exterior, interior, or in the vicinity of a motor vehicle may often have an important bearing on an investigation. Crime (such as murder, rape, or assault) may have been committed in a vehicle. A body may have been transported from the crime to another spot for disposition. Vehicles can be used as weapons or may have been used in hit-and-runs. The search for bodily fluid stains should be conducted on the exterior as well as the interior of the vehicle, with special attention to the undercarriage.

e. **Weapons**. Any object suspected of having been used to cut, stab, or strike a victim should be forwarded to a laboratory for blood examination. Sometimes, weapons are discarded at or near the scene with no attempt to remove evidence. Frequently, suspects retain weapons and try to destroy trace evidence by washing in water or other solvents. Even after such attempts, it may still be possible to detect bloodstains on the weapon. Blood may seep into cracks in wooden clubs or handles, between the blade and handle of a knife, or between the grip and the frame of a pistol or revolver. Blood may appear as a slightly glazed area that blends into the background on rusty metal, or rust may appear as blood when there is no blood present. Investigators should collect a liberal supply of suspected blood-stained objects, regardless of the subsequent work entailed in examining them.

f. **Plumbing**. Criminals sometimes try to dispose of biological stains by washing clothing and cleaning rags in kitchen or bathroom sinks. They may also dissect the bodies of their victims in bathtubs or showers. Merely washing blood from the hands may leave identifiable traces in a sink or washbowl. When these actions are suspected, towels and washcloths should be collected and submitted for examination. Drain pipes and joints in the plumbing fixtures should also be dismantled and examined.

g. **Rugs and Similar Material**. Any stain, wet or dry, on rugs, upholstery, tapestry, drapes, or similar fabrics, should be examined carefully and collected for analysis.

12. Interrupting Blood Stains

a. **Blood Near the Body**. A male body of 154 pounds contains approximately 123/4 pints of blood. A wound causing serious bleeding will activate defense mechanisms that lower the blood pressure to reduce the loss of blood. Evidence of bleeding indicates that death was not instantaneous. After death, the blood pressure drops to zero and bleeding ceases. Consequently, it may be said that dead bodies drain, they do not bleed.

When the amount of blood around the body is less than expected from the severity of the wounds, it is logical to assume the person was killed elsewhere. Every effort should be made to find the scene of the killing. The distance between the kill site and the dump site may indicate how the body was moved (dragged, carried, or transported by a vehicle). The nature of the terrain will indicate whether to search for tire tracks, bent or broken brush, a trail caused by dragging a body, or marks in the carpeting. Blood traces may be deposited when the body is moved.

b. **Clotting of Bloodstains**. When blood platelets are exposed to air, a fibrous coating forms. It becomes visible in a bloodstain in three to five minutes, and under normal conditions the entire process of clotting will be completed in ten to twenty minutes. The stain changes color from red to dark brown. Physically, the blood becomes a gelatinous mass surrounded by a wet area as the serum separates from other components. If the victim survives, the clotting and drying of blood in a wound creates a protective seal, or scab, in the process of healing.

c. **Drying of Bloodstains**. A bloodstain (or any biological stain) begins to dry at the edges and continues toward the center of the stain. The length of time required for the complete drying of the stain is governed by many conditions. The higher the *temperature* the faster the stain will dry. High *humidity* will slow down the drying speed. Stains dry faster on smooth and nonabsorbent surfaces. Exposure to the elements affects the rate of drying. Drying is speeded when the stains are exposed to wind and sunlight, and slowed when exposed to moisture from rain, snow, and so forth. The larger the size of the stain, the longer it will take to dry.

d. **Direction and Distance of Fall**. The shape and size of blood droplets reveal how they were created. The angle and height of the fall is reflected in the shape of the droplets. If a drop of blood falls from a low height at a 90 degree angle to the surface, it is characterized by a round drop. As the height increases, the edges become more jagged. Drops falling at an angle other than 90 degrees from the horizontal will be roughly oval or tear-shaped, with the point extended in the direction of fall. Depending on speed and force, these droplets may be elongated with small splashes from the parent drop. Investigators can use animal blood (from a forensic supplier, slaughterhouse, meat packing plant, etc.) to attempt to recreate the conditions that produced the droplets.

13. Collection and Transmission of Blood Specimens

Investigators' approach to collecting blood and body fluids must be, as with all evidence, methodical and meticulous. Biological evidence may change and deteriorate as it dries and be overlooked at the crime scene. Specimens submitted to forensic laboratories are often insufficient for analysis. Samples putrefy rapidly at high temperatures and excessive humidity. Dried stains are easily cracked, chipped away, and lost through improper handling and packing. Every effort must be taken to preserve specimens from the time of discovery to their ultimate disposition.

Documentation begins with copious notes. Notes should be made concurrent to the investigation rather than later from recollection. Notes should be specific and complete. Record the condition of a stain (liquid, moist, or solid) and its color. Describe the photographs taken and when sketches were made. Photographs and sketches should document not only location of stains but the size and shape of stains and droplets. Describe how the specimen was collected, removed, and marked for identification. Document the measures taken to protect the evidence and how it was transmitted to the laboratory.

If the object containing the stain can be sent to the laboratory, it should be submitted intact. If transporting the object is not practical, stains will need to be collected for shipment.

OTHER PHYSICAL EVIDENCE

14. Hairs and Fibers

During a violent confrontation, hairs and fibers are commonly transferred between victims and assailants. Because these items are light in weight and difficult to see, great care is needed in handling and packaging. Hairs and fibers from different locations at the scene should be placed in separate containers. They should be placed in a paper bindle or pillbox, sealed, and marked for identification. Where hairs are found attached to an object, such as a weapon, the object itself should be forwarded to the laboratory with the hairs in place. The area bearing the evidence should be protected by enclosing it in an evidence bag or wrapping it in paper before the object is transported. If the object is too large to forward to the laboratory, the hairs should be removed and submitted. Clothing of both victims and suspects should be collected and submitted to the laboratory.

a. **Standard Specimens**. DNA and mtDNA are now the definitive standard for hair analysis. Traditional hair analysis is used as an exclusionary step to save resources and reduce the backload of DNA cases. Hair samples from both the victim and suspect should be collected. Obtain several hairs from different regions of the body. For example, collect at least twelve to fifteen (preferably full length) hairs from various areas of the head. The characteristics of hair may vary across the scalp. If examining the hair of a victim with a scalp injury, several specimens should be taken from the vicinity of the wound.

15. Shoe and Tire Impressions

The movements of people through a crime scene must be restricted until the area has been thoroughly searched for shoe impressions, tire impressions, and other transient or fragile evidence. The approaches to the scene should first be examined. Impressions should be photographed and casted, and other evidence appropriately recorded and collected.

16. Shoe and Footprints

The floor (and any papers that may have been stepped on) should be searched for shoe prints. In wet weather, particularly, such prints may contain a wealth of detail. On tiled surfaces such as bathroom floors, there may be latent footprints that can be developed in the same manner as fingerprints. Foot and shoe prints should be first photographed with the axis of the camera perpendicular to the surface.

17. Clothing of the Deceased

The clothing of victims may be part of the *corpus delicti* and can yield valuable information about the manner of death. Garments should be described (including stains, cuts, and holes) and marked for identification. Clothing can be of great importance in shooting cases. For example, the medical examiner may be able to determine whether the firearm was discharged from a distance or close to the body. If the bullet has passed through the body, the holes in the clothing aid in establishing the direction of fire when the entrance and exit holes are not readily differentiable.

a. **Care of Clothing**. The clothing should be obtained from the morgue or hospital as soon as possible and preserved as evidence. If moist stains are present, garments should be placed on hangers to dry. When thoroughly dry, they should be placed in a large box, separated by layers of paper, with as little folding as possible or placed in paper evidence bags. Never put clothing in plastic bags.

18. Ligatures and Gags

All ligatures, gags, or wads found in the area of the neck and head, or in the mouth and throat should be carefully studied. In some cases, ropes, wires, tape, and improvised ligatures and restraining devices may be found on the limbs or body. These articles can sometimes be linked to their source or to similar items in the possession of the suspect.

19. Fingernail Scrappings

The fingernails of the victim sometimes contain evidence from the suspect. While struggling, victims may scratch or scrape the body or clothing of their assailants. Minute fragments of skin, strands of hair, cloth fibers, and other materials can provide valuable evidence. Fingernail scrapings are often productive in cases of strangulations, smothering, choking, and assaults. The medical examiner will ordinarily collect fingernail scrapings in these cases. Fingerprinting of the victim should be postponed until the scraping procedure has been completed. The scrapings from each fin-

gernail should be separately placed in filter paper and appropriately labeled.

POSTMORTEM EXAMINATION

The postmortem examination is performed by the medical examiner, coroner, or other qualified person in the investigation of a
death. It normally involves an examination of the crime scene,
identification of the body, external examination of the body, autopsy, and the analysis of samples, such as toxicological analysis.
A *medical examiner* is a physician appointed to oversee death investigations, and normally has at least some training in violent death
investigation. *Coroner* is a generic term for someone responsible for
death investigations, and it may have no requirements for education or skill. In some states a coroner is the equivalent of a medical examiner, while in others the coroner may be a layperson with
no special training. The postmortem examination may be performed by one physician or it may be conducted by a team (such
as pathologist, toxicologist, serologist, or histologist). The primary
purpose of a postmortem examination is to determine the cause of
death, while the primary function of investigators is to determine
who committed the offense.

20. Qualifications of the Examining Physician

The postmortem examination, especially the autopsy, should
ideally be performed by a forensic pathologist. Pathology is the
study of abnormal changes in bodily tissues or functions caused by
diseases, poisons, or other afflictions. Hospital pathologists are
trained to interpret the signs of disease, neglect, and the natural
death process. Forensic pathology is the study of sudden, unexpected, and violent death. A forensic pathologist receives additional training in the investigation of unnatural death. The forensic pathologist employs special techniques to gather evidence to
determine how, when, and where victims came to their deaths.
They investigate whether the nature of the violence employed was
suicidal, accidental, homicidal, or other.

Local laws and customs will determine who will perform the postmortem examination. Investigators will usually have to work with the personnel locally available. Obviously, an effort should be made to obtain the most qualified persons available. If qualified personnel are not available, investigators should seek a physician with some experience in postmortem work. State and federal agencies, also, provide forensic services to investigators. Organs and other specimens can be preserved and transmitted for examination by qualified persons.

21. When Should an Autopsy be Performed?

A postmortem examination (including an autopsy) should be performed in every death where there is a suspicion of homicide (including suicide). A physician experienced in death investigation should conduct a preliminary examination in cases of deaths from criminal violence, accidental deaths, suicides, sudden deaths where the person had been in apparent good health, deaths unattended by a physician, deaths occurring in prison, and deaths occurring in any suspicious or unusual manner. After considering the circumstances surrounding the death and an examination of the body, it can be determined if an autopsy is necessary. An autopsy is performed when the cause of death is in question or when there appears to be criminal violence.

Investigators should avoid the practice (common in some communities) of referring only the obviously violent or suspicious cases to medicolegally trained physicians. This practice leads to the exhumation of bodies (embalmed and buried too hastily) because the violence was not apparent at the time of death. Careful postmortem examinations can reveal violent deaths in cases not seen initially as suspicious.

22. Removal of the Body

A body should not be moved until released by the coroner or medical examiner. After completing the preliminary examination, the body is released to the morgue. An identification tag should first be attached to the body. In a criminal investigation, the body should be placed in a body bag and sealed by an investigator. The body is now evidence and must be treated as such. It should be carefully transported and handled to avoid new injuries that are not easily distinguishable from the antemortem injuries. In moving the body it is important to avoid contaminating the clothing with foreign dirt or body discharges. Powder marks, hair, dust, and other fragile evidence should not be disturbed.

23. Identifying the Body

The investigator needs to identify the body to the pathologist as the victim from the crime scene. This is an important procedure that may be overlooked. The results of a postmortem examination or autopsy can only be introduced into a criminal trial if the body is linked to the crime scene. If you cannot show that the body that was autopsied was the same body found at the crime scene, you have lost your chain of custody. Normally, the body will be identified by a law enforcement officer, who ideally sealed the body in a body bag at the scene and breaks the seal at the morgue. In cases where the victim survives for a period of time and later dies at the hospital, the identification is particularly important because the medical examiner/coroner/pathologist will have not first seen the body at the crime scene. The time, place, and manner of identification should be recorded in investigators' notes and reports.

24. The Autopsy

Investigators play a limited role at the autopsy. They should ensure the body is properly identified and then collect, label, preserve, package, and transmit evidence recovered from the autopsy. In some jurisdictions, investigators take the autopsy photographs. Investigators should also be capable of determining whether the medicolegal purposes of the autopsy are being served. Although not trained pathologists, investigators know the elements of the crime that will need to be proven in court. Investigators should ask questions during the autopsy. While personalities vary, it is the author's experience that most competent pathologists are willing to explain their procedures and teach others of their work.

Pathologists who refuse to answer questions or are dismissive are often covering for their own insecurities. Investigators should be wary of pathologists who rely more on their status than their knowledge. They may not be performing an adequate autopsy, and are likely to be poor witnesses in court.

a. **Autopsy Procedures**. The various lines of inquiry and directions the case may take are rarely known at the time of the autopsy. The autopsy must address future issues as well as the current ones, so it is important that it consist of a complete examination carried out in a systematic manner. The examination should not be limited to the suspected cause of death and ordinarily does not even begin in this area. Case requirements influence the process but a fixed routine should govern the procedure. The procedure should be based on anatomical features, mechanical efficiencies, and the general principle that tissues should be examined before they are disturbed. The customary order of procedure is: an external examination, head and brain, incision of the body, thorax, abdomen, pelvis, extremities, and an examination of the various regions. Samples for microscopic studies and toxicological analysis are normally collected.

b. **Reporting the Autopsy**. Along with a summary prepared by investigators, the pathologist performing the autopsy will prepare an autopsy protocol or record of the findings. The preferred procedure is for the pathologist to dictate findings as the examina-

Table 15-1. Possible Determinations of an Autopsy.

• Probable cause of death.	• Time between receiving the wound and death.
• Approximate time of death.	• Assessment of the victim's ability to move after receiving the wound.
• Number and nature of the wounds.	• Probable manner of death.
• Identity of the fatal wound.	• Blood types/DNA.
• Whether or not the wound was self-inflicted.	• Evidence of alcohol or drug use.
• Type of weapon used.	• Evidence of sexual assault.

tion progresses. Negative as well as positive findings are recorded. Many physicians use a prepared autopsy form that guides the procedure and assures a thorough examination.

c. **Legal Considerations**. An autopsy must be conducted in accordance with the laws of the jurisdiction. Generally, an unauthorized autopsy is a tort (the offending party is subject to civil suit for damages). Authorization for an autopsy may be made by consent of the person entitled to custody of the body, by the coroner or medical examiner, or by the will of the deceased. Since the dead have no right to privacy, the liability for an unauthorized autopsy is based on the outraged sensibilities of the person entitled to custody. The coroner or medical examiner can perform an autopsy only when authorized by statute. The unauthorized presence of spectators or use of photographs may constitute grounds for damage claims, but ordinarily the information obtained by an autopsy is not privileged.

The duty of burial is the responsibility of the next of kin who is given custody of the body. Interference with the rights of custody and interment of the dead may result in civil damages for mental pain and suffering. The regulations of the state department of health control the embalming, transportation, and interment of a body.

The principle of the sanctity of the tomb controls exhumation. The coroner or medical examiner may request in writing that the sheriff disinter a body for examination. A court order may be necessary to exhume a body.

TIME OF DEATH

25. Determining the Time of Death

Contrary to portrayals on television or in movies, there is no precise method of determining time of death. Good estimates, however, can be established by observing several postmortem conditions such as temperature, postmortem lividity, rigor mortis, and putrefaction. All of these factors are affected by time and ambient temperature becoming more pronounced with time and accelerating or slowing with the temperature. These observations may also help determine if the body was moved after death and whether the death was suicide or a murder. Other factors that can help to establish the time of death include factors that indicate the victim's activities immediately before death, examination of the stomach contents, insect activity, and chemical changes in the body.

a. **Temperature**. The average body temperature is 98.6 degrees Fahrenheit, but varies among people and in the individual throughout the day. Intense exercise or illness can raise a person's temperature. After death, the body begins to cool until it reaches the ambient temperature. The rate of cooling depends on a number of factors. The air temperature, amount and type of clothing, elevation, amount of body fat, and the composition of the surface in contact with the body all affect the rate of cooling. The bodies of two people killed in the same room at the same time could cool at very different rates. For example, the first victim hears a noise gets out of bed and is killed, and the perpetrator then kills the second victim who is still in the bed. The first victim is thin, lightly clad, and comes to rest on the tile floor. The second victim has more body fat, remains covered by blankets, and is at a higher elevation in the room. The first victim's body will cool at a much faster rate than that of the second victim even though they were killed at essentially the same time.

Investigators should be wary of attempts to calculate time of death using the temperature of the body. It is often claimed that a body will lose one or two degrees the first hour after death and one to one and one-half degree each succeeding hour. Such formulas can mislead because they appear quite precise, but do not account for the many variables involved in the cooling process.

b. **Postmortem Lividity**. After death the blood settles. This causes a dark blue discoloration on the parts of the body which are nearest the ground. The process begins after the heart stops (or CPR has been terminated). Lividity becomes observable in about two hours and fully developed in three to four hours. Once the blood has settled, it tends to clot in the tissues. In about 12 hours lividity is fixed. If the body is moved after this, the lividity remains. If a body is found with postmortem lividity on the upper surface, it can be concluded that the body was moved after death. If the body is moved before the lividity is fixed, there may be secondary staining as the blood again moves to the lowest position. This process can be accelerated by certain infectious diseases.

It is important to differentiate between discoloration due to lividity and that due to bruises. Close observation will reveal distinct differences. A bruise may have a swelling or an abrasion but lividity does not. The color of the bruise is variable while lividity is uniform. Lividity appears only on the low-lying parts of the body and bruises may appear on any part. An incision will reveal blood is still in the vessels with lividity and blood has broken out of the vessels in bruises.

c. **Rigor Mortis**. The muscles of the body stiffen after death because of chemical changes within the muscle tissue (the accumulation of waste products causes the coagulation of the myocin in the muscles). Immediately after death the body is limp and relaxed. The relaxing of the sphincters often leads to a release of the bladder. With the onset of rigor mortis, the body becomes stiff. The stiffening process is first detectable in the neck and lower jaw because these muscles tend to be short and powerful. With time, rigor can be detected in all the muscles.

Many variables affect the speed at which rigor mortis begins and disappears. Heat will accelerate the process by coagulating the proteins in the muscles. Individual differences such as muscular development affect the rate. In general, at normal room temperature rigor mortis may be detected in the neck and jaw in 15 minutes to one hour after death. In six to seven hours it should be detectable throughout the body, with the whole body becoming rigid in 12 to 18 hours after death. The stiffening should begin disappearing in about 36 hours after death.

1) *Cadaveric Spasm*. Sometimes, stiffening occurs in a localize area of the body immediately after death. This happens when there is a severe injury to the central nervous system or when there was great tension at the moment of death. A portion of the body becomes stiff rapidly. A hand may be found clutching a weapon. This spasm is strong presumptive evidence of suicide. Ordinarily,

the hand relaxes after death and the weapon falls away. If a weapon is subsequently placed in the hand of a dead person, it will lie loosely. It is not possible to force the hand to grasp the weapon tightly.

d. **Putrefaction**. The onset and rate of putrefaction are influenced by the temperature and oxygen level of the environment. Putrefaction may be well developed within a day in tropical surroundings or may be scarcely observable after months of exposure to a freezing atmosphere. A body that is buried or encased in a low oxygen environment will decompose at a slower rate. After death, gas-producing bacteria causes *bloating*. With the passage of time the gas escapes and the bloated tissues collapse. The rate of decomposition or desiccation depends on level of humidity. The *skin darkens* and the epidermal layer begins to separate from the dermas (*skin slip*). The skin of the abdomen experiences a green *discoloration*. *Blisters* filled with fluid or gas form on the skin.

26. Indicative Acts

Sometimes determining the victim's actions can help establish the time of death. A careful study of the crime scene may reveal what the victim was doing prior to death. Logical deductions may establish the victim was alive at a certain time. For example, whether the lights are on or off will suggest whether the crime occurred during the day or night. If the mail and newspapers are routinely collected at a particular time, their presence or absence from their place of delivery is significant. Meals prepared or eaten may indicate time intervals. Personal habits such as brushing of teeth, bathing, or preparing for work may be related to a definite time by one familiar with the habits of the deceased. The failure to perform customary acts indicates that death had already occurred.

Independent events that affect the crime scene can be used to establish timelines. For example, if the area beneath a body found outdoors is unaffected by a rainfall or snowfall, the body must have been there prior to the beginning of precipitation. Weather bureau statistics can establish a time frame.

27. Stomach Contents

Medical examiners can sometimes estimate the time of death from an examination of the stomach contents. It is necessary to know the time and size of the victim's last meal. It is helpful to know the specific food eaten and the interval between the last two meals.

Food travels through the stomach into the intestines. Digestion is the physical and chemical breakdown of food. There are a number of factors that will affect digestion, such as the kind of food eaten, the particle size, the amount of liquid consumed, and the strength of the stomach acids.

The rate of digestion depends primarily on the length of time the food is in the stomach and intestines. The stomach begins to empty approximately ten minutes after eating a meal. It may take up to two hours for a light meal to travel through the stomach and enter the intestines. A large meal may require up to six hours to completely pass through the stomach. At death, the stomach activity ceases. By knowing the size of the last meal and observing its position in the stomach, the medical examiner can approximate the number of hours between the deceased's last meal and death.

28. Insects

An entomologist can sometimes estimate the time elapsed since death by an examination of the insects present on the remains. Flies may lay eggs between the lips and eyelids within a few minutes of death. Maggots, the fly larvae, may be present within twenty-four hours. An entomologist who can determine the approximate *age of a maggot* can then make an estimate of the minimum time that could have elapsed since death. If the weather conditions during the entire period in question were conducive to insect activity (e.g., temperatures exceeding 40 degrees Fahrenheit), the entomologist can assume the minimum time elapsed is the probable time of death.

The types of insects that are attracted to a body change as decomposition progresses. An entomologist can identify the different species of insects on a corpse to approximate when death occurred. Furthermore, the presence of species not native to the area may indicate that the body was moved and provide a clue to the actual area of death.

29. Chemical Changes

Chemical analysis, especially for unputrefied bodies, may provide valuable information concerning the time of death. There are numerous chemical changes that take place in an orderly sequence that enable the pathologist to draw useful conclusions.

ASPHYXIA

Asphyxia or suffocation is a suspension of breathing due to a deficiency of oxygen in the red blood cells. Asphyxia includes drowning, hanging, strangulation, choking, and smothering. Death results if the oxygen supply to the blood and tissues falls below the level necessary to sustain life. The ability to move ceases if breathing stops for a period of three to four minutes, but the heart will continue to beat for another five minutes.

Asphyxia can occur in a number of ways, and there may be little to see at autopsy. At other times, a postmortem examination will reveal classic signs of asphyxia. Death from asphyxia may occur from disease such as pneumonia, cutting off air externally as in drowning or smothering, cutting off air in the throat by choking or hanging, breathing certain gases, poisoning, or wounds.

a. **Postmortem Appearance**. Signs of asphyxia include lividity of the mucous membranes, lip color ranging from pale blue to black, blue finger and toenails, usually calm or distorted facial expression, froth around the mouth, and well defined postmortem lividity (blood with a low oxygen content is darker in color). These postmortem conditions are also present if asphyxia was from natural causes. Death is caused by a lack of oxygen in the tissue, so finding the cause of asphyxiation is important.

b. **Hanging**. Hanging is usually suicide but sometimes accidental. Rarely is it used as a means of murder. It is not necessary that the body be suspended for death to take place. The body may be

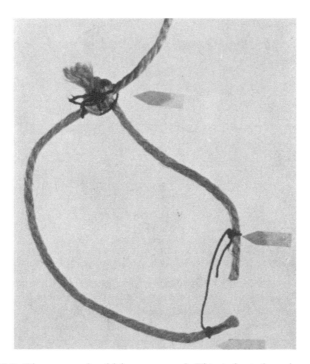

Figure 15-2. The noose should be preserved. This is best done by cutting the noose away from the knot and securing the ends with a string or wire. The knot also may be secured in this way. (Courtesy of Werner U. Spitz, M.D., from *Medicolegal Investigation of Death,* 3rd ed.)

half-prone, sitting, or in a standing position. The body weight provides the force necessary to cause death.

Asphyxia is commonly due to the tongue pressing upward and backward. The occlusion or tightening of the great vessels of the neck may cut off the blood to the brain. This may take place in a few seconds or several minutes and may be accompanied by the appearance that a minor effort would have freed the person. Disorientation from oxygen deprivation may preclude victims from taking simple, rational measures to free themselves. Heart failure may also occur from pressure on the vagus nerve. In legal executions by hanging, the fracture-dislocation of the spine is the most common cause of death.

1) ***Postmortem Appearance***. Hangings are characterized by a V-shaped wound from the rope or ligature. If a small rope is used a deep groove will be made in the neck, under the jaw bone. Black and blue marks are visible along the edges of the groove. After several hours, the tongue protrudes slightly from the mouth.

Hanging may be the result of an accident, suicide, or murder. Accidental hanging of adults is extremely rare and is more common for children. Unconsciousness takes place so rapidly that death occurs before discovery. Hanging is a common form of suicide. Victims may bind their hands or feet. When hands are not bound, scratches on the neck or even the deceased's fingers trapped between the neck and rope are common and do not indicate homicide. If the body is not completely suspended, it is usually a case of suicide, since a murderer will strive to achieve a complete suspension. Hanging as a form of murder is very infrequent. Ordinarily, it would be necessary for the victim to be unconscious from drugs, alcohol, or a blow before succumbing to the hanging. Evidence of a struggle is likely. A hanging may be staged after a murder to give the appearance of suicide. Other signs of violence may be visible about the neck to indicate prior strangulation.

2) ***Sexual Asphyxia***. Incidents of sexual asphyxia will appear to be suicide but are accidental hangings. In the typical case, a male body, sometimes dressed in female undergarments, will be found suspended in a closet, basement, or some other private place. The body may be bound with rope, usually in an elaborate interconnected fashion. There may be evidence of self-inflicted pain and ritualistic behavior. Pornography, literature, bondage equipment, or paraphernalia for sexual self-stimulation may be present. The term *autoerotic death* is frequently used in describing these cases. Victims enhance their sexual gratification by diminishing the oxygen supply to the brain. This is achieved using ligatures or by suspending themselves by rope around their necks to constrict the blood vessels. Victims experiencing light-headedness and euphoria may fatally neglect to unloosen the rope in time. Unconsciousness occurs and death follows shortly after. A death of this type is an accident and not a suicide because there is no intent to take one's life.

c. **Drowning**. In drowning death, the mechanism of asphyxia is fluids in the respiratory system. In the process of drowning the person takes some fluid in the mouth and begins to choke. Irritation of the mucous membranes results in the formation of a great deal of mucus in the throat and windpipe. Efforts to breathe produce sticky foam that may be mixed with vomit. The foam prevents the passage of air into the lungs.

1) *Postmortem Appearance*. The characteristic appearance of drowning can be observed if the body has not been in the water long. Fine foam accumulates about the mouth and nose, the body is usually pale, although some areas may appear red due to the sudden lowering of temperature in cold water.

Investigators must determine if death was due to drowning or if the victim was thrown into the water after death. This can sometimes be determined by an examination of the body. Drowning victims often have objects clutched in their hand, such as seaweed, twigs, or pebbles. They often have swelling of the lungs and other signs of asphyxia. There may be fluids in the stomach similar to the drowning environment. Their mouths are usually found open. A comparison of the chloride content and the magnesium content in the right and left ventricles of the heart may indicate drowning.

2) *Emergence of a Drowned Body*. A submerged body will invariably rise again. The bacteria in the body cause the formation of gases that accumulate until the body is again buoyant. The time required for emergence depends on the fat content of the body and the temperature of the water. Weights attached to the body will, of course, increase the required time. Eventually, the gas escapes from the tissues and the body sinks once again.

d. **Other Asphyxia Deaths**. There are many other forms of asphyxia death that will share some of the characteristics previously discussed.

1) *Strangulation*. There are two types of strangulation deaths—manual and ligature. They are often accompanied by scratches or bruising on the neck that may be more visible a day or two after death. In manual strangulation, the force or pressure comes from the hands or forearms of the perpetrator. Cyanosis and small hemorrhages in the face are common. In ligature strangulation, the ligature is forced or tied around the neck of the victim. Like hanging,

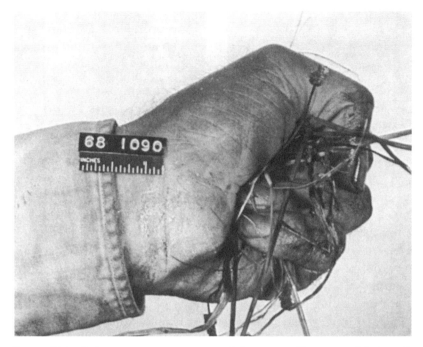

Figure 15-3. Cadaveric spasm in a case of drowning. (Courtesy of Joshua A. Perper, M.D., from *Medicolegal Investigation of Death,* 3rd ed.)

there may be ligature marks on the neck but without a classic V-shaped wound. The force causing death is supplied by the perpetrator and is not the weight of the body as in hanging.

2) **Smothering.** Smothering occurs when the respiratory passages are obstructed (e.g., a pillow forced over the face) or the victim is enclosed in a container with insufficient oxygen (plastic bag, refrigerator, etc.). It is difficult to smother a healthy adult without some signs of defensive wounds. If the victim is intoxicated, medicated, or frail from poor health, they may be unable to resist and there may be little to see at the crime scene or at autopsy. The mouth and lips should be carefully checked for injury.

3) **Choking.** Choking occurs when the airways are obstructed by food, foreign objects, swelling, or stomach contents. Furniture and other objects around victims may be overturned as they struggle to breathe. The obstruction is often found at autopsy but may be-

come dislodged at the scene. Investigators should search for possible obstructions at the scene.

4) ***Traumatic Crush Asphyxia***. Asphyxia may result when a compressive force that prevents respiration is applied to the chest. Accident victims are sometimes pinned by vehicles or victims can become partially buried and cannot expand their chests to breathe. Pressure lines are sometimes found on the victim's chests that are occasionally accompanied by rib fractures. Death can occur with no sign of injury.

5) ***Asphyxiating Gases***. High concentrations of certain gases can create an environment that cannot support life. For example, high levels of methane may develop in sewers killing utility workers or in barns killing farm animals. Carbon monoxide is the most common cause of asphyxiating gas death. These deaths are more common during heating season when people become victims of faulty heating appliances. Victims' skin often exhibits a range of reddish color depending on the concentration of carbon monoxide in the blood. (A more detailed discussion can be found later in this chapter in the section on poison gases.)

BURNING, LIGHTNING, AND ELECTRIC SHOCK

30. Fire Deaths

The discovery of a body in a burned building or vehicle presents a number of problems for investigators. The fire may be arson or accidental, the death may be accidental or intentional, and the death may be a result of the fire or other causes.

a. **Accidental Fire and Accidental Death**. This investigation is centered on the question of negligence. The improper storage of fuel, amateur electrical work, or other careless acts or omissions may point to negligence. Normal arson investigation techniques are applicable.

b. **Accidental Fire and Intended Death**. It this situation, the fire accidentally occurred after the commission of a homicide. The homicide investigation is hampered by the destruction of much of the evidence.

c. **Arson and Accidental Death**. Even if the arsonists were not aware a person was in the structure, they can be charged with murder if someone died because of the fire. Investigators must prove the elements of arson and that the victim's death was a result of the fire.

d. **Arson and Intended Death**. Criminals may use fire to kill someone and also to conceal a homicide. Suicide victims may use fire to cover the cause of their death.

e. **Arson and Death from Natural Causes**. Criminals may use fire to make a death by natural causes appear to be the result of an accidental fire to collect additional insurance.

1) *Cause of Fire Death*. To prove any situations involving both fire and death, it is important to establish the cause of death. Victims may die from direct exposure to the fire or from factors associated with the fire. During the course of a fire, noxious gases are generated. These gases can cause death either because the searing heat burns the skin and air passages, or because they are toxic. Less commonly, a vital organ is exposed to flames and damaged to the point where life can no longer be supported. While trying to escape, victims of a fire will take extraordinary risks climbing away from the flames and often fall to their deaths. Theater and auditorium fires may cause trampling or crushing deaths as panicked people try to force their way out. Sometimes, victims are killed from falling beams and masonry as the building loses structural integrity.

a. **Mechanisms of Death**. Investigators must not assume that victims died from exposure to the flames. They are much more likely to have died from toxic gases. There is a great amount of incomplete combustion in a building fire. Many victims die by asphyxiation or incapacitation due to carbon monoxide poisoning. There are many substances in factories, commercial establishments, and most homes that will produce toxic gases in a fire. Among the gases sometimes found in fires are oxides of nitrogen, acrolein, refrigerant gases (such as ammonia, freon, and methyl chloride), and phosgene (which is generated on burning carbon tetrachloride). The burning of four to five pounds of furniture stuffing in an average living room can produce lethal levels of toxic gas and carbon monoxide.

b. **Antemortem and Postmortem Changes**. The critical question is often whether the victim was alive at the time of the fire. The heat of the fire contracts the body into the *pugilistic posture.* The arms and wrists are flexed in a boxer's pose. Commonly skin splits and bones fracture may incorrectly be interpreted as wounds and injuries. Criminals using fire to conceal a homicide generally underestimate how difficult it is to incinerate a body. The underside of severely burned bodies may remain relatively protected from the fire. It takes a temperature of 1250 degrees Celsius for two hours to incinerate a body. Rarely will a victim's body be exposed to temperature that high for that amount of time. Bodies are astonishingly durable, and usually there is sufficient evidence remaining for the medical examiner to draw some useful conclusions. Some common indicators that the victim was alive during the fire include smoke stains in respiratory passages (about the nostrils, in the nose, and the air passages), carbon monoxide in the blood, and blistering and marginal reddening of the skin.

31. Death from Lightning

Being struck by lightning may result in death from either fibrillation of the heart (marked change in strength and rhythm of the heartbeat) or paralysis of the respiratory center. Victims have no characteristic appearance. People struck by lightning may be thrown into the air for a considerable distance resulting in fractures and lacerations. Burns may be observed particularly in the areas covered by metal objects worn near the skin, such as religious medals or belt buckles. At times, highly typical superficial burns may be observed in the shape of arborescent (treelike) markings caused by variations in skin conductivity.

Investigators may need to eliminate all other causes before determining the victim was struck by lightning. Interviews can help determine if there was storm and lightning activity in the immediate area. Look for signs of lightning strikes on trees and other tall objects near the scene.

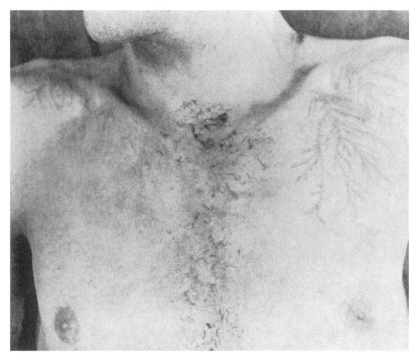

Figure 15-4. Fern-like red pattern due to lightning injury on shoulder. Note singeing of hair on the chest. (Courtesy of Barry D. Lifschultz, M.D., and Edmund R. Donoghue, M.D., *Medicolegal Investigation of Death,* 3rd ed.)

32. Electrocution

Deaths from electric shock are similar to those from lightning. A combination of small voltage and high current or high voltage and small current may cause death. A dosage of as little as 50 volts can be fatal. (The electric chair is ordinarily charged with 1700 volts.) Electricity becomes dangerous when the victim becomes a good ground for the current. Wet hands on plumbing fixtures while standing in water have caused many deaths in bathrooms. Fallen wires and pools of water present another hazard. A high voltage will send the heart into a spasm with death rapidly following. Low voltage (such as 110) volts can be fatal if the person is well grounded but death is not as rapid. Death results from fibrillation of the heart (the strength and rhythm of the heartbeat are altered) reducing the blood supply to the brain. The victim lapses into unconsciousness, and if this continues, the heart ceases to beat.

a. **Postmortem Appearance**. Although the resistance of the skin causes the electrical energy to be transformed into heat, an electrical burn is not always present. Often no mark is apparent at the point of contact or is not sufficiently characteristic to exclude other causes. Pulmonary edema (swelling) and the appearance of asphyxia are usually present. When present, an electrical injury has an elevated, round, grayish-white or yellow, wrinkled area. The dried skin may peel. The surrounding area may be black or may be burned. Matching entrance and exit lesions with the physical surroundings are helpful in forming a diagnosis.

WOUNDS IN GENERAL

33. Classification

Wounds are often classified according to the instrument that made them, for example, sharp force wounds (cutting, stabbing, chopping), blunt force wounds (bludgeoning with no blade), or gunshot wounds. The postmortem examination attempts to answer a variety of questions. What is the nature and extent of the wounds and the extent of damage to the organs? What is the cause of death? (It should not be assumed that the victim died as a direct result of the wounds. Although there are severe wounds, it is possible that death was caused by a fall or by heart failure.) How much time elapsed between the infliction of the wounds and death? Was the death accidental, suicide, or murder? After receiving the injury, could the victim move or talk?

34. Sharp Force Wounds

Sharp force instruments, such as knives, are commonly used in homicides but may also cause accidental or suicidal injuries.

The nature of a wound can be deceptive. Sometimes gunshot wounds striking the body surface at an angle may have the appearance of a slash. A head laceration may resemble a knife wound. The configuration of the weapon (shape and length of the blade, whether single- or double-edged, and its sharpness), and the manner it was used will affect the appearance of the wound. Stabbing (plunging the knife into the body) is usually accompanied by a cutting motion. The length of the entry slit or hole is larger than the blade of the knife. A careful examination of a sharp force wound will reveal the underlying tissue is incised, whereas in a blunt forced injury the underlying tissue is still connected by bridging material (capillaries, muscle, etc.).

The elasticity and thickness of the skin vary in different parts of the body affecting the size and shape of wounds. A pathologist may be able to estimate the length of a knife blade within some parameters. Stab wounds vary depending on how deeply the blade was inserted into the body. A wound could be less than the length of the blade if only part of the blade was inserted or more than the length of the blade if thrust forcefully enough to compress the tissues.

a. **Cause of Death**. The actual cause of death is determined by an autopsy. The wound may be the *primary cause* of death. For example, death could result from hemorrhage when a large artery is cut resulting in significant bleeding. The quantity of blood visible is an indication. A vital organ may have been injured. The victim may have been subjected to a number of small injuries with no single injury sufficient to cause death. In these cases the death may be attributed to shock. Fear, extent of area affected, trauma, and other considerations assist in the diagnosis of shock. Victims may also succumb to *secondary causes*. The victim may survive the attack but later die from an ensuing complication such as pneumonia or tetanus.

By observing the condition of the wound, a pathologist can estimate the elapsed time between receiving the injury and death. It is important also to determine whether a wound was received before or after death. Perpetrators may attempt to conceal the true causes of death by inflicting stab wounds. Wounds inflicted before death usually gape and bleed profusely, while wounds inflicted after death may not gape and will drain rather than bleed.

b. **Accident, Suicide, or Murder**. Most deaths by stabbing or cutting are murder or suicide and rarely accidents. When accidental, they are generally the result of a fall. For example, a person may fall on a pitchfork, picket fence, or against a long needle and puncture a vital organ.

Suicide victims most commonly attack the throat, left wrist, left chest, or femoral artery. A frequent method of suicide is to cut the throat with a razor or knife. The blade is usually held in the right hand (the dominant hand for most people) with the cut from below the left ear continuing under the chin to the right side. One common indication of suicide is the existence of superficial cuts, approximately one inch long, at the point of origin of the wound. These cuts are called *hesitation marks*. They indicate failed attempts before making the fatal slash. Most individuals underestimate the force and depth required to slash a throat or wrist and make a couple of unsuccessful attempts. Victims may have scars from previous unsuccessful attempts. The presence of the blade tightly clenched in the hand of the dead person is also considered strong evidence of suicide. Another indicator of suicide is finding the body at the place where the cutting or stabbing was done. Homicide victims often try to escape or pursue their assailant leaving blood drops and other evidence.

Victims who are attacked with a sharp force instrument generally take measures to defend themselves. Homicide victims are often injured by stabbing strokes. In defending themselves, victims may receive wounds on the palms of the hands and outer surfaces of the forearms. If the victim grasps the knife, deep gashes may be observed in the palm or undersurface of the fingers. The fatal wounds are usually in the neck or the upper chest. Wounds in the back are indicative of homicide.

c. **The Crime Scene**. In addition to the usual crime scene procedures, investigators need to document specific aspects of sharp force injuries. Note the condition of the clothing. Photograph the position of the hands. If a hand is gripping a knife, document the firmness of the grip, the direction of the blade in relation to the hand, the direction of the cutting edge, and the presence or absence of defensive wounds. The extent of the bleeding and a description of blood evidence should also be reported.

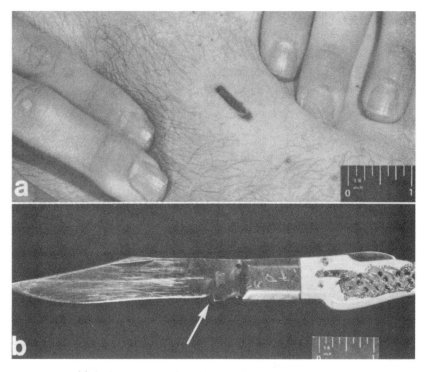

Figure 15-5. (a) Stab wound of the chest. The edges of the injury are approximated to overcome distortion produced by the inherent elasticity of the skin. The upper end of the wound corresponds to the width of the blade. (b) The lower end of the wound shows a patterned abrasion produced by the protruding portion of the blade near the hinge (arrow). The patterned abraded area is separated from the stab wound as a result of the notch between the cutting edge of the blade and the hinge portion. (Courtesy of Werner U. Spitz, M.D., from *Medicolegal Investigation of Death,* 3rd ed.)

d. **Information Obtained at Autopsy**. Ordinarily in cases where death appears to be from a knife wound, an autopsy is performed. The autopsy should assist in determining the *cause of death.* It should not be assumed that the victim died of the knife wounds. The *type of weapon* may be determined. An estimate of the size, shape, and sharpness of the knife or other weapon can be made from an examination of the wounds. The depth of penetration and the dimensions of the wounds are indications of the weapon. The autopsy may indicate the *circumstances surrounding the attack.* The character and location of the attack suggest the resistance offered by the victim.

35. Blunt Force Wounds

Blunt force wounds are caused by the application of direct force and constitute the largest portion of homicides. Clubbing over the head, kicking in the stomach, and hurling the victim to the ground or into some other stationary object are actions that cause blunt force injuries. Assaults, motor vehicle homicides, and negligent homicides frequently involve blunt force. Although crude, the cause of death may be difficult to establish. The external appearance of bruises is not a reliable indication of the seriousness of the internal damage. The location of the injury, instrument used, and the degree of force are factors.

a. **Head Injuries**. In approximately 45 percent of fatal motor vehicle accidents, the cause of death is an injury to the head. Similarly, death resulting from assaults and falls often involve head injuries. The scalp lying over the hard skull is easily lacerated by blunt force. The resulting wound may appear to be made by a sharp instrument. Injury to the scalp and consciousness are not reliable indications of possible damage to the brain. The pathologist by examining the injuries to the skull and brain often discerns the nature, extent, and direction of the force and the type of instrument used.

b. **Spine**. Fracture of the spine occurs most commonly in falls and motor vehicle accidents. Sometimes spine fractures are due to indirect violence such as a punch on the chin, diving into shallow water, or being struck in the head by a falling object.

c. **Neck**. A broken neck in itself is not a cause of death. Death will follow a broken neck if there has been sufficient damage to the spinal cord. A diagnosis of an injury of this type can only be made by an autopsy.

d. **Chest**. Blows or crushing wounds to the chest may result in death by a fractured rib piercing the lung or heart. If the driver of a motor vehicle is thrown against the steering wheel, the heart may be pressed between the sternum and the vertebral column causing heart failure. If the trauma is exceptionally severe, the heart may be crushed, ruptured, or torn out of place.

e. **Abdomen**. An injury to the abdomen may result from a fall, kick, or motor vehicle accident. Although only slight abrasions may be visible, the damage to the organs may be fatal. The liver, spleen, and kidneys may be ruptured, resulting in death from hemorrhage. A rupture of the stomach and intestines can follow a crushing blow to the spine. For example, in a street fight an assailant may drive a knee into the abdomen of the victim causing fatal injury.

GUNSHOT WOUNDS

The examination of a gunshot wound may help determine the type of weapon used, distance and direction of the shot, and the relative positions of the victim and the shooter. If the bullet is recovered, additional information can be obtained about the weapon. If a firearm is discovered, it may be possible to link or exclude as firing bullets found at the scene. All weapons, bullets, and shells should be submitted for forensic examination.

36. Nature and Extent of the Wound

It is not always possible to distinguish entry from exit wounds by visual inspection alone. The kind of ammunition, firing distance, ricocheting (striking another object before hitting the body), passage through clothing, and path through the body will affect the appearance of gunshot wounds.

a. **Entrance Wounds**. Some people erroneously believe that entry wounds are always smaller than exit wounds. The shape, size, and appearance of the entrance wound are greatly affected by the distance of discharge, the type of weapon, the nature of the gunpowder, and the area of the body. Entry wounds may be contact wounds (muzzle pressed against the skin), close shot wounds (muzzle within 18 inches), or distant wounds (muzzle more than 18 inches). If a black powder weapon was used, a gun fired from a distance of a few feet would leave evidence of a close discharge. With modern ammunition evidence of close discharge does not exceed a few inches. Wounds vary with the discharge distance and some useful conclusions can be drawn from characteristics of the wound.

When a bullet is fired from a close distance, it pushes against the tough, elastic surface of the skin. The skin will first stretch and indent before rupturing at the point of contact. As the bullet passes through the skin, grime from the sides of the bullet is deposited around the wound and forms a gray ring. Along with the bullet, the hot gases propelling the bullet are injected into the wound resulting in scorching and soot encompassing the wound. In the case of a contact wound over bone, there may be bruising or abrasions from the muzzle along with significant tearing of the skin in a star-shaped wound from the expanding gases. Powder, clothing, and, in cases of shotguns, a wad may be discovered in the wound. Burning and unburned gunpowder is driven into the skin by the explosive gases resulting in "tattooing."

Bullets fired from a greater distance reveal no discharge products such as tattooing or scorching around the entrance wound. Because the explosive gases dissipate before reaching the body, the wound is smaller than the bullet. The edges of the skin may be inverted.

Shotgun wounds are distinguishable by the presence of shot in the wound or the large diameter of the slug. A common type of shotgun found at murder scenes is the 12-gauge shotgun. This weapon, when fired from a distance of one to three feet, will make a hole in the body of one and one half to two inches in diameter. When fired from a greater distance the gun produces no central hole but rather a number of small wounds. The size of the pattern will depend on whether the shotgun has a normal bore or a choke-bore (narrowed slightly in the muzzle to concentrate the pattern).

The wadding provides a gas seal between the projectiles and the powder charge to ensure the burning gases push the projectiles rather than blow past them. It is generally made of paper or plastic. A search should always be made for the wadding since it gives an indication of the gauge of the gun. If the discharge distance is less than 10 feet, the wad will usually be found in the body. Outdoors the wadding can usually be found within 50 feet from where the weapon was fired.

b. **Exit Wounds**. If the bullet passes through the body unobstructed by bone, the typical exit wound is small and everted (skin edge turned out). When the bullet strikes bone, it may turn over on its axis, push fragmented matter ahead of its path, and produce a large exit wound. It is difficult to draw conclusions from the relative sizes of the entrance and exit wounds. If the weapon is fired from a distance, both entrance and exit wounds may be of the same size. At a close distance the relative size will depend on the path and construction of the bullet.

37. Accident, Sucide, or Murder

In the absence of eyewitnesses, determining whether a gunshot death is an accident, suicide, or murder may be difficult. Circumstantial evidence is helpful but may not be definitive.

a. **Accident**. Accidental gunshot deaths are quite common. Fatal accidents may occur from pulling a firearm through brush, carelessly cleaning weapons, pointing firearms at other people in jest, lackadaisical handling of weapons, and other misuse of a firearm. Questions of motive and opportunity must be investigated before rendering a judgment. One of the most important factors to be considered is the distance from which the shot was fired.

b. **Suicide**. A suicidal death can be contrived to appear accidental or as murder to defraud an insurance company or to spare family members concern or embarrassment. Uncovering the truth requires careful investigation.

The *position of the wound* in the body is of great importance. In murder, wounds may be found in any part of the body. Certain areas, however, are relatively inaccessible to suicide. Typically, suicide victims (if right handed) select an area such as the right temple, the mouth, the center of the forehead, beneath the chin, the left chest, behind the right ear, and in the center of the back of the head. The majority of suicide wounds are inflicted in the head, at the right temple. The firearm is usually held against the skin and may leave an imprint of the muzzle and the front sight. The next most popular area for suicides is to place the muzzle of the weapon in the mouth.

Without the aid of some mechanical device a person cannot commit suicide unless the weapon is within a few feet of the body. If the *weapon is fired close to the victim* (a distance less than 18 inches), a discoloration is visible on the exposed skin about the entrance wound. The discoloration may be smudging, tattooing, or both. These are not visible if the bullet has passed through clothing. Frequently suicide victims remove, rather than shoot through, clothing.

When the weapon is fired, unburned powder and particles of molten metal are also discharged. The size of the tattooed area is a function of the caliber, the powder charge, and the discharge distance from the victim. To estimate the distance of discharge, firearm examiners fire test shots from varying distances with the weapon and similar ammunition.

Useful conclusions can often be drawn from the *position of the body* in relation to other objects. In some cases it is obvious that death was planned. Victims may remove clothing to bare skin or may position themselves so they will fall on a bed. Preparations such as these reduce the probability of accident and point to suicide.

Victims' *actions after receiving the wounds are* often informative. Even fatally wounded victims may be capable of rational acts. Victims have shot themselves through the temple and still were able to move and alter the scene. Investigators cannot assume that the scene has not been altered by the victim or the person who discovered the body.

A strong indication of suicide is the presence of the weapon clenched in the hand (*cadaveric spasm*). It is impossible to reproduce this firmness of grip by placing the weapon in the hand after death. If the weapon lies loosely in the hand or has fallen away from the hand, no conclusion can be drawn.

c. **Murder**. For some homicides, murder is not obvious and needs to be determined by excluding the possibility of accident or suicide. Murder victims' injuries can be found on any part of the body, but wounds in the back are indicative of murder. In gunshot cases, the distance and position from where the shot was fired is important.

The body should be photographed from various angles to show its relationship to doors, windows, and furniture in the room. The distance of the body from these objects should be measured and sketched. The exact position of the body should be carefully documented.

Every attempt should be made to recover all fired bullets. The floor, ceiling, walls, and furniture should be examined for bullet holes, shell casings, fired bullets, and shotgun wadding. Recovered bullets or casings should be photographed, located in a sketch, and marked for identification.

Investigators should note the exact position of any weapon or firearm in photographs and sketches. The description of a firearm should include the type (automatic, revolver, shotgun, and rifle), caliber or gauge, make, model, and serial number.

38. Tests for Powder Residue

The discharge of a firearm may deposit certain gunpowder residues on the shooter. Several tests are available for the detection of powder residue. The gunshot primer residue analysis may be used to determine if an individual was recently in close proximity to a discharged firearm. Levels of trace elements associated with ammunition are dispersed on discharge of a firearm. The procedures are discussed in Chapter Five.

POISONING

A poison is a substance that causes harm or death when ingested in small quantities. The key is the relative term "small quantities." Many substances such as alcohol become poisons when consumed in excessive amounts. Alcohol, however, is not a substance likely to be used to commit a murder. Killers who use poison generally administer it surreptitiously. The substance is consumed before victims are aware they have been poisoned. The problem for investigators is to detect the poison. Substances toxic when taken in excessive quantities or after being contaminated are generally less difficult to detect and are more common in manslaughter and negligent homicide cases. Materials that are fatal when taken in small quantities are more likely to be used by murderers.

39. Classification of Poisons

Poisons can be classified as irritants, metallic poisons, organic poisons, gases, and food poisons.

a. **Irritants**. Irritants produce vomiting and acute pains in the abdomen. Redness or ulceration of the gastrointestinal tract is recognizable at autopsy. An extremely active irritant is termed a corrosive. Irritants are subdivided as *mineral* and *organic.*

There are many common mineral acids and alkalis that are effective poisons. Deaths from *sulphuric acid* (Vitriol) are usually accidental and occasionally suicide. In assaults motivated by jealousy and revenge, a bottle of this acid may be thrown at the victim. *Hydrochloric acid* (Muriatic Acid) is the most commonly used poison among the inorganic acids. It is a strong corrosive acid similar to but less destructive than sulphuric acid. *Nitric acid* (Aqua Fortis) is similar to hydrochloric acid. *Ammonia* is more commonly a cause of death in industrial accidents.

Organic acids include three of the quickest and most powerful poisons. *Carbolic acid* (Phenol, Creosote, Lysol®) is colorless in its pure state. For industrial use as a disinfectant, it is mixed with impurities and becomes a darker color. Carbolic acid is a common means of suicidal poisoning. The characteristic smell and the staining about the mouth are indicative of this poison. *Hydrocyanic acid* (Prussic Acid) is a colorless liquid commonly used in film photography and engraving. Its use as a gaseous disinfecting agent on ships occasionally results in accidental death. It is infrequently used in murders because the rapid onset of effects increases risk or exposure for the killer and decreases opportunities to flee before death occurs. *Oxalic acid* is used extensively in industry as an analytic reagent and as bleach. Printing, dyeing, cleaning, paper, photography, and rubber are some of the industries that use it. As a poison it is rapid and effective. Since it is inexpensive and easily obtained, it is often used for suicide. A burning of the throat and stomach, vomiting bloody matter, an imperceptible pulse, and a quiet spell followed by death in about twenty minutes are indications. The drinking vessels and vomit should be examined for characteristic white crystals.

b. **Metallic Poisons**. Two of the most common poisons used by murderers are arsenic and antimony. In suicides and in deaths from industrial diseases, mercury and lead are common. Traces of metallic poisons remain in the body long after death and have been found in exhumed bodies.

Arsenic is readily available, lending to its appeal to murderers. It is used as insecticides, rat poison, and for medicinal preparations. Arsenic is extremely effective in minute doses. As little as one and one half grains have been known to cause death. Murderers often induce chronic progressive poisoning rather than administer one large fatal dose.

Antimony is less commonly used and is available as tartar emetic and butter of antimony, a substance used by veterinarians. Unlike arsenic, its symptoms are immediate. The postmortem appearances are similar to those of poisoning by hydrochloric acid. The body remains in an excellent state of preservation for years after burial.

Mercury and lead are commonly used for industrial purposes. Accidental deaths may occur when used to prevent contraception or to induce abortion. These poisons are unlikely to be used by murderers and only occasionally are they used in suicide.

c. **Organic or Vegetable Poisons**. A large and effective group of poisons is extracted from plants. They may be classified as *alkaloids* and *non-alkaloids* and are sometimes called *neurotics* because they act mainly on the nervous system. The chief symptoms are drowsiness, delirium, coma, and sometimes convulsion and paralysis. Postmortem examination usually does not reveal any obvious physical effects on the organs as in the case of irritants.

Alkaloids are organic compounds with alkaline chemical characteristics. They are poisonous in small quantities.

At one time, *opium and its derivative alkaloids* were extensively used as a poison. Many suicides were committed by drinking laudanum. Although their popularity as poisons has diminished considerably, opium derivatives are still widely used. Opium itself is the dried juice of the opium poppy. Among the alkaloids it contains are morphine, codeine, and papaverine. Heroin, a synthetic derivative of morphine, is a commonly used narcotic but rarely used as a poison. Morphine is the most common of these poisons.

On absorbing a small amount of an opium derivative, such as morphine, the victim passes through a short period of mental excitement into a phase of nausea and finally into a coma. Convulsions may precede death. The skin becomes blue and clammy, bathed in sweat. Respiratory function ceases and death follows from asphyxia. The pin-point pupils, blue skin, gasping breath, and the odor of opium on the breath are the chief characteristics.

The Bellandona group includes atropine and scopamine or hyoscine. Symptoms develop in one-half to three hours and result in respiratory failure. The pupils become dilated, the throat husky, and the face flushed. A mild delirium precedes death. The drugs are extensively used in medicine and rarely employed in homicides. Accidental death is more likely.

Poisoning from *strychnine* is also likely to be accidental, since it is used in medicines such as cathartics. Strychnine is a deadly poison that rapidly affects the spinal cord and ultimately results in a cessation of breathing. It is characterized by extremely violent convulsions. In approximately fifteen minutes, muscular twitching begins, followed by a sensation of suffocation and constriction of the chest. Convulsions are accompanied by stiffening of the body and an apparent cessation of breathing. The head and feet are bent backward in a tetanic spasm, the face becomes blue, and the mouth is contracted in a fixed grin (*risus sardonicus*). Within a few minutes, the spasm passes and is succeeded by a relaxed exhaustion. After three or four increasingly severe convulsions, the victim dies of exhaustion and respiratory failure.

Non-Alkaloids in the form of soporifics (sleeping potions) are commonly used as poisons. Since their purpose is the inducement of sleep, an overdose produces unconsciousness.

Barbiturates or derivatives of barbituric acid are commonly used sleeping aids. They are produced under a variety of names by many pharmaceutical companies. Some popular brands include phenobarbital, Seconal, and Nembutal. They may appear as tablets or as white powders in colored capsules. At prescribe dosage levels, they induce a natural sleep. Excessive doses (eight or ten grams) result in a profound coma and subsequent death. They are often prescribed for sleep disorders and are a common means of suicide. They are practically tasteless. The first sensations are pleasant with a relaxing of inhibitions. Sleep overcomes the victim and death follows. The toxicity of barbiturates is considerably increased by the consumption of alcohol. A coma from an overdose may last several days.

Another widely used soporific is *chloral hydrate,* the active ingredient of the so-called "Mickey Finn." This is a white crystalline substance that is prescribed as a sedative. An overdose results in coma and shallow respiration.

d. **Gases**. *Hydrogen sulphide* is the toxic agent in sewer gas, but it can also be found in cesspools, privies, and other places where decayed animal or vegetable matter is present. In heavy concentrations, it produces immediate unconsciousness. Poisoning is almost always accidental.

Phosgene is a gas formed when chloroform or carbon tetrachloride is decomposed by heat. Using some fire extinguishers in confined spaces can result in the decomposition of the carbon tetrachloride and the formation of phosgene.

The most common cause of death from chemical asphyxiation is *carbon monoxide,* a colorless, odorless, and tasteless gas. Deaths are almost always accidental or suicide. Breathing the exhaust from an automobile was once a common means of suicide. The reduction in carbon monoxide and other toxic gases through improved emission control systems has greatly reduced its effectiveness as a means of suicide. It takes longer now to reach lethal levels and more likely the victim can be found before death but after suffering brain damage. Since carbon monoxide poisoning results in asphyxiation, it may be difficult to distinguish an accident from murder.

Carbon monoxide is the product of the incomplete combustion of carbonaceous materials such as wood, coal, and gasoline. Its toxicity stems from its great affinity for the hemoglobin of blood. By combining with the hemoglobin, carbon monoxide prevents the diffusion of oxygen to the cell tissues. As carbon monoxide levels rise in the blood, oxygen levels diminish and the victim suffocates. Factors include the *concentration* of the gas, *length* of exposure, *temperature* and *humidity* (insofar as they affect blood circulation), and *individual characteristics* (some people have greater resistance than others).

Death from carbon monoxide should be suspected if the victim's skin has a cherry red color. The source of the gas is usually from incomplete combustion in a defective heating system or gas appliance. On arriving at the scene, investigators should inquire whether any doors or windows were found open. In the excitement of the initial discovery of the body, the windows are usually opened for ventilation. This makes it impossible to determine accurately the original concentration of carbon monoxide. The original conditions may be recreated or appliances tested with the assistance of an expert. A concentration of forty parts of carbon monoxide to 10,000 parts of air is usually fatal if confined in an enclosed room for a period of an hour or more.

Carbon Dioxide may also cause death from asphyxiation. These deaths often appear as suspicious until the cause is determined. Death results from the depletion of oxygen. In rooms where heating and cooking appliances are being used without proper ventilation, the oxygen is depleted and carbon dioxide levels increase to a point that can no longer support life. Once again, investigators should determine if windows or doors were open, and if the room has been ventilated. In certain situations, the gas may still be present in lethal concentrations. In a manhole, the hold of a ship, or a silo, the original concentration may still be present and a sample of the air can be collected or tested.

e. **Food Poisoning**. Cases of accidental food poisoning are generally investigated by the local Department of Health or its equivalent. Police involvement centers on issues of negligence. The focus of the investigation is on discovery of the poison's origin, violation of health regulations in food service, and any failure to report disease. If the poisoning is not accidental, the case is treated in the same manner as other poison cases. When there are a large number of victims, investigators need to consider the possibility of sabotage or terrorism.

1) *Physical Effects*. Most cases of food poisoning involve bacterial contamination. The bacilli belong to the salmonella group and can affect food without any abnormal appearance or smell. The diagnosis is not difficult. Proof is established by isolating bacteria

from the excreta. In dead victims, the spleen, liver, and intestines are examined for bacteria.

Victims usually experience the onset of symptoms between six and twelve hours after ingestion. These can also occur as early as half an hour or as late as twenty-four hours after ingestion, depending on whether the poison was already formed in the food or was formed after eating or drinking. The postmortem appearance is similar to that of gastrointestinal irritation and toxemia.

2) **Botulism**. Bacterial food poisoning may also be due to eating sausages or canned food. The bacillus is *B.botulinus*. This anaerobic organism produces symptoms slightly different from those of ordinary food poisoning. There is no fever, pain, loss of consciousness, or vomiting. Partial paralysis occurs that may affect the respiratory muscles and heart leading to death.

Non-bacterial food poisoning is caused by eating plants and animals containing a naturally occurring poison. Foods include certain kinds of mushrooms (*Amanita muscaria* and *Amanita phalloides*), immature or sprouting potatoes, mussels (at certain times of the year), grain (especially rye contaminated with the ergot fungus), contaminated fruits (sprayed with metallic contaminants such as arsenic or lead) and food stored in cadmium-lined containers.

3) **Physical Evidence**. Investigators should consult the attending physician or a forensic chemist regarding the collection of physical evidence. Food, vomit, and feces should be collected in separate sealable jars. Utensils used in the preparation of the food should also be preserved. In some instances, kitchen fixtures such as faucets may contain evidence.

40. Investigative Techniques in Poisoning Cases

Frequently poisoning cases start with no witnesses or crime scene. It may not be known when or where the poison was ingested. The perpetrator may have planted the poison some time before it was consumed. Links between perpetrators and victims are commonly established by motives (revenge, profit, jealousy, or hate).

When known, investigators should visit the crime scene as soon as possible. Compile a detailed history of activities immediately preceding the death. The physical circumstances and details of the illness may aid the medical examiner in diagnosing the case as a poisoning and identifying the poison. Understanding the victim's activities may enable investigators to discover witnesses and suspects. Investigators should interview friends, relatives, and co-workers about the victim's life during the preceding year to identify possible motives.

Medical records are an important part of the investigation. Investigators should acquire reports from the physician who first examined the victim and the medical examiner who performed the autopsy. A toxicology report should be obtained, and the toxicologist should be interviewed about the poison identified (its common forms, its availability, the commercial sources, how it is administered, and the probability of accidental absorption).

Investigators' next task is to determine whether the poisoning was accidental, suicide, or homicide. From interviews (with the attending physician, medical examiner, and toxicologist), physical evidence, and practical experience an assessment of the nature of the death is made. The crime scene, if found, may reveal significant clues. Evidence for or against a suicide may be obtained from friends and relatives.

41. Physical Evidence

If poisoning is suspected, investigators should immediately begin collecting evidence. It may take several days or even months to confirm poisoning, and by that time evidence will have disappeared. In addition to the normal crime scene search, investigators should focus on likely sources of evidence.

a. **Bodily Substances**. If the victim vomited or defecated at the scene, the material should be collected in separate containers. Some poisons are volatile, so containers should be carefully sealed to avoid evaporation.

b. **Refuse**. The remains of meals should be collected and preserved. Garbage and cooking remnants may contain evidence. The container or pan should be taken along with its contents.

c. **Medicine Cabinets**. The entire content of the medicine cabinet should be collected for examination. Medicine containers may be incorrectly labeled.

d. **Food**. The kitchen should be searched for food that may contain poison. Intact foods and packaging are less likely sources. It is difficult to place poisons in food that is packaged in large quantities. For example, vegetables and fruits which appear intact are not likely carriers of poison. Prepared cereals should be inspected. Powdered or granulated foods are more likely candidates and should be collected. Flour, baking powder, sugar, salt, and spices can readily be diluted with a poison that is not detectable by visual inspection.

e. **Alcoholic Beverages**. An easy method for administering poison is to mix it in an alcoholic drink. The alcohol serves as an excellent solvent and the beverage dulls the senses of taste and smell. Liquor, wine, and beer bottles should be collected along with any glasses that may have been used.

f. **Insecticides**. Insecticides and vermicides should be collected. Plant sprays, roach powders, and rat exterminators are often used in poisoning cases.

g. **Clothes**. Garments, bedding, and similar articles should be thoroughly dried before they are packed. In packing, avoid folding any more than necessarily to prevent distributing or transferring stains. Tissue paper should be used to separate layers of clothing.

h. **Searches**. When there is sufficient evidence to obtain search warrants, suspects' residences and possibly workplaces should be searched for poisons. The search will be guided by the circumstances but should include the items and places discussed above. If the type of poison has been identified, the search is greatly simplified.

42. Special Points of Proof

In poisoning cases, investigators must show that suspects had the opportunity to commit the crime. Investigators need to show that suspects had *access to the poison*. This may be demonstrated in a number of ways. Is the poison a *common substance* and readily available to anyone? Did suspects *purchase* the poison? Investigators should canvass any location the suspect visited where the poison may have been purchased. Pharmacies, exterminator companies, garden supply companies, and chemical houses are the likely sources. A search of on-line suppliers will likely require a search warrant for suspects' computers, phones, and financial records. Suspects may also acquire poisons through their occupation or from acquaintances.

It must be shown that the suspects had *access to the victim.* Friends, relatives, or neighbors may be able to link suspects to victims. If the poison was sent through the mails, such as poisoned food, it may be possible to link the package to the sender. Fingerprints or DNA on the package are excellent proof. Wrapping paper, twine, and boxes may be linked to similar items possessed by suspects. Handwriting or printing on the package may be linked to suspects.

Along with evidence of motive and association, investigators must establish intent by demonstrating the suspect's knowledge of the poison. It is necessary to show that the suspect knew the substance was poisonous. This may be shown presumptively through the suspects' education, training, occupation, or through personal inquiries or on-line research concerning poisons.

43. Diagnosis of Poisoning

An extensive investigation is necessary to diagnose or confirm a case of poisoning. Actions preceding death must be studied, along with the manner of death and the nature of the illness. The symptoms of poisoning are similar to many other medical conditions, such as epilepsy, heart disease, uremia, gastric ulcer, gastritis, intestinal obstructions, and diseases of the central nervous system.

Poisoning may be acute or chronic. *Acute* poisoning is characterized by a sudden attack such as vomiting, convulsions or coma shortly after ingestion. Multiple victims are common in acute poisoning cases involving public health or deliberate contamination. *Chronic* poisoning occurs over a long period of time. The victim appears to suffer from malaise and ill health. Frequently, a medical diagnosis is difficult and inconclusive and the patient's condition improves when away from home if the caregiver is also the perpetrator.

44. Toxicology

Toxicology is the study of drugs and poisons, their effects and antidotes, and their detection. The toxicologist analyzes biological samples for chemical substances in the body.

a. **Autopsy**. A complete autopsy is always desirable and usually necessary in a case of suspected poison. If the autopsy reveals evidence of poisoning, organs and samples are collected and analyzed along with food and other substances suspected of containing poison. Generally, poison is administered surreptitiously and only small quantities are ingested. As a result, only microscopic quantities of the poison are found in the tissues and fluids of the body. The toxicological analysis requires an examination of the vital organs (liver, kidneys, heart, and brain) and samples of urine and blood. In certain instances, sections of the intestines and lungs are used.

Depending on the services available to the medical examiner, assistance in analyzing toxicological samples may be required from other agencies. State or federal forensic laboratories (such as the FBI laboratory) are often used. When using the services of a forensic laboratory, a copy of the autopsy report should accompany the specimens. The observations of the autopsy surgeon or the medical examiner are often useful to the toxicologist. Postmortem appearances such as discoloration of the skin, nails, and blood, unusual odors emanating from the body cavity, or charring, corrosion, and staining of tissues are all indicative of certain poisons.

SUICIDE

People who commit suicide become both perpetrator and victim as they voluntarily and intentionally end their own life. At one time suicide was considered a felony by common law and was punishable by ignominious burial and forfeiture of goods. An attempt at suicide was considered a misdemeanor by common law. In most states, suicide is no longer a crime and is treated as a mental health issue.

45. The Problem of Suicide

Investigators are often called upon to assist in deciding whether a death is murder, suicide, or accident. In the absence of eyewitnesses, a determination of suicide requires careful study of the injuries, the presence of the weapon or instrument of death, the existence of a motive, and the elimination of murder, accident, or natural causes. It is important that these cases are handled by investigators experience in death investigation, particularly suicide.

46. Type of Injury

The type or nature of the injury is not always a good indicator of suicide. Investigators must determine the cause of death.

a. **Position and Awkwardness**. In general, a wound produced by a suicide could also have been produced by a murderer. Certain types of wounds, however, are unlikely or impossible for suicide. For example, knife wounds in the back indicate murder, and cuts on the palm of the hands indicate a struggle against an assailant. Suicides are prone to select the front of the body for attack. The throat, wrist, and heart are generally targeted for sharp force injuries. The temple, forehead, center of the back of the head, mouth, and heart are targeted if a firearm is used. The position of the wound or the difficulty of self-infliction does not exclude suicide. There are cases of suicides where victims have shot themselves in the top of the head or multiple times in the head. There are also cases of victims tying weights to their bodies, and then binding their limbs to insure death by drowning.

b. **Combination of Methods/Previous Attempts**. Suicide should be considered if the victim used a combination of methods, injured multiple areas of the body, or there is evidence of previous wounds. For example, if a poisoning victim also made preparations for hanging or has a firearm close by, the death is probably a suicide. Indecision over methods or having an alternative plan is

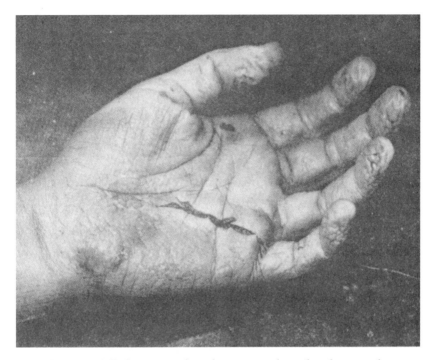

Figure 15-6. Defense wounds, indicating murder rather than suicide.

characteristic of suicide. Cutting of the wrist as well as the throat, for example, is another indication of suicide. Experimental wounds and hesitation marks are common in suicides using a knife. Many victims who successfully kill themselves failed in previous attempts. Look for evidence of previous attempts such as healed wounds.

c. **Extent of the Wound**. It is difficult to draw a conclusion from the extent or number of wounds. The means of death can be very violent. A deranged or determined individual may inflict a great number of very severe wounds. In one case, an aging World War II veteran disemboweled himself in his bathtub. In another case the victim failed in an attempt to cut his throat with a chainsaw (the chain jumped off the guide bar) before finishing the job with a razor blade. In other cases, victims have cut off body parts before slashing their throats or doused themselves with flammable liquids before setting themselves on fire. Do not rule out suicide merely because the method involves extensive pain and effort.

d. **Direction of the Wound**. In firearm deaths, investigators need to determine if the victim could have positioned the weapon (from the path of the wound track) to fire the shot. For stab wounds, non-fatal wounds may be indicative of an assailant trying to discover a vital spot. A series of parallel slashes on the left side of the head and neck would suggest suicide (if the victim is right-handed).

e. **Disfigurement and Clothing**. Many female victims purposely avoid disfiguring their faces. Suicide victims also tend to remove or push aside clothing so the weapon is in direct contact with the body.

f. **Incapacitating Sequence**. Certain combinations of wounds are very improbable for suicide. Two fatal shots that are some distance apart are not likely suicide. For example, shots through the heart and temple are unlikely self-inflicted.

47. Presence of Weapon

The means of death is generally apparent in cases of suicide. In firearm deaths, the weapon should be present. If the weapon is not found near the body, investigators should search adjoining areas. Even though mortally wounded, victims may be capable of considerable activity. Persons fatally shot through the head or heart have been known to travel as much as a hundred yards before succumbing.

a. **Concealment**. The weapon is sometimes deliberately concealed by the victim or by others. In one case, a banker arranged for the disappearance of the weapon so that his suicide would appear to be a murder committed during a robbery. In another case, the victim used a strong elastic band to pull the gun up the chimney after he had shot himself. If fragments of broken brick in the fireplace had not been noticed, this suicide may have been deemed a murder. Friends or relatives may conceal the weapon to collect insurance or to avoid unfavorable publicity.

b. **Accidental Disappearance**. The weapon is sometimes stolen. For example, after finding a gunshot victim in a deserted house, investigators assumed murder until it was discovered that the gun had been stolen by neighborhood children. Sometimes the weapon or instrument may not be apparent. In one case the victim committed suicide by hanging himself from the cord of a venetian blind. Death occurred quickly and the body slipped away from the unknotted cord. On finding the body on the floor with no obvious means of hanging, it was at first thought that strangulation by garroting was the cause of death.

48. Motive and Intent

Motive and intent can sometimes be discerned from statements or writings of victims. Suicide notes are left in about half of suicide cases. The absence of a note should not be considered suspicious.

Motive is deduced by discerning the victim's behavior during and just prior to death. Many victims are mentally unsettled or worried. Worry and alcohol account for a large percentage of suicides. Certain occupations that produce anxiety and tension, notably the medical and legal professions, are characterized by a higher incidence of suicides. Investigators should inquire into the state of mind of the deceased by interviewing members of the family, business associates, intimate friends, and social acquaintances. Focus on any domestic, business, or financial troubles. Anxiety over work and financial issues are common motivators for suicide. Interpersonal relationships are less likely motivators of suicide but may appear as excuses in suicide notes. Interviews should seek factual information rather than opinions concerning the deceased's state of mind. If a witness claims the deceased was depressed over professional failure or money, investigators need to substantiate a history of employment issues or financial troubles.

Any statements by victims of their intent to commit suicide are important to the investigation. It is falsely believed by some that people who talk about committing suicide never complete the act. Investigators should attempt to uncover such statements in the course of their interviews. A search should be made for diaries, letters or emails (sent or unsent), or other personal writings containing implicit or explicit references to suicide.

The most explicit expression of the intent to kill oneself is the suicide note. In its classical form, the suicide note contains a clear expression of both the motive and the intent. Suicide notes, however, should not be taken at face value either for content or authorship. Notes often cast blame upon a recent frustrating experience, but investigation often shows that this was a trigger and not a cause. Victims typically undergo a long series of disappointments that may be unrelated to the stated triggering event.

Investigators must also determine if the note was written by the victim. If written by the victim, was it written voluntarily? Physical notes should be processed for fingerprints and DNA, and also analyzed by a document examiner. Writing or printer samples are required along with samples of paper. Electronic notes will require the assistance of a forensic computer specialist.

49. Accidents

A fatal accident may involve injuries suggestive of suicide. If the injuries are consistent with suicide and the victim was in poor health or beset by financial or familial problems, the death may appear to be suicide. Sometimes the circumstances surrounding a death do not support any conclusion. Cases where persons fall from windows, step into traffic, drown, or are overcome by carbon monoxide often remain mysteries because of a lack of definitive evidence. Physical evidence may sometimes be helpful in these cases. For example, in a case involving a fall from a window the wall areas at the sides of the windows and the sill area should be processed for latent fingerprints and palm prints that may indicate preparations to jump. If a carbon monoxide death is intentional, evidence of tampering with a gas appliance may be discovered.

50. Natural Causes

Deaths from natural causes may also appear to be suicide. A person suffering from an undiagnosed disease may suffer an attack, fall from a balcony or fall into oncoming traffic. For workplace deaths, distinguishing between suicide and accidents could have great financial implications. A person can die from natural causes but there is an appearance of violence, just as a person can die from violence but it appears to be of natural causes.

a. **Appearance of Violence**. Investigators should not rule out the possibility of death from natural causes because of the appearance of violence. The appearance of a struggle can result from the thrashing of a person suffering from a painful attack. There are over seventy diseases that can produce sudden death. Victims of these sudden attacks may dishevel their clothing or severely injure themselves in a fall. Coronary distress is often precipitated by a sudden emotional crisis or physical exertion. When there are signs of violence, severe injury, and a victim with a fatal disease, the cause of death must be determined. How did these factors contribute to the death? Is the disease related to the injury? Could the disease by itself be the cause of death? Could the death be expected from the progression of the disease? Could the injury alone cause death? Is the disease merely a contributory factor, and death a result of the injury? Is the injury merely a contributory factor to a death caused by disease? An autopsy should assist in providing answers.

b. **Appearance of Natural Causes**. A death may be a suicide even though it appears to be from natural causes. Individuals may stage the scene to create the appearance of natural causes to defraud an insurance company or to protect the family reputation. For example, people have killed themselves by injecting alcohol into their veins then consuming alcoholic beverages to make it appear they died from drinking excessively. A more common example is to overdose on sleeping pills. In these cases, investigators should ascertain if the drugs were obtained legally and if the victim was aware of their lethal effect.

INTERVIEWING WITNESSES

51. Overview

The proper interviewing of witnesses is of equal importance to the proper examination of the physical evidence. Sometimes the scene of the crime offers only evidence of *corpus delicti,* and the identification of the perpetrators is obtained from witnesses. Most witnesses should be questioned as soon as possible. The passing of time permits a decline of memory and may diminish a witness' desire to participate in the investigation. The sequence for interviewing witnesses will depend on their availability and the development of information in the case. A logical order will begin to develop as the events of the crime unfold.

Witnesses can be classified according to the type of information they possess. An *eyewitness* is someone who observed the crime. Witnesses may also have information on the *circumstances* surrounding the crime, for example, the individual who sold the poison. An individual may be able to provide information concerning the *motive* for the crime. Others may be able to testify to acts of the accused subsequent to the crime and indicative of *flight*. A neighbor or roommate, for example, may testify that the suspect failed to return home after the crime. *Expert witnesses* are individuals qualified to give informed opinions on the significance of the physical evidence. *Suspects* are, of course, individuals believed to have perpetrated the crime and should be interrogated when investigators have sufficient information.

a. **Eyewitnesses**. Investigators must be patient and exhaustive in interviewing eyewitnesses. Develop a background history of eyewitnesses by asking for a brief history including any criminal record or involvement. Why were they at the scene, and do they know either the victim or the suspect? Witnesses should be asked to tell their story in their own way. Detailed questions should then be asked concerning the identification of the suspect and other aspects of the crime.

The specific questions will vary with the circumstances of the crime and the information of the witness. Typically, questions will test the knowledge of witnesses and their ability to observe what they report. Do you know the accused? Was this the first time you have ever seen the accused? How long did you observe him? From what position did you make your observations? What attracted your attention to the accused? What attracted your attention to the victim? Have you identified the accused since his or her apprehension? What were the circumstances surrounding that identification?

52. Circumstantial Testimony

Interviewing witnesses of circumstances surrounding the crime should consist of a comprehensive examination of details concerning the physical evidence and actions indirectly related to the crime. This type of evidence can be subdivided into several sometimes overlapping categories.

Corpus delicti evidence tends to show that a crime has been committed. In a murder, for example, it must be shown that a person died through the criminal action of another. This testimony is ordinarily given by the medical examiner.

Associative evidence can be used to link the suspect to the crime scene or with the crime in general. It includes diverse activities such as the suspect seen in the area before the crime or the suspect's vehicle seen fleeing the area.

Tracking evidence is objects and information that help to locate the suspect. Phone numbers in the memory of a cell phone dropped during the attack may help locate the perpetrator. Objects or botanical material found in the abandoned getaway car may help track the suspect to a particular area or region. A firearm found at the scene may be registered to the suspect or stolen. In either case, investigators would start by determining the last registered owner and may need to search available records for the history of the weapon.

Once suspects are identified, investigators look for circumstantial evidence that may link them to the crime. Are they familiar with the area? Do they know the victim or the victim's habits? If suspects do not know them, do they have acquaintances who could supply information concerning the victim? What are the normal lifestyle, activities, and income of each suspect, and have they changed since the crime? Do suspects have an alibi or have they tried to establish an alibi for the time of the crime?

53. Witnesses to Establish Motive

Although it is not necessary for the prosecution to prove motive in a homicide, juries are more likely to convict if they are provided a reason for the crime. Common motives include revenge, love, financial gain, and ego, but investigators must also accept that for some crimes motive cannot be determined.

A brutal, sadistic assault or a reckless drunken rage may provide a seemingly inexplicable problem for investigators if the suspect is now a calm and relatively pleasant person. Investigators must be particularly careful when questioning witnesses about a motive. For example, questioning the suspect's family requires courtesy, sympathy, and discretion. When the crime was part of a conspiracy, investigators who separate the members and imply knowledge of inside information may prompt suspects to compete for the best deal. In cases involving an illicit love affair, the third party should be questioned closely and persistently about his or her relations with the accused.

54. Witnesses to Flight

Disappearing after a crime may be a sign of guilt. The absence of suspects from their home or workplace can be interpreted as flight. Locate witnesses who can confirm that suspects are missing. Determine if the absence is unusual.

55. Assessing the Witness

Investigators should observe witnesses closely and classify their moral, intellectual, and psychological characteristics. Is their character weak and likely influenced by corruption, intimidation, or the solicitation of a friend? Are they aware of the seriousness of being a witness and of the responsibility of adhering to the truth? Are they honest but weak personalities likely to be easily led into confusion and vacillation? These and other factors will help investigators assess the strength of the case and the quality of the witnesses.

During interviews, investigators should observe the physical capabilities of witnesses. Direct questions can also be asked about their physical limitations. If witnesses make observations under difficult conditions, are their senses capable of detecting what they report? Do they have any impairment? Is their vision and hearing normal, corrected, or deficient? Investigators should be able to make some estimate of powers of observation and abilities to relate facts correctly and clearly. If limitations are detected, might they become worse by the time of a trial?

TRENDS AND PATTERNS IN HOMICIDE

56. Overview

Knowing your craft can provide certain advantages. Understanding the general patterns and trends of homicide will better prepare investigators to assess their cases and work more efficiently. The following discussion provides an overview of homicide trends in large urban, heterogeneous communities. Obviously, each case is unique and these generalizations are merely guidelines.

57. General Circumstances

a. **Time**. More than half of all homicides are committed over the weekend. Most homicides are committed during leisure hours, particularly between the hours of 8:00 p.m. and 2:00 a.m.

b. **Place**. Generally homicide rates are highest in areas with high crime rates, such as low-income residential areas surrounding industrial business areas. A significant number of homicides occur in the home.

c. **Weapon**. In the United States, most murders are committed using firearms. More than 65 percent of all murders are committed with firearms while less than 15 percent with cutting instruments. Both knives and firearms are often used in spontaneous murders, while firearms are prominently used in premeditated murder. Women are more likely than men to use a knife or ice pick rather than a firearm.

d. **Alcohol**. The majority of the homicide cases involve alcohol, with the assailant or the victim, or both, drinking heavily.

58. Victim-Offender Relationships

a. **Sex**. Males commit more than ninety percent of the homicides and comprise more than three-fourths of the victims.

Table15-2. Murder, Type of Weapon Used, 2010.

Total	12,996	100%
Total Firearms	8,775	67.5%
• Handguns	6009	
• Rifles	358	
• Shotguns	373	
• Other Guns	96	
• Firearm Not Stated	1939	
Knives or Cutting Instruments	· 1704	13.1%
Blunt Objects (clubs, hammers, etc.)	540	4.2%
Personal Weapons (hands, fists, feet, etc.)	745	5.8%
Unknown or Other Dangerous Weapons	884	13.6%
Poison	11	
Explosives	4	
Fire	74	
Narcotics	39	
Drowning	10	
Strangulation	122	
Asphyxiation	98	
Other Weapons Not Stated	874	

Source: FBI. *Uniform Crime Reports—2010.*

b. **Race**. Generally, whites murder whites and blacks murder blacks. African-Americans are more likely both to commit and be victims of murder.

c. **Acquaintance**. In over half of the cases, the victim knows the assailant. In about one-fourth of the cases, the victim is a member of the family. Over one-third of female victims are killed by boyfriends or husbands.

d. **Quarrels**. A significant number of murders stem from quarrels over relationships and romantic interests. These may include classic love triangles, unstable marriages, excessive jealousy, or trivial causes. Quarrels may also arise over gambling debts, disputed property claims, and apparent insults. Oddly enough, the most common causes of homicide are trivial in nature. A perceived insult, a jostle, or a profane slur when mixed with alcohol can readily lead to a fatal encounter.

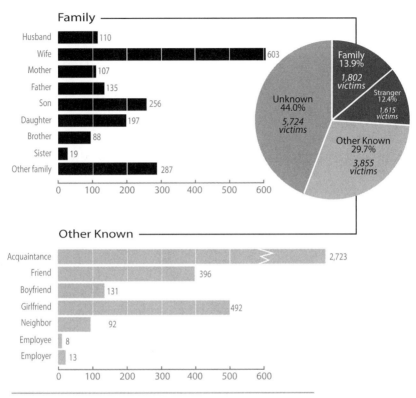

Figure 15-7. Source: FBI. *Uniform Crime Reports—2010.*

1 Relationship is that of victim to offender.
2 Due to rounding, the percentages may not ad up to 100.0.
NOTE: Figures are based on 12,996 murder victims for whom supplemental homicide data were received, and includes the 5,724 victims for which the relationship was unknown.

INFANTICIDE AND OTHER INFANT DEATHS

59. Overview

Infanticide is the slaying of a newborn infant between birth and the time required to report the birth to authorities. Sometimes the term *neonaticide* is used to refer to the killing of an infant in the first 24 hours of life. A killing of an infant after the time of reporting the birth is considered to be homicide. The slaying can be murder, manslaughter, or negligent homicide depending upon the circumstances. It is difficult to get an accurate figure because many of the bodies are not found, however, there were 186 murders of infants less than 1 year of age reported in 2010.

60. Motive

If the death is not accidental, the motive of infanticide is usually to be free of an unwanted child. Motives include embarrassment, economics, deformity of the baby, or mental derangement. Usually, infanticide follows a secret birth. The crime is almost always committed by the mother acting alone. Often she is young, isolated, and in denial about her pregnancy. After giving birth, she often panics and tries to quiet the baby by strangling, suffocating, or drowning in the toilet.

61. Autopsy Determinations

The discovery of a dead infant under suspicious circumstances does not automatically mean homicide. A higher probability of accidents is associated with secret births. A medical condition easily addressed by a physician can quickly result in death when an inexperienced woman gives birth under rigorous physical conditions without medical attention. The determination of homicide or accident can be made only after a careful postmortem examination.

The pathologist will need to determine the answers to a number of questions. Was the infant able or likely to live (*viability*)? It is necessary to show that the infant could have lived under normal care. The accepted criterion is normal formation and a gestation period of at least seven months in the uterus. Was the baby alive when born (*live birth*)? Pathological examination of the lungs will determine whether the infant actually breathed. Did the baby die of natural causes, accidental birth injuries, or criminal violence (*cause of death*)? Is the death due to *infanticide*? This is determined in the same manner as other homicides.

62. Innocent Deaths of Infants

Investigations of the deaths of children less than two years of age are difficult and may lead to erroneous conclusions of homicide. Knowledge of some of the more common causes of death can help to obviate unwarranted suspicions. Autopsies are necessary to confirm the cause of death.

a. **Sudden Infant Death Syndrome**. This is the sudden and unexpected crib deaths of seemingly healthy infants. It is the leading cause of death for infants from one week to one year of age afflicting two out of every 1,000 children. Sudden Infant Death Syndrome occurs at the highest frequency between the ages of two and four months. Though the mechanism of death is described as spontaneous cessation of breathing, the cause of this condition is mysterious. It is often accompanied by a minor viral infection and some congestion of the lungs. Neither of these conditions is considered sufficient to cause death. The infant, apparently in good health or suffering from a slight cold, is put to bed. Later, the child is found dead with little evidence of disturbance other than a spot of blood on the bed clothing or a slight discharge from the nose. Research shows an association between infants sleeping on their backs and a decline in SIDS death. Parents are now instructed to place their babies on their backs or sides when they put them to sleep.

b. **Disease**. Bacterial and viral infection can fatally overwhelm children in a short time because of their size and less effective immune system.

c. **Birth Defects**. The child may be afflicted at birth with some defect unknown to the parents. A variety of medical issues, such as a defective heart or a poorly functioning kidney or liver, may be the cause.

d. **Birth Injuries**. The child may have been injured during labor or delivery. Most commonly the brain is damaged by the compression and the subsequent release of pressure on the skull.

e. **Accidents**. A suspicious injury is sometimes the result of a fall from a bed. Asphyxia may result from food caught in the respiratory passages.

f. **Smothering**. In general, accidental suffocation is rarely the cause of death unless sleeping in the same bed as an adult who rolls over on the child. It very unlikely that a healthy infant, three weeks or older will be accidentally smothered by a pillow or bed clothing.

g. **Non-bacterial Food Poisoning**. Poisoning can occur from eating foods containing a naturally occurring poison. Common examples can be found in the preceding section on poisoning.

MOTOR VEHICLE HOMICIDES

63. Overview

When reconstructing motor vehicle accidents (particularly hit-and-run cases) the proper interpretation of physical evidence is often more important than the statements of witnesses. Accident investigation is unlike many other criminal investigations and requires special training for traffic accident investigators. Investigators should know the fundamentals of accident investigation as well as the forensic assistance available. The investigation should begin with standard crime scene procedures. Isolate and safeguard the scene of the accident. Interview witnesses and obtain statements. Photograph the scene of the accident and significant evidence. Evaluate evidence and transmit it for forensic examination.

64. Hit-and-Run Accidents

One of the tasks for investigations of a hit-and-run is to identify the missing vehicle and driver. In addition to motor vehicle violations pertaining to an accident, leaving the scene of a motor vehicle accident without properly identifying yourself is a violation of state laws.

65. Physical Evidence

Physical evidence, from broken vehicle parts to marks on the roadway, is of great importance in accident investigation. All materials, items, and conditions found at the scene that may be relevant to the investigation and should be recorded and preserved for further analysis. Evidence is used to identify vehicles that were at the scene, to establish that suspect vehicles were in an accident, to reconstruct the accident to identify the causative factors, and to corroborate or to disprove statements of suspects, victims, and witnesses.

There are many forensic techniques involved in accident investigation and reconstruction. Photography is important to document the scene, the location of evidence, and the appearance of skid marks. Casting is used to preserve tire and foot impressions. Measurements and sketches are used to estimate vehicle speed and maneuvers.

A variety of laboratory analysis may be needed. Physical comparison may link broken or missing parts to the suspect's vehicle. Chemical analysis and spectrographic examinations of paint and soil are commonly performed. Toxicology studies may be conducted on bodily fluids to determine levels of alcohol or drug use. An autopsy will determine the cause of death and help to recreate the accident.

66. Examination of the Scene

The scene investigation consists of three phases: the scene of the accident, the bodies of victims, and suspected vehicles. The scene of the accident frequently provides the only clues to the identity of hit-and-run vehicles. The scene may contain sufficient evidence to prove how the accident occurred and to support or dispute statements of those involved. Factors such as faulty perceptions, memory, levels of intelligence, and emotional stability affect the testimony of witnesses, so the physical evidence may be the only objective evidence available to investigators.

Every part of the scene must be examined, starting with the point of impact and moving to surrounding areas and the approaches to the scene. The search must be planned and systematic. The particular pattern of the search will vary with the individual case.

Several factors should be considered in a search plan. The scene should be secured so that fragile evidence is not destroyed. Evidence such as tire tracks, foot impressions, and stains should be preserved before addressing less destructible items. No significant area should be overlooked. The path of the hit-and-run vehicle should be examined for glass particles, metal fragments, and paint flakes that may have fallen from the vehicle. The approach to the point of impact should be examined for skid marks and tire impressions. Notes should be taken as the search progresses. Physical evidence should be marked for identification as it is picked up. The length of skid marks are an indication of the speed a vehicle was traveling. By knowing the coefficient of friction of the roadway and the length of the skid marks, an accident investigator can determine the minimum speed of the vehicle before the brakes were applied.

a. **Collecting and Marking Evidence**. After collecting and marking evidence, it should be documented in the investigator's notebook. The exact position of evidence should be recorded with reference to fixed objects and to the vehicle. Document the condition of the evidence (broken, dirty, etc.). Describe evidence and its probable source. Record the names of investigators who witnessed the finding of evidence.

The articles that can be removed should be placed in clean containers, envelopes, or cardboard boxes and properly marked. Large objects should be marked with an identifying mark, tagged, and secured.

b. **Photography**. All significant elements of the scene should be photographed. Several photos should be taken to insure complete coverage. Contributing factors such as foliage obstructing vision should be shown. Since perspective can influence accounts of what happened, the scene should be photographed from several different angles. Particularly important are the points of view of drivers, pedestrians, and any witnesses.

Photographs should portray a normal perspective. If the camera is too close or too distant, the relationship of objects will be distorted. As a general rule, the camera should be at eye level or positioned at the point of view of the observer. You should also strive to achieve great depth of field to better show relationships.

The scene should first be photographed to show general conditions, approaches to the point of impact, and the views of the different drivers. Vehicles should be photographed from all side with special attention to any damage. All tire tracks and skid marks should be documented with photographs.

c. **Evidence at the Scene**. Usually skid marks, tire tracks, and broken parts will be found. In addition, investigators may find mud and dirt that has fallen from the undersurface of the fenders of the vehicles. Dirt of this nature is easily recognized in the roadway. Samples should be collected and preserved for a possible later comparison with dirt obtained from the undersurfaces of the fenders of the suspected vehicle. Evidence of this nature is seldom conclusive because of the wide variety of soil that may be encountered in the vehicle's travels. Sometimes the shape of a piece of dirt may be significant. If the impact caused a large piece of dirt to fall intact it may be possible to find a corresponding cavity in the dirt remaining on the fenders.

It is sometimes possible to find small fragments of cloth, usually in the path of the skid marks. When the injured person is run over by the wheels of the vehicle, these small fragments of cloth are torn away and left in the roadway and on the striking vehicle. The tires and undercarriage of suspect vehicles should be examined for pieces of cloth or fibers.

When two cars collide it is to be expected that there will be an exchange of paint smears and small flakes of paint will be shaken loose and fall to the ground. It is possible from the examination of a flake of paint to determine the make and year of a car. If a vehicle has been repainted, the possibility of linking a paint sample to it improves. All samples of paint found at the scene of an accident should be collected.

67. Examination of the Victim

Victims may bear marks from the striking vehicle on their bodies or clothing. Both should be examined carefully. The clothing should be removed and studied for grease or oil (from the understructure of the vehicle), tire marks, and paint. There may be distinct tire or impact marks on the victim's back or chest. In addition, bone fractures may be distinctive to the type of accident.

68. Examination of the Suspected Vehicle

It may be difficult to determine whether a suspected vehicle has been in an accident. Often the body of the victim is cast aside on impact and leaves no evidence on the vehicle. If the vehicle collides squarely with a person, evidence is more likely.

It is not easy to determine the age of dents and scratches. The damage may have resulted from the accident or occurred earlier.

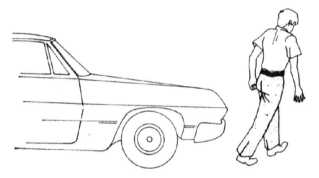

Figure 15-8. An adult pedestrian struck below the center of gravity sustains bumper injuries on his legs and an impact on the hip by the front of the hood.

Figure 15-9. At city speeds, the adult pedestrian is propelled upward after impact by the front of the vehicle and slides onto the hood. When the vehicle slows or comes to a halt, the victim rolls to the ground.

Figure 15-10. At highway speeds, the victim is thrown higher and on the roof or trunk of the automobile or strikes the rear bumper, from where blood or skin may be recovered. The victim may land on the road behind the car and be run over by other vehicles. (Courtesy of Werner U. Spitz, M.D., from *Medicolegal Investigation of Death,* 3rd ed.)

Pieces of glass and plastic may remain in recesses or cavities for lights or may fall into the engine compartment. A broken emblem or side mirror should be examined. The owner of the vehicle should be questioned concerning the damage and the story corroborated.

Trace evidence from the victim may be found on the suspect vehicle. Cloth or fiber may be found adhering to the vehicle body or undercarriage. If the victim is struck with sufficient force, an outline of the clothing pattern may be seen on the paint. In particularly violent accidents, bloodstains and tissue may be found on the radiator, the door handles, and other parts.

The undercarriage and tires of the vehicle should be examined for cloth, fibers, hair, blood, and tissue from the victim. Road dirt and soil should be examined on tires and under the fenders.

ADDITIONAL READING

Death Investigation

Browne, A.: *When Battered Women Kill.* New York: Free Press, 1987.

Catts, P.E. and Haskell, N.H. (Eds.): *Entomology and Death: A Procedural Guide.* Clemson, SC: Forensic Entomology Associates, 1990.

Copeland, A.R.: Accidental Death by Gunshot Wound. Fact or Fiction. *Forensic Science International, 26* (25), 1984.

——: Homicidal Drowning. *Forensic Science International, 31* (247), 1986.

DiMaio, D.J. and DiMaio, V.J.M.: *Forensic Pathology.* New York: Elsevier, 1989.

Duncan, T.S.: Death in the Office: Workplace Homicides. *FBI Law Enforcement Bulletin, 64* (4), 1995.

Eliopulos, L.N.: Death *Investigator's Handbook.* Boulder, CO: Paladin Press, 1993.

Erzinclioglu, Y.Z.: Forensic Entomology and Criminal Investigation. *The Police Journal, 64* (1), 1991.

Esposito, L., Minda, L., and Forman, C.: Sudden Infant Death Syndrome. *FBI Law Enforcement Bulletin, 67* (9), 1998.

Falk, G.: *Murder: An Analysis of Its Forms, Conditions and Causes.* Jefferson, NC: McFarland, 1990.

Fisher, B.A.J.: *Techniques of Crime Scene Investigation* (6th ed.). Boca Raton, FL: CRC Press, 1999.

Geberth, V.J.: Investigation of Drug-Related Homicides. *Law and Order, 38* (11), 1990.

——: *Practical Homicide Investigation* (3rd ed.). Boca Raton, FL: CRC Press, 1996.

——: Sex-Related Crimes. *Law and Order, 44* (8), 1996.

——: The Staged Crime Scene. *Law and Order, 44* (2), 1996.

Gormsen, H., Jeppesen, N. and Lund. A.: The Causes of Death in Fire Victims. *Forensic Science International, 24* (107), 1984.

Harries, K.D.: *Serious Violence: Patterns of Homicide and Assault in America.* Springfield, IL: Thomas, 1990.

Harris, R.I.: *Outline of Death Investigation.* Springfield, IL: Thomas, 1973.

Hazelwood, R.R., Dietz, P.E. and Burgess, A.W.: *Autoerotic Fatalities.* Lexington, MA: Lexington Books, 1983.

Hazelwood, R.R. and Douglas, J.E.: The Lust Murderer. *FBI Law Enforcement Bulletin, 49* (4), 1980.

Hughes, D.J.: *Homicide: Investigative Techniques.* Springfield, IL: Thomas, 1974.

Hunter, J.A., Hazelwood, R.R. and Slesinger, D.: Juvenile Sexual Homicide. *FBI and Law Enforcement Bulletin, 69* (3), 2000.

Johann, S.L. and Osanka, R.: *Representing . . . Battered Women Who Kill.* Springfield, IL: Thomas, 1989.

Kelleher, M.D.: *When Good Kids Kill.* Westport, CT: Praeger, 1998.

Lipskin, B.A. and Field, K.S. (Eds.): *Death Investigation and Examination: Medicolegal Guidelines and Checklists.* Colorado Springs, CO: Forensic Sciences Foundation Press, 1984.

Macdonald, J.M.: *The Murderer and His Victim* (2nd ed.). Springfield, IL: Thomas, 1986.

Morse, D. and Dailey, R.C.: The Degree of Deterioration of Associated Death Scene Material. *Journal of Forensic Science, 30* (119), 1985.

O'Dell, A.: Domestic Violence Homicides. *Police Chief, 63* (2), 1996.

Poole, H. and Jurovics, S.: Unsolved Homicides Team. *FBI and Law Enforcement Bulletin, 62* (3), 1993.

Regini, C.L.: The Cold Case Concept. *FBI and Law Enforcement Bulletin, 66* (8), 1997.

Ressler, R.K., Burgess, A.W., and Douglas, J.E.: *Sexual Homicide: Patterns and Motives.* Lexington, MA: D.C. Heath, 1988.

Revitch, E. and Schlesinger, L.B.: *Sex Murder and Sex Aggression: Phenomenology, Psychopathology, Psychodynamics and Prognosis.* Springfield, IL: Thomas, 1989.

Riedel, M. and Zahn, M.A.: *The Nature and Patterns of American Homicide.* Washington, D.C.: U.S. Government Printing Office, 1985.

Rodriguez, W.C. III and Bass, W.M.: Decomposition of Buried Bodies and Methods that May Aid in their Location. *Journal of Forensic Sciences, 30* (836), 1985.

Uniform Crime Reports, 2010. Available http://www.fbi.gov/about-us/cjis/ucr/crime-in-the-u.s/2010/crime-in-the-u.s.-2010/offenses-known-to-law-enforcement/expanded/expandhomicidemain.

Wagner, S.A.: *Death Scene Investigation.* Boca Raton, FL, CRC Press, 2009.

Wellford, C. and Cronin, J.: Homicide: What Police Can Do to Improve Homicide Rates. *National Institute of Justice Journal,* April 2000.

Multiple Murder

Brooks, P.R., et al.: Serial Murder: A Criminal Justice Response. *Police Chief, 54* (6), 1987.

Egger, S.A.: *The Killers Among Us: An Examination of Serial Murder and Its Investigations.* Upper Saddle River, NJ: Prentice-Hall, 1998.

——: A Working Definition of Serial Murder and the Reduction of Linkage Blindness. *Journal of Police Science and Administration, 12* (348), 1984.

Fox, J.A. and Levin, J.: *Mass Murder: America's Growing Menace.* New York: Plenum, 1985.

Geberth, V.J.: The Serial Killer and the Revelations of Ted Bundy. *Law and Order, 38* (5), 1990.

——: Psychopathic Sexual Sadists: The Psychology and Psychodynamics of Serial Killers. *Law and Order, 43* (4), 1995.

Goodroe, C.: Tracking the Serial Offender: The NCAVC Connection. *Law and Order, 35* (7), 1987.

Green, T.J.: VICAP's Role in Multiagency Serial Murder Investigations. *Police Chief, 60* (6), 1993.

Hickey, E.W.: *Serial Murderers and Their Victims.* Pacific Grove, CA: Brooks/Cole, 1991.

Holmes, R.M. and DeBurger, J.: *Serial Murder.* Newbury Park, CA: Sage, 1988.

Jenkins, P.: Serial Murders in England 1940-1985. *Journal of Criminal Justice, 16* (1), 1988.

——: Serial Murders in the United States 1900-1940: A Historical Perspective. *Journal of Criminal Justice, 17* (5), 1989.

Keppel, R.D.: *Serial Murder: Future Implications for Police Investigations.* Cincinnati: Anderson, 1988.

Kozenczak, J.R. and Henrikson, K.M.: In Pursuit of a Serial Murderer. *Law and Order, 35* (8), 1987.

Leyton, E.: *Compulsive Killers: The Story of Modern Multiple Murder.* New York: Columbia University Press, 1986.

McElhone, J.J.: Stopping a Serial Sniper. *FBI Law Enforcement Bulletin, 65* (4), 1996.

Terry, G. and Malone, M.P.: The "Bobby Joe" Long Serial Murder Case: A Study in Cooperation. Parts I and II. *FBI Law Enforcement Bulletin, 56* (11 & 12), 1987.

Suicide

Cimbolic, P. and Jobes, D.A.: *Youth Suicide: Issues, Assessment, and Intervention.* Springfield, IL: Thomas, 1990.

Fisher, D.: High School Suicide Crisis Intervention. *FBI Law Enforcement Bulletin, 59* (5), 1990.

Geberth, V.J.: Investigating a Suicide. *Law and Order, 36* (12), 1988.

Johnson, A.P.: Hammer Spur Impression: Physical Evidence in Suicides. *FBI Law Enforcement Bulletin, 57* (9), 1988.

Kennedy, D.B., Homant, R.J. and Hupp, R.T.: Suicide by Cop. *FBI Law Enforcement Bulletin, 67* (8), 1988.

Lester, D.: Suicide as a Learned Behavior. Springfield, Ill.: Thomas, 1987.

——: *Why People Kill Themselves: A 1990's Summary of Research Findings on Suicidal Behavior* (3rd ed.). Springfield, IL: Thomas, 1992.

——: *Why Women Kill Themselves.* Springfield, IL: Thomas, 1988.

Massello, W. III: The Proof in Law of Suicide. *Journal of Forensic Science, 31* (1000), 1986.

Stone, I.C.: Observations and Statistics Relating to Suicide Weapons: An Update. *Journal of Forensic Sciences, 35* (10), 1990.

Van Zandt, C.R.: "Suicide by Cop." *Police Chief, 60* (7), 1993.

Woods, D. & Polizzi, D.: Shoot Me! An Overview of Suicide by Cop. *Law Enforcement Executive Forum, 8* (2), 2008.

Bloodstain Evidence

Bevel, T. and Gardner, R.M.: *Bloodstain Pattern Analysis with an Introduction to Crime Scene Reconstruction.* Boca Raton, FL: CRC Press, 1997.

Cox, M.: A Study of the Sensitivity and Specificity of Four Presumptive Tests for Blood. *Journal of Forensic Sciences, 36* (1503), 1991.

——: Effect of Fabric Washing on the Presumptive Identification of Bloodstains. *Journal of Forensic Sciences, 35* (1335), 1990.

Eckert, W.G. and James, S.H.: *Interpretation of Bloodstain Evidence on Crime Scene.* New York: Elsevier, 1989.

Grispino, R.R.J.: Serological Evidence in Sexual Assault Investigations. *FBI Law Enforcement Bulletin, 59* (10), 1990.

Hunt, S.M.: *Investigation of Serological Evidence: A Manual for Field Investigators.* Springfield, IL: Thomas, 1984.

Laux, D.L.: Effects of Luminol on the Subsequent Analysis of Bloodstains. *Journal of Forensic Sciences, 36* (1512), 1991.

Lytle, L.T. and Hedgecock, D.G.: Chemiluminescence in the Visualization of Forensic Bloodstains. *Journal of Forensic Sciences, 23* (550), 1978.

MacDonell, H.L.: *Flight Characteristics and Stain Patterns of Human Blood.* Washington, D.C.: U.S. Government Printing Office, 1971.

Miller, L.S. and Brown, A.M.: *Criminal Evidence Laboratory Manual* (2nd ed.). Cincinnati: Anderson, 1990.

Murch, R.S.: The FBI Serology Unit: Services, Policies, and Procedures. *FBI Law Enforcement Bulletin, 54* (3), 1985.

Pizzola, P.A., Roth, S. and De Forest, P.R.: Blood Droplet Dynamics–Part I and II. *Journal of Forensic Sciences, 31* (36 & 50), 1986.

DNA Analysis

DNA Profiling Advancement. *FBI Law Enforcement Bulletin, 67* (2), 1998.

Fenton, J.: Baltimore Police to Develop Faster DNA Testing, Baltimore Sun, September 27, 2011. Available at www.baltimoresun.com/news/maryland/baltimore-city/bs-md-ci-dna-police-testing-20110927,0,6865075. story 10/18/20011.

Geberth, V.J.: Application of DNA Technology in Criminal Investigations. *Law and Order, 38* (3), 1990.

——: DNA Print Identification Test Provides Crucial Evidence in Lust Murder Case. *Law and Order, 36* (7), 1988.

Hicks, J.W.: DNA Profiling: A Tool for Law Enforcement. *FBI Law Enforcement Bulletin, 57* (8), 1988.

Miller, J.V.: The FBI's Forensic DNA Analysis Program. *FBI Law Enforcement Bulletin, 60* (7), 1991.

Saferstein, R.: *Criminalistics: An Introduction to Forensic Science* (7th ed.). Englewood Cliffs, NJ: Prentice-Hall, 2000.

Using DNA to Solve Cold Cases, NIJ Special Report, NCJ 194197, US Department of Justice, July 2, 2002.

Sylvester, J.T. and Stafford, J.H.: Judicial Acceptance of DNA Profiling. *FBI Law Enforcement Bulletin, 60* (7), 1991.

What Every Law Enforcement Officer Should Know About DNA Evidence. Washington, D.C.: National Institute of Justice, 1999.

Motor Vehicle Homicide

Badger, J.E.: Investigating Vehicular Homicide. *Law and Order, 36* (3), 1988.

Baker, J.S. and Lindquist, T.: *Lamp Examinations for On or Off in Traffic Accidents.* Evanston, IL: The Traffic Institute, Northwestern University, 1977.

Barrette, R.: Accident Scene Evidence: Placing the Driver behind the Wheel. Police: *The Law Officer's Magazine, 13* (12), 1989.

Basham, D.J.: *Traffic Accident Management.* Springfield, IL: Thomas, 1979.

Brown, J.F. and Obenski, K.S.: *Forensic Engineering Reconstruction of Accidents.* Springfield, IL: Thomas, 1990.

Collins, J.D.: *Accident Reconstruction.* Springfield, IL: Thomas, 1979.

Daily, J.: *Fundamentals of Accident Reconstruction.* Jacksonville, FL: Institute of Police Technology and Management, 1989.

von Breman, A.: The Comparison of Brake and Accelerator Pedals with Marks on Shoe Soles. *Journal of Forensic Sciences, 35* (14), 1990.

Woods, J.: Headlights are Tools in Traffic Accident Investigation. *Law and Order, 25* (6), 1977.

Zeldes, I.: Speedometer Examination: An Aid in Accident Investigation. *FBI Law Enforcement Bulletin, 49* (3), 1980.

Chapter 16

SEX OFFENSES

1. Overview

A VARIETY OF CRIMES are classified as sex offenses including rape, sexual assault, sexual abuse, and other deviant sexual practices prohibited by state laws. Investigations of these offenses are particularly demanding and require discretion and tact. Moreover, accusations of a sex offense can be easily made and often difficult to substantiate or disprove. Investigators are responsible for protecting the reputations of innocent subjects as well as prosecuting sexual predators.

RAPE AND SEXUAL ASSAULT

2. Overview

The terms rape, sexual misconduct, and sexual assault are often interchangeable and vary by state statute. Many states have incorporated the crime of rape into an encompassing statute of sexual assaults or sexual misconduct ranging from forbidden touching or fondling to penetration or intercourse. Acts that may be permissible between consenting adults become sexual assaults if the victim does not consent or cannot legally consent due to intoxication, unconsciousness, mental impairment, or age. The elements of proof required for conviction on the most serious degree of sexual assault often include intercourse or penetration, force, and the lack of consent.

Penetration, however slight, is sufficient to complete the offense. It must be shown that the genitals or an orifice of the body was penetrated. It is not necessary to prove emission. Penetration of the genitals can be accomplished by a finger, penis, or an object. Corroboration of the victim's testimony with respect to penetration is not required. Finally, penetration can be established in the absence of the victim's testimony by circumstantial evidence such as a medicolegal opinion of a qualified doctor or pathologist.

Of the major crimes, rape is the most underreported to the police. The FBI says only one offense in five is reported. Reluctance to report the crime is due in part to embarrassment, the fear of having one's prior sexual conduct explored in court, and skepticism about the legal system.

Most states have some form of rape shield laws to limit the introduction of information about a victim's personal sex life. These laws, however, afford only limited protection because the victim's past relationship with the accused is generally allowable. Furthermore, a skillful defense lawyer can circumvent the intent of these laws by impugning the victim's moral character with questions about lifestyle, living arrangements and marital status. For these reasons, many victims choose to spare themselves the embarrassment of prosecuting "date rape" and "acquaintance rape."

a. **Rape Crisis Counselor Privilege**. In a few jurisdictions, the confidentiality of the relationship between the victim and the professional rape crisis counselor is protected. It is considered a privileged communication similar to that between a psychiatrist and a patient and prohibits the disclosure of the counselor's notes and records in court. This permits victims to use crisis services without running the risk of their private statements appearing in court.

b. **Eased Evidence Requirements**. Many states have changed their law to ease the evidence requirements for a conviction of rape. Prior requirements of producing witnesses or proof of actual force (other than threats) have been stricken from the law. Some jurisdictions permit the courtroom use of video testimony of children who are victims of sexual offenses. This eliminates the requirement of confronting the assailant and spares the children further psychological trauma, eases some parental fears, and increases the likelihood that parents will allow their children to testify.

3. Characteristics of the Offense

Sexual assault tends to be intraracial with victims and perpetrators being of the same race. They tend to occur indoors in private places rather than outdoors in public places. Most perpetrators and victims are under 25 years of age.

a. **The Offender**. Many offenders are emotionally immature, with deep feelings of inferiority and a sense of inadequacy with respect to social relations. Some may be gentle and even naive about sex, living on fantasy and retreating from normal life to overcome feelings of inadequacy, while others are aggressive and brutal. Both can feel tremendous guilt and shame, and even concern for victims. Other offenders feel no guilt, have no concern, do not accept they are wrong, and are motivated by contempt and hostility.

4. Profiling Rapists

a. **Style of Attack**. The way that rapists approach their victims indicates something about their personally. Approaches can range from cunning to brutal. The *con approach* relies on subterfuge. The perpetrator openly approaches victims, initially appears friendly, and relies on an ability to interact with victims. The *blitz approach* rapist acts quickly to physically assault and subdue victims. Victims are often overcome before they can react. The perpetrator relies on force and physical injury to control victims, and may use gags, blindfolds, chemicals or gases to overcome victims. The *surprise approach* rapist generally hides in a secluded place before confronting the victim. The perpetrator moves in when there appears an advantage, such as the victim relaxes or even falls asleep. This perpetrator may make threats but is less likely to inflict injury.

b. **Types of Rapists**. There are four general categories of rapists. Each category reflects the personality of the rapist.

The *power-reassurance* rapists are the most common. About 81 percent of rapes are committed by this type. Their principle motive is to obtain power over the victim and establish their manhood. They often fantasize about having a sexual affair, plan their attack, observe their victim before the attack (and possibly stalk), and they may take souvenirs to remember and relive the experience. They are often shy and passive, have a low self-esteem, often live with a parent, likely unskilled or self-employed, and are the least likely to use violence. If not caught, though, the level of violence may increase in subsequent attacks. They are often polite, and may apologize to victims after the attack. They tend to select victims from their neighborhood who are of their own race and age group. They are easily intimidated, and investigators should take a friendly, low-key approach when interviewing. These offenders want to be understood and may respond to a sympathetic appeal to their manhood.

The *power-assertive* rapists are responsible for about 12 percent of rapes. They are motivated to demonstrate their manhood, have poor impulse control, and little appreciation for the rights of others. They seek to dominate and have little regard for others. They do not relate well to others and will exploit any vulnerability. These individuals are concerned about their image, often dress well, have nice cars, and are frequently loud and boisterous. They seldom plan their attacks, often hunt from bars, and are likely to use a con approach with moderate force but may use a blitz approach and rip the clothes from the victim. Their attack often combines both verbal and physical assaults. Levels of aggression tend to increase with each new victim. These rapists generally select victims of their age and racial group, and are likely to have a steady sex partner. They are generally intelligent and will exploit any weaknesses they perceive in the interrogator. The interrogation should be formal, serious, and based on facts. If the suspect detects a bluff or error by interrogators, there is little chance of gaining cooperation.

The *anger-retaliatory* rapists commit about 5 percent of rapes. They are easily angered and motivated by a desire to punish victims due to their anger and frustration toward women. They hate women, feel betrayed, and act from a sense of injustice. In spite of these feeling, they are generally considered socially competent. They are often married with a normal sexual relationship but are likely to be involved in extramarital affairs. Typically they are engaged in "macho" sports, hobbies, and occupations. Victims are generally selected from people close to the perpetrator's home. Victim may resemble someone who has significantly stressed the suspect. They seek to humiliate and harm their victims, tend to rely on blitz attacks, and are violent. Their attack is verbally (often profane) and physically aggressive and may escalate to murder. Investigators should take a low-key approach, be careful not to violate the subject's personal space, ask well-prepared questions, and try to conduct the interview in the evening (this affects the subject's sense of control). Subjects may identify better with male investigators, especially if the investigator shows a contrived dominance over female investigators or staff.

The *anger-excitation* rapists are dangerous individuals motivated by sadism and are likely to injure victims. Their attacks are planned after a period of fantasizing about sadistic sexual activity. Their methods are excessive and brutal, and they often use weapons. They are cruel, aggressive, and link sexual satisfaction with violence. They are often intelligent, well educated, middle class, and considered family oriented. Victims may resemble someone that perpetrators feel wronged them. Their goal is physical and psychological domination over victims that plays out in a ritualized fantasy that may include mutilation and overkill. They generally take victims to a reasonably secure place, within the offender's "comfort zone," where they can terrorize victims without interruption. Attacks are laced with profanity and the subject may call the victim by his wife's or mother's name. These offenders have no remorse. They believe they are smarter than investigators, so investigators need to appear knowledgeable and competent to prompt them to engage in conversation. Subjects may appear friendly, but will attempt to control the interview. They gain satisfaction from provoking investigators to anger.

5. Medical Examination of the Victim

Victims should receive a complete medical examination soon after the assault to address any health issues and to preserve any physical evidence of the attack. Hospital emergency rooms are staffed with individuals trained in the appropriate medicolegal procedures. Victims should be informed of the purpose of the examination and that the findings will be included in their medical report. Permission should be obtained from a parent or guardian if the victim is minor.

a. **Signs of Physical Resistance**. Physical signs of sexual assault will vary and may be absent even though the offense was committed. Investigators should be prepared for an examination that does not produce physical evidence. Where evidence does exist, it will vary according to the amount of force used in the assault. In the case of children or incapacitated adults, evidence of resistance may be absent while evidence of violation may be readily apparent. For most adult victims signs of violence such as wounds, bruises, and scratches will be present, and if absent an explanation should be sought. Fear and threats can sometimes render victims incapable of physical resistance. The acts and demeanor of victims immediately after the assault should be carefully examined.

b. **Examination Report**. Along with signs of force, the medical report should contain information about the attack. After describing the victim's recent medical history and previous sexual experience, the details of the assault should be recounted. The victim's general physical appearance and demeanor should be described along with the presence or absence of marks of violence on the body and their location. The examination should note the condition of the genitalia and the location of any bleeding, bruising, and abrasion. Finally, document the presence or absence of marks on the clothing.

c. **Evidence Collection**. Physicians in almost every hospital are supplied with a sexual assault evidence kit. It includes detailed

Table 16-1. Sexual Assault Evidence.

• Patients' clothing and underwear and foreign material dislodged from clothing; • Foreign materials on patients' bodies, including blood, dried secretions, fibers, loose hairs, vegetation, soil/debris, fingernail scrapings and/or cuttings, matted hair cuttings, material dislodged from mouth using dental floss, and swabs of suspected semen, saliva, and/or areas highlighted by alternate light sources;	• Hair evidence (including head and pubic hair samples and combings); • Vaginal/cervical swabs and smears; • Penile swabs and smears; • Anal/perianal swabs and smears; • Oral swabs and smears; • Body swabs; and • Known blood, saliva sample, or buccal swab for DNA analysis and comparison

Source: President's DNA Initiative.

instructions for collecting, preserving, securing, and transporting the physical evidence to a forensic laboratory. Evidence is collected to establish the *corpus delicti* and to identify the assailant.

6. Medical Examination of Suspect

Valuable evidence may be found if the suspect is examined by a physician soon after the crime. In addition to medical evidence of recent sexual activity, evidence may be found to link the suspect to the crime. A pubic hair combing may reveal foreign hair or fibers. Pulled pubic and head hairs should be collected for comparison with any that may be discovered on the victim or at the crime scene. Similarly, blood and saliva samples are obtained to compare with any fluids or stains connected to the crime. Fingernail scrapings may produce evidence to link the suspect to the victim.

7. Examination of Clothing

The clothing of suspects and victims should be examined for damage and the presence of trace evidence (bodily fluids, hairs, fibers, and when appropriate grass, weeds, seed, and soil). Trace evidence may link perpetrators to victims or the crime scene. Clothing is collected by having the subject disrobe while standing on a white sheet of paper. Each article of clothing is removed and packed in separate paper bags. The paper is then carefully folded to retain any trace evidence and placed in a bag. The bags are then sent to a forensic laboratory for examination.

8. Identification of Semen

Finding semen can corroborate the victim's account and identify the suspect. Semen is the grayish-white fluid produced by the male reproductive organs. It is a viscous adhesive fluid usually found as stains on clothing or bedding. Once dry it imparts a starchy stiffness to the fabric. If semen stains are not apparent, inspection of the evidence with an ultraviolet light or alternative light source can help locate them. Semen stains will display a bright luminescence under ultraviolet radiation. The Acid Phosphatase Color Test and microscopic examination remain useful screening devices, but DNA analysis has become the more useful investigative tool.

9. Evidence of Condom Use

In an effort to escape detection, some rapist use condoms during the assault. A recovered condom with semen in the interior and vaginal traces on the exterior would provide convincing DNA evidence. If the condom is not recovered, trace evidence of condom use might be present. Finely powdered particles are added to condoms to keep the latex from sticking together. Particle evidence found on a victim may be associated with a specific brand. Non-powdered latex gloves should be worn when collecting this evidence. Traces of spermicidal lubricants may also be used to identify the brand.

Trace evidence of condom use found on vaginal swabs can be used to establish penetration, part of the *corpus delicti* of the offense. If empty condom packages are found at the crime scene, the outside should be processed for fingerprints and the inside for trace evidence that may be recovered from the victim.

10. Interview of the Victim

Victims should be interviewed as soon as possible after their medical examinations. Gender should be considered, for it may be easier for victims to speak about their attack to someone of the same gender, but it should not be the determining factor. Victims should be questioned thoroughly concerning the attack, the circumstances surrounding it, and their activities before and after.

Determine whether the victim knows the perpetrator and evaluate the feasibility and consistency of the account. If there are discrepancies, are they explainable? If the victim knows the perpetrator, was there a prior sexual relationship? Was there a delay in reporting the crime, and if so, why? What transpired between the incident and reporting it to police? Who was the first person the victim told of the attack? Document any statements or actions that indicate a lack of consent, resistance, and force used to overcome the victim's resistance.

11. Examination of the Crime Scene

Generally there are no eyewitnesses and little direct evidence, so investigators must rely on circumstantial evidence. The scene should be carefully examined as soon as possible after the crime is reported. Investigators should use standard crime scene investigation procedures.

Photographs of the crime scene may be useful in verifying or disproving statements of victims or suspects. Outdoor scenes often include tire impressions and shoe impressions. Samples of soil, seeds, and pollen should be collected from the immediate scene for comparison with similar materials that may later be found on the suspect. Personal articles such as clothing, handkerchiefs, papers, or jewelry should be carefully collected and preserved. Surfaces that might bear latent fingerprints should be processed. Discarded matches, cigarette butts, bottles, and drink containers should be processed for fingerprints and DNA.

12. Neighborhood Canvas

Investigators should interview persons living and working near the crime scene for information about the crime. Did they see the victim or suspect, or hear any outcries or spontaneous utterances? Statements concerning the circumstances of a crime made while excited and without deliberation or design can be admitted into evidence as an exception to the hearsay rule.

13. Aiding and Abetting

Suspects who did not actually assault the victim may be guilty of sexual assault if they shared the criminal intent or purpose of the active perpetrators by aiding, encouraging, or inciting the crime. There must be intent to aid or encourage the perpetrator. There must be some participation or action to further the crime. For example, those who stand guard while companions commit a sexual assault are guilty as principals even though they did not have physical contact with the victim.

14. Drug-Facilitated Rape

Sexual assault is sometimes preceded by drugging the victim. Victims are incapacitated by an anesthetizing substance, usually slipped surreptitiously in their drinks. Typically, while victims are distracted or away from the table, a colorless and relatively tasteless substance is put in their drink. A few minutes after consuming the drug, victims appear intoxicated and then lose consciousness. In about four hours, they regain consciousness and have no memory of what happened. Often puzzled by the effect of a small quantity of alcohol, they may not know what happened to their clothing or why they are improperly dressed. Eventually victims become suspicious but remain confused and reluctant to notify police.

A delay in reporting may allow the drug to pass from the body. The two most commonly used drugs, GHB and Rohypnol, disappear in a relatively short period of time. GHB is undetectable in the blood after approximately five hours and in the urine after 12 hours. Rohypnol disappears from the blood in about 12 hours and from the urine in about 72 hours. Because of victims' inability to remember and the lack of witnesses, blood and urine samples may be the only way to establish a case. Both blood and urine samples should be taken from the victim during the medical examination. Because urine samples are not routinely collected in sexual assault cases, investigators should request them when it is suspected that victims have been drugged.

a. **GHB (Gamma Hydroxybutyrate)** is a central nervous system depressant. In the 1980s, GHB was available in health food stores as a body-building supplement and as a natural sleep aid. After it was banned in the 1990s, it became popular with party-goers for its euphoric and sedative effects. It is available on the Internet and can be purchased legally overseas. It is available as a colorless, odorless liquid or as a white powder. Incorrectly manufactured GHB is extremely dangerous, leading to a number of deaths each year.

b. **Rohypnol (Flunitrazepam)** is a central nervous system depressant used for sedation, presurgical anesthesia, and the treatment of severe sleep disorders. Although illegal in the United States and Canada, it is available in many other countries and on the Internet. It is manufactured in the form of a small white tablet that in some formulations is colorless and odorless when ground into a powder and dissolved in a liquid.

c. **Evidence Collection**. When the use of a date-rape drug is suspected, the crime scene should be examined not only for evidence of sexual assault but also for the presence of drugs. Urine and blood samples from the victim should be collected to determine the presence of drugs. Bottles and containers should be collected, along with any drinking glasses that may have been used by the victim. The suspect's residence should be searched for envelopes, mailing containers, or labels from medical or chemical supply sources. Computers, printouts, and storage devices should be examined for information on Internet suppliers or for receipts. Cameras and videotape equipment should be examined for pictures of the victim.

15. Statutory Rape or Sexual Assault

Victims who are not mentally competent or are too young to understand the nature of sexual intercourse are not considered legally capable of giving consent. The victim's inability to grant consent supersedes any questions of force or resistance. The investigation is similar but proof of victim's age or mental incapacity is necessary.

16. Attempt to Sexually Assault

An attempt to commit sexual assault is a lesser included offense of the crime of sexual assault. There must be a specific intent to commit sexual assault accompanied by an overt act to accomplish the crime. The elements of proof include an *act by* the suspect that was done with *specific intent* to commit sexual assault that was *more than mere preparation.*

a. **Specific Intent**. Specific intent is demonstrated by unlawful sexual misconduct with force and against the will of the victim. This may be established by direct evidence, such as statements by the suspect during the offense, or by circumstantial evidence, such as logical inferences based on the suspect's actions.

b. **Overt Act**. An overt act is more than mere preparation to commit an offense. It is an act that under the ordinary circumstances would further the commission of the offense. To constitute an attempt to commit sexual assault, the overt act must have helped to complete the crime if not for unforeseen intervention.

17. Assault with Intent to Commit Rape or Sexual Misconduct

An assault with intent to commit rape or sexual misconduct is not necessarily the equivalent of an attempt to commit rape or attempted sexual misconduct. An "assault with intent" differs from an "attempt" in that it lacks the overt act that would have completed the crime. The investigation is similar to that for a completed crime.

a. **The Assault**. The victim should be interviewed to obtain a complete and detailed description of the assault. Document the use of physical force, threats or menacing actions. If a weapon was used, obtain a detailed description. If a weapon is found, attempt to determine its owner and submit it for laboratory examination.

b. **The Intent**. The perpetrator's intent can be established by statements and indecent expressions, by gestures or intimate touching, and by the absence of any other rational motive. A thorough interrogation of the suspect can often eliminate other motives even without a confession or explicit admission.

c. **Use of Force**. It must be shown that the suspect planned to carry out the attack with force and against the will of the victim. Unless the suspect makes such a statement, it is likely this will need to be proven by circumstantial evidence. The use of force is established from the facts and inferred circumstances.

18. Indecent Assault

Indecent assault is the unlawful touching of another for erotic pleasure or in a sexually intimate manner. It is the indecent, lewd, or lascivious fondling of victims without consent and against their will for sexual gratification. Investigators should obtain complete and detailed descriptions of the incident from the victim, witnesses, and interrogation of suspects. In questioning suspects, determine their activities and location before, during, and after the incident. Any alibi should be thoroughly explored. Attempt to find witnesses to the suspect's actions preceding, during, and subsequent to the incident. Check background, criminal record, and involvement in any prior incidents of victims and suspects.

Table 16-2. Checklist for Rape and Lesser Included Offenses.

• Employment, marital status, and family relationships of the victim. • Previous history of similar occurrences or related offenses for victim and suspect. • Exact location of the offense. • Locations where preparations may have been made. • Places visited prior to the incident. • Persons seen prior to the incident. • Road followed in arriving at the place of incident. • Location of houses or establishments of possible witnesses who could have heard or seen the events. Names and addresses of occupants. • Was physical force used? • Description of any weapons used. • Areas of the body subjected to physical violence. • Statements or utterances of the suspect at the crime scene. • Resistance offered by the victim. • Duration of resistance. • Utterances of the victim at the time of the offense. • Screams or outcries of the victim. • Movements of the accused and the victim subsequent to the offense. Paths followed, roads used, places passed, and persons seen. • To whom did the victim make the first report of the offense? • Was the victim's report made voluntarily or was it the result of persuasion?	• Exact time of the victim's report. • Was the report made as soon as possible after the act took place? What reasons are given for any delay? • Results of the medical examination: Do they offer proof of the use of violence? Resistance? Penetration? Was the victim pregnant at the time of the offense, and if so, stage of pregnancy? • Reputation of the victim: Previously made similar complaints? Motive for false accusation? • Victim's relation to the accused: Were they previously acquainted? How long were they acquainted? How often did they see each other? What were the typical circumstances of their meetings? When did the accused make the first advance? Describe advances. What were the victim's overt reactions to these advances? • Statement of the accused: Suspect's responses to questions listed above, i.e., actions, movements at the scene, utterances, relationship with the victim, and so forth. Details of any alibi of the accused. Detailed log of suspect's movements during the broad period of time including the occurrence. Verification of details concerning alibi and movements.

If the victim is a minor, the investigation is similar except the victim cannot legally give consent. Parents should be interviewed to determine the child's credibility. Ordinarily the major difficulties encountered in the investigation lie in the testimony of the child. If the child is quite young, it may be difficult to obtain specific details. In addition, the identification of the offender may be a problem. Investigators should permit victims to give their accounts without interference or suggestion, and then cautiously elicited necessary information. Keep in mind that young children may be prone to tell what they believe investigators want to hear.

OTHER SEX OFFENSES

Society prohibits several activities it deems deviant, threatening to public decency and public health, or precursors to more serious criminal activity. Laws vary among the states as do enforcement practices. It is not possible to give a strict definition of the term *sexual deviance*. Some of the following practices are prohibited by statute while others are behaviors investigators may encounter in their investigations.

19. Indecent Exposure

Indecent exposure is the unwanted or public displaying of the genitalia to another. Usually this offense is committed by a male in the presence of one or more females. In psychiatry this compulsive neurosis is termed *exhibitionism*. Many exhibitionists are timid, lack aggressiveness, and are sexually dysfunctional. By exposing themselves, they irrationally hope that their victim will reciprocate. The practices of exhibitionists vary considerably. Some expose themselves at windows, others frequent parks, and still other expose themselves while seated in automobiles or on public transportation.

20. Voyeurism

A voyeur (from the French word meaning a "looker" or "viewer") is a "Peeping Tom." Sexual excitement and satisfaction are achieved by viewing others naked or undressing. Ordinarily the voyeur prefers to remain unseen, watch the victim disrobe, and may masturbate. Most voyeurs are a nuisance and do not move on to more serious criminal activity.

21. Sadism and Masochism

The sadist achieves sexual excitement by inflicting physical punishment on another. The masochist, on the other hand, derives pleasure from submitting to physical abuse at the hands of another. Some individuals derive pleasure from both practices. Whipping and biting are common. Both males and females engage in these practices.

22. Fetishism

This deviance usually involves the use of an object, commonly intimate apparel, of a person of the opposite sex to derive sexual satisfaction. Pure fetishism is rare in women. Fetishists sometimes break into houses to remove a certain type of article, such as shoes, lingerie, stockings, or other feminine apparel that they can possess or fondle to become sexually aroused.

23. Transvestitism

The transvestite achieves erotic pleasure through wearing the clothes of the opposite sex. Males occasionally dress up in feminine garments and solicit attention openly.

24. Frottage

Frottage is the practice of receiving sexual arousal and satisfaction by rubbing against the clothing or anatomical parts, usually the buttocks, of a person of the opposite sex. The frotteur is invariably a male. *Toucherism* is similar to frottage. The toucheur has irresistible impulses to touch the body of another person. They commonly work in large crowds, deriving sexual excitement from intimately touching, apparently inadvertently, their victims. Sometimes pinching or caressing are made to appear like a casual contact.

25. Tribadism

Tribadism is the mutual friction between women to achieve sexual excitement. The tribadist is often bisexual.

26. Sodomy

Sodomy is broadly defined in state laws. It is generally considered anal intercourse but may include bestiality, fellatio, and cunnilingus. Sodomy may take place between a male and a female as well as between two males or two females. Penetration, however slight, is sufficient to complete the act.

SEXUAL ABUSE OF CHILDREN

27. Pedophilia

Pedophilia is a psychosexual disorder involving gratification through sexual contact with children. Pedophiles are often males who are unable to find fulfillment in adult sexual relationships and prefer a less-threatening relationship with children. The abuse may involve a range of activities from displaying genitals, to fondling to intercourse. Abuse is largely unreported because children are silenced through bribes or threats. Abusers prey on the child's unfulfilled needs for food, shelter, toys, money, love, friendship, approval, or attention. The devastating effects of abuse may not be immediately apparent. Aside from the physical harm caused by sexual demands at too early an age, there is psychological harm expressed in confusion, depression, guilt, loss of self-worth, and a disruption in emotional development. Many of the effects of sexual abuse do not appear until later in life. Boys who have been molested tend to become sex offenders themselves. Sexually-abused girls will often adopt a self-destructive lifestyle manifested by substance abuse or prostitution.

28. Offenders

Pedophiles are compulsive and repetitive offenders. For confirmed pedophiles, the attraction to children can be as deeply ingrained in their personality as heterosexuality and homosexuality is to other people. The urge is often so powerful that the only answer is to isolate them from children. Many enjoy their habit and have no desire to change. The determined pedophile can molest literally hundreds of children over a lifetime punctuated by occasional short prison terms.

a. **Characteristics**. The vast majority of child molesters are male. Although a child molester may be of any age, the majority of those arrested are under the age of 35. Offenders usually possess normal intelligence and come from all walks of life. Ordinarily, they cannot be differentiated by occupation, income level, manner of dress, or lifestyle. The confirmed pedophile will often seek employment or do volunteer work for youth organizations to gain access to children. Their employment record may reflect many changes of address or occupation depending on how frequently they are discovered.

In the majority of cases, offenders are acquaintances of their victims, such as a neighbor, a relative, or a member of the immediate family. Pedophiles will often befriend neighbors that have children of the sex and age of their preference. They may subscribe to child pornography, chat rooms, websites, and maintain contact with other pedophiles through the Internet.

b. **Choice of Victim**. Child molesters may be attracted to girls only, boys only, or both. Female children are much more likely to be victims than male children. A girl is especially vulnerable in a dysfunctional family where she may be abused by her father, a stepfather, or an older brother.

c. **Sexual Orientation**. The majority of sex offenders are heterosexual and about half are married. Often they molest a son or daughter while maintaining normal marital relations with their wives. The others are true pedophiles and are sexually attracted to children with no desire for adult encounters. Men become pedophiles out of choice, not because of a lack of opportunity for sexual contact with adults. Often the pedophile who is attracted to boys will be completely heterosexual in his adult sexual encounters, or he may reject all adult sexual activity. It is not possible to deduce a pedophile's sexual preference (heterosexual, homosexual, or bisexual) from his choice of victims.

Offenders may be situational or preferential in their crimes. This distinction may be important in determining the direction and scope of an investigation.

1) **Situational**. This type of offender is primarily interested in adult sexual activity and uses children to substitute or supplement adult sexual activity. They are opportunistic and molest children when they are readily available. Frequently, they will molest their own children. They are commonly inadequate personalities with little self-esteem or self-control. They lack any moral sensitivity to abusing people in general or engaging in sex with whomever they choose. The majority of child molesters fit into this category. The activities of situational offenders are more limited in scope and with far fewer victims over their lifetime than the preferential offender.

2) **Preferential**. This offender prefers sexual relations with children. They have sex and age preferences in their victims and will continually seek out members of this group. They may be married or live with a woman who has children. Often, they are employed as teachers, ministers, camp counselors, hospital workers, or other occupations that bring them in contact with children. They may volunteer to help in youth organizations or sports programs. Because children grow up or leave their sphere of influence, they seek a steady supply of new recruits. Unlike situational offenders who will confine their attention to opportunistic victims, preferential offenders constantly look for new victims. They maintain contact with other pedophiles. These offenders are often skilled conversationalist who relate well to children. They are skilled manipulators. Through gifts, friendship, approval, and attention, they make their victims feel obligated to engage in sexual relations. Afterwards, they threaten victims to stay silent. Often the offenders express interest in the child, and victims may be reluctant to expose them. If discovered and prosecuted, they will often move to another state and again begin molesting children. State sex offender registries are an attempt to prevent such activities. During the course of a

lifetime, it is not extraordinary for offenders to have molested hundreds of children.

29. Pornography and Sex Rings

Because of the nature of their activities, pedophiles are, for the most part, secretive, but commonly share their experiences and fantasies with other pedophiles. They may initially make contact through underground magazines and the Internet. The Internet allows pedophiles to communicate anonymously, from the privacy of their homes, with children over a wide geographical area. They often misrepresent their age, interests, address, and even sex. Eventually they arrange to meet with the unsuspecting child.

Pedophiles may join associations dedicated to liberalizing the laws regarding child molesting such as the North American Man Boy Love Association. From organizations such as this, they make contact with other pedophiles. They may share photographs of their victims. Eventually, this may lead to exchanging victims. Occasionally, several pedophiles will band together to form a business devoted to producing pornography and providing children for sexual services.

30. Interviewing the Victim

Victims in sex offenses, particularly children, are difficult to interview. A tactful approach is necessary to avoid further psychological trauma. Interviews should be conducted in the presence of a parent, guardian, juvenile authority, or social service worker. Proceed in a slow, friendly manner. The child's account should be evaluated in light of the child's maturity and ability to distinguish between reality and fantasy.

Investigators need to take measures to facilitate communication. Children need to feel safe and comfortable before talking freely. The child's home is a good place for the interview as long as the abuse did not occur there. Younger children often have a language of their own. They may have unique terms for the various body parts or their own peculiar understanding of concepts such as time and place. For instance, "a long time ago" may mean a few days, weeks, or months depending on the child. Anatomically-correct dolls may be helpful for the child to point to when describing what has happened. Recording the session will free interviewers from the distraction of taking notes and enable them to concentrate on talking with the child.

Some children have difficulty distinguishing between right and wrong and have not yet developed a system of values. They may be genuinely fond of their abusers and do not want them disparaged or punished. Questions such as "Why did you do this?" may sound accusatory and should be avoided. Leading questions (questions that suggest a desired answer) may result in false accusations and should be avoided. Interviewers must be aware of these issues and adjust accordingly.

31. Interrogating the Offender

Because of the varieties of personality types encountered in these cases, it is not possible to prescribe fixed rules or even widely applicable principles of interrogation. The recidivist pedophile will by experience be able to resist the moral pressure of prolonged and vigorous questioning. On the other hand, the immature person who acted spontaneously and often under the influence of alcohol, may be remorseful and ready to confess. Pedophiles that are relatively young and inexperienced are more likely to respond to an approach free of animosity or hostility.

a. **Qualifications of the Interrogator**. Investigators assigned to interrogate pedophiles should be carefully selected on the basis of maturity, experience, and criminological knowledge. They should understand the various aspects and terminology of sex offenses and deviant sexual behavior. They must also be able to create and maintain rapport with the various types of individuals who perpetrate these crimes. Interrogators should convey the impression they want to understand the incident from the suspect's point of view or help with a problem, rather than prosecute the crime. Investigators must often mask their true feelings and appear sympathetic even as perpetrators blame their victims.

b. **Questions**. The choice of words and phrases used by the interviewer is important. Interrogators should project that they know of the suspect's involvement. For example, the question

"When did you first do this?" should be used rather than "did you ever do this?" If the suspect is shy or guilt-ridden, the order of questioning is important. Embarrassing questions about sex habits should not be asked too early in the interrogation. Critical questions should be preceded by a series of neutral inquiries concerning schooling, physical health, and relations with parents.

c. **Introduction**. Initially the interrogation should downplay the criminal investigation. Investigators should appear to be more interested in the subject's personal background. The conversation should be casual and related to everyday affairs, common acquaintances, or recreational interests. Experienced investigators will be able to establish rapport without an obvious attempt to put the subject at ease. As the subject begins to relax, investigators should slowly shift to more pertinent questioning.

The preliminary questions begin with the subject's *background history* including birthplace, family income during childhood, parents' educational background and compatibility, number of brothers and sisters, class of neighborhoods, type of dwellings, and other factors relating to childhood. Next, move to the *educational history* such as the types of schools attended, the courses pursued, academic success, relationships with instructors, and extracurricular activities. Inquire about the subject's social life including general background of friends, extent and nature of social activities, and club memberships. What are the subject's *recreational interests* such as types of sports, names of teams, and extent of athletic interests? Is there a *military history,* and what were the *circumstances* of separation from the service? Finally, gather the subject's *medical history* including any consultations with a psychiatrist or psychologist.

d. **Case Related Quesioning**. The most important part of the interrogation will deal with the subject's sexual activities with children and the offenses committed. The questioning should develop information about the specific incident as well as background information pertinent to sex offenses.

Several questions should be addressed. Does the subject have an *arrest record* for sexual offenses? Is there a history of sexual *activity with children?* What were the *circumstances surrounding his or her first sexual act with a child* (subject's age, age of the child, details of the incident, any rationalizations or explanations)? What was the *nature of subsequent acts?* What is the nature of the subject's *present sexual life?* What are the *identities of children* involved? Are *other pedophiles* involved? What *places* does the subject frequent for sexual activity or to associate with pedophiles? Does the subject use any *equipment* such as cameras, recordings, pornographic material, and sexual aids? Has the subject ever *tried to change* these behaviors (counseling, psychiatric treatment, avoiding high-risk situations)? What is the subject's *marital history* including number of children, compatibility, and desire for normal domestic life?

e. **Reactions of Subjects**. When first confronted with committing a sex offense, suspects typically act indignant and then deny all charges. It is imperative that investigators have a thorough knowledge of all the evidence and the suspect's criminal history. When questioning subjects, investigators should reveal only enough evidence to make any denials sound implausible. By withholding information, investigators can convey the impression that they know far more about suspects and their offenses than they actually do. Sometimes suspects will attempt to learn what investigators really know and, in the process, make careless admissions.

When denial is not believable, suspects often try to minimize their involvement. They will downplay either the number or the nature of their offenses. The extent of their activities is minimized, or multiple offenses and multiple victims are reduced to one or two. Penetration or intercourse is portrayed as merely touching. Sex offenders often blame their victims for luring them into the act. Any admission, no matter how small, or any inconsistency in subjects' accounts may be used by skillful interrogators to challenge the subjects' stories and elicit the truth.

32. Physical Evidence

Many pedophiles need to communicate with other pedophiles. Valuable evidence may be found in a computer's memory and storage devices, cell phones, trash, letters, address books, telephone bills, phone books, and classified advertisements cut from magazines. Photographs, videotapes, digital recordings, and film can be used to identify victims. Physical evidence may be used to establish the corpus delicti, identify victims, link suspects to victims, identify accomplices or associates, establish the suspect's sex and age preference in children, and establish the suspect's control of the premises and ownership of the equipment.

ADDITIONAL READING

Rape and Sexual Assault

Amir, M.: Patterns in Forcible Rape. Chicago: University of Chicago Press, 1971.

Asante, J.S.: GHB: Grievous Bodily Harm. *FBI Law Enforcement Bulletin, 68* (4), 1999.

Baker, T.: *Introductory Criminal Analysis: Crime Prevention and Intervention Strategies. Person Prentice Hall.* Upper Saddle, NJ: 2005.

Blackledge, R.D.: Condom Trace Evidence: A New Factor in Sexual Assault Investigations. *FBI Law Enforcement Bulletin, 65* (5), 1996.

Blair, I.: *Investigating Rape: A New Approach for Police.* Wolfboro, NH: Longwood Publishing, 1985.

Bradway, W.C.: Stages of a Sexual Assault. *Law and Order, 38* (9), 1990.

Burgess, A.W. (Ed.): *Rape and Sexual Assault: A Research Handbook.* New York: Garland, 1985.

Burgess, A. W., et al.: *Sexual Assault of Children and Adolescents.* Lexington, MA: Lexington Books, 1978.

Chapman, T.: Drug-Facilitated Sexual Assault. *Police Chief, 67* (6), 2000.

Fitzgerald, N. and Riley, K.J.: Drug-Facilitated Rape. *National Institute of Justice Journal,* April 2000.

Green, W.M., M.D.: *Rape: The Evidential Examination and Management of the Adult Female Victim.* Lexington, MA: D.C. Heath, 1988.

Griffiths, G.I.: Psychological Factors: The Overlooked Factors in Rape Investigations. *FBI Law Enforcement Bulletin, 54* (4), 1985.

Grispino, R.R.J.: Serological Evidence in Sexual Assault Investigations. *FBI Law Enforcement Bulletin, 59* (10), 1990.

Groth, A.N., et al.: Rape: Power, Anger and Sexuality. *American Journal of Psychiatry, 134:* 1977.

Groth, A.N.: *Men Who Rape: The Psychology of the Offender.* New York: Plenum, 1979.

Hazelwood, R.R.: The Behavior-Oriented Interview of Rape Victims: The Key to Profiling. *FBI Law Enforcement Bulletin, 52* (9), 1983.

——: The Criminal Sexual Sadist. *FBI Law Enforcement Bulletin, 61* (2), 1992. Hazelwood, R.R. and Burgess, A.W.: Introduction to the Serial Rapist: Research by the FBI. *FBI Law Enforcement Bulletin, 56* (9), 1987.

Hazelwood, R. and Burgess, A.W. (Eds.): *Practical Approach of Rape Investigation: A Multidisciplinary Approach.* New York: Elsevier, 1987.

Hazelwood, R.R. and Burgess, A.W.: Introduction to the Serial Rapist: Research by the FBI. *FBI Law Enforcement Bulletin, 56* (9), 1987.

Hazelwood, R. R. and Warren, J.: The Serial Rapist: His Characteristics and Victims. Parts I and II. *FBI Law Enforcement Bulletin, 58* (1 & 2), 1989.

Hazelwood, R. R. and Warren, J.: The Criminal Behavior of the Serial Rapist. *FBI Law Enforcement Bulletin, 59* (2), 1990.

Hertica, M.A.: Interviewing Sex Offenders. *Police Chief, 58* (2), 1991.

Holmes, R. & Holmes, S.: *Profiling Violent Crimes: An Investigative Tool* (4th ed.). Los Angeles, Sage: 2009.

Lanning, K.V. and Hazelwood, R.R.: The Maligned Investigator of Criminal Sexuality. *FBI Law Enforcement Bulletin, 57* (9), 1988.

Merrill, W. F.: The Art of Interrogating Rapists. *FBI Law Enforcement Bulletin, 4* (1), 1995.

Mills, J.K.: The Initial Interview of Sexual Assault Victims. *Police Chief, 56* (4), 1989.

Morneau, R.H., Jr.: *Sex Crimes Investigation: A Major Case Approach.* Springfield, IL: Thomas, 1983.

Olson, D.T.: Rape: Understanding Motivations an Aid in Investigations. *Law and Order, 37* (4), 1989.

Parrot, A. and Bechhofer, L. (Eds.): *Acquaintance Rape: The Hidden Crime.* Somerset, NJ: John Wiley, 1991.

Porrata, T.: Recognizing the Dangers of GHB. *Police Chief, 67* (4), 2000.

President's DNA Initiative. Sexual Assault Medical Forensic Examinations. Available http://samfe.dna.gov/operational_issues/evidence_collection_kit /minimum guidelines, 11/11/2011.

Stewart, G.D.: Sexual Assault Evidence Collection Procedures. *Journal of Forensic Identification, 40* (69), 1990.

Other Sex Offenses

Alicea-Diaz, A.: Child Sexual Abuse: Investigative Problems. *Police Chief, 57* (10), 1990.

Bierker, S.B.: *About Sexual Abuse.* Springfield, IL: Thomas, 1989.

Davidson, H.A.: Sexual Exploitation of Children: An Overview of Its Scope, Impact and Legal Ramifications. *FBI Law Enforcement Bulletin, 53* (2), 1984.

Goldstein, S.L.: Investigating Child Sexual Exploitation: Law Enforcement's Role. *FBI Law Enforcement Bulletin, 53* (1), 1984.

——: *Sexual Exploitation of Children: A Practical Guide to Assessment.* Investigation and Intervention. New York: Elsevier, 1986.

Goodwin, J.M.: Sexual Abuse: Incest Victims and Their Families. Littleton, MA: PSG Publishing, 1982.

Heck, W.P.: Basic Investigative Protocol for Child Sexual Abuse. *FBI Law Enforcement Bulletin, 68* (10), 1999.

Hertica, M.A.: Police Interviews of Sexually Abused Children. *FBI Law Enforcement Bulletin, 56* (4), 1987.

Holmes, R. and Holmes, S.: *Profiling Violent Crimes: An Investigative Tool* (4th ed.). Los Angeles: Sage, 2009.

Lanning, K. V.: *Child Molesters—A Behavioral Analysis—For Law Enforcement Officers Investigating Cases of Child Sexual Exploitation.* Washington, D.C.: National Center for Missing and Exploited Children, 1986.

Lanning, K.V. and Burgess, A.W.: Child Pornography and Sex Rings. *FBI Law Enforcement Bulletin, 53* (1), 1984.

Laws, M.E.: Substantiating Children's Statements in Sexual Abuse Cases. *Police Chief, 66* (9), 1999.

Lester, D.: *Unusual Sexual Behavior: The Standard Deviations.* Springfield, IL: Thomas, 1976.

Macdonald, J.M.: *Indecent Exposure.* Springfield, IL: Thomas, 1973.

McIlwaine, B.D.: Interrogating Child Molesters. *FBI Law Enforcement Bulletin, 63* (6), 1994.

Scholer, M.: Investigating Strip-Mall Brothels. Police Chief, 66 (9), 1999.

Underwager, R. and Wakefield, H.C.: *The Real World of Child Interrogations.* Springfield, IL: Thomas, 1990.

Wakefield, H.C., Underwager, R., et al.: *Accusations of Child Sexual Abuse.* Springfield, IL: Thomas, 1988.

Chapter 17

DRUGS

1. Overview

PERHAPS THE MOST DIFFICULT crimes to control are those involving drug abuse. Despite a policy of "zero tolerance" that included intercepting deliveries of illegal drugs, arresting and prosecuting dealers and users, expanding prisons, public education, and testing employees in the workplace, illegal drugs are still widely available. According to the 1970 *Uniform Crime Reports,* there were 322,300 arrests of adults for drug abuse violations. By 2010, the number of arrests had risen to 1,638,846. Drug arrests lead all other crimes followed by driving under the influence (1,412,223) and larceny-theft (1,271,410).

Illegal drug use has become a permanent feature of American life with serious effects on the health of the individual and the health of the nation. Users of illegal drugs face an increased risk of addiction, HIV infection, cardiovascular collapse, organ failure, and cancer. Increases in the cost of health care, crime, domestic violence, child abuse, workplace accidents, law enforcement, and prison are part of the price society pays for illegal drug use.

The failure of our national policies to control the use of illegal drugs raises a significant question. Are strict laws the best way to discourage drug usage? Drug laws are based on the belief that illegal drugs are detrimental to individuals, leading to medical problems and reduced productivity. Strict drug laws, however, often turn otherwise law-abiding citizens into criminals. When large numbers of people disagree with a law, the value of the law is diminished and respect for criminal justice declines. This presents a problem for society and for investigators.

2. Drug Addiction

Addicts, through repeated use of a drug, become dependent on it for their sense of well-being. If deprived of the drug, users suffer psychological cravings and withdrawal symptoms due to alteration of physiological processes.

a. **Causes**. Drug addiction is commonly attributable to both the availability of addicting drugs and personality disorders. Generally, individuals are introduced to a drug through a friend or acquaintance. Occasionally, they become addicted to a prescribed drug or through self-medication. The psychoneurotic individual will take drugs to relieve emotional or physical distress, while the psychopathic person resorts to them for their intoxicating effect. Early experimentation, however, is usually prompted by curiosity or a desire for adventure. Beginners may be confident they can avoid addiction but continued experimentation becomes habitual. Although starting as a pleasure-seeking curiosity or a quest for excitement, narcotic addicts soon seek only to ease their pain. Addicts soon need the drug just to stop hurting.

b. **Addicts**. Addicts habitually use illegal drugs and have lost the power of self-control. They may have a physical or psychological need for the drug.

c. **Physical Dependence**. Through continued use addicts gradually require the drug to maintain a normal sense of physical well-being. The need is attributable to physiological changes, particularly in the nervous system. It is more than a mere psychological craving. If deprived of the drug, addicts become physically ill and may turn to crime to procure drugs or money to buy drugs.

d. **Tolerance**. The body adjusts to repeated use of certain drugs so that addicts soon find that their customary dosage fails to give the expected effect. Increased quantities of the drug are required to give the needed stimulation or to feel normal. As the dosage is increased, the body correspondingly increases tolerance. In a short time addicts may find they can absorb dosages that previously would have been fatal.

e. **Social Degeneration**. Drug users and addicts find they must maintain some level of secrecy and isolation from mainstream society. Deceit, subterfuge, and evasion must be employed. Acquiring their drug is a crime, and users may find themselves associating with undesirable members of society. The cost of procuring their drugs may push them into crimes or questionable activities. Users and addicts may find they have marginalized themselves from the rest of society.

f. **Drug Dependence**. In addition to physical dependence, drugs can cause psychological dependence. From repeated use, they come to associate satisfaction and mental well-being with taking the drug. Physical and psychological dependence are closely related and may not be readily distinguishable. For this reason the World Health Organization introduced the broader concept of *drug dependence,* a state that may include either or both the physical and psychological dependence.

3. Narcotic

A narcotic is derived from opium, coca leaves, or opiates, and includes any compound produced from them or any substance chemically identical to any of these substances. An opiate is any drug derived from the opium poppy, such as opium, heroin, morphine, or codeine. The legal definition of narcotic has been expanded to include other substances having an addiction-forming or addiction-sustaining effect similar to morphine. Synthetic drugs are developed to be used medically as a substitute for morphine and placed under legal control. The Attorney General may declare new drugs to be within the meaning of the term "narcotic" and subject to the same regulations. Other drugs with abuse potential are similarly placed in the appropriate schedules of the Controlled Substances Act.

4. Legal Provisions

In general, federal and state laws forbid the unauthorized manufacture, sale, use, or possession of narcotics. There are several federal laws enacted before the Controlled Substance Act that regulated the sale and use of drugs. The *Harrison Act* (1914) taxed the importation, manufacture, distribution, and sale of narcotics. The *Narcotic Drug Import and Export Act* (1922) restricted the importation of opium and coca leaves to medical treatment and scientific research, and outlawed the importation and manufacture of heroin and the smoking of opium. The *Marihuana Tax Act* (1937) required the registration and taxation of marijuana, making it difficult to obtain legally. The *Drug Abuse Control Amendments* (1965) placed controls on amphetamines, barbiturates, and hallucinogens.

The *Controlled Substances Act* (1970) regulated narcotics and dangerous non-narcotic drugs as part of the Comprehensive Drug Abuse Prevention and Control Act. Title II is concerned with control and enforcement and is called the Controlled Substances Act. This act supersedes all other federal narcotics laws. It divides narcotics and other dangerous drugs into five schedules according to medical usage and abuse potential. Responsibility for enforcement is principally shared by the Drug Enforcement Administration and the Food and Drug Administration. Criminal penalties depend upon the classification of the drug, the nature of the offense (possession, sale, or manufacture), and whether it is a first or subsequent offense.

Because state laws are not always consistent with federal law, a violation in one state may not be a violation in another. The federal government encourages states to adopt similar laws to facilitate enforcement and provide consistency for manufacturers, pharmacists, doctors, and their patients. To assist states in developing consistent drug-control laws, the Uniform Controlled Substances Act was developed and adopted in many states.

5. Opium

Opium is derived from the poppy plant (*papaver somniferum*) that is grown chiefly in Asia but is found in other areas such as Mexico and Colombia. The plant is usually three or four feet high with smooth, dull foliage and flowers approximately four inches wide. The opium itself is a milky substance obtained by slitting open the capsules of the plant and scraping the sides. The substance is pressed into small cakes and shaped according to local custom. Raw opium is dark brown or black in color and is bitter to the taste. A number of alkaloids are derived from this substance, such as morphine, heroin, and codeine.

a. **Processed Opium**. Raw opium is boiled, fermented, and roasted to create a dark brown extract that may be smoked, chewed, or eaten. Medicinal opium may be a powder or liquid. In powder form, it is light brown or dark yellow in color. Solutions of opium such as laudanum were popular analgesics in Europe during the eighteenth and early nineteenth centuries when they could be readily purchased without prescription.

b. **Smoking Opium**. The opium pipe is more popular in Asia. It consists of a long stem and a detachable bowl with a narrow opening. Users usually lie down to smoke it. The opium is heated by a small lamp fueled with peanut oil to avoid smoking and unpleasant fumes. The lamp is covered by a cone-shaped device to direct the heat. The opium is heated to a viscous fluid. A long metal needle (yen hock) is dipped in the opium and a small pellet is gathered with a twirling motion. The pellet is cooked over the flame, kneaded against the lamp to express moisture, and then placed over the opening of the pipe. The user draws in the smoke with slow, deep inhalations. After smoking, a usable charcoal-colored residue remains in the pipe. This is called opium dross or yen shee and contains carbon, unburned opium, and morphine. After soaking in water, draining and evaporating, the yen shee can be smoked again. It may also be mixed with tea or wine, or may be injected.

c. **Effects**. Opium produces a feeling of well-being and relieves bodily pains. The drug is absorbed slowly into the body, gradually renders the smoker drowsy, and finally induces a deep sleep. Repeated use of opium results in addiction and physical dependency.

6. Opium Derivatives

Opium use is relatively uncommon in the United States, but its derivatives are a problem for law enforcement. The opium derivatives are a group of more than twenty alkaloids that are generally constituted as a white powder. The most common are morphine, heroin, and codeine. They are far more powerful in their effect and the addiction they produce.

a. **Morphine**. Morphine (morphine sulphate, morphine hydrochloride, and morphine tartrate) is widely used as a medical analgesic. About 12 percent of raw opium becomes morphine. Pharmaceutical morphine is usually produced in small white cubes or tablets approximately one gram in weight. Illegal morphine is usually sold in small quantities as white powder wrapped in a glassine paper. This quantity is referred to as a "deck," and is "cut" or diluted by the sellers to obtain greater profits. The actual amount of morphine in a deck may be as low as 3 percent and is mixed with a substance such as milk sugar.

1) ***Method of Use***. Morphine may be taken orally, but most addicts consider that wasteful. Typically, addicts inject it using a hypodermic needle or improvised equivalent. When used medicinally, the drug is injected under the skin or into the muscles. To achieve a more rapid and stimulating effect, addicts usually inject it directly into the blood stream (*mainlining*). A bent spoon, syringe or medicine dropper, needle, and rubber band constitute the addict's "kit." The drug is dissolved in water placed in a bent spoon. A match is used to heat the bottom of the spoon to accelerate the dissolving. A medicine dropper is often used as a substitute for a hypodermic syringe. The needle, attached to the dropper by the rubber band, is used to penetrate the skin. Sometimes, instead of a needle, the end of the dropper is broken and the jagged edge used to penetrate the skin. Addicts may also incise the skin with a sharp blade and insert the end of the dropper.

2) ***Effects***. Morphine produces a sense of euphoria and relaxed well-being. Addicts feel invigorated and mentally sharper, with increased self-confidence. The effect lasts for several hours, and then the effect gradually declines. With prolonged use, addicts develop tolerance and require a significantly larger dosage.

3) ***Identifying the Addict***. With access to their normal supply of drugs, addicts may appear quite normal. There is no irrational or exceptional behavior beyond possibly excess of enthusiasm. When the effects of the drug wear off, however, addicts may become unusually drowsy. Twenty-four hours after withdrawal, addicts will experience severe pains in the back and legs, their eyes and nose run continuously, and they may be overcome by nausea and stomach pain.

When under the influence of morphine, the pupils contract and do not react normally to changes of illumination. Because addicts inject the drug frequently, their arms are marked by punctures and scabs. A recent injection by a needle will appear as a small red spot with a small drop of coagulated blood. A scab will form and remain for approximately ten days. Dark blue scar tissue may appear where the vein walls have broken down from repeated punctures. To hide puncture marks, some addicts will inject in the back of the thighs and other concealed places.

b. **Codeine**. Methylmorphine or codeine is similar in many respects to morphine, but its effects are less intense. It is a natural alkaloid of opium with medical uses as a sedative (in cough mixtures) and an analgesic (in tablet form). In pure form, it is a crystalline powder or long, slender, white crystals. Although codeine, like all psychoactive drugs, represents a hazard for dependence-prone individuals, it is less addictive than morphine or heroin. Codeine dependence is rare. The danger of drug dependence when used in therapeutic dosages is slight. Instances of abuse of codeine cough syrups have been publicized by the news media but are not widespread.

c. **Heroin**. Heroin is a synthetic drug made from morphine as a diacetyl derivative. It is the most common drug of narcotic addiction. It is usually a white to brown (depending on impurities) crystalline powder but may be in the form of cubes or tablets. It is used similarly to morphine. The effects of heroin are the same as morphine but more intense. "Four times more powerful" is a phrase commonly used in comparing these two drugs. The withdrawal symptoms are similar. Heroin differs from morphine and codeine in that it cannot be legally manufactured or possessed in the United States, and is not authorized for medical use. The drug is, however, used legitimately by the medical profession in some other countries. It is considered a particularly effective analgesic for the terminal stages of such diseases as tuberculosis and cancer. Large quantities of heroin are manufactured abroad for illicit traffic in this country. Heroin is highly addictive and difficult to overcome.

7. The Heroin Problem

a. **The Changing Market**. Heroin is readily available in the United States and becoming increasingly popular in some markets. Prior to the 1990s, most of the heroin used in the United States originated from Southeast and Southwest Asia. In the early 1990s, the Colombian drug cartels, which controlled the world's cocaine market, began to smuggle homegrown Colombian heroin into the United States. They introduced a superior product, low-cost and high-purity, that quickly dominated the market. The Colombian drug dealers now offered a product sufficiently concentrated that could be sniffed or smoked rather than injected. This attracted new customers who would not otherwise use heroin, and drug dealers could offer it at a significantly lower price.

During this same period, Mexican dealers introduced "black tar" heroin that became widely available in the western United States. It derived its name from its unusual color and consistency (resulting from impurities in the manufacturing process). Black tar heroin is usually dissolved and then injected. Like Colombian heroin, it is low in price and high in purity. This higher-purity heroin has led to a dramatic increase in deaths from accidental overdoses. Mexican heroin production has increased substantially, and there are now indications they are using Columbian processing techniques to produce white heroin.

b. **The Problem of Addiction**. There are many health risks associated with heroin use. Heroin is a central nervous system depressant, and its immediate effects include euphoria, drowsiness, and the slowing down of the respiratory and the cardiac functions. When the purity of the drug is unknown, there is the potential danger of an overdose resulting in a cessation of breathing or cardiac arrest. Other dangers of heroin addiction include the contraction of diseases such as AIDS and hepatitis, collapsed veins, and infections of the heart lining and valves.

The addictiveness of heroin is a serious problem. Users become addicted after a few uses. Heroin addiction is characterized by compulsive drug seeking and use, physical dependence, and the development of tolerance. Depending on an individual's personality, almost any drug can produce psychological dependence. *Psychological dependence* leads a person to want to take a drug again and again, often simply because it feels good. For example, the psychological addiction of tobacco makes it difficult for smokers to quit the habit.

Physical dependence, on the other hand, involves actual biochemical changes in the body so that the brain cells appear to function normally only in the presence of the drug. Physical dependence means that the body has adapted to heroin use and that *withdrawal symptoms* will occur if usage is curtailed. These symptoms may include drug craving, restlessness, insomnia, diarrhea, and vomiting. Withdrawal symptoms peak around 48 hours after the last dose of heroin and persist for about a week. Another characteristic of heroin use is the development of tolerance, (the need to use an increased dosage to achieve the desired effect). Heroin addicts spend ever-increasing amounts of time and energy in seeking and using the drug. Eventually, their primary goal in life is a quest for their next fix.

c. **The Young Offender**. The popular portrayal of drug pushers luring young people into the drug market distorts reality. Most young people are introduced to drugs through friends and associates. Youthful enthusiasm and rebellion drive them to experiment and share their experience with friends. Users learn from each other. This is particularly true for heroin, where addicts teach new users how to use the needle.

Potential Pure Heroin Production in Mexico, in Metric Tons, 2004–2008.

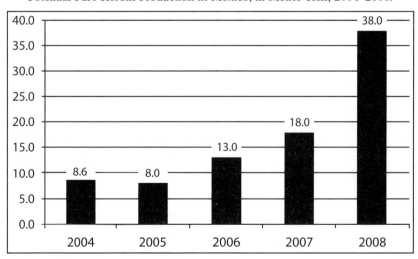

Figure 17-1. Source: Drug Enforcement Administration.

When the price of heroin falls and potency increases, a new and younger group of users emerge. They are attracted because the drug does not have to be injected but can be sniffed or smoked. They do not have to worry about contracting AIDS or hepatitis from contaminated needles or the social stigma of needle marks. Many of these users mistakenly believe that snorting or smoking heroin will not lead to addiction. While the "rush" from snorting or smoking is not as quick or intense as through injection, any form of heroin use can lead to addiction. These early exposures commonly lead to the more effective method of injection.

8. Synthetic Analgesics

Medical research has developed a series of drugs designed to replace opium derivatives. These chemically synthesized drugs produce the same effects as narcotics and are prescribed as analgesics (substances that relieve pain). Since their effects are similar to those of morphine, their manufacture, sale, and use are strictly regulated by the Controlled Substances Act. Among the more important synthetic analgesics are meperidine, methadone, Dilaudid, and Percodan.

a. **Meperidine**. Meperidine hydrochloride is also known as Demerol, Dolantin, Dolantol, Endolat, and the generic name, pethidine. It lies somewhere between morphine and codeine as a pain reliever. Opinions vary as to its capacity to develop physiologic dependence. The drug does have a moderate risk of addiction. Withdrawal symptoms are similar to morphine but considerably milder.

b. **Methadone**. Methadone hydrochloride is also known as Methadon, Amidone, Amidon, Dolophine, and Adanon. Its pharmacological effect is like morphine, except it does not produce a "high." Methadone is addictive, and its withdrawal symptoms are more gradual and less severe than those of morphine. In treating addiction to heroin, physicians commonly substitute methadone to alleviate withdrawal pains.

c. **Dilaudid (Dihydromorphinone Hydrochloride)**. Dilaudid is chemically similar to morphine and its physiological effects. It is effective in smaller dosages than morphine, with similar withdrawal symptoms.

d. **Percodan** (**Oxycodone Hydrochloride** and other analgesic ingredients). An effective and widely used pain reliever, Percodan has become popular in the illegal drug market. It is a semisynthetic opium derivative sold in yellow or pink pills. Percodan is similar to codeine but more addictive. Under the trade name of Percobarb it is combined with a barbiturate in a blue-and-white or blue-and-yellow capsule.

e. **OxyContin**. A powerful opioid to treat chronic pain, Oxy-Contin (oxycodone in a time-release form) was approved by the Federal Drug Administration in 1995. The time-release function allows patients to receive a larger dose of medicine and not run the risk of addiction. The rate the drug enters the brain determines the euphoric effect and its addiction potential.

Drug abusers circumvent the time-release mechanism by crushing the pill. It is snorted or injected for an immediate high. Commonly prescribed to reduce back pain, patients abuse the drug by taking it improperly or selling the pills to others. With OxyContin prescribed to one million patients and a thriving illegal market, it has become a significant problem for law enforcement (especially in rural areas). Because it is manufactured and distributed legally, it is not a crime to possess it with a prescription. Sometimes medically prescribed OxyContin is resold by users in the illegal market.

9. Cocaine

Cocaine is a white crystalline powder obtained from the leaves of the coca plant, *erythroxylon coca,* and was cultivated by Andean Indians before the Spanish occupation. The raw coca leaves are either chewed or brewed as a tea by the Indians to deaden pain, allay fatigue, diminish hunger, and relieve altitude sickness. Cocaine is derived from the coca leaves as an alkaloid powder or water-soluble hydrochloride. It is used as a surface anesthetic for medical purposes. Drug abusers inhale it through the nose or inject it into a vein. The effects are stimulation, pleasure, and increased self-confidence.

a. **Source**. Much of the world's supply of cocaine comes from Columbia, Peru and Bolivia. Production levels have declined in recent years due to successful enforcement efforts in Columbia. As a result, there is evidence that drug cartels are increasing their operations in Peru and Bolivia. The cartels are professionally run businesses that encompass every aspect of production and distribution. They protect the farmers, process the product, distribute it through smuggling, and supply drug dealers. Each drug cartel keeps a standing army to protect its operation.

b. **Trafficking**. Cocaine is principally smuggled into the United States across the border with Mexico. It is transported by land, sea, and air to California, Arizona, Texas, and southern Florida. Smugglers fly cocaine to northern Mexico where it is concealed in vehicles and then driven across the border. Smaller quantities are hidden on individuals (mules) who often walked across the border. It is smuggled into southern Florida by fishing boats and recreational craft. It is also hidden in cargo shipped to Miami.

c. **Ingestion**. Ordinarily, pure cocaine is diluted with lactose, dextrose, or quinine before being sold to customers. Users generally snort or inject the drug. Oral ingestion ordinarily remains limited to the coca leaf chewing or brewing practices of Indians. Most commonly, a small amount is snorted from the back of the hand, a small spoon, or through a straw. This direct application, however, can result in the erosion of the septum or middle part of the nose. Excessive use results in a characteristic deformity–the so-called "rat's nose." Injecting is done as with heroin. A water solution of cocaine is drawn into a hypodermic (or its equivalent) and injected into the vein. "Mainlining" produces an intense, quick-acting, and longer-lasting effect.

d. **Physical Effects**. Cocaine is an intense central nervous system stimulant affecting the higher brain centers. Users feel alert, restless, and more energetic. Fatigue is diminished and the appetite suppressed. In extreme cases, users experience paranoia and psychosis with nausea and hallucination. Although relatively rare, cardiac failure and subsequent death can result from an overdose of cocaine in the bloodstream.

e. **Mental Effects**. When injected, users experience great exhilaration and ecstasy, becoming restless and garrulous. With heavy use hallucinations and paranoid delusions may develop, and users lose contact with reality. The chief concern is the suppression of inhibitions resulting in reckless action, aggressive behavior, and confusion.

f. **Dependence and Withdrawal**. Tolerance and possibly physical dependence develops with the continued use of cocaine. It is not addicting in the same sense as opiates. There is no characteristic abstinence syndrome. Heavy users may experience severe depression, great fatigue, and confusion. The continued use of cocaine can produce a strong psychological dependence, leading to dangerous levels of abuse.

g. **The User**. There is no typical cocaine user profile. Users include young adults searching for new experiences and depressed individuals seeking to recapture an interest in life. As a stimulant, cocaine appeals to the imaginative but insecure person looking for self-confidence. Users are people trying to change how others perceive them or how they perceive themselves. Many well-known public personalities have been cocaine users, such as Sigmund Freud, Robert Louis Stevenson, Stephen King, and numerous other entertainers.

10. Crack

In 1983, "crack," a new form of cocaine, appeared on the streets of New York City. Within three years, more than half of all cocaine

Potential Pure Cocaine Production in Colombia, in Metric Tons, 2004–2008.

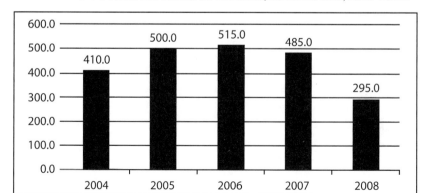

Figure 17-2. Source: National Drug Intelligence Center.

arrests involved crack. Crack immediately became attractive to drug dealers because it is easily prepared, low-cost, produces a euphoric effect, and is highly addictive. Its relatively low cost allowed dealers to offer free samples to attract new customers. Being highly addictive ensured users would become repeat customers. Many users turned to drug dealing, robbery, burglary, prostitution, and other crimes to support their habit. By 1986, a significant growth in crime in New York City was attributed to the spread of crack. Murder and assault also increased dramatically as drug dealers fought each other for control of the market.

Like most other fads, drug use fluctuates as times and tastes change. The 1990s witnessed a dramatic decrease in the use of crack. Some experts believe that the subsequent drop in the crime rate in New York City was attributable in part to the decline in the crack trade.

Crack is produced when cocaine (cocaine hydrochloride) is refined by a method called "freebasing" (the active cocaine is "freed" from its "base," the hydrochloride salt). The extraction technique involves dissolving the cocaine in water, adding a catalyst of either ammonia or baking soda, and then heating the mixture. This blend is then filtered and the precipitate is permitted to dry. This produces small yellow crystals that can be smoked in a pipe. The name "crack" is derived from the cracking sound heard when these crystals are heated. One gram of cocaine hydrochloride yields approximately one-half gram of crack.

a. **Characteristics**. Crack is 70 to 90 percent pure so it produces a more intense euphoria. When drawn into the lungs, it enters the bloodstream quickly and is carried to the brain in seconds. It is economical, because smaller amounts of cocaine are required. It is highly addictive because the intense euphoria is followed by severe depression. A susceptible individual can become a compulsive user in six to ten weeks.

b. **Distribution**. In a typical urban setting, the supplier hires dealers to sell the drugs. Dealers will often hire guards to keep them from being robbed by customers or other drug dealers. Frequent deliveries of drugs to dealers are essential. When dealers are arrested by police, they usually are carrying less than needed for a felony charge. Because crack cannot be smoked openly in the streets, they may go to a crack house, a structure where drugs can be purchased and consumed. Pipes for smoking crack are rented or sold there.

c. **Marketing**. Crack or "rock," as it is sometimes called, is most commonly sold in plastic vials or in self-sealing plastic bags. These vials are sometimes heat-sealed to prevent adulteration of its contents. To give the impression of quality control, they are often sold under brand names. This is important to insure customer satisfaction and repeat business. The vials are small enough so that they can be transferred from seller to buyer with a handshake. The typical crack user is a young lower-income urban male.

11. Marijuana

Marijuana *(cannabis sativa)* is the most widely used illicit drug. The smoking of marijuana cigarettes is especially popular among adolescents. The hemp plant from which the drug is obtained is a hardy weed which can be grown in a variety of climates. In warm regions the plant develops a resinous substance that has a strong effect. The hemp plant grows wild or is cultivated in Turkey, Greece, Syria, India, Africa, Brazil, Mexico, and the United States. The appearance of the plant varies widely depending on where it grows. It commonly grows to approximately five feet in height, but may grow taller. It is green in color with stalks fluted lengthwise. It has compound palmate leaves, with flowers in the male plant (greenish yellow sprays about 6 inches in length) and fruit or seed in the female plant (brown or greenish yellow moss enclosed in a green sticky pod).

a. **Preparation and Use**. Marijuana is made from the female hemp plant. As the plants ripen, their flower and seed heads exude a resin that contains the highest natural concentration of THC (delta-9-tetrahydrocannabinol), the chemical responsible for its psychoactive effects. The pure resin is called hashish and is more potent. The typical seizure of marijuana is a combination of female cannabis seed heads with leaves, chopped-up stalks, flowers, and hulls. Marijuana is illegally imported into this country, mainly from Mexico, either loose or pressed in bricks, called "keys" because each weighs one kilo (2.2 lb.). Marijuana is usually consumed by smoking it in a cigarette (*joint*), but may be eaten when mixed with foods and consumed as a beverage when steeped as tea.

b. **Identification**. The hemp plant is readily recognized by the serrations and vein structure of the leaf. Investigators should be familiar with its appearance. Prepared marijuana has the general appearance of catnip. In this form it may be identified by an experienced microscopist. Several chemical tests are available. One of these, the Duquenois test, is widely available as a prepackaged test kit that can be used as a field test prior to a seizure. Although not conclusive, it is a fairly reliable indication of the presence of marijuana. A small amount of the suspected material is placed in the test packet and if marijuana is present the solution will turn from pink, to violet, and then deep blue.

c. **Effects**. Using modern agricultural techniques (plant selection, cultivation, fertilization, and heated greenhouses), the United

Figure 17-3. Marijuana Leaf.

States now produces a highly potent form of marijuana. The THC content, the measure of its psychoactive potential, has increased significantly.

Among the short-term effects of marijuana smoking is the temporary impairment of visual and muscular coordination. Marijuana may also release inhibitions. The effect of the drug depends on the individual and the circumstances. It can produce hallucinations, distort perception, impair judgment and memory, create confusion and disorientation, cause difficulty in thinking and problem solving, and generate an increased heart rate, anxiety and panic attacks.

Serious health problems are associated with long-term marijuana use. Marijuana smokers tend to inhale deeply from unfiltered "joints," holding the smoke in their lungs for maximum absorption. This may explain why marijuana smokers develop many of the respiratory problems associated with tobacco smoking, such as bronchitis, emphysema, and bronchial asthma. Heavy marijuana use may impair mental activity, especially the critical skills related to attention, learning, and memory. Moreover, marijuana users have a greater risk for developing cancer. Marijuana contains known

Potential Marijuana Production in Mexico, in Metric Tons, 2003–2008.

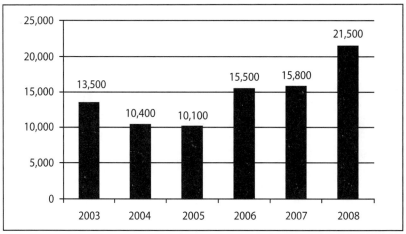

Figure 17-4. Source: National Drug Intelligence Center.

carcinogens that are stored in the body's fat cells for several months after using it.

d. **Addiction**. Polonged use of the more potent forms of marijuana can be addictive. According to the National Institute on Drug Abuse, 120,000 people enter treatment each year for primary marijuana addiction. Although withdrawal symptoms have been reported, they are relatively mild. Abstinence does not result in a severe withdrawal syndrome with intense physical suffering and craving that characterizes the opiates.

e. **Identifying the User**. It is not possible for investigators to visually identify marijuana users. Long-time users may develop yellowish skin particularly about the eyes, and may appear exophthalmic, i.e., "pop-eyed." After recent use a characteristic odor may be detectable on the breath.

12. Dangerous Non-narcotic Drugs

Many non-narcotic drugs are commonly abused and a considerable market and trafficking system has developed. Some can be obtained by prescription (tranquilizers and stimulants), while others (such as hallucinogens) cannot be legally obtained.

a. **Laws**. A collection of ineffective federal laws dealing with dangerous non-narcotic drugs was replaced by the Controlled Substances Act of 1970. It restricts the manufacture, sale, and distribution of any controlled drug to registered druggists and licensed physicians. It requires records of inventories, receipts, and dispositions. It also places restrictions on the refilling of prescriptions. The statute focuses on manufacturing and distribution and not possession of drugs for personal use.

All amphetamines and barbiturates are regulated by this statute. In addition, any other drug with potential for abuse (depressant, stimulant, or hallucinogenic) may be placed under the control of the act.

b. **Addictions, Tolerance, and Withdrawal**. Opinions vary regarding the addicting properties of dangerous non-narcotic drugs. The medical profession generally considers these drugs to be habit-forming but not addictive. Other than a possibility with excessive barbiturate use, no physical suffering follows withdrawal.

Very little tolerance to these drugs is developed even by prolonged use. While these drugs may not be considered addicting in the strict sense, they can produce psychological dependence and in some cases users may require medical treatment to break the habit.

13. Barbiturates

Barbiturates, or derivatives of barbituric acid, are commonly prescribed by physicians as soporifics or sedatives. When taken in correct dosages, barbiturates are a safe and invaluable treatment for insomnia, nervousness, and related conditions. They are readily obtainable and used in hospitals. An excessive dose is toxic and may cause death. Overdosing on barbiturates is a common method of suicide. At one time, the drug was overprescribed by some physicians who used it as they would a placebo.

a. **Identification**. Barbiturates may be dispensed as a white powder, tablets or capsules, or liquid. They are sold under many names, such as phenobarbital, Amytal®, Seconal®, Nembutal®, and Tuinal®. The various barbiturates are distinguishable by the colors used by the manufacturers. Amytal is usually found in a blue capsule, Seconal in red, Nembutal in yellow, and Tuinal in a capsule with a blue body and an orange cap. Phenobarbital is usually manufactured as a white tablet.

b. **Effects**. Barbiturates vary widely in their duration and the speed of action. Phenobarbital acts slowly but is effective for a long period of time. Seconal is felt within fifteen minutes but its effect is short-lived. Tuinal has a rapid onset and is relatively long lasting. All of the barbiturates affect the higher cortical centers lessening control of learned behavior and inhibitions governing instinctive behavior. In excessive dosage, users lose consciousness and the respiratory and circulatory systems are slowed. Death may ensue if the depression of the central nervous system is sufficiently severe. In medical dosages, the margin of error is sufficient to preclude accidental death. A fatal dose is usually fifteen times greater than the sleeping dose. As with many other poisons, the effect of barbiturates becomes more toxic with alcohol.

c. **Identifying the User**. According to the President's Commission on Violence, there is no reliable evidence to link tranquilizers (including barbiturates) with antisocial behavior. Although the use of barbiturates is not illegal, identifying users is sometimes helpful in an investigation. Habitual users are often maladjusted people seeking escape from reality. Occasionally, narcotic addicts will use barbiturates to relieve withdrawal symptoms. Barbiturate users experience a mild sense of well-being and may appear intoxicated and confused. Their speech is slurred, reflexes are diminished, and muscular control diminished. Tranquilizers can result in an impairment of driving ability. They may sleep for long periods depending on the type of barbiturate and their level of alcohol consumption. Upon awaking, users may demonstrate a lack of visual focus, imprecise movements, and difficulty articulating. Confirmed addicts sometime suffer from amnesia and may incur serious injuries from falls.

d. **Withdrawal Symptoms**. Usually there are no physical symptoms of withdrawal. Some medical authorities, however, have reported seizures if the drug was abruptly withdrawn from patients who had daily taken high dosages of barbiturates for a period of two months.

e. **Illegal Use**. Legal drugs, intended for medical treatment, are often diverted into the illegal drug market hindering attempts to control the illegal use of barbiturates. Some drugs are illegally manufactured in Mexico and California. Others reach the illegal market through forged prescriptions and drugstore burglaries.

14. Sedatives and Hypnotics

In addition to barbiturates, sedatives and hypnotics are behavioral depressants that reduce levels of alertness and activity. Sedatives are used to decrease anxiety and motor activity by depressing the central nervous system. Hypnotics go further by inducing a state resembling a normal sleep. Both are used for sleep or sedation by adjusting the dosage.

a. **Minor Tranquilizer**. Minor tranquilizers are used to relieve less severe psychological disorders. They are commonly prescribed for relief of anxiety, sedation, and as a muscle-relaxant. Included in this group are meprobamate (Miltown®, Equanil®), chlordiazepoxide (Librium®, Librax®), and diazepam (Valium®). Although these drugs are less powerful than barbiturates, abrupt withdrawal after an extended period of overuse may cause ill effects.

b. **Glutethimide**. Sold under the trade name Doriden®, this drug is used as a sedative and as a hypnotic. Its effects are similar to barbiturates, and it is used to treat insomnia.

c. **Methaqualone**. This is a powerful sedative-hypnotic sold under various trade names (most familiar are Sopor® and Quaalude®). It is used to treat insomnia and for daytime sedation. Recommended dosages for sleep are between 150 and 300 milligrams. Overdoses of the drug may lead to delirium and coma, progressing to convulsions. The effect of the drug is heightened when used with other sedatives or with alcohol.

d. **Chloral Hydrate**. This drug is sometimes used by criminals as "knockout drops" to sedate their victims. Chloral hydrate is colorless, transparent crystals with a strong odor and sharp taste. It is highly soluble in water and alcohol and readily mixes in a drink. It depresses the central nervous system, and as the pulse and respiration slows, the victim quickly sinks into a deep sleep. When combined with alcohol the effect of the drug is considerably enhanced. An overdose may paralyze respiration or the heart and result in death. Chloral hydrate is legitimately used as a sedative or soporific (in tablets or capsules).

15. Amphetamine (Benzedrine)

The use of amphetamines is widespread in the United States and represents a broad class of stimulants known as "pep pills." Ephedrine and epinephrine may also be placed in this category. Amphetamines raise the spirit, dispel fatigue, and impart a sense of energy. If used without medical supervision, there is a danger of overwork because of the absence of the normal signals of fatigue. During World War II, they were used to instill energy and confidence in the troops and to assist pilots on long bomber missions.

a. **Appearance**. Amphetamine may be found as a colorless liquid with a burning taste and a strong odor, or as a white, crystalline powder. As a prescription drug, it is commonly manufactured as orange or green, heart-shaped tablets but may be found in other forms as well.

b. **Effects**. The effects are similar but less intense than cocaine. Users experience increased muscular efficiency, exhilaration, sleeplessness, and loss of appetite. Persons with unstable personalities may experience problematic reactions. Habitual and excessive use can result in overexertion and collapse. Little tolerance is developed.

16. Methylphenidate (Ritalin)

This central nervous system stimulant is prescribed by doctors to treat attention-deficit/hyperactivity disorder (ADHD) in children. Sold under the trade name Ritalin, it helps to calm and improve concentration of hyperactive children. It is stronger than caffeine but weaker than amphetamines. Ritalin is abused for its stimulating effects that suppress appetite, reduce need for sleep, create euphoria, and improve concentration. Typically, abusers take Ritalin tablets orally or crush the tablets and snort the powder. Less frequently, they will dissolve the tablets in water and inject the liquid. Students may use Ritalin tablets to help them concentrate and to stay awake to study for exams.

17. Methamphetamine

Methamphetamine abuse has become a serious drug problem in United States. "Meth" is a dangerous, highly-addictive drug that has spread across the country. It may cause violent behavior and creates serious health problems besides addiction.

Until 1994, methamphetamine was manufactured and distributed by west coast motorcycle gangs. In 1994, experienced Mexican drug traffickers (who previously dealt in marijuana, heroin, and cocaine) saw a potential market and quickly moved in. They established larger production laboratories in both Mexico and the United States. Mexican drug gangs continue to control a large portion of meth production and distribution. (Although as can be seen in the number of labs seized, some states have significant problems with small local labs.) In 1995, meth abuse began spreading from the western states to the Midwest and the Southeast.

Methamphetamine is the drug most often synthesized in clandestine labs. Meth labs are operated by individuals with little or no chemical training, using easily obtained chemicals and recipes passed along in the meth community or by the Internet. With little investment, a meth laboratory operator or "cook" can produce thousands of dollars worth of the drug.

a. **Characteristics**. Methamphetamine is a highly addictive central nervous system stimulant. It is chemically related to amphetamines but is much more powerful. Like amphetamines, it has legitimate medical uses, particularly for treating obesity and narcolepsy.

Meth comes in two forms that may be ingested in a variety of ways. The most common form is methamphetamine hydrochloride or "crystal meth" (clear crystals resembling rock candy) that is smoked in a pipe. It also appears as a water soluble, white, bitter-tasting, odorless powder. This form can be snorted, taken orally, or injected.

b. **Effects**. The immediate effects of methamphetamine use are euphoria, increased energy, and hyperactivity. Chronic users may inject or smoke meth and sometimes stay awake for a week at a time. This may cause nervousness, irritability, paranoia, and violent or erratic behavior. Withdrawal is accompanied by severe depression. Methamphetamine abuse can produce anorexia, respiratory problems, strokes, cardiovascular collapse, and death.

c. **Clandestine Labs**. The violent and erratic behavior of the chronic user is only one of the dangers. A more significant threat is the clandestine laboratories that produce meth. The flammable, explosive, and toxic nature of the chemicals used to manufacture meth makes police raids very dangerous. In some instances, labs are booby-trapped. New "recipes" for meth allow it to be produced in small, highly portable containers. Unless investigators have training in the handling of chemicals, fires, bombs, and hazardous waste, a raid on a meth lab should not be undertaken.

Because these laboratories are located in apartments, motel rooms, garages, storage lockers, motor homes and other vehicles, police may inadvertently come into contact with them. Labs may be discovered when making traffic stops or responding to domestic disputes.

In addition to the immediate danger to the police officer, the clandestine meth lab can produce long-term environmental dam-

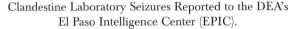

Clandestine Laboratory Seizures Reported to the DEA's
El Paso Intelligence Center (EPIC).

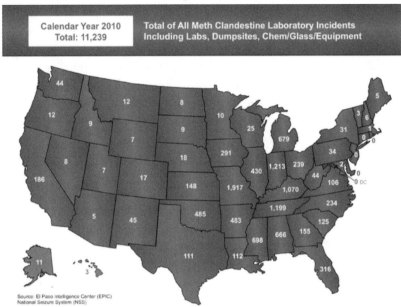

Figure 17-5. Drug Enforcement Administration.

age to the community. For each pound of meth produced, approximately five pounds of toxic waste is created. Lab operators usually have no concern for the environment or the threat that these toxins pose to people and animals. They routinely dump their chemical contaminants in the soil, in streams, or in the sewer system. The closing of a meth lab may require thousands of dollars of cleanup costs.

18. MDMA (Ecstasy)

Ecstasy, 3, 4-Methylenedioxymethamphetamine (MDMA), is a stimulant with hallucinogenic effects. It was patented in Germany in 1914 as a weight-loss drug but was not marketed because of its side effects. Users experience heightened awareness, lessened anxiety, relaxed inhibitions, with empathy and emotional closeness to others. Ecstasy is usually taken orally as a tablet or capsule, but it can be snorted or injected in powder form. It is commonly used during all-night dance parties or "raves" and its effects last about four to six hours. Its stimulant effect suppresses the need to eat, drink, or sleep and allows users to party or celebrate for several days.

Although a few clandestine labs in the United States produce MDMA, most is produced in the Netherlands and Belgium and smuggled into the United States. Ecstasy is usually not taken with alcohol, which would diminish its effect. This drug is especially popular with white middle-class young adults.

Ecstasy can damage the neurons that control the release of serotonin in the brain. Serotonin is thought to play an important part in regulating memory, mood, aggression, sleep, and sensitivity to pain. MDMA damage to the neurons is long-lasting, leading to memory and cognitive loss. Psychological effects include confusion, depression, anxiety, and paranoia that can occur at the time of use or weeks later. Hyperactivity coupled with dehydration from the stimulant effects of MDMA could result in kidney or heart failure.

19. Hallucinogens

Hallucinogens cause profound distortion of sensory perception, and include several natural chemicals (mescaline, psilocybin, and psilocin) and a number of synthetics (LSD, DOM, and DMT). Under the influence of these drugs, users may see, hear, and sense objects that do not exist. Time, space, color, sound, and physical shapes may change and take on a dramatically new appearance and significance.

Historically, various religions and cultures used hallucinogenic plants to induce a mystical state to provide insight into a spiritual world beyond ordinary experience. When synthetic hallucinogens became popular in the United States in the late 1960s, they were extolled by proponents for their "mind-expanding" potential. Use of hallucinogens often produced terrifying experiences or "bad trips," requiring hospital treatment. As hazards were recognized and preferences changed in the drug culture, the use of hallucinogens declined. In the 1990s, however, LSD (the most popular and most powerful of the synthetic hallucinogens) reemerged in a significantly less potent form. The average dosage in the 1960s of about 250 micrograms is now more commonly about 50 micrograms.

a. **Natural Hallucinogens**. Natural hallucinogens are relatively mild when compared to the synthetics. Discovered by Native Americans, *mescaline* or *peyote* has religious and cult associations in northern Mexico and southwestern United States. Mescaline is taken from the spineless peyote cactus in the form of a flower or "button," which resembles a dried brown mushroom, about the size of a half dollar and a quarter-inch thick. The button is eaten or brewed for drinking. The drug produces hallucinations, described by some as an appearance of geometric figures against a kaleidoscopic background of colors. Although bitter in taste and tending to produce nausea, the drug does not appear to have any serious after effects. Users experience a sense of well-being and are not incited to violence. Mescaline can also be produced synthetically.

Psilocybin and *Psilocin* are chemicals extracted from Mexican and Central American mushrooms. They are more powerful than mescaline and are used in traditional native rituals. These drugs are often found in capsules containing either spores or dried, ground mushrooms. Psilocybin and Psilocyn may also be produced synthetically.

b. **Synthetic Hallucinogens**. There are several synthetic hallucinogens with varying effects depending on their purity and dosage. In smaller dose, they do not produce hallucinations but alter mood, thought, and sensory perceptions. In larger doses, they may produce hallucinations lasting up to 12 hours.

LSD (Lysergic Acid Diethylamide) or "acid" was originally developed by Dr. Albert Hoffman, a Swiss chemist, in 1938. It has no accepted medical use and cannot be legally manufactured in the United States. It is, however, widely available and produced in clandestine laboratories.

LSD is sold most commonly in the form of "blotter acid," sheets of colorfully decorated paper soaked in the hallucinogen and perforated in 1/4-inch squares. Each square is an individual dose. It is also sold as tablets, or "microdots," and squares of gelatin called "window panes." The effects of LSD depend on the amount taken and on the personality and mood of the user. The physical effects often include an increased heart rate, elevated blood pressure, dizziness, nausea, dilated pupils, changes in body temperature, and sweating. The most significant danger comes from personal injury due to impaired judgment.

Tolerance develops quickly. It will dissipate if the user stops taking the drug for a few days. There is no evidence of withdrawal symptoms. Most users stop voluntarily. LSD is not considered addictive because it does not produce a compulsive need for the drug.

Psychological effects can vary widely, with some users reporting an enjoyable and mentally stimulating experience and others reporting it as unpleasant and terrifying. The effects are unpredictable for each person and for each experience.

Short-term effects may include hallucinations involving distortions of time, space, and perception of objects. Users may experience slow motion movement and the changing shape of their own body. One phenomenon often described is the feeling of "hearing colors" or "seeing sounds." These distortions of reality may be frightening and cause intense emotional reactions.

Long-term effects include a number of psychological disturbances that persist long after the drug is used, such as psychosis, depression, dramatic mood changes, hallucinations, and schizophrenia. Hallucinogen Persisting Perception Disorder (HPPD) is the spontaneous and recurring perceptual effect of LSD that occurs a long time after the drug has been used. These "flashbacks" may take the form of hallucinations or more commonly visual disturbances, such as bright flashes of light or light trails that follow moving objects.

DOM or *STP, DMT, DOB,* and *MDA* are some other synthetic hallucinogens that are produced and sold illegally. They are usually taken orally. These drugs vary widely in their ability to cause hallucinations and alter perceptions, thoughts, or moods.

20. Dissociative Drugs

Dissociative drugs produce feelings of detachment from self and the environment. The experience may vary from feeling distant or estranged, to floating alongside one's body, or of complete sensory detachment. Originally developed as surgical anesthetics, PCP and ketamine produce a trance-like state in which users may not be aware of pain or injury. Dissociative drugs also distort sight and sound, and sometimes produce hallucinations of short duration.

a. **PCP (Phencyclidine)**. The popularity of PCP or "angel dust," is limited because it often produces terrifying side-effects such as acute anxiety, panic, fear of impending doom, and violent or suicidal behavior. It is a dangerous drug with unpredictable effects. Some people have a bad reaction and use it only once, while others experience a sense of power and invincibility and become regular users.

Phencyclidine is manufactured in make-shift laboratories by people with little knowledge of chemistry. Normally PCP is a white crystalline powder but can vary in color and consistency due to contaminants in manufacturing. It may be sold in tablets, capsules, powder, or liquid that may be swallowed, snorted, or smoked. Sometimes PCP is dissolved in ether and sprayed on vegetative matter, such as marijuana, mint, or parsley, and then smoked.

b. **Ketamine**. Ketamine hydrochloride, or "special k" or "k," is a veterinary anesthetic that is manufactured as a liquid for injection. Because it is difficult to synthesize, it is not produced in clandestine labs but rather stolen from veterinarians' offices or supply houses. The liquid may also be evaporated into a powder to be snorted. Both the liquid and the powder form may be sprinkled on vegetative matter and smoked. Ketamine is sold in small plastic bags, in folded paper, or in aluminum foil.

Ketamine has effects similar to PCP but less potent and of shorter duration. Users may experience trance-like states, detachment from one's body, sensory distortions, and hallucinations. It is often consumed at all-night dance parties called "raves." Ketamine has been used in drug-facilitated rapes because it is odorless and tasteless, mixes readily with alcohol, and induces amnesia.

c. **Dextromethorphan**. This is a widely available cough suppressant found in cough medicine. When taken at recommended dosage, dextromethorphan is safe and effective. In large doses, it will produce effects similar to PCP and ketamine, such as a sense of dissociation from one's body.

21. Inhalants

Inhalants are volatile substances that produce intoxicating chemical vapors. These psychoactive agents are found in over 1,000 household products. Inhalants comprise a wide range of substances that include *volatile solvents* (liquids that vaporize at room temperature, such as paint thinner, glue, and gasoline), *aerosol sprays* (containing propellants and solvents, such as paint, hair, and deodorant sprays), and *gases* (medical gases, such as ether and nitrous oxide, and household products, such as butane lighters and whipped cream dispensers). The common characteristic of all of these substances is that they can be inhaled.

a. **Problem**. Inhalants are a significant health concern because of their toxicity and their widespread abuse by children. They often represent a child's introduction to the world of drugs. Inhalants are abused more by younger children than by older children. Usage typically peaks around the eighth grade. The household products are inexpensive, readily available, and easy to conceal, making it difficult to prevent their misuse by children.

Table 17-1. Commonly Abused Commercial Products.

Adhesives	Model airplane glue, rubber cement, household glue.
Aerosols	Spray paint, hair spray, air freshener, deodorant, fabric protector.
Anesthetics	Nitrous oxide, ether, chloroform.
Cleaning agents	Dry cleaning fluid, spot remover, degreaser.
Food products	Vegetable cooking spray, dessert topping spray (whipped cream), "whippets" (nitrous oxide).
Gases	Nitrous oxide, butane, propane, helium.
Solvents and gases	Nail polish remover, paint thinner, paint remover, typing correction fluid and thinner, toxic markers, pure toluene, toluol, lighter fluid, gasoline, carburetor cleaner, octane booster.

Source: National Inhalant Prevention Coalition.

Table17-2. Recognizing Inhalant Abuse.

• Chemical odors on breath or clothing • Paint or other stains on face, hands, or clothes * Hidden empty spray paint or solvent containers and chemical-soaked rags or clothing	• Drunk of disoriented appearance • Slurred speech • Nausea or loss of appetite • Inattentiveness, lack of coordination, irritability and depression

Source: National Institute on Drug Abuse. Early identification and intervention are the best ways to stop inhalant abuse before it causes serious health consequences. Parents, educators, family physicians, and other health care practitioners should be alert to the following signs of a serious inhalant abuse problem.

b. **Uses**. Inhalation can be through the nose or the mouth. Sniffing from an open container or "huffing" from a rag soaked in the inhalant and held to the mouth are common. Alternatively, an open container or an inhalant-soaked rag may be placed in a bag to concentrate the vapors which are then inhaled.

c. **Effects**. Inhaled vapors are rapidly absorbed through the lungs into the bloodstream, producing an alcohol-like inebriation. Dizziness, lack of coordination, euphoria, hallucination, and drowsiness often result. Prolonged inhalation of highly concentrated solvents can lead to heart failure, even in healthy first-time users. Inhalants are highly toxic to the lungs, liver, and kidneys and can cause permanent brain and neurological damage.

Signs of inhalant abuse include: chemical odors on the clothes, skin, or breath; a drunk, dazed, or dizzy appearance; and a characteristic "glue sniffer's rash" around the nose and mouth.

22. Anabolic Steroids

Anabolic steroids are synthetic drugs, chemically related to testosterone, that promote muscle growth. Body builders, distance runners, cyclists, and other athletes use these drugs to enhance their performance or to improve their physical appearance. Anabolic steroids are usually taken orally, but can be injected or rubbed onto the skin as a cream or gel. These drugs are obtained through illicit sales at gymnasiums, athletic events, mail order, or the Internet. There are more than 100 different anabolic steroids that require a prescription to be used legally. The majority of illicit sales are from supplies smuggled in from other countries. Occasionally, steroids are diverted from U.S. pharmacies or are produced by clandestine laboratories.

a. **Physical Effects**. Anabolic steroids do promote rapid muscle growth and have affected the outcome of sporting events. The short-term gains are far outweighed by the debilitating long-term effects. The physical side effects include elevated blood pressure and cholesterol, liver and kidney tumors, premature balding, acne, and reduced sexual function. In males, steroid use may lead to abnormal breast development. In females, there is a masculizing effect, resulting in a deeper voice and excess facial hair. Some of these effects are irreversible.

b. **Psychological Effects**. Steroid use in high doses has been associated with increased irritability and aggressiveness, leading to crimes such as assault and armed robbery. Addiction is possible. Withdrawal symptoms include depression that may last for a long period after ceasing drug use and sometimes result in suicide.

c. **Prevention**. Because steroid abuse is often part of a pattern of high-risk adolescent behavior, it is difficult to discourage and control. Efforts by professional sports to eliminate steroid use have brought increased awareness. Education of coaches, trainers, and athletes, and increased testing of athletes may help in prevention.

23. Investigative Methods

Drug crime may include possession, use, sale, or manufacturing of a prohibited controlled substance. Investigators will need to establish the specific elements of the crime, suspects' actions, and the circumstances of the incident.

a. **The Nature of the Substance**. An essential step in the investigation is to establish that the substance is a narcotic or other controlled drug. The *corpus delicti* must be proved independently of any confession. If the subject was deceived into buying a harmless white powder instead of a narcotic, they cannot be prosecuted for possessing a controlled substance. A laboratory analysis must confirm the identity of the suspected drugs.

b. **The Unlawful Act**. Investigators must prove that the subjects' actions were illegal, i.e., that they possessed, sold, or used an illegal drug. These may not be mutually exclusive acts.

1) ***Possession***. It is necessary to prove that the drug was in the possession of the accused. Possession of contraband is presumed to be wrong unless the possessor can prove otherwise. The possession is legal if the drug has been prescribed by a physician, when it is possessed by medical or police personnel in performance of their duty, or when possessed through accident or mistake. When possible, subjects should be searched in the presence of witnesses. If drugs are found, the person should be confronted to obtain an admission. Occasionally, investigators will discover a cache of drugs. Experienced users or sellers will usually have several places where they hide drugs. The problem for investigators is to connect subjects to the hidden drugs. Sometimes investigators can show that only the suspects had access to the drugs or there is physical evidence linking the drugs to the suspects. Surveillance may be necessary to implicate suspects when they return for the drugs.

2) ***Use***. Determining use of drugs may be important in some employment situations or to corroborate a charge of possession. For example, subjects may claim that they are in possession by some accident or mistake or that the drug was prescribed by a physician. A thorough questioning at the time of arrest may result in admissions or limit later excuses or alibis.

Subjects may be in possession of apparatus or paraphernalia associated with drug use (e.g. hypodermic needles, medicine droppers, bent spoons, pipes, etc.). These should be submitted for laboratory analysis to determine the presence of any residual drugs. The possession of the apparatus cannot by itself support a charge of use of drugs unless some residue is present on the instrument.

Information about the habits of suspects may be helpful. It is possible there may be witnesses to their drug use. Suspects may have confided in friends or acquaintances about their drug use.

Suspects should be examined by a physician for physical marks, conditions, and symptoms of addiction. Analysis of the urine, blood, or hair may reveal the use of drugs. Withdrawal syndrome is a reliable indication of addiction.

3) ***Selling***. The illegal sale of drugs is a more serious offense than possessing or using them. Investigators should attempt to identify the source or at least the immediate seller in drug cases. A drug

sale may be established if investigators or witnesses observed the exchange. Several states have enacted legislation that creates a presumption of intent to sell if a specific amount of drugs are possessed. In some states there is a presumption of possession by all persons in a motor vehicle when drugs are found. Although both presumptions are rebuttable, the burden of proof shifts to the defendants. In addition, the need for drug buys is reduced since the mere possession of a specified amount is *prima facie* evidence of intent to sell.

Intensive questioning of users often leads to the identity of the seller. In most cases, users know only the sellers' nicknames and places they frequented. Showing users photographs of known drug sellers may help to identify their sources.

Investigators may be assigned to work undercover, posing as drug users. After locating the seller they should arrange to make a buy. This, of course, is not a simple matter and the assistance of informants may be needed. Investigators may make purchases but it is preferable to have an informant make purchases with investigators witnessing the sales. It may also be possible for investigators to witness sales to other users. This helps to avoids charges of entrapment.

Fixed and moving surveillances are sometimes needed to witness sales and to gather other evidence. Binoculars, marked buy money (recorded serial numbers or tracing powder), telephoto photography, and video recordings are commonly used.

Suspects should be thoroughly searched when apprehended for drugs and drug paraphernalia. Since these items can be very small, exceptional care and considerable ingenuity must be employed whenever searching for drugs. Suspects can be very ingenious in hiding drugs. Hollow bedposts, false-bottomed stoves, hollow heeled and soled shoes, toilet tanks, hidden compartments in furniture, inside of stereo speakers or clocks, sealed tubes or pockets in automobile tanks, whiskey, food packaging, coffee, hollowed-out candles, specially constructed underclothing, belts tied to various parts of the body beneath clothing, rolled-up magazines and newspapers, and in fraudulently manifested packages are some of the methods that have been used. Heroin has been stuffed inside animals and toys. The various body orifices, between toes, underarms and fingernails are places where drugs may be hidden. Drugs carried openly in the guise of familiar and legitimate objects is perhaps the most subtle means of avoiding detection.

24. Laboratory Examination

A laboratory analysis is necessary to conclusively identify a substance as a drug subject to the Controlled Substances Act. An admission by a suspect is not sufficient. Several field tests are available, but they are not conclusive or entirely reliable. In addition, a field test is only useful if investigators' suspicions are correct and they use the proper test for that specific drug. The substance may be a prohibited drug, but not the one suspected by investigators.

Evidence should be forwarded to a laboratory along with a letter containing case identification information, a summary of the case, any statements of suspects regarding the nature of the substance, and any other information as to the type of drug suspected. This information is particularly valuable when the evidence sample is small. Sellers may have adulterated the drug by adding an innocuous substance such as milk sugar or aspirin. This adulteration adds to the difficulty of analysis. When analysts are provided with information concerning the suspected identity of the substance, a more efficient approach can be used that will consume less of the evidence.

25. Care of Evidence

The handling of drug evidence requires exceptional care because the quantity is often limited and investigators must account for all of the evidence. All evidence forwarded to the laboratory must be protected from contamination.

a. **Original Container**. Ordinarily, the evidence should not be removed from its original container. It may need to be removed to inventory but then should be returned to the container. Mark and preserve any boxes, cans, bottles, envelopes, or wrappers connected with the evidence and processed for additional physical evidence. In addition, containers may be linked to the seller. In one case, the user confessed to illegally buying the drug from a drugstore, and after the druggist's denials, it was shown that glue spots and paper cutter marks on the glassine envelope matched envelopes found in the store.

b. **Inventory**. All suspected drug evidence should be accurately weighed or counted in the presence of a witness. Tablets and capsules should be both counted and weighed since it is possible to remove some of the drug without altering the number of items. A record of the inventory should be made in the investigator's notebook and report.

c. **Packaging**. When the inventory is completed, the evidence should be placed in a suitable container. Tablets, pills, capsules, and powders can be placed in small envelopes or in pillboxes and liquids in appropriate bottles. Seals should be placed across the flaps of envelopes and the edge of bottle caps. Seals should bear the investigator's name. If the evidence is to be shipped to a laboratory, it should be placed in an appropriate box with precautions taken to prevent breakage or loss.

d. **Labeling**. A label should be affixed to containers before packaging. The information on labels should include the case number, name, and title of the investigator, weight and substance or number of items, time and date of seizure, and place of seizure.

26. Medical Examinations

Medical examinations of suspects may provide corroboration of drug use, but must comply with the laws of the jurisdiction and with the rights of the accused. A physician experienced in drug cases should conduct the examination. Signs of use and addiction include contracted pupils, withdrawal syndrome, needle scars, and ulcerations on the arms and legs. Urine, blood, and hair analysis provide the best evidence of drug use. A physician or a qualified medical technician should draw samples of the suspect's blood and urine to be used for toxicological analysis. Specimens should be properly sealed and labeled.

27. Drugs and Crime

The exact relationship between drug addiction and crime is unclear, but it is well accepted that drug addicts are often involved in crime. Drug users' involvement in non-drug offenses cannot be estimated with any great degree of accuracy.

a. **Drug Offenses**. Although addiction in itself is not a crime under either federal or state law, it inevitably leads to violations of the drug laws. To maintain their habit, users must buy and possess the drugs. Unauthorized purchase and possession are violations of both federal and state laws. Moreover, to finance an expensive habit users may becomes drug sellers, greatly increasing their liability for arrest. In many states the non-medical use of controlled drugs and the possession of a hypodermic needle or equivalent paraphernalia such as a needle and syringe is an offense.

b. **The Cost**. Many addicts cannot afford the expense of their drug supply and must supplement their income through crime. They find themselves drifting into crimes (larceny, burglary, selling drugs, procuring, prostitution, and other offenses) to support their habit. For the most part they concentrate on theft of cash or property that can be easily converted to cash.

Drug users are responsible for a substantial amount of crime. If the cost of the crimes committed by drug users to obtain their daily drug supply could be accurately calculated, the sum would be considerable. The cost to society in loss of productivity, health care, and other costs run into many billions of dollars a year.

Table 17-3. Jail Inmate Dependency and Abuse.

	Alcohol	Drugs	Alcohol or Drugs
Any Dependency or Abuse	47%	53%	68%
Dependency	23%	36%	45%
Abuse only	24%	18%	23%
No Dependency or Abuse	53%	47%	32%

Source: Substance Dependence, Abuse, and Treatment of Jail Inmates, 2002.

Table 17-4. Commonly Abused Drugs.

Substance: Category & Name	Examples of Commercial & Street Names	DEA schedule/ How Administered	Effects & Health Risks
Cannabinolds			
Marijuana	Blunt, dope, ganja, grass, herb, joint, bud, Mary Jane, pot, reefer, green, trees, smoke, sinsemilla, skunk, weed	I/Smoked, swallowed	**Acute Effects**— Euphoria; relaxation; slowed reaction time; distorted sensory perception; impaired balance and coordination; increased heart rate and appetite; impaired learning, memory; anxiety; panic attacks; psychosis
Hashish	Boom, gangster, hash, hash oil, hemp	I/Smoked, swallowed	**Health Risks**— Cough, frequent respiratory infections; possible mental health decline; addiction
Opiods			
Heroin	*Diacetyl-morphine:* smack, horse, brown sugar, dope, H, junk, skag, skunk, white horse, China white; cheese (with OTC cold medicine and antihistamine)	I/Injected, smoked, snorted,	**Acute Effects**— Euphira; drowsiness; impaired coordination; dizziness; confusion; nausea; sedation; feeling of heaviness in the body; slowed or arrested breathing **Health Risks**— Constiptation, endrocarditis; hepatitis; HIV; addiction; fatal overdose
Opium	Laudanum, paregoric: big O, black stuff, block, gum, hop	I Injected, smoked	

continued

Table 17-4—*Continued.*

Stimulants

Cocaine	*Cocaine hydro-chloride:* blow, bump, C, candy, Charlie, coke, crack, flake, rock, snow, toot	II/snorted, smoked, injected	**Acute Effects—** Euphoria; drowsiness; impaired coordination; dizziness; nausea; sedation; feeling of heaviness in the body; slowed or arrested breathing
Amphetamine	Biphetamine, Dexedrine: bennies, black beauties, crosses, hearts, LA turnaround speed, truck drivers, uppers	II/swallowed snorted,	**Health Risks—** Weight loss, insomnia; cardiac or cardiovascular com-plications; stroke; seizures; addiction
Meth-amphetamine	*Desoxyn:* meth, ice, crank, chalk, crystal, fire, glass, go fast, speed	II/swallowed snorted, smoked, injected	**Also, for cocaine—** Nasal damage from snorting **Also for metham-phetamines—**Severe dental problems

Club Drugs

MDMA (methylenedioxy-methamphetamine)	Ecstasy, Adam, clarity, Eve, lover's speed, peace, uppers	I/swallowed snorted, injected	**Acute Effects, for MDMA—**Mild hallu-cinogenic effects; increased tatile sensitivity; empathic feelings; lowered inhibition; anxiety; chills; sweating; teeth clenching; muscle cramping
Flunitrazepam	*Rohypnol:* forget-me pill, Mexican Valium, R2, roach, Roche, roffies, roofinol, rope rophies	IV/swallowed, snorted	**Also, for Flunitraze-pam—**Sedation; msucle relaxation; confusion; memory loss; dizziness; impaired coordination

continued

Table 17-4—*Continued.*

GHB	*Gamma-hydrooxybutyrate:* G, Georgia home boy, grievous bodily harm, liqud ecstasy, soap, scoop, goop, liquid X	I/swallowed	**Also, for GHB—** Drowsiness; nausea; headache; disorientation; loss of coordination; memory loss **Health Risks for MDMA—**Sleep disturbances; depression; impaired memory; hyperthermia; addiction **Also, for Flunitrazepam—**Addiction **Also, for GHB—**Unconsciousness; seizures; coma

Depressants

Barbiturates	*Amytal, Nembutal, Seconal, Phenobarbital:* barbs, reds, red birds, phennies, tooies, yellows, yellow jackets	II, III, V/injected swallowed	**Acute Effects—** Sedation/drowsiness, reduced anxiety, feelings of well-being, lowered inhibitions, slurred speech, poor concentration, confusion, dizziness, impaired coordination and memory
Benzodiazepines	*Ativan, Halcion, Librium, Valium, Xanax:* candy, downers, sleeping pills, tranks	IV/swallowed	**Health Risks—**lowered blood pressure, slowed breathing, toleance, withdrawal, addiction; increased rish of respiratory distress and death when combined with alcohol

continued

Table 17-4—*Continued.*

Sleep Medications	*Ambien (zolpidem), Sonata (zaleplon), Lunesta (eszopiclone):* forget-me pill, Mexican Valium, R2, Roche, roofies, roofinol, rope, rophiesing	IV/swallowed, snorted	**Also, for barbiturates**— euphoria, unusual excitement, fever, irritability/life-threaten- withdrawl in chronic users

Dissociative Drugs

Ketamine	Ketalar SV: cat Valium, K, Special K, vitamin K	III/injected, snorted, smoked	**Acute Effects**— Feelings of being separated from one's body and environ- ment; impaired motor function
PCP and analogs	Phencyclidine: angel dust, boat, hog, love boat, peace pill	I, II/ swallowed smoked, injected	**Also, for ketamine**— Analgesia; impaired memory; delirium; respiratory depression and arrest; death
Salvia divinorum	Salvia, Shepheredess's Herb, Maria Pastora, magic mint, Sally-D	Not scheduled/ chewed, swallowed, smoked	**Also, for PCP and analogs**—Analygesia; psychosis; aggres- sion; violence; slurred speech; loss of coor-
Dextro- methorphan (DSM)	Found in some cough and cold medications: Robotripping, Robo, Triple C	No scheduled/ swallowed	dination; hallucina- tions
			Also for DSM— Euphoria; slurred speech; confusion; dizziness; distorted visual perceptions
			Health Risks— Anxiety; tremors; numbness; memory loss; nausea

continued

Table 17-4—*Continued.*

Hallucinogens

LSD	*Lysergic acid diethylamide:* acid, blotter, cubes, microdot yellow sunshine, blue heaven	I/swallowed, absorbed through mouth tissues	**Acute Effects—** Altered states of perception and feeling; hallucinations; nausea
Mescaline	Buttons, cactus, mesc, peyote	I/swallowed smoked	**Also, for LSD—** Increased body temperature, heart rate, blood pressure; loss of appetite; sweating; sleepless- ness; numbness, dizziness, weakness, tremors; impulsive behavior; rapid shifts in emotion
Psilocybin	Magic mush- rooms, purple passion, shrooms, little smoke	I/swallowed	**Also, for Mescaline—** Increased body temperature, heart rate, blood pressure, loss of appetite; sweating; sleepless- ness; numbness; dizziness, weakness; tremors; impulsive behavior; rapid shifts in emotion
			Also, for Psilocybin— Nervousness; paranoia; panic
			Health Risks for LSD—Flashbacks, Hallucinogen Persisting Perception Disorder

continued

Table 17-4—*Continued.*

Other Compounds

Anabolic steroids	*Anadrol, Oxandrin, Durabolin, Depo-Testosterone, Equipoise:* roids, juice, gym candy, pumpers	III/injected, swallowed, applied to skin	**Acute Effects, for Anabolic steroids—** No intoxication effects **Also for Inhalants (varies by chemical)—** Stimulation; loss of inhibition; headache; nausea or vomiting; slurred speech; loss of motor coordination; wheezing
Inhalants	Solvents (paint thinners, gaso-line, glues); gases (butane, propane, aerosol propellants, nitrous oxide); nitrites (isoamyl, isobutyl, cyclo-hexyl): laughing gas, poppers, snappers, whippets	No scheduled/ inhaled through nose or mouth	**Health Risks, for Anabolic steroids—** Hypertension; blood clotting and cho-lestoral changes; liver cysts; hostility and aggression; acne; in adolescents—pre-mature stoppage of growth; in males—prostate cancer, reduced sperm pro-duction, shrunken testicles, breast enlargement; in females—menstrual irregularities, develop-ment of beard and other masculine characteristics **Also, for inhalants—** Cramps; muscle weakness; depres-sion; memory impair-ment; damage to cadiovascular and nervous systems; unconsciousness; sudden death

Source: National Institute on Drug Abuse

ADDITIONAL READING

Drug Investigation

Beary, K., Mudri, J.P., and Dorsch, L.: Countering Prescription Fraud. *Police Chief,* 63 (3), 1996.

Benson, C.C.: K-9 Sniffers. *Law and Order, 39* (8), 1991.

Bradenstein, A.E.: Advanced Technologies Bolster Law Enforcement's Counter-Drug Efforts. *Police Chief, 64* (1), 1997.

Brown, L.P.: Strategies for Dealing with Crack Houses. *FBI Law Enforcement Bulletin, 57* (6), 1988.

Bulzomi, M.J.: Drug Detection Dogs: Legal Considerations. *FBI Law Enforcement Bulletin, 69* (1), 2000.

Cameron, J.: Pressure Point: One City's Solution to Crack Cocaine. *Law and Order, 36* (6), 1988.

Carroll, P.J.: Operation Pressure Point: An Urban Drug Enforcement Strategy. *FBI Law Enforcement Bulletin, 58* (4), 1989.

Cashman, M.: Meth Labs: Toxic Timebombs. *Police Chief, 65* (2), 1998.

Commonly Abused Drugs. National Institute of Drug Abuse. Available www .drugabuse.gov/ on 2/13/2012.

Doane, G. and Marshall, D.: Responding to the Methamphetamine Problem. *Police Chief, 65* (2), 1998.

Entrapment Defense in Narcotics Cases: Guidelines for Law Enforcement. Washington, D.C.: Institute for Law and Justice, 1991.

EPIC.: Clandestine Laboratory Seizures. Available http://www.justice.gov /dea/concern/ map_lab_seizures.html, 2011.

Florez, C.P. and Boyce, B.: Laundering Drug Money. *FBI Law Enforcement Bulletin, 59* (4), 1990.

Hargeaves, G.: Clandestine Drug Labs. 69 *FBI Law Enforcement Bulletin, 4,* 2000.

Hendrie, E.M.: Proving Guilty Knowledge: Caught Red-Handed or Empty-Headed? *FBI Law Enforcement Bulletin, 69* (4), 2000.

Hermann, S.: Clandestine Drug Lab Raid. *Law and Order, 38* (9), 1990.

James, R.D.: Hazards of Clandestine Drug Laboratories. *FBI Law Enforcement Bulletin, 58* (4), 1989.

Karberg, J. and James, D.: *Substance Dependence, Abuse, and Treatment of Jail Inmates, 2002.* Bureau of Justice Statistics Special Report. NCJ 209588. National Institute of Justice, Washington D.C., 2005.

Kingston, K.A.: Hounding Drug Traffickers: The Use of Drug Detection Dogs. *FBI Law Enforcement Bulletin, 58* (8), 1989.

Lyman, M.D.: Minimizing Danger in Drug Enforcement. *Law and Order, 38* (9), 1990.

Role. *FBI Law Enforcement Bulletin, 53* (1), 1984.

——: *Practical Drug Enforcement: Procedures and Administration.* New York: Elsevier. 1989.

Macdonald, J.M. and Kennedy, J.: *Criminal Investigation of Drug Offenses: The Narcs' Manual.* Springfield, IL: Thomas, 1983.

Mahoney, P.T.: *Narcotics Investigative Techniques.* Springfield, IL: Thomas, 1992.

Mangan, R.J.: Exploiting the Financial Aspects of Major Drug Investigations. *FBI Law Enforcement Bulletin, 53* (11), 1984.

McCormack, W.U.: Detaining Suspected Drug Couriers: Recent Court Decisions. *FBI Law Enforcement Bulletin, 60* (6), 1991.

Meyers, M.A.: Operation Clean Sweep: Curbing Street-Level Drug Trafficking. *FBI Law Enforcement Bulletin, 69* (5), 2000.

Moore, M.H.: *Buy and Bust.* Lexington, MA: Lexington Books, 1977.

Moriarty, M.D.: Undercover Negotiating: Dealing for Your Life. *Police Chief, 57* (11), 1990.

Narcotics Investigator's Manual. Washington, D.C.: Drug Enforcement Administration, 1978.

National Drug Intelligence Center.: National Drug Threat Assessment 2010.: Available at http://www.justice.gov/ndic/pubs38/38661/index.htm#Contents, 2010.

Office of National Drug Control Policy (2004). *The Economic Costs of Drug Abuse in the United States, 1992–2002.* Washington, DC: Executive Office of the President (Publication No. 207303)

Ross, C. and Block, J.M.: K-9 Narcotics Detection Training. *Police Chief, 55* (5), 1988.

Snow, R.L.: Street Level Narcotics Environment. *Law and Order, 38* (7), 1990.

Wade, G.E.: Undercover Negotiating: Flashrole Management. *Police Chief, 57* (11), 1990.

Role. *FBI Law Enforcement Bulletin, 53* (1), 1984.

——: Undercover Violence. *FBI Law Enforcement Bulletin, 59* (4), 1990.

Uniform Crime Reports: Crime in the United States 2010. Available http://www.fbi.gov/about-us/cjis/ucr/crime-in-the-u.s/2010/crime-in-the-u.s.-2010/index-page.

U.S. Government's Cocaine Production Estimates, Just the Facts. Available http://justf.org/blog/20111/01/20/us- governments-cocaine-production-estimates, 1/20/2011.

Warshaw, B. and Daly, P.: Drug Trafficking in the United States. *Police Chief, 63* (3), 1996.

Chapter 18

THE INVESTIGATOR IN COURT

RULES OF EVIDENCE

1. Overview

THE SUCCESS of a criminal prosecution depends upon the thoroughness of the investigation and the quality of evidence presented in court. Months of labor must be effectively presented. Mistakes through ignorance or carelessness may lead to the rejection of vital evidence and suspicion of the competency or prejudice of investigators. It is essential that investigators understand the purpose of evidence and the rules that control its admissibility. Only then can they serve the cause of justice efficiently.

Evidence can be anything that establishes or disproves a relevant fact. The purpose of evidence is the discovery of the truth. The laws of evidence are the rules governing its admissibility. Certain types or forms of information may be irrelevant or tend to confuse rather than assist in determining truth. The primary aim of the rules of evidence is to remove these risks from influencing the jury and court members. The rules of evidence differ among the states.

2. Classifications and Definitions

Direct evidence establishes a main point or issue (elements of the crime). For example, eyewitness accounts of a crime are direct evidence. Witnesses are describing an event they actually observed.

Circumstantial evidence supports a fact or situation by inference. Where direct evidence is the immediate experience of a witness, circumstantial evidence requires a presumption. For example, X and Y enter a closet, close the door, a shot is heard, Y rushes out with a smoking gun in his hand, and *X* is found lying on the floor. An eyewitness relaying this event would be offering circumstantial evidence that *Y* shot *X* since the actual shooting was not seen. From the facts, it may reasonably be inferred that *Y* shot *X.*

Real evidence is comprised of tangible objects introduced to prove or disprove a fact in question. The evidence speaks for itself. It requires no explanation, merely identification. Examples of real evidence are guns, fingerprints, and bloodstains. Real evidence may be direct or circumstantial.

3. Admissibility of Evidence

To be admissible, evidence must be material and relevant. The rules of evidence address the admissibility of facts and materials and not their weight as evidence. The weight to be given evidence is a question for the judge or jury to determine.

a. **Materiality**. Evidence is material if it tends to prove a fact at issue in the case. Evidence that proves something that is not part of the case is immaterial. To be material the evidence must significantly affect an issue of the case. For example, if the suspect is being tried for larceny of a crate of oranges, testimony about the color of the oranges is immaterial. Such evidence is unimportant, so it is immaterial.

b. **Relevancy**. Evidence that tends to prove the truth is relevant. In a case of murder with a crossbow, it is relevant to show that the defendant knew how to use a crossbow. It would be irrelevant to show that he or she was skilled with firearms.

4. Competency of Witnesses

To be eligible to testify, a witness must be competent. It is presumed a witness over thirteen years of age is competent. Mental competency refers to the ability to see, recall, and relate. Moral competency implies an understanding of the truth and the consequences of a falsehood. The competency of children may be shown by apparent understanding and recognition of the importance of telling the truth. A previous conviction is unrelated to competency but may affect credibility.

5. Impeaching a Witness

Impeachment is the discrediting of a witness. A witness may be disqualified by showing mental deficiency, immaturity, previous criminal conviction, or a reputation for untruthfulness.

6. Judicial Notice

Certain facts can be recognized by the court without the formal presentation of evidence. This recognition is called *judicial notice.* In general, the court need not require proof in matters of common knowledge (e.g., historical and geographical facts, a state's own laws, weights and measures, etc.).

7. Burden of Proof

No one is required to prove his or her innocence. The burden of proof for a conviction rests solely with the prosecution. In criminal cases, the prosecution has the burden of proving guilt beyond a *reasonable doubt.* The accused, however, must prove any allegations they make such as alibis, claims of self-defense, and insanity.

8. Presumptions

A presumption is a justifiable inference. It is a logical conclusion drawn from the existence of two or more facts based upon previous experience of their connection. Presumptions generally shift the burden of proof to the other party who must then establish contradictory facts.

a. **Conclusive Presumption**. A conclusive presumption is considered final, unanswerable, and cannot be overcome by contradictory evidence. For example, everyone is presumed to know the law, and children under seven years are presumed to be incapable of committing a crime.

b. **Rebuttable Presumptions**. A rebuttable presumption can be overcome by proof. There are many examples. Everyone is presumed to be innocent and presumed to be sane. People are presumed to be of good character, chaste, or sober. There is a presumption that police officers properly perform their tasks. It is presumed that someone is dead after an unaccounted absence of seven years. There is a presumption of legitimacy of children and validity of marriage. All of these can be rebutted by evidence to the contrary.

9. Rules of Exclusion

Rules of exclusion define circumstances when evidence will *not* be admissible. They are often technical and obscure, and have evolved to control the presentation of evidence to juries. Because jurors are inexperienced in legal matters, it is sometimes difficult to separate immaterial and unimportant matters from germane issues. It is feared that laypersons may not discriminate properly between gossip and fact, or between allegation and truth.

Rules of exclusion limit witnesses' testimony to things about which they have direct, sensory knowledge. Witnesses may relate what they saw, felt, and smelled. The jury then tries to evaluate the reliability of the witness. Generally, all direct and circumstantial evidence (that is material and relevant) is admissible except for opinion evidence, evidence concerning character and reputation, hearsay evidence, privileged communications, and secondary evidence. (There are exceptions, however, to the admissibility all of these categories of evidence).

10. Opinion Evidence

a. **The Opinion Rule**. Generally, opinion evidence is not admissible in a trial. Witnesses may testify only to facts, not to their conclusions or opinions. They are limited only to those facts they have observed, directly through their senses - sight, hearing, touch, taste, or smell. It is the function of the jury to weigh the evidence and to draw conclusions. If witnesses add opinions, confusion may arise as to what was observed and what was interpreted.

b. **Exceptions to the Opinion Rule**. There are exceptions to the opinion rule for judgments that tend to be reliable common practices or the opinions of trained specialists.

1) *The Lay Witness*. There are many observations that the average person is qualified to express. Laypersons may give opinions

on matters of common experience such as physical properties like color, weight, size and visibility. Estimates of a person's age, race, nationality, language or emotional state are permissible. A person's apparent physical condition or state of intoxication can be reported. The approximate speed of a vehicle can be estimated by a lay witness. These opinions are permitted only for issues within the knowledge and experience of the average person.

2) ***Expert Testimony***. Experts are persons skilled in some art, trade, or science and possess information not within the common knowledge of the average person. Medical doctors, fingerprint specialists, and collectors may be considered experts. Experts can provide interpretations of technical issues to assist the judge and jury reach a correct conclusion. Expert testimony is not proof, but is an informed opinion that is weighed for credibility by each member of the court.

Experts must satisfy the court that they have the proper skill, knowledge, and experience or education to render an opinion. In other words, they must possess qualifications beyond the average person and limit their opinions to subject matters within their qualifications. The rationale is that facts that support the expert's opinion are of such a technical nature that the judge and jury may not be expected to have sufficient knowledge, skill, and understanding of the subject matter.

The circumstances of the case will determine which areas of expertise are relevant. The possibilities are innumerable. Some common areas include medical matters, fingerprint identification, DNA analysis, and blood-alcohol content. In traffic accident cases, experts might testify, based on skid marks, as to the movement of a vehicle or the minimum distance required to stop it from a certain speed.

11. Character and Reputation

As a general rule, testimony concerning a person's character and reputation cannot be introduced to imply guilt. This exclusion is based on the difficulty that the jury may encounter separating the defendants' criminal record or moral conduct from the question of their guilt in the current crime.

Defendants may introduce evidence of their own good character and reputation to show the probability of innocence. Such testimony may either be given by themselves or by character references and may deal with specific character traits such as sobriety and chastity. If such testimony is offered, though, the "door is open" for the prosecutor to introduce evidence to rebut the character of the defendant. If the defendant introduces testimony concerning sobriety, the prosecution may then produce evidence relating to instances of drunkenness.

a. **Exceptions**. Previous crimes may be introduced into evidence if they tend to link defendants to the crime currently at trial.

1) *Modus Operandi*. The prosecution may show that the patterns of previous crimes are similar to the present crime, i.e., they may show that "this is the way the defendant operates."

2) *Previous Acts*. These may be brought in to rebut a defense of *mistake* or *ignorance*. For example, if a wife claims that the arsenic in the meal that caused her husband's death was the result of a mistake, the fact that three previous husbands died of arsenic poisoning would be admissible.

3) *Identifying Evidence*. Evidence is admissible if it serves to identify the defendant as the perpetrator of the crime. If a pistol found at the scene of a burglary was stolen previously by the defendant, this evidence can be designed to show that the pistol was in the possession of the defendant before the crime and not to show guilt of a theft.

4) *Guilty Knowledge or Intent*. An example of this would be if the defendant had previously been a fence of stolen goods, he or she should have known from the circumstances that the property in the present case was stolen.

12. Hearsay Evidence Rule

Hearsay evidence is not the personal knowledge of the witness but a repetition of what the witness has heard from others. Its value and credibility cannot be derived from the witness but rests mainly on the veracity or competency of some other person. For example, a witness states, "I know Bob hit Jim because Bill told me." This statement would be hearsay.

Hearsay applies to both oral and written statements. It is excluded for a number of reasons. The author of the statement is not present and under oath. There is no opportunity to confront or cross-examine the person making the assertion. There is no opportunity for the court to observe the author's or speaker's demeanor. There is a possibility of error in the passage of information from one person to another.

a. **Exceptions to the Hearsay Rule**. There are numerous exceptions to the exclusion of hearsay evidence. The circumstances surrounding these exceptions tend to minimize the possibility of error or fraud.

1) *Confessions*. Since a confession is a direct acknowledgment of guilt, it is not likely that individuals would make untrue statements against their own interests.

2) *Conversations in the Defendant's Presence*. If before apprehension, the defendant was confronted with an accusation of guilt and failed to deny it, the circumstances can be offered in evidence.

3) *Dying Declaration*. In a trial for criminal homicide, the dying declaration of victims about actions or circumstances of their injuries (including the identity of the perpetrator) is admissible in evidence to prove such circumstances.

There are several conditions that must be met. The evidence must be given in a trial for homicide. The statement must be that of the victim. The statement must concern the circumstances of the act causing death. The victim must believe he or she is dying. The victim must in fact have died. The victim must have been competent at the time the statement was made.

b. **Spontaneous Exclamations**. When people speak without time to reflect or to fabricate a lie, they often speak the truth. The element of surprise tends to minimize the possibility of design or deliberation.

A spontaneous exclamation is an utterance by an individual who is excited, shocked, or surprised concerning the circumstances of a crime. These statements are admissible by anyone who heard it. The spontaneous exclamation can either support or jeopardize the interests of the speaker. They can be made by anyone present, not simply by the victim or suspect. Such statements are part of the *res gestae* (things which happened) but are related specifically to the hearsay rule.

A spontaneous exclamation must be carefully examined before it is admitted into evidence. The statement or action should be close in time to the act (precede, follow, or be concurrent). The spontaneous character of the statement should clearly be without fabrication or deliberation. The declaration should not have been made in response to a question. The statement should tend to illuminate or explain the character of the act. In general, only a person who committed, participated in, or witnessed the act may be the declarant.

A similar concept is the *fresh complaint*. In some jurisdictions the fact that the victim reported a sexual offense shortly after the crime is admissible to bolster the credibility of the claim. For these fresh complaints, only the victim's statement is considered. The statement may only relate to *who* was responsible and *what* happened.

c. ***Documentary Evidence***. Documents may be introduced in evidence as an exception to the hearsay rule. Their submission is controlled by several rules, but principally by the "best evidence" rule. Basically, this rule requires that persons bring into court the best evidence available to them. Whenever possible, the original written document should be produced.

Secondary evidence (copies, carbons, and other duplicates of the original) is not ordinarily admissible. Secondary evidence may be admissible when the original is lost or destroyed, when it is in the hands of the defendant (who refuses to surrender it), when its value is such that its production in court is not deemed advisable, when there is some other valid reason for which it cannot be produced.

Authenticated copies of *official records* can be introduced because their maintenance is required by law, regulation, and custom, and they can be attested to by their custodians. It would disrupt the operation of government to require officials to appear each time records are required.

Investigators' notes and memoranda, made contemporaneous to the activities they describe, may be used by investigators to refresh their memory in testifying. They may also be entered into evidence under the certain conditions.

Former recorded testimony under certain conditions may be admissible. If the witness who gave the testimony is not available and the former trial involved the same or similar defendants and substantially the same issues, the testimony can be admitted.

The testimony of a witness who will not be available at the time of trial may be formally recorded, as a *deposition,* and is ordinarily admissible. Witnesses may be questioned through written interrogatories or by direct questioning by both prosecution and defense, and their answers to both parties and any cross-examination is recorded. Special requirements are placed on the qualifications of the persons taking the depositions.

Regular entries in the course of business may be admissible. It is reasoned that an entry made in the course of regular business is sufficiently credible to be admissible as evidence. The entry must have been made at a time close to the occurrence of the fact in issue. The entry must have been made by someone with personal knowledge of the event or transaction or as a regular part of the bookkeeping process, such as a sales receipt. The original entry must be offered in court.

13. Privileged Communications

Information obtained in certain confidential relationships is considered to be privileged communication and not admissible as evidence. The court may, however, receive this evidence from a person not bound by the privilege.

a. **State Secrets and Police Secrets**. Some confidential information is essential to the functioning of the state and considered privileged. Examples include informants who provide information about crime to public officers, deliberations of petit and grand juries, diplomatic correspondence, and official communications whose disclosure would be detrimental to the public interest.

b. **Personal Privileged Communications**. At the trial of a *husband or wife,* neither can divulge confidential information they shared, unless both consent to the disclosure. The person entitled to the benefit is the spouse who made the communication. (This exclusion is generally negated for crimes within the family.) Communication between an *attorney and client* is privileged if part of the attorney-client relationship. Communication between *penitent and clergy* is privileged if it is part of a religious practice or while seeking spiritual advice on a matter of conscience. Confidential information between *doctor and patient* is privileged in some jurisdictions.

14. Real Evidence and Admissibility

Real evidence is not generally protected by the privilege against self-incrimination. The privilege is primarily based on the Fifth Amendment restriction that individuals shall be compelled to give testimony against themselves in a criminal case. This privilege extends to any person who is called as a witness and protects against being compelled to give verbal or other communication of involvement in a crime.

The privilege usually does not apply to physical evidence such as clothing, fingerprints, or biological samples. In most jurisdictions, for example, suspects may be required to try on clothing or shoes, place their feet in impressions, produce a sample of handwriting, and utter words for voice identification. They may be required to give a sample of DNA, blood, urine, saliva, and breath tests for forensic analysis. These practices, however, vary with jurisdictions.

15. Entrapment

Investigators cannot incite someone into committing a crime. *Entrapment* occurs when peace officers or agents of the government induce individuals (for the purpose of prosecuting them) to commit crimes they had *not contemplated* committing. It is not entrapment, though, to furnishing an opportunity to commit a crime when the criminal intent was already present in the suspect's mind. For entrapment, the officer plants the seed or "puts the idea" into the suspect's mind. The danger of entrapment is more likely to arise in an undercover assignment, and investigators must avoid becoming accessories to a crime. They may pretend to participate with the criminal's plans, but they should never render active assistance in the preparation or commission of the offense. A defense of entrapment may be used if the crime was actually planned and instigated by officers and the accused was lured into its commission by persuasion or fraud. Investigators may, however, employ decoys and supply opportunities to commit crimes. Investigators can facilitate but cannot originate or substantially motivate someone to commit a crime.

16. *Corpus Delicti*

Corpus delicti (the body of the crime) consists of all the facts relating to the commission of a particular crime. In a criminal trial, it is necessary to first establish the *corpus delicti,* or actual elements of the offense committed, and then identify the perpetrator.

There are several rules related to *corpus delicti.* A confession cannot be used to establish the corpus delicti, but the confession of co-defendants may be used. *Corpus delicti* must be established before there can be a conviction. The *corpus delicti* does not have to be proved beyond a reasonable doubt, but substantial corroborative evidence of the offense must be presented. Direct, real, or circumstantial evidence can be used to establish *corpus delicti.* Negative proof of the *corpus delicti* is sometimes permitted. For example, in arson it can be shown negatively that the fire was a criminal act by eliminating all natural or accidental causes.

TESTIMONY IN COURT

17. Overview

Appearing as a witness in court is the final and most demanding test of an investigator's work. The quality of the case preparation, along with the skill, professionalism, fairness, and character of the investigator is also on trial. The precautions taken at the crime scene, the preservation of the evidence, the information from witnesses, the search for the fugitive, the interrogation of the suspects, the preparation of exhibits, and the report of investigation are all evaluated in the trial. The probative value of the evidence depends on how it is presented to the jury. The effectiveness of the evidence is a function of the impression investigators make as witnesses.

Since the reputations of investigators rest in part on their courtroom performance, they should develop their skills as witnesses. They should project dignity and behave with professional decorum. On the witness stand investigators represent the agency that employs them. Deficiencies or irregularities in their behavior will reflect upon the organization. Errors of judgment and misrepresentations may undermine the pursuit of justice.

When taking the witness stand, investigators are subject to critical review. They are no longer dealing with friendly supervisors. They must contend now with the objective and critical eye of the court and at times with the outright animosity of the defense counsel. Regardless of the proficiency of the investigation, a failure on the witness stand may render worthless much of the work performed in the case. The trial results are weighed heavily by the public and by organizational supervisors. Although the substance of testimony is important, equal significance is attached to investigators' conduct and manner of testifying. Investigators can develop skills to become effective witnesses, and will improve with time and experience.

18. Training in Laws of Evidence and Court Procedure

To become skilled in testifying on the witness stand, investigators should first be familiar with the laws of evidence. This will guide their investigations and better prepare them to testify in court. It will give investigators insight into what is taking place in the courtroom at any given time. Investigators will understand what the attorneys are attempting to achieve by their tactics. Finally, investigators will be able to avoid the pitfalls and traps of cross-examination.

a. **Rules of Evidence.** Knowledge of the rules of evidence helps investigators to recognize relevant and material evidence, and the admissibility of evidence. They may testify only to what they have learned through their own senses and to facts that are part of their personal knowledge: they cannot give opinions. If asked a question by counsel that would require an inadmissible answer, investigators should pause to give opposing counsel an opportunity to object.

b. **Knowledge of Court Procedure**. Investigators should know the jurisdiction of the various courts and have an understanding of the court procedure. They should understand the function of the judge and the other courtroom participants.

19. Preparation

When testifying, investigators should appear prepared but not rehearsed. Strive to be sincere and credible. You want to be perceived as a fact-finder, not a persecutor.

Prior to testifying, investigators should anticipate the questions they may be asked. Investigators should review their notes and case reports to be familiar with the highlights of the case. Be mindful of the rules of admissibility and the probative value of the evidence. Investigators should be able to readily recount the full history of the evidence. They must be prepared for trickery and deception from opposing counsel while expressing themselves in a fair, convincing, and forceful manner. They must avoid errors, confusion, and inconsistencies that can result in a loss of composure that will undermine their credibility with the jury.

Although investigators are permitted to use their notes in court, they will convey a better impression if able to narrate the facts without reference to documentation. When witnesses must look up each point in their notebooks, their testimony loses force and effectiveness. They should know the case well enough to report all facts without reference to notes except data such as numbers, dates, addresses, and the spelling of names. Their appearance on the stand must be preceded by a conscientious, thoughtful review of the facts. An inadequate review will result in misstatements, omissions, and contradictions. Often investigators must recall actions from several months in the past.

20. On the Witness Stand

When called to testify, investigators should promptly step up to the stand and be sworn in. Sit in a comfortable but straight posture; do not slouch. Identify yourself and your agency. Speak in a slow, audible, and distinct manner. Address your testimony to the jury and not to the attorneys.

Ordinarily investigators are asked to relate a series of observations or activities. Using straightforward language, describe the events observed in the order they took place. Your narrative should enable the jury to clearly understand what happened.

The prosecuting attorney is prevented from asking leading questions, so investigators may need to anticipate the line of questioning. Place appropriate emphasis on important highlights. The narration should be designed to cover the elements of proof.

While testifying, investigators should present a modest demeanor and display a sincere interest in accuracy and truth. Any sign of bias, prejudice, or antipathy will diminish the impact of your testimony. Investigators must appear to be focused on the presentation of the facts, not convicting the defendant.

Investigators must remain mindful of their role in the dynamics of the trial. Although they may see themselves as objective collectors of facts, others will try to portray them as overzealous and unfairly trying to convict the defendant. The defense counsel may portray investigators as seizing the nearest suspect based on little evidence. Investigators must not display extraordinary motivation to convict when presenting their testimony. They must play the part of impartial, conscientious public servants endeavoring to achieve the aims of justice. A calm and forthright presentation is more likely to win over the judge and jury and project honesty and integrity.

a. **Personal Knowledge**. Investigators must tell only what they know from personal knowledge to be the truth. The sole function of the witness is to assist the court in arriving at a just decision in the case. The truth is told by an accurate choice of words and careful control of emphasis and tone to avoid exaggeration or underestimation.

b. **The Appearance of Candor**. Professional investigators should perfect their presentation and demeanor to give the impression of telling the truth. (No suggestion of duplicity is intended by this statement.) Unfortunately, some truthful individuals do not project honesty well. Nervousness and timidity make them appear evasive. Such mannerisms are detrimental to investigators who must testify in court. They need to learn to project poise, confidence, and a forthright demeanor.

c. **Courtesy**. Investigators must display courtesy and respect. They must avoid sarcasm, witticisms, or ridicule. Even obviously absurd questions should be answered seriously and temperately.

d. **Direct Answers**. Witnesses must answer the questions they are asked. Their answers must be responsive. Listen to the question and gather its exact meaning. If you do not understand, ask for clarification. When the answer is known, offer it without hesitation. The answer should do no more than reply to the question. It should not express a view of the case, draw a conclusion, or present an argument. Further, it should not provide "ammunition" for opposing counsel.

e. **Control**. Witnesses who become angry or otherwise lose control of their emotions are easy prey for astute counsel. Emotional composure is a necessity. Investigators must ignore insults, badgering, and innuendoes and maintain a professional demeanor. Appearing contentious can easily be turned against a witness.

21. Expert Testimony

Even though investigators may not have the specialized training of a forensic laboratory expert, they may occasionally be asked to offer opinions in a limited area of expertise. After questioning them on their background, counsel (either prosecution or defense) may receive permission from the judge to request an opinion. Investigators may know a number of crime scene techniques and technical procedures that qualifies them to offer expert testimony on limited topics.

a. **Common Evidence**. Expert testimony is a valuable means of arriving at the truth, and may be derived from experiments conducted to prove or disprove a fact or statement. Some possible examples include visibility (the possibility of seeing one place from another), the length of time required to go from one place to another, the distance traveled in going from one place to another, the nature and audibility of a sound, the length of time required for a candle to burn or ice to melt, the results of firing a given weapon, or whether a particular firearm will give a visible flash with certain ammunition. Facts such as these can be proved by experiments conducted by investigators, if made under substantially the same conditions as those existing at the time of the crime.

b. **Professional Experts**. In matters requiring extensive technical knowledge, investigators will need assistance from professional experts. Trying to give opinions beyond one's area of expertise is a dangerous practice. For example, questions relating to microscopy, biology, handwriting, fingerprint identification, or DNA identification should be left to experts. Investigators can assist the expert by acquiring an understanding of the scope and limitations of the expert's scientific knowledge. Investigators should know what can be fairly expected of science and what is out of the realm the expert's field. This will help investigators to collect, preserve, and properly transmit evidence to the expert so it can be properly analyzed.

c. **Expert Investigative Techniques**. Investigators need to show on the witness stand that they possess the necessary training, experience, and knowledge of the literature in their field. Photography, casting, and the development of latent fingerprints are subjects commonly mastered by investigators. Before testifying concerning these matters, investigators should review some standard literature on the particular technique used in acquiring the evidence. They should inform the prosecutor of their qualifications and previous experiences testifying in similar matters.

ADDITIONAL READING

Rules of Evidence

Chamelin, N.C. and Evans, K.R.: *Criminal Law for Police Officers* (6th ed.). Englewood Cliffs, NJ: Prentice-Hall, 1995.

Donigan, R.L., et al.: *The Evidence Handbook* (4th ed.). Evanston, IL: Traffic Institute, Northwestern University, 1980.

Hanley, J.R. and Schmidt, W.W.: *Legal Aspects of Criminal Evidence.* Berkeley, CA: McCutchan, 1977.

Inbau, F.E., Aspen, M.E. and Carrington, F.: *Evidence Law for the Police.* Philadelphia: Chilton Book, 1972.

Kaplan, E.J.: *Evidence: A Law Enforcement Officer's Guide.* Springfield, IL: Thomas, 1979.

Klein, T.J.: *Law of Evidence for Police* (2nd ed.). St. Paul: West Publishing, 1978.

Klotter, J.C.: *Criminal Evidence* (6th ed.). Cincinnati: Anderson, 1995.

Klotter, J.C. and Meier, C.L.: *Criminal Evidence for Police* (4th ed.). Cincinnati: Anderson, 1986.

Murphy, D.: Hearsay: The Least Understood Exclusionary Rule. *Journal of Criminal Justice, 17* (265), 1989.

Pellicciotti, J.M.: *Handbook of Basic Trial Evidence.* Lanham, MD: University Press of America, 1985.

Schloss, J.D.: *Evidence and Its Legal Aspects.* Columbus, OH: Merrill, 1976.

Weston, P.B., et al.: *Criminal Evidence for Police* (4th ed.). Englewood Cliffs, NJ: Prentice-Hall, 1994.

Entrapment

Callahan, M.: Predisposition and the Entrapment Defense. Parts I and II. *FBI Law Enforcement Bulletin, 53* (8 & 9), 1984.

Entrapment Defense in Narcotics Cases: Guidelines for Law Enforcement. Washington, D.C.: Institute for Law and Justice, 1991.

Hardy, B.A.: The Traps of Entrapment. *American Journal of Criminal Law, 3* (165), 1975.

Heydon, J.D.: The Problems of Entrapment. *Cambridge Law Journal, 32* (268), 1973.

Miller, J.D.: The Entrapment Defense. Parts I and II. *FBI Law Enforcement Bulletin, 42* (2 & 3), 1973.

——: Entrapment. *FBI Law Enforcement Bulletin, 42* (10), 1973.

Park, R.: The Entrapment Controversy. *Minnesota Law Review, 60* (163), 1976.

Courtroom Testimony

Anderson, P.R. and Winfree, L.T., Jr. (Eds.): *Expert Witnesses: Criminologists in the Courtroom.* Albany: State University of New York Press, 1987.

Bratton, W.J. and Esserman, D.M.: Post-Arrest Training. *FBI Law Enforcement Bulletin, 60* (11), 1991.

Burke, J.J.: Testifying in Court. *FBI Law Enforcement Bulletin, 44* (9), 1975.

McDonald, W.F. (Ed.): *The Defense Counsel.* Beverly Hills, CA: Sage, 1983.

Mogil, B.M.: Maximizing Your Courtroom Testimony. *FBI Law Enforcement Bulletin, 58* (5), 1989.

Petersen, R.D.: *The Police Officer in Court.* Springfield, IL: Thomas, 1974.

Reynolds, D.W.: *The Truth, the Whole Truth, and Nothing But . . . A Police Officer's Guide to Testifying in Court.* Springfield, IL: Thomas, 1990.

Rutledge, D.: *Courtroom Survival: The Officer's Guide to Better Testimony.* Costa Mesa, CA: Custom Publishing, 1984.

Stutler, T.R.: Stand and Deliver: Cross-Examination Strategies for Law Enforcement. *FBI Law Enforcement Bulletin, 66* (9), 1997.

Tierney, K.: *Courtroom Testimony: A Policeman's Guide.* New York: Funk & Wagnalls, 1970.

Whitaker, M.W.: *The Police Witness: Effectiveness in the Courtroom.* Springfield, IL: Thomas, 1985.

EPILOGUE

THE CHALLENGE OF CRIMINAL INVESTIGATION

A DVANCES IN FORENSIC SCIENCE, computer processing, electronically retrievable data, and mass communication have transformed criminal investigation. Investigators must constantly keep pace with changes in technology and the way people communicate. The Internet and social media will continue to expand as a resource to be mined by astute investigators.

Most technological advances come in small steps. With each step we become more efficient and effective. Some advances are transformational. Advances in DNA analysis changed crime scene practices, laboratory procedures, and investigative strategies. Minute traces of biological evidence can now link suspects to crimes. It has also helped overturn convictions of individuals imprisoned based on less reliable evidence.

Investigators are still learning how to fully use the resources of the Internet. Communications and information sharing has increased dramatically. Investigators can now access in seconds information that once required hours or days to acquire. In the next few years, research currently in progress should help investigators better utilize the extensive information available on social networking sites. Investigators will also reap benefits from apps that sort through and process the myriad of electronic data.

At the same time, many of the fundamentals of criminal investigation presented over 50 years ago by Charles O'Hara are still valid and effective. While some of the tools have changed, the basic methods of criminal investigation remain legitimate and useful.

Good investigators seek the truth through careful, methodical, and painstaking procedures. At times luck may play a role, but successful investigators continually place themselves in positions to exploit good fortune. The path to justice is a slow, deliberate, and cautious collection and analysis of facts. The rush to judgment is fraught with mistakes and peril. A false conviction punishes the innocent, empowers the guilty, and often results in additional victims.

Effective investigators understand the crimes they investigate and the people who commit them. The strength of O'Hara's original work was to describe how crimes were committed and guide investigators in dealing with perpetrators. Each crime and individual is different, but by studying patterns, investigators can begin to develop investigative strategies. For each crime, investigators draw from their experience to look for what they expect to find, note what they did not expect to find or what is missing, and then proceed to explain why the crime unfolded as it did. In a similar manner they assess personality to understand motivation in suspects and witnesses. When the consistencies are documented and the oddities explained, the investigation is well on the way to finding the truth.

GLOSSARY

ABC method. A three-man tail used to minimize the risk of detection.

accelerant. Highly combustible liquids used by the arsonist to make a fire spread rapidly.

acid phosphatase color test. A field test for the presence of semen.

addiction. The condition of habitually using a narcotic drug and of having lost the power of self-control with respect to it.

admission. A self-incriminatory statement by the subject falling short of an acknowledgment of guilt. It is an acknowledgment of a fact or circumstance from which guilt may be inferred.

alligatoring. The pattern of crevices on the surface of charred wood that is similar in appearance to the skin of an alligator.

amnesia. Loss of memory and with it the knowledge of one's identity.

amphetamines. Stimulants that are used to uplift the spirit, dispel fatigue, and impart a sense of great work capacity.

analgesic. A drug used to relieve pain.

anthropometry. A method of physical identification based on body measurements, developed by Alphonse Bertillon (1853-1914).

arson. The malicious burning of another's house.

aspermia. The condition of lacking any sperm.

asphyxia. Suffocation. The suspension of breathing due to a deficiency of oxygen in the red blood cells.

assault. The willful attempt or immediate threat to do physical harm to another.

associative evidence. Objects or substances that link the suspect to the crime scene or the offense.

autopsy. A postmortem medical examination to determine the cause of death.

barbiturate. A commonly abused drug prescribed by doctors to treat insomnia and nervousness and sold in the form of a white tablet or capsules in a variety of colors.

battery. The unlawful application of force to another.

bertillonage. See anthropometry.

"best evidence" rule. A rule governing the admissibility of documents in court which requires that, where available, the original of a document should be submitted.

borescope. A lighted fiber-optic instrument designed to be inserted into small holes, useful for examining the contents of a safe.

brushing. Developing fingerprints by the application of powder by brush.

bug. A miniature electronic device concealed in a room that receives and transmits the sound of voices.

"bumper-beeper." A battery-operated transmitter that is attached to the underside of a vehicle which permits the surveillant to receive radio signals and thereby track its movements.

burglary. The breaking and entering of a person's dwelling at night with intent to commit a crime therein.

burning bar. See thermal lance.

cadaveric spasm. A stiffening occurring immediately after death. A tenacious grasp of a weapon by the deceased is evidence of suicide.

canvass. The technique of systematically interviewing the people living near or frequenting the vicinity of the crime scene in order to locate someone who can provide information about the crime.

chain of custody. Protecting evidence by recording and receipting each change of possession.

chemical etching. A method used by investigators to restore serial numbers on metal objects that have been filed away.

"chopping." Cutting a hole through the bottom of a safe with hammer and chisel or an ax.

circumstantial evidence. A fact or circumstance from which one may infer another fact at issue.

class characteristic. An attribute of evidence which serves to identify the kind, make, or model of the object associated with it. A tread pattern or a brand name are class characteristics.

"close tail." Surveillance in which extreme precautions are taken against losing the subject.

cocaine. A white crystalline powder made from a derivative of coca leaves. It is inhaled or injected as a stimulant.

coercion. Compelling behavior by physical force or threat.

cognitive interview. A series of interviewing techniques designed to help the witness enhance his memory recall in order to recollect the details of a crime.

concentric fractures. Secondary cracks in glass that appear as a series of lines connecting the radial lines in circular patterns around the point of impact.

conclusive presumption. In a court of law, a justifiable inference considered final and not overturned by contradictory evidence.

confidential informant. A person who provides an investigator with information concerning a past or projected crime and does not wish to be known as the source of this information.

confession. An oral or written acknowledgment of guilt to the crime charged or to an essential element of the crime.

constructive breaking. The use of collusion, trick, ruse, intimidation, or impersonation to gain entry.

convoy. A person who follows the subject to make sure he is not being followed.

core drill. A tool used to create a circular hole in a safe large enough to reach in and remove its contents.

corpus delicti. The fact that a crime was committed.

corpus delicti **evidence.** Objects or substances that tend to establish that a crime has been committed.

crack. A highly addictive form of cocaine that is usually smoked in a pipe.

crazing. The pattern of thin irregular lines found in glass that has been exposed to high temperatures.

criminal homicide. The killing of a human being that is not excusable or justifiable.

criminal investigator. A person who collects facts concerning a crime in order to identify and locate the guilty party and to provide evidence of his guilt.

cyanoacrylate (Super Glue) method. A fuming technique for developing fingerprints on nonporous surfaces such as glass, metal, tin foil, leather, and is especially useful on plastics and plastic bags.

data surveillance. Collecting information on what a person has done or thought. It consists of official records as well as personal data collected by government and corporate computers.

"day-lock." The practice of closing the safe door and turning the combination dial slightly.

deductive reasoning. Applying a general theory to a particular instance in order to explain that instance. Proceeding from the general to the particular.

deposition. Sworn testimony obtained by questioning in the presence of an official who can administer oaths, and presented in written form in court in lieu of an appearance by the witness.

depressant. A drug that sedates the central nervous system. Barbiturates and valium are depressants.

developing a fingerprint. Converting a latent fingerprint into a visible image.

direct evidence. Evidence which directly establishes the main fact at issue, such as an eyewitness account of a criminal act.

DNA. Deoxyribonucleic acid. The complex genetic material found in the cells of every organism that can be used to uniquely identify a person.

double strip method. A crime scene search pattern in which the area to be searched is blocked out in the form of a rectangle and the searchers proceed along paths parallel to the base of the rectangle and then parallel to its side.

"druggist fold." Filter paper folded into thirds in both directions forming a square interior compartment.

duress. Compelling behavior through the imposition of restrictions on physical liberty; for example, deprivation of food or sleep.

EDTA. A chemical preservative added to blood when DNA analysis is to be performed.

elements of the offense. The conditions that must be fulfilled by the evidence in order to establish the guilt of the accused.

embezzlement. The fraudulent appropriation of money or goods by a person to whom they are entrusted.

entrapment. The act of a police officer in inducing a person to commit a crime not previously contemplated, for the purpose of prosecuting this person.

excusable homicide. A homicide which is the outcome of an accident while doing a lawful act in a lawful manner, or a homicide committed in self-defense.

felony. A crime of a serious nature that is usually punishable by a prison term of more than one year.

fencing. Receiving stolen property.

fibrillation. A marked change in the strength and rhythm of the heartbeat.

field of view. The area included in a photograph.

fingerprint camera. A fixed-focus camera used to copy fingerprints on flat surfaces.

finished drawing. A drawing of the crime scene based on the rough sketch, drawn to scale by a skilled draftsman.

forgery. The making or altering of a document with the intent to defraud.

fresh complaint. A statement by the victim made within a short time after a sexual offense that is admissible as evidence.

fuming. Developing a fingerprint by exposing it to chemical vapor.

grid method. See double strip method.

hackle marks. Minute irregular lines found on the edge of glass that has been broken by a sudden powerful force.

hallucinogens. A group of drugs named for their capacity to cause hallucinatory or delusional effects. It includes natural chemicals, such as mescaline or peyote and psilocybin, and synthetic chemicals, such as LSD, DOM or STP, and DMT.

hematoma. An accumulation of blood in the tissues following a rupture of the blood vessel.

heroin. An opium derivative in the form of a white crystalline powder usually injected by hypodermic needle. It is highly addictive and characterized by severe withdrawal symptoms.

hesitation marks. Superficial cuts, approximately one inch long at the point of origin of the wound, made by testing a razor on the skin. It is a common indication of suicide.

high-torque drill. A tool, equipped with carbide or diamond-tipped bits, used to pierce the drill-resistant metal of a safe.

homicide. The killing of a human being.

housebreaking. The unlawful entering of the building of another with intent to commit a crime therein.

hypnosis. A sleep-like state of heightened awareness and concentration in which the subject becomes aware of those experiences, stored in his subconscious memory, that were repressed, forgotten, or that he was not fully conscious of at the time of their occurrence.

hypnotic. A drug used to induce a sleep-like state by depressing the central nervous system.

identifying evidence. Objects and substances that tend to establish directly the identity of the perpetrator.

impeachment. The discrediting of a witness in a court of law.

individual characteristic. An attribute of evidence which serves to identify the specific object associated with it. A manufacturing defect or accidental damage, such as a nick or a cut, may be an individual characteristic.

inductive reasoning. Forming a general theory from an examination of particular details. Proceeding from the particular to the general.

informant. A person who gives information to the investigator.

information. The knowledge that the investigator gathers from other persons.

instrumentation. All the technical methods by which the investigation is advanced.

intent. The desire to accomplish an act.

intuition. A sudden and unexpected insight that clarifies a problem.

involuntary manslaughter. An unlawful homicide committed without an intent to kill or inflict great bodily harm; it is an unlawful killing by culpable negligence.

iodine method. A fuming technique used for developing fingerprints on porous surfaces such as paper and cardboard.

justifiable homicide. A killing of a human being that is authorized or commanded by law, such as a soldier killing an enemy on the battlefield.

kleptomania. A psychological disturbance that impels one to steal.

larceny. The taking of someone else's property with the intent of permanently depriving him of its use.

laser method. Using laser light to cause latent fingerprints to become luminescent, providing a nondestructive method of viewing them.

latent fingerprints. "Hidden" or relatively invisible fingerprints that must be developed by special methods.

lead. A possible source of information pertinent to the investigator.

legend. The explanation of symbols used to identify objects in the sketch.

lifting. The physical removal of a latent fingerprint from its original surface.

lineup. A police identification procedure in which a suspect is exhibited with a number of similar-looking persons so that a witness can identify him.

loan sharking. The lending of money at exorbitant rates of interest backed ultimately by the threat of violence in the event the debtor defaults.

location markers. White arrows or numbered signs placed in the field of view of a photograph in order to draw attention to significant points of evidence.

"loose tail." A type of shadowing employed where only a general impression of the subject's habits and associates is required.

"lost." Eluded by the subject during surveillance.

luminol. A chemical applied by aerosol spray, useful for detecting minute traces of blood while searching large areas, such as walls or carpeting.

"made." Recognized as a shadow by the subject.

Magna-Brush. The method of developing fingerprints on paper that uses a magnet to move ferromagnetic powder across the paper.

"mainliner." A user who injects a drug directly into the bloodstream.

malice. A legal term for the intent to do injury to another.

manipulation. The art of opening a safe without prior knowledge of the combination using only the senses of sight, hearing, and touch.

manslaughter. An unlawful homicide without premeditation.

marijuana. *Cannabis sativa.* The most widely used illicit drug, derived from the hemp plant and smoked as a cigarette.

markers. Devices placed in the field of view which aid in the interpretation of a photograph.

material. Tending to prove a fact that is a significant issue in a legal case.

mental reconstruction. Developing a theory concerning the actions of the criminal at the crime scene, using the accounts of witnesses and the arrangement of objects.

mescaline. Peyote. An hallucinogen found in the flower of a spineless peyote cactus.

methadone. A synthetic analgesic used in the treatment of heroin addiction.

***Miranda* warnings.** Advising a suspect of his right to remain silent and to have an attorney present as a necessary preliminary step before an investigator can interrogate a person in custody.

missing person. Anyone reported missing who is under eighteen or anyone missing who is eighteen or over and either: (1) seriously affected mentally or physically, or (2) absent under circumstances which would indicate involuntary disappearance.

MO. See *modus operandi.*

modus operandi. Method of operation.

morphine. An opium derivative used by the medical profession as a pain reliever.

motive. That which induces the criminal to act.

night-viewer. A binocular-type instrument that uses infrared radiation for surveillance operations in the dark.

ninhydrin. A chemical, often sprayed on documents, useful for developing old fingerprints on paper.

nitroglycerine. An explosive substance used for blowing safes.

notebook. The investigator's record of the relevant details of the case.

odontologist. A dentist trained in the recovery and analysis of dental evidence.

oligospermia. The condition of having a low sperm count.

opium. The juice of the oriental poppy which is dried to a brown, gummy substance and smoked in an opium pipe.

oxyacetylene torch. An industrial welding tool that can be used to burn a hole in a safe.

pathology. The study of abnormal changes in bodily tissues or functions caused by diseases, poisons, or other bodily afflictions.

pedophilia. A psychosexual disorder in which an individual receives gratification through sexual contact with children.

"peel." A safebreaking method that involves separating the metal layers on the door and then curling back the top layer with a pry bar to expose the lock or bolt.

pen register. A device that is attached to the telephone line which records every number dialed from a particular phone, as well as the date, time and duration of the call.

Petrographic File. A file, maintained by the FBI, containing samples of and data concerning safe insulations.

photographic identification. An identification procedure in which a witness selects a photograph of a suspect from a series of photographs of similar-looking persons.

physical dependence. A condition in which a drug is needed to maintain well being due to physiological changes brought about by using the drug.

physical evidence. Articles and materials found in connection with an investigation which assist in the discovery of the facts.

physical reconstruction. Reproducing the positions of articles and the actions of the persons at the crime scene.

physical surveillance. Observing what a person is doing and saying by means of activities such as shadowing, wiretapping, hidden videotaping and spying.

"plant" (arson). A device which is designed to ignite combustible material sometime after the arsonist has left the premises.

plastic fingerprints. Impressions, depressed below the original surface, that are found on such objects as soap, butter and putty.

point of origin. The place where the fire began.

poison. A substance that, when introduced into the body in small quantities, causes a harmful or deadly effect.

portrait parlé. The systematic procedure for the verbal description of persons.

postmortem lividity. The dark blue discoloration that is observable on the parts of the body which are nearest the ground, caused by blood settling under its own weight.

presumption. In a court of law, a justifiable inference which shifts the burden to the opposing party to establish contradictory facts.

privileged communication. Information obtained in certain confidential relationships that will ordinarily not be admissible in court. For example, the relationship of husband and wife or attorney and client.

psilocybin. An hallucinogen extracted from a Mexican mushroom.

psychological constraint. Compelling behavior by instilling fear in the subject that harm will befall him, his family or his property if he does not cooperate.

psychological dependence. The association of a sense of satisfaction and mental well-being with the periodic administration of a drug, leading a person to want to take that drug again and again because it feels good.

psychological surveillance. Recording what a person is thinking and feeling by means of equipment such as lie detectors, employment forms and personalitytests.

public safety exception. When there is an immediate threat to public safety, an arresting officer may question a suspect without first giving *Miranda* warnings.

pugilistic posture. The position of the body with arms and wrists flexed in a boxer's pose which sometimes results from the exposure of a dead body to fire.

"punch job." A safebreaking method that involves knocking off the dial with a hammer and then driving the spindle back through the locking mechanism, thus releasing the lock.

pyromania. An uncontrollable impulse to start fires.

radial fractures. Spoke-like cracks in glass emanating from the area of impact.

rape. The act of having sexual intercourse with a female without her consent.

rape shield laws. Laws prohibiting courtroom inquiry into the prior sexual conduct of the victim.

rape trauma syndrome. Characteristic behavior patterns frequently exhibited by rape victims, such as fear of men, fear of the offender, fear of being alone, shame and repression of the incident.

real evidence. Tangible objects, such as guns, fingerprints, and bloodstains, introduced at a trial to prove or disprove a fact at issue.

rebuttable presumption. In a court of law, a justifiable inference that can be overcome by proof of its falsity.

receiving stolen property. The crime of buying or accepting stolen goods with the intention of converting them to your own use.

reconstructing the crime. The process of determining what happened at the crime scene.

relevant. Tending to prove a fact related to an issue in a legal case.

report. A permanent official record of the relevant information obtained in an investigation.

rib marks. The curved lines of stress that are faintly visible on the edge of a piece of broken glass.

rigor mortis. The stiffening of the body after death caused by chemical changes in the muscle tissue.

"ripping." Cutting a hole through the metal layers of a safe with a hammer and chisel or an ax.

robbery. The taking of property from another, in his presence and against his will.

rolling. The method of developing fingerprints on paper, which involves tilting the paper back and forth to spread the powder.

"rough shadowing." Tailing a subject without special precautions. It is used when the subject must be shadowed and is aware of that fact.

rough sketch. A drawing of the crime scene made by the investigator at the scene.

rules of evidence. Laws governing its admissibility in court.

secretors. Individuals whose blood group can be determined by an analysis of their body fluids.

sedatives. Drugs used to decrease anxiety and motor activity by depressing the central nervous system.

shadowing. Tailing; following a person.

showup. The confrontation of a single suspect by a witness for the purpose of identification.

silver nitrate method. An immersion technique used to develop fingerprints on paper.

"sniffer." A portable hydrocarbon vapor detector used to determine their presence at fires of suspicious origin.

spalling. The chipping, flaking and discoloration of concrete or brick due to intense heat.

spermatozoa or sperm. The male reproductive organisms in semen.

spiral method. An outdoor crime scene search pattern in which the searchers, following each other, begin in an outside circle and spiral in toward the center.

spontaneous exclamation. An utterance concerning the circumstances of a startling event by an individual in a condition of excitement, shock, or surprise, that is admissible as evidence.

stimulant. A drug that acts on the central nervous system to produce greater alertness and excitement. Cocaine and amphetamines are stimulants.

streamer. A length of candlewick, rope or cloth, saturated with an flammable liquid that is strung from room to room to provide a path for the fire.

strip method. An outdoor crime scene search pattern in which the area to be searched is blocked out in the form of a rectangle and the searchers proceed along paths parallel to the base of the rectangle.

subject. In a criminal investigation, the person being interviewed, interrogated or observed.

Super Glue. See cyanoacrylate.

surveillance. The covert observation of places, persons and vehicles for the purpose of obtaining information concerning the identities or activities of subjects.

surveillance log. A description of the activities taking place in the establishment under surveillance, with the time of arrival and departure of each person noted.

surveillant. The person who maintains the surveillance or performs the observation.

suspect. A person whose guilt of an offense is considered on reasonable grounds to be a practical possibility.

synthetic analgesics. Drugs used as substitutes for opium derivatives to reduce pain.

tailing. Shadowing; following a person.

"testing for a tail." A subject determining whether or not he is being shadowed.

thermal lance. A tool used in construction, capable of reaching temperatures in excess of 7000 degrees, that can penetrate any metal surface.

tolerance. The adaptation of the body to the use of a drug, making it necessary to increase the dosage to achieve the same result.

tool mark. The result of a metal instrument being applied to a relatively hard surface.

toxicology. The science which deals with poisons, their effects and antidotes, and recognition.

tracing evidence. Articles that assist the investigator in locating the suspect.

tranquilizer. A drug commonly prescribed for relief of anxiety, sedation, and as a muscle-relaxant.

trial combination. The safe combination set by the manufacturer.

undercover work. A form of surveillance in which the investigator assumes a different and unofficial identity in order to obtain information about a criminal activity.

undeveloped lead. An uncontacted possible source of information.

unidentified dead. Dead persons whose true identities are unknown and whose friends and relatives cannot be located.

unidentified person. One who has been physically or mentally affected to a degree or in a manner requiring the attention of the police and who cannot be identified, or whose friends and relations cannot be immediately located.

"V" pattern. A characteristic of fire that it burns upward and outward in a "V"-shaped pattern from the point of origin.

visible fingerprints. Those left by fingers covered with a colored material such as paint, blood, grease and ink.

voiceprints. The visual representation of characteristics of the human voice that permit identification by comparison.

voluntary manslaughter. An unlawful killing committed in the heat of sudden passion caused by adequate provocation.

waiver of rights. A declaration by a suspect in custody that he understands his *Miranda* rights but chooses to forgo them. He is willing to make a statement and does not want an attorney present.

wheel method. An outdoor crime scene search pattern in which the searchers begin at the center of a circular area and proceed outward along radii or spokes.

wiretap. An electronic device that is attached to a telephone wire which allows the investigator to hear both ends of a conversation.

zone method. An outdoor crime scene search pattern in which each searcher is assigned a subdivision of a quadrant to search.

INDEX